THE LAW
RELATING TO
CHILDREN

By

H. K. BEVAN, LL.M. (*Wales*)

*of the Middle Temple, Barrister, Professor of Law and Head of the
Department of Law in the University of Hull*

LONDON

BUTTERWORTHS
1973

ENGLAND:	BUTTERWORTH & CO. (PUBLISHERS) LTD.
	LONDON: 88 KINGSWAY, WC2B 6AB
AUSTRALIA:	BUTTERWORTHS PTY. LTD.
	SYDNEY: 586 PACIFIC HIGHWAY, CHATSWOOD, NSW 2067
	MELBOURNE: 343 LITTLE COLLINS STREET, 3000
	BRISBANE: 240 QUEEN STREET, 4000
CANADA:	BUTTERWORTH & CO. (CANADA) LTD.
	TORONTO: 14 CURITY AVENUE, 374
NEW ZEALAND:	BUTTERWORTHS OF NEW ZEALAND LTD.
	WELLINGTON: 26-28 WARING TAYLOR STREET, 1
SOUTH AFRICA:	BUTTERWORTH & CO. (SOUTH AFRICA) (PTY.) LTD.
	DURBAN: 152-154 GALE STREET

ISBN Casebound: 406 11700 4

Limp: 406 11701 2

Printed in Great Britain
at the St Ann's Press, Park Road, Altrincham, Cheshire WA14 5QQ

To My Family

Preface

This book is an attempt to reflect the growing and sustained attention which the last decade or so has given to the protection of the interests and welfare of children. Much of the relevant law is embodied in enactments which have yet to receive the authority of higher judicial interpretation and, partly for this reason, it has not, until quite recently, sufficiently excited academic interest. Insofar as the syllabuses of Family Law courses at university law schools have dealt with the parent-child relationship, the emphasis has very largely been on custody disputes in matrimonial proceedings, guardianship, wardship and adoption. These matters will continue to figure prominently, but the controversial Children and Young Persons Act 1969 has emphasised, in a way which the earlier legislation did not, that the breakdown of the family is not limited to those circumstances where the relationship between the parents is severed and where there is a dispute *inter se* over the upbringing of their children. A breakdown of another kind, but with no less profound consequences for the child, occurs where his welfare demands intervention by the courts or government agencies because of the parents' failure to discharge their obligations to him. If the student is to have a composite understanding of the law as it affects the family, this area requires as close an examination as the traditionally recognised ones. I have attempted to signify its importance by devoting the earliest chapters to much of it.

Although I have written with students primarily in mind, I have also attempted to attract a wider variety of readership. I recognise the dangers in such a policy, but the demarcation between the academic and the practical and between substantive law and procedure is artificial and arbitrary. I hope therefore that those directly and indirectly engaged in the

Preface

administration of child law be they the Bench, practitioners, probation officers or social workers will also find the work of some benefit.

The numerous footnote references to *Clarke Hall and Morrison on Children*, especially in the earlier chapters, will indicate my indebtedness to that treatise, but they cannot adequately reveal the extent to which it has reduced my labours in consulting and checking sources. I owe much to it. My thanks are due to my colleague, Mr. G. R. Rudd, for readily undertaking the task of reading the whole of the proofs and, in so doing, for saving me at the eleventh hour from certain errors and infelicities; to my secretary, Miss Belinda Bailey, for her seemingly boundless patience in transforming an untidy manuscript into type-written form; and to my publishers for their forbearance over my delay in submitting it and for their many kindnesses in helping to publish it.

I have tried to state the law as it was at October 1, 1972. The final Report of the Departmental Committee on the Adoption of Children appeared too late for inclusion in Chapter 10, but it is hoped that the reader may still find a useful comparison between it and the Committee's earlier provisional proposals, which have been noted.

October 1972   H. K. BEVAN

Contents

Contents

CHAPTER 4. CARE PROCEEDINGS AND CRIMINAL PROCEEDINGS
IN JUVENILE COURTS – III. ORDERS

CHAPTER 5. CHILDREN IN THE CARE OF LOCAL AUTHORITIES

CHAPTER 6. THE PENAL PROTECTION OF CHILDREN – I. PHYSICAL
HARM

Contents

Contents

Contents

Contents

Table of Statutes

References in this Table to "Stats." are to Halsbury's Statutes of England (Third Edition) showing the volume and page at which the annotated text of the Act will be found.

Table of Statutes

Table of Statutes

Table of Statutes

Table of Cases

In the following Table references are given where applicable to the English and Empire Digest where a digest of the case will be found.

Table of Cases

Table of Cases

Table of Cases

PAGE

xxxiv

PAGE

C

PAGE

Table of Cases

Table of Cases

Table of Cases

Table of Cases

Table of Cases

Table of Cases

Table of Cases

Table of Cases

xlix

Table of Cases

1

Table of Cases

Table of Cases

Table of Cases

Table of Cases

CHAPTER I

The Juvenile Court

A. ITS HISTORY

In spite of the centuries-old jurisdiction of justices of the peace over young offenders, the juvenile court dates only from 1908. Its modernity is partly explained by the fact that individual philanthropists and voluntary organisations of the eighteenth and nineteenth centuries were, rightly, directing their main energies to securing reform of the substantive law relating to the care and protection of children and to the treatment of convicted juvenile offenders. For them the establishment of a distinctly constituted tribunal to deal with the young was not a priority, although some recognised the moral dangers arising from young offenders having to associate with hardened criminals while they were awaiting trial.

But the main reason for the late appearance of the court was the persistent belief that the improvement of the administration of the criminal law with respect to young offenders lay, not in the establishment of a separate process of trial, but merely in the enlargement of the summary jurisdiction of the justices. Some expansion of that jurisdiction, over adult and young offenders alike, had taken place in the eighteenth century, but in 1800 there were still many offences which were triable only on indictment even though they were of a minor nature, petty larceny being the most common. Henry Fielding, who had been Chief Magistrate of Bow Street (1748-54) had advocated a simpler process of trial in cases of petty theft, and in 1819 the Select Committee on Criminal Laws made a similar recommendation, a proposal which "doubtless . . . had juvenile offenders particularly in mind".[1] But it was the Commissioners on the Criminal Law, who, in 1836, came down firmly against the idea of a distinction being drawn in the mode of trial of adult and of juvenile offenders and were content to see the

[1] Radzinowicz, *A History of English Criminal Law*, Vol. I, p. 551, n. 85.

1

summary jurisdiction of justices over young offenders extended.[2] This opinion prevailed. Following the recommendations of a Select Committee of the House of Lords, an Act of 1847 provided that offenders under the age of 14 years who were charged with petty larceny could be tried summarily by two justices who could discharge the accused if they thought it expedient not to inflict any punishment.[3] The Act was replaced by the much wider provisions of the Summary Jurisdiction Act 1879, which distinguished between children, *i.e.*, persons under 12, and young persons, *i.e.*, those who were at least 12 but under 16.[4] It provided that the former could be dealt with summarily when charged with any indictable offence other than homicide if the court thought it expedient and providing that the parent or guardian did not object. Young persons charged with certain indictable offences (mainly stealing or receiving stolen goods) could be tried summarily if they consented and the court thought it expedient.[5] This distinction was later widened and to some extent remains a feature of the present law.[6]

It was only when this extended jurisdiction was well established that attention was really turned to the problem of minimising contact between juvenile and adult criminals pending trial by the establishment of separate courts for dealing with the former. The suggestion that there should be separate courts seems to have been first put forward much earlier by Sir Eardley Wilmot, a Warwickshire justice of the peace,[7] when Sir Robert Peel was preparing his programme of reform of the criminal law and penal administration. His proposal was that there should be special courts each consisting of two justices to deal with young offenders. It is noteworthy that just about the same time, in 1828, Joseph Parkes, a leading advocate of reform of the Court of Chancery, published his *History of the Court of Chancery* in which he recommended[8] a separate court

---

[2] Third Report from the Commissioners on Criminal Law, British Sessional Papers, (1836) [79] xxxi, p. 1.
[3] 10 and 11 Vict., c. 82, s. 1.
[4] 42 and 43 Vict., c. 49, s. 49.
[5] *Ibid.*, ss. 10 and 11.
[6] See *post*, Chapter 2, p. 40.
[7] In *A Letter to the Magistrates of England on the Increase of Crime: and An Efficient Remedy Suggested for their Consideration* (2nd edn., 1827); see Radzinowicz, *op. cit.*, p. 571, n. 12, who describes this and other proposals of Wilmot as "remarkably progressive suggestions".
[8] At pp. 402-404.

to exercise wardship and guardianship jurisdiction over infants. But these were lone voices, and it seems that it was not until some fifty years later that the idea of separate courts was again seriously canvassed, when Benjamin Waugh in his book, *The Gaol Cradle*, published in 1873, advocated it. Eventually at the turn of the century, courts in some cities, probably influenced by the practice which had already obtained for some years in some of the States of America,[9] began to arrange special sittings to hear juvenile cases, and this procedure soon received legislative approval when the Children Act 1908,[10] provided that a court of summary jurisdiction, when dealing with persons under 16, must sit in a different building or room or on a different day or at a different time from the ordinary sittings of the court.

Significant though this provision was in establishing a separate court to deal with juveniles, it simply provided for the separate venue of the court, and nothing was done to prescribe rules for its constitution. The Royal Commission on the Selection of Justices of the Peace, which reported in 1910,[11] was silent on the matter, partly, it would seem, because there must have been some doubt about whether the composition of juvenile courts was within its terms of reference,[12] and partly because the new system had been in existence for too short a time to evoke criticism. It is likely that some juvenile courts followed the practice which had been adopted in the experimental courts[13] existing at the date of the Act, notably in the court in Birmingham. The practice was to call on particular justices to sit in rotation in the court. The first step to lay down statutory rules was taken with regard to the metropolitan area of London when the Juvenile Courts (Metropolis) Act 1920 required each juvenile court in the area to consist of a metropolitan stipendiary magistrate, who was to preside, and two lay justices, one of whom was to be a woman and both of whom

[9] Orphan courts had long existed in some States; Parkes, *supra*, referred to them. Still, it was not until 1899, in Illinois, that the first specialised court to deal with juvenile offenders was established.
[10] Section 111 (1).
[11] Cmnd. 5250.
[12] The Commission was asked to "consider and report whether any and what steps should be taken to facilitate the selection of the most suitable persons to be Justices of the Peace, irrespective of creed and political opinion".
[13] *Supra.*

were to be chosen from a panel of justices nominated by the Home Secretary. Nothing was done about the rest of the country until the Children and Young Persons Act 1932, accepting the recommendations of the Departmental Committee on the Treatment of Young Offenders,[14] introduced a system of selecting for juvenile court work those justices who were specially qualified for it. As will be seen,[15] the system remains basically unaltered.

Under the Children Act 1908, the newly established court was not only to hear charges against children and young persons,[16] but was also to assume the civil jurisdiction which justices of the peace had already been exercising under legislation, beginning with the Industrial Schools Act 1857, with regard to children who were vagrants or were found begging or destitute or who, being inmates in a poor law institution, were refractory or whose parents were unable to control them or who, under the Elementary Education Act 1876, failed to comply with a school attendance order. Under the nineteenth century legislation such children could be sent to an Industrial School for care, education and training.[17] The Act of 1908 widened the class of children in respect of whom this power could be exercised and also gave the court additional powers to deal with them.

B. THE CONSTITUTION AND ORGANISATION OF JUVENILE COURTS

A juvenile court usually consists of three justices of the peace who are specially qualified to deal with cases concerning juveniles. Certainly there can never be more than three and so far as concerns lay justices, as opposed to stipendiary magistrates, there must be at least two, since a juvenile court is a court of summary jurisdiction and is deemed to be a petty sessional court, which by definition requires the presence of two or more

[14] (1927) Cmnd. 2831, pp. 26-28.
[15] *Infra.*
[16] Then defined respectively as persons under 14 and those 14 but under 16.
[17] See further Chapter 2, p. 19.

lay justices.[18] Save in exceptional circumstances, the court must include a man and a woman "on the analogy that it requires a parent of either sex to bring up a child properly."[19] With regard to detailed organisation and the methods of selection of the chairmen and justices it is, however, still necessary to distinguish between the courts in the Metropolitan area and those elsewhere,[20] but new rules relating to juvenile court panels and the composition of juvenile courts are contemplated by the Children and Young Persons Act 1969.[1]

Courts Within the Metropolitan Area[2]

For the purpose of juvenile court jurisdiction the area comprises the Inner London area[3] and the City of London. It is split up by the Home Secretary into a number of divisions with juvenile courts sitting in these divisions but "without prejudice . . . to their jurisdiction with respect to the whole area."[4] The members of the courts are chosen from a panel nominated by the Lord Chancellor from the lay justices of the Inner London area. Nominations are for a specified period but are revocable at any time. The Lord Chancellor[5] also nominates the chairman of each court, who must be either one of the lay justices on the panel or a metropolitan stipendiary magistrate.[6] If, because of

---

[18] See C. & Y.P. Act 1933, s. 45 and the Interpretation Act 1889, s. 13(11) and (12), and compare the definition of "magistrates' court" in the Magistrates' Courts Act 1952, s. 124.

[19] John Watson, *The Child and The Magistrate*, 3rd edn., p. 55.

[20] *Cf. supra*, p. 4.

[1] Section 61, *infra*, p. 10.

[2] The relevant rules are contained in the C. & Y.P. Act 1933, s. 45; the C. & Y.P. Act 1963, Sched. 2, Part II; the Administration of Justice Act 1964, ss. 12, 39 and Sched. 3; the Juvenile Courts (London) Order 1965, S.I. 1965 No. 584, as amended by S.I. 1965 No. 1362, and S.I. 1968 No. 592; and the Juvenile Courts (Constitution) (Metropolitan Area) Order 1965, S.I. 1965, No. 830.

[3] Defined by the Administration of Justice Act 1964, s. 2(1) (a), as consisting of the Inner London boroughs. It corresponds with what was formerly the metropolitan stipendiary courts area.

[4] 1963 Act, Sched. 2, Part II, para. 14.

[5] Prior to the Act of 1964 the Home Secretary nominated the panel and chairman.

[6] Under the Juvenile Courts (Metropolis) Act 1920, (*ante*, p. 3.) only a stipendiary magistrate could preside, but the Children and Young Persons Act 1932 empowered the Home Secretary to nominate a lay justice as chairman, and since 1936 lay justices have usually been appointed chairmen, although the Chief Metropolitan Magistrate is still the head of the panel and some other stipendiary magistrates are in practice also appointed chairmen.

"illness or other emergency",[7] the chairman is not available, any metropolitan stipendiary magistrate or, with the Lord Chancellor's consent, any other justice on the panel may temporarily act as chairman. If a chairman considers that a court cannot be fully constituted and that an adjournment would not be in the interests of justice, he may sit with one other member (whether a man or woman), except that if he is a metropolitan stipendiary magistrate he may, in such circumstances, sit alone.

Courts Outside the Metropolitan Area[8]

(1) *Juvenile Court Panels*

In these courts, too, a justice is not eligible to sit unless he is a member of a juvenile court panel. Normally there is a panel for each petty sessions area, but the Home Secretary can create a combined panel for two or more areas.[9] Combination is desirable where the number of juvenile cases in one area is too small to enable members of the court to gain adequate experience of their work. Moreover, it is more likely to ensure that there will be enough justices among those for the combined areas who are suitably qualified for appointment to the panel. In spite of these advantages combined panels were until recently uncommon, this being partly explained by the Home Office's inadequate knowledge of local conditions. To meet this difficulty and to encourage the establishment of such panels, particularly in rural areas, the Children and Young Persons Act 1963, adopting substantially the recommendations of the Ingleby Committee,[10] empowers magistrates' courts committees, or requires them when so directed by the Home Secretary, to submit to him recommendations for the formation (or dissolution) of combined panels. Where the committee is directed to report but does not put forward any recommendations, its report must give reasons for not doing so.

Before it submits any recommendations a committee must consult the justices for every petty sessions area concerned

---

[7] 1963 Act, Sched. 2, Part II, para. 16.
[8] The rules are to be found in the 1933 Act, s. 45; the 1963 Act, Second Sched., Part I; and the Juvenile Courts (Constitution) Rules 1954, S.I. 1954, No. 1711.
[9] He can also correspondingly dissolve a combined panel.
[10] See Cmnd. 1191, paras. 163-166. The Royal Commission on the Justices of the Peace had already stressed the need for combined panels; see (1948) Cmnd. 7463, paras. 179-180.

which is within the committee's area, and also any other committee whose area is wholly or partly concerned.[11] The committee will also have to notify all those persons of the recommendations eventually submitted and they (the justices or other committee) or any juvenile court panel concerned are entitled to make representations to the Home Secretary within one month from the time when the notice was given.

The Home Secretary may then make an order[12] giving effect, with or without modifications, to the committee's recommendations. If, however, the committee fails to submit a report within six months of being directed by him to do so, or if he is dissatisfied with its report, he may make whatever order[12] he deems fit. Where he proposes to make an order which departs from the committee's recommendations or which is being made in the absence of recommendations, a copy of it must first be sent to the justices and any magistrates' court committee concerned to enable them or any panel concerned to make representations to him within one month from the date when the copy was sent.

(2) *Membership of a Panel*

Hitherto membership of a panel and the composition of the court have been determined in the following ways.[13]

The members of a panel are not nominated by the Lord Chancellor, as they are in the Metropolitan area, but are chosen by the justices for the particular petty sessions area (or combined areas) from amongst their own number.[14] Appointments are made at their annual meeting in October in every third year.[15] Members then serve for a period of three years, beginning 1st November following the date of appointment, but are eligible for re-appointment: indeed, were they not so, it would not be possible to produce a body of justices with wide experience of juvenile court work. There is no fixed number of

---

[11] That committee must in turn consult the justices within its own area.
[12] No order can be made providing for the formation of a combined panel for an area which includes (a) a county or part of a county and the whole or part of another county or (b) two county boroughs.
[13] For future procedure see *infra*.
[14] Exceptionally justices for a petty sessions area of a county may appoint a justice from another area of the county.
[15] The first appointments were made in October 1955, as required by the Juvenile Court (Constitution) Rules, 1954.

members of a panel, but justices are directed to appoint as many as they think sufficient for the juvenile courts in their area, and they may at any time make additional appointments and fill vacancies. There are, however, two limits on the kinds of justices who may be appointed. They must be specially qualified for dealing with juvenile cases, a requirement considered below; and they must at the date of appointment be under the age of 65. On attaining that age membership automatically ceases unless the Lord Chancellor directs that the particular justice shall continue to serve for a specified period.[16] This age limit does not apply to a stipendiary magistrate who may remain a member of a panel so long as he holds office.[17]

(3) *Composition of the Court*

A juvenile court panel must meet at least twice a year to make arrangements with regard to the holding of juvenile courts and to discuss questions concerning their working, but its first function after being established is to appoint a chairman and deputy chairmen. These are elected by secret ballot by the members of the panel from amongst themselves and they must choose a sufficient number to ensure that each juvenile court in the area will sit under a person so elected. For this reason the panel can elect additional deputy chairmen and fill vacancies. A stipendiary magistrate is not entitled *ex officio* to be a chairman or deputy chairman: he must be elected to that position.

As with juvenile courts in the Metropolitan area, exceptions are allowed to the normal requirements that the court must consist of a chairman, or deputy chairmen, and two other justices, and must include one man and one woman. If the chairman or deputy chairman is not available "owing to circumstances unforeseen when the justices to sit were chosen",[18]

---

[16] Application for a direction must be made some time before the justice is due to reach retirement age; see H.O. Circular No. 126/1967.

[17] The age of compulsory retirement was formerly 72 but this is reduced to 70 in respect of appointments made since the Justices of the Peace Act, 1968.
     The Ingleby Committee (para. 156) recommended that stipendiary magistrates should, like lay justices, cease to be members of juvenile court panels when they reach 65.

[18] The Juvenile Courts (Constitution) Rules 1954, r. 13(2).

or if he cannot properly sit as a member,[19] members of the court can choose one of their own number to preside at a particular sitting. If, for the same reasons, no man or no woman is available or properly entitled to sit, the other members may proceed to sit if they think it inexpedient in the interests of justice to adjourn the case. Moreover, where a stipendiary magistrate finds that he is the only member present at a sitting he may sit alone if he considers adjournment inexpedient. These exceptions will only be allowed on the ground of "unforeseen" circumstances if at the time of arranging the composition of the court the panel took steps to "ensure"[20] that the court would be fully composed in accordance with the normal requirements. Merely giving notice to a woman justice to attend without inquiring whether she can do so is not ensuring her attendance, so that proceedings held by two male justices in her absence are void.[1] It cannot be said that they are entitled to proceed because the circumstances of her absence are unforeseen when they have no evidence as to what those circumstances are.

A comparison of these exceptions with those applicable in the Metropolitan area shows that while there are basic differences there are some unjustifiable distinctions which might have been removed by the 1963 Act when it amended the rules of composition of courts in that area. It is difficult to see why the power to choose a temporary chairman should depend in that area on the chairman's not being available because of "illness or other emergency",[2] whereas elsewhere it depends on his absence being due to unforeseen circumstances.[3] These respective provisions are almost certainly intended to cover the same contingencies. They should be expressed in the same terms. To the rules governing the Metropolitan juvenile courts there ought expressly to be added a provision that the power to appoint a temporary chairman is exercisable where the chairman "cannot properly sit as a member of the court"[3]. These

[19] Clarke Hall and Morrison on *Children*, 8th edn., p. 475, instance the case of a chairman disqualified under the Justices of the Peace Act 1949, s. 3, because he is a member of a local authority which is a party to the proceedings. Another example would be a chairman having a personal interest in the case.

[20] See the 1954 Rules, *supra*, r. 11.

[1] *Re J.S. (an Infant)* [1959] 3 All E.R. 856.

[2] 1963 Act, Sched. 2, Part II, para. 16.

[3] As in the Juvenile Courts (Constitution) Rules 1954, r. 13(2).

are just two examples to show that there is room for greater uniformity in the two sets of rules.[4]

That result might be achieved when effect is given to the new procedure allowed by the Children and Young Persons Act 1969. Section 61 (which is operative) enables rules to be made with regard to (a) the formation and revision of juvenile court panels and the eligibility of justices to be members; (b) the appointment of chairmen of juvenile courts; and (c) the composition of those courts. They may confer on the Lord Chancellor powers with respect to any of those matters and may, in particular, provide for the appointment of panels by him instead of by the justices themselves. It is likely that in exercising his powers he will be guided by the advice of local committees of justices. Different provisions may be made for different areas, but the section does not affect the present system concerning the areas for which panels are formed and juvenile courts constituted or the formation of combined panels.[5]

The Qualifications and Training of Juvenile Court Justices

(1) *Qualifications*

When nominating members of the juvenile court panel the justices, or, in the case of the Metropolitan area, the Lord Chancellor, are required to choose justices who are specially qualified for dealing with juvenile cases.[6] The rules provide no criteria for determining what are special qualifications, but the general terms in which the provision is expressed have been defended on the ground that it is not practicable for "the elements of what constitutes suitability [to] be expressed in

---

[4] As another example compare the following: R. 12(1) of the 1954 Rules states: "Each juvenile court shall be constituted of not more than three justices and, subject to the following provisions of this Rule, shall include a man and a woman". But para. 15 of the Second Schedule of the 1963 Act provides: "Subject to the following provisions of this Schedule – (a) each juvenile court shall consist of a chairman and two other members and shall have both a man and a woman among its members". For yet a further illustration, see *infra*, n. 6.

[5] *Supra*, p. 6.

[6] See the Juvenile Courts (Constitution) Rules, 1954, r. 1(1) and, for the Metropolitan area, the C. & Y.P. Act 1963, Sched. 2, para. 18. The latter provision also expressly instructs the Lord Chancellor to take account of "the previous experience of the persons available". It is suggested that this factor is equally considered when nominations are made to panels outside the Metropolitan area. Guidance is given in H.O. Circular No. 193/1970.

any short phrase or definition".[7] Still, a clear indication of the basic principles to be borne in mind when nominating was given by Viscount Caldecote in words which remain as true today as when they were written – thirty years ago:[8]

> "The magistrates themselves can make or mar the system established by the [Children and Young Persons Act 1933]. If the magistrate is not endowed with qualities which enable him to understand the workings of a child's mind, and, if he has no practical acquaintance with the conditions in which large numbers of the children who will come before him are reared, he will fail. Even if it is no longer true that half of England has no knowledge of the life lived by the other half it is certainly true to say that no magistrate can be properly equipped as a member of a juvenile court unless he knows for himself something about the appalling conditions in which so many children live."

The Royal Commission on Justices of the Peace 1946-48 and the Ingleby Committee were generally satisfied with the present system of selection,[9] but both stressed the desirability of justices being normally between 30 and 40 years of age when first appointed to the juvenile court panel although it was recognised that there could not and should not be an inflexible rule. Both, too, affirmed the principle that a person's occupation must be neither a qualification nor a disqualification, and for that reason were opposed to the suggestion that teachers as such were specially suitable for selection. The Royal Commission also saw practical objections to the appointment of teachers. There is a distinct danger of a conflict of interests arising, since most teachers are employees of a local authority and, as will be seen,[10] the local authority occupies a special position, with many responsibilities, in relation to juvenile courts.

---

[7] The Report of the Royal Commission on Justices of the Peace, 1946-48, Cmnd. 7463, para. 187.

[8] In his Introduction to the first edition of Watson, *The Child and the Magistrate* (1942). The learned author himself, with a wealth of experience, stresses (at p. 130) the need for a juvenile court magistrate to have foresight, imagination and intuition and the ability "to try to recognise at an early stage those children of whom a diagnostic examination by the psychiatrist may be revealing".

[9] For their respective views see (1948) Cmnd. 7463, paras. 184-190 and (1960) Cmnd. 1191, paras. 154-162; but see *infra*, n. 11.
     In all, there are about 16,000 Justices in Great Britain, but only about one quarter are under 50 years of age.

[10] See especially Chapter 3.

11

Since the members of the juvenile court panel are drawn from the justices of the particular area, it is essential that when advisory committees are submitting to the Lord Chancellor nominations for appointment as justices they include in their list a sufficient number of persons who will be specially qualified to sit in the juvenile court.[11] At the same time it is generally undesirable that persons should be appointed solely for that purpose. Certainly the demands of the juvenile court are heavy, with its special jurisdiction and, to some extent, distinctive procedure and methods of treatment, and justices appointed to the panel should, it is suggested, largely devote themselves to the work of that court; but some experience in adult courts, particularly in adjudicating in matrimonial cases, will give justices insight into the various causes of the break up of the matrimonial home, which in turn so often accounts for juvenile delinquency and the need for children to be given care or control. Outside the Metropolitan area nearly all of them do in practice also sit in the adult courts.[12]

(2) *Training*

The need for justices of the peace to undergo some form of training has long been recognised but its implementation has been a slow process.[13] Finally, however, a system of compulsory training was introduced in 1966, in the sense that every prospective justice, unless exempted by the Lord Chancellor, must give an undertaking that, if appointed, he will complete a prescribed course of basic training within a year after his appointment.[14] In addition every justice who is elected to the

---

[11] Notwithstanding the general satisfaction expressed by the Royal Commission and the Ingleby Committee, the system of appointing justices has not escaped criticism, partly on the ground that it may be used as a method of political patronage. In so far as this is a defect, it may adversely affect the composition of juvenile court panels, a significant factor bearing in mind that almost a half of the lay justices sit in the juvenile court. The composition of advisory committees, other than that for the Inner London area, is still shrouded in secrecy.

[12] See W. E. Cavenagh, *Juvenile Courts, The Child and the Law*, p. 13.

[13] See the Government White Paper on "*The Training of Justices of the Peace in England and Wales*", (1965) Cmnd. 2856, and Watson *op. cit.*, pp. 355-359.

[14] The course combines theoretical and practical training and is in two stages, the first of which is to be completed before the appointee sits to adjudicate and the second within a year after his appointment. For details see Appendix A of the White Paper.

Juvenile Court Panel must, unless exempted, undergo a special course of instruction within a year after election. This latter training is designed to enable juvenile court justices

(a) to understand the place of the juvenile court in the judicial system and certain special aspects of procedure in that court;

(b) to appreciate the social and educational background of juveniles before the court;

(c) to know the services available to them, particularly the educational, medical and psychiatric services; and

(d) to learn the various courses which may be taken in dealing with juveniles who are brought before the court because they are in need of care or control, so that they understand the nature and purpose of the methods of treatment which they may use and their effect.[15]

The training is carried out in two stages. In the first the justice attends the juvenile court as an observer: in the second he receives instruction in a number of subjects and visits the kinds of institutions to which as the result of exercising his judicial powers the juvenile is likely to be sent.

These arrangements for obligatory training are only the beginning, and the National Advisory Council on the Training of Magistrates is required to report from time to time to the Lord Chancellor on the working of the present system; but there are no signs that we are moving towards the principle that the juvenile court shall have a legally qualified chairman, as obtains in some other legal systems.

C. JURISDICTION

Subsequent chapters deal at length with the different kinds of jurisdiction exercised by a juvenile court. The present purpose is merely to outline them and consider a general principle applicable to all.

(1) Care Jurisdiction and Criminal Jurisdiction Over Juveniles[16]

A juvenile court has power to make various orders where children and young persons are found to be, within prescribed

---

[15] *Ibid.*, Appendix B.
[16] *Post*, Chapters 2-4.

conditions, in need of care or control or, in criminal proceedings, guilty of an offence.

Some reference has already been made to the emergence of separate civil and criminal jurisdiction, which the Children Act 1908 recognised.[17] The Children and Young Persons Acts 1933 and 1963 extended the civil jurisdiction but preserved the duality. The Children and Young Persons Act 1969 to some extent blurs the distinction by allowing the juvenile offender to be dealt with in the same way as other kinds of juveniles who need care or control, but, even if the relevant provisions were fully implemented, they would only "represent a compromise between the [former] procedure and the abolition of the juvenile courts, for which many reformers still press".[18] As it is, they will hardly achieve even this result. It will be some time before the abolition of criminal proceedings in respect of all children under 14, for which the Act provides,[19] will be given full effect, and the introduction of rules[20] severely restricting the prosecution of young persons is only a remote possibility. Consequently, either the care jurisdiction or the criminal jurisdiction may be invoked to deal with juveniles aged between 10 and 16 inclusive[1] who are suspected of having committed an offence, other than homicide (prosecution for which is not affected by the 1969 Act) or, in the case of young persons, other than certain other grave crimes.

Care and criminal jurisdiction over juveniles[2] extends not only to the making of original orders and to their variation or discharge but also to incidental matters; for example, the

---

[17] *Ante*, p. 4.
[18] O. M. Stone, *Children Without A Satisfactory Home*, 33 M.L.R. 649 at p. 653.
[19] Section 4.
[20] Section 5.

[1] The minimum prosecutable age is soon to be raised to 12.
[2] Unless the particular context otherwise requires, the term "juvenile" is used throughout this book as a collective term for children (*i.e.*, persons under 14) and young persons (*i.e.*, those who have attained 14 but are under 17). Unaccountably the Legislature has been reluctant so to use it.

In other contexts the term child may have different meanings; *e.g.*, for the purpose of the Children Act 1948 it means a person under 18.

For a composite historical picture of the fixing of age limits for various purposes (*e.g.*, education, employment, protection, methods of treatment) see James, *The Age of Criminal Responsibility*, [1959] Crim. L.R. 497, who refers to "the random fixing of ages bestowing capacities without regard to any specific test". See also Glanville Williams, *Criminal Law, The General Part*, 2nd edn., p. 804; Stone, 33 M.L.R. 649, n. 4.

power to order that a young person, who is in the care of a local authority under a care order, be removed to a borstal institution because of his behaviour.[3]

(2) Children in Care Under the Children Act 1948
If a parent objects to a resolution of a local authority that it shall assume all the rights and powers of the parent, the authority must obtain an order of the juvenile court authorising the resolution to remain operative.[4]

(3) Foster Children
A juvenile court has jurisdiction under the Children Act 1958 to order the removal of a foster child from a foster parent on the complaint of the local authority. On the other hand, a foster parent can appeal to the court against any requirement or prohibition imposed by the authority with regard to the keeping of the foster child.[5]

(4) Adoption
Next to care jurisdiction and criminal jurisdiction, jurisdiction to make orders for the adoption of minors[6] ranks as the most important in the work of juvenile courts; but practice varies considerably. Most adoption applications are heard by county courts, but in some areas the juvenile court is the more popular.[7]

Under the Adoption Act 1958 the court also has jurisdiction with regard to "protected children", *i.e.*, children under the upper school age limit who are waiting to be adopted or who have been placed with strangers in circumstances defined by the Act.[8]

The Welfare of the Minor
In cases concerned with the custody, guardianship or wardship of a minor the court is statutorily directed to regard his welfare as the paramount consideration in reaching its decision.[9]

[3] See *post*, p. 132.
[4] *Post*, Chapter 5.
[5] *Post*, Chapter 11.
[6] *I.e.*, persons under 18; Adoption Act 1958, s. 57(1); Family Law Reform Act 1969, ss. 1(3), 12 and Sched. 1.
[7] *Post*, Chapter 10.
[8] *Ibid.*
[9] Guardianship of Minors Act 1971, s. 1.

In adoption proceedings, while an adoption order is not to be made unless it is for the minor's welfare, the principle of paramountcy is not expressly accepted because of the importance attached to the need for the parent to consent to an order being made. However, where no dispute over consent arises, there is no obstacle to the application of that principle and the court should follow it.

As with adoption, the principle is not expressly enacted for the purpose of jurisdiction over children and young persons and it is uncertain how far it is applicable thereto. Section 44(1) of the Children and Young Persons Act 1933 provides:[10]

> Every court in dealing with a child or young person who is brought before it, either as an offender or otherwise, shall have regard to the welfare of the child or young person and shall in a proper case take steps for removing him from undesirable surroundings and for securing that proper provision is made for his education and training.

It is submitted that the nature of care jurisdiction, as defined in s. 1 of the Children and Young Persons Act 1969, is such that, once the conditions prescribed by that section have been proved, the juvenile's welfare becomes not merely the paramount but the exclusive consideration in deciding upon the order to be made in respect of him, and it would have been better if that Act had expressly so provided. It is with regard to criminal jurisdiction that uncertainty surrounds s. 44, owing to differing opinions as to how far criminality should involve the interests of the public as well as those of the juvenile. Juvenile courts are divided between the view that the effect of the section is to make the juvenile's welfare the paramount, even the sole, factor irrespective of the nature of his delinquency and that which relates his welfare to the delinquency and to the public interest.

> "The existence of the two views . . . means therefore that, even though the justices have had the benefit of expert opinion about the nature of the defendant and his needs before making an order, the kind of recommendations which would involve serious interference with personal liberty, or the gravity of which appear

---

[10] As amended by C. & Y.P. Act 1969, s. 72(4) and Sched. 6.

disproportionate in relation to the triviality of the offence or record, may be acceptable to some justices and not to others."[11]

Although the 1969 Act allows the juvenile offender to be dealt with under care proceedings as an alternative to prosecution, it sheds no light on how the conflict between these views is to be resolved.

D.   APPEALS FROM JUVENILE COURT

(1) Criminal Cases and Care Cases

A juvenile may, in the same way as an adult who has been convicted and sentenced by a magistrates' court, appeal against his conviction or sentence or both, or, where he pleaded guilty, against his sentence.[12]

Similarly he may appeal against an order made in care proceedings under s. 1 of the Children & Young Persons Act 1969,[13] and, where a court finds the offence condition[14] satisfied with respect to him but no order is made, he can appeal against the finding.[15] However, no appeal lies, either at the instance of the juvenile or his parent, against an order requiring the latter to enter into a recognisance to take proper care and exercise proper control over the juvenile. The reason for this rule, which equally applies where the parental recognisance has been entered into as the result of criminal proceedings against the juvenile,[16] is that the order could not have been made without the parent's consent. For the same reason there is no right of appeal by a juvenile against an order, made in care proceedings based on the offence condition, that he enter into a recog-

---

[11] W. E. Cavenagh, *Juvenile Courts, the Child and the Law*, pp. 189-190.
[12] Magistrates' Courts Act 1952, s. 83. Appeal also lies against a hospital order or guardianship order even though made without a conviction and it may be brought by the juvenile or his parent on his behalf (Mental Health Act 1959, s. 70(1) and (3)).
[13] See s. 2(12).
[14] For the offence condition see *post*, Chapter 2, p. 29.
[15] Section 3(8). The rule equally applies where one court has found the condition proved and has remitted the case (in accordance with ss. 2(11) and 3(5)) to another court which decides not to make an order. For the right of appeal where a juvenile offender is in criminal proceedings remitted by a court to a juvenile court see C. & Y.P. Act 1933, s. 56(2) and *post*, Chapter 2, p. 43.
[16] C. & Y.P. Act 1969, s. 7(7), *post*, p. 116.

nisance to keep the peace or be of good behaviour.[17] But a
parent who is ordered to pay a fine, compensation or costs in
criminal proceedings against a juvenile, or to pay compensation
where the offence condition is proved in care proceedings, has
a right of appeal.[18]

(2) Foster Children and Protected Children

An appeal lies from an order of a juvenile court made under
the Children Act 1958 with regard to foster children[19] or under
the Adoption Act 1958 in respect of "protected children".[19]

In all these cases appeal formerly lay to quarter sessions, but
since the Courts Act 1971 appellate jurisdiction is exercised
by the Crown Court, which is normally composed of between
two and four magistrates sitting, not as assessors[20] but as
full members, under the chairmanship of a professional judge
or recorder.[1] These changes do not affect the right of a person
to appeal by way of case stated to the High Court.

(3) Adoption Cases

Appeals are heard by a single judge of the Family Division
of the High Court.[2]

---

[17] *Ibid.*, s. 3(7), *post*, p. 95. But where such an order is made in criminal
proceedings there is a right of appeal (Magistrates' Courts (Appeals from
Binding Over Orders) Act 1956).
[18] See respectively C. & Y.P. Act 1933, s. 55(5) and C. & Y.P. Act 1969,
s. 3(8).
[19] *Supra*, p. 15.
[20] As formerly under C. & Y.P. Act 1963, s. 19.
[1] Section 5. Appeals are decided on a majority decision, but in the event
of equal division the judge or recorder has a second, casting vote.
[2] Adoption Act 1958, s. 10; Administration of Justice Act 1970, s. 1. and
Sched. 1.

CHAPTER 2

Care Proceedings and Criminal Proceedings in Juvenile Courts — I Jurisdiction

A. CARE PROCEEDINGS

I. DEVELOPMENT OF CARE JURISDICTION

It has already been briefly noted[1] that the civil jurisdiction of the juvenile court is traceable to nineteenth century legislation dealing with juveniles who for various reasons were living in undesirable conditions. The provisions of the Industrial Schools Act 1866[2] were re-enacted and extended by the Children Act 1908 to cover further categories of juveniles "at risk".[3] Broadly, the effect was that the court could send to an industrial school, or place into the care of a fit person, a child under 14 (1) who was found begging or, having no parent or no parent or guardian exercising proper guardianship, was a vagrant, or, because his parent was in prison, was destitute; or (2) who was in moral danger because he was in the company of a thief or prostitute or, in the case of a girl, because her father had been convicted of a sexual offence against her;[4] or (3) whose parent because of criminal or drunken habits was unfit to have care of him. A young person in similar circumstances could be the subject of a fit person order.[5]

The Act also repeated the earlier provisions of the 1866 Act concerning the child whose parent was unable to control him and the refractory child who was being maintained in a Poor Law institution, and it re-enacted those dealing with the truant whose parent did not comply with a school attendance order made under the Elementary Education Act 1876.[6]

---

[1] *Ante*, p. 4.
[2] Replacing the earlier Act of 1857, as amended.
[3] Section 58.
[4] *Viz.*, under s. 4 or s. 5 of the Criminal Law Amendment Act 1885.
[5] Children Act 1908, s. 59.
[6] Children Act 1908, s. 58(4)-(6).

Since 1908 there have been three major changes in the legislation affecting juveniles needing care and control, the direct results of Reports of Departmental Committees or White Papers.

The Committee on the Treatment of Young Offenders[7] drew attention to many instances of juveniles in physical or moral danger who could not be brought before the court under the 1908 Act, and its main recommendations were given effect by s. 61 of the Children and Young Persons Act 1933,[8] which re-cast the law by defining three classes of juveniles who were "in need of care or protection", *viz.*,

> (a) Those who, having no parent or guardian or having a parent or guardian who was unfit to exercise guardianship or was not properly exercising it, were falling into bad associations or were exposed to moral danger or were beyond control. The fact that a juvenile was found destitute, wandering or begging was evidence of moral danger.
> To this category was later added[9] those who were ill-treated or neglected in a manner likely to cause them unnecessary suffering or injury to health.
> (b) Those who required care or protection because they were the victims of specified offences (which involved cruelty or neglect or were sexual offences) or were living in homes where any of those offences had been committed in respect of other juveniles.
> (c) Those who were prevented from receiving education because they were in the care of vagrants.

The 1933 Act continued the jurisdiction to deal with those beyond parental control, refractory juveniles in the care of Poor Law authorities and truants.[10] It also allowed for a juvenile who was not responding favourably to supervision to be brought back before the court.

The next major review was undertaken by the Ingleby Committee on Children and Young Persons whose Report[11] in 1960 led to, *inter alia*, the Children and Young Persons Act 1963. Experience had shown that it was paragraph (*a*) of the definition in s. 61 of the earlier Act which caused the greatest difficulty,

---

[7] (1927) Cmnd. 2831.
[8] Re-enacting provisions in the C. & Y.P. Act 1932.
[9] By the C. & Y.P. (Amendment) Act 1952, s. 1.
[10] *Supra.*
[11] Cmnd. 1191.

the essential criticism being[12] that, by insisting on the fulfilment of two conditions where there was a parent or guardian,[13] a number of juveniles were being deprived of treatment which otherwise the juvenile court could have beneficially ordered. On the one hand, it was often impossible to prove that a very young child was falling into bad associations or being exposed to moral danger: on the other hand, where those matters could be proved with regard to an older juvenile there were many cases where it was impossible to prove the shortcomings of the parent. The Ingleby Committee recognised the difficulties, but the suggestion that the two sets of criteria should be made alternative requirements was rejected as being too wide:

"Many children are capable of looking after themselves even though their parents are 'unfit'; and it would be harsh to put a parent in danger of losing the custody of his child where there was no evidence that the parent was neglectful or irresponsible."

The Committee sought to overcome the difficulties by proposing a compromise definition.[14] A juvenile would be in need of protection or discipline if either (i) he is exposed to physical, mental or moral danger; or (ii) is in need of control, *and*, in any such case, needs care, protection, treatment, control or discipline which is likely to be rejected or unobtainable except by order of a court.[15]

The definition had the advantage of avoiding any direct reference to the parent or guardian, and it is noteworthy that s. 1 of the Children and Young Persons Act 1969 follows similar lines.[16] Had s. 2 of the 1963 Act, which partly gave effect to the Ingleby proposals, done so, it might have resulted in a less complicated provision. It divided juveniles who were "in need of care, protection or control" into two categories, *viz.*,

(i) those who were beyond parental control; but with regard to them it introduced the important change that the juvenile was to be brought before the court by the local authority, the police or an authorised person and not by the parent;

---

[12] See Appendix III of the Report, p. 170.
[13] *I.e.*, (1) that the parent is unfit, or is failing, to exercise proper care and guardianship and (2) that the juvenile is falling into bad associations etc.
[14] Para. 86 and Appendix IV.
[15] The Committee added a third category, *viz.*, a child under 12 who acts in a manner which would render a person over that age liable to be found guilty of an offence; see *post*, pp. 28 *et seq.*
[16] See *infra*.

(ii) those who were not receiving such care, protection and guidance as a good parent may reasonably be expected to give and (*a*) were falling into bad associations or were exposed to moral danger or (*b*) the lack of care, protection or guidance was likely to cause them unnecessary suffering or seriously affect their health or proper development or (*c*) were the victims of serious offences or were living in homes where any of those offences had been committed in respect of other juveniles.[17]

Supportive and preventive work was the main philosophy underlying the two White Papers, "The Child, the Family and the Young Offender"[18] and "Children in Trouble",[19] which led to the third major change in the law, now embodied in the Children and Young Persons Act 1969. As will be seen,[20] under the new law greater emphasis is placed on consultation between parents, the local authority, the police and teachers; but, if this policy should fail, the aid of the court will have to be sought. For example, there may be a poor response from the home and the parents may be unwilling to allow the juvenile to be received into the care of the local authority under section 1 of the Children Act 1948.[1] Again, the juvenile may have committed an offence and the police may insist on court proceedings.

II. GROUNDS ON WHICH ORDERS MAY BE MADE

Section 1 of the 1969 Act preserves the principle that State intervention against the wishes of the parent and juvenile can be justified only on specific grounds of neglect or misbehaviour, and denies to juvenile courts a general guardianship jurisdiction, based solely on the welfare of the juvenile. Nevertheless, most of the grounds for intervention are so widely expressed that they minimise the differences between a specific and a general jurisdiction.[2] The court can make an order if one or more of the following conditions is satisfied with respect to the juvenile and there is need for care or control:

(*a*) his proper development is being avoidably prevented or neglected or his health is being avoidably impaired or neglected or he is being ill-treated;

---

[17] *Cf.* s. 61 of the C. & Y.P. Act 1933, *supra.*
[18] (1965) Cmnd. 2742.
[19] (1968) Cmnd. 3601.
[20] *Post*, Chapter 3.
[1] *Post*, Chapter 5.
[2] But see *post*, p. 29, for the "offence" condition.

22

or (*b*) it is probable that the condition set out in the preceding paragraph will be satisfied in his case, having regard to the fact that the court or another court has found that that condition is or was satisfied in the case of another child or young person who is or was a member of the household to which he belongs;

or (*c*) he is exposed to moral danger;

or (*d*) he is beyond the control of his parent or guardian;

or (*e*) he is of compulsory school age within the meaning of the Education Act 1944 and is not receiving efficient full-time education suitable to his age, ability and aptitude;

or (*f*) he is guilty of an offence, excluding homicide,

and also he is in need of care or control which he is unlikely to receive unless the court makes an order under s. 1 in respect of him. Care includes protection and guidance; control includes discipline.[3]

The Six Conditions

The condition relating to guilt of an offence is considered below[4] and that concerned with lack of education in a later chapter.[5] The remainder incorporate the essentials of the former law,[6] but that offers little guidance on the likely interpretation of the new provisions, since it itself was rarely subjected to interpretation by the superior courts.

The condition contained in sub-para. (*a*) is clearly in very wide terms. It covers, for example, both physical and mental health and development, and it is enough to show some impairment or neglect, whereas s. 2 of the Act of 1963 referred to "unnecessary suffering" or serious consequences to health or development. On the other hand, s. 1 of the present Act does call for proof of actual impairment or neglect, while the earlier enactment needed only proof of the likelihood of suffering or injury, although it is doubtful to what extent in practice juvenile courts were willing to act on that alone.

In one respect sub-para. (*b*) is too restrictive in that the condition therein must be satisfied with regard to another *juvenile*,

[3] C. & Y.P. Act 1969, s. 70(1).
[4] *Post*, p. 29.
[5] Chapter 13.
[6] C. & Y.P. Act 1963, s. 2, *supra*, p. 21.

but there could be occasions when neglect or ill-treatment of an older member of the household (*e.g.*, a twenty year old son who is mentally infirm) could equally lead to the probability of the condition being satisfied in relation to the juvenile who is before the court.[7] The words "was satisfied" in the paragraph cover the case of a person who has ceased to be a juvenile or who has died.

Cases of those offences of a violent or sexual nature affecting juveniles, which the old law specifically marked out,[8] may, according to the circumstances, fall under one or more of sub-paragraphs (*a*), (*b*) or (*c*) and those where juveniles are "falling into bad associations" under any of the six sub-paragraphs, but most likely under (*a*) or (*c*). If there has been a conviction, that fact is admissible evidence and, in the absence of rebuttal, is proof that the convicted person committed the offence.[9] But difficulties may arise where there has not yet been a prosecution, and it has been suggested[10] that in order to avoid the risk of inconsistent findings "magistrates should decline to entertain applications which would lead to concurrent jurisdiction in different courts". Until the criminal case is heard the juvenile court can make interim orders[11] to protect the child.

Sub-para. (*d*) is also potentially wide in view of the definition of a guardian for the purposes of the Children and Young Young Persons Acts.[12] The term is not limited to a person so appointed by law, but includes anyone who for the time being has the charge of or control over the juvenile. The definition is particularly important in relation to the putative father, because the term "parent" is not for present purposes defined, so that the common law presumption excluding him from it applies,[13] although possibly he may be treated as a parent if he has custody under an order of a court.[14]

The Need for Care or Control

The additional requirement that there is a need for care or

[7] The court must consider the probability on the assumption that no order is going to be made (s. 2(7)).
[8] C. & Y.P. Act 1933, Sched. I, which is still operative for other purposes.
[9] Civil Evidence Act 1968, s. 11.
[10] Clarke Hall and Morrison on *Children*, 8th edn., 131, 132.
[11] See *post*, Chapter 5.
[12] C. & Y.P. Act 1933, s. 107(1); C. & Y.P. Act 1969, s. 70(1).
[13] *Re M. (An Infant)*, [1955] 2 Q.B. 479; [1955] 2 All E.R. 911.
[14] Holden, *Child Legislation* 1969, p. 108.

control which the juvenile is unlikely to receive unless an order is made lays down an objective test. That was the nature of the test in s. 2 of the Children and Young Persons Act 1963, under which it had to be shown that the juvenile was "not receiving such care, protection and guidance as a good parent may reasonably be expected to give", but that provision was capable of creating a difficulty which the present one avoids, namely, in the case where a parent in good faith does not obtain medical treatment for his child. His conduct may have been prompted by a genuine belief that the child's welfare was best served without such treatment (*e.g.*, a belief in spiritual healing). That would not necessarily relieve him of criminal liability, but that is due to a narrow interpretation of the relevant statute.[15] It could still have been argued however, under the former law that he was a "good parent", so that the court would not have been entitled to intervene.[16] A more general objection to the former enactment was that it "directed attention solely to the quality of parental care", whereas s. 1 of the 1969 Act makes the quality of parental care, protection and guidance an important but not conclusive factor in deciding whether to make an order.[17]

Proof of one or more of the six conditions will be at least presumptive evidence that the child needs care or control, but, since the conditions refer to past or present circumstances whereas the question of the need for care or control necessarily also involves future considerations, the court may and should call for wider evidence. However, where the evidence is sufficient to satisfy the condition in sub-para. (*d*), little, if any, further evidence will normally be needed or, indeed, be avail-

[15] See *post*, Chapter 6.
[16] In the case where the parent refuses consent to a life-saving operation the Ministry of Health and the Home Office have advised that hospital authorities should "rely on the clinical judgment of the consultants concerned after full discussion with the parents". Care proceedings should not be instituted with a view to a care order being made and the consent of the local authority being obtained. There are obvious practical objections to that procedure, since an order may not be made in time, but it is submitted that there are not, as the Ministry suggests, legal difficulties, since the effect of a care order is that the local authority assumes almost all parental powers including that of giving assent to medical operations upon juveniles under 16. (See Ministry of Health Circular F/P9/1B dated April 14, 1967, and Home Office Circular No. 63 (1968)).
[17] See Home Office Guide on Part I of the Act, para. 25. Watson, *The Juvenile Court*–1970 *Onward*, p. 8.

able, to satisfy the additional test; but occasionally this may not be so. For example, if the father is temporarily living away from the home and the child is meanwhile beyond his mother's control, it might be possible to show that on his father's imminent return he will be likely to "receive" control without any order having to be made.

III. THE OFFENCE CONDITION

The Emergence of Care Jurisdiction Over Juvenile Offenders

From the fourteenth century, if not earlier, the common law gradually accepted the principle that children of tender years should not be the subject of criminal liability. Initially, no minimum age was prescribed, but eventually it came to be established at seven years. The precise origin of this fixed rule has not been traced, but Hale stated it to be the law[18] and it was not subsequently questioned. It remained unaltered until the Children and Young Persons Act 1933[19] raised the age to 8 and then the Children and Young Persons Act 1963[20] further raised it to the present minimum of 10. Though a rule of substantive law, it is one of those which are unhappily described in the form of irrebuttable presumptions.[1]

It was also accepted by the common law that a rebuttable presumption of innocence applied in respect of children between 7 and 14.[2] Subject to the statutory increase of the minimum age, this presumption still operates. A child over 10 but under 14 is in law not capable of committing a crime unless it is proved that at the time of the act he knew that it was wrong. The scope of the presumption is considered later.[3]

The *raison d'être* of these rules of absolute protection from criminal responsibility and presumption of inability to commit a crime lay in the desire to avoid the infliction of punishment on children. This view prevailed whether punishment was regarded as deterrent or retributive. However, after the institu-

---

[18] I P.C., 27-28.   [19] Section 50.   [20] Section 16(1).

[1] Section 50, as amended by s. 16, states: "It shall be conclusively presumed that no child under the age of 10 years can be guilty of any offence."

[2] Here, too, the upper age limit was not firmly laid down until the 17th century when Hale (I P.C., 22 *et seq.*) following Coke (Littleton, §. 405, f. 247 b) accepted 14 as the "age of discretion".

[3] See *post* p. 33.

tion of juvenile courts and especially following the Children and Young Persons Act 1933 and the Criminal Justice Act 1948, the reformative powers of those courts over juvenile offenders were considerably widened, with correspondingly less emphasis being placed on their punitive powers. Consequently, the lower the minimum age of criminal responsibility and the greater the insistence on the presumption of innocence the more restricted the court has been in its ability to invoke its powers of correction and treatment, since the establishment of the child's guilt is a prerequisite to the exercise of those powers if the court is relying on its criminal jurisdiction. In some cases the difficulty has been obviated by invoking the civil jurisdiction, since a child who commits an act which, if done by an adult or young person, would render him criminally liable, very often does so as the result of his needing care or control. But this depends upon the attitude of those who are responsible for instituting proceedings. The more radical reform which would raise the minimum age of criminal responsibility and simultaneously bring more juvenile offenders under the care or control procedure has long been advocated. Its acceptance, however, is proving to be a slow process.

It was the Committee on the Treatment of Young Offenders which in this country first focused public attention on the problem by pointing out that there was "little or no difference in character and needs between the neglected and the delinquent child".[4] But the Committee rejected proposals for abolishing criminal jurisdiction over children up to the age of 14, partly because the child offender should be made conscious of his wrong doing. Instead, it contemplated reform along the lines of new methods of treatment.[5]

The proposals of the Ingleby Committee were more far-reaching. It recommended an increase in the minimum age of criminal responsibility, initially to 12 (with the possibility of a further increase to 13 or 14) and the abolition of the presumption of innocence, so that all children of and over that age would be fully responsible for their criminal acts. But these

---

[4] (1927) Cmnd. 2831, especially at pp. 17-20. See also Clarke Hall, *Children's Courts*, (1926), pp. 55 *et seq.*

[5] It was for this reason that the Committee recommended the abolition of the distinction between Reformatory Schools and Industrial Schools, a proposal which the C. & Y.P. Acts 1932 and 1933 adopted by creating Approved Schools.

changes were to depend on a fundamental change in the jurisdiction and procedure of the juvenile court.[6] It "should get still further away from the conceptions of criminal jurisdiction, while keeping as far as practicable the sanctions and methods of treatment at present available".[7] There should be "a special jurisdiction designed for the particular purpose and not a modified version of something that is essentially meant for adults".[8] Accordingly, it was recommended that the jurisdiction over children in need of care or control be widened to include a child under 12 who commits an act which would render a person over that age liable to be found guilty of an offence, and that a new procedure for exercising the jurisdiction be introduced with wider powers to deal with children in need of protection or discipline.

None of these proposals was implemented by the Children and Young Persons Act 1963,[9] but the Government in its White Paper, *The Child, the Family and the Young Offender*[10] introduced fresh proposals. In one respect these followed basically the same line as those of the Ingleby Committee in that it was recommended that juvenile offenders under 16 should be removed from the sanctions of the criminal law and dealt with as needing care or control. Like that Committee the White Paper also saw the need for greater emphasis on supportive and preventive social work, but it was the radical methods which it recommended to achieve these objects that were questioned. A major proposal would have abolished the juvenile courts,[11] replacing them with "family councils" and "family courts". To the former could be brought all juveniles under 16 who had committed what would in an older person be an offence or who were in need of care or control, and, after social inquiries had been made, the family council[12] would discuss with the parents the most suitable method of dealing

[6] Cmnd. 1191, paras. 78-94.
[7] *Ibid.*, para. 77.
[8] Para. 83.
[9] The only relevant change was to raise the minimum age of criminal responsibility from 8 to 10; see *supra*.
[10] (1965) Cmnd. 2742.
[11] The Ingleby Committee (paras. 67-77) considered this possibility but rejected it.
[12] A number of family councils would be appointed for each local authority area, with each consisting of social workers of the children's service and others with understanding and experience of children.

with the child. If agreement could not be reached, the matter would then have to be referred to a family court for determination, the court being a special magistrates' court constituted from panels of justices selected for their capacity to deal with juveniles.

So vehement was the criticism generated by the White Paper, especially among magistrates, that its proposals were dropped and fresh ones put forward in a new White Paper, *Children in Trouble*.[13] These had the same fundamental objective of keeping children so far as possible out of court, but, as a compromise, offered different methods of achieving it. They abandoned the idea of the family council, preferring young offenders and those needing care and control alike to be dealt with informally by social workers within the family, with the parents being helped and encouraged to fulfil their responsibilities.[14] If, however, after consultation it was thought necessary to bring the offender before the court, this should be done on the basis that he was deprived, not depraved. Criminal proceedings against persons under 14 should therefore be abolished (except in cases of homicide) and child offenders should be treated as being in need of care or control. Young persons should normally be treated in the same way, but criminal proceedings could be instituted against them in certain defined circumstances for serious offences. These, like other fundamental changes proposed, should be introduced gradually over a period of years as and when sufficient staff and resources became available. How far has the Children and Young Persons Act 1969 implemented them?

The Scope of the Offence Condition

Care proceedings may be brought in respect of an offender if, as with each of the other conditions in s. 1(2) of the Act, a double test is satisfied. It must be proved not only that the juvenile has committed an offence but also that he needs care or control which he is unlikely to receive unless the court makes an order.

As for the former, the rules relating to the age of criminal responsibility apply as they do where there are criminal pro-

[13] (1968) Cmnd. 3601. For the main objections to the earlier proposals see Stone, *Children Without A Satisfactory Home – A Gap Family Law Must Fill*, (1970) 33 M.L.R. 649, 652.
[14] On this aspect of the new law see *post*, Chapter 3.

ceedings[15] and the general safeguards against liability provided by the criminal law are also extended to the condition[16]. Thus, in accordance with the principles of *autrefois acquit* or *autrefois convict*, no account shall be taken of an alleged offence which was the subject of earlier criminal proceedings, and by analogy no reliance can be placed on it if it was alleged in previous care proceedings based on the offence condition.[17] Conversely, a person cannot be charged with an offence which was alleged in care proceedings in order to satisfy that condition.[18] If the offence is a summary one, the time limit of six months on prosecution for such an offence[19] is extended to the care proceedings.[20] Section 3 of the 1969 Act also provides that the burden of proof is the same as in criminal proceedings, which means a heavier burden than that required to establish any of the other conditions in s. 1 of the Act.

The above restrictions only operate, however, for the purpose of determining whether the offence condition is satisfied. They do not restrict the admissibility of evidence of an offence, which was the subject of earlier proceedings, for the purpose of proving any other condition in s. 1 (*e.g.*, that the juvenile is exposed to moral danger) or that there is need for care or control.[1]

The additional test relating to care or control has raised a storm of criticism in some quarters on the ground, *inter alia*, that it discriminates against the offender who comes from an unsatisfactory home and in favour of one from a more secure background, since the latter is likely to be able to receive the care or control of which the former may well be deprived. The argument is *prima facie* attractive, bearing in mind especially the extensive powers of the local authority once a care order

[15] See *infra*, p. 33.   [16] By s. 3(1) to (3) of the 1969 Act.

[17] See s.3(1) paras. (c) and (a) respectively.

Although the subsection does not expressly so provide, it is submitted that if the offence had earlier been alleged to try to prove a condition other than the offence condition, *e.g.*, that the juvenile was exposed to moral danger, it ought similarly not to be admissible in later proceedings to satisfy the offence condition.

[18] Section 3(4).

[19] See Magistrates' Courts Act 1952, s. 104.

[20] C. & Y.P. Act 1969, s. 3(1) (b).

[1] *Ibid.*, sub.-s. (2). But see Clarke Hall and Morrison, *op. cit.*, 140, who warn that "great care must be taken to avoid hearing any evidence on this point which would not be admissible in relation to the offence, until that condition is found to be satisfied".

has been made. But the argument ignores the spirit of the legislation, which is to bring before the courts, and then to help, only those juveniles who are in fact in trouble through lack of care or control. If the powers which the Act confers are too wide, the remedy lies in modifying them and in providing further safeguards against abuse, not in depriving juveniles of their benefits.[2]

Children as Offenders

Having resisted the pressures to raise the minimum age of criminal capacity above 10, the Act accepts the principle that criminal proceedings against offenders between that age and 14 should be abolished and that such persons should be subject only to care proceedings, primarily by virtue of the offence condition but possibly under one of the others. Section 4 therefore provides that a person shall not be charged with an offence, except homicide, by reason of anything done or omitted while he was a child. However, the section is to be brought into operation only gradually, through orders prescribing from time to time the minimum age for instituting criminal proceedings.[3] No order has yet been made, and, until the section becomes wholly operative, the effect of the Act is to produce an uncertain compromise and to make care proceedings and criminal proceedings alternative procedures where a child between 10 (or whatever higher age may later from time to time be specified) and 14 is alleged to have committed an offence. The need for consultation among those involved in bringing children before the court, which is a salient feature of the new legislation, is therefore vitally important. The present dichotomy should further encourage the use of cautioning offenders,[4] but, if proceedings are thought to be necessary, the following factors should especially be borne in mind in deciding

[2] For a summary of the opposing views as to the need for a double test where care proceedings are based on the offence condition see Watson, *op. cit.*, pp. 9-15. See also Stone, (1970) 33 M.L.R. at p. 657.
[3] Orders are to be made by the Secretary of State, but any specifying a minimum age above 12 requires an affirmative resolution of both Houses of Parliament; see s. 34(1) (4) and (7). The present Government's intention is not to make any orders until satisfied that local authorities have sufficient care facilities to cope with the change.
[4] In 1967 no less than 17,000 out of 47,000 offenders aged between 10 and 14, and 13,000 out of 73,000 between 13 and 17, were cautioned with no further steps being taken against them.

whether to invoke the care jurisdiction or the criminal jurisdiction, *viz.*, (1) the additional methods of dealing with the child if reliance is placed on the latter jurisdiction;[5] (2) the seriousness of the offence;[6] and (3) the likelihood of proving the offence, since, if there is real doubt on this but there is evidence of disturbed family circumstances, it would be wiser to rely on the care jurisdiction, alleging in the alternative the offence condition and another appropriate condition on which that jurisdiction might be based.

Young Persons as Offenders

Section 5 of the Act does not abolish, but imposes severe restrictions on, criminal proceedings against the offender who is a young person. But the section is not likely to be brought into force for some years[7] and, until it is, care proceedings and criminal proceedings will be alternative procedures as they now are where a child is an alleged offender.

When the section does begin to operate it will mean that private prosecutions of young persons will not be permitted. The only persons who will be able to lay an information against a young person will be "qualified informants", *i.e.*, a servant of the Crown, a police officer, a member of certain other designated police forces (such as the British Transport Police), a local authority or any body designated by the Home Secretary as a public body for the purpose.[8] The Act also preserves the power for a person to lay an information with the consent of the Attorney-General or the Director of Public Prosecutions.

The right of the qualified informant to prosecute will be strictly limited. He will be allowed to do so only if he is of the opinion that the case is of a description which comes within Regulations to be made by the Home Secretary[9] and that it

---

[5] See *post*, Chapter 4.
[6] Recent research shows that most offences committed by juveniles are not very serious; see D. J. West, *The Young Offender* (1967).
[7] Except for sub-ss. (8) and (9), see *post*, Chapter 3, p. 52.
   The Act (s. 34(1) (b)) enables s. 5. to be introduced piecemeal to apply to young persons below the maximum age, *e.g.*, to those under 16. Moreover, until s. 4 becomes fully operative, s. 5 may be extended to children outside s. 4; for example, if an order were to prescribe a maximum age of 12 for the purpose of s. 4, s. 5 could be made to apply to 13-year-olds.
[8] Likely bodies are the Post Office and certain Government Departments such as Customs and Excise.
[9] If and when Regulations are made, they are likely to be on the lines laid down in the White Paper, *Children in Trouble*, Appendix A, para. 2(1).

would not be adequate for the case to be dealt with either (1) outside the court by a parent, teacher or other person or by a police caution or by the local authority or a body such as the National Society for the Prevention of Cruelty to Children or (2) in the court by way of care proceedings. Before coming to a decision he must tell the appropriate local authority[10] that a prosecution is being considered and must give the authority an opportunity to state their views on the case, unless he considers such steps are not essential, as, for example, where the offence is a serious one.[11] Usually the informant will be a police officer and one of the main objects of s. 5 is to give, what previous legislation has never done, statutory guidance to the police on the criteria they should follow when deciding whether to prosecute young persons. One of its defects is its failure to impose a time limit for consultation between the police and the authority, so as to avoid the possibility of delay in prosecution.

B. CRIMINAL PROCEEDINGS

I. THE CRIMINAL RESPONSIBILITY OF CHILDREN

Presumption of Innocence

The limits of the criminal liability of children have already been briefly noted.[12] One consequence of the rule prescribing 10 as the minimum age of criminal capacity[13] is that a child under that age who commits conduct which in an older person would constitute an offence can be brought before the juvenile court only under care proceedings.[14] If he is between 10 and 14,

---

[10] This means the local authority for the area in which it appears to the informant that the young person resides or, if there is apparently no residence, the local authority in whose area the relevant offence is alleged to have been committed (s. 5(9)).

[11] The C. & Y.P. Bill as originally drafted required the consent of a juvenile court magistrate for the prosecution of young persons, but professional opinion was so sharply divided that the requirement was withdrawn from the Bill and the discretion to prosecute left with the police; see Watson, *op. cit.*, pp. 17-18.

[12] *Ante,* p. 26.

[13] C. & Y.P. Act 1933, s. 50, as amended by C. & Y.P. Act 1963, s. 16(1)

[14] Another consequence of the rule is that anyone who arrests a child under 10 for what in a person over that age would be an alleged arrestable offence (as defined by the Criminal Law Act 1967, s. 2) may render himself liable to an action by the child for false imprisonment; see *Marsh* v. *Loader* (1863), 14 C.B. N.S. 535. Damages are not likely to be more than nominal, but this is not necessarily so. In *Marsh* v. *Loader* the court declined to upset a jury's award of £20 damages.

he is presumed not to have the capacity, unless it is proved that at the time of the act he knew that it was wrong.[15] But, in addition to proof of knowledge, it must, of course, be shown that the child had *mens rea*.[16] The point tends to be overlooked when stating the presumption, but is particularly relevant in cases of homicide where it sometimes happens that a child charged with murder is convicted of manslaughter because of the absence of "malice aforethought". A child may, for example, know that it is wrong to use violence on another, but he may not be expected, in the absence of further evidence, to have foreseen that death would or might be caused by his conduct,[17] whereas the foresight might be attributed, without further evidence, to an adult or young person acting in similar circumstances.

The presumption is undoubtedly anachronistic, its scope uncertain and its application variable.[18] In the juvenile courts it is often given little attention; indeed, possibly in the majority of courts. Its operation is, however, significant in the case of the child who, because he is charged with homicide or because he has been committed for trial jointly with an adult charged with an indictable offence,[19] is being tried by a jury. Then, again, there are some doubts about the nature of the knowledge needed to rebut the presumption. This matter has never been fully analysed by the courts, but it is now commonly accepted by commentators, particularly since the decision

---

[15] The presumption has been stated in this form since the first half of the 19th century (*R.* v. *Owen* (1830), 4 C. & P. 236; *R.* v. *Manley* (1844), 1 Cox C.C. 104; *R.* v. *Smith* (1845), 5 L.T. O.S. 393); but it is also commonly described in the terms that the child is presumed to be *doli incapax*. This latter form of stating it has been criticised on the ground that the child may act with a mental state involving *dolus* (fraud or intention) without necessarily knowing that his act is wrong; see Williams, *Criminal Law: The General Part*, 2nd edn., p. 815, n. (8) where other ways of expressing the rule are criticised because they do not necessarily import the need for knowledge of wrongness.

[16] If the offence is one which, in the case of an adult, does not require proof of *mens rea*, it is apparently still necessary in the case of a child to prove that he knew his act was wrong; see Howard, *Strict Responsibility*, p. 192.

[17] *R.* v. *Vamplew* (1862), 3 F. & F. 520.

[18] For its history see Kean, 53 L.Q.R. 364. Stephen, *History of the Criminal Law of England*, ii, 98, did not take kindly to it: "the rule is practically inoperative, or at all events operates seldom and capriciously".

One of its chief modern critics has been Professor Glanville Williams, and much that follows in the present section embodies his basic comments and criticisms; see *Criminal Law: The General Part*, 2nd edn., pp. 814–821 and [1954] Crim. L.R. 493.   [19] See *post*, p. 41.

in *R.* v. *Windle*,[20] that the child's knowledge that his act was legally wrong, that it would excite the attention of a policeman, is a sufficient rebuttal, even though there was no knowledge that the act was morally wrong. So, a 10-year-old boy who shoplifts while looking over his shoulder for any shop-walker but who does so because he believes that he is morally justified in so acting in order to provide the necessities of life for his widowed mother will be held to be guilty. But, alternatively, is it enough to prove that a child knew that his act was morally wrong, even though unaware of its legal wrongness?[1] Certainly, some earlier statements about the presumption infer knowledge of a moral wrong. Thus, Hale in speaking of the need for proof of "mischievous discretion" insisted that it must be proof that the child could "discern between good and evil".[2] In *R.* v. *Gorrie*[3] it was said that he must know that his act was "gravely wrong, seriously wrong", and it has been suggested[4] that this test contemplates moral and not legal knowledge, since a child may be able to classify moral wrongs according to their seriousness but can scarcely be expected to distinguish crimes according to their gravity. "The most he knows of the law is whether the policeman will or will not take him to court for it".[4] Although the matter is not wholly free from uncertainty, it is, with respect, suggested that the law has been accurately stated in the following terms:[5]

> "Proof that the child knew that the act was against the law – he would not have done it if a policeman had been watching – is undoubtedly sufficient; but it also seems clear that knowledge of legal wrongness is not necessary, if the child knew that the act was morally wrong".

The rules as to the kind and amount of evidence needed to establish the requisite knowledge are also to some extent

---

[20] [1952] 2 Q.B. 826 (C.C.A.); [1952] 2 All E.R. 1. The case established the rule that, for the purpose of the M'Naghten rules as a defence to a criminal charge, "wrong" means legal wrong.
[1] When, prior to *Williams* v. *Williams*, [1964] A.C. 698; (H.L.); [1963] 2 All E.R. 994, the M'Naghten rules were a complete defence to a charge of matrimonial cruelty, it was held that for that purpose "wrong" could include not only that which was punishable by law but also what was morally culpable; see *Sofaer* v. *Sofaer*, [1960] 3 All E.R. 468; [1960] 1 W.L.R. 1173.
[2] 1 P.C. 26. Similarly Plowden, 1, 19 n. (f) and Blackstone, *Commentaries*, iv, 23.   [3] (1918), 83 J.P. 136.
[4] *R.* v. *Williams*, [1954] Crim. L.R. at p. 494.
[5] Smith and Hogan, *Criminal Law*, 2nd edn., p. 112.

uncertain and unsatisfactory.[6] The courts have spoken of the evidence having to be "strong and pregnant" or "clear and beyond all probability of doubt", but such criteria seem to be ignored, except that the younger the child and (or) the more serious the offence the stronger must be the rebutting evidence. What is certain is that the prosecution must adduce some evidence that the child knew he was doing wrong: mere proof that he committed the act is not enough.[7] But a plea of guilty by the child may be held sufficient to rebut the presumption.[8] So, too, may be the evidence of a police officer that the child admitted the offence under interrogation.[9] Another form of evidence which the court is ready to admit is that of the child's home background. In *B. v. R.*[10] evidence that a boy, aged just under 9, came from a respectable family, had been properly brought up and was generally well behaved was held sufficient to prove that he knew that house-breaking and theft were wrong, and in *F. v. Padwick*[11] the Divisional Court went further by emphasising the general desirability of admitting evidence of the child's home background "and all his circumstances",[12] even at the risk of disclosing information highly prejudicial to him. Wide though this discretion is, it does not, it is submitted, allow the admissibility of evidence of every previous finding of guilt. It would have to be shown that the earlier finding was in respect of an offence of the same kind as that now charged, and even then the evidence would have to comply with the general rules concerning the admissibility of similar fact evidence.[13] These considerations are relevant where the question of admissibility of evidence of family and other circumstances relate to rebuttal of the presumption of innocence, but they do not affect the admissibility of such

---

[6] On the practical difficulty of attributing to a child knowledge of wrongness see Cavenagh, *Juvenile Courts, the Child and the Law*, pp. 149-152.

[7] *R. v. Kershaw* (1902), 18 T.L.R. 357.

[8] *R. v. Thomas* (1947), 111 J.P. 669.

[9] *W. (An Infant) v. Simpson*, [1967] Crim. L.R. 360.

[10] (1960), 44 Cr. App. Rep. 1; *sub nom. X. v. X.*, [1958] Crim. L.R. 805. This case was, of course, decided when the minimum age of criminal responsibility was 8.

[11] [1959] Crim. L.R. 439.

[12] But the demeanour of the child and his parent in court, if it is a matter of evidence (which is doubtful), is of very little weight in rebutting the presumption; see *ex parte N.*, [1959] Crim. L.R. 523.

[13] For these rules see *Makin v. A.-G. of N.S.W.*, [1894] A.C. 57, (P.C.); [1891-94] All E.R. Rep. 24; and treatises on the law of evidence.

evidence in care proceedings to prove the need for care or control or in those proceedings or criminal proceedings to assist the court in deciding upon the appropriate method of dealing with the juvenile.

Sexual Offences

A boy under the age of 14 cannot be found guilty of committing rape[14] or of assault with intent to commit rape[15] or of offences involving carnal knowledge;[16] and it is not certain whether he can be held guilty of an attempt to commit any of these offences.[17] In spite of the fact that these rules rest on the principle of physical impossibility, no evidence is admissible to prove that the particular boy had attained puberty before the age of 14[18] and that the act did take place.[19] However, he can be convicted of indecent assault[20] or of common assault[1] and while these two offences are less serious than some of the above from the point of view of punishment of an adult offender, the distinction is of minimal significance in relation to the boy under 14. It may be relevant to any future record of his previous convictions,[2] but otherwise it would not matter

---

[14] *R.* v. *Groombridge* (1836), 7 C. & P. 582; *R.* v. *Brimilow* (1840), 2 Mood. C.C. 122.

[15] *R.* v. *Eldershaw* (1828), 3 C. & P. 396; *R.* v. *Philips* (1839), 8 C. & P. 736.

[16] For example, unlawful sexual intercourse with a girl under 13; *R.* v. *Jordan and Cowmeadow* (1839), 9 C. & P. 118; *R.* v. *Waite*, [1892] 2 Q.B. 600 (C.C.R.).

So far as it concerns rape the rule is an old one; see Hale, 1 P.C. 630.

[17] See the conflicting dicta in *R.* v. *Williams*, [1893] 1 Q.B. 320 (C.C.R.). Smith and Hogan, *op. cit.*, p. 294, persuasively suggest that "in principle he should not be so convicted, for, if he completes the act, it is not a crime", and cite in support the cases which decide that a boy under 14 cannot be convicted of an assault with intent to commit rape.

[18] *R.* v. *Jordan and Cowmeadow*, *supra*; *R.* v. *Philips*, *supra*.

[19] *Cp. R.* v. *Brimilow*, *supra*, where the report speaks of the "commission of the act [being] proved".   [20] *R.* v. *Williams*, *supra*.

[1] *R.* v. *Philips*, *supra*; *R.* v. *Brimilow*, *supra*.

[2] Even in this respect its importance has been much diminished by the C. & Y.P. Act 1963, s. 16(2), which provides that in any criminal proceedings against a person over the age of 21, any offence of which he was found guilty while under 14 is to be disregarded for the purposes of any evidence relating to his previous convictions, and he cannot be asked or compelled to answer any question relating to such an offence. The finding of guilt of that offence should be included in the proof of evidence of the police officer when in the later proceedings he gives evidence of the offender's antecedents; but the finding must not be included in the factual statement of previous convictions and findings of guilt which is attached to the proof of evidence; see *Practice Direction* of the Court of Criminal Appeal, [1966] 2 All E.R. 929.

whether he was charged with, for example, rape, if that were possible, or with indecent assault. If he could be charged with the former it would still be the juvenile court who heard the case and their powers of dealing with him would be the same as if he were found guilty of assault.

There is, however, nothing in the above rules to prevent a boy under 14 from being found guilty as an aider and abetter if he assists another to commit rape[3] or, *semble*, any of the other offences which he himself cannot in law commit.

How far he can be liable for buggery is by no means clear. It is commonly stated that he cannot, either as agent or patient. There is no direct authority for the view that he cannot be liable as an agent, but his exemption is usually said to rest on the same conclusive presumption of physical incapacity as exempts him from liability for rape and other offences involving unlawful sexual intercourse.[4] As for non-liability where he is the patient, the Court of Criminal Appeal in *R. v. Tatam*[5] had no doubt that "he was unable at law to commit [the] offence", but offered no reason for its conclusion. There is a conflict of authority and opinion[6] as to whether he can abet buggery. The point arose in *Tatam* and in *R. v. Cratchley*[7] in relation to the question of the need for corroboration of the boy's evidence. In *Cratchley* a 10-year-old boy was told to keep a look-out while the accused, an adult, committed buggery upon a 13-year-old boy. The Court of Criminal Appeal held that he was not an accomplice but this was on the ground that there was no evidence of his having guilty knowledge, and it is clear that it recognised that, with such evidence, he could have been liable. But in *Tatam* the Court held that three boys under 14 were not accomplices to buggery committed upon themselves. These cases must either be regarded as in conflict or distinguishable on the ground that in the one the patient was a third person and in the other the boys themselves.[8] It

---

[3] *R. v. Eldershaw, supra* [obiter]; *cf. R. v. Ram* (1893), 17 Cox C.C. 609, [a woman can be convicted of abetting rape].
[4] But if he in fact performs the act and the pathic is an adult, the latter can be convicted; *R. v. Allen* (1848), 1 Den. 364.
[5] (1921), 15 Cr. App. Rep. 132.
[6] *Cf.* Hogan, [1962] Crim. L.R. 683, and Glanville Williams, [1964] Crim. L.R. 686.   [7] (1913), 9 Cr. App. Rep. 232.
[8] But the distinction is tenable only if it is assumed that in *Tatam* none of the boys abetted the buggery of another; see Smith and Hogan, *op. cit.*, p. 321, n. 9.

can at least be said in favour of *Cratchley* that it is logically consistent with the rule relating to rape that a boy under 14 can abet that offence even though he cannot in law himself commit it. On the other hand, although current opinion increasingly recognises that protection of the child should be a basic feature of the law, it is not possible to explain *Tatam* on the ground that, in relation to the young boy, the sole object of the law relating to buggery is to protect him and not to render him criminally liable for offences committed upon himself.[9] There is no such suggestion in the judgment, which was based simply on the principle that since the boy cannot commit the offence he cannot be an accomplice. It seems that his total exemption from liability as a patient has arisen from a mis-interpretation of what was written by Coke, Hale and East on the subject.[10] All that they seem to have said is that there was no liability without proof of mischievous discretion: in other words, that the normal presumption of innocence should operate if the boy was between the minimum age of criminal responsibility and 14.

But the question arises: even as the law stands, need the juvenile court really concern itself with these uncertainties and niceties of distinction? It clearly need not, because, as we have seen,[11] its care jurisdiction, apart from that part of it which is based on the offence condition, is sufficiently comprehensive to include all cases where a child has been a party to an act of buggery, whether as agent or patient or look-out.

II. THE SCOPE OF THE CRIMINAL JURISDICTION

Since the creation of the juvenile court it has, with two slight qualifications,[12] been consistently recognised that adult[13]

---

[9] *Cf.* the rule which prevents a girl under 16 who consents to a male having unlawful sexual intercourse with her from being liable for abet-ting or inciting the particular sexual offence because the statute (formerly the Criminal Law Amendment Act 1885, s. 5, now the Sexual Offences Act 1956, s. 6) is designed to protect her from such conduct; see *R. v. Tyrrell*, [1894] 1 Q.B. 710 (C.C.R.); [1891-4] All E.R. Rep. 1215.

[10] See respectively 3 Inst. 59; 1 P.C. 670 and 1 P.C. 480, and see Smith and Hogan, *op. cit.*, p. 321.

[11] *Ante*, p. 24.

[12] C. & Y.P. Act 1933, s. 48(1) and (2), *post*, pp. 47 and 49 n. 3.

[13] For the purpose of the jurisdiction of the juvenile court the term "adult" is here used to mean a person who has attained the age of 17 years.

offenders are to be excluded from its jurisdiction;[14] but the principle that that court alone should deal with juveniles has required some modification, partly in order to meet the case where a juvenile and adult are jointly involved in the commission of an offence and partly in the past because of an unwillingness to abolish the young person's right of election to trial by jury.

In practice that right was seldom exercised; when it was, it was usually on the advice of a parent or solicitor. It was therefore represented to the Ingleby Committee that the right should be abolished as it had been in respect of children by the Children and Young Persons Act 1933,[15] but the Committee, while acknowledging that abolition would not cause great hardship, thought it would have little effect.[16] The principal argument in favour of abolition was that by retaining the right the young person would be deprived of the specially qualified experience which the court had in dealing with persons of that age, but against that it was argued that the principle of exclusive jurisdiction over young persons had in any event been qualified where there were joint charges and there seemed no overriding reason why a fundamental right like that of election for jury trial should not also be a recognised exception, particularly in view of the power of an adult court which finds a juvenile guilty to remit him to the juvenile court to be dealt with by that court.[17] The former view has finally prevailed in the Children and Young Persons Act 1969.

Leaving aside for the moment cases of joint charges, every child must be tried summarily by the juvenile court for all offences, summary and indictable; other than homicide for which he must always be committed for trial. Jurisdiction over summary offences rests on the fact that the court is by definition a court of summary jurisdiction.[18] That over indictable offences is now conferred by the 1969 Act.[19] The same rules apply to

---

[14] While generally approving this exclusion the Ingleby Committee was prepared to allow an exception to enable the court to deal with an adult who failed to secure his child's attendance at school; see Cmnd. 1191, para. 181.

[15] Following the recommendations of the Departmental Committee on the Treatment of Young Offenders, Cmnd. 2831, pp. 30-31.

[16] Cmnd. 1191, para. 239.

[17] See *infra*, p. 43.

[18] See C. & Y.P. Act 1933, s. 45; and see s. 46(1), *infra*.

[19] Section 6(1).

a young person, except that if he is charged with a serious indictable offence of the kind which, if he were convicted of it, would render him liable to be sentenced to be detained for a long period,[20] he must be committed for trial, provided that there is sufficient evidence to put him on trial.[1]

Joint Charges

Where a juvenile is charged jointly with an adult[2] and the offence charged is an indictable one, other than homicide, the magistrates' court must, if it considers it necessary in the interests of justice and there is sufficient evidence, commit them both for trial.[3] But the 1969 Act fails to deal with the case of a child who allegedly commits an offence with a young person and the offence is of the kind which, if the young person had alone committed it, the court would have committed him for trial.[4] Apparently in such a case there cannot be a joint charge and the child will have to be dealt with separately in the juvenile court. It seems strange that a child may be jointly committed for trial with an adult but not with a young person, even though the offence committed in the latter case may be very much more serious than the one committed with the adult.[5]

Section 46(1) of the Children and Young Persons Act 1933 establishes the general principle that the criminal jurisdiction over juvenile offenders is to be exercised by a juvenile court and not by any other court of summary jurisdiction, but the following exceptions to this principle are admitted so as to

[20] Under C. & Y.P. Act 1933, s. 53(2); see *post*, Chapter 4, p. 136.
[1] C. & Y.P. Act 1969, s. 6(1); and see sub.-sec. (2) which amends ss. 25 (1) and 18(1) of the Magistrates' Courts Act 1952 so as to abolish respectively in relation to young persons the right to claim trial by jury and the alternative procedures for trying "hybrid" offences (*i.e.*, those triable either on indictment or summarily in accordance with s. 18).
See *R. v. Coleshill Justices, ex parte Davies*, [1971] 3 All E.R. 929 [1971] 1 W.L.R. 1684, (D.C.), *infra*, n. 3.
[2] For meaning of adult in the present context see *supra*, p. 39, n. 13.
[3] C. & Y.P. Act 1969, s. 6(1). Where the offence is homicide both must be committed if there is *prima facie* evidence.
The juvenile court must be satisfied that there is sufficient evidence to put the juvenile on trial and therefore there cannot be committal under s. 1 of the Criminal Justice Act 1967 on the strength of written statements which have not been considered; *R. v. Coleshill Justices ex p. Davies; R. v. L. and W.*, [1971] Crim. L. R. 481.
[4] *Supra.*
[5] This anomaly can hardly be explained on the ground that s. 4 of the 1969 Act provides for the abolition of criminal proceedings for offences by children, since, as we have seen (*ante*, p. 31) the Act contemplates only the gradual implementation of the section.

enable an adult court to hear the charge. These exceptions occur where the juvenile is involved with an adult in the same or an allied offence. They are designed to keep the adult offender out of the juvenile court, but at the same time to avoid separate trials. The first exception is mandatory, the other permissive.

A charge made jointly against a juvenile and an adult must be heard by an adult court.[6] Such a court may hear a charge against a juvenile (1) if an adult is charged at the same time, with aiding or abetting the offence with which the juvenile is charged,[7] or (2) if, conversely the charge against the juvenile is one of aiding or abetting an offence with which an adult is charged at the same time,[8] or (3) where the offence with which he is charged arises out of circumstances which are the same as or connected with those giving rise to an offence with which an adult is charged at the same time,[9] for example, in a case where there are cross summonses for assault.

In addition to these cases where there are joint charges, the Children and Young Persons Act 1969 admits a further exception to the principle in s. 46(1) of the 1933 Act that criminal jurisdiction over juveniles must be exercised by a juvenile court. It arises where an adult court of summary jurisdiction, mistakenly assuming that a young person is 17 years of age or over, summons him to appear before the court and he pleads guilty by post under the Magistrates' Courts Act 1957. Any consequent order is valid and will not be invalidated on discovery of the true age.[10]

C. THE POWER TO REMIT JUVENILES TO JUVENILE COURTS

(a) Criminal Proceedings

While the effect of some of the above rules is to confer on adult courts jurisdiction over juvenile offenders,[11] the Children and Young Persons legislation does seek to ensure that normally such offenders are not deprived of the benefit of the special experience which juvenile courts have in dealing with

---

[6] Para. (a) of the proviso to s. 46(1).   [7] *Ibid.*, para. (b).
[8] C. & Y.P. Act 1963, s. 18, sub-para. (a).   [9] *Ibid.*, sub-para. (b).
[10] Sub-s. (1A) of s. 46 of the C. & Y.P. Act 1933, as added by C. & Y.P. Act 1969, s. 72(3) and Sched. 5, para. 4.
[11] See also Part D, *infra*.

persons like them. Accordingly, once the adult court has found the child or young person guilty of the offence,[12] it must remit the offender to a juvenile court "unless satisfied that it would be undesirable to do so". [13] The exception adopts a recommendation of the Ingleby Committee,[14] but it is difficult to justify and it gives no indication of what is to be regarded as undesirable. Would it, for example, be undesirable to remit because of the limited experience which the appropriate juvenile court has in dealing with the particular type of offender?

However the Children and Young Persons Act 1969 has now specified circumstances which are undesirable where the adult court is a magistrates' court and the offender is a young person or was a young person when the proceedings in question were begun.[15] The court must remit unless it decides to deal with the case by exercising its powers to make an order for absolute or conditional discharge, for the payment of a fine, damages or costs, for a recognisance to be entered into by the parent or guardian or for disqualification or endorsement under the Road Traffic Act 1972.[16] This provision applies also to children aged 10 or over so long as they remain liable to criminal prosecution.[17]

The case will be remitted to a juvenile court acting for the place where the offender was committed for trial, or, if he was not committed, to a juvenile court acting either for the same place as the remitting court or for the place where the offender habitually resides.[18] The juvenile court may then deal with him in any way in which it might have dealt with him if he had been tried and found guilty by that court, but apparently

[12] This excludes homicide, which, as already noted, is entirely outside the jurisdiction of a juvenile court.
[13] C. & Y.P. Act 1933, s. 56(1), as amended by C. & Y.P. Act 1963, s. 64 and Sched. III, para. 14(1) and by C. & Y.P. Act 1969, s. 72(3) and Sched. V, para. 6. [14] Cmnd. 1191, para. 176.
[15] For the time factor see Part D, *infra.*
[16] C. & Y.P. Act 1969, s. 7(8), as impliedly amended by the Road Traffic Act 1972.
[17] See C. & Y.P. Act 1969 (Transitional Modifications of Part I) Order 1970, S.I. 1970 No. 1882.
[18] The remitting court may remand him in custody or on bail until he is brought before the juvenile court (s. 56(3)).
There is no right of appeal against the order of remission; see C. & Y.P. Act 1933, s. 56(2)(a), as substituted by C. & Y.P. Act 1963, s. 64 and Sched. III, para. 14(2).

it may allow the juvenile to change a plea of guilty before the remitting court to one of not guilty.[19]

The remitting court must send to the juvenile court a certificate stating the nature of the offence, the fact that the offender has been found guilty and that an order for remission has been made. This is evidence on which the juvenile court can act[20] and there is no need to call witnesses to prove the offence. However, their appearance may sometimes be desirable to assist the court in deciding how best to deal with the particular offender.[1]

Before the Act of 1963 it was very uncertain whether one juvenile court could remit a case to another juvenile court. Section 56(1) of the 1933 Act is so amended as to make it clear that this is now possible,[2] but remission is entirely discretionary and not, as it is with an adult court, compulsory in the absence of special reasons. A likely instance is where the remitting juvenile court considers remission administratively convenient for the purpose of obtaining background information about the offender.

(b) Care Proceedings

Where a juvenile is brought before a court in care proceedings and it appears that he resides in a petty sessions area other than that for which the court acts, the court must, unless it dismisses the case, direct that he be brought before a juvenile court acting for the area in which he resides. In addition it must either make an interim order[3] and inform the other court of the remission or inform the local authority, in whose area the juvenile lives, of the case, whereupon the authority must bring him before the appropriate court within 21 days.[4] If, however, the care proceedings are based on the offence condition, the remitting court may first determine whether the condition is satisfied and any determination is binding on the court to which the case is remitted.[5]

---

[19] S. (*An Infant*) v. *Manchester City Recorder*, [1971] A.C. 481 (H.L.) [1969] 3 All E.R. 1230.
[20] See C. & Y.P. Act 1933, s. 106(2) (a).
[1] Clarke Hall & Morrison, *op. cit.*, p. 61.
[2] "Any court . . . may and, if it is not a juvenile court, shall unless satisfied that it would be undesirable to do so, remit the case . . .".
[3] For interim orders see *post*, Chapter 5. The maximum duration of an order is 28 days but further orders are permitted.
[4] C. & Y.P. Act 1969, s. 2(11), replacing C. & Y.P. Act 1963, s. 4.
[5] *Ibid.*, s. 3(5). Cf. the position in criminal proceedings, *supra*, n. 19.

This provision, designed to encourage the almost exclusive jurisdiction of the court of residence, is administratively desirable, since those persons and administrative bodies most familiar with the juvenile and his background are very likely to come from the area in which he lives. Nevertheless, it does not wholly eliminate a defect to which the former law was also subject.[6] Since some evidence will apparently have to be adduced to enable the directing court to form an opinion that the case should not be dismissed, the procedure will involve some witnesses, at least, in attending both courts to give evidence.

D. THE APPLICATION OF THE UPPER AGE LIMIT

(a) Attaining the Age of 17 before Commencement of Proceedings

Since the jurisdiction of the juvenile court depends upon the person who is the subject of care proceedings or criminal proceedings being below the age of 17, problems may arise where he attains that age before or during the course of the proceedings. But when do proceedings begin, or, more precisely, when does the court begin to exercise jurisdiction? Various provisions in the Children and Young Persons Acts show that the relevant date is that when the person first appears before the court, and, if at that time the person has attained the age of 17 and the court knows this, there is no jurisdiction. That, it is submitted, was the true effect of the decision in *R. v. Chelsea Justices, ex parte Director of Public Prosecutions.*[7] There a 16-year-old boy was charged with wounding with intent. He appeared before the juvenile court and was remanded, at first in custody, and then on July 3, 1963, on bail until July 31, with a view to being tried summarily for the indictable offence.[8] On July 28 he attained the age of 17. Immediately before the hearing on July 31 the police preferred a further charge of attempted murder which was based on the same facts as those alleged in respect of the earlier charge.

[6] See Clarke Hall and Morrison, 8th edn., p. 137.
[7] [1963] 3 All E.R. 657; [1963] 1 W.L.R. 1138.
[8] In accordance with s. 20 of the Magistrates' Courts Act 1952. With the introduction of summary trial in nearly all cases of indictable offences committed by young persons (*supra*, p. 41), s. 20 has been repealed.

The justices, knowing his age, decided that they would at a later date hear both offences summarily. An order for prohibition was issued to prevent them from dealing with the charge of attempted murder. References in the judgment of ROSKILL, J., to the fact that the charge was preferred after the 17th birthday might suggest that that is the moment for determining whether *criminal* jurisdiction exists rather than the date of first appearance before the court,[9] but those references are to be read within the context of the particular facts. The preferring of the charge of attempted murder and the appearance of the juvenile before the court in connection with that charge were virtually simultaneous. Had the charge been preferred between July 3 and July 28 the court, it is submitted, would still not have been able to assume jurisdiction in view of its knowledge at the date of appearance that the defendant was no longer a young person. The statutory jurisdiction on which the jurisdiction was based supported this conclusion, for as ROSKILL, J., recognised, "it was clearly intended to apply only where a person not yet 17 appears or is brought before the court on a particular charge".[10] The same conclusion is to be drawn from s. 6 of the Children and Young Persons Act 1969, which supersedes the earlier provision and allows for summary trial of an indictable offence "where a person under the age of 17 appears or is brought before a magistrates' court", and it is submitted that the same rule applies where the offence is a summary one. As for care proceedings, s. 2 of the Act expressly provides that the date when the child is first brought before the court is the relevant one.[11]

---

[9] The conflict between these views can be avoided by making the date of appearance to be the date when the charge is preferred. That was the line adopted by STREATFEILD, J., in *R.* v. *Rider*, [1954] 1 All E.R. 5; [1954] I.W.L.R. 463 when dealing with a defence under s. 2 of the Criminal Law Amendment Act 1922 [see now s. 6(3) of the Sexual Offences Act 1956] to a charge of unlawful sexual intercourse with a girl under 16, *i.e.*, that the accused, being under 24, believed her to be over 16. That defence is valid only on the first occasion on which such a person is charged with that offence. It was conceded by counsel that "within the meaning of [section 2] a charge is not that which is stated by a police officer verbally to a man when he is charging him with an offence". The learned judge went on to hold that "the proper construction to put upon the word 'charge' is that a man is charged before a court which has jurisdiction to determine the matter in question".

[10] [1963] 3 All E.R. at p. 658; [1963] 1 W.L.R. at p. 1140.

[11] Section 2(14) provides: "For the purposes of this Act, care proceedings in respect of a relevant infant are begun when he is first brought before a juvenile court . . ."

Any doubt about this being the appropriate time in criminal proceedings is removed by s. 99(1) of the Children and Young Persons Act 1933, for, in laying down for both criminal proceedings and care proceedings the rules for presuming or determining whether a person is within the statutory age limit of a child or young person, it requires the court to presume or determine what his age is at the time when he is brought before the court.[12]

The question of fixing the time of commencement of jurisdiction is particularly relevant in interpreting the rather vague provisions of s. 48(1) of the 1933 Act.

This enactment, as amended, states:

> A juvenile court sitting for the purpose of hearing a charge against a person who is believed to be a child or young person may, if it thinks fit to do so, proceed with the hearing and determination of the charge, notwithstanding that it is discovered that the person in question is not a child or young person.

The situation apparently contemplated by this provision is one where the person has in fact attained the age of 17 when jurisdiction is first assumed but because of some mistake or misrepresentation the court initially believes that he has not and only in the course of the proceedings finds out his actual age.[13] The effect of the subsection seems to be that on discovery of the age the court may either refer the case to an adult court of summary jurisdiction or, at its discretion, continue to hear the charge. In the latter event it seems that it must proceed as if it were now itself an adult court. It could not therefore make an order which is within the exclusive jurisdiction

---

[12] The age presumed or declared by the court is deemed to be the true age and any order or judgment of the court is not invalidated if it is subsequently proved to be otherwise.

In trying to decide the age the court may admit the evidence of a welfare officer; see *R. v. Cox*, [1898] 1 Q.B. 179 (C.C.R.); [1895-9] All E.R. Rep. 1285, where evidence of an officer of the N.S.P.C.C., a police constable and a schoolmistress was admitted and held sufficient.

[13] The subsection is not, it is submitted, open to the interpretation that, if the court proceeds to deal summarily with a person charged with an indictable offence of a kind within the meaning of s. 53(2) of the 1933 Act on the mistaken assumption that he is a child, it has the right to continue to do so on finding that he is a young person. In such a case, in accordance with s. 6 of the 1969 Act (*supra*, p. 41) the young person must be committed for trial, providing that there is sufficient evidence to put him on trial.

of a juvenile court, *e.g.*, a supervision order or care order.[14] If, however, the discovery is not made until after the juvenile court has made an order, the validity of the order is expressly preserved by s. 99(1) of the 1933 Act.[15]

If this is the scope of the subsection and if the date of first appearance before the court is the date of commencement of jurisdiction, the court would not be entitled to proceed with the hearing of a charge against a person who was already 17 when the charge was preferred and whose true age is discovered by the time when he first comes before the court, even though when the charge was preferred he was believed by those preferring it to be still a young person.[16]

The subsection as originally enacted also extended to care jurisdiction, but the Children and Young Persons Act 1963[17] restricted it to criminal cases. This distinction is preserved by the Children and Young Persons Act 1969, but, as will be seen,[18] where the young person attains the age of 17 after proceedings have begun, there is jurisdiction in both criminal proceedings and care proceedings.

The 1933 Act provides a corollary to s. 48(1). Where an adult court of summary jurisdiction is dealing with a person and in the course of the proceedings it appears that he is a child or young person, the court may, nevertheless, continue the hearing, instead of transferring the case to a juvenile court.[19] Its object is thus to provide for the situation where the adult court was mistaken about the person's age when it assumed jurisdiction. The rule is wider than s. 48(1) in that it is not limited to the hearing and determination of a charge but applies

[14] *Cf., infra,* the case where a young person attains the age of 17 during the course of the proceedings.
[15] See *supra.*
[16] In *R. v. Chelsea Justices ex parte Director of Public Prosecutions, supra,* ROSKILL, J., said ([1963] 3 All E.R. at p. 658):
"Further s. 48(1) . . . does not in my view, apply to a case where a defendant appears before the court on a charge preferred for the first time after his 17th birthday and which *the court then* knows to have been so preferred". (Italics supplied). "Then" refers to the moment of appearance and not, as the headnote to the report suggests, "when the charge was first preferred". Because of the special circumstances of that case the court happened to know of the age at the latter date, but in the normal case how could it possibly know of the matter at that date when it had not yet itself been convened?
[17] Section 64, Sched. III and Sched. V.
[18] *Infra.*
[19] Para. (c) of the proviso to s. 46(1).

to "any proceedings". However, apart from adoption proceedings, it is difficult to conceive of any other kind of civil jurisdiction of the juvenile court being assumed by an adult court.

(b) Attaining the Age of 17 during the Course of Proceedings

Where proceedings in respect of a young person are begun but he attains the age of 17 before they are concluded, the court may nevertheless deal with the case and make any order which it could have made if he had not attained that age. This rule formerly applied only to care proceedings but has been extended by the 1969 Act to criminal proceedings.[20] Before the amendment it seems to have been accepted that the court could either remand the person to an adult court or continue to deal with him as though it were an adult court;[1] but it could not make an approved school order or a fit person order.[2] The effect of the amendment is that the court can now make a care order or a supervision order in such circumstances.[3]

---

[20] C. & Y.P. Act 1963, s. 29(1), as amended by C. & Y.P. Act 1969, s. 72(3) and (4) and Sched. 5, para. 49 and Sched. 6.

[1] *Cf.* s. 48(1), *supra.*

[2] *Hamlyn* v. *Pearce*, [1962] 2 Q.B. 346, (D.C.); [1962] 2 All E.R. 436.

[3] It may be conveniently noted here (but see further, *post*, Chapter 4, p. 115) that the powers of a juvenile court in respect of the commission of a further offence after an order for conditional discharge are not affected by the fact that the young person in respect of whom the order was made has since the date of the order attained the age of 17 (C. & Y.P. Act 1933, s. 48(2)).

CHAPTER 3

Care Proceedings and Criminal Proceedings in Juvenile Courts — II Procedure

A. THE DECISION TO INSTITUTE PROCEEDINGS

I. PERSONS WHO MAY BRING PROCEEDINGS

(a) Care Proceedings

Except where they are based on the offence condition, care proceedings may be brought by a local authority, a constable[1] or a person authorised to do so.[2] Under the old law the only recipient of the specific authority was the National Society for the Prevention of Cruelty to Children.[3] That Society has now been authorised to bring proceedings under the new Act,[4] but no further authorisation seems to be contemplated. Proceedings alleging that the offence condition is satisfied (and that there is need for care or control) must be instituted by a local authority or constable.[5] This limitation takes account of the past practice of the N.S.P.C.C. not to prosecute juveniles.

In the majority of cases proceedings are likely to be brought by a local authority,[6] although it remains to be seen how far the

---

[1] Invariably he is a member of a police force, but the term has a wider meaning; see Holden, *Child Legislation* 1969, pp. 105-106.
[2] C. & Y.P. Act 1969, s. 1(1).
   An "authorised person" means a person authorised by order of the Secretary of State to bring such proceedings and any officer of a society who is so authorised (s. 1(6)).
[3] Including the Liverpool and the Birkenhead and Wirral Societies.
[4] C. & Y.P. Act 1969 (Authorisation for the purposes of s. 1) Order 1970, S.I. 1970, No. 1500.
[5] C. & Y.P. Act 1969, s. 3(2). The Ingleby Committee recommended that in *all* cases authority should be given only to the police and local authorities to bring juveniles before the court and that where the N.S.P.C.C. was involved it should report the facts to one of those bodies for them to take appropriate action; see Cmnd. 1191, paras. 87 and 88.
[6] For the purpose of the Children and Young Persons Acts this means the council of a county, county borough or London borough or the Common Council of the City of London, except that where proceedings are based on s. 1(2)(e) of the 1969 Act the appropriate body is the local education authority; see *ibid.*, ss. 2(8) and 70(1).

introduction of the offence condition into the law will lead the police to assume the responsibility. Very much will depend upon the degree of liaison between the police and the local authority in the particular locality.[7] It is clear that the 1969 Act intends that the main responsibility should lie with the local authority, because it not merely allows but requires the authority to bring the juvenile before the court, unless satisfied that bringing proceedings is neither in his interest nor the public interest or that some other person is about to do so or is to charge him with an offence.[8] Moreover, if the authority receives information suggesting that there are grounds for bringing care proceedings it must see that inquiries are made unless it considers them unnecessary.[9]

In the case of the juvenile who is beyond parental control the local authority may still feel that care proceedings are not the appropriate method of tackling the problem, but the parent may think otherwise. If he does, he can by written notice request the authority to bring him before the court, and the former right of the parent himself to commence proceedings[10] has not been wholly superseded in that, if the authority should refuse, or fail to do so within 28 days from the date of request,[11] the parent may apply to a juvenile court for an order directing it to do so.[12] When an application is made the authority must provide the court with full information about the home surroundings, school record, health and character of the juvenile.[13] This may require preliminary investigations to be made. A parent who lives apart from the complaining parent (or guardian) must be notified by the latter of the time and place of the

---

[7] See further the question of Consultation, *infra*, p. 53.

[8] C. & Y.P. Act 1969, s. 2(2).

[9] *Ibid.*, sub-s. (1).

[10] Conflicting views had been expressed to the Ingleby Committee on the desirability of the parental right. One was that, if a parent took the step of bringing his own child before the court this was very likely to lead to an irreparable breach of the parent-child relationship. On the other hand, it was suggested that such a drastic step sometimes had the reverse, salutary effect of strengthening that relationship. The former opinion prevailed with the Committee (Cmnd. 1191, paras. 129-134) and was given effect by the Children and Young Persons Act 1963.

[11] In reckoning this period the date on which notice was given is to be ignored; *Goldsmiths' Co.* v. *The West Metropolitan Rail. Co.*, [1904] 1 K.B. 1, (C.A.); [1900-3] All E.R. Rep. 667.

[12] C. & Y.P. Act 1963, s. 3(1), as amended by C. & Y.P. Act 1969, s. 72(3) and Sched. 5.

[13] *Ibid.*, sub-s. (2).

hearing, since he is entitled to be heard.[14] The juvenile must not be present at the hearing,[15] and, if the court directs the local authority to institute care proceedings, any justice who was a member of that court is precluded from sitting at the subsequent proceedings.[16]

Either the local authority in whose area the juvenile resides or that in whose area he is found may commence care proceedings. Usually it is the former, and, in the case of a juvenile beyond the control of a parent who insists on his being brought before the court, it must be the "residential" authority, since it is only to that authority that the parent can make his written request.[17]

The local authority or its social services committee may empower its clerk or chief education officer to exercise in its name any of its powers with regard to the institution of care proceedings, but the power to act can only be conferred in a case which appears to the officer to be one of urgency.[18] It would seem, however, that this express limitation does not override the general power conferred on a local authority by the Local Government Act 1933[19] to authorise any of its members or officers to institute proceedings before a court of summary jurisdiction. Thus, an authority is entitled to authorise its director of social services to act in its name.

(b) Criminal Proceedings

Until s. 5 of the Children and Young Persons Act 1969 becomes wholly operative and private prosecutions of juveniles are abolished,[20] any person may lay an information against a juvenile, but, if he decides to do so, he must give notice of his decision to the appropriate local authority, unless that authority itself is laying the information. The appropriate authority is that for the area in which the juvenile appears to reside or, if he appears not to reside in a local authority's area,

[14] Magistrates' Courts (Children and Young Persons) Rules 1970, r. 22(1).
[15] C. & Y.P. Act 1963, s. 3(3); but *quaere* this rule prevents him from being called as a witness; see Clarke Hall and Morrison, 8th edn., p. 93.
[16] Magistrates' Courts (Children and Young Persons) Rules 1970, r. 22(2).
[17] C. & Y.P. Act 1963, s. 3(1), *supra.*
[18] C. & Y.P. Act 1933, s. 96(7) and (8). The former subsection is amended by the Local Authority Social Services Act 1970, s. 14 and Sched. 2, para. 1.
   Semble, the officer may be given a general authority to act in cases of urgency and not merely in respect of a particular case; see Clarke Hall and Morrison, *op. cit.,* p. 76.
[19] Section 277.   [20] See *ante,* Chapter 2, p. 32.

that within whose area it is alleged that the offence was committed.[1] Until criminal proceedings in respect of children are
abolished the above rule applies to children as to young persons.[2]

II. CONSULTATION

Co-operation on a voluntary basis resulting from close consultation between the parents, the local authority, the police and
the school authorities lies behind the recent legislation concerning juveniles in trouble. Yet, the Children and Young
Persons Act 1969 is very largely silent on how the policy is to
be carried out. The statutory requirement that a person, other
than the relevant local authority, who decides to institute care
proceedings[3] or criminal proceedings[4] must notify the local
authority of that decision should result in consultation with the
authority before the decision is reached. This is especially so in
respect of care proceedings. Inquiries will usually need to be
made with the authority about the home background, so that
those instituting the proceedings will be able to satisfy the court
of the present lack of care or control of the juvenile. In practical
terms the need is most likely to arise where the police are contemplating care proceedings based on the offence condition, but
there is no statutory duty to consult the authority. Nor, until
ss. 4 and 5 of the 1969 Act are given effect, is there any statutory restriction on their right to institute criminal proceedings
instead of civil proceedings based on that condition. The desirability of a statutory code for consultation between the various
agencies, especially between the police and local authorities,
seems to be reflected in the detailed guidance which the Home
Office has already proposed.[5] This, coupled with local arrange-

---

[1] C. & Y.P. 1969, s. 5(8) and (9).
[2] C. & Y.P. Act 1969 (Transitional Modifications of Part I) Order 1970.
[3] C. & Y.P. Act 1969, s. 2(3); Magistrates' Courts (Children and Young
Persons) Rules 1970, r. 14.
[4] *Ibid.*, s. 5(8), *supra*.
   Where care or criminal proceedings are brought in respect of a juvenile
aged 10 or over, notice must also be given to a probation officer, (s. 34(2);
C. & Y.P. Act 1969 (Transitional Modifications of Part I) Order 1970).
If the probation service is already obliged to provide the court with
information service they will continue to do so; see *post*, p. 80.
[5] See the Guide to Part I of the Children and Young Persons Act 1969,
paras. 83-107.
   No code, formal or informal, will, however, ensure consultation in
all cases so long as social service departments are understaffed, and the
position will worsen when supervisors will have to assume additional
responsibilities for intermediate treatment under s. 12 of the 1969 Act.

ments existing before 1971, may ultimately lead to a national pattern, and it also seems likely that larger issues will eventually have to be settled by statute, for example, the question whether social workers are to be integrated into the educational system.

Consultation may lead to various forms of informal action. In the case of an offender, the police may feel that a caution is sufficient or, if there is a police juvenile liaison officer scheme operating in the area, that the juvenile should be admitted to it.[6] In other cases the local authority or the police may see the best solution in encouraging parental responsibility, and the local authority, in accordance with its statutory obligation, must give advice and help to that end. However, the circumstances may warrant the removal of the juvenile from his present surroundings and the local authority may assume care under s. 1 or s. 2 of the Children Act 1948.[7] If these or other measures are considered inappropriate, care proceedings or criminal proceedings should then be instituted.

B. THE INSTITUTION OF PROCEEDINGS

(a) Care Proceedings
Summons or Warrant

The statutory provisions for securing the attendance of a juvenile before the court and, where necessary, for his prior temporary detention are complicated and derived from several sources.

In the case of care proceedings he may be brought before the court by way of summons or by warrant for his arrest[8] or as a result of his having been taken to a place of safety. In most cases proceedings are commenced by summons, and a warrant may only be issued where a summons cannot be served, or, if it has been served, where the juvenile has failed to answer it, or where he has failed to appear at an adjourned hearing after receiving adequate notice of the time and place.[9] If a warrant has to be issued but he cannot immediately on arrest be brought before the court, he must be detained in a place of safety for a maximum period of 72 hours, unless the warrant is endorsed

---

[6] For these schemes see the Ingleby Committee, Cmnd. 1191, paras. 138-149; Cavenagh, *Juvenile Courts, the Child and the Law*, Chapter 7.
[7] See *post*, Chapter 5. [8] C. & Y.P. Act 1969, s. 2(4).
[9] C. & Y.P. Act 1969, s. 2(4); Magistrates' Courts Act 1952, s. 47(3) and(4).

for bail. Within that time he must be brought before the court or, failing that, before a justice.[10] In the latter event the justice must either direct his release or make an interim order committing him to the care of a local authority for a specified period not exceeding 28 days and beginning with the date when he was taken into custody.[11] On the expiration of the order the local authority must bring him before the court specified in the order unless that court fixes an earlier hearing.[12] The juvenile must be present when the interim order is made unless the justice is satisfied that he is under the age of five or cannot be present because of illness or accident.[13]

Detention in Place of Safety

The "place of safety" to which the juvenile can be taken under the above power may be "a community home provided by a local authority or a controlled community home, any police station or any hospital, surgery or any other suitable place, the occupier of which is willing temporarily to receive a child or young person".[14] It will be seen that an assisted community home is not explicitly included but may come within the definition as a "suitable place". However, those responsible for running that kind of community home[15] are not subject to the statutory duty which is imposed on a local authority[16] with regard to a local authority community home or a controlled community home, namely, to make special provision therein for the reception and maintenance of juveniles who are removed to a place of safety under, *inter alia*, the Children and Young Persons Acts.

In addition to the above power the Children and Young Persons Acts give other, wider powers to detain juveniles in places of safety before they are brought before the court.

[10] *Cf. infra.*, p. 61, the duty to bring a juvenile arrested for an offence before a magistrates' court within the same period (s. 29(5)).
[11] C. & Y.P. Act 1969, ss. 2(5) and 20(1).
[12] Section 22(2).
[13] Section 22(1). For interim orders see further Chapter 5, *post*, pp. 152 *et seq.*
[14] So defined by C. & Y.P. Act 1933, s. 107(1), as amended by C. & Y.P. Act 1969, s. 72(3) and Sched. 5, para. 12(2).
  Since a juvenile cannot be sentenced to imprisonment (see *post*, Chapter 4, p. 127), a prison is obviously outside the definition.
[15] For community homes and their classification see *post*, Chapter 5.
[16] By the Children Act 1948, s. 51(1), as amended by C. & Y.P. Act 1969, s. 72 (3) and Sched. 5, para. 20(1).

(i) *Section 28 of the Children and Young Persons Act* 1969. Section 28(1) enables a justice to order a juvenile to be so detained for a specified period not exceeding 28 days if he has reasonable cause to believe that any of the conditions (other than the offence condition) prescribed by s. 1 of the 1969 Act[17] is satisfied or that a court would find the condition in s. 1(2)(b) relating to the probability of neglect or ill-treatment so satisfied.[18] Any person may apply for authority to detain and take the juvenile to a place of safety. Usually it will be an officer of the local authority or a constable, but s. 28(2) confers additional powers on the latter in that he may detain a juvenile without the authority of a justice if he has reasonable cause to believe that any of the conditions in s. 1 (other than the truancy and offence conditions) is satisfied or that a court would find the condition in s. 1 (2)(b) satisfied.[19] If he does act under s. 28(2), he must ensure that as soon as practicable a police officer[20] inquires into the case, and, in the light of the inquiry, the latter must either release the juvenile or, if he considers further detention is in the juvenile's interests, arrange for him to be kept in a place of safety. The maximum period of detention is eight days from the date when the juvenile was first detained by the constable, but he or his parent (or guardian)[1] can apply to a justice for earlier release, which must be granted unless further detention is in his interests.[2]

The person who detains a juvenile under s. 28(1) or (2) must notify him and his parent (or guardian) of the reason for the detention and, where he is further detained in a place of safety under sub-s. (4), they must be told of the right to apply for earlier release.[3] While the juvenile is being detained at the place

[17] *Ante*, Chapter 2, pp. 22 *et seq.*
[18] An order may similarly be made where it is reasonably believed that the juvenile is about to leave the United Kingdom in contravention of the restrictions on juvenile entertainers going abroad.
[19] It has been pointed out (see Home Office Guide to Part I of C. & Y.P. Act 1969, para. 182) that the reason for excluding the truancy condition from the terms of s. 28(2) is that truancy does not require the immediate removal of the child. But s. 28(2) does apply where a vagrant is guilty of the offence of preventing his child from receiving education; see further Chapter 13, p. 437, n. 3.
[20] He must be at least an inspector or be the officer in charge of a police station.
[1] C. & Y.P. Act 1969, s. 70(2).
[2] *Ibid.*, s. 28(4) and (5). His parent or guardian must be told of his right to apply.
[3] Sub-sections (3) and (4).

of safety it may be found necessary to detain him beyond the period authorised by the justice, or, as the case may be, beyond that of eight days, before he can be brought before the juvenile court under s. 1. An application for this purpose may be made to a magistrates' court (which need not be a juvenile court) or to a justice, who may make an interim order committing him to the care of a local authority, the latter being then responsible for bringing him before the juvenile court.[4]

Section 28 is intended to cover cases of detention of juveniles who, if they are subsequently to be brought before the court, can *only* be brought by way of care proceedings. The prior detention of juvenile offenders who may be the subject matter either of criminal proceedings or, by virtue of the offence condition, care proceedings is governed by s. 29.[5] At present children aged 10 or over are to be treated in the same way as young persons so that the latter section will apply to them, and a child between 10 and 14 who is arrested without a warrant will have to be brought before the court within 72 hours.[6] However, as and when children cease to be prosecutable, a child arrested without a warrant for an offence other than homicide will be kept in a place of safety under s. 28 for the maximum period of eight days in the same way as a child or young person who is detained by virtue of sub-s. (2) of that section may be kept there for that period.

(ii) *Section 40 of the Children and Young Persons Act* 1933. A constable may in certain circumstances be given special authority by a justice to take a juvenile to a place of safety. The power is conferred by s. 40 of the Children and Young Persons Act 1933 and may be exercised where, as a result of an information,[7] the justice reasonably suspects that the juvenile is the victim either (1) of such assault, ill-treatment or neglect as is likely to cause unnecessary suffering or injury to health or (2) of one

[4] Sub-section (6). If an interim order is refused, the juvenile may be released forthwith.
The sub-section does not state who may apply; presumably it is any person who may apply for a care order under s. 1.
[5] See *infra*, p. 60.
[6] C. & Y.P. Act 1969, s. 29(5); C. & Y.P. Act 1969 (Transitional Modifications of Part I Order 1970).
[7] The information may be laid by anyone who in the justice's opinion is acting in the juvenile's interests.

of the offences listed in Sched. 1 of the 1933 Act.[8] Refusal to allow a foster child or a "protected child" as defined by the Adoption Act 1958 to be visited, or premises to be inspected, by an officer of the local authority is a reasonable cause to suspect for the purpose of the section.[9] If the justice is of that opinion, he may issue a warrant authorising the constable either to search for the juvenile and, if he finds that the latter is the victim of ill-treatment or an offence, to take him to a place of safety or to remove him with or without search to such a place.[10] It has been suggested[11] that the second alternative should be employed unless the evidence of ill-treatment or an offence is not strong. The warrant may direct that the constable be accompanied by a doctor; and, as for the informant, he may accompany the constable except where the warrant otherwise directs.

Where a juvenile is removed to a place of safety he must be brought before a juvenile court within the period specified in the warrant, which must not be more than 28 days, unless he has been released or received into the care of a local authority.[12]

If he is "not otherwise brought before the court", the responsibility for doing so lies with the local authority in whose area the place of safety is situated. In such a case the court may order his release or make an interim order committing him to the care of a local authority.[13] If the juvenile is under the age of five or cannot be brought before the court because of illness or accident, an application may be made for one or other of those orders to be made without the juvenile being present.

(iii) *Section 43 of the Sexual Offences Act* 1956. Apart from the powers conferred by s. 40 of the Children and Young

---

[8] For ill-treatment of children see *post*, Chapter 6, pp. 188 *et seq.*

[9] Children Act 1958, s. 8; Adoption Act 1958, s. 45. See also C. & Y.P. Act 1969, s. 59(3).

[10] The warrant may also authorise the arrest of a person accused of any offence in respect of the juvenile.

[11] Clarke Hall and Morrison, *op. cit.*, p. 48.

[12] C. & Y.P. Act 1963, s. 23(1), as amended by C. & Y.P. Act 1969, Sched. 5, para. 48. The section does not indicate the circumstances which would justify the juvenile being received into care, but it is submitted that they must be the same as those which would require a local authority to receive a child into care under s. 1 of the Children Act 1948, *post*, Chapter 5, p. 144.

[13] C. & Y.P. Act 1963, s. 23(3) and (5). Sub-s. (3) is expressed ambiguously and is open to the interpretation that the power to release or make an interim order is not available where the juvenile is "otherwise brought before the court", *e.g.*, by a constable.

Persons Act 1933, a constable may be authorised by a warrant issued under s. 43 of the Sexual Offences Act 1956 to search for and remove to a place of safety a woman who is being detained for the purpose of having unlawful sexual intercourse with men. She must then be brought before a justice of the peace. If she is under the age of 17 one of the ways in which she might be dealt with is to bring her before the juvenile court under s. 1 of the Children and Young Persons Act 1969.[14]

(b) Criminal Proceedings

Summons, Warrant or Summary Arrest

A juvenile offender, like an adult, comes before the court as the result of a summons or of a warrant for his arrest or of his being arrested without a warrant and charged with the offence.[15] Summonses are far more common than warrants, but the choice between proceeding by way of a summons and arresting and charging the juvenile (where the latter procedure is permissible) is wholly within the discretion of the police. The Ingleby Committee rejected the suggestion that "a child ought never to be arrested unless a breach of the peace is threatened or the offence is so grave that the child charged with it ought never to be left at large", and felt that "it would be neither practicable nor desirable to restrict by statute the manner in which proceedings should be started".[16] This unfettered discretion may be questioned. A justice of the peace when considering whether to issue a summons or warrant is expected to apply the principle that the latter should not be issued where a summons will be equally effective, except where the charge is of a serious nature.[17] It is not unrealistic to impute to a police officer equally an ability to assess the gravity of an offence,[18] so that a similar principle should operate when he has to decide whether proceedings be set in motion by the issue of a summons or by arrest and charge. Moreover, where the juvenile is a child, as opposed to a young person, there should be a particu-

[14] See further Chapter 7, *post*, p. 232.
[15] For the powers of arrest without warrant the reader is referred to works on constitutional law and criminal law, and to the Criminal Law Act 1967, ss. 2 and 3. [16] Cmnd. 1191, para. 117.
[17] *O'Brien* v. *Brabner* (1885), 49 J.P. Jo. 227.
[18] Compare the more difficult matters he may have to determine under s. 28(2) or s. 29(1) of the C. & Y.P. Act 1969, *supra*, p. 56, and *infra*, respectively.

larly strong presumption that a summons will suffice to secure attendance. After all, it has been laid down that he shall be tried summarily for all offences except homicide. Since the summons is the normal method of instituting proceedings against adults in respect of summary offences, it ought to be the common method for ensuring the child's appearance in respect of all offences other than homicide. Its one disadvantage[19] compared with the method of proceeding by way of summary arrest is that it can sometimes lead to delay in bringing the juvenile before the court, especially if the prosecutor does not promptly apply for a summons; whereas the juvenile who is summarily arrested is normally released on bail and will then appear at the next sitting of the juvenile court.[20]

Release or Detention of Arrested Juveniles

Section 29 of the Children and Young Persons Act 1969 is concerned with the release or continued detention of juveniles who, whether arrested with or without a warrant, cannot be brought immediately before a magistrates' court. The section operates in respect of young persons arrested for any offence and, by its terms, is intended to apply only to children arrested for homicide. However, so long as children aged 10 or over remain prosecutable, it will apply to them as it does to young persons.[1]

After the arrest a police officer[2] must inquire into the case and must then release the juvenile unless there are specific grounds for his continued detention. If he (1) considers that the juvenile ought in his own interests to be further detained,

---

[19] The same can be said of the warrant for arrest.

[20] The need to avoid delay in bringing the juvenile before the court prompted the Ingleby Committee [Cmnd. 1191, para. 118] to recommend that normally criminal proceedings should be instituted not more than 28 days after the identity of the offender first becomes known to the prosecutor, but this proposal has not been adopted.

On the other hand, the Committee saw no justification for altering, in its application to juveniles, the general rule contained in s. 104 of the Magistrates' Courts Act 1952 that, unless a particular enactment otherwise provides, an information alleging a non-indictable offence must be tried within six months from the time when the offence was committed. It rejected a suggested limit of three months.

[1] C. & Y.P. Act 1969, s. 34(1)(c) and C. & Y.P. Act 1969 (Transitional Modifications of Part I) Order 1970.

[2] He must be the officer in charge of the station to which the juvenile is brought or must have the rank of inspector or above.

for example, to remove him from undesirable associations or
(2) reasonably believes that the latter has committed homicide
or another grave crime[3] or that his release would defeat the
ends of justice,[4] or, where he has been arrested without a
warrant, that he would fail to appear to answer the charge, the
officer must arrange for him to be taken into the care of, and
detained by, the local authority, unless the juvenile is of so
unruly a character as to make it inappropriate to do so.[5] But
he must be brought before a magistrates' court within 72 hours
from the time of his arrest, unless a police officer[6] certifies to
the court that because of illness or accident he cannot be
brought within that period. In either event, if the court does
not then proceed to inquire into his case, it must order his
release except where he was arrested with a warrant or where
detention is in his own interests or where any of the other above
grounds which would lead a police officer to arrange for detention by a local authority exist. In any of those cases he must be
remanded in custody or on bail; and if bail is refused he must
be informed of his right to apply to a High Court judge for it
and the reason for the refusal.[7]

One of the main objects of s. 29 is to ensure that there shall
not be delay in bringing before some judicial authority an
arrested juvenile to whom the police have refused bail.[8] It
could be said that a maximum period of 72 hours' detention is
too long, but the rule may be explained by a desire to afford

[3] Not defined for the purpose of s. 29.
[4] *E.g.*, where the juvenile is charged jointly with an adult and the latter
is likely to bring pressure on him to falsify evidence. *Cf.* the power
under s. 13(2) of the C. & Y.P. Act 1933 to detain a person charged with
any of the offences, listed in the First Schedule to that Act, against a
juvenile, which may be used to prevent contact between the person and
the juvenile.
[5] If and when the restrictions on bringing criminal proceedings against
a young person become operative under s. 5 of the 1969 Act (*ante*,
Chapter 2), the police officer will be required to notify him that a decision
will have to be taken in accordance with that section whether to lay an
information against him. This duty will arise where the young person is
detained after being arrested without a warrant (s. 29(4)).
[6] Not below the rank of inspector.
[7] For the corresponding right of a person aged 17 or over who is refused
bail by a magistrates' court see the Criminal Justice Act 1967, s. 18(7)
and (8).
    Apart from s. 29, the C. & Y.P. Act 1933, s. 46(2) expressly preserves
the power of any justice to grant bail or to remand in custody.
[8] Re-enacting in substance s. 22 of the C. & Y.P. Act 1963, s. 29(5) adopts
a recommendation of the Ingleby Committee (para. 122).

reasonable time for steps to be taken to see that the magistrates' court before whom he is brought is either a juvenile court (which even within that time may in some areas be difficult to arrange) or at least that it includes a justice or justices who are members of a juvenile court panel.

The duty under s. 29 to release the juvenile when first arrested is subject not only to the above grounds which justify detention but also to the rule that where he has been arrested in pursuance of a warrant he can be released only on recognisances being entered into in his own name or that of his parent or guardian[9] and either with or without sureties.[10] The recognisance may also be conditioned for the attendance of the parent or guardian. The relationship between this power of a police officer to release on bail and that of a justice to authorise bail when issuing a warrant for arrest is not clear.[11] Where a warrant is endorsed the terms of the recognisance will be specified so that when the juvenile is arrested the police officer must release him on his entering into the recognisance. *Semble*, the police officer could not then rely on s. 29 of the 1969 Act and insist on a recognisance also being entered into by the parent or guardian to secure the juvenile's attendance. But when the warrant is not endorsed, then, apparently s. 29 may operate.

Where the juvenile has been arrested without a warrant, s. 29 does not enable the police officer to insist on recognisances as a condition for release, but, under s. 38(2) of the Magistrates' Courts Act 1952, release can be made subject to a recognisance for the juvenile to report to a police station, if necessary.[12] The recognisance may be taken from the parent or guardian with or without sureties.[13]

Separation of Juveniles from Adult Defendants

Whenever a juvenile is arrested and detained in a police

---

[9] For meaning of guardian see C. & Y.P. Act 1933, s. 107(1).
[10] If a person has entered into a recognisance but fails to surrender to his bail, a magistrates' court can issue a warrant for his arrest (Magistrates' Courts Act 1952, s. 97). This rule applies to juvenile offenders as to adults.
[11] For the powers of a justice see the Magistrates' Courts Act 1952, s. 93.
[12] See Home Office Guide, para. 208.
[13] Magistrates' Courts Act 1952, s. 38(3).

station the police must make sure that he or she is not able to associate with adult defendants and, if the juvenile is a girl, she must, while detained, be placed under the care of a woman.[14] Separation is not, however, obligatory where the adult and the juvenile are related or where they are jointly charged, although in both cases it may be desirable.

Taking Finger-prints

A magistrates' court may order the taking of the finger-prints (including palm-prints) of a person not less than 14.[15] An order may be made where he is summoned to appear before the court "for any offence punishable with imprisonment"[16] or he is arrested and brought before the court charged with any offence. The finger-prints will be taken by a police constable who may, if necessary, use reasonable force for the purpose. They must be taken on the court premises or at the place where the person is being remanded in custody. In the event of his being acquitted or the information against him being dismissed or, where there are committal proceedings, his not being committed for trial, the finger-prints with all copies and records must be destroyed.[17]

The jurisdiction to make an order does not extend to children between 10 and 14, even though they are still subject to criminal proceedings; but apparently the view taken by police authorities is that their finger-prints may lawfully be taken with the consent of the parent. The assumption seems to be that the giving of consent is incidental to the right of custody and is analogous to that of giving consent to medical treatment

---

[14] C. & Y.P. Act 1933, s. 31. For the application of this section when the juvenile is attending a court, see *post*, p. 67.

[15] Magistrates' Courts Act 1952, s. 40, as extended by the Criminal Justice Act 1967, s. 33. An application for an order must be made by a police officer not below the rank of inspector.

[16] Section 33. These words are, it is submitted, to be read as "any offence punishable with imprisonment in the case of an adult"; *cf*. s. 8(1) (a) of C. & Y.P. Act 1969, *infra*. A young person (14-17) is not so punishable, but under s. 33 he may be finger-printed.

[17] When the restrictions imposed by s. 5 of C. & Y.P. Act 1969 with regard to instituting criminal proceedings against a young person become operative, it will be possible to make an order for him to be finger-printed so as to assist in deciding whether to prosecute or to rely on other methods of dealing with him; see s. 8. The decision calls for the maximum relevant information being available. This includes the possibility of the young person having been involved in other offences and an order to fingerprint may thus be helpful. See Holden, *op. cit.*, p.134.

for the child. On this basis it is equally lawful to take the finger-prints of a young person with parental consent and without the need for an order of the court. The taking of finger-prints is such a serious interference with individual liberty that it is surprising that the legislature has not dealt comprehensively with it in relation to juveniles.

C. THE HEARING

There is no distinct code of procedure exclusively applicable to the trial of a juvenile offender. The rules governing criminal proceedings in a juvenile court are an adaptation of those followed in an adult court exercising summary jurisdiction. Nor is there an exclusive procedure in care proceedings, although their special nature does mark them off more sharply from other civil proceedings in magistrates' courts. The provisions of the Magistrates' Courts Act 1952 which are applicable to the adult magistrates' court operate, therefore, in the juvenile court, except in so far as they are modified or excluded by special enactments.[18] These are to be found in the Children and Young Persons Acts 1933 to 1969 and the Magistrates' Courts (Children and Young Persons) Rules 1970.[19] As will be seen, they seek to modify the formalities that have to be observed in the hearing of an adult case and to provide a greater degree of simplicity in the juvenile court proceedings. But they can only provide the framework within which the juvenile court must work. The extent to which formality and intricacy give way to informality and simplicity depends very much on the experience and practice of the particular court and on the age and character of the juvenile before it.

Sittings of the Court
(a) Frequency

Juvenile courts must sit as often as necessary to exercise their jurisdiction.[20] In many areas it is usual to sit at least

[18] Section 130 of the Act states that its provisions "relating to the constitution, place of sitting and procedure of magistrates' courts shall, in their application to juvenile courts, have effect subject to any provision contained in the rules or any enactment regulating the constitution, place of sitting or procedure of juvenile courts".
[19] The Home Office has recognised the need for a thorough review of the Rules and intends to institute it "in due course"; see H.O. Circular No. 267/1970.   [20] C. & Y.P. Act 1933, s. 47(1).

once a week, but in London and some of the large cities sittings are much more frequent, and with the increase in the number of cases that are adjourned for further inquiries[1] this trend is certain to continue. Elsewhere, practice varies considerably according to the amount of business of the courts. It is obviously desirable that delay in bringing the juvenile before the court should be avoided, so that even in rural areas the periods between sittings should not be too long. Moreover, there should be a readiness to convene the court *ad hoc*, if this would avoid delay.[2]

(b) Place

The Children Act 1908[3] gave juvenile courts considerable latitude in the choice of place and time of their sittings. It enabled them to sit in a different building or room or on different days or at different times from the sittings of other courts. The Children and Young Persons Act 1933[4] abolished the right to sit merely "at different times", but otherwise preserved the earlier rule. Now, however, since the Children and Young Persons Act 1963,[5] there is simply a general prohibition that juvenile courts "shall not sit in a room in which sittings of a court other than a juvenile court are held if a sitting of that other court has been or will be held there within an hour before or after the sitting of the juvenile court". The reason for this change was to overcome the problem of shortage of court accommodation that exists in many areas, but that point could have been met by a simple amendment which restored the words "at different times"[6] and returned to the original rule laid down in 1908. That method would, it is suggested, have been preferable because it might have emphasised that it is still desirable whenever practicable that the juvenile court should sit in a different building or room or on different days from any other court.

[1] See *post*, p. 86.
[2] The Ingleby Committee (Cmnd. 1191, para. 195) felt that a number of juvenile courts should sit more often, and earlier, in 1955, a Home Office Circular (No. 19/1955) pointed out to juvenile court justices that if proceedings are delayed "the memory of the occurrence that occasioned them may often have little connection in the child's mind with the steps that are being taken".   [3] Section 111(1).
[4] Section 47(2), re-enacting the C. & Y.P. Act 1932, s. 1(4).
[5] Section 17(2).
[6] With the addition that there should be a minimum interval between the sitting of a juvenile court and any other court.

Accommodation

Of those three possibilities the ideal solution is clearly the first provided that there are suitable buildings. But of these there are few,[7] and the national picture is a depressing one of courts in many areas being held in the most deplorable conditions. Unfortunately, the provision of improved accommodation has not been regarded as a high priority in the expenditure on social services, although the need is gradually coming to be recognised.[8] Future improvements, particularly in urban areas, could well develop along the lines of the realistic suggestion of the Ingleby Committee that juvenile courts should form a part of a "multi-purpose" centre, used also for other local authority services.[9] The re-organisation of some of those services under the Local Authority Social Services Act 1970[10] may eventually encourage this development.

The accommodation provided for juvenile courts should be such as to meet the following requirements.[11] Even where existing facilities are wholly inadequate there should be adaptation to secure as far as possible this object.

(1) The court room should be so arranged and furnished as to create an atmosphere of dignity but simplicity.

This effect is more likely to be produced if the "trappings" of an adult court room such as the raised bench and the dock are excluded.[12]

(2) There should be adequate ancillary accommodation in the forms of:

(i) waiting and interviewing rooms which should be so arranged that juveniles remanded in custody are kept separate

---

[7] In one or two places, notably Birmingham and Liverpool, there are buildings specially designed for juvenile courts.

[8] See the Report of the Ingleby Committee, Cmnd. 1191, para. 191. In 1961 the Home Office set up a Working Party to consider the question of accommodation for London juvenile courts. For its most recent pronouncement see H.O.C. No. 39/1971.

[9] Cmnd. 1191, para. 193. [10] See *post*, Chapter 5.

[11] For a fuller examination see Watson, *The Child and the Magistrate*, 2nd edn., pp. 62-69.

[12] Hence the desirability of avoiding, if possible, the use of an adult court room. If it has to be used, it should be re-arranged so as to make it as informal as possible.

Opinion on the use of the witness box is divided. Its retention is commonly defended on the ground that it can help to impress on the juvenile witness the seriousness of the oath.

The dock may well disappear from the criminal court; see Rosen, (1966) 29 M.L.R. 289.

from those who have been summoned or remanded on bail and
that boys are kept separate from girls;

(ii) separate rooms for each of the following, namely,
the magistrates, their clerk, witnesses, probation officers and
officers of the local authority and the police;

(iii) lavatory accommodation.

(3) The whole of the accommodation should be so arranged as
to provide a separate entrance to the court and a separate exit,
so that the juvenile who has appeared before the court should
not encounter those still to be called. This can be an important
consideration where the juvenile or parent is leaving it in a
distressed condition.[13]

(4) The arrangements must be such as to ensure compliance
with the rule that juveniles must, while being conveyed to the
court and while waiting before or after attendance in court, be
kept apart from adult defendants.[14] This requirement can be
especially significant if an adult court room is used for juvenile
court proceedings, even allowing for the rule that there must
be a minimum period of one hour between the sittings.

Persons Present

The Children and Young Persons Act 1933,[15] restricts the
classes of persons allowed to attend juvenile court proceedings
to the following.

(a) Members and officers of the court.

The clerk to the magistrates, probation officers, officers of
the Social Services Department of a local authority, a court
usher and police officers are allowed to be present. Apart from
the prosecuting police officer and police witnesses, an inspector
of police is also normally present, and it is desirable, if practicable, that a woman officer should be there.[16]

[13] See Watson, *op. cit.*, p. 64.
[14] C. & Y.P. Act 1933, s. 31, which also requires girls to be under the
care of women; and see *ante*, p. 63. The rule applies to juvenile witnesses as well as juvenile offenders and extends to attendance before any
criminal court, not merely a juvenile court.
[15] Section 47(2). These restrictions do not apply to proceedings brought
in a juvenile court in connection with children in care and possession
pending adoption proceedings or with foster children; see respectively
the Adoption Act 1958, s. 47 and the Children Act 1958, s. 10.
[16] A police officer often acts as usher.
It is a matter for the Bench whether the police are allowed to appear
in uniform. Opinion is divided, but with the current trend in favour of
the juvenile court's discarding its "criminal" features, the uniform is
best avoided. For a different view see Watson, *op. cit.*, p. 68; Ingleby
Committee, para. 185.

(b) The parties to the case before the court, their solicitors and counsel and witnesses and other persons directly[17] concerned in the case.

It is only exceptionally, in serious cases or where a difficult point of law is involved, that a solicitor, or even less frequently counsel, represents the person bringing the proceedings or the juvenile.

(c) *Bona fide* representatives of newspaper or news agencies.

Although the press can be present in a juvenile court, the right to publish reports of the proceedings is subject to certain restrictions, imposed primarily by s. 49 of the Children and Young Persons Act 1933, which aim to preserve the anonymity of the juvenile. These restrictions also apply to radio and television broadcasts.[18] Unless the court itself or the Home Secretary gives express permission to do so, a newspaper report or broadcast must not reveal the name, address or school of a juvenile or any other details which are likely[19] to lead to his identification, and a newspaper must not carry a picture of him.[20] If there is publication, it is no defence to show that there were irregularities in the conduct of the proceedings.[21] Even these restrictions may not always guarantee complete protection from publicity: enough may be published for the juvenile to be identified by those living in the immediate neighbourhood.[1] Permission to disclose is uncommon and may only be given where it is "appropriate to do so for the purpose of avoiding injustice to a child or young person".[2] Its object

[17] For the attendance of parents see *infra*.
[18] C. & Y.P. Act 1933, s. 49, as amended by C. & Y.P. Act 1963, s. 57 and C. & Y.P. Act 1969, s. 10 and Sched. 5, para. 53.
  The provisions extend to the publication in England of reports and broadcasts of proceedings in Scottish juvenile courts and *vice versa*.
[19] Section 49(1) of the 1933 Act speaks of the disclosure of details which are "calculated" to lead to identification. It has been pointed out that "calculated" apparently means "likely" rather than "intended"; see Clarke Hall and Morrison, *op. cit.*, p. 56.
[20] Wrongful disclosure is a summary offence carrying a penalty of a fine of up to £50. It is also a matter which may well be brought to the attention of the Press Council.
[21] *Roberts* v. *Dolby* (1935), 80 Sol.Jo. 32. (Juvenile court was held in an ordinary court room but not on a different day from sittings of the adult magistrates' courts, so that the hearing was contrary to s. 47(2) of the C. & Y.P. Act 1933, as it then stood. *Held*, that this did not excuse disclosure of the name of the juvenile's school in a newspaper report).

[1] See Cavenagh, *Juvenile Courts, The Child and the Law*, pp. 220-221.
[2] C. & Y.P. Act 1933, s. 49(1), as amended by C. & Y.P. Act 1969, s. 10(1) (c).

is to exculpate a juvenile who, but for the disclosure of the name of the offender, might himself be wrongly identified as the offender.

These provisions relate to criminal and civil proceedings alike and they apply to persons who are witnesses as well as to those against or in respect of whom the proceedings have been taken; but, as originally enacted, s. 49 extended only to persons under the age of 17, even though the juvenile court exceptionally had jurisdiction beyond that age; *e.g.*, where a young person attained that age during the proceedings.[3] The Children and Young Persons Act 1969 has widened the jurisdiction of the court so as to enable it to deal with persons even over the age of 18, especially with regard to the variation and discharge of supervision orders and care orders,[4] and s. 10 of that Act has extended the restrictions of s. 49 of the 1933 Act so as to take account of the wider jurisdiction. Thus the latter section also now applies to (1) persons aged 17 but under 18 who may be the subject of proceedings in a juvenile court and (2) persons of any age in respect of whom proceedings under Part I of the 1969 Act are brought in that court.

Section 10 also extends s. 49 to certain proceedings held in an adult magistrates' court. As will be seen,[5] such a court may, under ss. 15 and 16 of the 1969 Act, vary or discharge a supervision order where the supervised person has attained the age of 18 Since this jurisdiction is essentially a continuation of the juvenile court jurisdiction, the extension is logical and desirable, but the court must announce in the course of the proceedings that s. 49 is applicable, otherwise no liability under it will arise for any disclosure.

Section 49 applies to proceedings on appeal (whether to the Crown Court or by case stated) as it does to those at first instance, and, in the case of committal proceedings in respect of a juvenile, the publication of the notice of the result of those proceedings[6] must not disclose the name and address of *any* juvenile,[7] unless the examining justices are of the opinion that disclosure would avoid injustice to him.[8] But the section does

---

[3] See *ante*, Chapter 2, p. 49.
[4] *Post*, Chapter 4.   [5] *Ibid.*
[6] In accordance with s. 4 of the Criminal Justice Act 1967.
[7] *I.e.*, not only the juvenile charged with the offence.
[8] C. & Y.P. Act 1969, s. 10(3).

not apply to the trial of a juvenile who has been committed. There is, however, a general power, conferred by s. 39 of the 1933 Act,[9] for *any* court to direct that the matters stated above shall not be disclosed in a newspaper report or broadcast of its proceedings, civil as well as criminal, in which a juvenile has been concerned whether as the party by or against or in respect of whom the proceedings were taken or as a witness.[10] Both s. 39 and s. 49[11] rest on the principle that publicity may not be in the interests of the juvenile,[12] but there is a difference of emphasis. Under s. 49 the publication of details of identification is intended to be exceptional, whereas under s. 39 it is the restriction on publication that is the exception: if the court does not prohibit, the details are freely publishable, subject, however, to the general law relating to the publication of judicial proceedings.[13] It is submitted that s. 49 should be extended to all criminal proceedings in any court[14] on the ground that it is inherent in their nature that there is real risk of harm to the juvenile offender by identification. The onus should, therefore, in such proceedings always be placed on the court to decide whether in the exceptional case to allow publication. With a uniform rule of this kind there would also be less chance of the court's overlooking the question of publicity.[15] As for civil proceedings outside the juvenile court, identification is not likely to be harmful and s. 39 should continue to apply thereto.

(d) Other persons specially authorised by the juvenile court to be present.

This power of the court is particularly useful to enable

---

[9] As amended by C. & Y.P. Act 1963, s. 57.
[10] Until it was amended s. 39 was limited to proceedings arising "out of any offence against, or any conduct contrary to, decency and morality", and was probably intended to relate mainly, if not wholly, to proceedings concerning sexual offences. This is the kind of case in which it is still most likely to be invoked.
[11] Section 39 carries the same penalty for breach of it as s. 49 and the relevant provisions extend to publication in England of reports and broadcasts of proceedings in Scottish courts and *vice versa*.
[12] For the merits of the principle see Cavenagh, *op. cit.*, pp. 146-147.
[13] For example, photographs, portraits and sketches of persons involved in judicial proceedings cannot be taken in a court (Criminal Justice Act 1925, s. 41).
[14] The Ingleby Committee (Cmnd. 1191, para. 260) saw no reason for extending even s. 39 to all criminal proceedings; see *supra*, n.10 for the original scope of the section.
[15] *Cp.* s. 10(2) of C. & Y.P. Act 1969, *supra*, which allows for oversight.

students of social welfare to attend, and with the need for increased recruitment of social workers and for much more research into the working of juvenile courts it must be hoped that justices will never be impressed by the narrow view adopted by the Departmental Committee on the Treatment of Young Offenders[16] that the practice of allowing students to be present is "prejudicial to the interests of the young people concerned". Provided that their presence is made inconspicuous and their number is strictly limited to one or two to each sitting, the experience gained must surely be valuable.

Attendance at Court of Parents of Juvenile

Any court before whom a juvenile is being brought, whether as an alleged offender or for any other reason, can insist on his parents or guardians[17] being present during the whole of the proceedings. Alternatively, it can require attendance at a particular stage; for example, after an offender has pleaded guilty to a charge and the court is inquiring into his antecedents and family background.[18] The requirement for attendance is enacted by s. 34(1) of the Children and Young Persons Act 1933,[19] but until the law was amended by the 1963 Act the court could only compel the attendance of the parent who had "the actual possession and control" of the juvenile, except that, if that person was not the father, the latter could also be compelled to attend. Furthermore, a parent's attendance could not be required where the juvenile had, before the institution of the proceedings, been removed from the custody or charge of the parent by an order of the court. By its terms this latter rule was applicable even though the parent had been deprived only temporarily of his parental rights and duties and might still have some concern, at least, for the welfare of his child; for

[16] Cmnd. 2831, p. 37.
[17] For the purpose of the C. & Y.P. Acts a guardian includes not only a legal guardian appointed by deed or will or order of a court, but also one who in the opinion of the court "has for the time being the charge of or control over" the juvenile; C. & Y.P. Act 1933, s. 107(1).
Subsequent references within the present topic to a parent include, unless the context otherwise requires, references to a guardian.
[18] Such an inquiry is a distinct stage in the proceedings; see *R. v. Wheeler*, [1917] 1 K.B. 283 (C.C.A.); [1916-17] All E.R. Rep. 1111.
[19] As substituted by s. 25(1) of the C. & Y.P. Act 1963 and amended by the C. & Y.P. Act 1969, Sched. 6.

example, where the juvenile was already the subject of a fit person order or an approved school order. Under the present law the court is given a general power to compel the attendance of "any person who is a parent or guardian", but it would, it is suggested, have been better had it also been expressly enacted that both parents should normally be required to attend. Attendance of both is certainly desirable in the vast majority of cases where they are living together and are jointly responsible for bringing up their children; but it is equally so in many cases where they are living apart. In the latter circumstances as much as in the former, unless both attend, the court may not be able to have proper regard to the welfare of the juvenile as it is statutorily directed to do[20] when deciding how to deal with him. In these cases of separation very much will depend on the present custody, care and control of the child. If only one parent has these or has been entrusted with them by a court and the other has totally abdicated his parental responsibilities, it is most unlikely that the court will want to see that other. But the court may well take a different view if the other parent has been granted access and is in fact seeing the juvenile regularly. Again, where a court has made a "divided" order giving, say, care and control to the mother and custody to the father,[1] both should normally be asked to be present. So, too, the stepparent who has accepted the child as a member of the family should normally attend. His responsibilities have already been recognised in matrimonial proceedings,[2] and there is no legal obstacle to similar recognition for the purpose of juvenile court jurisdiction, since the stepparent who has accepted the juvenile as a member of the family may be a guardian within the meaning of the Children and Young Persons Acts as one having "for the time being the charge of or control over" the juvenile.[3]

The attendance of the parents can be important for various reasons. There is, firstly, the obvious one that appearance before the court, particularly if it is a first appearance, is for

---

[20] C. & Y.P. Act 1933, s. 44, *ante*, Chapter 1, p. 16.

[1] For divided orders see *post*, Chapter 9, p. 263.

[2] Matrimonial Proceedings and Property Act 1970, and the Matrimonial Proceedings (Magistrates' Courts) Act 1960.

[3] *Supra.*

many juveniles an ordeal which is likely to be more resolutely faced if there is accompanying parental support and comfort. Secondly, unless the juvenile is legally represented, his parents ought to be there to help him conduct his case. But there is the further advantage that attendance often enables the court to bring home to the parents their own responsibilities concerning the upbringing of their child and to point to their past failures in this respect. Consequently, the court's discretion under s. 34 not to require attendance if that is unreasonable ought to be exercised sparingly.

The importance of parental attendance under s. 34 is reflected in the measures which can be taken to ensure it. It can be enforced by summons or warrant and the former can be included in a summons to the juvenile to attend.[4] Moreover, when a juvenile is arrested steps must be taken by the person arresting him to inform at least one of the parents.[5] A similar duty is imposed on a police officer who decides to detain a juvenile in a place of safety in accordance with s. 28 of the Children and Young Persons Act 1969.[6] We have also seen[7] that when a juvenile is arrested for an offence and is remanded on bail on a recognisance entered into by his parent, the recognisance may be conditioned for the attendance of the parent as well as the juvenile.[8]

Apart from s. 34, there are other provisions which may make the attendance of the parent essential. One of the features of the Children and Young Persons Act 1969 is that it enables care proceedings to be brought in respect of children under five

[4] Magistrates' Courts (Children and Young Persons) Rules 1970, r. 26, (replacing the Summary Jurisdiction (Children and Young Persons) Rules 1933, r. 30). The Ingleby Committee pointed out (Cmnd. 1191, para. 202) that the rule does not make clear whether a warrant can be issued without an information on oath and recommended amendment to ensure that such an information was necessary. The proposal has not been implemented by the 1970 Rules.

[5] C. & Y.P. Act 1933, s. 34(2), as substituted by C. & Y.P. Act 1963, s. 25 (1), and amended by C. & Y.P. Act 1969, Sched. 5, para. 3 and Sched. 6.

The subsection in its present form does not make clear of what the parent must be informed. Presumably it means information not only of the juvenile's arrest but also of the need for the parent to attend court. As originally enacted, it expressly required the parent to be warned to attend.

[6] See sub-s. (4), *ante*, p. 56.

[7] C. & Y.P. Act 1969, s. 29(2), *ante*, p. 62.

[8] The terms of the Magistrates' Courts Act 1952, s. 96, are such that the juvenile court itself can enforce the recognisance against the parent.

without their presence in court. The procedure is wholly within the court's discretion, but a prior condition is that either notice of the proceedings was served on the parent or he is in fact present before the court. In either event the court may direct that the proceedings continue, subject to the parent (if present) being given an opportunity to be heard.[9]

Again, in criminal proceedings, if a parent has not been required to attend the court but the court is contemplating imposing a fine to be paid by the parent instead of by the juvenile or requiring him to give security for the juvenile's behaviour, he must be given the opportunity of being heard.[10] Presumably, the court would follow the same procedure where, in care proceedings, it is thinking of making an order requiring the parent to enter into a recognisance to take proper care of the juvenile and exercise proper control over him;[11] but the 1969 Act is silent on the point.

All the above provisions are concerned with the power of a court to compel or enable attendance. Whether a parent has a general *right* in all cases to attend the *juvenile* court is another question, and the answer depends upon whether he can claim to be a person "directly concerned" in the case within the meaning of s. 47(2) of the Children and Young Persons Act 1933.[12] This provision has not been judicially interpreted, but it is submitted that in care proceedings he does have the right, since the requirement in s. 1 of the 1969 Act that the juvenile is in need of care or control is a matter with which the parent is directly concerned.

The Conduct and Order of the Proceedings

It is essential not only that there should be simplicity in juvenile court procedure but also that the juvenile and his parents should have a clear understanding as to what is actually happening. The Ingleby Committee suggested that it is well worth explaining to them beforehand what they can expect,[13] and some courts try to do this, useful methods being the poster displayed in waiting rooms and the explanatory leaflet out-

---

[9] C. & Y.P. Act 1969, s. 2(9). The effect of the direction is that the child is deemed to have been brought before the court under s. 1 of the Act.
[10] C. & Y.P. Act 1933, s. 55(3).
[11] C. & Y.P. Act 1969, s. 1(3) (a); see *post*, Chapter 4, p. 96.
[12] *Supra*, p.68   [13] Cmnd. 1191, para. 186.

lining the order and conduct of proceedings.[14] Nevertheless, the onus of making clear by means of the simplest language what is going on rests mainly on the chairman of the court throughout the proceedings. His role has been well described by one with considerable experience of the office:[15]

> "The efficient working of a juvenile court largely depends upon a suitable person being appointed to this office. The chairman, it is submitted, should personally conduct the proceedings: he should be the mouthpiece of the court and be experienced, not merely in talking to children, but in persuading children to talk to him. He should be sympathetic, but not complacent; patient but not easy-going; firm but not unkind. He must ever distinguish between sentiment and sentimentality, be prone to the one but shun the other. He must be willing to work as one of a team, listen always to his clerk's advice, lead his colleagues without overbearing them."

(a) Criminal Proceedings[16]

Proceedings begin with the court, through its clerk, explaining to the juvenile in simple language suitable to his age and understanding the substance of the charge and then asking him whether he admits it.[17]

Plea of guilty.—If he pleads guilty, the prosecution then relates the facts of the case, but, unlike the trial of an adult, the magistrates should hear what the juvenile has to say about the events, even though he has pleaded guilty.[18] This is desirable not only in case the juvenile did not understand the nature of the charge[19] but also because it will help the Bench to assess the character and background of the juvenile and, where

---

[14] See *ibid.*, Appendix V, which reproduces a leaflet introduced by Croydon Juvenile Court.

[15] Watson, *The Child and the Magistrate*, pp. 359-360.
And for the relationship and rapport which should exist between the chairman and his fellow magistrates see *ibid.*, pp. 360-362.

[16] Since certain aspects of the procedure in criminal cases are directly relevant to care proceedings based on the offence condition, the order followed in earlier sections of this chapter is reversed.
For a practical account of criminal proceedings in a juvenile court see especially Watson, *op. cit.*, pp. 71-85, and for rules of procedure see the Magistrates' Courts (Children and Young Persons) Rules 1970, Part II. Within the present topic subsequent citations of rules refer to Part II.

[17] Rules 6 and 7. The duty to explain does not mean that in all cases the court must go into details about the essential features of the offence; *R. v. Blandford Justices, Ex parte G. (Infant)* [1967] 1 Q.B. 82; [1966] 1 All E.R. 1021.

[18] Watson, *op. cit.*, p. 73.

[19] See *R. v. Blandford Justices, Ex parte G. (Infant)*, *supra*.

there is more than one alleged offender, the extent of his participation in the commission of the offence.

The Magistrates' Courts Act 1957,[20] which allows a person charged with a minor summary offence[1] to plead guilty in his absence, does not apply to juvenile courts, and the Ingleby Committee after careful consideration came down against extending the Act to those courts.[2] One of the main arguments in support of this view is that when the court is dealing with a juvenile offender it must have regard to his welfare,[3] and this it may not be able to do without first having the benefit of seeing him and questioning him. Furthermore, the commission of a trivial offence is often indicative of deeper troubles, which a personal appearance might reveal.[4]

Plea of not guilty.—If the juvenile does not admit the charge, the court will then hear the evidence of the witnesses for the prosecution and each witness may be cross-examined by or on behalf of the juvenile.[5] Where he is not legally represented the court must allow his parent or guardian[6] to assist him in cross-examining and in generally conducting his defence, and if the parent or guardian cannot be found or cannot in the court's opinion reasonably be required to attend,[7] the court may allow his place to be taken by any relative or other responsible person.[8]

When a juvenile is not legally represented and not assisted in his defence the Chairman is often hard put to it to control him in conducting his cross-examination. Invariably when the

[20] Section 1.
[1] *I.e.*, a summary offence other than a summary offence also triable on indictment or for which a sentence of more than three months' imprisonment may be imposed.
[2] Cmnd. 1191, paras. 240-246.   [3] C. & Y.P. Act 1933, s. 44(1).
[4] Cmnd. 1191, para. 245 (d).
[5] Rule 8(1). The order of evidence and speeches is the same as in criminal proceedings against an adult; see Magistrates' Courts Rules 1968, r. 13.
[6] For the meaning of guardian see *ante*, p. 71, n. 17.
[7] See *ante*, p. 71.
[8] Rule 5. The rule equally applies where the juvenile court is acting as examining justices.
    The term "relative" is not defined for the purpose of the Children and Young Persons legislation; (*cf.* the definitions in the Children Acts, 1948 and 1958, *post*, pp. 145 and 376, respectively; the Nurseries and Child-Minders Act 1948, s. 13(2), and the Adoption Act 1958, *post*, p. 321). Taken in conjunction with the term "other responsible person" (also not defined), it ought, it is submitted, to be construed liberally so as to include not only, as it *prima facie* means, legitimate relatives (see *Seale-Hayne* v. *Jodrell*, [1891] A.C. 304 (H.L.)) but also illegitimate.

juvenile does ask questions they will include irrelevant ones, as is readily to be expected in view of the difficulties in the art of cross-examination; but it frequently happens that he asks few or no questions, preferring at this point to give his own version of the story and then not always coherently. Should this happen the court must on his behalf put to the witness such questions as it deems necessary, and in order to do this it can question the juvenile so as to clarify any point arising from the assertions he has made.[9]

If, at the conclusion of the case for the prosecution, the court decides that there is a case to answer, it must tell the juvenile that he may either give evidence or make an unsworn statement.[10] The distinction and its effect, namely, of course, that adoption of the former but not of the latter alternative renders him liable to cross-examination, must be clearly and simply explained.[11]

When a child is called as a witness in any criminal proceedings and he is too young to understand the nature of an oath but is sufficiently intelligent and does understand the duty of telling the truth,[12] he may be allowed to give unsworn evidence, as opposed to making an unsworn statement.[13] If he does he can be cross-examined on it. This provision applies to children "of tender years". This term is not defined,[14] but with 10 being the minimum age of criminal responsibility, it is unlikely that a child of or just above that age who is charged with an offence will come within it. He, like any other alleged juvenile

---

[9] Rule 8(2). The rule also applies where the juvenile court is acting as examining justices.   [10] Rule 9.

[11] For the way in which this ought to be done see Watson, *op. cit.*, p. 79, and for the form of oath to be used by juveniles see C. & Y.P. Act 1963, s. 28, amending the Oaths Act 1909, s. 2. A juvenile, like an adult, may, however, be allowed to affirm.

[12] The court should put a few preliminary questions so as to be able to form an opinion on these matters; see *R.* v. *Lyons* (1921), 15 Cr. App. Rep. 144 (C.C.A.); *R.* v. *Reynolds*, [1950] 1 K.B. 606, (C.C.A.); [1950] 1 All E.R. 335.

[13] C. & Y.P. Act 1933, s. 38(1). *Quaere* whether the unsworn evidence can be corroboration of sworn evidence given by another person; *cf. R.* v. *Campbell*, [1956] 2 Q.B. 432 (C.C.A.); [1956] 2 All E.R. 272 with *R.* v. *E.*, [1964] 1 All E.R. 205; [1964] 1 W.L.R. 671. Certainly, under the proviso to s. 38(1), a person cannot be convicted on a child's unsworn evidence unless it is corroborated by other material evidence; *R.* v. *Hester*, (1972) 2 All E.R. 1020, (C.A.). On corroboration see Clarke Hall and Morrison, *op. cit.* p. 46.

[14] In *R.* v. *Wallwork* (1958), 42 Cr. App. Rep. 153 (C.C.A.), it was thought to be undesirable for a child as young as five to give evidence.

offender, will have to choose between giving his evidence on oath and making an unsworn statement.

Subsequent stages in the hearing of the case for the defence follow the same lines as in the summary trial of an adult. Witnesses for the defence are heard[15] and the juvenile or the parent or other person assisting him in his defence or, where he is legally represented, his advocate may address the court on the evidence. The magistrates then decide whether the juvenile is guilty of the offence.

Where the juvenile is found guilty, whether after a plea of guilty or a plea of not guilty, he and (if present) his parent or guardian must be given the opportunity to make a statement.[16] The court must then take into consideration various reports before making its order, and this may mean adjournment and remand of the juvenile.[17]

(b) Care Proceedings

Just as criminal proceedings follow the same pattern as they do in an adult magistrates' court, so care proceedings are broadly similar to those by way of complaint in that court. But, as in criminal cases, the procedure is also designed to some extent to make itself intelligible to the juvenile and his parents.[18]

Thus, at the outset of the hearing the court must inform the juvenile of the general nature of the proceedings and the grounds on which they are brought,[19] and this must be done in terms suitable to his age and understanding. If, because of his age and understanding or his absence, this is impracticable, any parent[20] who is present must be informed.[1] Unless the juvenile or his parent is legally represented or the care proceedings are brought at the parent's request (or under an order resulting from a request) on the ground that the juvenile is beyond his control[2] or unless the juvenile otherwise requests, the court must allow the parent to conduct the case.[3] It may, where it considers it appropriate, allow a relative or some other

[15] Rule 9.   [16] Rule 10(1) (a).
[17] See *post*, pp. 86 *et seq.*
[18] The procedure also applies to the variation and discharge of supervision orders and care orders and to the removal of persons in care to Borstal; r. 13(1).
[19] The duty to inform him does not arise where he is the applicant (which, in effect, means where he is applying for variation or discharge of an order) or where the court is allowed to proceed in his absence.
[20] Or guardian; see *supra*, p. 71, n. 17.
[1] Rule 16(1).   [2] See *ante*, p. 51.   [3] Rule 17(1).

responsible person to do so as the juvenile's "friend", unless he otherwise requests.[4]

The order of the evidence and speeches is the same as in the case of a complaint,[5] and, being a civil case, both the juvenile and his parents are compellable witnesses. When the case for the applicant has been heard and the court considers that a *prima facie* case has been made out,[6] the juvenile or the person conducting the case on his behalf must be told of his right to give evidence or make a statement and to call witnesses.[7]

Except where the juvenile is conducting his own case, evidence may be given in his absence, if this is thought to be in his interests; but he must be present to hear evidence of his character or conduct. This power to exclude is often necessary to avoid embarrassment when the parent's conduct is being considered on the question whether the juvenile is in need of care or control. Conversely, the parent may in special circumstances be required to withdraw while the juvenile is giving evidence or making a statement, although, should the juvenile make any allegation against him he is entitled to meet it by calling evidence or otherwise.[8]

All care proceedings involve two stages:[9] proof of one of the conditions prescribed by s. 1 of the 1969 Act, followed by proof of the need for care and control. In most cases the evidence necessary for the latter will have been very largely adduced when establishing the particular condition, but where the proceedings are based on the offence condition it is essential that the two stages are clearly distinguished.[10] The Act and the Magistrates' Courts (Children and Young Persons) Rules 1970 partly recognise this but do not draw the attention of the court or the parties to the distinction with sufficient particularity.

[4] Rule 17(2). *Cf.* r. 5 in relation to criminal proceedings (*supra*, p. 76) which is in rather different terms.
[5] Magistrates' Courts Rules 1968, r. 14.
[6] It is significant that the Rules do not (as they do in criminal proceedings under r. 8(2)) expressly impose on the court a duty to put questions in cross-examination on the juvenile's behalf. Nevertheless, it is submitted that the court may and ought to do so.
[7] Rule 19. There is the same power to issue a summons or warrant to secure attendance as there is for the hearing of a complaint (C. & Y.P. Act 1969, s.2(6)).
[8] Rule 18(1) and (2).
[9] See *ante*, Chapter 2, p. 22.
[10] See Watson, "*The Juvenile Court* – 1970 *Onward*", pp. 28-31.

When a juvenile is brought before the court under s. 1 for an alleged offence, and the nature of the proceedings is explained to him, it must be made clear that a finding of guilt does not mean criminal liability. Nevertheless, the first stage in the procedure then follows the same lines as that in criminal proceedings, depending upon whether there is a plea of guilty or not guilty,[11] with the same burden of proof and rules of evidence applicable.[12] Moreover, there is no power as in other care proceedings to require a parent to withdraw while the juvenile gives evidence or makes a statement.[13] Once it is decided whether or not the offence condition is satisfied the juvenile must be informed of the finding,[14] and, if it is satisfied, the court must then proceed to consider in accordance with the civil burden of proof whether he is in need of care or control, as it would do if the care proceedings were based on one of the other conditions.

D. INQUIRIES AND REPORTS

In deciding how to deal with the juvenile after he has been found guilty of an offence or, in care proceedings, after the applicant's case has been proved, the court must not only have regard to his welfare but also, where the circumstances so warrant, see that he is removed from undesirable surroundings and that proper provision is made for his education and training.[15] The court cannot properly discharge these duties unless it is fully informed about such matters and about his background and antecedents.

The responsibility for providing the necessary information falls upon the local authority[16] who have instituted the proceedings or, as the case may be, have been notified that proceedings are being brought.[17] They must investigate, and report on, the home surroundings, school record, health and character of the juvenile, unless they consider it unnecessary.[18] They are also relieved of the obligation where the juvenile has reached the age of 10 and, by a direction of justices or a probation and after-care committee, arrangements are in force

---

[11] *Supra*, pp. 75-78.   [12] C. & Y.P. Act 1969, s. 3(1) and (3).
[13] *Supra*. See r. 16(2) (c).   [14] Rule 16(2) (d).
[15] C. & Y.P. Act 1933, s. 44(1), as amended by C. & Y.P. Act 1969, Sched. 6.
[16] Or the local education authority where care proceedings are based on s. 1(2) (e) of the 1969 Act (*ante*, p. 50, n.b.).
[17] For the duty to notify see *ante*, p. 53.   [18] C. & Y.P. Act 1969, s. 9(1).

for information with respect to his home surroundings to be furnished to the court by a probation officer.[19] However, in areas where such arrangements exist it might instead be arranged that in the case of proceedings brought by a local authority (as opposed to any other person) the authority will investigate instead of a probation officer, unless the latter is expressly requested to do so by the court.[20] Apart from the normal duty of the local authority to investigate, the court may request them to make inquiries, whether the latter have done so or not,[1] and it may seek information from other sources if it so wishes.

All information presented must be considered by the court and, if it is thought desirable, the juvenile may be remanded for further inquiries to be made,[2] the most likely instance being for a medical report on the juvenile. In most cases, however, remand will not be necessary. This is especially so in care proceedings. Pre-trial enquiries are essential in order that oral evidence may be adduced to prove the need for care or control and the subsequent information in the form of a written report (and, if need be, an oral statement in support) which is presented to assist the court in deciding upon how to deal with the juvenile may be simply a "follow-up" of that evidence.[3] In criminal proceedings evidence of background and antecedents is not admissible until proof of the offence,[4] except where it is necessary to rebut the presumption of innocence,[5] and, although there are objections to pre-trial inquiries, on balance they seem desirable, especially where the juvenile admits the offence and provided that they do not delay the hearing.[6]

The social inquiry report[7] furnished by the local authority

---

[19] *Ibid.*, s. 34(3).   [20] See Home Office Guide, para. 104.

[1] C. & Y.P. Act 1969, s. 9(2).

[2] Magistrates' Courts (Children and Young Persons) Rules 1970, rr. 10(1) (b) and (c) and 20(1) (a) and (b).

[3] Watson, *The Juvenile Court* – 1970 *Onward*, p. 39.

[4] This is true also of care proceedings based on the offence condition, but in that case oral evidence of background, *etc.*, will then be necessary to satisfy the condition of need for care or control.

[5] See *ante*, Chapter 2, p. 36.

[6] See Williams, *Criminal Law: The General Part*, pp. 823-824; Ingleby Committee, Cmnd. 1191, paras. 219-220.

[7] For accounts of the preparation and contents of reports see Watson, *The Child and the Magistrate*, Chapters 5 to 8, and *The Juvenile Court* – 1970 *Onward*, Chapter 4.

through their social worker or by a probation officer is the most comprehensive which the court receives. It should deal with, *inter alia*, (1) the juvenile's antecedents, especially any record of illnesses and of offences of which he has previously been found guilty, together with the kinds of treatment then ordered; (2) his family, particularly its composition and income, the home and the relationship between him and the other members; (3) his general activities or the lack of them. The reporting officer should finally express his opinion on whether supervision is likely to be successful and put forward a general recommendation on the treatment the court should order.[8]

The report of the juvenile's school record ought to include a record of his attendance over a period of some two months with reasons for any absences, his conduct in relation to his teachers and to other children, his state of health, his ability and aptitude to deal with school work and the attitude of his parents to his education. These matters should be dealt with fully, but the stereotyped form in which reports are usually given and the fear of some teachers that their reports may be read out before the juvenile and the parents militate against frankness.[9]

If the court decides that a psychiatrist's report should be obtained it will remand the juvenile for psychiatric examination at a child guidance clinic. These clinics exist to deal with a wide class of children who are delinquent, maladjusted or educationally disabled or who have serious psychological difficulties in relation to their own family. Like many other social and welfare services they owe their origin to the efforts of voluntary organisations, the first independent clinic being set up in 1927 in the East End of London by the Jewish Health Organisation of Great Britain. But their value was soon recognised by local education authorities. Since 1946 a number have also been established by Regional Hospital Boards under the National Health Service Act 1946, each of these forming a

---

[8] But courts vary in their views on whether it is part of the functions of a reporting officer to make recommendations; see Cavenagh, *op. cit.*, pp. 55-60 and the Report of the (Streatfeild) Interdepartmental Committee on the Business of the Criminal Courts (1961) Cmnd. 1289, paras. 343-346.

[9] For a criticism see Kirk, *School Reports to the Juvenile Courts*, (1968) 132 J.P. 27.

psychiatric unit within a particular hospital. Of the local authority clinics[10] some are run entirely by local authorities, but the remainder are joint clinics with medical staff provided by regional hospital boards.[11]

The essential organisation of these clinics has been described in the following terms:[12]

"From their early days a characteristic feature of child guidance clinics has been their team-work. In a clinic run on classical lines the team consists of a psychiatrist, an educational psychologist and a psychiatric social worker. The psychiatrist seeks to discover and understand the child's emotional difficulties and conflicts, and helps to deal with them, the psychologist tests his intellectual capacity and educational attainments, and where necessary and possible helps him to overcome any special scholastic difficulties and deficiencies, while the psychiatric social worker is primarily concerned to assess and, if necessary, modify the social factors in his environment which affect his behaviour. In particular she helps the parents to a better understanding of the child's difficulties and of their own relationships with him.

This pattern has now been modified in many clinics and the whole approach appears to be more flexible. New methods of treatment, for example group therapy, are also being used, and new kinds of workers, such as child therapists, are coming in, but whatever the modifications made the work is still essentially team work."

The juvenile court may remand a juvenile for psychiatric examination either on bail or to a community home provided by a local authority or a controlled community home.[13] A juvenile remanded on bail or in a home without its own clinic will have to attend for examination at an outside clinic provided by the local authority or at a hospital unit or at a clinic attached to some other community home. This may well mean delay in the examination.

Besides an examination of physical health, there is an assessment of the juvenile's intelligence, character and emotions and an inquiry into his home environment, with particular reference

[10] There are approximately 500 child guidance clinics, of which about 400 are local authority clinics.
[11] The joint clinic was recommended by the Report of the Committee on Maladjusted Children (Underwood Report), (1953).
[12] Hall, *The Social Services of Modern England*, 6th edn., p. 219, and *The Social Services of England and Wales* (1969), pp. 149-150.
[13] On community homes see *post*, Chapter 5.

to the relationship between him and his parents who, unless unwilling to co-operate, are invariably interviewed. To assist in the examination the court should ensure that copies of social inquiry reports, which the local authority or the probation officer have submitted, are provided. The subsequent report of the psychiatrist ought to refer to any causal connection between the juvenile's health and his delinquency (if any) and proceed to make recommendations as to the most suitable treatment.

Disclosure of Contents of Reports

The juvenile court may consider any written report of a probation officer, local authority, local education authority or medical practitioner without having it read aloud, but, unless it is impracticable to do so in view of his age and understanding, the juvenile must be told the substance of any part of the report concerning his character or conduct which the court considers material to the manner in which he should be dealt with. So, too, the parent[14] must, if present, be informed of the substance of any part of the report which refers to his own character or conduct or to the character, conduct, home surroundings or health of the juvenile, in so far as these matters are similarly considered material. The juvenile or the parent will be allowed to produce rebutting evidence concerning the matters so disclosed to him, if the courts think it would be material, and for this purpose the proceedings will be adjourned and the court can require the person who made the report to attend the adjourned hearing, when (although the rules do not expressly so provide) the juvenile and the parent will have the opportunity to cross-examine him.[15]

The Ingleby Committee[16] was told that these rules were observed in different ways, that "in some courts the whole of the reports were read aloud, even in the presence of the child; in some copies were handed to parents; in some very little or even nothing of the reports was disclosed; and in some the chairman summarised the reports, omitting or paraphrasing items that he considered it unnecessary or harmful to reveal,

[14] Or guardian. For the meaning of guardian see *ante*, p. 71, n. 17.
[15] Magistrates' Courts (Children and Young Persons) Rules 1970, rr. 10(1) (d), 10(2), 20(1) (c) and 20(2).
[16] Cmnd. 1191, paras. 207-217.

or to reveal in the form in which they were reported". The basic difficulty is to avoid indiscriminate disclosure of the contents of a report which could cause distress to the juvenile, harm the relationship between him and his parents and, in the long run, deter reporting agents from producing frank reports without, on the other hand, concealing from the juvenile and the parents material information which they should have the opportunity to challenge. Anxious to avoid these consequences courts are just as insistent that full disclosure shall not be made to the advocate appearing on behalf of the juvenile.[17]

The Committee recognised that there is not a perfect solution to the problem, but felt that the difficulty can be considerably minimised by skilled summarising of reports by the chairman; this was a matter of experience and administrative guidance rather than formal regulation.[18] But while the Committee declined to make any formal recommendation, it did suggest that reporting agents should be encouraged to submit in a separate section of their reports confidential matters which they think should not be disclosed or disclosed only after careful consideration. If it is accepted that skilful summarising, coupled with separation of confidential material, is the best procedure, there is no justification for continuing to allow the court a discretion to read aloud the whole of the report, and the present rules should be amended accordingly.

The difficulties to which disclosure of reports can give rise can also be partly avoided by the court's relying on its power to require the juvenile or his parent or guardian to withdraw from the court. This it can do whenever it considers the step necessary in the juvenile's interests.[19] Thus delicate matters in a report which could distress him (for example, that his parent has previous convictions) could be mentioned and discussed with the parent in his absence. But this power should be exercised with care, and the court should weigh against it the

---

[17] See Richardson, *Social Inquiry Reports and the Juvenile Court*, 136 J.P. 74.

[18] For a similar suggestion see Watson, *The Juvenile Court – 1970 Onward*, pp. 40-43; see also Richardson, *supra*.

[19] Magistrates' Courts (Children and Young Persons) Rules 1970, rr. 10(1) (e) and 20(1) (d). The rule requiring withdrawal can be invoked at any stage subsequent to the court's finding the juvenile guilty of the offence or, as the case may be, finding the conditions of s. 1 of the 1969 Act satisfied.

possibility of the juvenile's feeling a sense of injustice if he is excluded. Certainly, if he is asked to withdraw, it ought normally to be only after he has been heard in the parent's absence.[20] Where a report has been considered in a person's absence he must be told the substance of it and allowed to produce further evidence.

E. ADJOURNMENTS, REMAND AND INTERIM ORDERS

I. CRIMINAL PROCEEDINGS

In criminal cases the juvenile court may at any time before or during the trial adjourn it and may remand the juvenile in custody or on bail.[1] Adjournments and remand are most likely to occur after the court has found the offence proved and it wants further information about the juvenile before deciding on the method of dealing with him; but sometimes, for example, when the facts are complicated, the court may have to adjourn before it has reached the stage where it can determine whether the juvenile is guilty.

Where the adjournment is without a remand, the court need not, but in practice does, fix the time and place at which the trial is to be resumed,[2] but, whether it does so or not, there should be no avoidable delay in resuming. Where, however, a remand is ordered, the time and place of resumption must be fixed when adjourning. If there is an adjournment before the offence is proved, the remand must not be for more than eight clear days,[3] unless it is on bail and the juvenile and prosecutor consent to a longer period.[4] An adjournment after proof of the offence may be for up to four weeks, unless there is a remand

[20] Watson, *The Child and the Magistrate*, p. 93.
[1] Magistrates' Courts Act 1952, ss. 14, 105 and 106.
 For the power to adjourn and remand where the court is sitting as examining justices see s. 6.
[2] Section 14(2).
[3] *I.e.*, not including the day of remand and the day on which the juvenile is again to appear before the court.
[4] Magistrates' Courts Act 1952, s. 105(4), proviso (a).
 Where a person is remanded on bail for such longer period but is initially committed in custody because the recognisances of his sureties have not yet been taken, he must be brought before the court at the end of eight clear days or at such earlier time as may be specified in the warrant of commitment, unless in the meantime the sureties have entered into their recognisances (Magistrates' Courts Rules 1968, r. 22).

in custody when the maximum period allowed is three weeks.[5]
This latter distinction seems unjustified in view of the power in
care proceedings to detain for up to 28 days under an interim
order.[6]

Where there is a remand for obtaining information with
respect to a juvenile the court may extend the period of remand
in the juvenile's absence, providing that he appears before the
court or a justice at least once in every 21 days.[7] It seems that
this provision is limited to a remand after the case has been
proved. There are other similar powers to order further
remands in the juvenile's absence but apparently these may be
exercised before or after the case is proved. Thus, if illness or
accident prevent his appearance when the period of remand has
expired, he can be further remanded in his absence and
(where it is before he has been found guilty) for more than
eight clear days, if the court wishes.[8] Moreover, a juvenile, who
has been remanded on bail and who fails to appear before the
court, whether because of illness, accident or any other reason,
may in his absence have his recognisance and those of his
sureties enlarged to a later time.[9] There is one further exceptional situation which allows further remand in the juvenile's
absence, namely, where the Secretary of State has made a
transfer direction under the Mental Health Act 1959 in respect
of a juvenile who has been remanded in custody, *i.e.*, a direction that, because he is mentally ill, he be removed to and
detained in a hospital.[10]

The court has a complete discretion, provided that it is

---

[5] Section 14(3), as amended by the Criminal Justice Act 1967, ss. 30,
130 and Sched. VI.
[6] Compare the view of the Ingleby Committee (Cmnd. 1191, paras. 226-
227) who regarded a period of three weeks as normally reasonable for
completing inquiries and reports and opposed any extension, since the
courts and reporting agents would tend unnecessarily to work to the
new maximum.
[7] C. & Y.P. Act 1933, s. 48(3) (a). Notice must be given to him and his
sureties (if any) of the date when he is to appear; see Magistrates'
Courts (Children and Young Persons) Rules 1970, r. 12.
[8] Magistrates' Courts Act 1952, ss. 105(2) and 106(1).
[9] Section 106(2) and (3). Where the absence is not due to illness or
accident (so that s. 106(1) does not apply) the enlargement is deemed
to be a further remand.
[10] Mental Health Act 1959, s. 72(6) (a) (as amended by C. & Y.P. Act
1969, Sched. 6) and s. 77(3).
The clerk of the court must notify the managers of the hospital of the
further remand (Magistrates' Courts Rules 1968, r. 24).

judicially exercised, to remand in custody or on bail[11] and can choose the former even though sworn evidence connecting the juvenile with the crime has not yet been given.[12] If the remand is in custody but for a period not exceeding 24 hours, the juvenile may be committed to the custody of a constable,[13] but otherwise it must be to the care of the local authority for the area where he resides or where the offence was committed, unless he is aged 14[14] or over and the court certifies that he is so unruly that he cannot safely be committed to their care, in which case he will be sent to a remand centre or, if that is not available, to a prison.[15] An unruly young person already remanded to the care of a local authority may, on their application, similarly be committed to a remand centre or prison for the remaining period of remand. Until criminal proceedings against children are abolished,[16] the power to commit to the care of a local authority applies to all juveniles charged with or convicted of an offence or committed for trial or sentence,[17] except that a young person committed to the Crown Court with a view to a borstal sentence must be committed to a remand centre, if available, or otherwise to a prison.[18]

The power to remand in custody for inquiries and reports

---

[11] With the rare qualification that, if the adjournment is due to the non-appearance of the prosecutor, the remand must not be in custody unless the accused has been brought to the court from custody or cannot be remanded on bail because of his failure to enter into a recognisance or to find sureties (Magistrates' Courts Act 1952, s. 16(2)).

[12] *R. v. Guest, Ex parte Metropolitan Police Commissioner*, [1961] 3 All E.R. 1118.

[13] Magistrates' Courts Act 1952, s. 105(5), as amended by C. & Y.P. Act 1969, s. 23 (5).

A magistrates' court that has power to commit to prison a person convicted of an offence can order his detention in the court house or at a police station up to 8 p.m. of the day on which the order is made (Magistrates' Courts Act 1952, s. 110(1)), but since the court cannot impose imprisonment on a juvenile (s. 107(2)), this power cannot be exercised in respect of a juvenile, and reliance must instead be placed on s. 105(5).

[14] There is power to raise the age (C. & Y.P. Act 1969, s. 34(1) (e)).

[15] C. & Y.P. Act 1969, s. 23. This enactment has meant the substitution of a new s. 27 in the Criminal Justice Act 1948 empowering remand of persons aged 17 to 20 to remand centres or prisons; (see C. & Y.P. Act 1969, Sched. 5, para. 24).

[16] See s. 4 of the 1969 Act, *ante*, Chapter 2, p. 31.

[17] When s. 4 comes into operation the power will apply to a child (as opposed to a young person) only if convicted of homicide or committed for trial for that offence.

[18] Magistrates' Courts Act 1952, s. 28(1) and (4), as amended by the Criminal Justice Act 1967, s. 103, Sched. 6, para. 11; Courts Act 1971, s. 8 and Sched. I.

after the juvenile has been found guilty must not be used as a means of punishing the offender. In *R.* v. *Toynbee Hall Juvenile Court Justices, Ex parte Joseph*[19] a boy aged 16 was charged with having travelled on a railway without having paid his fare, the maximum penalty for the offence being a fine of 40 shillings. On February 7, 1939, he was found guilty of the offence, but the hearing was adjourned and he was sent to a remand home for seven days, an application for bail being refused. On February 14 he was remanded in custody to the remand home for a further seven days. The chairman said that the boy was a liar, that he had to learn not to defraud the railway company, that his father had prompted him to lie and that for his own good he ought to go to a remand home. On his third appearance[20] before the court, on February 21, the charge was dismissed on payment of 40 shillings costs.[1] On an application to have the orders of February 14 and February 21 quashed it was held as to the former that it was invalid because the observations made by the chairman showed that the boy was being remanded for the indirect purpose of punishing him. The case is particularly strong because the court was detaining him as punishment for an offence for which only a fine could be inflicted, but the principle established is equally applicable where the offence is one for which an order for detention could be made on conviction.

Apart from the above considerations, the court in deciding whether to remand on bail or in custody should take account of the same factors as it would when considering the remand of adult offenders, namely, the likelihood of appearance at the adjourned hearing and the risk of interference with witnesses.[2] But, more importantly, in juvenile cases much weight should be given to the circumstances of the juvenile's home and his interests. They may be so bad as to warrant his immediate removal pending the final order of the court. If there is to be a

---

[19] [1939] 3 All E.R. 16. See also *R.* v. *Brentford JJ., Ex parte Muirhead* (1941), 166 L.T. 57.
[20] Between the date of his first and second appearamce and between his second and third appearance the boy had in fact been released on bail on the order of a judge in chambers.
[1] Under the Probation of Offenders Act 1907.
[2] *Cf.* the factors to be taken into account when deciding whether to detain a juvenile who has been arrested until he can be brought before the court; see C. & Y.P. Act 1969, s. 29(1), *ante*, p. 60.

remand for medical examination, the court will have to consider whether the facilities are more suitable and more readily available at a community home or an outside child guidance clinic. A distinct advantage of remand in a home – and this applies to remands in custody generally – is that the juvenile's behaviour is being observed by trained staff who, through the superintendent of the home, will report thereon to the court.

Remand for Medical Examination

When the court considers a medical examination is needed it will adjourn the case and must[3] then remand the juvenile. The maximum period of adjournment is four weeks at a time where there is a remand on bail, three weeks if a remand in custody. The duty to adjourn and remand is imposed by s. 26 of the Magistrates' Courts Act 1952[4] on every magistrates' court which is trying an offence punishable on summary conviction with imprisonment;[5] but if the offence being tried is not punishable by imprisonment the court can exercise its powers under s. 14(3) of the Act.[6]

When the juvenile is remanded on bail under s. 26 it must be made a condition of the recognisance that he will undergo medical examination by a duly qualified medical practitioner or, if it relates to his mental condition and the recognisance so specifies, two practitioners; that he will attend at a particular place for the examination; and, where the inquiry is into his mental condition, that he will comply with any directions concerning the examination. There may also be a condition that for the purpose of the examination he reside at a particular institution for a specified period or until he is discharged.[7] In such cases further remand will obviously be necessary.

A court proceeding under s. 26 must send to those respon-

---

[3] *Cf.* s. 14 of the Magistrates' Courts Act 1952, *supra*, p. 86, where on adjournment remand is discretionary.

[4] As amended by the Mental Health Act 1959, Scheds. 7 and 8, and the Criminal Justice Act 1967, ss. 30 and 130 and Sched. 6.

[5] A magistrates' court cannot impose imprisonment on a person under 17, but the application of s. 26 to a juvenile court is preserved by s. 126(8) of the Magistrates' Courts Act 1952 which provides that "references in [the] Act to an offence punishable on summary conviction with imprisonment shall be construed without regard to any prohibition or restriction imposed by or under this or any other Act on imprisonment of young offenders".

[6] *Boaks* v. *Reece*, [1957] 1 Q.B. 219; [1956] 3 All E.R. 986 (C.A.).

[7] Magistrates' Courts Act 1952, s. 26(3).

sible for the examination a statement of its reasons for the examination together with information about the juvenile's physical and mental condition.[8]

II. CARE PROCEEDINGS

The rules relating to adjournment and the detention of the juvenile follow a similar pattern in care proceedings, but are not so disparate as they are in criminal cases.

An adjournment may be ordered before or during the hearing[9] and an interim order may be made placing the juvenile in the care of the local authority for a maximum period of 28 days.[10] The order is permitted if the court "is not in a position to decide what order, if any, ought to be made" under s. 1 of the 1969 Act.[11] It is submitted that this provision is wide enough to enable an interim order to be made before, and not merely after, the court has found that the conditions of s. 1 have been satisfied.[12] For example, it might not be possible to prove the need for care or control without further inquiries and reports, but the evidence already before the court may presumptively indicate that the circumstances of the home are such that it would be safer to place the child in care until completion of the inquiries.

As in criminal proceedings, there is the alternative possibility of a juvenile aged 14 or over being committed to a remand centre, where the court certifies him to be so unruly that he cannot safely be committed to the care of a local authority. Should he already be in their care under an interim order, they may apply for committal to a remand centre for the remainder of the period specified in the order, with the possibility of detention there for further periods of up to 28 days, corresponding to those allowed under interim orders.[13]

[8] Magistrates' Courts Rules 1968, r. 23.
[9] Magistrates' Courts (Children and Young Persons) Rules 1970, r. 15(1).
[10] C. & Y.P. Act 1969, ss. 2(10) and 20(1). For interim orders see further *post*, Chapter 5, p. 152.
[11] See s. 2(10) *supra*.
[12] The wording of the former corresponding enactment (s. 67(2) of C. & Y.P. Act 1933) which s. 2(10) replaces is in this respect to be preferred: "If a juvenile court before which any person is brought is not in a position to decide whether any and, if so, what, order ought to be made . . ."
[13] C. & Y.P. Act 1969, s. 22(5) and (6). The age of 14 may be raised (s. 34(1) (f)).

III. CONSTITUTION OF COURT AT RESUMED HEARING

When there has been an adjournment, whether before or after the court has found the case proved, there is the possibility that at the date of the resumed hearing one or more of the justices cannot attend. The Juvenile Courts (Constitution) Rules 1954 go far to meet this situation, because those[14] which allow exceptions to the general requirement that the court shall consist of not more than three justices and shall include a man and a woman, apply to "any sitting of a juvenile court" and, therefore, it is submitted, include a sitting at a resumed hearing of a criminal case or care case. These exceptions, it will be remembered,[15] allow the court to be constituted without a man or without a woman or allow a stipendiary magistrate to sit alone, in each case if it is inexpedient in the interests of justice for there to be an adjournment.

In criminal proceedings, as an alternative it may be possible to rely on s. 48(3) of the Children and Young Persons Act 1933. This allows, *inter alia*, a juvenile court other than that which remanded the juvenile finally to deal with him. Its terms show[16] that it is intended primarily to apply where there has been adjournment and remand under s. 14 of the Magistrates' Courts Act 1952 for inquiries after a finding of guilt,[17] but it is submitted that it can also be invoked where there has been a remand for medical examination under s. 26 of that Act.

Whether or not it has this additional scope, it must be read in conjunction with s. 98(7) of the 1952 Act. The latter, while permitting a magistrates' court, which has adjourned the trial of an information after the accused has been convicted, to be differently constituted when it comes to sentence or deal with him, does require the court firstly to inquire into the facts and circumstances of the case so as to enable the justices who were not sitting when the offender was convicted to be fully acquainted with them.

---

[14] Rule 12(2) and (3).   [15] See *ante*, Chapter 1, p. 8.
[16] "When a juvenile court has remanded a child or young person for information to be obtained with respect to him, any juvenile court acting for the same petty sessional division or place . . .
      (b) when the information has been obtained, may deal with him finally;"
[17] It does not apply to any adjournment before such finding.

Invariably every effort is made to see that the court as originally constituted finally deals with the juvenile, because the justices who have already had the opportunity of making some assessment of the juvenile and his background during the course of the trial are likely to be best suited to determine the final order. For that reason and in view of the additional requirement imposed by s. 98(7), if all members of the court cannot be present at the resumed hearing, reliance should, when possible, be placed on the Juvenile Courts (Constitution) Rules 1954 rather than on the provisions of the Acts of 1933 and 1952.

CHAPTER 4

Care Proceedings and Criminal Proceedings in Juvenile Courts — III Orders

After inquiries and reports have been completed, the court must tell the juvenile and his parent or guardian,[1] if present, of the way in which it proposes to deal with the case, except that it must not so inform the juvenile where it considers disclosure undesirable or, in care proceedings, impracticable because of his age and understanding. Those informed are then allowed to make representations.[2]

On making an order the court must normally explain to the juvenile its general nature and effect;[3] but the rules do not expressly require information to be given about the right to apply for discharge or variation of supervision orders or care orders. This is a serious omission in view of the wide powers of local authorities under those orders, and courts ought always to refer to the matter. Where the order is one requiring the parent or guardian to enter into a recognisance there is no obligation to explain this to the juvenile, if it is considered undesirable. The court is similarly relieved of the obligation in care proceedings where the age and understanding of the juvenile make an explanation impracticable.

A. ORDERS IN CARE PROCEEDINGS

The orders which may be made under s. 1 of the Children and Young Persons Act 1969 are:

    (a) an order requiring the parent or guardian to enter into a recognisance to take proper care of the juvenile and exercise proper control over him;

---

[1] In criminal proceedings it must also inform anyone assisting the juvenile in his defence.

[2] Magistrates' Courts (Children and Young Persons) Rules 1970, rr. 11(1) and 21(1).
    A duty to disclose also arises if the case is to be remitted to another court; for remittal see *ante*, Chapter 2, p. 42.

[3] Rules 11(2) and 21(2).

or (b) a supervision order;

or (c) a care order (other than an interim order);

or (d) a hospital order within the meaning of Part V of the Mental Health Act 1959;

or (e) a guardianship order within the meaning of that Act.

Save that a care order and a hospital order may be combined[4], not more than one of the above may be made; and, if the court makes an order of a kind already in force in respect of the juvenile, it may discharge the earlier one.[5] However, in a case where the offence condition is satisfied, certain other orders which are similarly available in criminal proceedings may be made. Thus, where the offence is an indictable offence,[6] the court can, whether or not it makes an order under s. 1, order the payment of compensation up to £100.[7] It may, if the offender is a young person, and must, if he is a child, order the parent[8] instead of the juvenile to pay the amount, unless the parent cannot be found or has not conduced to the commission of the offence by neglecting to exercise due care or control. Unless the parent has failed to comply with a request to attend the court, no order is to be made without giving him an opportunity of being heard.[9] In an "offence condition" case there is also power to order the juvenile, providing that he is a young person and consents, to enter into a recognisance for an amount not exceeding £25 and for a period not exceeding a year to keep the peace or be of good behaviour. But such an order is permissible only if an order under s. 1 is not made,[10] and it is not likely to be made often.

---

[4] This may be desirable to ensure that the juvenile has someone to visit him in hospital and to receive him on discharge. *Semble*, so far as concerns the place of accommodation, the hospital order prevails over the care order; see Home Office Guide to Part I of the 1969 Act, para. 53.

[5] C. & Y.P. Act 1969, s.1(4) and, with regard to hospital and guardianship orders, see the Mental Health Act 1959.

As part of the transitional provisions of the 1969 Act the court may discharge a fit person order (other than one committing a juvenile to a local authority, which by virtue of the Act became a care order on 1 January 1971), supervision order or order to enter into a recognisance made under the C. & Y.P. Act 1933; see C. & Y.P. Act 1969, Sched. 4, para. 1.

[6] C. & Y.P. Act 1969, s. 3(6).

[7] Compare the maximum of £400 in criminal cases; see *post*, p.118.

[8] Or guardian as defined in the C. & Y.P. Acts.

[9] C. & Y.P. Act 1969, s. 3(6).

[10] *Ibid.*, sub-sec. (7). The order under the sub-section is deemed to be an order under s. 1, but without a right of appeal to the Crown Court.

There is one general restriction relating to orders under s. 1. None of them may be made if the juvenile has attained 16 and is or has been married, whether in England or abroad and whether monogamously or polygamously.[11] But a person under 16 who is a party to a valid foreign marriage can be the subject of care proceedings. The point arose in *Mohamed* v. *Knott* under the former enactments relating to care, protection and control proceedings. The parties to a potentially polygamous marriage, celebrated in Nigeria and valid by their personal law, were a girl then aged just over 13 and a man almost twice her age. Soon after the marriage they came to England but within six months a juvenile court made a fit person order in respect of the girl on the ground that she was in moral danger by living with her husband, even though they were happily married. The court found *inter alia* that immediately after the marriage the parties had sexual intercourse when "almost certainly" the girl had not reached puberty; the husband later contracted gonorrhoea from a prostitute; he had then abstained from intercourse with his wife, but now that he was cured of the disease he was intending to resume intercourse with her once she was fitted with a contraceptive. In these circumstances, the court concluded, "a continuance of such an association, notwithstanding the marriage, would be repugnant to any decent minded English man or woman. Our decision reflects that repugnance".[12] The Divisional Court reversed the decision on the ground that the justices had failed to take account of the customs and way of life in which the parties had been brought up, but it recognised that the circumstances of a marriage might be such as to justify intervention and make an appropriate order; for example, if there was evidence of ill-treatment of the wife by the husband or of introducing her to drugs or of similar conduct, it would be proper to make a supervision order or care order. *Mohamed* v. *Knott* is an illustration of the problems (already found elsewhere)[13] of balancing the recognition of foreign family customs with English notions of protection of the child.

1 Recognisance of the Parent

The order requiring the parent to enter into a recognisance

---

[11] *Mohamed* v. *Knott*, [1968] 2 All E.R. 563; [1968] 2 W.L.R. 1446, *infra*.
[12] [1968] 2 All E.R. at p. 568; [1968] 2 W.L.R. at p. 1457.
[13] See *post*, Chapter 6, p. 212; and Chapter 7, p. 225.

to take proper care of the juvenile and exercise proper control over him[14] has hitherto not been widely used either in the former care, protection or control cases or in criminal cases;[15] but, since one of the purposes underlying the 1969 Act is to encourage the family to assume responsibility for the juvenile rather than to remove him from them, the order may become more common. Its very nature, however, is such that its efficacy depends upon the co-operation of the parent and the making of it is therefore subject to his consent.[16] The Act recognises the difficulty which the parent may have in bringing up the juvenile by fixing a maximum amount of £50 in which the parent may be bound. There is also a maximum duration of either three years or until the juvenile attains 18, whichever is the shorter period.[17]

2 Supervision Orders

The statutory recognition which the Probation of Offenders Act 1907 eventually gave to the long established voluntary practice of supervision of offenders[18] was immediately extended

[14] Under the former enactment, s. 62(1) (c) of C. & Y.P. Act 1933, the recognisance was "to exercise proper care and guardianship". Section 1(3) (a) of the 1969 Act, with its reference to "care" and "control" is much to be preferred, partly because it avoids the ambiguity of the term "guardianship" as found in the C. & Y.P. Acts and partly because it indicates that the Legislature is slowly moving towards uniformity in terminology relating to the legal relationship between an adult and a child.

[15] For criminal cases see McLean and Wood, *Criminal Justice and the Treatment of Offenders*, pp. 202-203.

[16] C. & Y.P. Act 1969, s.1(5) (a). The former enactment did not require consent.

[17] Section 2(13). The forfeiture of a recognisance is on the same conditions as forfeiture of a recognisance to keep the peace under s. 96 of the Magistrates' Courts Act 1952.

[18] The supervisory system, it is widely acknowledged, originated in the practice of Warwickshire justices passing a sentence of one day's imprisonment upon a young offender on condition that he returned to the care of his parent or master, by whom he was to be carefully supervised. The practice dates from about 1820 and commended itself to Matthew Davenport Hill, Recorder of Birmingham, who, some 20 years later, strengthened it by ordering inquiries concerning the offender to be made before deciding whether to order his release, by requiring the parent or master to acknowledge his obligation to supervise the juvenile and by requesting the police to follow up cases to see how the juvenile was behaving and whether the parent was fulfilling his obligation. The next stage of development is when the duty of supervision is undertaken by religious workers, known as "court missionaries", who became increasingly active from 1890 onwards. So much so that some courts, with Home Office encouragement, made use of them to advise and befriend offenders who had been bound over under the Summary Jurisdiction Act 1879 or the Probation of First Offenders Act 1887.

to juveniles who were not offenders but who were for various reasons in need of care or control.[19] One of the additional powers conferred by the Children Act 1908 in relation to them was that which enabled the court to make an order under the former Act placing under the supervision of a probation officer a juvenile who was being committed to the care of a relative or other fit person.[20] The Children and Young Persons Act 1933[1] went further by enabling the court to make a supervision order not only in addition to a fit person order but also without the latter order being made, and the Children and Young Persons Act 1963[2] brought supervision orders very largely into line with probation orders. The 1969 Act completes the unifying process by abolishing the probation order in relation to juvenile offenders and making the supervision order available both for them and for juveniles who are the subject of care proceedings. In one or two respects, however, the distinction between the offender and the juvenile found to be in need of care and control is still relevant.

Apart from orders being made in the first instance in care proceedings and criminal proceedings, they may also be made on the discharge of care orders.[3]

The Choice of Supervisor

Under the 1933 Act the supervisor could be either a probation officer or "some other person appointed by the court".[4] but the 1963 Act recognised the rapid expansion of the child care service after 1948 by expressly providing that a local authority could be so appointed.[5] The 1969 Act shows a further shift towards local authorities, the policy being to make them very largely responsible for the supervision of *children*. Thus, while a supervisor may be either an authority or a probation officer,[6] the latter may only be appointed in respect of a child, as opposed to a young person, if the authority whose area is to be named in the order[7] so request and a

---

[19] See *ante*, Chapter 2, p. 19.
[20] Children Act 1908, s. 60. A child (*i.e.* a person under 14) beyond parental control could also be placed under supervision (s. 58(4)).
[1] Section 62.   [2] Section 5 and Sched. I.
[3] C. & Y.P. Act 1969, s. 21(2).
[4] C. & Y.P. Act 1933, s. 62.
[5] C. & Y.P. Act 1963, s. 5(3).   [6] Section 11.
[7] A supervision order must name the area of the local authority and the petty sessions area in which it appears that the supervised person resides or will reside (s. 18(2) (a)); residence means habitual residence (s. 70(1)).

probation officer is, or has been, concerned with supervising[8] another member of the same household.[9] Initially this limitation is to relate to children under 10[10] but, when the further expansion of the social services so permits, it will extend to all under 14. The continued use of the probation service for the supervision of children in such circumstances recognises that it is normally undesirable and unnecessary to have two social workers involved with the same family. It has also been pointed out[11] that in any event the local authority will wish to consult the probation officer who is already working with the family before deciding whether to recommend to the court that, if a supervision order is made, a probation officer be appointed as supervisor. It remains to be seen whether, in cases where there is no legal restriction on the appointment of a probation officer, the courts will nevertheless favour the local authority as supervisor.

Normally the appropriate authority to act as supervisor is that within whose area the supervised person resides or will reside, but it may be another if it agrees to be designated.[12] The probation officer must be one who is assigned to the petty sessions area named in the supervision order.[13] The order does not have to name him, but the juvenile should be told his name if the court knows it.[14]

The Nature and Contents of a Supervision Order

A supervision order operates for three years or for any shorter period it specifies. Terms of one year or two are the most common. However, where the order is made under s. 1 of the 1969 Act or when a care order is discharged, it automatically ceases when the juvenile becomes 18, although the full period has not expired.[15] However, when it is made in criminal proceedings it may continue beyond that age.

So long as an order is in force the supervisor must "advise, assist and befriend" the juvenile.[16] These are his basic functions

---

[8] *I.e.*, by virtue of para. 3(5) and 6(b) of Sched. 5 to the Criminal Justice Act 1948.
[9] C. & Y.P. Act 1969, s. 13(2). The term "household" is not defined, but no doubt means a group of persons sharing a common home and life; *cf.* the Divorce Reform Act 1969, s. 2(5).
[10] C. & Y.P. Act 1969 (Transitional Modifications of Part I) Order 1970, para. 2. [11] Home Office Guide to Part I of the 1969 Act, para. 112.
[12] C. & Y.P. Act 1969, s. 13(1). [13] Sections 13(2) and 18(2)(a).
[14] *Cp.* Watson, *The Child and the Magistrate*, pp. 164-165.
[15] C. & Y.P. Act 1969, s. 17. [16] *Ibid.*, s. 14.

and to facilitate the performance of them the order may and should include a provision (1) that the juvenile inform his supervisor of any change of residence or employment, and (2) that he keep in touch with his supervisor as the latter so instructs and, in particular, that he receive visits from the supervisor at his home.[17] In all cases regular contact is essential, especially during the early part of the period of supervision, and the frequency of meetings will depend partly on the behaviour and progress of the juvenile.[18] Given the wide powers which the 1969 Act entrusts to a supervisor where the order authorises "intermediate treatment",[19] the need to establish an early personal relationship is all the greater.

Section 12 of the 1969 Act also confers on the court the power to include certain requirements relating to residence and treatment. In many respects they will have far-reaching consequences, but there is no longer the general power, as there was under the former law governing supervision orders[20] and as there still is in respect of probation orders,[1] to include such provisions as the court, in the circumstances of the case, considers necessary for fulfilling the purposes of the order.

(1) *Residence with an individual.*—Under subsection (1) of s. 12 an order may require the juvenile to reside with a named individual, such as a relative or friend. Its purpose is to allow residence in the household[2] of a private person and, to some extent, is a substitute for the former order which enabled a juvenile to be placed in the care of an individual as a fit person, but with the essential difference that the juvenile remains subject to the general control of the supervisor. It does not authorise residence at a specified place and, therefore, if the court considers residence at an institution is desirable, it may either rely on subsection (2) and give the supervisor a discretion to direct residence in such a place[3] or make a care order.[4] The latter has the advantage that, unlike subsection (2) and unlike a probation order, which cannot require a probationer to reside

---

[17] Section 18(2) (b) and the Magistrates' Courts (Children and Young Persons) Rules 1970, r. 28(2).
[18] *Cp.* the Probation Rules 1965, r. 35.
[19] See *infra.*
[20] C. & Y.P. Act 1963, Sched. I, para. 1.
[1] Criminal Justice Act 1948, s. 3(3).
[2] For the meaning of a household see *supra*, p. 99, n. 9.
[3] See *infra.*   [4] *Post,* Chapter 5.

at an institution for more than 12 months,[5] it is not subject to limitations on the period of residence. It also allows for flexibility in moving the juvenile from one institution to another.[6]

A requirement relating to mental treatment or to intermediate treatment overrides a residence requirement in so far as they conflict.

(2) *Treatment for a mental condition.*—Where the court has medical evidence that the mental condition of the juvenile needs treatment but does not warrant the making of a hospital order, it may include in the supervision order a requirement that for a specified period he submit to treatment by a named doctor or at a hospital or nursing home as a resident or out-patient.[7] The requirement need not be limited to a maximum period of 12 months, as it must where a similar provision is included in a probation order,[8] but it is automatically terminated when the juvenile becomes 18. This latter restriction is in effect relevant only to criminal proceedings, since, as we have seen,[9] a supervision order made under s. 1 of the 1969 Act or on the occasion of the discharge of a care order itself comes to an end on that date. The requirement is subject to two further restrictions, namely, that before including it the court must be satisfied that arrangements for treatment can be made and, where the juvenile is a young person, he consents to the inclusion. In the latter respect the requirement differs from those concerning residence and intermediate treatment, whose inclusion in the order does not, as it formerly did with regard to residence,[10] need the young person's consent.

It has been pointed out[11] that a juvenile who is a resident patient has no right to have his case periodically reviewed. The reason given for not granting him the right is that he is free at any time to leave the hospital. That is so, and there is

---

[5] Criminal Justice Act 1948, s. 3(4) (b).
[6] See Home Office Guide to Part I of the 1969 Act, para. 119.
[7] C. & Y.P. Act 1969, s. 12(4).
[8] Criminal Justice Act 1948, s. 4(1). A similar restriction applied to supervision orders under the former law; C. & Y.P. Act 1963, Sched. I, para. 8.
[9] *Supra*, p. 99.
[10] See C. & Y.P. Act 1963, Sched. I, para. 7 (supervision orders) and Criminal Justice Act 1948, s. 3(5) (probation orders). For a criticism of the change in the law see Watson, *The Juvenile Court – 1970 Onward*, p. 53.
[11] See Holden, *Child Legislation* 1969, pp. 141-142.

also the possibility of his seeking variation or cancellation of the requirement,[12] but it is essential that when the requirement is inserted these matters should be made clear to him. So, too, should the fact that, if he leaves, the supervisor may bring him back before the court, with the possible result of a care order being substituted.

(3) *Intermediate treatment.*—One of the major changes proposed by the White Paper, *Children in Trouble*, was that there should be "new forms of treatment, intermediate between supervision in the home and committal to care"[13] which would enable the juvenile to be brought under different environmental influences. The proposal was not entirely novel. The Advisory Council on the Treatment of Young Offenders had been asked to consider the possibility of introducing a system of training centres where juvenile offenders, especially those who might otherwise be sent to an approved school, detention centre or borstal institution, could over a reasonably long period receive intensive and constructive training without being removed from their homes. The Council considered a number of proposals,[14] including the following: the proposed centres should provide physical education and handicraft or similar forms of occupation and should arrange group counselling; there should be evening attendance on two or three nights a week; each centre should be run by experienced social workers; and attendance at a centre should be made a requirement of a probation order. However, the Council for various reasons came down firmly against such a system. Its own preference was for increased efficiency in the use of the existing methods of treatment coupled with experimentation "within the framework of the existing services that are designed to provide for the general and social education of young people in the community as a whole". Local authorities, it was suggested,[15] could specifically relate to delinquent and other "difficult" young people their duty[16] to provide leisure time occupation for persons over compulsory school age by paying more attention to "social and psychological education [which would] cover group counselling and any other methods that depend directly for their effective-

[12] *Infra.* p. 106. [13] Cmnd. 3601, para. 21.
[14] See the Report on *Non-Residential Treatment of Offenders Under 21*, (1962).
[15] Para. 51. [16] Imposed by the Education Act 1944, s. 41.

ness on the interplay of human relationships". There was, it was thought, also room for closer co-operation between the probation service and the youth service and further education service, and, although attendance at youth clubs, evening institutes or similar organisations depended on a probationer's voluntary acceptance, it could sometimes be advisable to make attendance a requirement of the probation order.

Activities of the kind described by the Advisory Council, and others such as adventure training and social work, will eventually form part of the new forms of intermediate treatment contemplated by the 1969 Act, but the Act goes very much further. Sections 12(2) and (3) and 19 provide for a system which will

> "make available to supervisors additional resources, sufficient finance for the use of these resources, and compulsory powers for use where necessary. The aim is to take action which is constructive and remedial, not punitive, by extending the preventive approach, by making the maximum possible use of the existing resources of each local community, and by spending relatively small sums for this purpose so as to avoid, where possible, the need for more expensive measures later on".[17]

The decision whether a supervision order should include a requirement relating to intermediate treatment is solely a matter for the court. The order may authorise the supervisor to give to the juvenile directions of the kind specified in para. (a) or para. (b) of s. 12(2) or both. But the decision whether they should be given, and, if so, their precise form and date of commencement is one for the supervisor.

If he is authorised to give directions under para. (a), he can require the juvenile to live for a specified *single* period at *a* place specified by him; for example, in a community home[18] or a boarding school. The period which he specifies must not exceed 90 days or such lesser maximum period as the court has laid down in the order, and it must not begin more than one year after the date of the order, except that if the supervisor gave directions which were to begin within the year but the juvenile did not begin to comply with them within that time, he may direct that they start to operate after the year has expired.

---

[17] Home Office Guide to Part I of the 1969 Act, para. 121.
[18] For community homes see *post*, Chapter 5.

If the order enables him to give from time to time directions of the kind prescribed by para. (b), he may require the juvenile to do all or any of the following:

(i)   to live at a specified place or places for a specified period or periods;

(ii) to present himself to a specified person or persons at a specified place or places on a specified day or days;

(iii) to participate in specified activities on a specified day or days.

The places, periods, persons and days are specified by the supervisor. The aggregate of the periods must not in any one year exceed 30 days or such lesser maximum period as the supervision order prescribes, but there is no need for any directions to be given in the first year of supervision.[19]

Where the court authorises directions to be given under paragraphs (a) *and* (b), the aggregate of the periods which the supervisor may specify must not exceed 90 days or any shorter period fixed by the order. For the purpose of calculating the periods under the paragraphs the supervisor may disregard any day on which the directions were not complied with.[20]

Section 12(2) only provides a bare legal framework. Its effectiveness depends upon the establishment by the children's regional planning committees of schemes for their respective planning areas,[1] and a court cannot include a requirement that the juvenile comply with para. (a) or para. (b) directions given by his supervisor unless there is a scheme in force for the regional planning area in which the juvenile resides or will reside or that the date on which it is to begin has been determined.[2] The scheme will embody arrangements which the planning committee has made "with such persons as it thinks fit" for the provision of facilities enabling directions under s. 12(2) to be carried out effectively.[3] These will include arrangements with the local authorities within the planning area,[4] the probation service, the police and various voluntary bodies. Once arrangements have been made with a local

[19] Compare a direction under paragraph (a), *supra*.
[20] Section 12(3).
[1] For the system of planning committees and planning areas see *post* Chapter 5.
[2] Section 19(6). Schemes are not likely to operate before the beginning of 1973.
[3] Section 19(1).   [4] "The relevant local authorities" (s. 35(3)).

authority, the authority must provide the facilities so long as they are specified in the scheme,[5] but the continued provision of facilities by a voluntary organisation will depend upon the terms of the agreement between it and the planning committee.

The responsibility for providing facilities is thus mainly one for each planning area and they may vary from area to area; but some central control is exercised, since facilities must be approved by the Secretary of State who must also determine the date on which a scheme is to come into force.[6] It is intended that most facilities will be generally rather than specifically approved, *i.e.*, general criteria will be formulated with which proposed facilities will have to comply.[7] Any alterations in arrangements will similarly need approval, but not the date of their commencement.

The discretion which may be conferred on a supervisor is limited by three factors. It depends upon the terms of the requirement for intermediate treatment laid down in the supervision order; if there is also included a requirement relating to mental treatment that takes precedence;[8] and the supervisor may only give directions to use facilities which are available under the relevant planning area scheme.[9] Moreover, there are limits to the sanction behind a direction. If the juvenile refuses to comply with it, the only effective step open to the supervisor is to take him back to the court and seek a care order.[10] Nevertheless, the discretion is wide enough to cause some concern.[11] The fear is that with his varied powers

---

[5] Section 19(5). The local authority in whose area the juvenile resides or will reside is responsible for any expenditure incurred by the supervisor for the purpose of directions, whether he is the local authority or a probation officer (s. 18(4)).

[6] Section 19(2) and (5).

[7] Home Office Guide to Part I of the Act, para. 130.

[8] Section 12(2).   [9] Section 19(6).

[10] But see *post*, p. 120 for the powers of a court where there is non-compliance with a requirement imposed by s. 12 in a supervision order made in criminal proceedings and the juvenile has attained the age of 18.

The Act does not make clear the extent to which a supervisor can withdraw a direction. Supposing that he directs the juvenile to attend an establishment, in accordance with s. 12(2) (b), for a specified period but later decides that a shorter period would be more in the juvenile's interests, may he shorten it or must he turn to the court and seek a variation of the supervision order? The fact that s. 12(2) (b) enables him to give directions "from time to time" might support the former view, but if the residence were directed under s. 12(2) (a) it seems that he would have to rely on variation by the court.

[11] See Watson, *The Juvenile Court – 1970 Onward*, pp. 56-59.

to direct residence or attendance the supervisor may come to be regarded by the juvenile as one fulfilling a punitive function rather than being a friend and adviser. However misconceived the notion is, often it may not easily be corrected, and it is therefore imperative that the court patiently explains to the juvenile and his parent the nature of intermediate treatment and his right to seek variation or cancellation of a requirement relating to it.

Variation and Discharge of Supervision Orders

Either the supervisor or the juvenile or his parent or guardian may apply for the supervision order to be discharged or varied.[12] If the supervisor does so, he may bring the juvenile before the juvenile court and, if necessary, may apply for a summons or warrant to secure his attendance.[13] Normally the juvenile must be present before the court but orders concerned only with the following matters may be made in his absence:[14]

(a) discharging the supervision order;

(b) cancelling a provision included by virtue of sections 12 or 18(2) (b);

(c) reducing the duration of the order or any provision made under s. 12;

(d) altering the name of any area;

(e) changing the supervisor.

Where the supervision order has been made in care proceedings by virtue of s. 1 of the 1969 Act or on the occasion of the discharge of a care order, the juvenile must be under 18 to enable the court to exercise its powers of discharge and variation,[15] for, as we have seen, [16] an order made in either of those circumstances automatically ceases on attainment of that age.

---

[12] Sections 15(1) and 70(2).

[13] Section 16(1) and (2). If the juvenile is arrested in pursuance of a warrant and cannot immediately be brought before the court, he may be detained in a place of safety for up to 72 hours, by which time he must be brought before a justice who must release him forthwith or make an interim order. Compare the similar provisions in s. 2(4) and (5), *ante*, Chapter 3, p. 54.

In criminal cases, if the juvenile has attained the age of 18, instead of making an interim order the court must remand him (s. 16(3)).

[14] Section 16(5).

[15] Section 15(1). If while an application for variation or discharge is pending the juvenile becomes 18, the court must proceed with the case as if he were still under that age (s. 16(11)).

[16] *Ante*, p. 99.

Wider powers exist where the order has been made in criminal proceedings.[17]

The court[18] may under s. 15(1) vary the order by cancelling any requirement included under s.12 or s.18(2)(b) or by inserting any provision which could have been included in the order if the court had then had power to make it and were exercising the power; but there is no power to insert, after the expiration of 12 months from the date of the original order, a requirement relating to residence in pursuance of s. 12(2) (a) or, after the expiration of three months from that date, one relating to treatment for a mental condition, unless in either case it is in substitution for such a requirement already included in the order. If it discharges the order, the court may make a care order, other than an interim order.[19] In the event of dismissal of an application for discharge, no such further application may be made by any person (whether the original applicant or not) for at least three months from the date of dismissal unless the court otherwise consents.[20]

The power to order variation or discharge is subject to the same basic principle as applies to care proceedings under s. 1 of the 1969 Act, namely, that the court's decision must be governed by the juvenile's need for care or control. Thus, it must not substitute a care order, discharge a supervision order or insert, vary or cancel a requirement authorised by s. 12 unless it is satisfied that the juvenile either is unlikely to receive the care or control he needs unless the court makes the order or is likely to receive it notwithstanding the order.[1]

There are special limitations on the variation of a mental treatment requirement. If the doctor responsible for the treatment is unwilling to continue it or is of opinion that (a) it should be continued beyond the period specified in the order or (b) that different treatment is needed or (c) that the juvenile is not susceptible to treatment or (d) does not further require it, he must so report to the supervisor who must then refer the

[17] See *post*, p. 120.
[18] The appropriate juvenile court is one acting for the petty sessions area named in the supervision order (under s. 18(2) (a)); see s. 16(11).
[19] Where there is an application for variation or discharge the court may, however, make an interim order if it wants further information before coming to a decision (s. 16(4) (b)).
[20] Section 16 (9).
[1] Section 16(6) (a).

107

matter to the court, which in turn may cancel or vary the requirement,[2] subject to the above principle that an order is needed in the interests of the juvenile's proper care or control[3] and to the juvenile's consent if he is a young person and the order is to alter the mental treatment requirement otherwise than by removing it or reducing its duration.[4] Consent is similarly needed to insert into the order by way of variation a mental treatment requirement.[5]

The juvenile has a right of appeal to the Crown Court against an order for variation except one which could have been made in his absence or one relating to mental treatment and he consented to the variation. He also has a right to appeal against the dismissal of an application to discharge the supervision order.[6]

(3) Care Orders

Under a care order the juvenile is committed to the care of a local authority. Its nature, scope and effects are fully examined in Chapter 5.

(4) and (5) Hospital Orders and Guardianship Orders

Because of his mental condition the court may order the juvenile to be detained in a specified hospital or placed under the guardianship of a local health authority or a person approved by the authority.[7] Under the Local Authority Social Services Act 1970 the welfare of mentally disordered persons while in hospital and the guardianship of such persons by the authority are functions of the social services committee,[8] discharged primarily through its mental welfare officers. There are three main restrictions on the making of these orders.

Firstly, there must be the evidence of two doctors that the

---

[2] Section 15(5), re-enacting the provisions of Sched. I to the C. & Y.P. Act 1963, para. 10. Compare the power of a doctor under the Criminal Justice Act 1948, s. 4(5) and (6) to change arrangements for the treatment of a probationer without the court's approval.

[3] Section 16(6) (b).   [4] Section 16(7).

[5] *Ibid.* The same medical evidence is required as would be necessary to include the requirement in an order in the first instance (s. 16(6)(c)); see *supra*, p.101.   [6] Section 16(8); Courts Act 1971, Sched. 9.

[7] C. & Y.P. Act 1969, s. 1(3) (d) and (e) and (5) (b).

[8] Section 2(1) and Sched. I.

juvenile is suffering from a particular kind of mental disorder[9] and that it is such as to warrant his detention in a hospital or reception into guardianship.[10] The evidence may be oral or written. Where a written report is submitted (otherwise than on the juvenile's behalf) and the juvenile is legally represented, only the substance of the report need be disclosed to him or, if present in court, to his parent.[11] It will be seen that these rules are wider than the general rules relating to disclosure,[12] in that the rights of the advocate are wider; but it is questionable whether the distinction drawn for present purposes between the advocate and the juvenile and parent is a valid one, since even if the advocate must withold the copy from the juvenile (which is doubtful) the juvenile may require the doctor to be called to give oral evidence, which may result in the whole of the written report in effect coming to the knowledge of the juvenile. The precise relationship between these rules and the general rules is uncertain. For example, is that contained in the latter, which enables the court to require the juvenile to withdraw,[13] overriding even though the Mental Health Act 1959 is silent on the point?

Secondly, the court must be satisfied that a hospital order or guardianship order is "the most suitable method of disposing of the case". In determining this, it is directed to have regard to all the circumstances including the nature of the offence[14] and the character and antecedents of the juvenile and the other available methods of dealing with him.[15] So far as concerns juveniles this statutory direction might be said to be superfluous. They are all matters of which a juvenile court should always take cognisance, if it is to discharge its general duty[16] of having regard to the juvenile's welfare when deciding how to deal with him.

Thirdly, no hospital order can be made unless the court is

---

[9] The different kinds of mental disorder are mental illness, psychopathic disorder, subnormality and severe subnormality. Each of these, except the first, is defined by the Mental Health Act 1959, s. 4.
    The doctors must be agreed about the kind of disorder from which the juvenile is suffering.   [10] Mental Health Act 1959, s. 60(1).
[11] *Ibid.*, s. 62.   [12] *Ante*, Chapter 3, p. 84.
[13] Magistrates' Courts (Children and Young Persons) Rules 1970 rr. 10(1) (e) and 20(1) (d), *ante*, p.85.
[14] This factor is relevant not only in criminal proceedings but also where care proceedings are based on the offence condition.
[15] Mental Health Act 1959, s. 60(1) (b).
[16] Under C. & Y.P. Act 1933, s. 44, *ante*, Chapter 1, p. 16.

satisfied that arrangements have been made for the juvenile's admission to a hospital within 28 days of the order.[17] It is obviously preferable to place the juvenile in a hospital near to his residence so that relatives may visit him, but it is not necessary that there should be a vacancy in a hospital in a particular region. The court should not be deprived of the power to make an order if there is no such vacancy, because there is no statutory or administrative rule or order or, indeed, administrative way of thinking which precludes a person in respect of whom an order ought to be made being sent to any vacancy existing in any part of the country.[18] A guardianship order may only be made if the court is satisfied that the local health authority or other person is willing to receive the juvenile into guardianship.

The effect of an order is that the juvenile is very largely treated as if he had been compulsorily admitted to hospital or guardianship, as the case may be, under Part IV of the Mental Health Act 1959. The order is for an indefinite period but lapses after one year[19] unless renewed for a further period of one year and, if necessary, thereafter at two-year periods. A hospital order may, however, be discharged at any time by the responsible medical officer or the hospital managers and a guardianship order by the medical officer or local health authority.[19] But there is no power, as there is in cases under Part IV, for the nearest relative to order discharge.[20] Instead he may apply to a Mental Health Review Tribunal once a year for an order. The juvenile may himself apply once he attains the age of 16.[1] These rules and the nature of the orders perhaps show more than any other kind of order which may be made in respect of a juvenile the need for tact and patience on the part of the Bench when their effect is being explained to the juvenile and his parent.

[17] Mental Health Act 1959, s. 60(3).
    If an order is made, the court may give directions for the juvenile to be kept in a place of safety pending his admission to the specified hospital within the 28-day period (s. 64(1)).
[18] *Per* SACHS, L. J. in *R. v. Marsden*, [1968] 2 All E.R. 341; [1968] 1 W. L.R. 785.
    If an order is made, but for some special reason it is not practicable for the juvenile to be received into the hospital named within 28 days, the Minister may name another hospital (s. 64(2)).
[19] For special restrictions in criminal cases see *post*, p. 138.
[20] Mental Health Act 1959, s. 63(3).   [1] *Ibid.*, sub.-s. (4).

B. ORDERS IN CRIMINAL PROCEEDINGS

I. INTRODUCTION

Whatever view earlier law or practice may have adopted concerning the punishment of juveniles – and there are indications of some mitigation in their favour[2] – certainly by the 17th century the principle of equality was firmly established, with no distinction being drawn between juvenile and adult offenders in the forms of punishment that could be inflicted. Depending upon the penalties attaching to the particular offence committed, juveniles, like adults, could be hanged, transported, imprisoned, subjected to various forms of corporal punishment[3] or fined.

In the 18th century cases of juveniles being sentenced to death were quite common and sometimes the sentence was carried out.[4] Nevertheless, there was a distinct reluctance to execute children, save for a period at the beginning of the 19th century when there was apparently some readiness to do so in

[2] As early as the 10th century Aethelstan decreed that an offender under 15 should not be slain for any offence unless he chose to defend himself or tried to escape and refused to give himself up; Ordinance VI cap. 12 1 and 2; see Attenborough, *The Laws of the Earliest English Kings*, p. 169. The various ways in which the child could be dealt with if he did surrender show that this enactment was one of the more sophisticated of the Anglo-Saxon laws. The child on giving himself up must be imprisoned, but, if no prison is available, his relatives must stand surety for him to the full amount of his wergeld (the price to be paid for the offence) for his future good behaviour. If they would neither redeem him nor stand surety he had to "swear, as the bishop directs him, that he will desist from every form of crime, and he shall remain in bondage until his wergeld is paid. If he is guilty of theft after that, he shall be slain or hanged as older offenders have been". There were also other enactments of Aethelstan the effect of which was that thieves not over the age of 12 were spared from capital punishment; see Ord. II, cap. 1, VI cap. 1 1 (Attenborough, pp. 127 and 157).
The Report of the Departmental Committee on the Treatment of Young Offenders (1927) Cmnd. 2831, p. 7, cites a case in the Year Books (Y.B. 32 Ed. I., rot. 13) where judgment for burglary was spared to a boy of 12. The significance of this isolated reference to medieval leniency is uncertain but it suggests a willingness to distinguish between juvenile and adult offenders.

[3] "The records show that in the 17th century the pillory was one of the milder ways in which the country sought to deal with some of its juvenile delinquents . . ." (Eddy, *Justice of the Peace*, p. 45, referring to an entry in Pepys Diary).

[4] The youngest recorded instance seems to be that of a seven-year-old boy who was hanged in 1708; see Kenny, *Outlines of Criminal Law*, 19th edn., p. 80, n. 4.

111

order to try to check the practice of parents ordering their children to steal on the assumption that the latter would escape the penalty because of their age.[5] This stricter attitude seems to have been short lived; yet, it was only with the passing of the Children Act 1908 that sentence of death was abolished in respect of persons under the age of 16.[6]

The steep rise in the number of juvenile offenders from 1800 onwards is, however, only partly explained by parental pressures. The main cause lay in the new social conditions created by the Industrial Revolution. Overpopulated urban areas soon became fertile breeding grounds for juvenile offenders, many of whom, especially in London, frequented the notorious "flash houses", which served as social centres for debauchery and the organisation of criminal activities.[7] That juvenile delinquency was one of the main social problems is evidenced by the formation in quick succession of two reforming bodies both of which devoted much of their work to inquiries into the reasons for its widespread existence. These were the Society to Inquire into Causes of Juvenile Delinquency, founded in 1815, and the Society for the Improvement of Prison Discipline and for the Reformation of Juvenile Offenders, founded in 1818. But the solutions to the problem would not be found merely in inquiries of this kind. Reformers recognised also the need for mitigation of the severity of the criminal law and the introduction of separate methods for dealing with juvenile offenders. The immediate response of the legislature was modest. As we have seen,[8] its relevant contri-

---

[5] See Radzinowicz, *A History of English Criminal Law*, Vol. I, p. 523, n. 4.
[6] Subsequent legislation raised the age to under 18. See now C. & Y.P. Act 1933, s. 53(1), as substituted by the Murder (Abolition of Death Penalty) Act 1965, s. 1(5).
[7] For an account of these dens of vice see Radzinowicz, *op. cit.*, Vol. II, pp. 297-306.
   A glimpse at contemporary social life of young people is shown by the Third Report of the Commissioners on Criminal Law (1836) [British Sessional Papers, 79, xxxi, p. 11]:
   "We are persuaded that it is desirable that increased powers should be given to the police to withdraw young persons from public-houses, beer-shops, penny theatres and other notorious places of meeting for the idle and dissolute. Much advantage also might be derived from giving to the police a more distinct authority than they now possess to disperse or apprehend as vagrants boys wandering in companies in the streets or loitering around theatres and other places of public amusement without any ostensible employment."
[8] *Ante*, Chapter I, p. 1.

bution to the substantive law was essentially to extend summary jurisdiction over young offenders, but gradually much more began to be done with regard to the treatment of young offenders. It will be seen that some of the orders which a court may make today owe their origin to 19th century legislation.

In addition to those orders which may be made in care proceedings the following are available as methods for dealing with the offender: (1) discharge, (2) binding over, (3) fine and compensation, (4) attendance centre order, (5) detention centre order, (6) borstal, (7) order under s. 53 of the Children and Young Persons Act 1933.

II. NON-CUSTODIAL ORDERS

(1) Discharge

The Larceny Act 1827 empowered a justice of the peace to discharge a first offender who was summarily convicted for an offence under the Act upon his making to the aggrieved party satisfactory payment for damages and costs. Although not confined to the young offender, this enactment seems to have been mainly intended for him.[9] An Act of 1847[10] went further. When a juvenile who was not more than 14[11] was found guilty of simple larceny, the justices could discharge him, if they thought it expedient not to inflict any punishment. Subsequently, under the Summary Jurisdiction Act 1879,[12] discharge became bound up with orders for release during good behaviour and then, under the Probation of Offenders Act 1907, with the new system of probation. So it remained until the Criminal Justice Act 1948 firmly distinguished between discharge and probation.

An order for the absolute or conditional discharge may be made when the court is "of opinion, having regard to the circumstances including the nature of the offence and the character of the offender that it is inexpedient to inflict punishment and that a probation order is not appropriate".[13] Since the supervision order has replaced the probation order in

[9] The Act was part of Peel's programme of reform, none of which, however, was exclusively directed to the young offender.
[10] 10 and 11 Vict., c. 82, s. 1.
[11] An Act of 1850 (13 and 14 Vict. c. 37) raised the age to 16.
[12] Section 16.　　[13] Criminal Justice Act 1948, s. 7(1).

respect of juvenile offenders, the above enactment must, it is submitted, be construed accordingly. The court has a complete discretion whether to make the discharge absolute or conditional. It can additionally order the offender to pay damages and compensation,[14] but not a fine since that is a form of punishment,[15] and it can allow any person who consents to do so to give security for the good behaviour of the offender.[16] Discharge cannot be ordered where the offence is one the sentence for which is fixed by law. So it cannot be made in a case where the court must detain the juvenile during Her Majesty's Pleasure.[17]

Absolute Discharge

This is a dismissal after proof of guilt. Unless the offence is trivial and is a first offence, the court will rarely order it. Even in trivial cases some courts are reluctant to make use of it because of a feeling that more harm than good may be done if the juvenile and his parents are left with the mistaken idea that he has "got away with it"; but this wrong impression may sometimes be corrected if the court explains the reasons for its leniency.[18]

Conditional Discharge

This means that the offender is discharged subject to the condition that he commits no offence during a specified period not exceeding three years. Before making the order the court must in ordinary language explain to him that if he does commit another offence during that period he will be liable to be dealt with for the original offence, quite apart from his liability for the later offence.[19]

The appropriate court for dealing with him for the original offence is normally that which made the order for conditional discharge but complicated provisions recognise other possibilities.[20] The rules apply to juvenile cases as follows:

---

[14] *Ibid.*, s. 11(2). It can also at its discretion order the payment of costs.
[15] *R.* v. *McClelland*, [1951] 1 All E.R. 557.
[16] Criminal Justice Act 1948, s. 11(1).
[17] See C. & Y.P. Act 1933, s. 53(1), *post*, p. 137.
[18] See Watson, *op. cit.*, p. 154.
[19] Criminal Justice Act 1948, s. 7(3), as amended by the Criminal Justice Act 1967, s. 52.
[20] *Ibid.*, s. 8, as amended by the Courts Act 1971, s. 56 and Sched. 8.

(a) Where the original order was made by the Crown Court. That Court has exclusive jurisdiction to deal with the original offence. So, where the juvenile is found guilty by a juvenile court in respect of the later offence, that court commits him in custody or on bail to the Crown Court to be dealt with for the original offence.[1]

(b) Where the original order was made by a juvenile court. That court normally deals with the original offence, but if the court which finds him guilty of the later offence is another juvenile court the latter may, with the consent of the first court, deal with him for the original offence.[2] A juvenile court may deal with him for that offence as if he had just been found guilty of it[3] and it still has jurisdiction even though he has attained the age of 17 since the original order.[4]

Where the juvenile is found guilty of the further offence by the Crown Court the latter may deal with him for the original offence instead of the juvenile court; but the sentence which it can impose is limited to that which the juvenile court could itself impose.[5]

(2) Binding Over

(a) *The juvenile*[6].—One of the effects of the Criminal Justice Act 1948 was to incorporate into the new order the principle of binding over to be of good behaviour, but without the need for a recognisance. There is still, however, the possibility of justices relying on the ancient powers of ordering a person to enter into a recognisance with or without sureties to keep the peace or to be of good behaviour. The exact scope of the powers is uncertain, as are the sources,[7] but they may be invoked where it is apprehended that a person may commit a breach of the peace or some other offence or may incite others to do so.[8] Juvenile courts rarely rely on it,[9] but exceptionally

[1] Sub-section (4).   [2] Sub-section (7).
[3] Sub-sections (5) and (7).   [4] C. & Y.P. Act 1933, s. 48(2).
[5] Criminal Justice Act 1948, s. 8(6), as amended by the Courts Act 1971, s. 56 and Sched. 8.
[6] Compare *ante*, p. 95, the power to bind over a young person in care proceedings based on the offence condition.
[7] It is not clear how far the powers are derived from the common law, from the commission of peace held by justices or from the Justices of the Peace Act 1361.
[8] *R.* v. *Sandbach, ex parte Williams*, [1935] 2 K.B. 192.
[9] The power of the Crown Court to release an offender upon a recognisance to come up for judgment if called upon is also very rarely exercised in respect of a juvenile.

it can be a useful method of dealing with a juvenile whose aggressive conduct is such as to warrant a supervision order. For example, the 16-year-old political extremist who, with a reputation for obstructing the police at public meetings, is threatening similar behaviour might be dealt with in this way. If an order is made and not complied with, the juvenile may be committed to custody for a period of not more than six months or until he sooner complies with it.[10]

(b) *The parent (or guardian)*.—The Children and Young Persons Act 1933[11] enabled the court to bind over the parent or guardian, *i.e.*, to order him to give security for the juvenile's good behaviour. The 1969 Act[12] substitutes a power to require the parent to enter into a recognisance to take proper care of the juvenile and exercise proper control over him. The same limits apply as in care proceedings.[13]

(3) Fines and Other Pecuniary Payments

A juvenile may be ordered to pay a fine, damages for injury, compensation for loss[14] and costs, but the powers of a court to make any of these orders in respect of him differ in two respects from its corresponding powers in relation to an adult. Firstly, if the court is a magistrates' court there are limits on the amounts of the payment that can be ordered. Secondly, whatever kind of court makes such orders the parent or guardian can be ordered to make the payment instead of the juvenile.

Lack of data precludes any firm conclusion about the extent to which the fine was used historically as a method of dealing with juveniles. It seems that, whatever the age of the offender, Assizes and Quarter Sessions made little use of it. The position

---

[10] Magistrates' Court Act 1952, s. 91(3).   [11] Section 55(2).
[12] Section 7(7). The power extends to young persons which at present includes children aged 10 to 14 (C. & Y.P. Act 1969 (Transitional Modifications of Part I) Order 1970).   [13] See *ante*, p. 97.
[14] But where property has been stolen an order for restitution may be made; Theft Act 1968, s. 28. Note also the power of a magistrates' court to order delivery to the person who appears to be the owner of the property which has come into the possession of the police in connection with any criminal charge. This power may also be exercised where the juvenile has been brought before the court under care proceedings based on the offence condition (Police Property Act 1897, s. 1; C. & Y.P. Act 1969, Sched. 5, para. 1); but the 1969 Act confers no power to make orders for restitution where neither criminal proceedings nor care proceedings are instituted because the police and local authority consider it desirable to keep the juvenile out of court.

in courts of summary jurisdiction was even more uncertain until the Summary Jurisdiction Act 1879 restricted the power of those courts to impose fines on juveniles.[15] The maximum fines permitted were 40 shillings in respect of a child and £10 in respect of a young person. These amounts remained unaltered until the Criminal Justice Act 1961 raised them respectively to £10 and £50, which remain the present limits.[16]

The fine is mainly used to deal with first offences which spring from mischievous juvenile behaviour rather than from more deeply seated causes. Otherwise, its exclusively punitive nature renders it of limited value as a method of dealing with juveniles, and even the punitive effect may be lost on the juvenile if the parent is required to pay the fine. Where he is personally required to pay he ought generally to be ordered to do so by way of instalments.[17] The penalty is likely to have a more salutary effect where it has to be met by him over a period of time from his pocket money or wages. There is a further advantage in that a juvenile court can then also order him to be supervised until completion of payment.[18] The supervisor is likely to be a probation officer, but it may be that in future more use will be made of the local authority. This supervision is a modest but useful substitute for supervision under a supervision order, and can also be ordered where there is an order to pay costs, damages or compensation.

The payment of damages and compensation can be ordered whenever a court makes an order for discharge, whether absolute or conditional,[19] but where the order is made by a magistrates' court the total amount must not exceed £100, unless some special enactment allows a greater sum. There

[15] Sections 10(1), (11)(1) and 15.
  When in 1847 juveniles were allowed to be tried summarily for simple larceny, the court was given power to fine the offender up to £3; see *ante*, p. 2.
[16] For the relevant enactments see the Magistrates' Courts Act 1952, s. 32; the Criminal Justice Act 1961, s. 8(1) and (3); and the Children and Young Persons Act 1969, ss. 6(3) and 34(5).
[17] The power to do this is conferred on magistrates' courts by the Magistrates' Courts Act 1952, s. 63(1) and on the Crown Court by the Criminal Justice Act 1948, s. 14(1) as amended by Courts Act 1971, Sched. 8.
[18] Magistrates' Courts Act 1952, s. 71. The person appointed must advise and befriend the juvenile with a view to inducing him to pay the fine and thereby avoid committal to custody, and, if required, must inform the court about the juvenile's conduct and means (Magistrates' Courts Rules 1968, r. 46(2)).
[19] Criminal Justice Act 1948, s. 11(2).

are other provisions which also allow orders for compensation, but these are rarely invoked against juveniles. Thus, where a juvenile court finds a juvenile guilty of an indictable offence it can award a sum not exceeding £400 to any person who as a result of the offence has suffered loss or damage to property, just as an adult magistrates' court or the Crown Court has the power.[20] Again, if a juvenile is found guilty by a magistrates' court of criminal damage to property, he may be ordered to pay such compensation as is just but not exceeding £400.[1] These powers may be compared with that which may be invoked in care proceedings.[2]

The only statutory limit on an order for costs made against a juvenile is that, where a fine is imposed on him by a magistrates' court and is to be paid by him personally, the amount of the costs must not exceed the amount of the fine.[3]

Ordering Parent or Guardian to Pay Fine, etc.

The power of a court to order the parent or guardian instead of the juvenile to pay a fine, damages, compensation or costs first appeared in the Youthful Offenders Act 1901. It was introduced mainly because it was recognised that juveniles invariably lacked the means to pay the fines themselves, but it was also seen as a way of making the parent aware of his parental responsibilities. It is difficult to determine how far these objects have been kept in mind. The Criminal Statistics have shown that only in a small percentage of cases where fines have been imposed have the parents been ordered to pay, but this result is partly to be explained by a substantial failure to record such orders.[4]

Under the present law the court may, if the offender is a

[20] Magistrates' Courts Act 1952, s. 34 and Forfeiture Act 1870, s. 4, as amended by the Criminal Law Act 1967, s. 10(1) and Sched. 2, para. 9.
These provisions do not extend to loss or damage due to an accident arising out of the presence of a motor vehicle on a road.
[1] Criminal Damage Act 1971, s. 8.
[2] *Ante*, p. 95.
[3] Costs in Criminal Cases Act, 1952, s. 6(1). No such limit applies to orders for costs made by the Crown Court.
[4] The problem is of long-standing. The Committee on the Treatment of Young Offenders reported in 1927 (Cmnd. 2831, p. 66) that "nearly a third of the charges heard in juvenile courts are disposed of [by fines] every year, though the available figures do not show in how many of those cases the fine is imposed on the parent".

young person, and must, if he is a child, make an order against the parent or guardian,[5] unless it is satisfied that the latter cannot be found or that he has not conduced to the commission of the offence by neglecting to exercise due care or control of the juvenile.[6] Except where the parent or guardian has failed to comply with a request to attend the court, no order is to be made without giving him an opportunity of being heard.[7]

Enforcement of Fines, etc.

(a) *Against the juvenile.*—Under the former law a juvenile who defaulted in paying a fine, etc., could be committed to a remand home or required to attend an attendance centre, or, if he was a young person, could be committed to a detention centre.[8] These powers were rarely invoked and have been abolished by the Children and Young Persons Act 1969.[9] Ignoring as fanciful the possibilities of enforcement by levying distress[10] or by civil proceedings in the High Court or a county court,[11] the only method of enforcement is the attachment of earnings order[12] which by its nature is limited to the young person who is working. However, once a young person attains the age of 17 it will be possible to commit him for default in payment of a fine imposed when he was under that age.

(b) *Against the parent or guardian.*—When the parent or guardian is ordered to pay the fine, the amount thereof may be recovered from him as if the order had been made on his being convicted of the offence with which the juvenile was charged.[13]

(4) Supervision Orders

Although the Children and Young Persons Act 1969 has

---

[5] "Guardian" has the wide meaning given by C. & Y.P. Act 1933, s. 107(1).
[6] C. & Y.P. Act 1933, s.55(1), as amended by the Criminal Justice Act 1961, s. 8(4) and C. & Y.P. Act 1969, Scheds. 5 and 6.
[7] C. & Y.P. Act 1933, s. 55(3).
[8] C. & Y.P. Act 1933, s. 54; Criminal Justice Act 1961, s. 5; Criminal Justice Act 1948, s. 19.
[9] The enactments cited in the previous footnote have been respectively repealed or amended by the following provisions of the 1969 Act: s. 72(4) and Sched. 6; ss. 7(4), 72(3) and Sched. 5; and s. 72(1) and (2) and Sched. 4, para. 6.
[10] Magistrates' Courts Act 1952, s. 64.
[11] Criminal Justice Act 1967, s. 45.
[12] Attachment of Earnings Act, 1971, s. 1.
[13] Administration of Justice Act 1970, s. 41 and Sched. 9.

abolished the probation order in relation to the juvenile offender[14] and substituted the supervision order, the distinction between him and the juvenile who is found to be in need of care or control is still relevant, partly because the Act has, in respect of the offender, incorporated provisions which generally correspond to those relating to breach of a probation order,[15] and partly because in criminal proceedings the supervision order does not automatically cease to operate when the juvenile attains the age of 18.[16]

Once he attains that age the powers to discharge or vary the order become exercisable, on the application either of the supervisor or the supervised person, by an adult magistrates' court[17] instead of a juvenile court, but the powers, so conferred by s. 15(3) of the Act, are not as wide as those of the latter court under s. 15(1)[18] in that (1) if the order is discharged, a care order cannot be substituted since the latter is appropriate only to persons under 18 and (2) for the same reason no requirement relating to residence or intermediate treatment which s. 12(1) and (2) allows[19] may be added to the order.

Where the supervised person has failed to comply with a requirement which has been included in the supervision order in accordance with s. 12 or s. 18(2)(b) the adult court may, on the application of the supervisor, invoke other powers under s. 15(4), and it is immaterial whether the breach of the order occurred before or after the person attained the age of 18. Additionally or alternatively to its powers to discharge or vary, it may impose a fine of up to £20 or make an attendance centre order, if a centre is available to the court and provided that the juvenile has not previously been sentenced to borstal training or detention in a detention centre or ordered to an approved school.[20] But if the court *discharges* the supervision order it can impose "any punishment" which it could have imposed had it just been convicting him as an 18-year-old of the offence for which that order was made. The terms in which

---

[14] Section 7(2).
[15] See Criminal Justice Act 1948, s. 6, as amended by Criminal Justice Act 1967, s. 54.   [16] C. & Y.P. Act 1969, s. 17, *ante*, p. 99.
[17] *I.e.*, a court acting for the petty sessions named in the order (s. 16(11)). That court alone has jurisdiction even if the supervision order was made by a court other than a juvenile court; *e.g.*, the Crown Court.
[18] For s. 15(1) see *supra* p. 107.   [19] *Supra* pp. 100 *et seq.*
[20] For attendance centre orders see *infra* and for their application to breaches of supervision orders see C. & Y.P. Act 1969, s. 16(10).

s. 15(4) confers this power suggest that the court cannot discharge him absolutely or conditionally, as it can where there is a breach of a probation order, and it is doubtful whether it can make a probation order. It is expressly provided that the punishment cannot exceed imprisonment for a term of six months and a fine of £400.[1]

Should there be a reasonable chance that the supervised person may still respond to supervision the court should vary rather than discharge the supervision order and rely on its additional power of imposing a fine or making an attendance centre order.

Where the supervised person is still under 18 the jurisdiction to discharge or vary resides exclusively with the juvenile court, whichever court made the original order, and it may exercise its powers under s. 15(1) as it can where a supervision order is made in care proceedings. However, if that person is between the ages of 17 and 18 or becomes 18 in the course of the proceedings for discharge or variation,[2] the court can alternatively exercise the above powers which an adult magistrates' court has over a person who has attained that age. The practical importance of the rule is that it enables, within the age limits, the juvenile court to make the additional orders where there has been a breach of the supervision order. For the juvenile under 17 who commits a breach the only effective sanction seems to be an application by the supervisor to discharge the supervision order with a view to a care order being substituted.

It should be noted that a juvenile who commits a further offence during the period of supervision can only be dealt with for that offence and the special powers which the juvenile court has where a juvenile commits a further offence during the period of an order for his conditional discharge (or which it also formerly had when probation orders could be made in respect of juveniles) do not apply to the supervised juvenile.

(5) Attendance Centre Order

The Departmental Committee on Corporal Punishment in its Report in 1938[3] drew attention to the need for juvenile

---

[1] These are the limits of jurisdiction of a magistrates' court trying an indictable offence summarily.
[2] C. & Y.P. Act 1969, s. 15(2) and s. 16(11).   [3] Cmnd. 5684, para. 31.

courts being given further powers enabling them to deal with juveniles whose behaviour did not warrant institutional treatment but rather some form of short and sharp punishment which would act as a deterrent. The outcome was a provision in the Criminal Justice Bill of that year which would have authorised compulsory attendance at centres at week-ends where the offender would be required to do schoolwork or manual labour. The Bill had to be shelved because of the war, but the attendance centre order appeared a decade later in s. 19 of the Criminal Justice Act 1948. The need for it was made greater by the abolition of corporal punishment of juveniles, for which the Act also provided, although it would be wrong to think that the order was created simply as a substitute for such punishment: it was designed to serve a distinct purpose of its own. This, at least, seems to be the view taken by magistrates.[4]

The Nature, Scope and Purpose of the Order[5]

An order may be made by any magistrates' courts[6] in respect of any person under the age of 21. Attention is here directed only to juveniles, but the Children and Young Persons Act 1969[7] provides for the future abolition of the order in respect of them. This is likely to happen as and when facilities for intermediate treatment under supervision orders become available.

The order has two basic uses. First, it can be made whenever the court has, or would have but for the restrictions upon the imprisonment of young offenders, power to impose imprisonment. Thus, it is available as a method of dealing not only with a juvenile found guilty of an offence punishable with imprisonment but also with one who defaults in complying with an order of the court, for example, in paying a fine. Its most frequent use as a means of dealing with an offender, as opposed to a defaulter, is in connection with various forms of theft,

---

[4] See McClintock in the *Report of the Cambridge Institute of Criminology on Attendance Centres*, (1961), p. 25. This is subsequently referred to as "the Cambridge Report".

[5] See McLean and Wood, *Criminal Justice and the Treatment of Offenders*, pp. 203-209.

[6] This includes the Crown Court in the exercise of its appellate jurisdiction and when an offender is committed to it for sentence.

[7] Section 7(3); Sched. 4, para. 6 and Sched. 5, para. 23.

burglary, criminal damage to property and driving a vehicle.[8] Its other function is, as we have seen,[9] to deal with a supervised person who fails to comply with requirements in a supervision order.

Because the times of attendance must be such as to avoid, so far as practicable, interference with the offender's school or working hours,[10] Saturday attendance is invariably ordered. This is preferred to evening attendance on other days because it is felt to be more punitive; for example, in respect of the hooligan at football matches. The aggregate number of hours for which attendance may be ordered must (a) be not less than 12, except where the juvenile is under 14 and the court considers that period is excessive, and (b) must not exceed 12 unless the court considers that that is inadequate, in which case it may be for up to 24 hours.[11] The first date and time of attendance is fixed by the court, but all subsequent attendances by the officer in charge of the centre. The juvenile cannot be required to attend on more than one occasion on any day or for more than three hours on any occasion.[12] On the other hand, so far as practicable an attendance must not be for less than one hour.[13] Within these limits the officer has an unfettered discretion and as a method of punishment may increase the number of attendances by reducing each to one hour.

The Home Secretary is responsible for seeing that centres are provided[14] and does this by arranging with local authorities or police authorities for them to be established.[15] Because of central government responsibility the cost of running centres is borne by the Exchequer and therefore the Home Office conducts regular inspections. In deciding whether to establish a centre the Home Office consults the local juvenile court panel, the social services department of the local authority and the probation service.

[8] See Cambridge Report, pp. 51, *et seq.*   [9] *Supra*, p. 120.
[10] Criminal Justice Act 1948, s. 19(2).
[11] Criminal Justice Act 1961, s. 10(2).
   Increasing use has been made of the maximum; see McLean and Wood, *op. cit.*, p. 208.
[12] Section 19(2).
[13] Attendance Centre Rules 1958, r. 4(2), (s.i. 1958, No. 1990).
[14] Criminal Justice Act 1948, s. 48(2).
[15] Most centres are run by the local police authority with an inspector or person of higher rank in charge. There are only two centres for offenders over 17 and there is none for girls.

The use of the order is considerably restricted by the rule that it can only be made if the court has been notified by the Home Secretary that a centre is available for the reception of persons of the offender's class or description[16] and that it is "reasonably accessible having regard to his age, the means of access available to him and any other circumstances".[17] It seems that a court usually regards 10 miles or a travelling time of 45 minutes as a reasonable maximum to travel.[18] It is mainly for this reason that centres are in practice confined to urban areas.

The order is intended for "young people who are only on the threshold of a criminal career and are either first offenders or have been dealt with for previous offences by being discharged, placed on probation (or supervision) or fined".[19] That it is not designed for the recidivist is clear from the rule which prevents an order being made in the case of an offender who has been previously sentenced to imprisonment, borstal training or detention in a detention centre or sent to an approved school.[20] There is, however, a conflict of opinion about the main purpose of the order, although the preponderant view has been that it is punitive rather than reformative.[1] The statutory provisions can hardly be said to resolve the conflict. On the one hand those relating to the hours of attendance clearly contemplate that the usual aggregate shall be 12, and this tends to support the view that the order is intended as a form of sharp punishment depriving a person of his leisure hours. On the other hand, the rule that the occupation and instruction given at a centre "shall be such as to occupy the persons attending there . . . in a manner conducive to health of mind and body"[2] tends to support the contrary opinion. It certainly seems that those responsible for centres differ in the emphasis to be put on occupation and instruction. Some insist

[16] Section 19(1). [17] Criminal Justice Act 1961, s. 10(3).
[18] See Clarke Hall and Morrison, *op. cit.*, p. 375, referring to a Home Office letter.
   The Ingleby Committee (para. 291) thought that for 10 and 11-year-olds the distance and time should be less.
[19] Watson, *The Child and the Magistrate*, p. 204.
[20] Criminal Justice Act 1948, s. 19(1).
[1] Most magistrates seem to regard it as mainly punitive; see the Cambridge Report, p. 15. That, too, was the opinion of the Ingleby Committee (para. 288). See also McLean and Wood, *op. cit.*, p. 204.
[2] Attendance Centre Rules 1958, r. 2(1).

more on the strictness of the discipline; others are more concerned with providing training which will help to reform the offender. Making due allowance for variation in the facilities in different centres, it does seem surprising, in view of the statutory requirement that "the occupation and instruction shall be in accordance with a scheme approved by or on behalf of the Secretary of State"[3] that the central government has not given more guidance as to the emphasis to be given respectively to discipline and training, thereby achieving greater uniformity in this form of treatment.

Breach of Rules Relating to Attendance

Whenever an offender has failed without reasonable excuse to attend the centre as required or has while attending committed a breach of the Attendance Centre Rules 1958, for which under those Rules he cannot adequately be dealt with, a magistrates' court may revoke the order and deal with him in any way in which the court making the original order could have dealt with him had it not made the order.[4]

It is, however, very uncommon to bring an offender back before the court for a breach of the 1958 Rules. Instead, the officer in charge may exercise various disciplinary powers; for example by separating the offender from others and giving him less pleasant tasks, or by requiring him to leave the centre and discounting his attendance on that occasion, or by reducing the duration of each period of attendance and correspondingly increasing the number of attendances.

Reports

Although an attendance centre must keep certain records (*e.g.* of attendance and breach of rules), there is no statutory duty to provide the centre with reports on the offender before his first attendance. Nor is there a duty for the centre to report on him when his attendance ends. The need to provide the officer in charge with records relating to previous appearances in court, a social enquiry report and a school record was stressed in the Cambridge Report.[5] In most cases these documents are forwarded and correspondingly many officers in

[3] *Ibid.*, r. 2(2).
[4] Criminal Justice Act 1948, s. 19(7) and (8).
[5] Pages 41-42.

125

charge report to the court; but the importance of these measures is self-evident and they ought to be made compulsory.

Discharge and Variation of Orders

The offender or the officer in charge may apply for the order to be discharged or varied, but the only variation permissible is the day or hour specified for the offender's first attendance at the centre.[6] Either the court that made the order or a justice acting for the division for which that court acts may discharge or vary it.

III. CUSTODIAL ORDERS

The Children and Young Persons Act 1969 allows for extensive changes with regard to custodial orders. It has already abolished the fit person order, the approved school order and the order committing to a remand home,[7] substituting therefor the flexible care order, and it provides for the eventual abolition of the detention centre order and the sentence to borstal training in respect of juveniles.[8]

(1) Care Orders

A care order may be made where the juvenile is found guilty of an offence which in the case of an adult would be punishable with imprisonment. As will be seen,[9] one of the effects of the care order is to enable the local authority to curtail the liberties of the juvenile; another is to enable them to move him within the various community homes available without any need to resort to the juvenile court for permission. Both these powers are particularly relevant where the care order is the result of criminal proceedings.

(2) Detention Centre Orders

In spite of the barbaric conditions which prevailed in English prisons throughout the 18th century, Parliament refused to do anything to provide for the separate detention of juvenile and adult offenders. Even when the influence of Howard and Bentham began to be felt soon after 1800 the

---

[6] Criminal Justice Act 1948, s. 19(3).
[7] Section 7(5) and (6); S.I. 1970 No. 1499. Temporarily, approved schools and remand homes will continue as such until absorbed into the system of community homes; see *post*, Chapter 5.
[8] *Ibid.*, sub-ss. (3) and (1) respectively.   [9] *Post*, Chapter 5.

early reforms of the prison system did not include special provisions for young offenders.[10] It was only as the result of the persistent efforts of voluntary organisations that Parliament finally accepted what had come to be known as the reformatory movement. Under the legislation relating to reformatory schools and industrial schools[11] young offenders could be sent to those schools, but an initial defect in the legislation was that a school order could only be made if the offender first served a term of imprisonment and not until 1899 was it enacted that an order was to be a substitute and not an addition to imprisonment. The process of restricting the imprisonment of juveniles was carried much further by the Children Act 1908 which abolished imprisonment of children and only allowed it with regard to young persons (then 14 to 16) in exceptional cases of unruliness or depravity.[12] The total abolition of imprisonment of juveniles was finally achieved by the Criminal Justice Acts 1948 and 1961.[13]

The effect of the above provisions of the Act of 1908 was that, unless some other form of detention was introduced, the reformatory or industrial school order would be the only method of detaining juveniles; but such an order must, as the law then stood, be for a training period of three to five years, so that there was no power to detain for a short period of strict discipline even though that might be the most appropriate way of dealing with the juvenile. To fill this gap the Act created the remand home and, *inter alia* provided for the punitive detention of juvenile offenders there for a maximum period of one month. As a substitute for imprisonment these homes proved, however, to be of limited value, and the Criminal Justice Act 1948 sought partly to meet the deficiency by providing for the establishment of a new type of institution which would permit a somewhat longer period of detention.

---

[10] As late as 1849 more than 10,000 juveniles were imprisoned or transported during that year; see the Report of the Committee on the Treatment of Young Offenders (Cmnd. 2831 at pp. 7-8).

[11] The first Reformatory Schools Act was in 1854 and the first Industrial Schools Act in 1857.

[12] Children Act 1908, s. 102. The Act also abolished penal servitude in relation to juveniles.

[13] Under the 1948 Act magistrates' courts were not to impose imprisonment on anyone under 17 and courts of assize and quarter session on anyone under 15. The later Act brought the latter courts into line with magistrates' courts.

Detention centres are available for the detention of offenders between 14 and 21 "under discipline suitable to persons of their age and description".[14] They are here examined in relation to young persons.

A detention centre order may be made whenever a young person could, but for the statutory prohibition, be sentenced to imprisonment.[15] But an order is only possible if the court has been notified by the Home Office that a centre is available.[16] The period of detention must be three months, except that where the finding of guilt is by the Crown Court and the maximum term of imprisonment for which the court, were the offender not a young person, could pass sentence of imprisonment exceeds three months, the period may be not less than three nor more than six months.[17] A remission of one-third of the period may be granted for industry and good conduct. There is no longer any power to make an order in respect of a young person who is a defaulter.[18]

Nature of Detention Centres

The administration and management of centres, the discipline, training and welfare of inmates and a variety of kindred matters are very largely governed by the Detention Centre Rules 1952.[19]

Centres are classified into junior and senior. The former are provided for those under 17, the latter for those over that age,[20] but the Prison Department of the Home Office may excep-

[14] Prison Act 1952, s. 43 (1), as amended by the Criminal Justice Act 1961; s. 41(1) and Sched. IV.

[15] Criminal Justice Act 1961, s. 4.

[16] Before making an order a court should inquire from the warden of the centre whether a vacancy is available. The C. & Y.P. Act 1969, s. 7(3) (which is not yet operative) will enable the Secretary of State to notify a court that a detention centre will not be available for a particular class or description of juveniles.

[17] Criminal Justice Act 1961, s. 4(2), as amended by Courts Act 1971, Sched. 8, para. 41.

Where a young person is tried summarily by a juvenile court for an indictable offence and reaches the age of 17 in the course of the proceedings, the term of a detention centre order still cannot exceed three months. This is the effect of s. 6(3) of the C. & Y.P. Act 1969 read with s.4(2) of the 1961 Act. See H.O. Guide to Part I of the 1969 Act, para. 219.

[18] For the power to make an order where a defaulter has attained the age of 17 see s. 5 of the Criminal Justice Act 1961, sub-s. (1), of which has been substituted by the C. & Y.P. Act 1969, Sched. 5, para. 44.

[19] S.I. 1952, No. 1432, as amended by the Detention Centre (Amendment) Rules 1972 (No. 1012).

[20] There are no longer centres provided for girls.

tionally direct that, having regard to a person's mental or physical development, he should be detained in a senior rather than a junior centre or *vice versa*. Each centre is administered by a Board of Visitors, whose members are appointed by the Home Secretary for a period of up to three years. They are required to visit and inspect the centre frequently and they have free access to all parts and the right to see all inmates. Over-all control lies with the Prison Department, to whom the Board owes a variety of duties; for example it must submit annual reports and reports of any abuses of which it becomes aware.

Although increasing use has been made of the detention centre order, it remains a controversial method of treatment.[1] The uncertainty as to the kinds of offenders for whom it is intended is basically due to the contradiction in its aims. Introduced as a punitive measure, it has retained that primary purpose. The discipline at centres is severe and, some would claim, still too military in outlook. The emphasis is heavily on manual work, physical training and strict supervision, and, although corporal punishment of inmates is unlawful, allegations of it are not unknown. Gradually its reformative aims have come to be recognised. Some educational and training facilities, especially for young persons, must be made available and opportunities provided for establishing a personal relationship between staff and inmates; but critics have doubted whether these functions are consistently and positively discharged. That it is not intended as a suitable substitute for long-term training is partly shown by the statutory restriction that, unless there are special circumstances, an order should not be made if the young person has already served a sentence of borstal training.[2] Similarly, it generally is unsuitable for the

---

[1] Much has been written about it. See especially 5 B.J.D. 207 and 10 B.J. Crim. 178; Dunlop & McCabe, *Young Men in Detention Centres;* Banks, *Boys in Detention Centres;* Thomas, *Principles of Sentencing*, pp. 233-236; McLean and Wood, *op. cit.*, pp. 232-239; Hall Williams, *The English Penal System in Transition*, pp. 330-343; *Report of the Advisory Council on the Penal System*, HMSO 1970.

[2] Criminal Justice Act 1961, s. 4(4).
  Even where exceptional circumstances (whether relating to the offence or the offender) warrant the making of an order, the court must first consider any report made by the Prison Department. This will mean that the juvenile court will have to adjourn the hearing and remand the offender in custody for a report to be made.

juvenile who has previously been in an approved school[3] or (in future) in a community home under a care order or has previously been the subject of a detention centre order.[4] Nor ought it normally to be invoked in the case of the first offender, although its use in such cases is quite common.

Curiously, there is no rule preventing an order being made on the ground of the offender's physical or mental disability, nor is there any duty to consider reports on his health.[5] Nevertheless, the court should inquire into such matters and refuse an order where it considers the offender's health will be unable to withstand the rigorous demands of the regime of a centre. Thus in *R. v. Jobes*[6] the Court of Criminal Appeal released from a detention centre a 20-year-old under-developed offender who had been in and out of hospital with spinal tuberculosis between the ages of 3 and 16.[7]

After-Care

Prior to the Criminal Justice Act 1961 an inmate on release from a centre could voluntarily submit to after-care, but the response was poor. Where an offender was guilty on two counts a probation order and detention centre order might be combined, but when this combination was held illegal[8] the Act introduced compulsory after-care under a probation officer for a period of 12 months, subject to a power to recall the released person to the centre for the period of remission or for 14 days, whichever is the longer, if he fails to comply with any requirements imposed when he was first released.[9]

[3] *R. v. Nolan*, [1967] Crim. L.R. 117.
[4] *R. v. Moore*, [1968] 1 All E.R. 790; [1968] 1 W.L.R. 397. A second order is unlikely to have an immediate impact on the offender, which is an essential feature of the order.
[5] But before making an order a juvenile court should call for social inquiry reports.   [6] [1962] Crim. L.R. 714.
[7] There are unsatisfactory features about this case. The Board of Visitors must have known of the inmate's state of health, since every person on admission to a detention centre must undergo a medical examination within 24 hours. Indeed, it is reported that the inmate was excused physical activities because of his condition. Yet, there is no indication of the Board's having complied with the duty of informing the Prison Department that the inmate's health was such as was likely to be injured by the conditions of his detention. If they did, there is no evidence of prompt measures being taken to secure the inmate's release. There was certainly ample time for someone to have acted – the offender had already been in the centre seven weeks before the decision of the Court of Criminal Appeal.
[8] *R. v. Evans*, [1959] 3 All E.R. 673; [1959] 1 W.L.R. 26.
[9] Section 13 and Sched. I.

(3) Borstal Training
Nature of Training

The system of Borstal institutions was established by the Prevention of Crimes Act 1908.[10] Like that of the reformatory schools it was inspired by the need to separate young offenders from adults and give them specialised treatment. Indeed, basically it started as an extension of the reformatory principle to young offenders, *i.e.,* persons no longer juveniles but still under 21. Subsequent legislation[11] has, however, extended it to young persons who have attained the age of 15 and, as with the detention centre order, it is here examined primarily with regard to them.[12] The term "juvenile" in the present context therefore means a person aged between 15 and 17.

For the juvenile Borstal training is a form of medium term custodial training which is most likely to be ordered where neither the long-term care order nor the short-term detention centre order is considered suitable.

"The emphasis in Borstal training is on remedial and educational treatment based on close study of the individual. Borstals are organised so as to facilitate individual study, personal training and wise leadership. Standardisation is not sought. The system of training seeks the all-round development of character and capacities – moral, mental, physical and vocational – and is based on progressive trust demanding increasing personal decision, responsibility and self-control. Opportunities are given to practise these qualities, and the conditions in borstals are sufficiently various and elastic to suit different characters and different stages of development".[13]

The Borstal Rules 1964 contain detailed provisions concerning the treatment, employment, discipline and control of inmates, and Borstals vary widely in their facilities and training from open establishments[14] to those with a regime of strict

---

[10] Following an experiment at the Borstal prison, Rochester.

[11] Criminal Justice Act 1948, s. 20, as amended by the Criminal Justice Act 1961, s. 1.

[12] On Borstals generally see especially Hood, *Borstal Re-assessed;* McLean and Wood, *op. cit.,* pp. 239-250; Thomas *op. cit.,* pp. 236-246; Hall Williams, *op. cit.,* Chapter 22.

[13] *The Sentence of the Court,* para. 111 (H.O. Handbook on the Treatment of Offenders).

[14] *Quaere* how far the decision of the House of Lords in *Home Office* v. *Dorset Yacht Co.,* [1970] A.C. 1004; [1970] 2 All E.R. 294 may affect such establishments. There it was held that Borstal officers owe a duty to a member of the public to take care to prevent trainees under their

security where the punitive element of the sentence is also present.[15] In order that the individual offender may receive the training best suited to his age, ability, character and other needs,[16] he is after sentence first sent to a classifying centre where he undergoes examination and scrutiny by a specialist staff before being allocated to a particular institution.

Jurisdiction

A juvenile court is empowered to remove a juvenile to a Borstal from a community home in which he is accommodated under a care order if his behaviour there is detrimental to the other inmates. The responsibility for bringing him before the court lies with the local authority, subject to Home Office consent.[17] If the court is not in a position to decide whether to order removal, it may temporarily order detention in a remand centre for up to 21 days, with power to vary or extend the detention, provided that it does not exceed 8 weeks in all.[18] When the minimum age for sentencing to Borstal training under the following jurisdictional rules is raised to 17[19] (or possibly initially to 16[20]), it will still be possible to exercise the above powers of removal unless and until a higher age than 15 is specified.[1]

Removal is exceptional, and most inmates at a Borstal are there as a result of a sentence imposed by the Crown Court. The Court may so sentence an offender whom it has found

---

control or supervision from injuring him or his property and that there is no ground of public policy for granting to the Home Office or its officers complete community from liability in negligence. Will this mean that Borstal staff will exert stricter control and that establishments will *de facto* cease to be "open"?

[15] For this reason, when a court is sentencing an offender to Borstal training because it considers that he needs punishment, it ought to give the reason so that those responsible for choosing a suitable institution may take account of it; see LORD PARKER, C. J. in *R.* v. *Lowe*, [1964] 2 All E.R. 116; [1964] 1 W.L.R. 609.

[16] And see the previous footnote.

[17] C. & Y.P. Act 1969, s. 31 (1) and (2).

A similar power formerly existed with regard to juveniles who were guilty of serious misconduct in, or absconding from, approved schools or whose detention there was detrimental to other inmates.

[18] *Ibid.*, sub-ss. (4) and (5).

The power to vary or extend may also be exercised by any other magistrates' court and not necessarily by a juvenile court; but except where illness or accident prevents it, the juvenile's attendance in court is essential.

[19] Section 7(1).   [20] Section 34(1) (d).

[1] Section 34(1) (f). But the likelihood is that the power to remove will simultaneously be brought into line with the power to sentence.

guilty of an offence punishable with imprisonment, but cases
of juveniles appearing before it on indictment are not frequent
and, in any case, a sentence to Borstal training is only to be
passed as a last resort when no other appropriate order can be
made. A juvenile offender is more likely to be sentenced to
Borstal training where he has been found guilty by a juvenile
court and then committed to the Crown Court under s. 28 of
the Magistrates' Courts Act 1952[2] with a view to such a sentence being imposed. In considering whether Borstal training
is expedient, the Court must have regard to the circumstances
of the offence[3] and the offender's character and previous conduct.[4] In practice, the juvenile court, when deciding whether
to commit, will itself also consider those matters, but it would
be as well if this were made an express statutory duty.

An offender may be committed for sentence either on bail
or in custody. Committal on bail is a fairly recent innovation,[5]
and juvenile courts should have it much in mind. But where
committal in custody is considered desirable it must be to a
prison, unless the court has been notified by the Home Secretary that a remand centre is available. The juvenile cannot be
committed to the care of a local authority and sent to a community home. His position differs from that of a juvenile found
guilty of an offence by the Crown Court who is remanded in
custody while the court decides how to deal with him, because,
as already seen,[6] he is to be remanded to the care of a local
authority unless, because he is unruly or depraved, it is necessary to remand him in a remand centre or prison.[7]

---

[2] As amended by the Criminal Justice Act 1961, s. 41 and Scheds. IV, V
and VI, and the Courts Act 1971, Sched. 8. Section 28 applies, of course,
to all magistrates' courts.
[3] In R. v. Gooding (1955), 39 Cr. App. Rep. 187, it was held to be inappropriate to sentence to Borstal training an offender, who had just been
released from a detention centre, in respect of offences committed before
the offence for which he was sent to the centre.
[4] There is no reason why an offender guilty of a homosexual offence should
not be sentenced to borstal training if he is otherwise suitable for such
a sentence; R. v. Gardiner (1957), 41 Cr. App. Rep. 95.
    On the other hand the offender's criminal record may be so bad that
it would be expedient not to send him to a borstal institution because of
the risk of corrupting others, but rather to sentence him to imprisonment; R. v. Kneale (1931), 23 Cr. App. Rep. 73. But where he is a
juvenile that possibility is not open and the court could scarcely do other
than send him for Borstal training.
[5] Criminal Justice Act 1967, s. 103 and Sched. VI, para. 11, amending
s. 28 (2) and (4) of the 1952 Act.
[6] Ante, Chapter 3, p. 88.   [7] C. & Y.P. Act 1969, s. 23(1) and (2).

If the Crown Court decides that Borstal training is not suitable, it may deal with the juvenile in any manner in which the juvenile court might have dealt with him when they decided to commit.[8] The need to relate the powers of the Crown Court to the date of committal is illustrated by *R. v. Hammond*[9] where it was held that, since the committing court had been precluded from making a detention centre order in respect of an offender under 17 because they had not been notified that a centre was available for the detention of persons of his age, it was not open to quarter sessions to do so, and *a fortiori* the latter court could not adjourn the proceedings until the offender attained 17 in the hope that a senior centre would then be available so as to permit the making of an order.

The Ingleby Committee strongly recommended that juvenile courts should be given a general power to order Borstal training. It relied on two arguments.[10] First, transfer of the power to those courts would avoid the need for young persons to be detained in prison or a remand centre while waiting for the next sitting of quarter sessions. The Courts Act 1971 does not remove the need, but it does enable the period of detention to be kept to a minimum, since the Crown Court sits continually at many places and frequently and regularly at others, so that the system is sufficiently flexible to enable committal to be made, if necessary, to the Court at a sitting outside the area over which the juvenile court has jurisdiction.[11] The second argument of the Committee was that the reports on juveniles prepared for juvenile courts are fuller than those dealing with offenders aged 17 or over, and therefore, together with the report from the Prison Department,[12] would provide firmer guidance as to the suitability of Borstal training; but there is no reason why the Crown Court should not ensure that it has

---

[8] Criminal Justice Act 1948, s. 20(5) (a) (ii).
[9] [1963] 2 Q.B. 450, (C.C.A.); [1963] 2 All E.R. 475.
[10] Cmnd. 1191, paras. 353-357.
[11] Previously the hardship was mitigated by the Criminal Justice Administration Act 1962, s. 15, which allowed an offender to be committed to quarter sessions other than those for the county or borough for which the committing court acted, if it was unlikely that he would otherwise be dealt with within one month of committal and provided that he would not suffer hardship by a change of venue.
[12] This must be prepared for the Crown Court when considering a sentence of Borstal training; Criminal Justice Act 1961, s. 1(3); but the Court is not precluded from passing that sentence without it being available (*R. v. Lowe*, [1964] 2 All E.R. 116; [1964] 1 W.L.R. 849).

the same information as the juvenile court when it is dealing
with a juvenile. Nevertheless, it is disappointing that the Committee's recommendation has not been accepted in view of the
wider experience of juvenile courts in dealing with juveniles
than that of the Crown Court and its predecessors.[13] Instead,
the Courts Act 1971 makes the concession that, in the absence
of waiver by the Lord Chancellor, not less than two and not
more than four justices must sit with a judge of the Crown
Court in proceedings on committal for sentence.[14]

Duration of Detention; Release and Supervision; Recall and Return
The sentence to Borstal training is a quasi-indeterminate
sentence, because while statute prescribes detention for a
minimum period of six months and a maximum of two years
from the date of sentence,[15] the Home Secretary has an unfettered discretion to release at any time within the two years,
even within the first six months of detention.[16] The exercise of
this discretion will depend upon the progress report made by
the Board of Visitors. The discretion may never be exercised
or may be long delayed, so that the sentence may well deprive
the offender of his liberty for a period longer than the maximum
prison sentence which could have been passed for the particular
offence had he not been a juvenile. Yet, the fact that this may
happen is a relevant consideration, but no more, in deciding
whether to impose the sentence.[17]

When an order is made removing a juvenile from a community home to a Borstal institution,[18] the care order ceases to
have effect and he is treated as being sentenced to Borstal
training from the date of the order of removal; but he cannot
be detained after the date when the care order would in the
normal way have come to an end,[19] if that date is less than two
years from the date of the removal order.[20]

[13] See Samuels [1961] Crim. L.R. 755.
[14] Section 5(1) and (5). Prior to the Act, in borough quarter sessions two
members of the juvenile court panel had, if practicable, to sit with the
Recorder as assessors (C. & Y.P. Act 1963, s. 19).
[15] Prison Act 1952, s. 45(2), as amended by the Criminal Justice Act 1961,
s. 11.
[16] The average period of training is about 14 months. (See "The Sentence
of the Court", para. 107).
[17] *R.* v. *Amos*, [1961] 1 All E.R. 191 (C.C.A.); [1961] 1 W.L.R. 308; cf.
R. v. *James*, [1960] 2 All E.R. 863; [1960] 1 W.L.R. 812.   [18] See *supra.*
[19] For the duration of care orders see *post*, Chapter 5, p. 152.
[20] C. & Y.P. Act 1969, s. 31(3) (a).

Upon his release the inmate is placed under the supervision of a probation officer for a period of two years, but the Home Secretary may bring it to an end at any time.[1] Supervision may be subject to specified conditions which he may later modify or cancel, and if he is satisfied that the supervisee has failed to comply with any of them he may order his recall to a Borstal where he may be further detained until two years have elapsed from the date of the original sentence[2] or six months from when he was taken into custody under the order, whichever is the later. An order for recall ceases to be operative, however, at the end of two years from the date of his release, unless at that time he is already in custody. Any one who is detained after recall may later again be released and placed under supervision, with the possibility of further recall within the remaining period of two years from the date of his original release.

A supervisee, found guilty of an offence for which the court has, or, but for the statutory restrictions upon imprisonment of young offenders, would have power to sentence to imprisonment, may, instead of otherwise being dealt with, be ordered to be returned to a Borstal.[3] The rules relating to the period of further detention follow those applicable to cases of recall.

(4) Detention for Grave Crimes

A child or young person who is found guilty of an offence which, in the case of an adult would be punishable with imprisonment for 14 years or more (the sentence being a fixed one) may be sentenced to be detained for a specified period[4] at such place and on such conditions as the Home Secretary may direct.[5] Until criminal proceedings against children are abolished (except for homicide), these powers will be exercised

[1] Prison Act 1952, s. 45.
[2] For the case where the supervisee had been removed from a community home see C. & Y.P. Act 1969, s. 31(3) (b).
[3] Criminal Justice Act 1961, s. 12. A similar rule applies to an absconder from the institution.
    If anyone while under supervision or after recall or after being ordered to be returned to a borstal is sentenced by any court in Great Britain to borstal training, his original sentence of borstal training ceases to operate (Prison Act 1952, s. 45(5)).
[4] The period must not exceed the maximum term of imprisonment which could be imposed on an adult in respect of the particular offence. It must be a determinate period (*R.* v. *McCauliffe*, [1970] Crim. L.R. 660), but this includes detention for life (*R.* v. *Abbott*, [1964] 1 Q.B. 489; [1963] 1 All E.R. 738).
[5] C. & Y.P. Act 1933, s. 53(2).

by a juvenile court if the offender is a child, but, if he is a young person, he will be committed for trial and the trial court will be responsible for sentencing him. In either case, this form of detention should only be ordered if none of the other methods of dealing with the juvenile is considered suitable.[6]

Many of those sentenced under s. 53 will be detained in the newly established Youth Treatment Centres,[7] but the Home Secretary has power to direct detention by a local authority in a community home provided by the authority or in a controlled community home,[8] although in such cases the person cannot be detained there after attaining the age of 19.[9] He may also be able to arrange with the managers detention in an assisted community home[10] or, so long as they continue to exist, in an approved school.[11]

Section 53 of the 1933 Act[12] also provides that a person found guilty of murder committed when he was under 18 must be sentenced to detention during Her Majesty's pleasure in such places as the Home Secretary may direct. The Youth Treatment Centre or the community home will also be available for that kind of offender.

The Home Secretary may on the recommendation of the Parole Board release on licence a person detained under s. 53, but, in the case of detention during Her Majesty's pleasure or for life, he must also first consult the Lord Chief Justice and the trial judge if available.[13] The release may be made subject to conditions and the Home Secretary may revoke the licence and recall the person to detention.[14]

(5) and (6) Hospital Orders and Guardianship Orders

These have been examined as methods of treatment of

---

[6] In considering suitability the court should remember that there is no possibility of aftercare and supervision where there is an order under s. 53. For this reason a care order may be more appropriate, especially where the juvenile is already being detained in a community home under a s. 53 order and is progressing well in the home; see *R.* v. *G., Times,* 27 September 1971, (C.A.). But the Court of Appeal seems to have overstated the significance of aftercare and supervision following a care order; see *post,* Chapter 5, p. 172.

[7] See *post,* Chapter 5.   [8] For community homes see *ibid.*

[9] C. & Y.P. Act 1969, s. 30. The local authority is entitled to be reimbursed by the Home Office for any expenses reasonably incurred.

[10] For assisted community homes see Chapter 5.

[11] C. & Y.P. Act 1933, s. 58 (not yet repealed).   [12] Sub-section (1).

[13] Criminal Justice Act 1967, s. 61.   [14] Section 62.

juveniles found to be in need of care or control.[15] The following additional matters should be noted:

(1) In criminal proceedings the Crown Court may make either order where the offence is other than one for which the sentence is fixed by law, and a magistrates' court where it is one punishable on summary conviction with imprisonment.[16]

(2) If an order is made in respect of a juvenile, the court cannot impose a fine or make a supervision order or an order that the parent enter into a recognisance to take proper care of him and exercise proper control over him or any order for his detention. But a care order may be combined with either a hospital order or a guardianship order.[17] In care proceedings it may only be combined with a hospital order,[18] but the distinction, it is submitted, is academic. Since the guardian is the local health authority or a person approved by them no practical purpose would be served in additionally making a care order.

(3) When a hospital order is made by the Crown Court, an order restricting the discharge of the offender may also be made if this is considered necessary for the protection of the public.[19] A magistrates' court cannot make a restriction order. If it considers such an order should be made, it may, instead of making a hospital order or otherwise dealing with him, commit him to the Crown Court to be dealt with.[20]

---

[15] *Ante*, p. 108.
[16] Mental Health Act 1959, s. 60(1), as amended by the Courts Act 1971, Sched. 8.
[17] *Ibid.*, sub-s. (6), as amended by C. & Y.P. Act 1969, Scheds. 5 and 6.
[18] See *ante*, p. 95.
[19] See Mental Health Act 1959, s. 65 as amended by the Courts Act 1971, Sched. 8; *R.* v. *Gardiner*, [1967] 1 All E.R. 895; [1967] 1 W.L.R. 464.
[20] Section 67, as so amended.

CHAPTER 5

Children in the Care of Local Authorities

A. ORGANISATION AND ADMINISTRATION

Before 1948 children deprived of a normal home-life were dealt with under a variety of statutes, depending upon the reason for the deprivation.[1] The largest group were the destitute children, cared for either, as part of the Poor Law, by local authorities under the general control of the Ministry of Health or by voluntary organisations who were subject to inspection by that Ministry or, in some cases, the Home Office. Children under nine could be fostered for reward and were then supervised by local authorities, also under the direction of the Ministry. By virtue of the Children and Young Persons Act 1933 juveniles could be committed to the care of a local authority or sent to approved schools,[2] and, finally, children who were physically or mentally handicapped could be placed in local authority or voluntary institutions inspected by the Board of Control or the Ministry of Education.

These several methods of providing a substitute for home life involved considerable variation in the degree of responsibility, both at central and local government level, and the Curtis Committee, which was the first thorough inquiry into the care of deprived children, in recommending a large extension of public care, stressed the need for concentrating responsibility for it, though not for all aspects of the child's life, in one central department, with immediate responsibility to be undertaken by the local authority, working through a specialised committee. The Committee's recommendations were given effect by the Children Act 1948.

---

[1] For a detailed account see the Report of the Care of Children Committee (Curtis Committee), (1946), Cmnd. 6922, paras. 12-99, and for a learned historical survey of the care of the deprived child see Heywood, *Children in Care*.

[2] See *ante*, Chapter 4.

The Act makes county councils and county borough councils[3] responsible for the care of deprived children, subject to some central control by the Department of Health and Social Security and, in Wales, by the Welsh Office. Their functions are mainly derived from the Act itself, but also partly from a number of other statutes. Thus, they have been the appropriate local authorities for the purpose of those Parts of the Children and Young Persons Acts 1933 and 1963 which have dealt with remand homes, approved schools and fit persons.[4] They are responsible for ensuring the well-being of foster children under Part I of the Children Act 1958[5] and of protected children within the meaning of Part IV of the Adoption Act 1958.[6] By virtue of Part II of the latter Act they are able to serve as adoption agencies,[7] and by the Mental Health Act 1959,[8] obligations are imposed on them with regard to accommodating and looking after mentally disordered children. They may also be made responsible for supervising children under supervision orders made under the Matrimonial Causes Act 1965,[9] the Matrimonial Proceedings (Magistrates' Courts) Act 1960[10] and the Family Law Reform Act 1969.[11] Moreover, children may be committed to their care under those three Acts,[12] in which case, with qualifications, the provisions in the Children Act 1948 relating to care become applicable. They also supervise nurseries and child-minders.[13]

As earlier chapters have partly shown, the Children and Young Persons Act 1969 introduces far-reaching changes with regard to some of these functions. The gradual implementation of the Act means additional responsibilities for local authorities in the supervision and care of juveniles, in the arrangement of facilities for supervision,[14] in the planning of an integrated

[3] Children Act 1948, s. 38. See also now the Local Authority Social Services Act 1970, s. 1. The London borough councils and the Common Council of the City are the authorities for the London area.
[4] *Ante*, Chapter 4.
  These functions will gradually be replaced by those laid down by the Children and Young Persons Act 1969, *infra*.
[5] *Post*, Chapter 11.   [6] *Post*, Chapter 10.
[7] *Post*, Chapter 10.   [8] Sections 9 and 10, *post*, p. 173.
[9] Section 37.   [10] Sections 2(1) (f) and 3(7).
[11] Section 7(4).
[12] Section 36; ss. 2(1) (e) and 3(1) to (5); and s. 7(2) respectively; see *post*, pp. 154-156.
[13] Nurseries and Child-Minders Regulation Act 1948, *post*, Chapter 11.
[14] *Ante*, Chapter 4.

system of community homes to accommodate children in care[15] and in the protection of foster children.[16]

In the past, a local authority normally discharged those several functions through its children's committee, sub-committees and the Children's Officer at the head of what was in effect a separate department of local government.[17] The practice was for the committee to concern itself with issues of general policy, leaving more detailed administration and supervision to its sub-committees, with the department being responsible for the day to day exercise of the functions of the local authority and the committee.

But the re-organisation of the child care service by the Children Act 1948 still left other departments of the local authority, mainly the health and education departments, to deal with other aspects of child care, and the need for local authorities to co-ordinate those of their services connected with the family gradually became apparent.[18] The problem of co-ordination was examined generally by the Younghusband Working Party on social workers in the local authority health and welfare services (1959) and specifically in relation to child neglect by the Ingleby Committee.[19] The latter recognised the possibility of a long-term solution in a re-organisation of the services into a unified family service,[20] but foresaw formidable difficulties. The Seebohm Committee, to whom the matter was eventually referred,[1] did not find them insurmountable. Admitting that many changes were necessary before an effective family service could be created, it saw as "the first necessity" the establishment of a new department of local government – a unified social service department within each major local authority, which would merge the existing children's department, welfare department and some sections of the health

---

[15] *Post*, pp. 158 *et seq.*   [16] *Post*, Chapter 11.
[17] Children Act 1948, ss. 39–41.
[18] To avoid overlapping of functions legislation has been necessary; see the Local Authorities and Local Education Authorities (Allocation of Functions) Regulations 1951 (S.I. 1951 No. 472), made under s. 21 of the Children Act 1948.
[19] (1960) Cmnd. 1191.
 The White Paper, *"The Child, the Family and the Young Offender"*, also referred to the matter; see (1965) Cmnd. 2742, para. 7.
[20] Cmnd. 1191, para. 47.
[1] The Report of the Committee on Local Authority and Allied Personal Social Services, (1968) Cmnd. 3703.

department. The new department should be run by a separate committee of the local authority, with a principal officer at its head, and it should have area offices, with each office serving a population of 50,000 to 100,000 and having a team of at least 10 to 12 social workers. The Local Authority Social Services Act 1970[2] implements some of these proposals.

Each local authority must have a social services committee through whom it discharges, *inter alia*, the functions formerly discharged by the children's committee.[3] The authority must refer every matter relevant to those functions to the committee, unless it also relates to a general service of the authority, in which case the authority may, after hearing the views of the social services committee, refer it to another committee. Except in urgent cases no action can be taken by the authority on any matter referred to the social services committee until the committee has reported on it, but alternatively the authority can delegate to the committee any of its "social service" functions. Subject to any restrictions imposed by the authority, the committee may establish sub-committees and authorise them to exercise any of its functions.[4]

A social services committee may either be composed exclusively of members of the local authority or include other persons providing they form a minority.[5] In practice they are likely to be persons specially qualified in matters relating to the committee's functions.[6] A sub-committee or joint sub-committee must include at least one member of each of the local authorities concerned. Two or more authorities may combine to appoint a joint social services committee,[7] which in turn may appoint sub-committees, provided, again, that each local authority is represented thereon.

Under the new system the children's officer and the director of welfare services are replaced by the director of social services, whose appointment by the local authority must be in accordance with qualifications prescribed by the Secretary of

---

[2] The Act is gradually being brought into operation.
[3] Section 2 and Sched. I.
[4] Section 4(2). Indeed, social services committees of two or more local authorities may appoint joint sub-committees (s. 4(3)).
[5] Section 5. There is also a power to co-opt.
[6] They must not be disqualified under s. 59 of the Local Government Act 1933, *e.g.* as local government officers.
[7] Section 4(1).

State.[8] A director may be appointed to act for two or more authorities, but, whether appointed for one or more, he must not be employed in any other capacity except with the consent of the Secretary of State.

Central control is exercised in various ways. Treasury grants are made for the purpose of training persons in child care and the form of training is subject to Home Office approval.[9] The local authorities come under the general guidance of the Secretary of State[10] and are subject to inspection by the Department of Health and Social Security.[11] The Secretary is advised by the Advisory Council on Child Care,[12] which is composed of persons specially qualified to deal with matters affecting the welfare of children, those having experience in local government and those with other special qualifications. The Council advises him on any matters relating to his functions under the Children and Young Persons Acts 1933 to 1969, the Children Act 1948, the Children Act 1958 and the Adoption Act 1958.[13]

A potentially far-reaching change, introduced by the Children and Young Persons Act 1963,[14] was that which authorises both the Home Office and local authorities to conduct or assist in conducting research into any of their functions under the Children and Young Persons Acts, Children Acts or Adoption Acts, but this enactment, like so many others affecting the social services, has been hit by economic restrictions.

B. ADMISSION OR COMMITTAL TO CARE

Children may come into the care of local authorities through

[8] Section 6. Until regulations come into force, appointments are subject to prior consultation with the Secretary.
[9] Children Act 1948, s. 45, as amended by the Local Authority Social Services Act 1970, s. 14 and Sched. 2, para. 5. Grants may also be made by the Department, as well as by local authorities, to voluntary organisations concerned with child care.
  Note also the general power under the Local Government Grants (Social Need) Act 1969, s. 1, to provide grants to local authorities who in exercising any of their functions are required to incur expenditure by reason of the existence of any social need in any urban area.
[10] Local Authority Social Services Act 1970, s. 7.   [11] See *post*, p. 161.
[12] Children Act 1948, s. 43, as amended by C. & Y.P. Act 1969, s. 72(3) and Sched. 5.
[13] But excluding s. 32 which empowers the Secretary of State to make regulations relating to the functions of local authorities as adoption agencies.
[14] Section 45, as amended by C. & Y.P. Act 1969, s. 72(3) and Sched. 5.

various enactments, of which the Children Act 1948 and the Children and Young Persons Acts are by far the most important.

I. CHILDREN ACT 1948

(1) Receiving into Care under Section 1

Section 1(1) imposes on a local authority the duty to receive a child into their care if it appears to them:

> "(a) that he has neither parent nor guardian or has been and remains abandoned by his parents or guardian or is lost;
>
> or (b) that his parents or guardian are, for the time being or permanently, prevented by reason of mental or bodily disease or infirmity or other incapacity or any other circumstances from providing for his proper accommodation, maintenance and upbringing;
>
> and (c) in either case, that the intervention of the local authority is necessary in the interests of the welfare of the child".

This is an ambiguous provision. On the one hand, sub-para. (b) gives it wide scope, for there may be a variety of "other circumstances" which will justify intervention by the local authority; the child of the homeless family is a common example.[15] On the other hand, the subsection is so worded, particularly in its reference to "either case" in sub-para. (c), that it suggests that sub-paras. (a) and (b) are mutually exclusive and, therefore, that it would not be open to the local authority to say that one of the conditions in sub-para (a) is satisfied in relation to the one parent and one of those in sub-para. (b) to the other. Supposing, for example, that on a decree of divorce the father were granted custody by the court and the mother, who then remarried, did not maintain contact with the child. The father deserts the child by going abroad and the mother now wants to bring him into her present family but her second husband will not allow her. It is difficult to see how the case can come wholly within sub-para. (a). Accepting that abandonment has the same meaning in that sub-para. as it has in s. 1 of the Children and Young Persons Act 1933[16] and s. 5 of the Adoption Act 1958[17] and amounts to leaving the child to his fate in such circumstances as to render the parent

---

[15] For other instances see Leeding, *Child Care Manual*, p. 13.

[16] See *post*, Chapter 6, p. 194, for further discussion of the term, where, however, it will be seen that "abandonment" probably has a wider meaning for the purpose of s. 1 of the 1948 Act.

[17] *Post*, Chapter 10, pp. 341-342; but see *ibid.*, also for a possibly wider meaning.

144

criminally liable, the father has abandoned the child but the mother can hardly be held to have done so, since he was in the father's custody by order of the court. Equally, the circumstances do not wholly fall within sub-para. (b) in view of the father's abandonment. But, clearly, sub-para. (a) does cover the father and sub-para. (b) the mother[18] The narrow construction of mutual exclusion would certainly conflict with the social policy underlying s. 1 and until there is judicial authority to support that construction, local authorities are likely to intervene in cases of this kind.

It is obvious that a local authority will have to inquire into the circumstances of each case to decide whether the conditions laid down by sub-para. (a) or (b) are fulfilled, but neither the Act nor any Regulation imposes any requirements as to the method or extent of their investigations. Moreover, the question of the necessity for intervention is a matter for the authority to decide and, providing that its officers act with propriety, the wisdom of their decision will not be reviewed by the court.[19] We shall deal with this matter in the chapter on Wardship,[20] when we consider the relationship between the prerogative jurisdiction of the court and the statutory powers of the local authorities under ss. 1 and 2 of the Children Act 1948, especially in the way in which it may affect the natural parent and the foster parent.

The duty of the local authority extends to any child appearing to them to be under 17, but, once received into care, they must keep him so long as his welfare appears to them to require their care, and this can continue, if necessary until he is 18. Nevertheless, they must, if they think it consistent with the child's welfare, try to secure that care is taken over either (a) by a parent or guardian or (b) by a relative[1] or friend, who must,

---

[18] The "other circumstances" being the second husband's attitude.
[19] *Re M. (an infant)*, [1961] Ch. 81; [1961] 1 All E.R. 201.   [20] Chapter 12.
[1] By s. 59(1) this means a grandparent, brother, sister, uncle or aunt, whether of the full blood, of the half blood or by affinity, and includes –
  (a) where an adoption order has been made in respect of the infant or any other person, any person who would be a relative of the infant within the meaning of this definition if the adopted person were the child of the adopter born in lawful wedlock.
  (b) where the infant is illegitimate, the father of the infant and any person who would be a relative of the infant within the meaning of this definition if the infant were the legitimate child of its mother and father. *Cf.* the definition for the purposes of the Adoption Act 1958 (s. 57(1)) which is in almost identical terms.

where possible, either be of the same religious persuasion as the child or give an undertaking that the child will be brought up in that persuasion.[2]

Section 1, however, only empowers the local authority to receive into care, not to take the child against the wishes of the parent or guardian. If they feel that the circumstances justify taking him into care they will have to institute care proceedings under the Children and Young Persons Act 1969.[3] On the other hand, if they do receive into care but the parent wants the child returned to him, they are not under an absolute duty to return him regardless of the circumstances, even though s. 1 directs that "nothing in [the] section shall authorise a local authority to keep a child in their care under this section if any parent or guardian desires to take over the care of the child".[4]

For the purposes generally of the Children Act 1948 the term "parent" refers to the father and mother of a legitimate child but only to the mother of an illegitimate, and in relation to an adopted child it means his adoptive parents. "Guardian" is used in the strict sense of one so appointed by deed or will or order of the court.[5] However, for the purposes of ss. 1 to 4 of the Act, if there is an order of a court in force giving custody to any person, for references in any of those sections to parents or guardian there must be substituted references to that person.[6]

Should a local authority receive into care a child who is then ordinarily resident in the area of another authority, the latter may agree, but cannot be compelled, to take over the care of the child.[7] If they do,[8] the first mentioned authority "may recover" from the other the expenses which they incurred in caring for the child. It is submitted that this means that they are legally entitled to payment, not that payment is in the discretion of the other authority. Ordinary residence can be

---

[2] Section 1(3).   [3] *Ante*, Chapter 2.
[4] See *Re K.R. (An Infant)*, [1964] Ch. 455; [1963] 3 All E.R. 337; *Krishnan v. London Borough of Sutton*, [1970] Ch. 181; [1969] 3 All E.R. 1367, (C.A.); see further Chapter 12, p. 415.
[5] For these rules see s. 59(1).   [6] Section 6(2).
[7] Section 1(4). The "resident" authority cannot be compelled to take the child even though they may know far more about him and his family than the "receiving" authority does.
[8] They must do so not later than three months after the determination of the child's ordinary residence, unless the authorities agree to a later date.

notoriously difficult to determine[9] and if the authorities cannot agree about it, the question must be settled by the Secretary of State.

(2) Assumption of Parental Rights

Section 1 entrusts to the local authority care and control,[10] but s. 2 goes much further, because it empowers them to pass a resolution vesting in themselves almost all parental rights and powers over a child after he has been received into their care. This they may do if any of the following conditions are satisfied:

(i) The child's parents are dead and he has no guardian.

(ii) A parent or guardian of his has abandoned him.
Abandonment doubtless means the same as it does in s. 1, but for the purpose of s. 2 if the whereabouts of a parent or guardian have remained unknown for not less than 12 months he is deemed to have abandoned the child.[11]

(iii) The parent or guardian suffers from some permanent disability rendering him incapable of caring for the child. The disability may be physical or mental.

(iv) The parent or guardian suffers from a mental disorder as defined by the Mental Health Act 1959 (or the Mental Health (Scotland) Act 1960) which renders him unfit to have the care of the child.[12] This ground supplements (iii), and applies to temporary as well as permanent disorder.

(v) The parent or guardian is of such habits or mode of life as to be unfit to have the care of the child. This in itself is a wide provision but it has been further strengthened by the following ground.

(vi) The parent or guardian has so persistently failed without reasonable cause to discharge the obligation of a parent or guardian as to be unfit to have the care of the child.[13]

---

[9] In determining it for present purposes no account is to be taken of any period during which the child resided at a school or other institution or at any place in accordance with the requirements of a supervision order or the conditions of a recognisance or while boarded out by a local authority under various enactments; see s. 1(5).

[10] Although the section refers only to care, the term, it is submitted, is used comprehensively for care and control in the sense in which they are now commonly used, *viz.*, to denote the parental duties to protect the child and regulate his conduct.   [11] C. & Y.P. Act 1963, s. 48(1).

[12] C. & Y.P. Act 1963, s. 48(2) (a).

[13] *Ibid.*, s. 48(2) (b). *Cf.* the similar ground for dispensing with parental consent to adoption; Adoption Act 1958, s. 5(2), *post*, p. 349.

We have just seen that these provisions correspondingly apply where a person other than a parent or guardian has been given custody by the court.[14] If any of the conditions (other than the first) relates to him, then, apart from the right of the local authority to pass a resolution, the circumstances would obviously be appropriate for the custody order to be revoked. However, it is another matter whether there is adequate machinery for doing so. Supposing, for example, that a stepmother is granted custody under the Matrimonial Proceedings (Magistrates' Courts) Act 1960 and later becomes unfit to have the care of the child, whose parents by that time are dead. It seems that the only person then entitled to seek revocation is one "who seeks the legal custody of the child".[15] Although, presumably, the local authority could itself apply, this it would regard as unnecessary, since it will have obtained care and control by virtue of the resolution. If the stepmother had obtained custody under an order under the Matrimonial Proceedings and Property Act 1970,[16] it seems that not even the authority could apply, for while the Act empowers the court to make further orders with respect to custody, it seems that only the parties to the original matrimonial proceedings may do so. It is suggested that in all cases of this kind the authority should be empowered and required to apply for revocation of the custody order.

Duration of Resolution

Often the parent or guardian may agree to the resolution being passed, but sometimes he will be opposed or indifferent to it. Unless his prior written consent has been given, the authority must, if they know his whereabouts, forthwith after passing the resolution give him written notice of the fact. He is then entitled to object in writing within a month.[17] If he does so, the resolution will lapse after 14 days from the service of the notice of objection, unless meantime the authority complain to a juvenile court, in which case it remains in force until the court decides whether it should lapse. This it must order unless it is satisfied that the child has been, and when the

[14] Children Act 1948, s. 6(2), *supra*.
[15] See s. 10(1) of the 1960 Act.   [16] See s. 18.
[17] The notice from the authority must inform him of his right to object. It must be sent by registered post.

resolution was passed remained, abandoned by the objector
or that the latter is unfit to have care because of his mental
disorder or his habits or mode of life or his persistent failure
to discharge the obligations of a parent.[18]

If there are no parents and no guardian or if a parent or
guardian consents or if the court orders that the resolution is
not to lapse, it continues in force until the child attains 18,
unless in the child's interests it is earlier rescinded by a further
resolution of the local authority or determined by an order of
a juvenile court on the complaint of the parent or guardian
on whose account the original resolution was passed or, where
it was passed on the ground that there were no parents and no
guardian, on the complaint of a person claiming to be a parent
or guardian.[19]

A court may appoint a guardian for a child who has no parent
or guardian or anyone else having parental rights with respect
to him and this may be done even though a resolution under s. 2
is in force. Such an appointment, however, brings the resolution to an end.[20] So, too, does an adoption order.[1] On the other
hand, the marriage of the child apparently does not have this
effect any more than it causes a child to cease to be in care
where he is the subject of a care order or where he has been
received into care under s. 1.[2]

Effects of Resolution

When a resolution is passed because the parents are dead
and there is no guardian the local authority acquires the rights

---

[18] See the proviso to s. 2(3) of the Children Act 1948, as amended by
  C. & Y.P. Act 1963, s. 48(2).
    It will be seen that these grounds for continuing the resolution are not
  identical with those on which the authority may pass it (leaving aside the
  case where there are no parents and no guardian) in that they do not
  include that of a parent suffering from some permanent disability. The
  reason for the omission is obscure but probably not material, since a case
  of permanent disability could, it is submitted, be brought within one of
  the grounds mentioned in s. 2(3).
[19] Section 4, as amended by C. & Y.P. Act 1969, s. 72(3) and (4) and
  Scheds. 5 and 6.
[20] Guardianship of Minors Act 1971, s. 5; see *post*, Chapter 12, p. 401.
[1] Adoption Act 1958, s. 15(4).
[2] But marriage may well lead to rescission or determination of a resolution
  or revocation of a care order or to the local authority's entrusting the
  child to his or her spouse (presumably as "a friend"!) under s. 1(3) of
  the 1948 Act, as the case may be. Such consequences are particularly
  likely in view of the rule that no order can be made under care proceedings in respect of a juvenile who is or has been married; see *ante*, p. 96.

and powers which the deceased parents would have had were they still alive, but when passed for any of the other reasons, the authority assumes the rights and powers of the person on whose account the resolution was passed.[3] Where both parents are alive, and especially if they are living together, the resolution is likely to relate to both of them, but this is not necessarily so. For example, if there is a divided order[4] in force giving custody to the father and care and control to the mother, it may be that her conduct or disability alone led to the resolution. The father may be abroad, so that no blame attaches to him. In such a case, because he retains custody, the local authority would, it is submitted, be required to consult him on the child's upbringing, for example, on his training for a trade or profession.[5]

The assumption of parental rights and powers is subject to two qualifications, both of which are open to criticism. Firstly, the power to consent to adoption is not transferred to the local authority.[6] Consequently, if the child is an orphan and has no guardian, no one's consent to his being adopted is necessary, and, if s. 2 has been invoked for any other reason, it is very likely that the court hearing the adoption application will be able to dispense with the consent of the parent or guardian.[7] In either type of case it seems desirable that the local authority's consent should be required. Certainly, in both the guardian *ad litem* has a particularly vital role to play. Secondly, the authority must not cause the child to be brought up in any religious creed other than that in which he would have been brought up but for the resolution.[8] a restriction which can place the authority in difficulties if there has been uncertainty or dispute over religious upbringing, for example, where an Anglican father and Roman Catholic mother of a young child are killed in an accident.

---

[3] Children Act 1948, s. 3. This includes the power to give consent to the marriage of a child under the Marriage Act 1949. If that Act (see Sched. 2) gives that power to the person to whose custody the child is committed when the parents are deprived of custody, *a fortiori* does it pass to a person who is expressly stated to acquire the rights and powers of parents.

[4] For divided orders see *post*, Chapter 9.

[5] On the question of religious upbringing see *infra*.

[6] Adoption Act 1958, s. 4(3) (c).

[7] For the grounds on which this may be done see *post*, Chapter 10, pp. 341 *et seq.*, and compare the grounds on which a resolution may be passed.   [8] Children Act 1948, s. 3(7).

Nor, again, does the transfer of the parental rights relieve any person from any liability to maintain, or contribute to the maintenance of, the child.[9] Primarily, this provision ensures the continued duty of the father and mother to provide maintenance under the Children Act 1948,[10] but it may have wider effect; for example, the stepfather of a child in care will remain liable under a matrimonial order made under the Matrimonial Proceedings (Magistrates' Courts) Act 1960.

The reception of a child into care under s. 1 and the passing of a resolution under s. 2 do not affect any supervision order previously made with respect to him,[11] but they may persuade the court to revoke the order.[12]

(3) Children in Unregistered Voluntary Homes

As will be seen[13] the Children Act 1948 introduced compulsory registration of voluntary homes. If a home, not being a community home under the Children and Young Persons Act 1969,[14] is not registered or is removed from the register the Secretary of State for Social Services may require the local authority in whose area the home is situated to remove from the home and receive into care under s. 1 of the 1948 Act the children accommodated therein. The authority must comply with the request whether or not the circumstances fall within that section and even if the children appear to be over the age of 17.[15]

II. CHILDREN AND YOUNG PERSONS ACT 1969

As already noted,[16] one of the orders which this Act enables the juvenile court to make in care proceedings and criminal proceedings is that committing a juvenile to the care of a local authority.[17] It may also be made when a supervision order is

[9] *Ibid.*, s. 3(6). [10] Sections 23 and 24, *post*, p. 494.
[11] *Ibid.*, s. 6(1). [12] See Leeding, *op. cit.*, p. 45.
[13] *Post*, p. 166. [14] *Post*, p. 158.
[15] Children Act 1948, s. 29(6). [16] *Ante*, pp. 108 and 126.
[17] Sections 1(3) (c), 7(7) (a) and 20(1). The appropriate local authority is that in which the juvenile habitually resides or, if he appears not to reside in the area of a local authority, any local authority in whose area the offence was committed or any circumstances arose in consequence of which the order is made. Where an interim care order (*infra*) is made, the court may choose any of the above authorities, but that of residence is the most likely.

discharged.[18] Subject to the power to discharge the order,[19] the juvenile remains in care until he is 18 or, if the order was made when he had attained the age of 16, until he is 19; but an order which otherwise would expire at 18 may, on the application of the local authority, be extended to 19, if, because of his mental condition or behaviour, this is in his or the public interest.[20] The extension could in exceptional cases be crucial for the juvenile's future.[1]

The effect of a care order is that the local authority will have the same powers and duties as the parent or guardian would have if the order had not been made, but the Act expressly adds that they may restrict the juvenile's liberty as they consider appropriate.[2] The assumption of parental powers is subject to the same qualifications as apply where there is a resolution in force under s. 2 of the Children Act 1948, *viz.*, that the power to consent to adoption is not transferred to the local authority,[3] and that the authority must not cause the juvenile to be brought up in any religious creed other than that in which he would have been brought up apart from the care order.[4]

Interim Orders

Committal to care under the Act includes the temporary committal of a juvenile under an interim order for a period of 28 days or for such shorter period as the order specifies;[5] but such an order cannot be made unless the juvenile either (a) is present before the court or justice or (b) is under five or cannot be present because of illness or accident.[6] At the end of the period the local authority must normally bring the juvenile

---

[18] Section 15(1). [19] *Infra.*
[20] Sections 20(3) and 21(1). An extension can only be ordered if the juvenile is present before the court, and he must at the time be accommodated in a community home or a home provided by the Secretary of State and not be boarded out or maintained in a voluntary home (other than a community home). However, no extension is allowed where a fit person order was converted by the Act into a care order, (Sched. 4, para. 11).
[1] See Home Office Guide to Part I of the 1969 Act, para. 169, and on the maximum period of care orders generally see Holden, *op. cit.*, pp. 160-161.
[2] Section 24(2).
[3] Adoption Act 1958, s. 4(3) (a), as amended by C. & Y.P. Act 1969, s. 72(3) and Sched. 5.
[4] C. & Y.P. Act 1969, s. 24(3).
[5] Section 20(1). If the order is made by a court, the period begins when the order is made: if made by a justice, with the date when the juvenile was first in legal custody.
[6] Section 22(1).

before the court, but if he is under five or incapacitated by illness or accident it must do so only if the court so requires.[7]

Discharge of Care Orders

A juvenile court may, on the application of the local authority or the juvenile or his parent or guardian[8] discharge a care order. If it does, it may substitute a supervision order, unless the care order was an interim order or the juvenile has attained 18.[9] Where the discharge of an interim order is refused, no further application can be made without the consent of a juvenile court. In the case of other care orders no further application will be entertained for a period of three months, unless the court consents.[10] The juvenile or the parent or guardian may appeal to the Crown Court against the dismissal of the application or against any supervision order which is made.[11] The High Court may also discharge an interim order on the application of the juvenile, parent or guardian.[12]

A local authority must review the case of every child who has been in their care throughout the preceding six months, if a review was not held during that period, and where he is in care as the result of a care order they must in reviewing the case consider applying for discharge of the order.[13] The duty to review is important in the light of the wider powers of local authorities under the 1969 Act.

Remand to Care of Local Authorities

This and the power to detain juveniles in a place of safety have already been considered.[14]

[7] *Ibid.*, sub-s. (2).
[8] For the meaning of guardian for the purpose of the Children and Young Persons Acts see *ante*, p. 71. For present purposes it includes any person who was guardian to the juvenile when the care order was made; see C. & Y.P. Act 1969, s. 70(2).
[9] Section 21(2).
[10] Sub-section (3).
[11] Sub-section (4), as amended by the Courts Act 1971, Sched. 9. It has been pointed out that, since the sub-section allows appeal by "the person to whom the relevant care order relates or related" the wording "seems to imply the possibility of appeal against an order which has expired"; see Clarke Hall and Morrison, *op. cit.*, 164.
[12] Sections 22(4) and 70(2). The procedure is prescribed by R.S.C. O.94, r. 13; see Rules of the Supreme Court (Amendment No. 4) 1970.
[13] Section 27(4).
[14] *Ante*, Chapter 3, pp. 55 and 88.

III. MISCELLANEOUS ENACTMENTS

There are five other statutes which provide for reception into care as though this has occurred under s. 1 of the Children Act 1948.

(1) Adoption Act 1958

On the complaint of a local authority a protected child within the meaning of the Act[15] may be ordered by a juvenile court or a magistrate to be removed from unsuitable surroundings to a place of safety and the local authority *may* then receive him into care under s. 1 of the 1948 Act, whether or not the conditions of that section apply and notwithstanding that he may appear to the authority to be over 17.[16]

(2) Children Act 1958

A similar provision governs the removal of a foster child from unsuitable surroundings, but here, too, the local authority has a discretion whether to receive into care.[17]

(3) Matrimonial Causes Act 1965

Under s. 36 of this Act, on the other hand, the authority is under a *duty* to receive into care. When the High Court or a county court, having jurisdiction in a matrimonial cause[18] to make an order for custody of a child,[19] considers that there are exceptional circumstances making it impracticable or undesirable for him to be entrusted to either of the parties to the marriage or to any other individual it may order him to be committed to the care of the local authority[20] until he is 18 (subject to the power to vary or discharge the order), providing that at the date of the order he is under 17. With certain qualifications[1] the child is then to be treated as if he had been received into

---

[15] For the meaning see *post*, Chapter 10, p. 330.
[16] Section 43(1) and (3).   [17] Section 7(1) and (4).
[18] *I.e.*, in proceedings for divorce, nullity of marriage, judicial separation, or wilful neglect to maintain.
[19] See *post*, Chapter 9, pp. 279 *et seq.* for the scope of this jurisdiction.
[20] *I.e.*, the authority for the area in which the child was resident before the order to commit to care is made. The local authority is entitled to make representations on the matter and on the question of payments for the maintenance and education of the child. They must therefore be given 14 days' notice of the intention to commit to care (M.C. Rules, 1971, r. 93 (1)); *cf. R. v. Falmouth Borough Justices* (1962), 61 L.G.R. 179 (D.C.).
[1] *Infra*, p. 156.

care under s. 1 of the Children Act 1948. While the order is in force the child remains in the care of the authority notwithstanding any claim by a parent or any other person, but the authority does not assume parental rights and powers.

Section 36 offers no guidance as to what are exceptional circumstances, but it is suggested that the court ought to be guided, though not bound, by the same considerations as would lead a local authority to act under s. 1.[2] In deciding, however, whether the circumstances are exceptional they should be considered in their totality. Thus the fact that a parent is living in adultery is only one factor.[3]

(4) Matrimonial Proceedings (Magistrates' Courts) Act 1960

A similar power is conferred on a magistrates' court under this Act,[4] but it is limited to children under 16. It also differs in other details from the power of committal under s. 36 of the 1965 Act. Thus, it is expressly enacted that a provision for committal cannot be included in a matrimonial order if there is already in force a custody order made by an English court or if the child is already in the care of a local authority.[5] Since the 1965 Act and the Matrimonial Causes Rules are silent on both points, presumably no such limitations apply to an order under s. 36. A provision for committal may be revoked on the complaint of the parties to the marriage or the local authority or any person to whose legal custody the child is for the time being committed by the order or who by the same complaint also seeks the legal custody,[6] but it cannot be varied and cannot be revived once it has ceased to be in force.[7] Nor can the matrimonial order itself be varied by the *addition* of such a provision.[8] An order for committal under s. 36 is subject to a

---

[2] *Cf. F. v. F.*, [1959] 3 All E.R. 180; [1959] 1 W.L.R. 863, where it was held that the fact that a parent, who is otherwise a fit person to have custody, is living under conditions which make it impossible or even undesirable for the child to live with him or her is in itself an exceptional circumstance entitling the court to commit to care.

[3] *G. v. G.* (1962), 106 Sol. Jo 858.

[4] Section 2(1) (e), s.3.   [5] Section 2(4) (a) and (b).

[6] Section 10(1).   [7] Proviso to s. 8(1).

[8] *Ibid.* But this last mentioned restriction, like the others in the proviso, must be read subject to s. 4, the effect of which is that if a complaint is made to vary a matrimonial order by revoking a provision granting legal custody, then, even if it is not revoked, a provision for committal to care could be added, (s. 4(1)).

general power to vary or discharge.[9] Moreover, since the 1960 Act, unlike s. 36, does not empower the court to make express provision with regard to the child's education the local authority has no right to make representations on payments for education.[10]

An order providing for committal to care, whether made under the 1965 Act or the 1960 Act, cannot at the same time include a provision that the child be placed under supervision or a provision for access to the child.[11]

(5) Family Law Reform Act 1969

A further power similar to that conferred by s. 36 of the Matrimonial Causes Act 1965 is given by this Act enabling the High Court to commit a ward of court to the care of a local authority.[12]

C. TREATMENT OF CHILDREN IN CARE

When a child is in care for any of the reasons considered in the previous section, he must be treated in accordance with Part II of the Children Act 1948,[13] subject, in the case of committal to care under s. 36 of the Matrimonial Causes Act 1965, to any directions given by the court.[14] Part II imposes on the local authority a general duty to exercise their powers so as to further the child's best interests and afford him opportunity for the proper development of his character and abilities,[15] but the Children and Young Persons Act 1969[16] enables them and the Secretary of State to act inconsistently with those objects in order to protect members of the public; for example, by

---

[9] Sub-section (7).
[10] For the purpose of hearing other representations the period of notice is 10 days; *cf. supra.*
[11] Both restrictions are imposed by the 1960 Act (s. 2(4) (c)), but only the first by the 1965 Act (s. 37(4)). It is, nevertheless, submitted that by analogy a divorce court is equally precluded from dealing with access in such cases. The policy of the Children Act 1948 is to leave it to the local authority to maintain contact between the parent and the child.
[12] Section 7(2) and (3).
[13] With the introduction of care orders and community homes Part II has been amended by C. & Y.P. Act 1969. For the purposes of Part II a child means a person under 18 and one who has attained that age and is the subject of a care order (C. & Y.P. Act 1969, s. 70(1)).
[14] See also the emigration of children in care, *post*, p. 168.
[15] Section 12(1).   [16] Section 27(2) and (3).

restricting his liberty in a community home. The powers conferred by the Acts of 1948 and 1969 are very wide, but the
local authority should always subordinate them to their duty
of trying to bring the period of care to an end if the child's
welfare is likely to be best served in that way.[17] However, so
long as he is in their care, their main specific duty is to provide
accommodation and maintenance for him.

I. ACCOMMODATION AND MAINTENANCE

Section 13 of the 1948 Act, as originally enacted, required
accommodation and maintenance to be provided either by
boarding the child out with foster parents or, where that was
not practicable or desirable, by maintaining him (1) in a home
provided by the local authority under the 1948 Act[18] or (2)
in a voluntary home[19] or (3) in certain other ways. These
other methods of accommodation included the following.
Children in care who were over compulsory school age could
be accommodated in a hostel which was wholly or mainly intended for persons who were over that age but under 21,
whether the hostel was provided by a local authority[20] or by a
voluntary organisation. Residential nurseries set up under the
National Assistance Act 1948 could accommodate children in
care under three years of age, while those over that age could
temporarily be put into other accommodation provided by that
Act. Moreover, a local authority could with the authorisation
of the Secretary of State make use of other kinds of accommodation provided by that or another local authority (*e.g.*, the
residential school of an Education Authority).

A new s. 13, substituted by the Children and Young Persons
Act 1969, further illustrates the wide discretions which the
latter Act confers on a local authority, since it no longer insists
on priority for boarding out but enables the authority to choose
as it thinks fit any of the forms of accommodation allowed by

---

[17] See s. 1(3) of the Children Act 1948, *ante*, p. 145, (duty of trying to
have the care of the child taken over by the parent, guardian, relative or
friend) and s. 1 of C. & Y.P. Act 1963, *post*, p. 171, (duty of diminishing
the need to receive into, or keep in, care). Note also the power of the
local authority to apply for discharge of an order committing a child to
care.
[18] Section 15. See further *post*, p. 163.
[19] For the definition of a voluntary home see *post*, p. 166.
[20] Children Act 1948, s. 19. For the right of local authorities to provide
similar accommodation under the new system of community homes see
post, p. 160, n. 16.

157

the new section.[1] Apart from boarding out, which is considered in a later chapter,[2] accommodation can be provided (1) in a community home or (2) in a home provided by the Secretary of State and offering specialised facilities or (3) in a voluntary home (other than a community home) whose managers are willing to receive the child or (4) by making such other arrangements for him as seem appropriate to the local authority. Of these methods it is in the community home system that the main interest and changes lie.

(1) Community Homes

Part II of the Children and Young Persons Act 1969 provides for the creation of a comprehensive and integrated system of community homes. These are gradually to supersede local authority children's homes and hostels, many of the children's homes of voluntary organisations, residential nurseries, remand homes, approved schools, approved hostels and approved homes and, in so far as they accommodate persons under 17, detention centres and Borstal institutions.[3] This, as we have seen,[4] means the replacement of certain kinds of orders dealing with juveniles by the comprehensive care order.

The system is being planned by local authorities on a regional basis through children's regional planning committees.[5] Twelve planning areas have been created by the Secretary of State,[6] with a children's planning committee established for each by the local authorities whose own areas are wholly or partly within the particular planning area. The size of a committee is determined by the relevant local authorities, who then nominate the members.[7] Subject to any directions given by the relevant authorities, the nominated members decide upon the

[1] Notwithstanding the amendment, it is suggested that emphasis will in practice continue to be placed on private fostering.

[2] Chapter 11.

[3] The changes with regard to detention centres and Borstal institutions are not likely in the foreseeable future.

[4] *Ante*, Chapter 4.

[5] Section 35.

[6] Children and Young Persons (Planning Areas) Order 1970 (S.I. 1970, No. 335).

[7] C. & Y.P. Act 1969, Second Sched. A Home Office Circular (No. 44/1970) suggests that it may be sufficient for each authority to be represented by one or two nominated members rather than having representation proportionate to such factors as population, rateable value or number of children in care.

procedure and quorum of the committee and have power to co-opt. The majority of the committee must be members of the relevant authorities.

A committee must prepare for the approval of the Secretary of State a regional plan for the provision and maintenance of community homes.[8] Committees are currently preparing their first regional plans.[9] A community home is either one provided by a relevant local authority[10] or a voluntary home provided by a voluntary organisation[11] but with a relevant authority participating in the management of it.[12] The latter kind of community homes are classified into "controlled" homes and "assisted" homes, according to the extent of that participation. A home is "controlled" when the responsibility for its management, equipment and maintenance lies with the local authority and, under its instrument of management,[13] two-thirds of the body of managers are appointed by the authority with the remainder appointed in accordance with the instrument from among those who are managers of the voluntary home. The latter, known as "the foundation managers", are to represent the interests of the voluntary organisation providing the home and to see that, as far as practicable, the character of the home as a voluntary home is preserved and the terms of any trust deed relating to it are observed.[14] When the responsibility is undertaken by the voluntary organisation and the foundation managers constitute two-thirds of the management, with one-third appointed by the local authority, the home is an assisted home.[15] Whether the home is controlled or assisted the premises provided by the voluntary organisation remain vested in it.

The regional plan must also contain proposals with regard

---

[8] Section 36.
[9] The Secretary of State may approve only part of a plan, in which case the committee will have to submit a supplementary plan. It is open to a committee later to submit a further plan replacing or varying the plan previously approved (s. 37).
[10] Sections 36(2) (a) and 38.
[11] For the definition of a voluntary home see *post*, p. 166.
[12] Section 36(2) (b) and (3).
[13] An instrument is drawn up by the Secretary of State.
[14] Section 39(3) (a) and (4). If there should be any inconsistency between the instrument of management and the trust deed, the former prevails (s. 40(3)); it is up to the voluntary organisation to apply under the law relating to charities to seek amendment of the deed.
[15] Section 39(3) (b).

to the nature and purpose of each of the community homes,[16] and for providing facilities for observing the physical and mental condition of children in care and for assessing the most suitable accommodation and treatment for them.[17] These requirements go to the very heart of the new system and should at an early stage test its soundness. It remains to be seen how far existing homes will change in substance and not merely in name; how far they will produce flexibility and provide adequate facilities and trained staff for widely differing classes of children; and how far local authorities and voluntary organisations are prepared from the outset to co-operate, because no local authority home or voluntary home is to be included in a regional plan as a proposed community home without the consent of the local authority or the voluntary organisation.[18] Moreover, where the home is a controlled or assisted home, the voluntary organisation may, by giving two years' notice to the Secretary of State, cease to provide the home as a community home, although the requirement that the organisation must make repayment for any increase in the value of the premises and other property belonging to it which is due to the expenditure of public money while the home was a community home may prove a strong disincentive against taking that step.[19]

The co-operation of local authorities and voluntary organisations is implicit not only in the willingness to make homes available but also in their mutual relationship in the successful running of controlled and assisted homes. The Act, however, anticipates possible disputes by conferring on the Secretary of State power to determine these whenever they arise[20] (1) in

---

[16] When an instrument of management is drawn up by the Secretary of State for a controlled or assisted community home it may include, *inter alia*, provisions specifying the nature and purpose of the particular home and the number of places in it to be made available to local authorities (s. 40(2)).

A local authority is allowed to provide hostel accommodation in a community home for a person over compulsory school age but under 21 if the home is provided for children over the compulsory school age and is near that person's place of employment, education or training; see s. 19 of Children Act 1948, as substituted by s. 50 of C. & Y.P. Act 1969.

[17] Section 36(4).

[18] Section 36(5). The preparation of the regional plan obviously calls for close consultation between the children's planning committee and local authorities and voluntary organisations having institutions in the planning area. [19] See ss. 47 and 48.

[20] The need for his intervention is likely to be exceptional.

respect of controlled homes, between the local authority specified in the instrument of management and either the voluntary
organisation providing the home or any local authority who
place a child in their care in the home, and (2) in respect of
assisted homes, between the voluntary organisation and a local
authority placing a child there.[1]

Like local authority homes and voluntary homes, community
homes are to come under inspection[2] and if the Secretary of
State considers that premises used as a community home are
unsuitable or that the home is not being run according to
regulations governing them or is otherwise unsatisfactory he may
direct that the premises are not used as a community home.[3]

Change of Status of Existing Approved Institutions

Section 46 and Sched. 3 of the 1969 Act provide a scheme
for converting an existing approved school, approved probation
hostel or approved probation home into a community home
as and when the future of the particular approved institution
is determined.[4] The change of status is effected by an order
made by the Secretary of State directing that the establishment
shall cease to be an approved institution. The order may also
include provisions relating to the transfer of existing staff to
the employment of the local authority or voluntary organisation
responsible for running the new community home.[5] If the
home is a controlled community home, the order will also provide for the rights, liabilities and obligations of the voluntary
organisation providing the home to be transferred to the local
authority responsible for its management.[6] No question of
transfer arises in the case of an assisted community home unless
the voluntary organisation responsible for providing and maintaining it does not consist of the persons who carried on the
former institution. If an approved institution is provided by a

---

[1] Section 45.
[2] Section 58(1) (a) and (b). The inspectorate has been transferred from the Home Office to the Department of Health and Social Security and, in Wales, to the Welsh Office.   [3] Section 43(4).
[4] An approved institution may alternatively be changed to a county school, a voluntary school which is a controlled or aided school or a maintained or non-maintained special school.
[5] Schedule 3, paras. 1 and 2.
    A s. 46 order may be made relating to an approved institution which is not to be included in a regional plan. If so, the institution ceases to exist as an approved institution and the Secretary of State may assume financial liabilities owed to existing staff.   [6] *Ibid.*, para. 10(2).

voluntary organisation and previously there has been an obligation to repay exchequer grants,[7] the obligation ceases when
the institution becomes a community home (subject to the
right of the Secretary of State to call for part repayment of
capital grants), but if the home ceases to be a community
home, the organisation becomes liable to repay that part of
the value of the premises attributable to public expenditure
before the establishment ceased to be an approved school,
probation hostel or probation home. It will similarly be liable
for public expenditure on the establishment during the period
that it has served as a community home.[8]

A voluntary organisation may not wish itself to participate
in the system of community homes, but it may be willing to
sell premises, hitherto used as an approved institution, to a
local authority so that the latter may run it as a community
home.[9] Alternatively if the premises have to a substantial extent
been provided with exchequer grants, the Secretary of State
can make a s. 46 order and authorise the transfer of the premises
to a local authority for use as a community home on such terms
as to payment and other matters as may be agreed between the
local authority and the voluntary organisation. The authority
becomes responsible for the repayment of capital grants.[10]

Transitional Provisions

It will be some time before any regional plan for community
homes comes fully into operation.[11] During the interim period
children in the care of local authorities will continue to be
accommodated in local authority homes and local authority
hostels[12] and similarly any approved school may be used for
that purpose until it ceases to be such an institution.[13]

[7] Under s. 104 of C. & Y.P. Act 1933 (approved schools) or s. 77 of the
Criminal Justice Act 1948 (approved probation hostels and homes).
[8] See C. & Y.P. Act 1969, s. 48 and Sched. 3, para. 9.
[9] Or it may transfer the establishment to another voluntary organisation
with a view to the latter bringing it into the community home system.
[10] Schedule 3; paras. 6 and 9.
[11] The Home Office estimated that regional plans would become effective
during the period April 1971 to April 1972; see H.O.C. No. 237/1969,
para. 30. [12] Schedule 4, para. 13.
[13] Schedule 3, para. 3. For the position which approved schools are to
occupy during the transitional period see Home Office Circular No.
184/1970. The fact that a child who is accommodated in an approved
school will be in the care of a local authority and not of the Managers of
the school has necessitated minor amendments of the Approved School
Rules 1933 (see Approved School Rules 1970).

The conduct of local authority homes is to some extent
regulated by the Administration of Children's Homes Regulations 1951[14] which are aimed at securing the well-being of
children there. The local authority must, for example, ensure
that each child receives instruction appropriate to his religious
persuasion; they must make adequate arrangements for protecting the health of the children, including the appointment
of a medical officer; and they are only allowed to administer
corporal punishment within strict limits, no such punishment
being permitted in respect of girls aged ten or over or boys who
have reached the school leaving age.[15] However, the Regulations
provide only part of the answer. They do not, for example,
prescribe rules about the size of homes, this being left to the
authority's discretion.[16] Nor do they lay down conditions about
staffing. Nevertheless, these are matters which the authority
cannot ignore if they are to fulfil their general duty of furthering
the child's best interests and affording him opportunity for the
proper development of his character and abilities.[17] That duty
requires them to run a home as an effective substitute for a
normal home. This, as the Curtis Committee pointed out,[18]
means giving the child affection and personal attention, stability,
the opportunity to make the best of his ability, and a share in
the common life within a homely environment.

To ensure compliance with the 1951 Regulations and fulfilment of the general duty, local authority homes must be visited
at least monthly on behalf of the authority by a member of the
Social Services Committee or one of its sub-committees or by
an officer of the authority.[19] They are also subject to Central
Government inspection,[20] and, if it appears to the Secretary
of State that premises used as a home are unsuitable or that
the home is not being run in accordance with the Regulations
or is otherwise unsatisfactory, he may direct that the place
shall not further be used as a home.[1]

[14] S.I. 1951, No. 1217.   [15] See Regs. 4, 5 and 11.
[16] For the most part they range from small communities of about eight
children to larger ones comprising 25. For the way in which homes are
run see Leeding, *op. cit.*, pp. 35-38.
[17] Children Act 1948, s. 12(1), *supra*, p. 156.
[18] See para. 427 of its Report, Cmnd. 6922.
[19] Reg. 2.
[20] C. & Y.P. Act 1969, s. 58(1) (c).
[1] Children Act 1948, s. 15(5). Such direction may be revoked (sub-s. (6)).

The Community Homes Regulations 1972 follow the pattern of the 1951 Regulations and leave much to the discretion of the local authority or voluntary organisation responsible for the community home. But as these Regulations show by their provisions concerning secure accommodation, regulations governing the conduct of community homes will have to take some account of the differing kinds of homes.

In *Re Cole (deceased)*[2] a majority of the Court of Appeal[3] held that, while a gift for the endowment or maintenance of a local authority home might be charitable, one for "the general benefit and general welfare" of the children for the time being living there could not, mainly on the ground that, since the residents might include delinquent or refractory children, a gift for their general benefit (*e.g.*, a television set) would not come within the definition of a charity.[4] Lord EVERSHED, M.R., however, took the view that the reference in the Charitable Uses Act 1601 to maintenance of "houses of correction" supported the contrary conclusion and the definition could extend to such children as well as to those in care as being in need of care or control:

> "After all, the notion underlying the relevant provisions of the [Children and Young Persons Act 1933 and the Children Act 1948] is surely that children of the delinquent class have fallen into their bad habits and associations through lack of care and protection which a home of the kind contemplated by the Acts can provide: and because, in the absence of such care and protection, they, as children, are defenceless against the temptations to which they are exposed".[5]

This reasoning is more in line with the thinking underlying the White Paper, *Children in Trouble*,[6] to which the Children and Young Persons Act 1969 gives effect, and it is submitted that a gift, in the terms of those in *Re Cole (deceased)*, to a community home should be held to be charitable.

---

[2] [1958] 3 All E.R. 103.
[3] ROMER and ORMEROD, L.JJ.
[4] "If it were, then I suppose a gift to provide the inmates of a Borstal Institution with amenities would be charitable, which would appear to me to be an impossible contention". – *per* ROMER, L.J., at p. 107.
[5] *Ibid.*, at p. 112.
[6] Cmnd. 3601.

(2) Homes With Specialised Facilities

The Children and Young Persons Act 1969[7] recognises the need for new kinds of homes to deal with the special problems of severely disturbed children who are in care and empowers the Secretary of State to provide such establishments. A beginning has been made. For such persons there are to be three Youth Treatment Centres,[8] each accommodating about 100 boys and 100 girls, aged between 12 and 19. It is planned that the Centres should "combine the training and treatment facilities of a school, a children's home and a hospital" and should also provide "substantial provision for psychiatric observation and treatment and an element of secure accommodation".[9] For the most part they will be available only to children who are in care as the result of an order of the court (usually but not necessarily a care order) but who because of their disturbed condition cannot be adequately managed and treated at a community home. But they will also be used to accommodate some of the juveniles found guilty of certain serious offences.[10] These Centres are under the control of the Department of Health and Social Security, which will determine the terms on which a child may be admitted, accommodated and maintained there.[11]

(3) Voluntary Homes (Other than Community Homes)

The various possibilities open to a voluntary organisation which has an approved institution[12] are similarly available where the establishment is a voluntary home, except that the Secretary of State has no power to authorise its transfer to a local authority for the purpose of being used as a local authority community home. Thus, the voluntary organisation may agree to its being used as a controlled or assisted community home under a regional plan or they may sell the premises to a local authority to be used as a community home. But there is nothing in the Children and Young Persons Act 1969 to prevent a

[7] Section 64.
[8] The one at Brentwood, Essex, is already in use. One is being planned in the Midlands and one in the North of England.
  An explanatory guide has been published by the Department of Health and Social Security.
[9] See H. C. Debs., Vol. 779, No. 787, col. 1183.
[10] Under C. & Y.P. Act 1933, s. 53(1) and (2); see *ante*, Chapter 4.
[11] Children Act 1948, s. 13(3), as substituted by C. & Y.P. Act 1969, s. 49.
[12] See *supra*, p. 162.

voluntary home from continuing, outside the community home system, to be used to accommodate children in care.

A local authority may place a child who is in their care in a voluntary home, if the managers are willing to receive him.[13] A voluntary home is widely defined.[14] It is any home or other institution for the boarding, care and maintenance of poor children or young persons,[15] which is supported wholly or partly by voluntary contributions or by endowments, but not being a school and not including any mental nursing home or residential home for mentally disordered persons. Since 1948 every voluntary home has had to be registered with the Home Office,[16] and its name may be removed from the register if it is not conducted in accordance with the Administration of Children's Homes Regulations 1951 or is otherwise unsatisfactory.[17] With one or two additional provisions,[18] those Regulations apply to voluntary homes as to local authority homes and their conduct, too, comes under Central Government inspection.[19] However, neither the Regulations nor the rules of registration affect a voluntary home so long as it is a community home.

When a child in care is placed in a voluntary home (other than a community home) the local authority must arrange for him to be visited there in the interests of his well-being.[20] If

---

[13] Children Act 1948, s. 13(1) (c), as substituted by C. & Y.P. Act 1969, s.49.

[14] C. & Y.P. Act 1933, s. 92, as amended by the Children Act 1948, s. 27 and the Mental Health Act 1959, s. 19(3).

[15] The term includes for present purposes any person up to the age of 18 (Children Act 1948, s. 28).

[16] Children Act 1948, s. 29. Application for registration must be made in accordance with the Voluntary Homes (Registration) Regulations 1948 (S.I. 1948 No. 2408).

    Every year the person in charge of the home must send to the Secretary of State particulars relating to the home as prescribed by Regulations (C. & Y.P. Act 1933, s. 32; Children Act 1948, s. 32; and the Voluntary Homes (Return of Particulars) Regulations 1949, 1950 and 1955).

[17] There is a right of appeal to a tribunal against a refusal to register or a removal from the register (Children Act 1948, s. 30 and the Children Act (Appeal Tribunal) Rules 1949).

[18] For example, the Secretary of State, may give directions limiting the number of children who may be accommodated in a voluntary home (Reg. 12).

[19] C. & Y.P. Act 1969, s. 58(1) (b).

[20] Children Act 1948, s. 54(3) and (4), as amended by C. & Y.P. Act 1969, s. 72(3) and Sched. 5, para. 21.

    These provisions, inspection under the C. & Y.P. Act 1969, s. 58, and the 1951 Regulations do not apply to a voluntary home which is, as a whole, subject to inspection by or under the authority of a government department otherwise than under the C. & Y.P. Act 1969.

they are not satisfied about his welfare, they presumably have power to remove him.[1]

(4) Other Arrangements

Section 13 of the Children Act 1948 now enables a local authority to make such other arrangements as seem appropriate to them for accommodating a child in their care, but it gives no indication as to what forms these may take.[2] Whatever they may be, neither they nor the other forms of accommodation specifically provided by the section affect the general power of a local authority to make use of any of the facilities and services available for children in the care of their own parents.[3] Thus, they may, for example, put the child into lodgings or residential employment or, in the case of a handicapped child, in a suitable home or hospital. Moreover, an authority may allow a child in their care to be under the charge and control of a parent, guardian, relative or friend for a fixed period or until the authority otherwise determine,[4] except that where the High Court has refused an application to discharge an interim order the local authority may exercise its powers only with the consent and under the directions of that court.[5] At the end of the fixed period or, where no period is fixed, at any time, it is open to the authority in a case where the child is in care by virtue of a resolution under s. 2 of the Children Act 1948[6] to give written notice to the parent *etc.* requiring him to hand back the child to them. If he or anyone else should then harbour or conceal the child or prevent his return, he is guilty of an offence.[7]

II. MISCELLANEOUS POWERS AND DUTIES OF THE LOCAL AUTHORITY

Apart from those relating to accommodation, there are few specific powers and duties given to a local authority for dealing with children in their care. Instead, within the limit of the

[1] The 1969 Act repeals s. 16(1) of the Children Act 1948 which conferred a power to remove without re-enacting its provisions.
[2] The use of approved schools as an interim measure is separately covered; see Schedule. 3, para. 3, *ante*, p. 162.
[3] Children Act 1948, s. 12(2).
[4] *Ibid.*, s. 13(2).   [5] C. & Y.P. Act 1969, s. 22(4).
[6] See *ante*, pp. 147 *et seq.*
[7] C. & Y.P. Act 1963, s. 49(1), as amended by C. & Y.P. Act 1969, s. 72(3) and Sched. 5, para. 52. The penalty, on summary conviction is a fine of up to £20 or imprisonment for two months or both.

general duty to exercise their powers so as to further the child's interests and enable him to develop his character and abilities,[8] they are left with a wide discretion. We have just seen[9] how they may avail themselves of various facilities, especially those for education, training and employment, as parents may do for their own children; but, in assisting a child in care to establish a career they are also expressly empowered to enter into a guarantee under a deed of apprenticeship or articles of clerkship and may extend the guarantee beyond the period of care.[10]

Arranging for the emigration of a child in care is another specific power,[11] but this may only be done with the consent of the Secretary of State who will only allow it if he is satisfied that emigration would benefit the child, that suitable arrangements for his reception and welfare in the country to which he is going are made and that, where practicable, the parents or guardian[12] have been consulted. The child must also consent, if old enough to express an opinion on the matter. If he is not, the consent of the Secretary of State may still be given, provided that the child is emigrating with a parent, guardian or relative or is to join any of them or a friend abroad.[13] Arrangements may be made even though it is intended that the child be adopted abroad: a provisional adoption order[14] is not needed.[15] The power is exercisable where a child is in care by virtue of s. 1 of the 1948 Act or under a care order,[16] but not where the committal to care is ordered under the Matrimonial Causes Act 1965 or the Matrimonial Proceedings (Magistrates' Courts) Act 1960.[17]

Running through the legislation relating to children is the principle that those who become responsible for looking after

---

[8] Children Act 1948, s. 12(1), *ante,* p. 156.   [9] *Supra.*
[10] C. & Y.P. Act 1963, s. 47.   [11] Children Act 1948, s. 17.
[12] "Parents" or "guardian" here refers to all persons who are such (s. 17(3) and s. 9). Thus, a parent deprived of parental rights will have to be consulted. See Leeding, *op. cit.,* p. 29.
[13] Why a child may be given consent to join a friend in a foreign country, but not to emigrate in his company is difficult to justify. Indeed, where the friend is in this country the Secretary of State may well be better informed about him.
[14] *I.e.,* under s. 52 of the Adoption Act 1958, *post,* Chapter 10, p. 371.
[15] C. & Y.P. Act 1963, s. 55, as amended by C. & Y.P. Act 1969, s. 72(4) and Sched. 6.
[16] Regulations may be made to control arrangements for emigration made by voluntary organisations (Children Act 1948, s. 33(1) and (2)).
[17] See respectively s. 36(5) (b) and s. 3(2) (a) of the Acts.

the child must take account of his religious persuasion, but, as will be seen,[18] the various enactments do not impose a uniform obligation. The principle also underlines the rule which forbids a local authority to order the cremation of a deceased child if this is contrary to his religious persuasion.[19]

Maintaining Contact with the Family

Both the Children and Young Persons Acts and the Children Act 1948 encourage a local authority to bring the period of care to an end as soon as the child's welfare permits. Hence the duty of the authority to try to arrange for a child received into care under s. 1 of the 1948 Act to be taken over by the parent or guardian or, at least, a relative or friend;[20] and, whether the child is in care under that section or s. 2 of that Act or as the result of a care order or other order committing to care, he may be allowed temporarily to be under the charge and control of such a person.[1] If the experiment is successful, the authority may well rescind its resolution under s. 2[2] or, as the case may be, seek revocation of the order.

In order to facilitate the child's return to his family, whether for a trial period or permanently, it is desirable that the family should keep in contact with him while he is in care, and visiting should be encouraged.[3] Therefore, the local authority may make payments to any parent or guardian "or any other person connected with" the child, in respect of travelling, subsistence or other expenses incurred by him in visiting the child, if the authority considers that such visits would otherwise not be possible without undue hardship and that the circumstances warrant the making of the payments.[4] There is no specific authorisation for payments for visits made by the child to his family, but it is submitted that this is permitted by virtue either of the general duty to further the child's best interests[5] or that

[18] *Post*, Chapter 13, p. 431.
[19] See Children Act 1948, s. 18(1), which empowers the authority to arrange for the burial or cremation of the child.
[20] Sub-section (3), *ante*, p. 145.
[1] *Ibid.*, s. 13(2) as substituted by C. & Y.P. Act 1969, s. 49, *ante*, p. 167.
[2] See s. 4(2) and note also the right of a juvenile court to determine the resolution at the instance of the parent or guardian (s. 4(3)).
[3] Regularity of contact with the family is an important factor in helping to create stability for the child in residential care; see Kellmer Pringle and Clifford, *Conditions Associated with Emotional Maladjustment Among Children in Care*, (1962), Vol. 14 Educational Review.
[4] Children Act 1948, s. 22.　　　　[5] *Ibid.*, s. 12(1), *ante*, p. 156.

of diminishing the need to keep the child in care.[6] With regard to the visiting of children in voluntary homes, the Secretary of State may from time to time call upon those carrying on the home to inform him of the facilities for visiting.[7]

Contact between the child and his family may be negligible or non-existent. The Children and Young Persons Act 1969[8] partly meets the problem by the introduction of the "visitor" in certain circumstances where a child or young person is the subject of a care order. His duties are to visit, advise and befriend the juvenile and, if he considers it appropriate, to apply on his behalf for the discharge of the order. In view of the immense powers of local authorities over persons in their care, the last mentioned function is of cardinal importance, and the Act recognises that both this and the other functions can be properly discharged only if an "independent person" is appointed visitor, *i.e.*, one who is independent of the local authority appointing him and is unconnected with any community home. To secure independence, regulations have prescribed the conditions for eligibility for appointment.[9] The new requirement will probably lead to a new kind of voluntary social worker,[10] but it may be some time before they appear in appreciable numbers. This may account for the present restrictions on appointment. The local authority is under a duty to appoint only if all the following conditions are applicable: (1) there is a care order; (2) the juvenile has attained the age of five; (3) he is accommodated in a community home or other establishment which he has not been allowed to leave during the preceding three months for the purpose of ordinary attendance at an educational institution or at work and (4) it appears to the local authority that either (a) communication between him and his parent or guardian has been so infrequent that the appointment is appropriate or (b) he has not lived with or visited or been visited by either of his parents or his guardian

[6] C. & Y.P. Act 1963, s. 1, *infra*. See also Leeding, *op. cit.*, p. 46, supporting the latter alternative.
[7] Administration of Children's Homes Regulations 1951, reg. 14. The regulation refers, however, only to visits by parents and guardians and does not include anyone else who may be connected with the child.
[8] Section 24(5).
[9] Children and Young Persons (Definition of Independent Persons) Regulations 1971.
[10] A visitor is entitled to recover reasonable expenses from the appointing local authority.

during the preceding twelve months.[11] It is suggested that the visitor should be available in respect of all persons in care who have lost contact with their families.

Preventive Work of Local Authorities

Although the Children and Young Persons Act 1933 and the Children Act 1948 required a local authority to try to secure the child's return to the family, neither Act gave them power to give positive assistance to the family to rehabilitate the child. Nor were they empowered to help families to prevent the need for children to be received into care. Nevertheless, both objects were pursued by some local authorities "on the fringe of their statutory responsibilities",[12] and preventive work was encouraged by the Home Office. Following the recommendations of the Ingleby Committee, the Children and Young Persons Act 1963 gave a legal basis upon which such work could be undertaken.

Section 1 requires a local authority "to make available such advice, guidance and assistance as may promote the welfare of children[13] by diminishing the need to receive children into or keep them in care . . . or to bring children before a juvenile court". Assistance may be given in kind (*e.g.*, food or clothing) or in exceptional circumstances in cash (*e.g.*, to pay arrears of rent or fuel bills). It may be given directly by the local authority or through voluntary organisations or "other persons". The most effective methods of advice may be through family advice centres or the individual social worker, depending upon the circumstances.

The Seebohm Committee was "impressed by the amount of preventive work amongst families accomplished by children's departments since the Children and Young Persons Act 1963";[14] but s. 1 is wide in its terms and it seems that policies and practices of local authorities in giving effect to it vary considerably.[15] Home Office statistics have shown that since 1963 the number of children in the care of local authorities

---

[11] An appointment comes to an end when the care order ceases to operate or it may earlier be terminated by the authority or the visitor (s. 24(6)).
[12] Report of Seebohm Committee, Cmnd. 3703, para. 182.
[13] For the purpose of the section a child means a person under 18 (s. 1(5)).
[14] Cmnd. 3703, para. 430.
[15] Research into the operation of the section is currently being undertaken by some University Departments of Social Administration.

has slightly fallen each year and this might suggest that the policy of the section is having some effect. Providing a unified social services department should, in the view of the Seebohm Committee, accelerate the reduction in numbers.

III. CONTRIBUTIONS TOWARDS MAINTENANCE OF CHILDREN IN CARE

This subject is considered in the chapter on Financial Provision for Children.

IV. AFTER-CARE

When it comes to the knowledge of a local authority that there is in their area a child who, when he ceased to be of compulsory school age or subsequently, was in the care of a local authority under s. 1 of the Children Act 1948 but is no longer so, they must advise and befriend him until he is 18, unless they are satisfied that his welfare does not require it. They are under the same duty if he is in the care of a voluntary organisation, but if they are satisfied that the organisation have the necessary facilities for advising and befriending they can arrange for them to discharge those functions. Provision is also made to ensure after-care in cases where the child moves to the area of another local authority or ceases to be in the care of a voluntary organisation.[16]

Further powers have been conferred by the Children and Young Persons Act 1963 to visit and befriend a person formerly in care and in exceptional circumstances to give him financial assistance, but these are only to be exercised at the request of that person. The powers relate to anyone who was, at or after the time when he became 17, in the care of the local authority by virtue of the Children Act 1948, the Children and Young Persons Act 1933, the Matrimonial Causes Act 1965 or the Matrimonial Proceedings (Magistrates' Courts) Act 1960, and they may be exercised until he attains 21.[17] This provision has not, however, been expressly or, it is submitted, impliedly amended by the Children and Young Persons Act 1969,[18] so

[16] Children Act 1948, s. 34; see further Clarke Hall and Morrison, *op. cit.*, p. 913.   [17] C. & Y.P. Act 1963, s. 58.
[18] Section 27(1) of the 1969 Act merely provides that s. 11 of the Children Act 1948 is to be amended so that Part II of that Act extends also to children in care under a care order. Nor has s. 58 been extended to the ward of court who has been in care (see *ante*, p. 156).

that no power exists to provide for the after-care of a child formerly the subject of a care order. However, when such an order is discharged, a supervision order can be made.[19]

V. CARE AND AFTER-CARE OF MENTALLY DISORDERED CHILDREN

Section 9 of the Mental Health Act 1959 gives to a local authority, as the children authority, power to accommodate in their homes[20] a child under 18 who is not in their care within the meaning of Part II of the Children Act 1948 but who is, or has been, mentally disordered and whose care or after-care is being undertaken by that or any other local authority as a local health authority.[1] This rule is apparently not abrogated by the re-organisation of the social services under the Local Authority Social Services Act 1970, but the power under the section will in future be exercised on behalf of the local authority by its social services committee.[2] The section does not, however, impose any duty on the local authority to provide residential accommodation for mentally disordered children, and it is to be regretted that the Children and Young Persons Act 1969 does not insist that a regional plan for community homes shall include provision for accommodating children who are mentally disordered but whose mental disorder is not so serious as to require the care and treatment provided by the National Health Service hospitals.

The power conferred by s. 9 does not preclude a local authority as children authority from receiving mentally disordered children into their care under s. 1 of the 1948 Act, a point which further justifies imposing on local authorities a duty to provide accommodation for such children. Nor does the enactment prevent a local health authority from accommodating a child who is in the care of that or any authority as a children authority.[3]

[19] C. & Y.P. Act 1969, s. 21(2), *ante*, p. 153.
[20] *I.e.*, homes hitherto provided by the authority under s. 15 of the Children Act 1948, (*ante*, p. 163) or in future, community homes provided by them under s. 38 of the C. & Y.P. Act 1969, (*ante*, p. 158).
[1] Where such an arrangement is made and the same authority is involved as children authority and local health authority, the cost of accommodating the child may be charged against the authority in its latter capacity; see Mental Health Act 1959, s. 9(2).
[2] See Local Authority Social Services Act 1970, s. 2 and Sched. 1.
[3] Mental Health Act 1959, s. 9(3).

When a local authority assumes parental rights and powers over a child or young person as a result of his being committed to their care by a care order under the Children and Young Persons Act 1969, or as a result of a resolution passed under s. 2 of the Children Act 1948, and he is a mentally disordered patient, then, if he is admitted to a hospital or nursing home (whether for treatment for mental disorder or for any other reason), the authority shall arrange for him to be visited and take such other steps as would be expected to be taken by his parents; for example, the provision of additional comforts and presents.[4] These functions are now undertaken by the Social Services Department of the authority.

An authority who has for either of the above reasons assumed parental rights and powers is then deemed to be the juvenile's nearest relative, except for his or her spouse and, where the assumption was by resolution under the 1948 Act, except also for a parent whose rights are not affected by the resolution.[5]

---

[4] Mental Health Act 1959, s. 10, as amended by C. & Y.P. Act 1969, s. 72(3) and Sched. 5.
    These duties are also imposed on an authority where, as local health authority, they have assumed guardianship of a person (whatever his age) under the 1959 Act or where the functions of his nearest relative have been transferred to them under the Act.
[5] Mental Health Act 1959, s. 50, as amended by C. & Y.P. Act 1969, s. 72(3) and Sched. 5.

CHAPTER 6

The Penal Protection of Children
1. Physical Harm

A. INTRODUCTION

Protection of children from physical and moral harm is, to a considerable extent, secured by the sanctions of the criminal law. Its provisions dealing with offences against the person apply generally to children as they do to adults, but some of them have special application where the victim is a child. In addition, there are certain offences specifically created to protect children. Most are concerned with protection from physical harm, some from moral harm and others from both. They are dealt with in this and the next chapter under the broad classification of Physical Protection and Moral Protection, with "mixed" offences being placed into the one or other category according to whether their emphasis is, in the author's view, on the one form of protection or the other. Sexual offences are, however, separately treated, as, in a later chapter,[1] are those relating to the employment of children.

A parent may render himself criminally liable by inflicting upon his child physical injury which exceeds the bounds of reasonable chastisement[2] or by failing to fulfil his duty to protect the child from physical harm, especially by failing to provide it with the necessities of life. This duty to protect, a natural incident of parenthood, is not, however, restricted to the parent-child relationship. At common law it arises whenever anyone old enough to be held legally responsible assumes the care of someone who, because of immaturity or disability, is unable to look after himself. Thus, for example, it is imposed on the step-parent or the foster parent[3] or on the spouse who nurses

---

[1] Chapter 13.
[2] For the parental power to administer corporal punishment see *post*, p 210.
[3] *R. v. Bubb* (1850), 4 Cox C.C. 455; *R. v. Gibbins and Proctor* (1918), 13 Cr. App. Rep. 134, (C.C.A.).

his or her sick partner.[4] Moreover, as the last illustration indicates, the duty does not depend on the age of the person to be protected. Obviously, it exists in relation to children of tender years,[5] but it does not apply to those who, though still minors, are sufficiently equipped to look after themselves.[6] On the other hand, exceptionally, children who have attained majority may need protection.[7]

The common law duty has been immensely reinforced by statute. The need for this was due to the inability or unwillingness to enforce the duty rigorously. Even where the failure to protect had caused the death of the child juries were either ready to acquit[8] or, at least, inclined to convict for manslaughter rather than murder. The reluctance to hold the parent liable is demonstrated by *R. v. Renshaw*.[9] In that case a ten-day-old illegitimate baby had been left by its mother in a large piece of flannel at the bottom of a dry ditch in a field, but was found alive soon after it had been left. The mother was acquitted of attempted murder because of lack of evidence of the necessary intent, an understandable verdict in the circumstances. She was, however, also acquitted of common assault, for a reason which the court expressed in the following terms:[10]

> "There were no marks of violence on the child, and it does not appear in the result that the child actually experienced any injury or inconvenience, and it was providentially found soon after it was exposed; and therefore, although it is said in some of the books that an exposure to the inclemency of the weather may amount to an assault, yet if that be so at all, it can only be when the person exposed suffers a hurt or injury of some kind or other from the exposure."

Moreover, the common law insisted that the injury suffered was serious.[11]

---

[4] *R. v. Bonnyman* (1942), 28 Cr. App. Rep. 131 (C.C.A.).
[5] Apart from the parent-child relationship, historically the duty was most apparent in connection with apprentices and servants; see, for example, *R. v. Friend* (1802), Russ & Ry. 20 (neglect of master to provide for 13-year-old girl apprentice).
[6] *R. v. Shepherd* (1862), Le. & Ca. 147, (mother of 18-year-old pregnant girl under no duty to send for a midwife).
[7] *R. v. Chattaway* (1922), 17 Cr. App. Rep. 7 (C.C.A.).
[8] This was particularly common where the death of a newly born child was caused by the mother's post-natal neglect.
[9] (1847), 2 Cox C.C. 285.
[10] *Ibid.*, at p. 287. See also *R. v. Friend* (1802), Russ. & Ry. 20.
[11] *R. v. Phillpot* (1853), Dears, C.C. 179.

Introduction

The inadequacy of a rule which was prepared to punish neglect of children only if there was proof of actual, serious harm was eventually acknowledged. A series of statutes creating offences relating to cruelty to children has successively embodied the principle that neglect in itself is punishable provided that there is a likelihood of resultant harm. The first notable step was taken by the Poor Law Amendment Act 1868, s. 37 of which made it an offence for a parent wilfully to neglect to provide adequate food, clothing, medical aid or lodging for his children, who were under 14 years of age and in his custody, so that their health "shall have been or shall be likely to be seriously injured".[12] This enactment was repealed and replaced by the more comprehensive provisions of the Prevention of Cruelty to, and Protection of, Children Act 1889, which not only made the ill-treatment and neglect of children a statutory offence, but also made provision for children who were ill-treated and neglected to be removed from the parent, or anyone else having custody or control, and entrusted to a fit person. This Act was amended,[13] but was at once replaced by the Prevention of Cruelty to Children Act 1894. The effect of the changes was to extend the legislation to cases of assault as well as ill-treatment and neglect. It was also specifically provided that a parent would be neglecting his child if, being without means to maintain him, he failed to provide for his maintenance under the Poor Law,[14] and the power to deal with the child and commit him to the charge of a fit person was no longer limited to cases of assault, ill-treatment and neglect under the 1894 Act, but also applied where various offences under the Offences Against the Person Act 1861 had been committed in respect of the child.[15] The Act of 1894 was in turn replaced in 1904 by an Act of the same name and this remained the Principal Act[16] until the Children and Young Persons Act 1933,

---

[12] Even before this enactment it was an offence for anyone unlawfully to abandon or expose a child under two years of age so that his life was endangered or his health was or was likely to be permanently injured; Offences Against the Person Act 1861, s. 27. See *post*, p. 195.

[13] By the Prevention of Cruelty to Children (Amendment) Act 1894.

[14] *Cf. R.* v. *Hogan* (1851), 2 Den. 277, where it had been held that to be liable the parent must have had the means of supporting the child.

[15] For example, an offence under s. 27, *supra*, n. 12. Other sections dealt with assault (s. 43), sexual offences (s. 52), and unlawful removal of children (ss. 55 and 56).

[16] It was amended by the Children Act 1908, and the Children and Young Persons Act 1932.

placed the law on its present footing. This will be considered later.[17]

B. HOMICIDE OF CHILDREN

The law of homicide has special application to children in two ways: in relation to childbirth and to the breach of the duty to protect, although, as will be seen,[18] the two are sometimes inter-related.

I. HOMICIDE AND CHILDBIRTH[19]

(1) Murder and Manslaughter

The law of murder and manslaughter in its application to the newly-born child has been narrowly construed and reluctantly enforced. These offences are only possible if the child is born alive. The conditions necessary for live-birth are that the child must be alive after complete extrusion from the mother[20] and must have an existence independent of her.[1] The legal test of separate existence is whether the child is carrying on its being without the help of the mother's circulation,[2] but physiologically it may not be possible to determine the precise moment of dissociation of the foetal and parental circulations.[3] Furthermore, while on the one hand a child may be born alive without having breathed, on the other hand it may have breathed at some stage in the process of birth and yet not be born alive.[4] For a live-birth it is not, however, necessary that there should have been expulsion of the after-birth or that the umbilical cord should have been severed.[5]

Although live-birth is a prerequisite to murder or manslaughter, the act causing death may have been committed while the child was *en ventre sa mere* or may occur while it is in the process of being born, as happened in *R. v. Senior*,[6] where a man who practised midwifery was convicted for the manslaughter of a child which had died immediately after birth

---

[17] *Post*, pp. 188 *et seq.*   [18] See *post*, p. 186.
[19] See Atkinson, *Life, Birth and Live-Birth* (1904) 20 L.Q.R. 134; Seaborne Davies, *Child-killing in English Law, Modern Approach to Criminal Law*, p. 301.
[20] *R. v. Poulton* (1832), 5 C. & P. 329; *R. v. Sellis* (1837), 7 C. & P. 850.
[1] *R. v. Enoch* (1833), 5 C. & P. 539; *R. v. Wright* (1841), 9 C. & P. 754.
[2] *Per* Wright J. in *R. v. Pritchard* (1901), 17 T.L.R. 310.
[3] See 20 L.Q.R. at p. 145.   [4] *R. v. Brain* (1834), 6 C. & P. 349.
[5] *R. v. Reeves* (1839), 9 C. & P. 25; *R. v. Trilloe* (1842), 2 Mood. 260.
[6] (1832), 1 Mood. 346.

because its skull had been negligently broken and compressed by the accused during the birth. Moreover, a person who causes a pre-natal injury will, depending upon the mental element, be guilty of murder or manslaughter if the injury results in a premature birth which thereby renders the child much less capable of surviving and it in fact dies soon afterwards.[7] The courts have declined, however, to extend these principles to the case where the death after birth has been caused by gross pre-natal neglect by the mother, so as to render her liable for the manslaughter of her child.[8] This refusal to hold the mother liable for pre-natal neglect[9] has been paralleled by the unwillingness of juries to convict her for manslaughter of her newly-born child where there has been post-natal neglect. Such deficiencies in the law and its administration have emphasised the need for other offences concerning childbirth.

(2) Abortion

Although the common law insisted on live-birth for the purposes of murder and manslaughter, it did apparently recognise that it was a misdemeanour to destroy a child when it was quick in its mother's womb.[10] An Act of 1803[11] made it an offence to administer a poison to a woman with intent to procure her miscarriage, and the offence was made punishable by death if she was in fact quick with the child and by transportation or imprisonment if she was not. In 1828 the offence was extended to any means of procurement.[12] but the distinction between the quick and the non-quick woman was retained until the Offences against the Person Act 1837,[13] recognising the difficulty of sometimes drawing the distinction, abandoned it. The present governing statutes are the Offences Against the Person Act 1861 and the Abortion Act 1967. Under s. 58 of the earlier Act procuring or attempting to procure abortion is punishable with imprisonment for life and may be committed by the woman herself, provided that she is in fact pregnant, or

---

[7] *R.* v. *West* (1848), 2 C. & K. 784.
[8] *R.* v. *Knights* (1860), 2 F. & F. 46; *R.* v. *Izod* (1904), 20 Cox 690.
[9] For abortive 19th century attempts to fill this gap in the law of manslaughter see Seaborne Davies, *op. cit.*, p. 309.
[10] For the history of abortion see Seaborne Davies, *The Law of Abortion and Necessity*, (1938-39) 2 M.L.R. at pp. 130-135.
[11] 43 Geo. 3 c. 58.
[12] By the Offences against the Person Act 1828 (9 Geo. 4 c. 31) which replaced the earlier Act.   [13] 1 Vic. c. 85.

by a third person whether the woman is pregnant or not. But even where she is not pregnant, she herself may be guilty of conspiring to procure her own miscarriage[14] or of aiding and abetting in the commission of abortion.[15]

The offence may be committed by unlawfully administering a "poison or other noxious thing"[16] or by unlawfully using any instrument or other means to procure the miscarriage. The fact that the method used could not produce a miscarriage is not material, providing that there is the necessary intent.[17] Moreover, it is an offence[18] for anyone to supply or procure[19] any poison, noxious thing, instrument or other thing knowing that it is intended to be unlawfully used with intent to procure a miscarriage. This offence has been widely construed, for it is sufficient to show that the accused intended that the particular thing should be used to abort even if the person supplied did not intend so to use it[20] or even if the woman for whom it was intended was not in fact pregnant.[1]

Section 58 excludes from its provisions lawful acts to terminate pregnancy, but this exemption has been limited to therapeutic abortion undertaken by the medical profession. The exemption, which is based on the doctrine of necessity, was not judicially recognised until 1938[2] in the well-known case of *R. v. Bourne.*[3] As a test case the facts could scarcely have been stronger. A 14 year old girl was the victim of a brutal and horrifying rape which left her pregnant. A distinguished gynaecologist openly performed an operation in a hospital to terminate the pregnancy because he was of the opinion that otherwise the girl would probably become a physical and mental wreck. He was acquitted of an offence under s. 58, but the precise effects of the case were uncertain. It was made

---

[14] *R. v. Whitchurch* (1890), 24 Q.B.D. 420, (C.C.C.R.).
[15] *R. v. Sockett* (1908), 1 Cr. App. Rep. 101, (C.C.A.).
[16] The words "noxious thing" are not limited to a noxious thing which is an abortifacient; see *R. v. Marlow* (1964), 49 Cr. App. Rep. (C.C.A.). The same principle applies to the word "poison"; see *ibid.*
[17] *R. v. Spicer* (1955), 39 Cr. App. Rep. 189 (manual interference such as not to be able to cause a miscarriage).
[18] Under s. 59 of the Offences Against the Person Act 1861. The offence is punishable by imprisonment for not more than five years.
[19] The word "procure" here means "getting possession from someone else"; see *R. v. Mills,* [1963] 1 Q.B. 522, (C.C.A.); [1963] 1 All E.R. 202.
[20] *R. v. Hillman* (1863), 9 Cox C.C. 386, (C.C.C.R.).
[1] *R. v. Titley* (1880), 14 Cox C.C. 502.   [2] But see *infra*, n. 4.
[3] [1939] 1 K.B. 687; [1938] 3 All E.R. 615.

abundantly clear by MACNAGHTEN, J., that if an operation was performed in good faith in order to preserve the mother's life it was lawful. Whether it was enough to show that the object was protection of her health was left open to doubt, although subsequent cases supported this wider principle.[4]

The Abortion Act 1967 has in this respect clarified the law, for it allows termination of a pregnancy whenever medical opinion[5] considers that its continuance would involve a greater risk to the woman's life or to her physical or mental health than if it were terminated. But the Act also adds two other grounds for lawful termination, namely, where the continuance would involve greater risk of injury to the health of any existing children of the woman's family and where there is a substantial risk[6] that if the child were born it would suffer from such physical or mental abnormalities as to be seriously handicapped.[7] The addition of the latter ground meets a demand of the medical profession,[8] the former introduces into the law of abortion a novel aspect of child protection. Both cut deep inroads into the traditional principle that the protection which the law gives to human life extends to the unborn child.[9]

---

[4] *R.* v. *Bergmann and Ferguson*, 1948 (unreported); see Williams, *The Sanctity of Life*, p. 154: *R.* v. *Newton and Stungo*, [1958] Crim. L.R. 469.
   Medical textbooks had long taken the view that acts done to preserve either the life or health of the pregnant woman were lawful.
[5] See *infra*, n. 9.   [6] See *infra*.   [7] See s. 1(a) and (b).
[8] See Havard, *Therapeutic Abortion*, [1958] Crim. L.R. 600, at p. 606.
   This ground for termination is likely to be increasingly significant in view of the new technique (known as amniocentesis) for screening pregnancy, which may disclose, *inter alia*, that the baby is likely to be born with a serious congenital abnormality.
[9] The above are the only grounds on which termination of pregnancy is allowed by the Act; see s. 5(2). But it has been argued that this provision does not entirely eliminate the operation of general defences to crime; see Smith and Hogan, Criminal Law 2nd edn., p. 247.
   The termination must be performed by a registered medical practitioner and normally only if two such practitioners are of the *bona fide* opinion that one of the grounds exists. Normally, too, treatment for termination must be carried out in a National Health Service hospital or in a place approved by the Secretary of State for the Social Services. However, where a practitioner is of the opinion that the termination is immediately necessary to save the woman's life or to prevent grave permanent injury to her health it may be carried out in another place and without a second concurring opinion; see s. 1(3) and (4). No-one is compelled to participate in treatment *authorised by the Act* if he has conscientious objections to it, (s. 4(1)), but this does not affect any duty to participate which is necessary to save the life or to prevent grave permanent injury to the health of the woman, (s. 4(2)), and it has been argued that there may be a common law duty on a doctor to act in such circumstances; see Smith and Hogan, *ibid.*, p. 248.

Due to the wide terms in which these last two grounds are stated there is some uncertainty about their scope.[10] It is impossible to lay down precise criteria for determining whether the risk of abnormality is substantial or the resultant handicap serious, and the court will have to rely solely on medical opinion. Equally it may be difficult for a doctor to decide whether the continuance of the pregnancy would involve greater risk[11] of injury to the health of any existing child of the family. Although it is clear that something more will have to be shown than a mere reduction in the standard of living of the family which an addition to it would entail, it is suggested that in most cases the question for consideration is whether the addition would seriously handicap the woman's ability to take care of her children. This may more readily be proved if any existing child is suffering from a serious physical or mental disability.

In calculating the risk of injury to the health of the woman or of an existing child account may be taken of her "actual or reasonably foreseeable environment".[12] The main matters to be considered here are the woman's place and mode of living and presumably[13] the people with whom she is living. This last factor would enable account to be taken not only of their financial resources (as well as the woman's) but also their views about the proposed abortion. The point is of special importance in relation to the husband, since the Act does not expressly require him to consent or even be consulted. It may well be that if he is consulted he will be able to satisfy the doctors that, contrary to what the mother may say, no great strain will be imposed on her health or that of the existing children if there is an addition to the family.

Another difficulty created by the Act is its failure to define the term "any existing children of her family". It is to be hoped that it will be widely construed. It does, it is submitted, include not only any natural or adopted child but also one who is in fact a member of the woman's family, even though not a natural or adopted child of her or of her husband.[14] Nor

---

[10] For a close analysis of the Act see Hoggett, [1968] Crim. L.R. 247.

[11] But the Act does not say that the increase in the risk has to be substantial.

[12] Section 1(2).   [13] See Hoggett, [1968] Crim L.R. at p. 251.

[14] *Cf.* the definitions of "child of the family" in the Matrimonial Proceedings and Property Act 1970, s. 27(1), and the Matrimonial Proceedings (Magistrates' Courts) Act 1960, s. 16(1); see *post*, Chapter 9.

should the term necessarily be restricted to children under the age of majority: the true test, it is suggested, is the child's dependence on the woman, not its age.

Problems may also arise over the woman's giving consent to the termination of her pregnancy. These are part of the general uncertainty about the law relating to consent to medical treatment. Normally her consent is necessary as it would be if she were undergoing any other surgical operation, but in a case of emergency (*e.g.*, where her life is in danger) the abortion without consent would be justified on the ground of necessity. The Family Law Reform Act 1969[15] enables a girl who is 16 or over to give a valid consent to surgical and medical treatment, so that only her consent to the termination of her pregnancy is necessary. Nevertheless, it is submitted that, if she is still under 18 and unmarried the doctor ought, with her permission, to consult her parent or guardian about the proposed abortion, especially in view of the desirability of taking into account her environment.[16] If, however, she forbids him to do so, her right to privacy should be regarded as paramount. If she is under 16, parental consent must be sought, but, if this is not granted, pregnancy may still lawfully be terminated if the doctors consider it necessary to protect the girl's life or health.[17]

The 1967 Act leaves a wide discretion with the medical profession and it is uncommon to establish in the courts breach of its provisions. There are, however, clear indications of marked divergence in operating it within the National Health Service, while, on the other hand, abuse of the powers conferred has made it necessary to tighten up on Ministerial approval of private clinics. Such concern and doubts about its operation have already led to inquiry by a Departmental Committee.[18]

(3) Child Destruction

Closely related to abortion is the offence of child destruction, created by the Infant Life (Preservation) Act 1929, because of

[15] Section 8. The section gives effect to a recommendation of the Committee on the Age of Majority (1967), Cmnd. 3342, paras. 474-484.
[16] *Cf. supra* the position of the husband.
[17] The younger the girl the easier it may be to show risk of injury to her mental health if the pregnancy continues.
Semble the necessity to protect life or health is also overriding in those cases where the parent demands abortion but the girl objects.
[18] Under the Chairmanship of LANE, J.

the restrictive rule that murder is only possible if the child is born alive.[19] Under s. 1 it is an offence wilfully to cause a child, which is capable of being born alive, to die before it has an existence independent of its mother, and evidence that the mother has been pregnant for 28 weeks or more is *prima facie* proof that the child is capable of being born alive. Before a person can be convicted of the offence it must be proved that the act causing the child's death was not done in good faith for the purpose only of preserving the life of the mother. However, although this offence and abortion overlap,[20] the wider defences provided by the Abortion Act 1967, have not been extended to child destruction and that Act is limited to the case of a foetus not yet viable.[21]

(4) Infanticide[1]

This offence owes its origins to the notorious unwillingness to apply the full rigour of the law of murder to cases of killing by mothers of their very young children. Even if in such cases juries could be persuaded to convict of murder, the death sentence was invariably commuted.

Section 1(1) of the Infanticide Act 1938 provides that, where a woman wilfully causes the death of her child who is under the age of 12 months and but for that section the circumstances would have amounted to murder, she will be guilty of infanticide if at the time of her act or omission the balance of her mind was disturbed because she had not fully recovered from the effect of giving birth to the child or because of the effect of lactation consequent upon the birth. She may then be dealt with as if she had been guilty of manslaughter of the child. Theoretically, therefore, she may be sentenced to life imprisonment, but imprisonment for even a short period has become much less common and frequently she is put on probation or even granted a conditional or absolute discharge.

[19] See *ante*, p. 178.
[20] In *R. v. Bourne*, [1939] 1 K.B. 687, at p. 691, MACNAGHTEN, J., stated *obiter* that child destruction deals with the case where the child is killed while it is being delivered, but there is nothing in the 1929 Act so limiting the offence.
[21] An advisory body has recommended to the Secretary of State for Social Services that a foetus should be regarded as viable at 20 weeks; *The Use of Foetus and Foetal Material for Research* (H.M.S.O. 1972).
[1] See Seaborne Davies, *Child-killing in English Law, Modern Approach to Criminal Law*, p. 301; Williams, *The Sanctity of Life*, pp. 25-45.

The readiness to treat the offence as a minor one gives added force to the view that it "is an illogical compromise between the law of murder and humane feelings".[2]

(5) Concealment of Birth

"The offence most pressed into service to fill part of the gap later to be largely closed by the creation of Child Destruction and Infanticide was that of concealment of birth".[3]

But the gap filling was a gradual process. The offence originated in an Act of 1623,[4] passed because of the difficulty of proving live-birth in a charge of murder of a newly-born child. In practice the person who for that reason most commonly escaped liability was the mother who killed her illegitimate child and tried to conceal its death by secretly disposing of its body, and it was against her alone that the Act was aimed. Although the Act required the child to have been born alive, all that was needed to be proved was the secret disposition of the body, because then the onus was put on the mother to prove that it was born dead. Eventually the offence acquired its modern features[5] and under the present provisions[6] it relates to legitimate and illegitimate children alike, may be committed by the mother or by anyone else and applies whether the child died before, at or after its birth. It is, however, necessary that the foetus shall have become a child, but the legal test for determining this is uncertain. It seems that it is not sufficient for the foetus to have the outward appearance of a child,[7] but that the child must have "arrived at that stage of maturity at the time of birth that it might have been a living child".[8]

II. BREACH OF THE DUTY TO PROTECT

If a parent fails to fulfil his duty of protecting his child and it

---

[2] Williams, *op. cit.*, p. 37. An Infanticide Bill, in 1970, would have made the offence a summary one.
[3] Seaborne Davies, *Child-killing in English Law, Modern Approach to Criminal Law*, at p. 312.
[4] 21 Jac. I, c.27. See Radzinowicz, *History of English Criminal Law*, Vol. I, pp. 430 *et seq.*
[5] For its subsequent history see 43 Geo. 3, c.58, s.2, and 9 Geo. 4, c.31, s. 14, as amended by 10 Geo. 4, c.34, s. 17(1).
[6] Offences Against the Person Act 1861, s. 60.
[7] *R. v. Colmer* (1864), 9 Cox C.C. 506, to the contrary is a doubtful authority; see *Russell on Crime*, p. 611.
[8] *Per* ERLE, J. in *R. v. Berriman* (1854), 6 Cox C.C. 388 at p. 390.

consequently dies, he may be guilty of murder or manslaughter.[9] As already noted,[10] the duty at common law has been largely replaced by statute. The breach of the duty may take various forms.[11] Usually it is neglect by the parent, or whoever else has the charge or care of the child, to provide the child with the necessities of life, for example, adequate food or medical aid. If his neglect is wilful, that is to say, he deliberately and not accidentally or inadvertently omits to supply the particular necessity, he is guilty of an offence under s. 1 of the Children and Young Persons Act 1933.[12] If such neglect results in the child's death and the parent intended to kill it or, at least, cause it grievous bodily harm or knew that his neglect would probably cause death or such harm,[13] he is guilty of murder. In the absence of such intention or knowledge he will for the following reasons be guilty of manslaughter.

Although its exact scope was disputed, it was a long accepted principle that the commission of an unlawful act resulting in death in itself constituted manslaughter and neither motive nor state of mind was material. Its application to the present topic is illustrated by the case of refusal to obtain medical aid for one's child. Thus, in *R.* v. *Senior*,[14] which is a leading authority on the general principle, the parent belonged to a religious sect, known as "The Peculiar People", whose tenets did not permit him to seek medical aid. It was, nevertheless, held that, whatever his motive, his deliberate refusal to do so was a statutory misdemeanour,[15] and, therefore, since it had caused or accelerated the child's death, he was automatically guilty of manslaughter. The general principle has, however,

---

[9] A detailed analysis of the mental element in homicide is outside the scope of this book. The reader is referred to textbooks on the criminal law. See especially Smith and Hogan, *op. cit.;* Williams, *Criminal Law, The General Part.* [10] *Ante*, p. 177. [11] See further *post*, pp. 188 *et seq.*

[12] *R.* v. *Senior*, [1899] 1 Q.B. 283, (C.C.C.R.). See further *post*, p. 189.

[13] In *R.* v. *Walters* (1841), C. & M. 164, a case of a mother abandoning her newly born child by leaving it naked on the side of a road where it died from the cold, COLTMAN, J., in his directions to the jury spoke of the parent having to know that the result would be death, but it is now well settled that knowledge of grievous bodily harm is sufficient *mens rea* for murder.

[14] [1899] 1 Q.B. 283, *supra*. The principle had already been applied to refusal of medical aid in *R.* v. *Downes* (1875), 1 Q.B.D. 25 (C.C.C.R.); *cf. R.* v. *Morby* (1881), 8 Q.B.D. 571 (insufficient evidence of causal connection between the refusal and death).

[15] Under s. 1 of the Prevention of Cruelty to Children Act 1894, which then operated.

been qualified by *R. v. Church*[16] in that, where an unlawful act causes death, to constitute manslaughter it "must be such as all sober and reasonable people would inevitably recognise must subject the other person to, at least, the risk of some harm resulting therefrom, albeit not serious harm". But this objective test requires only a recognition of the risk of some harm; there is no need to prove risk of death or of grievous bodily harm.[17] This being so, it is submitted that whatever effect *Church* may have in relation to other types of unlawful acts resulting in death it will make no practical difference to the operation of the law in the kind of case under consideration. It is no more necessary now than it was before *Church* to prove anything more than the parent's wilful neglect, because if a child is deprived of a necessity of life a sober and reasonable man would be bound to realise that it runs the risk of suffering some harm. The conduct is such that it admits of no other conclusion.[18]

The circumstances may be such that the parental neglect could not amount to an offence under the Act of 1933. Thus, the child may have attained the age of 16, or the neglect may be inadvertent and not "wilful", as already defined. Reliance will then have to be placed on the common law duty.[19] If, in the former case, the breach of that duty is deliberate and causes the child's death, it seems clear that the above principles will apply for determining whether murder or manslaughter has been committed, as they do in cases of "wilful" neglect.[20]

[16] [1966] 1 Q.B. 59, (C.C.A.); [1965] 2 All E.R. 72.

[17] The court stressed that it was not considering the essential elements of other forms of manslaughter. For example, in manslaughter based on criminal negligence the negligence must relate to death or, at least, to grievous bodily harm. Nevertheless, in laying down the objective test in relation to manslaughter arising from the commission of an unlawful act, the court did speak in terms of a degree of *mens rea* being essential. In so far as it did, the decision has met with the disapproval of the Court of Appeal in *R. v. Lipman*, [1969] 3 All E.R. 410, which has rejected any assumption that *Church* introduced a new element of intent or foreseeability in this latter type of manslaughter.

[18] But see *R. v. Hayles*, [1969] 1 Q.B. 364, (C.A.); [1969] 1 All E.R. 34, *post*, p.188. [19] See *ante*, p. 175.

[20] Most of the relevant authorities were decided before wilful neglect became a statutory offence in 1868 (see *ante*, p. 176). They should be treated cautiously in view of subsequent changes in the law relating to the mental element in murder and manslaughter. Those which may usefully be referred to are *R. v. Bubb* (1851), 4 Cox C.C. 455, (starvation); *R. v. Walters* (1841), C. & M. 164, (abandonment and exposure); and *R. v. Wagstaffe* (1868), 10 Cox C.C. 530, (refusal of medical aid). The common law position on refusal of medical aid is rather uncertain; see the doubts expressed in *R. v. Downes* (1875), 1 Q.B.D. 25 (C.C.C.R.) and *cf.* Lord RUSSELL, C. J., in *R. v. Senior*, [1899] 1 Q.B. 283 at p. 292.

Where, however, the neglect is inadvertent it will have to be shown that the inadvertence amounted to gross negligence, in which case in accordance with general principles of the law of manslaughter the parent would be guilty of that offence. Refusal to provide food, clothing or shelter is almost certain to be deliberate, but refusal to seek medical aid may sometimes be due to gross negligence.

C. PHYSICAL HARM NOT CAUSING DEATH

(1) Cruelty to Children under 16

We have already seen[1] how the weakness of the common law in protecting children led in the second half of the nineteenth century to a series of statutes which dealt with neglect and ill-treatment of children and also with other aspects of protection from physical and moral danger. The relevant law is now to be found in Part I of the Children and Young Persons Act 1933, of which s. 1[2] is undoubtedly the most far-reaching provision. Sub-s. (1) provides:

> If any person who has attained the age of 16 years and has the custody, charge or care of any child or young person under that age, wilfully assaults, ill-treats, neglects, abandons or exposes him, or causes or procures him to be assaulted, ill-treated, neglected, abandoned, or exposed, in a manner likely to cause him unnecessary suffering or injury to health (including injury to or loss of sight, or hearing, or limb, or organ of the body, and any mental derangement) that person shall be guilty of [an offence] . . .

This provision is doubly comprehensive: in the nature of the conduct which may give rise to liability and in the kinds of persons who may be held liable for it.

Nature of the Conduct

Sub-section (1) shows that the cruel conduct may take one of five forms, but these are not five mutually exclusive offences. In *R. v. Hayles*[3] the three-year-old son of the defendant fell and sustained serious injuries. The defendant put him to bed,

---

[1] *Ante*, p. 177.
[2] As amended by C. & Y.P. Act 1963, ss. 31, 64, 65 and Sched. III.
[3] [1969] 1 Q.B. 364; (C.A.); [1969] 1 All E.R. 34.

but did not obtain medical aid. The child died. The Court of Appeal held that, although the defendant's conduct was essentially neglect, the neglect was such that it could properly be described as ill-treatment, and that therefore he could be convicted of the offence of wilfully ill-treating the child, with which he was charged in the indictment.[4]

Whichever form the conduct may take it must be "wilful" and must be such as is likely to cause unnecessary suffering or injury to health.[5] This is a flexible term which leaves to the court a wide discretion. As for the term "wilful", as already noted, it here means that "the act is done deliberately and intentionally, not by accident or inadvertence, but so that the mind of the person doing the act goes with it";[6] but it does not require the parent (or whoever else has charge or care) to know of all the circumstances and consequences of his *actus reus* before he can be held liable. To take the type of case in which this meaning was formulated, if a parent, having considered the matter, decides not to seek medical aid for his child, that fact and the consequent likelihood of unnecessary suffering or injury to health – which is to be determined objectively – are all that have to be proved. It is not necessary to show that he knew that his failure to seek aid was likely to have that result. A parent who does not obtain the aid because he thinks that it is not necessary for the child's health or believes it to be in the child's best interests not to have the aid[7] is, nevertheless, wilfully neglecting him. The emphasis throughout sub-s. (1) is on the protection of the child not on the limitations of the parent's liability.[8] For this reason, too, there can be no doubt

---

[4] An alternative count for manslaughter based on the allegation that the defendant had occasioned the son's injury was withdrawn. But could not manslaughter have been alternatively based on his wilful neglect to seek medical aid? *Cf. supra*, p. 186.

[5] The specific reference in sub-s. (1) to injury to or loss of sight, hearing, limb or organ of the body and any mental derangement is supererogatory. The mention of mental derangement has tended to imply the need for proof of severe mental cruelty and the Ingleby Committee (para. 535) recommended an amendment to make it clear that sub-s. (1) covers mental suffering falling short of mental derangement. Surely the solution is a straightforward reference to "suffering or injury to health, whether physical or mental".

[6] *R. v. Senior*, [1899] 1 Q.B. 283 (C.C.C.R.), *ante*, p. 186.

[7] For example, because of a religious conviction that those interests would be best served by spiritual healing.

[8] For a criticism of the narrow meaning given to wilfulness in the sub-s. see Williams, *Criminal Law, The General Part*, (2nd edn.), ss. 53 and 241.

that there is imported into that sub-section the common law principle that a parent is himself guilty of wilful neglect if he knows that the other parent is wilfully neglecting the child but does nothing himself about it.[9]

Where the conduct is in the form of an assault it usually involves the use of personal violence to a degree that proof of unnecessary suffering or injury to health or both will not be difficult.[10] But under s. 1 it is not necessary to show actual suffering or injury: it is enough that the juvenile was treated "in a manner likely to cause" either result. So, where there is an assault without an accompanying battery, it will still be possible to prosecute under s. 1 if the likelihood of unnecessary suffering or injury to health can be proved. Proof of the likelihood may, however, be difficult, because, although it is an essential element of assault that the victim should fear that personal violence is about to be used against him, his fear may be too superficial or transient to produce the consequences which s. 1 requires.[11] An assault without battery is most likely to be by way of confinement of the juvenile or threatening him with some instrument or by means of words (for the better opinion is that threatening language may amount to an assault).[12] In deciding whether the particular assault comes within the section much will depend on the age of the juvenile and also on his peculiar sensibilities, because, although the wording of s. 1 suggests that the likelihood of suffering or injury is to be determined objectively, that standard must, it is submitted, be related to the particular individual. For example, to keep a three-year-old child locked in a dark room for an hour is a traumatic experience likely to cause him unnecessary suffering

[9] See *R. v. Hook* (1850), 4 Cox C.C. 455 (a case of homicide).

[10] *Cf. R. v. Hatton*, [1925] 2 K.B. 322 (C.C.A); (and preferably) 19 Cr. App. Rep. 29, where only slight force was used in that the accused, the stepfather of a 12-year-old girl, put his hand over her mouth to stop her screaming after he had committed an indecent act, not against her, but in her presence. It was held that, although his conduct prior to the act of force was "likely to cause, if not suffering, at any rate no little agitation of mind and astonishment and disgust", the only assault was his act of putting his hand on her mouth and the question for the jury was whether that constituted a wilful act likely to cause unnecessary suffering.

[11] For this reason it has been suggested that the parent should also alternatively be charged with common assault under s. 42 of the Offences Against the Person Act 1861; see Clarke Hall and Morrison, *op. cit.*, pp. 13-14.

[12] See Smith and Hogan, *Criminal Law*, 2nd edn., pp. 250-251 and references therein.

and possibly also affect his health. On the other hand neither effect is normally likely if he is a fourteen-year-old; but it would be otherwise if he were of an abnormally nervous disposition.

An assault without, or with only slight, violence may, therefore, be outside the scope of s. 1. but if the conduct is repeated over a period of time the point may be reached where it is likely to cause unnecessary suffering or injury to health; for example, repeated threats of violence. If so it would constitute ill-treatment, a term which is not defined by the Children and Young Persons Act 1933, but which, it has been suggested, means any course of conduct likely to cause injury to a child.[13] Continuity in the conduct seems to be the essence of ill-treatment.[14] Thus nagging of a juvenile, though not an assault, would be within the meaning of the term.

Most charges are based on neglect. This is also not statutorily defined, but the 1933 Act does enact certain rules with regard to it and there has been some judicial interpretation. In *R. v. Senior* Lord RUSSELL, C.J., said:[15]

"Neglect is the want of reasonable care – that is, the omission of such steps as a reasonable parent would take, such as are usually taken in the ordinary experience of mankind – that is, ... provided that the parent had such means as would enable him to take the necessary steps."

The Act[16] prescribes some of the steps expected of a parent or whoever else is legally liable to maintain the juvenile by providing that he is deemed to have neglected him in a manner likely to cause injury to his health[17] if he has failed to provide adequate food, clothing, medical aid or lodging for him.[18] Apart from the Act, it is also wilful neglect to omit to pay part

---

[13] See Clarke Hall and Morrison, *op. cit.*, pp. 15, 16. This view is now supported by *R. v. Hayles*, (C.A.), *supra*, p. 188.
[14] See also *ibid.*, p. 15.
[15] [1899] 1 Q.B. 283 at p. 291.   [16] Section 1(2) (a).
[17] Why the Act should be silent on the alternative effect of unnecessary suffering is impossible to determine.
[18] Apart from liability under s. 1 of the 1933 Act, a parent is liable under s. 30 of the Ministry of Social Security Act 1966, and s. 51 of the National Assistance Act 1948, (which s. 30 largely supersedes) if social security benefits have to be provided for his child because of persistent refusal or neglect to maintain it. But the penalties for that offence are not so severe as those for neglect under the 1933 Act.

of one's earnings towards the support of one's child.[19] Moreover, contrary to what the dictum of Lord RUSSELL might suggest, a person is equally deemed to be guilty of neglect if, not having the means for providing those necessities, he fails to take steps to procure their provision under the appropriate legislation. Obvious examples are not seeking medical aid under the National Health Services Acts or failing to claim unemployment benefits for the child under the National Insurance Acts.

A nice but uncertain point is whether a parent can be held liable under s. 1 if he deliberately refuses to accept suitable employment and relies on the benefits for children provided by the national insurance and supplementary benefits schemes. Even if it were shown that by his refusal their standard of living was markedly reduced, could he successfully plead that he was adequately providing for them, since it must be taken that the Legislature has enacted what is to be regarded as the minimum financial provision needed to provide adequately the necessities of life so as to prevent unnecessary suffering or injury to health? There are two possible answers. First, it is a rule that a person may still be liable under s. 1 even though actual or likely suffering or injury was obviated by the action of another person,[20] and it is arguable that this could apply where intervention is by way of State-provided financial benefits. Secondly, though more doubtfully, it is arguable that for the purpose of s. 1 adequacy is to be given a relative meaning, depending upon the standard of living to which the juvenile has hitherto been accustomed. If so, and if there is a sharp drop in that standard, he may well be said to suffer thereby, and, since this is due to conduct which the parent could have avoided, the suffering may be said to be unnecessary.

[19] *Cole* v. *Pendleton* (1896), 60 J.P. 359; *R.* v. *Connor*, [1908] 2 K.B. 26, (C.C.C.R.). *Semble*, in the light of the latter case and the narrow definition of "wilful", there is no need to prove that the parent knew that the child needed support; the omission to provide is enough.
But, for the purpose of liability in matrimonial proceedings brought on the ground of wilful neglect to provide reasonable maintenance, knowledge that the child needed support is, apparently, necessary. That has been the view taken, at least, with regard to the husband's duty to maintain the wife; see *Jones* v. *Jones*, [1959] P. 38; [1958] 3 All E.R. 410, (D.C.); *Lilley* v. *Lilley*, [1960] P. 169, (C.A.); [1959] 3 All E.R. 283.
[20] Section 1(3) (a). The rule applies to any kind of conduct and not only to neglect. See, for example, *R.* v. *Falkingham* (1870), 11 Cox C.C. 475, (C.C.C.R.), (intervention of relieving officer); *R.* v. *White* (1871), 12 Cox C.C. 83, (C.C.C.R.), (police constable).

We have already seen[1] that problems can arise concerning the provision of medical aid where there are religious objections to it. Another difficulty is where the parent, though agreeable to some such aid being given, refuses to allow an operation on the juvenile. In such a case the test of wilful neglect depends on the nature of the operation and the reasonableness of the refusal to allow it. Thus, in *Oakey* v. *Jackson*[2] it was held to be wilful neglect to refuse to let a thirteen-year-old daughter have her adenoids removed.

One kind of neglect singled out by the Act is where a child under three years of age dies as the result of suffocation[3] while he is in bed with a person over the age of 16 and it is shown that that person was under the influence of drink when he went to bed. He is in those circumstances deemed to have neglected the child in a manner likely to cause injury to its health.[4] But the neglect must be wilful in the meaning earlier explained,[5] and the drunkenness may be such as to negative that *mens rea*. If a parent was so drunk that when he went to bed alongside a child he did not know what he was doing he cannot, it is submitted, be liable under s. 1, but *quaere* whether it is enough to show that he knew that he was going to bed or that he must also have known that the child was in bed.[6] Whichever be the answer to this last question, the relationship between this offence and manslaughter is uncertain.[7] The answer may depend on whether the drunkenness was self induced and whether the parent knew that later he was going to share his bed with a child. If it was and if he did, it is submitted that he would have behaved with gross negligence so as to render him liable for manslaughter; otherwise he would be liable only for an offence under s. 1.

For the purpose of s. 1, to abandon a juvenile means to

---

[1] *Ante*, p. 189.   [2] [1914] 1 K.B. 216, (D.C.).
[3] But not suffocation caused by disease or the presence of a foreign body in the child's throat.
[4] Section 1(2) (b). It is suggested that the rule ought to be extended to a person under the influence of drugs.
    Section 1(3) (b) expressly provides that the death of a juvenile does not prevent conviction of an offence under s. 1. See further *infra*. To describe, as s. 1(2) does, conduct resulting in death as being likely to cause injury to health is not a very felicitous use of language!
[5] *Ante*, p. 189.
[6] Logically and morally it ought to be the latter, but the wording of s. 1 tends to favour the former construction.
[7] Prosecutions are rare.

leave it to its fate[8] and the fact that a parent takes some measures to avoid this result may not be enough to escape liability. This principle, which was affirmed in *R. v. Boulden*,[9] is illustrated by a comparison of that case with *R. v. Whibley*.[10] In the latter case a father, who took his five children with him when he had to attend a children's court and then in a moment of passion left them there, was held not to have abandoned them, since he had not left them in a place which would expose them to injury. They could have immediately been put in the care of a society or, today, received into the care of a local authority under the Children Act 1948.[11] On the other hand, in *Boulden*, after the mother had left the matrimonial home one afternoon to return to her parents in Scotland to seek assistance for her children, the father about 9 p.m. that evening telephoned to the headquarters of the N.S.P.C.C. to inform them that the children were alone in the house and asked them to send someone to look after them. When asked why he could not look after them he gave a false excuse. Shortly afterwards a policewoman arrived and found the house in darkness and the children alone there, with only a small quantity of food. The following night the father followed the mother to Scotland. It was held that there was evidence on which the jury were entitled to find abandonment and neglect of the children. It would seem in the light of these cases that the test is whether the parent has taken all reasonable steps to ensure that the juvenile has been received into care.[12]

Often the abandonment is accompanied by exposure of the juvenile, a typical illustration being the mother who leaves her

---

[8] *Cf.* s. 1(1) of the Children Act 1948 where the term is given the same meaning; see *ante*, p. 144.   [9] (1957), 41 Cr. App. Rep. 105, (C.C.A.).
[10] [1938] 3 All E.R. 777, (C.C.A.).
[11] *Ante*, Chapter 5. The Ingleby Committee rejected a proposal which would have widened the meaning of abandonment so as to empower a local authority to prosecute a person who abandoned his child in such circumstances that the authority had to receive the child into their care under s. 1 of the Children Act 1948, even though, as in *Whibley* it cannot be said that the parent left the child to its fate. It was felt that to extend criminal liability to such and similar cases might cause parents, through fear of prosecution, to keep in unsatisfactory conditions children who should have been received into care. See Cmnd. 1191, paras. 538-540.
[12] In *Boulden* the father said that he watched the arrival of the policewoman from the other side of the street and that, had he not seen her take the children away, he would have returned to the house himself. It is submitted that if the jury believed that statement he could not have been found guilty of abandonment.

young baby on the doorstep of a house.[13] But a parent may
sometimes expose a juvenile to suffering or injury without ever
having abandoned it; for example, by depriving it of shelter
which has been made available to them both[14]

Apart from s. 1, a person may be convicted of abandoning
or exposing a child under s. 27 of the Offences Against the
Person Act 1861. This section, however, is limited to children
under two years of age, and it must be shown that the abandonment or exposure is such that the life of the child is endangered
or his health has been or is likely to be permanently injured.
This imposes a heavier burden of proof than does s. 1 of the
1933 Act and probably accounts for the fact that s. 1 has virtually superseded it, even though conviction on indictment for
an offence under the latter carries a heavier maximum penalty.[15]

Persons Who May Be Liable

One of the less satisfactory features of much of the legislation
relating to children[16] is the involved use of varied terminology
to describe the relationship which may exist between an adult
and a child. The terms "custody", "charge", "control", "care"
and "possession" all appear, with much overlapping and im-
precision.[17] It is suggested that the law could be simplified
without being strait-jacketed if the terms custody, care and
control were alone relied on, as the courts have done in exercising matrimonial jurisdiction. Certainly the continued use of
"possession", with its normal associations with property and
not persons, seems unnecessary; at one time, for example, it
produced unfortunate effects in the law of adoption.[18]

[13] If she should leave it outside the father's house and he will have nothing
to do with it, he, too, is guilty of abandonment and exposure; *R.* v. *White*
(1871), 12 Cox C.C. 83, (C.C.C.R.). For another illustration of abandonment and exposure see *R.* v. *Falkingham* (1870), 11 Cox C.C. 475,
(C.C.C.R.) (mother sending baby by rail in a hamper to the father).
    Both the cases cited were concerned with an offence under s. 27 of the
Offences Against the Person Act 1861, *infra*, but the principles therein
would apply equally for the purpose of s. 1 of the 1933 Act.
[14] *R.* v. *Williams* (1920), 4 Cr. App. Rep. 89, (C.C.A.).
[15] *I.e.*, imprisonment for not more than five years, compared with two
under s. 1.
[16] The word is here used in its widest sense and not in the narrower one
adopted in the C. & Y.P. legislation.
[17] The same comment may sometimes be made of the common law; see
the judgments in *Urmston* v. *Newcomen* (1836), 4 A. & E. 899.
[18] See *post*, Chapter 10.
    One of the earliest statutory references to possession in relation to
the person is to be found in an Act of 1558 which dealt with abduction
of girls under 16; see *post*, p. 228.

Nowhere is the complication more apparent than in Part I of the Children and Young Persons Act 1933, which extends some of its provisions, including s. 1, to any person over 16 who has custody, charge or care of a juvenile. None of these three terms is defined and certain rules in the Act tend to confuse rather than clarify them.

Section 17 lists the following presumptions:

> Any person who is the parent or legal guardian of a child or young person or who is legally liable to maintain him shall be presumed to have the custody of him, and as between father and mother the father shall not be deemed to have ceased to have the custody of him by reason only that he has deserted, or otherwise does not reside with, the mother and the child or young person;
>
> Any person to whose charge a child or young person is committed by any person who has the custody of him shall be presumed to have charge of the child or young person;
>
> Any other person having actual possession or control of a child or young person shall be presumed to have the care of him.

An additional and, it is submitted, unnecessary complication is the distinction drawn by the Act [19] between a "legal guardian" which means a person appointed to be guardian by deed or will or order of a court (which is the normal meaning of a guardian) and a "guardian" who, for the purpose of the Act includes anyone who in the opinion of the court has for the time being the "charge of or control over" the juvenile.

Let us examine the three terms more closely.

(i) *Custody*. This term is commonly used in the narrow sense to mean *de facto* care and control of a juvenile and is often then described as "actual custody", but it is also used in a wide sense to denote the sum of a number of parental rights and powers of which care and control are two. If the parent surrenders those to another, the residuary rights which he retains, notably the right to determine the juvenile's education and upbringing, are collectively described as constituting custody. The presumption relating to custody in s. 17 recognises this wider meaning. Thus if, for example, a magistrates' court made a divided order under the Guardianship of Minors Act 1971, whereby care and control is entrusted to the mother but custody to the father, he could be liable under s. 1 for wilful

---

[19] Section 107(1).

neglect if he did not maintain the juvenile.[20] If, as is almost certain, he is ordered to maintain, there will be no problem of proving that his neglect is wilful (assuming that he has the financial ability to do so), but, even in the very exceptional case where there is no order to maintain because of the mother's financial ability, if he knew that she was not in fact adequately maintaining the juvenile and he did nothing about it, he could by virtue of his custody be liable under s. 1. Where he is living apart from the mother and juvenile and there is no order granting him custody, he is still deemed to have custody whatever the cause of the separation may be. Section 17 expressly says so, and the above principles will apply just as they do where there is a custody order in his favour. It is not possible for him by his own act, for example by an agreement giving sole custody to the mother, to get rid of the legal presumption; he must be deprived of custody by an order of a competent court.[1] Moreover, even if he sends the mother an adequate amount for the juvenile's support, but he learns that she is neglecting the juvenile, he is still liable. The rule has been based on the doubtful premise that she is acting as his agent,[2] but the better explanation, it is submitted, is that under s. 17 the father is deemed still to have custody. In those circumstances he should take the children away, or, if this is opposed, seek an order of custody. If he cannot himself provide accommodation he should take all reasonable steps to ensure that the juvenile is received into care.[3]

The presumption concerning custody in s. 17 operates in relation not only to the parent or the legal guardian[4] but also to any person who is "legally liable to maintain the juvenile". There is nothing in the Act to suggest that these words are to be interpreted restrictively, and their effect, it is submitted,

---

[20] Because of his neglect he would very likely be deprived of custody, but that would not affect any prior liability under s. 1.

[1] *Brooks* v. *Blount*, [1923] 1 K.B. 257. See also *R.* v. *Connor*, [1908] 2 K.B. 26, (C.C.C.R.).   [2] *Poole* v. *Stokes* (1914), 110 L.T. 1020, (D.C.).

[3] See *ante*, p. 194. In *Poole* v. *Stokes*, *supra*, the father went to the N.S.P.C.C. and drew their attention to the facts, but it was held that this did not relieve him of the duty of protecting his children and seeing that they were properly clothed and fed. There was nothing, so far as the court could see, to prevent him from taking his children away from his wife. But supposing that he could not have accommodated them, what more could he have reasonably been expected to do?

[4] For the definition see *supra*.

is to give "custody" an even wider meaning than the one already stated. For example, a step parent who has entered into an agreement with his wife to maintain her child will be presumed to have custody, even though at common law he would not be accorded custody.[5] Another example is the step parent ordered by a court in exercise of its matrimonial jurisdiction to maintain a child of the family. But it is in respect of the father of an illegitimate child that the test of legal liability to maintain is specially relevant. In *Butler* v. *Gregory*[6] it was held that the father of an illegitimate daughter whose mother was dead and who was not living with him could not be presumed to have custody of her, since no affiliation order had been made against him. The decision has been firmly accepted as establishing that in the absence of such an order the presumption of custody cannot operate.[7] Where there is an order, the existence of the presumption is not to be explained on the ground that the father is a "parent", because there is nothing in the 1933 Act to rebut the common law presumption that that term does not include the father of an illegitimate child.[8] It is due to the fact that the order renders him "legally liable to maintain".[9] In *Butler* v. *Gregory* Lord ALVERSTONE, C.J., urged a statutory amendment "to throw the obligation on parents who were in fact fathers", a reform which is still awaited. This gap is consistent with a general unwillingness of the law to impose liability on the father of a bastard.[10]

[5] For example, he would not have the right to determine the child's education and upbringing.   [6] (1902), 18 T.L.R. 370, (D.C.).
[7] But this would not, it is submitted, prevent him from being liable under an agreement to maintain; *cf.* the step parent, *supra*.
[8] See *Re M.*, [1955] 2 Q.B. 479, (C.A.); [1955] 2 All E.R. 911 and compare the Children Act, 1948, s. 59, which expressly excludes the father.
[9] The point needs emphasising because *Butler* v. *Gregory* was decided under the Prevention of Cruelty to Children Act 1894. Section 23, a predecessor of s. 17 of the 1933 Act, laid down the presumption relating to custody and applied it to the "parent", a term there defined as including "every person who is by law liable to maintain the child". The ambiguous statement of the Divisional Court that the term "parent" should refer "to a person declared to be the legal parent by proceedings instituted for that purpose" does not make it clear whether the father was held not liable in that case because he was not a parent or specifically because he was not legally liable to maintain. Section 17, it will be noted, treats parents and those legally liable to maintain disjunctively and it is into the latter category that the father of an illegitimate child is to be brought, if brought at all.
[10] *Cf.* (1) the former miserable limitation of liability to £2. 10. od. weekly under an affiliation order, now removed by the Maintenance Orders Act, 1968 and (2) the limitation of the father's liability to maintain his child under the Ministry of Social Security Act 1966, s. 22, to the case where he has been adjudged to be the putative father.

It must be stressed, however, that it is only where the father and child are not living together that the presumption of custody cannot arise unless an affiliation order is in existence. If he has *actual* custody, charge or care he may be liable under s. 1 of the 1933 Act.[11]

(ii) *and* (iii) *Charge and Care*. It is very difficult to know exactly what these terms mean. It has been suggested that the "test of charge seems to be immediate control".[12] If it is, it makes it very difficult to distinguish it from care, bearing in mind the presumption relating to the latter in s. 17, with its reference to "actual possession or control".[13] Possibly "charge" is intended to emphasise the power of the adult to control the juvenile's conduct in the latter's interests; "care" to emphasise the responsibility of the adult to protect the juvenile from harm. Whatever the distinction may be, it is better to treat them as going hand in hand and to recognise that they may be simultaneously entrusted to more than one person, either generally or specifically. For example, a parent may during his absence abroad generally commit his child to the charge and care of a relative who in turn for a limited period may delegate the charge and care to another, *e.g.*, a baby sitter.

Prosecutions and Penalties

Prosecutions of an offence under s.1 or of any other offence under Part I of the 1933 Act are usually brought by the police or the National Society for the Prevention of Cruelty to Children, but a local authority (*i.e.*, a county or county borough council) may do so either as the local education authority or, through its social services committee (formerly its children's committee).[14]

At one time objections were taken to the latter procedure on the ground that if the committee acted as prosecutor it would make it more difficult when dealing with the juvenile to secure the parents' co-operation, but that argument seems to have

---

[11] *Liverpool S.P.C.C.* v. *Jones*, [1914] 3 K.B. 813.
[12] Clarke Hall and Morrison, *op. cit.*, p. 12.
[13] The question is further complicated by the fact that s. 1(7) of the 1933 Act, *post*, p. 211, apparently treats control and charge as distinct concepts.
[14] See C. & Y.P. Act 1933, s. 98 and C. & Y.P. Act 1963, s. 56. These provisions also empower an authority to prosecute for an offence under Part II of the two Acts, as to which see *post*, pp. 446 *et seq.*

lost its force.[15] The express power given to a local education authority is justified since it emphasises the vital part schools have to play in helping to protect juveniles from parental harm.[16]

An offence under s. 1 is triable on indictment or summarily. For conviction on indictment the maximum penalties are a fine of £100 or two years' imprisonment or both; on summary conviction they are respectively £100 or six months' or both;[17] but in either case heavier penalties can be imposed if the person convicted stands to gain financially by the juvenile's death.[18] The Ingleby Committee,[19] while recognising the need to retain the power to impose imprisonment (especially in cases of calculated cruelty) recommended that the courts should make full use of the facilities available for the rehabilitation of the family through residential training or skilled social help.

(2) Miscellaneous Offences under the Offences Against the Person Act 1861

(i) *Assaults*

This Act may be invoked to deal with more or less serious cases of assault than those contemplated by s. 1 of the Children and Young Persons Act 1933.[20] Moreover, only the former Act is available if the accused did not have custody, charge or care of the child. Of the more serious cases the most likely to arise are offences under ss. 18, 20 and 47 of the Act of 1861[1]: *i.e.*,

---

[15] See Report of Ingleby Committee, paras. 542-543.

[16] So amply illustrated by Clegg and Megson in *Children in Distress* (1968).

[17] Section 1(1) (a) and (b) of 1933 Act, as amended by the 1963 Act, s. 31.

[18] *Ibid.*, s. 1(5) and (6).
    In the case of a conviction on indictment the maximum fine is £200, but in lieu of awarding any other penalty the court may impose up to five years' imprisonment. On summary conviction it may take into consideration the fact that the person had a financial interest and knew of it.   [19] Para. 549.

[20] Because the victim is too young or too afraid to complain it is difficult to estimate the incidence of serious cruelty to children, but the indications are that it is high. This has been shown to be the American experience (see Helfer and Kempe, *The Battered Child*), while in England it has been regarded as sufficiently widespread to lead the N.S.P.C.C. to set up a "Battered Baby Unit" to investigate the causes underlying parents' cruelty towards their children. For its first report see "78 *Battered Children: A Retrospective Study*". See also Stark, (1969) Public Law, p. 48.

[1] Other offences which on rare occasions may be charged are attempts to choke, suffocate or strangle a child in order to commit an indictable offence (ss. 21 and 22, and *cf.* the Sexual Offences Act 1956, *post*, p. 219); and unlawfully and maliciously administering poison to it (ss. 23 and 24).
See also child-stealing under s. 56, *infra*.

unlawfully and maliciously wounding or causing grievous bodily harm to the child with the intention of doing such harm to it[2]; the lesser offence under s. 20, of unlawfully and maliciously wounding or inflicting grievous bodily harm upon the child; and assault occasioning actual bodily harm.[3] Where any of these offences are charged there may be an additional charge of an offence under s. 1 of the 1933 Act.[4]

Where, on the other hand, the assault is not sufficiently serious to be likely to produce the unnecessary suffering or injury which s. 1 requires, common assault under s. 42 of the 1861 Act[5] may be charged.[6] If the assault is of an aggravated nature and is committed against a boy under fourteen or against a girl of any age, proceedings may be instituted under s. 43[5] but, except where the accused does not have custody, charge or care, they should be taken under s. 1 of the 1933 Act, since the penalties thereunder are heavier.

(ii) *Child-Stealing*

The general lack of concern for children shown by the early law is illustrated by the fact that it was only after child-stealing had long been a widespread social evil that eventually in 1814, it was made a crime;[7] and even then was introduced, and ever since been primarily regarded, as an offence against the rights of the parent rather than against the child.[8] It is now governed by s. 56 of the Offences Against the Person Act 1861,[9] which makes it an offence[10] if a person unlawfully, by force or fraud,

[2] Section 18, as amended by the Criminal Law Act 1967, s. 10(2) and Sched. III, Part III.

[3] See, for example, *R. v. Frank Beanland* (1970), 54 Cr. App. Rep. 289, (C.A.).

[4] If a person is charged with an offence under s. 1 of the 1933 Act and elects trial by jury, the facts disclosed at the preliminary examination may justify other counts being added in the indictment charging, for example, offences under ss. 18 and 20 of the 1861 Act; see *R. v. Roe*, [1967] 1 All E.R. 492, (C.A.); [1967] 1 W.L.R. 634.

[5] As amended by the Criminal Justice Act 1925, s. 39 and the Criminal Justice Act 1967, s. 92 and Sched. III, Part I.

[6] It may often be desirable to prosecute both offences; see, for example, *ante*, p. 190.

[7] 54 Geo. 3, c. 101. The law reports do not show any readiness to rely on the common law offence of kidnapping, *i.e.*, "the stealing and carrying away or secreting of some person" (East 1 P.C. 430).

[8] *Cf.* abduction of girls, *post*, pp. 228 *et seq.* See also enticement, etc., of children in care, *post*, p. 231.

[9] As amended by the Criminal Justice Act 1948, s. 83(2) and (3) and Sched. X, Part I.

[10] Punishable with up to seven years' imprisonment. See *R. v. Jones* (1971), 56 Cr. App. Rep. 212, (C.A.).

leads or takes away or decoys or entices away or detains a child under 14 with intent to deprive the parent, guardian, or other person having lawful care or charge of it, of its possession or with intent to steal any article upon or about the person of the child. Anyone who with the same intent receives or harbours the child knowing it has been led away, *etc.*, is also guilty.[11] There is no need to prove that the accused intended to deprive the parent, *etc.*, permanently of the possession of the child,[11a] and the force or fraud may be exercised on the parent instead of on the child itself.[12] Thus, a person who persuades the parent to let him take his son off for the day and then promptly whisks him away on a week's holiday would be guilty of the offence. Moreover, a person is deemed to be still detaining the child, even though no longer in his possession, if he hands him over to a third person without the consent of the parent.[13] Where fraudulent means are employed there is no need to show whether those means affected the mind of any person.[14]

An odd feature of s. 56 is its proviso which states:

> No person who shall have claimed any right to the possession of such child or shall be the mother or shall have claimed to be the father of an illegitimate child shall be liable to be prosecuted . . . on account of the getting possession of such child, or taking such child out of the possession of any person having the lawful charge thereof.

Under the original enactment[15] the proviso was limited to protecting the father of the illegitimate child. Since he was not himself a parent, guardian or other person having the lawful care or charge of the child, his taking the child away from the mother would otherwise have been child-stealing. The law was not prepared to go to this length in its non-recognition of the putative father. Why the mother should have later been included in the proviso is not easy to decide. One would have thought that, since she is a parent, whether her child is legiti-

---

[11] *Cp. R.* v. *Pryce* [1972] Crim. L. R. 307.
[11a] *R.* v. *Powell* (1914), 24 Cox C.C. 229. *Cf.* abduction of girls *post*, p. 228.
[12] *R.* v. *Bellis* (1893), 17 Cox C.C. 660 (C.C.C.R.).
   If there is no fraud or force at all and the child goes off with the accused willingly but without the consent of the parent or guardian, it would constitute kidnapping.
[13] *R.* v. *Johnson* (1884), 15 Cox C.C. 481.
[14] *R.* v. *Smith* (1965), 115 L.J. 628 (C.C.A.).
[15] 54 Geo. 3, c. 101, s. 2.

mate or illegitimate,[16] she could not be guilty of child-stealing, so that the protection given by the proviso is unnecessary.[17] If, however, s. 56 would *prima facie* be available against her where she, having been deprived of custody, takes the child away from, say, the guardian, then the proviso has meaning. But if it has, the same argument could be advanced in respect of the father of a legitimate child; yet, he is not expressly included in the proviso. Probably the inclusion is to be explained by the fact that in 1861 rights of custody were only beginning to be accorded to the mother. The proviso, in so far as it refers to her, may have been intended to bolster her rights by protecting her from criminal liability if she took her legitimate child away from the father.

It has been pointed out[18] that the proviso strangely does not extend to cases of detaining the child, an omission which robs it of much of its value.

(3) Exposing Children under 12 to Risk of Burning

This and the following offence[19] deal with specific instances of lack of reasonable steps being taken to protect children from harm. It is concerned with children under the age of 12, an age limit higher than is generally realised. As with s. 1 of the 1933 Act, the duty is imposed on a person who, being 16 or over, has the custody, charge or care of the child, and the offence is committed if the child is allowed to be in a room containing an open fire grate or any heating appliance liable to cause injury by contact with it and the grate or appliance is not sufficiently protected to guard against the risk of his being burnt or scalded, with the result that the child is killed or suffers serious injury. Notwithstanding the need to prove such serious consequences the offence is only a summary one with a

[16] The proviso is not free from ambiguity. Presumably it refers to the mother of any child, but it is open to the possible interpretation that it means only the mother of an illegitimate child.

[17] In *R.* v. *Duguid* (1906), 21 Cox C.C.200, Lord ALVERSTONE, C. J. would have relied on the proviso for the mother's immunity from prosecution had it been necessary to do so. There it was held that such immunity did not prevent a person who conspired with the mother to remove her child from the possession of the lawful guardian from being guilty of conspiracy. *Quaere* whether the mother could also be convicted of conspiracy; see Smith and Hogan, *op. cit.*, p. 156.

[18] Smith and Hogan, p. 277.

[19] See ss. 11 and 12 respectively of the C. & Y.P. Act 1933. The former is amended by the C. & Y.P. (Amendment) Act 1952, ss. 8 and 9 and Sched. I.

maximum penalty of £10 fine, but this does not prevent prosecution for any appropriate indictable offence, *e.g.*, manslaughter if there has been gross negligence.

(4) Failure to Provide for Safety of Children at Entertainments

Anyone who provides in a building an entertainment for children[20] under 14 at which more than one hundred of them are present, must post there a sufficient number of adult attendants in order to prevent more persons being admitted than the building can accommodate, to control the movement of the children and others admitted while they enter and leave, and generally to take all other reasonable precautions for the children's safety. The occupier of the building, who for hire or reward permits the building to be used for entertainment must take all reasonable steps to see that the above precautions are observed. The offence is a summary one punishable with a fine,[1] but, in addition, if the building is licensed as a cinema, theatre or place for music or dancing, the licence is liable to be revoked.

Further control is exerted through the Cinematograph Act 1952[2] which requires the licensing authority to give its consent to the holding of any cinematograph exhibition organised wholly or mainly as an exhibition for children under 16. In so doing, the authority may impose conditions.[3]

(5) Supplying Intoxicating Liquor and Tobacco to Children and Cognate Offences

(i) *Intoxicating Liquor*

Most of the offences relating to this subject are primarily designed to protect the child from physical harm, but some are also concerned with moral protection. The big question mark to be placed against them is the extent to which they are observed and enforced.

---

[20] Or an entertainment at which the majority of those attending are children.
[1] Up to £50 for a first offence and up to £100 for a second or subsequent offence.
[2] Section 4. See also the Cinematograph (Children) (No. 2) Regulations 1955, S. I. 1955, No. 1909.
[3] Another kind of statutory provision concerned with the safety of children which may be noted here is that which empowers, though not compels, local authorities to provide school crossing patrols to control road traffic at places where children cross roads on their way to and from school; see the Road Traffic Regulation Act 1967, ss. 24 and 25.

The most widely known provisions are to be found in section 169 of the Licensing Act 1964, which makes it an offence (a) for a licensee knowingly to sell intoxicating liquor, or allow it to be sold, in licensed premises to a person under 18[4] or knowingly to allow such a person to consume liquor[5] in a bar, (b) for anyone to buy liquor for consumption in a bar by such a person and (c) for such a person to buy or consume liquor in those circumstances.[6] An exception is allowed enabling the sale of beer, porter, cider or perry to a person who has attained 16 for consumption at a table meal. For the licensee to be liable he must know[7] that the person has not attained 18, so that an honest belief that he has done so is a good defence.[8] It seems certain that anyone who buys liquor for consumption in a bar by a person under 18 must also have the knowledge, even though s. 169 does not expressly say so.[9]

Similar provisions forbid the delivery to a person under 18 of intoxicants to be consumed off the licensed premises, except where the delivery is made at the residence or, oddly, the working place of the purchaser, and forbid anyone to send such a person to obtain intoxicants for consumption off the premises.

[4] Evidence of age should be given, but the court may be able to act on its own visual evidence of the person; see *Wallworth* v. *Balmer*, [1965] 3 All E.R. 721, (D.C.).

[5] Since shandy is partly composed of beer, the sale or consumption of it may be contrary to s. 169; see *Hall* v. *Hyder*, [1966] 1 All E.R. 661, (D.C.).

[6] An offence under (a) and (b) is subject to a maximum fine of £25 on a first conviction and £50 on any further conviction, providing that for this purpose a conviction that took place more than five years previously is to be disregarded [s. 194(2)]). In the latter event, if the defendant is the licensee his licence may be forfeited. For an offence under (c) the maximum fine is £20.

[7] The knowledge of another person, *e.g.* a servant, will not be imputed to the licensee (*Emary* v. *Nolloth*, [1903] 2 K.B. 264; [1900-3] All E.R. Rep. 606, (D.C.), unless he has delegated his power and authority to the servant (*Allen* v. *Whitehead*), [1930] 1 K.B. 211; [1929] All E.R. Rep. 13, (D.C.); *Howker* v. *Robinson*, [1972] 2 All E.R. 786; [1972] 3 W.L.R. 234, (D.C.). [8] *Groom* v. *Grimes* (1903), 20 Cox C.C. 515, (D.C.).

[9] Compare sub-ss. (1) and (2) of s. 169 with sub-paras. (a) and (b) of s. 172, with the reference in sub-sec. (1) and para. (a) to knowledge and with no such reference in sub-s. (2) and para. (b). In *Sherras* v. *De Rutzen*, [1895] 1 Q.B. 918, (D.C.), which was concerned with interpreting provisions which para. (b) re-enacts, it was held that, notwithstanding the absence of express mention of knowledge, that was an essential element. But the further conclusion of DAY, J. that the effect of the omission was to shift the legal burden of proof on to the defendant to show that he did not have knowledge has been doubted; see DEVLIN, J. in *Roper* v. *Taylor's Central Garages, Exeter, Ltd.*, [1951] 2 T.L.R. 284. It would seem that the first principle, though probably not the second, enunciated in that case would apply to s. 169(2).

These provisions do not apply where the person under 18 is a member of the licensee's family or is his servant or apprentice and is employed as a messenger to deliver intoxicants.[10]

The Licensing Act 1964 also imposes restrictions on the employment and presence of children in a bar. A person under 18 cannot be employed there even if he receives no wages for his work,[11] and a child under 14 is not allowed to be there during the permitted hours of sale and consumption, unless he is the licensee's child or resides in the premises but is not employed there or uses the bar merely as a means of transit to other parts of the premises.[12] Proof of the child's presence renders the licensee liable unless he shows that he used due diligence to prevent the child's admission or that the child had apparently attained 14.

Other relevant offences affecting children are:
to give intoxicating liquor to a child under five unless ordered by a doctor or in a case of sickness, apprehended sickness or other urgent cause;[13]
to sell intoxicating liquor in confectionery to a person under 16, knowing him to be so;[14]
to be drunk in any highway or other public place or on any licensed premises while in charge of a child under seven.[15]

(ii) *Tobacco*

It is an offence to sell tobacco or cigarette papers to a person who is apparently under the age of 16.[16] Where cigarettes[17] or

---

[10] Licensing Act 1964, s. 169 (5) to (7).
[11] Section 170. The licensee may be fined up to £5 for a first conviction and, subject to s. 194(2) [*supra*, n. 6], £20 for a subsequent conviction.
[12] Section 168. The maximum fine is 40 shillings and, subject to s. 194(2), £5 for a subsequent conviction.
  Apart from any other person a local education authority may institute proceedings under this section.
[13] C. & Y.P. Act 1933, s. 5, as amended by the Criminal Justice Act 1967, s. 92 and Sched. III, Part I. The maximum penalty is a £10 fine.
[14] Licensing Act 1964, s. 167(2). The maximum penalty is a £10 fine or, on subsequent conviction, [subject to s. 194(2)], a £25 fine.
[15] Licensing Act 1902, s. 2, as amended by the Penalties for Drunkenness Act 1962, s. 1, which imposes a maximum penalty of £10 or one month's imprisonment.
[16] C. & Y.P. Act 1933, s. 7, as amended by C. & Y.P. Act 1963, s. 32.
  The maximum penalties are £25, £50, £100 for a first, second and subsequent offence respectively.
[17] The term covers cut tobacco rolled up in such form as to be capable of immediate use for smoking.

cigarette papers are sold the liability is strict in that it makes no difference whether they were for the buyer's use or not and whether or not the seller knew by whom they were to be used, but in the case of a sale of tobacco in any other form it is only when it is for the buyer's use and the seller knows or has reason to believe this that he will be liable. This, it is submitted is the construction to be put on the uncertain terms of the enactment.[18]

In order to counter partially the evasive effect which the widespread use of automatic vending machines has on the enactment, a magistrates' court, in a case where a machine is being extensively used by persons apparently under 16, may order the owner of the machine or the person on whose premises it is kept to take precautions to prevent it being so used or, if necessary, to remove it.[19]

Another power[20] conferred is that on a constable or uniformed park-keeper to seize any tobacco or cigarette papers in the possession of anyone apparently under 16 whom he finds smoking in any street or public place. It seems rarely to be exercised.

(6) Restrictions on Possession and Handling of Firearms by Juveniles

The main object of these restrictions, imposed by the Firearms Act 1968, is to protect others from the juvenile's inexperience in the use of firearms, but they also serve to protect him from possible harm to himself and may therefore be conveniently noted here.

The Act distinguishes shot guns and air weapons (*i.e.*, an air rifle, air gun or air pistol not of a type declared to be speci-

---

[18] Section 7(1) states:
"Any person who sells to a person apparently under the age of 16 years any tobacco or cigarette papers, whether for his own use or not, shall be liable . . .
Provided that a person shall not be guilty of an offence under this section in respect of any sale of tobacco otherwise than in the form of cigarettes, if he did not know and had no reason to believe that the tobacco was for the use of the person to whom it was sold."

[19] The maximum penalty for non-compliance is a fine of up to £50 and a further fine not exceeding £10 for each day during which the offence continues.

[20] C. & Y.P. Act 1933, s. 7(3).
None of the provisions in s. 7 applies to persons apparently under 16 who are employed by a manufacturer or dealer in tobacco.

ally dangerous) from all other firearms,[1] and the restrictions imposed on the acquisition, handling and possession of firearms by a juvenile depend partly on this classification and partly on the juvenile's age.[2] Thus,

- (i) no-one under 17 may purchase or hire any firearm or ammunition;
- (ii) subject to certain exceptions, no-one under 14 may have in his possession any firearm or ammunition. This restriction does not apply to a shot gun or air weapon;
- but (iii) no-one under 15 may have with him an assembled shot gun except while under the supervision of a person aged 21 or over or while the gun is so covered that it cannot be fired;
- and (iv) no-one under 14 may have with him an air weapon (or ammunition for it) except while under supervision or while using it at a rifle club or shooting gallery; and, subject to similar exceptions, this restriction extends to persons under 17 so far as having such a weapon in a public place.

The remarkable feature of these provisions is that they carry with them penalties imposable by magistrates' courts which conflict with basic rules relating to methods of dealing with juvenile offenders. As we have seen,[3] no imprisonment may be imposed by such (or any other) court on any juvenile under 17 and the maximum fine imposable by those courts is £10 on a child and £50 on a young person. Yet, offences under sub-paragraphs (i) and (ii) above are punishable with six months' imprisonment or a fine of £200 or both and under (iii) and (iv) with a fine of £50.

There are also provisions essentially corresponding with the above which create various offences for supplying firearms to juveniles, but they are subject to the general defence that the supplier reasonably believed that the juvenile was not under the age prescribed.[4]

---

[1] For this classification see s. 1, which, along with s. 2, makes the lawful possession of a firearm other than an air weapon normally depend on the holding of a firearm or shotgun certificate.
[2] See ss. 22 and 23.
[3] *Ante*, pp. 127 and 117.
[4] Firearms Act 1968, s. 24.

(7) Tattooing of Children

Many people, women as well as men, have grown up to regret the tattooist's needle. Its ultimate effects are surprisingly varied.[5] It may lead to social ostracism; it may cause difficulties over obtaining employment; it may impede the rehabilitation of prisoners; it may even create matrimonial problems; and, with the increasing demand for operations, under the National Health Service, to remove tattoos, it can be an additional charge on the taxpayer.

Until the Tattooing of Minors Act 1969, the tattooing of a consenting child was an offence[6] only if he was unable to appreciate the nature of the Act, in which case his consent was held to be ineffectual,[7] but the Act imposes a general prohibition on the tattooing of any person who is under 18, unless performed for medical reasons by a qualified medical practitioner or a person working under his direction. It is, however, a defence that the person charged had reasonable cause to believe and did believe that the person tattooed was of or over that age.[8]

This is the most recent statute designed to save the child from physical harm. Two other matters urgently calling for protective legislation concern drug addiction and the use of poisons in homes. It is remarkable that, while elaborate provisions are enacted with regard to consumption of alcohol and tobacco, there is nothing in the Drugs Acts 1965 and 1967 or in the Misuse of Drugs Act 1971, which is to replace those Acts, which imposes stiffer penalties on those who supply drugs to children.[9] In the same vein one may criticise the fact that while special provision is made for protection against fires in the home, there is no similar restriction on parents to ensure that their young children are protected from access to poisonous substances.[10]

---

[5] See Post, *Relationship of Tattoos to Personality Disorders*, 59 J. Crim. L., Criminol & P.S. 516.

[6] *I.e.*, assault or assault causing actual bodily harm.

[7] *Burrell* v. *Harmer* (1966), 116 New L.J. 1658 (D.C.).

[8] The penalty on summary conviction is a fine of up to £50, or for a further conviction, £100.

[9] There is evidence of increasing incidence of drug addiction among children under 16, even as low as the age of 12.

[10] The Royal Society for the Prevention of Accidents has estimated that in 1966 over 12,000 children were admitted to hospital after ingesting poison and that 20 times that number were treated at home.

D. LAWFUL CORRECTION OF CHILDREN

Even the crude Anglo-Saxon laws did not give the head of the family powers of life and death over his children, but that was about the limit to the control which he exercised over them. Gradually, but by a process that has not been traced, his powers were attenuated and the common law came to accept the principle that the father was entitled to administer reasonable corporal chastisement over his legitimate children as an incident of his right of custody.

This right to punish is shared by the mother, but it is equally uncertain when this came to be so. So long as the parents lived together the question would not, in practice, arise, since correction was a matter for the father. On his death, however, the mother was entitled to the custody of her infant children for nurture[11] – unless, after 1660, the father appointed a testamentary guardian[12] – and, therefore, the right to punish them apparently became exercisable by her. Exceptionally, too, where the marriage broke up and the father had grossly ill-treated the children, she might acquire custody. Whatever the origin of her right it is clear that, once the mother's claims to custody began to be recognised by equity and then by legislation, the recognition of the incidental right to punish would necessarily follow, and her present equality with the father in respect of the one extends to the other. As for the mother of the illegitimate child, the recognition of her right to punish has, it seems, in a similar way depended on the gradual, but late, recognition of her right to custody.

A person *in loco parentis* also has this right to punish.[13] The test for determining whether anyone stands in that relationship to a child may vary in emphasis for different legal purposes. In the present context the test seems to be whether the care and control[14] of the child has been entrusted to the person by the parent or, where the parent is absent or there is

---

[11] *R. v. Clarke* (1857), 7 E. & B. 186, 200.

[12] By virtue of the Tenures Abolition Act 1660.

[13] As did the master over his apprentice, but his right is obsolete.

[14] The law reports usually refer to the "charge" of the child, but for reasons advanced earlier, (*ante*, p. 195), the term "care and control" is, it is suggested, preferable. See also *ante* p. 199.

In relation to raising the presumptions of satisfaction and ademption in equity the emphasis is on whether the donor has taken upon himself the duty of a parent to make provision for the child; see JESSEL, M. R., in *Bennet* v. *Bennet* (1879), 10 Ch. D. 474, 477, citing with approval Lord Eldon in *Ex parte Pye* (1811), 18 Ves. 140 and Lord COTTENHAM in

no parent, is assumed by that person.[15] But anyone living with the parent cannot assume his rights without his authority, even though the parent may temporarily be absent. Thus in *R.* v. *Woods*[16] an elder brother was held not to be entitled to punish a younger, since the father had not placed him *in loco parentis*. With that case may be compared that of the step parent who, with the natural parent's consent, assumes care and control. In addition to delegation or assumption, the right to punish will arise wherever custody and/or care and control are entrusted by an order of the court to any person. Accordingly the right may, for example, be exercised by an adoptive parent, guardian or local authority.

It is on the principle of parental delegation that the right of a school authority to inflict corporal punishment has been traditionally explained, but more recently it has been suggested that the authority's right is an independent one.[17] The point is important because on it depends whether a parent can lawfully forbid the school to administer punishment. It must be remembered that the older view was formulated before the introduction of compulsory education,[18] in cases where a contractual relationship existed between the parent and school authority and there could fairly be said to be delegation,[19] but to rely on that principle now is unrealistic in view of the parental duty to secure the child's education. Nevertheless, modern authorities have reaffirmed the old principle.[20]

Powys v. *Mansfield* (1837), 3 My. & Cr. 359, 367. The same test seems to be used in deciding whether a presumption of advancement has displaced a presumption of resulting trust where property is purchased in the name of a child.

[15] As, for example, in the case of a foster parent; *cf. R.* v. *Cheeseman* (1836), 7 C. & P. 455, (assumption of care and control by an aunt).

[16] (1921), 85 J.P. 272.

[17] See Street, *Torts*, 5th edn., pp. 87-88. See also Smith and Hogan, *op. cit.*, p. 257.   [18] By the Elementary Education Acts 1870 and 1876.

[19] For the principle of delegation much reliance has been placed on the judgments of COCKBURN, C. J. in *R.* v. *Hopley* (1860), 2 F & F. 202, 206 and *Fitzgerald* v. *Northcote* (1865), 4 F. & F. 656, 689; but see the footnote to the latter case where it is pointed out that Hawkins (P.C. 150) seems to place the parent, master and schoolmaster "on the same footing" with regard to the right to punish. This suggests an early willingness to treat the teacher independently. *Cf.* the same tendency in s. 1(7) of C. & Y.P. Act 1933, which expressly refers to the teacher: "Nothing in this section shall be construed as affecting the right of any parent, teacher or other person having the lawful control or charge of a child or young person to administer punishment to him".

[20] See *Mansell* v. *Griffin*, [1908] 1 K.B. 160 (D.C.); *R.* v. *Newport (Salop) Justices*, [1929] 2 K.B. 416 (D.C.).

The teacher's power, be it delegated or independent, is not limited to the conduct of a pupil on the school premises, but may extend to acts done while on the way to and from school[1] and even beyond,[2] and it includes not only the power to inflict corporal punishment but also to detain, save that detention after school hours for not doing home lessons is not permitted, at least if the school is administered by a local authority under the Education Act 1944, since that Act does not authorise the setting of home lessons.[3]

Punishment may only be lawfully administered if it is moderate and reasonable. If these standards are broken the parent *etc.* is criminally and tortiously liable.[4] In applying the standards obviously relevant factors are the nature and degree of the punishment. Thus, for example, caning is regarded as a proper method,[5] providing that it is not excessive,[6] but boxing on the ear is not.[7] It is also excessive if administered for the gratification of passion or rage or protracted beyond the child's powers of endurance.[8] If it results in death it almost inevitably means that it was immoderate, although that would not necessarily follow if the child's constitution was abnormally sensitive[9] and the parent *etc.* did not know this. In the case of the teacher-pupil relationship it is submitted that it would be unreasonable to inflict physical chastisement for breach of an unreasonable school rule, even though the degree of force used was not unreasonable.[10] In addition to moderation and reasonableness, punishment is only lawful if the child is capable of appreciating correction.[11]

[1] *Cleary* v. *Booth*, [1893] 1 Q.B. 465.
[2] *R.* v. *Newport (Salop) Justices, supra,* (smoking in street having left school for the day).
[3] *Hunter* v. *Johnson* (1884), 13 Q.B.D. 225.
[4] Immigrants must conform to the standard of behaviour acceptable in England, and it is thus not a defence to a charge of assault to show that the standard of parental correction is harsher in the foreign native country; *R.* v. *Derriviere* (1969) 53 Cr. App. Rep. 637, (C.A.).
[5] *Gardner* v. *Bygrave* (1889), 6 T.L.R. 23, (D.C.).
[6] *R.* v. *Cheeseman* (1836), 7 C. & P. 455.
[7] *Ryan* v. *Fildes*, [1938] 3 All E.R. 517.
[8] See COCKBURN, C. J. in *R.* v. *Hopley* (1860), 2 F. & F. 202, 206.
[9] *Cf. R.* v. *Woods* (1921), 85 J.P. 272, where such a condition existed, but in any event the chastisement was not justified; see *supra.*
[10] *Cf. R.* v. *Newport (Salop) Justices*, [1929] 2 K.B. 416, (D.C.), (school rule against smoking held not unreasonable).
[11] *R.* v. *Griffin* (1869), 11 Cox 402, where a child two and a half years old was held not to be capable. Similarly there would be no right to punish a child who was mentally disordered.

CHAPTER 7

The Penal Protection of Children
11. Moral Harm

A. OFFENCES OTHER THAN SEXUAL OFFENCES

Under this heading are grouped various statutory provisions, most of which are aimed at protecting the juvenile from influences which may harm his character and moral upbringing but a few of which are designed to save him from mental strain and embarrassment. One or other object is to be found in the first group to be mentioned.

I. PROTECTION OF JUVENILES IN RELATION TO JUDICIAL PROCEEDINGS

This protection is given by a number of provisions in Part III of the Children and Young Persons Act 1933,[1] some of which have already been noted.

(1) Separation of Juveniles from Adults

Thus, we have seen[2] that, in order to minimise the risk of contact with hardened criminals, arrangements must normally be made for keeping juveniles apart from adult defendants both while they are at a police station and during the course of attending any criminal court.[3] Moreover, during such times a girl must be under the care of a woman,[4] and if the juvenile is attending as a witness he should have a trusted adult close at hand at all times, especially when giving evidence.[5]

(2) Provisions Relating to the Attendance of Juveniles at Court

No child[6] (other than an infant in arms) is allowed to be

---

[1] As extended by C. & Y.P. Act 1963.
[2] *Ante*, pp. 62 and 67.
[3] C. & Y.P. Act 1933, s. 31.
[4] *Ibid.*
[5] Home Office Circular No. 208/1964.
[6] The rule does not apply to a young person.

present in court during the trial of any other person who is charged with an offence or during any proceedings preliminary thereto, except during such time as his presence is required as a witness or otherwise for the purpose of justice.[7]

There are also provisions designed to minimise tension and embarrassment when a juvenile has to give evidence in adult courts. If the proceedings relate to an offence or conduct contrary to decency or morality, which, it seems, here means sexual morality or decency, the court is empowered, though not compelled, to hear his or her evidence in camera, with only those directly concerned in the case and newspaper representatives being present.[8] It is advisable that the court be cleared before the juvenile enters.[9] This protection extends to anyone who, in the court's opinion, is a child or young person. It is suggested that this procedure should be made compulsory and not left to the court's discretion. The interests of the juvenile will always be best served by it, without those of the parties to the case being prejudiced.

Where the offence is a sexual one (which for this purpose means any offence under the Sexual Offences Act 1956 or the Indecency with Children Act 1960 or any attempt to commit such an offence)[10] and it is to be tried on indictment, a child, as opposed to a young person, who is to be called as a witness for the prosecution must not normally be called to give oral evidence at the committal proceedings. Instead, at that stage a written statement by him is admitted,[11] in so far as it complies with the rules of admissibility of evidence. This leaves him to give his oral evidence at the trial itself[12] and saves him a

---

[7] C. & Y.P. Act 1933, s. 36.
There is a proviso that the rule does not apply to messengers and the like who are required to attend court for purposes connected with their employment, but it is very doubtful whether children are ever so employed; in any event they would have to be at least 13 years old (see *post*, p. 449). There ought to be an absolute prohibition on such employment.

[8] Section 37.   [9] Home Office Circular No. 208/1964.

[10] For these offences see *post*, pp. 219 *et seq.*

[11] The officer who took the statement should be called to produce it and prove that it was made by or taken from the child; see H.O. Circular No. 17/1964.

[12] C. & Y.P. Act 1963, s. 27.
Since this enactment wider recognition has been given to the use of written statements before examining justices; see Criminal Justice Act 1967, s. 2.

double appearance in court.[13] The procedure is not, however, permitted if the defence objects to it, or the prosecution requires the child's attendance in order to identify a person, or the inquiry into the offence takes place after the court has discontinued to try it summarily and the child has given evidence in the summary trial, or the child is being called as a witness for the defence.

Other provisions of the 1933 Act relieve a juvenile of the duty of giving oral evidence where he has been the victim of any of the offences listed in Schedule I to that Act. In such a case the court may wholly dispense with the child's attendance if satisfied that it is not essential to the just hearing of the case,[14] but its discretion should be exercised cautiously, since it is more likely than not that the juvenile's evidence will be essential for a just hearing, especially as otherwise the accused is deprived of the opportunity of cross-examination. Special powers also exist concerning the use of depositions where his attendance "would involve serious danger to his life or health". Section 42 of the Act empowers a justice, who is satisfied on medical evidence that there would be such a danger, to take a deposition of the juvenile, which, under s. 43, is then admissible in evidence without further proof if the court of trial is similarly satisfied of the danger.[15] However, the deposition is not admissible *against* the accused unless he had reasonable notice of the intention to take the deposition and he or his legal representative had had an opportunity to cross-examine the juvenile.

There is room for further protecting the juvenile who has to give evidence. The Home Office has recommended,[16] at least in a sexual case, that the hearing should be on a fixed

---

[13] But the child must give oral evidence on at least one occasion. Hence the provision (in s. 27(3)) that s. 23 of the Magistrates' Courts Act 1952 shall not apply to any statement admitted under s. 27 of the 1963 Act. S. 23 of the former Act provides that, in a case where an inquiry into an offence is followed by summary trial, evidence given for the purposes of the inquiry is treated as having been given for the purposes of the trial.

[14] C. & Y.P. Act 1933, s. 41. See *R.* v. *Hale*, [1905] 1 K.B. 126, (C.C.C.R.).

[15] The court may similarly admit under s. 43 a deposition taken in the ordinary way in committal proceedings under the Magistrates' Courts Act 1952. Since the First Schedule to the 1933 Act includes some of the offences in the Sexual Offences Act 1956 and offences under the Indecency with Children Act 1960 the powers conferred by ss. 42 and 43 must, it is submitted, in relation to those offences be read subject to the overriding ones of s. 27 of the 1963 Act, *supra*.

[16] Home Office Circular No. 208/1964.

215

date, as early as possible in the day's list, with the juvenile giving his evidence early in the proceedings and then being released from attendance. But these admirable arrangements ought not to be left to the discretion and goodwill of those who arrange the court's business: they should be the subject of a statutory duty in all cases. Another defect in the present rules is that they do not place on the prosecution a duty to draw the court's special attention to them. Again, ss. 42 and 43 are too restrictive and ought, as the Ingleby Committee recommended,[17] to be amended so that the powers thereunder may be invoked where the juvenile's attendance "would involve injury to his health". Improvements of this kind can be made without disturbing the balance between the welfare of the juvenile witness and the right of the accused to receive a fair trial.[18] The problem of cross-examination is, however, a different matter and may give rise to a sharp conflict between the respective interests of the juvenile and the accused. To deny any cross-examination would clearly favour the one but prejudice the other. On the other hand to allow it to proceed too far may place an unbearable strain on the juvenile, particularly if he is a young child. The court should, therefore, be ready to impose limits. Of course, if the juvenile is himself the defendant any limit imposed will work in his favour. Still, the point may be reached where he is so distressed that to permit further questioning would be "a travesty of justice".[19] It is difficulties of this kind which bolster the argument for abolishing the criminal prosecution of children under fourteen.

(3) Protection Against Publicity

We have already considered[20] the restrictions on newspaper and broadcast reports of proceedings in, or on appeal from,

---

[17] Cmnd. 1191, para. 261.
[18] See, as illustrations of the protection given to the accused, his right to object to a written statement under s. 27 of the 1963 Act, *supra*, and the rule that depositions are not admissible against him under ss. 42 and 43 of the 1933 Act, *supra*, if he has not had the chance to cross-examine. Note also the rule that if a child of tender years gives unsworn evidence (under s. 38 of the 1933 Act) on behalf of the prosecution there must be corroborative evidence.
[19] So described by CUSACK, J. during the trial at Newcastle Assizes of two girls, aged 13 and 11 who were jointly accused of murdering two small boys; see *The Guardian Newspaper*, 12 December 1968.
[20] *Ante*, p. 68.

magistrates' courts[1] or of proceedings in any court in which a juvenile has been concerned whether as a party or a witness.[2]

II. PROTECTION FROM HARMFUL PUBLICATIONS

The law of obscenity to some extent protects juveniles and adolescents from the corrupting influences of certain kinds of publications, but no more than it protects the public at large. The test of obscenity is whether the article is such as to tend to deprave and corrupt persons who are likely to read, see or hear it.[3] In applying this test the possible effect of the work on young people is an important factor,[4] but it is not overriding, unless the work is primarily intended for them, because as STABLE, J., put it:[5]

"A mass of literature, great literature, from many angles is wholly unsuitable for reading by the adolescent, but that does not mean that a publisher is guilty of a criminal offence for making those works available to the general public."

Even if the work is mainly intended for the young it may still be doubtful whether it is obscene. The scope of the offence is notoriously uncertain and it was for this reason that it was found necessary to enact the Children and Young Persons (Harmful Publications) Act 1955 in order to put a stop to the widespread publication of "horror comics", ghoulish pictorial publications which were calculated to stimulate brutish emotions in young people. The Act accordingly applies to any "book, magazine or other work" having the following characteristics.[6]

(i) It is of a kind likely to fall into the hands of a juvenile.

(ii) It consists wholly or mainly of stories told in pictures, whether with or without written matter: the picture tells the story.

---

[1] C. & Y.P. Act 1933, s. 49, as amended by C. & Y.P. Act 1969, s. 10.
[2] *Ibid.*, s. 39.
[3] Obscene Publications Act 1959, s. 1(1) A number of other enactments also forbid publication of harmful material. These include the Vagrancy Act 1824, s. 4 and the Vagrancy Act 1838, s. 2; The Metropolitan Police Act 1839, s. 54(12) and the Town Police Clauses Act 1847, s. 28; the Indecent Advertisements Act 1889; the Judicial Proceedings (Regulation of Reports) Act 1926; and the Post Office Act 1953, s. 11.
[4] *R. v. Reiter*, [1954] 1 All E.R. 741 (C.C.A.).
[5] In *R. v. Martin Secker and Warburg Ltd.*, [1954] 2 All E.R. 683, 686.
[6] Section 1.

(iii) The story portrays the commission of crimes, acts of violence or cruelty or incidents of a repulsive or horrible nature.

(iv) The portrayal is in such a way that the work as a whole would tend to corrupt a juvenile into whose hands it might fall.

Anyone who prints, publishes, sells, lets on hire or has in his possession[7] any such work is guilty of an offence, but it is open to him to prove that he had not examined its contents and had no reasonable cause to suspect that the work was one to which the Act applies.[8] The efficacy of the Act is shown by the fact that horror comics are now unknown; indeed, even while the Bill was before Parliament there was a dramatic decline in circulation. Today it is other forms of "publication" which raise questions of possible harmful effects on the young.[9]

III PROTECTION FROM GAMBLING

Certain provisions in the Betting, Gaming and Lotteries Act 1963 are specifically aimed at protecting the young from the temptations of gambling. Thus, the Act[10] makes it an offence for anyone to effect with or through a young person any betting transaction[11] or to employ him in a licensed betting office. A young person here means one who either (a) is under 18 and whom the other person knows or ought to know is under that age or (b) is apparently under 18. No betting circulars may be sent to anyone known to be under 18 and, if such a circular is sent to a person at a place of education and he is under that age, the sender is deemed to have known that the addressee is under age, unless he proves that he has reasonable grounds for believing the contrary.[12]

The Gaming Act 1968 forbids anyone under 18 taking part in certain forms of gaming in public houses in which adults are allowed to participate,[13] and no one under that age is allowed

---

[7] There is a power to search for and seize any offending work (s. 3).

[8] Section 2.

[9] But present evidence throws doubt on the view that the representation of violence on television is a main cause of juvenile delinquency. Compare the second and third reports of the Television Research Committee (1969-70, Leicester University Press).

[10] Section 21.

[11] Using a young person to effect such a transaction by post is, however, permitted.

[12] Section 22, as amended by the Family Law Reform Act 1969, s. 1(3) and Sched. I.   [13] Section 7.

in a room in licensed premises, clubs or institutes while gaming takes place.[14] A licensing authority must refuse to register, or to renew registration of a club or institute for the use of gaming machines if the premises are frequented wholly or mainly by persons under 18.[15]

IV. MISCELLANEOUS FORMS OF PROTECTION FROM MORAL HARM

There are a few enactments contained, or originating, in the Children and Young Persons Act 1933 which offer special protection to juveniles. They are not directly inter-related but may be grouped together on the basis that they all seek to prevent juveniles from participating in undesirable dealings.

Thus, it is an offence[16] for anyone to cause or procure a juvenile under 16 to be in a street, premises or place for the purpose of begging.[17] This is also committed by anyone who, having custody, charge or care of the juvenile, allows him to be in such places and it is proved that the juvenile was there for the purpose of begging. The onus is on the defendant to prove that he did not allow the juvenile to be there for that purpose. Apart from criminal liability, in such circumstances it may be appropriate to bring the juvenile before the juvenile court as being in need of care or control.

Pawnbrokers are forbidden to take an article in pawn from anyone apparently under 14[18] and scrap metal dealers must not acquire scrap metal from those apparently under 16.[19] It is a defence to prove that the juvenile was of or over the specified age.

B. SEXUAL OFFENCES

Further penal protection of children is provided by the sanctions imposed in respect of sexual offences, almost all of which are to be found enacted in the Sexual Offences Acts 1956 and 1967. Most of these relate to adults and children alike, but

[14] Section 17. They may, however, attend bingo clubs provided they do not participate (ss. 20(6) and 21(4)).   [15] Section 30 and Sched. 7, para. 7.

[16] Maximum penalty on summary conviction is £25 fine or three months' imprisonment or both.

[17] C. & Y.P. Act 1933, s. 4, as amended by C. & Y.P. Act 1963, s. 64(1) and Sched. III, para. 3.

[18] *Ibid.*, s. 8. There is a similar offence under s. 50 of the Metropolitan Police Act 1839 which applies to transactions in the Metropolitan area involving juveniles apparently under 16.

[19] Scrap Metal Dealers Act 1964, s. 5(1), replacing C. & Y.P. Act 1933, s. 9.

others are concerned only with children. They are dealt with on that basis and also according to whether the victim is a girl or boy.

I. PROTECTION OF GIRLS

General Protection

Many of the provisions of the Act of 1956 apply whatever the age of the woman victim may be. They include those dealing with rape and kindred offences involving unlawful sexual intercourse by force, intimidation or fraud (ss. 1-4), or with mental defectives (ss. 7 and 9,)[20] incest (s. 10), indecent assault (s. 14), abduction (ss. 17 and 21) and offences relating to prostitution (ss. 22, 24, 27 and 29).[1] But even some of these may have special application if the victim is a girl.

Thus, while every successful prosecution of rape requires proof of absence of consent, in the case of a girl under 16 who is not proved to have physically resisted the act it will be enough to show that her understanding and knowledge were such that she was not in a position to decide whether to consent or resist[2] and for this purpose she may be so young that little, if any, evidence other than her age will be required,[3] although there is not a prescribed age limit below which rape must be held to have been committed.[4]

Incest carries a heavier maximum penalty, of imprisonment for life instead of for seven years, if it is committed with a girl under 13 and is so charged in the indictment.[5] If committed or attempted with a girl under 18, the trial court may divest the man of "all authority" which he has over her.[6] Where she is under 17, the effective method of doing this would, it is sug-

---

[20] See also the Mental Health Act 1959, s. 128 (member of hospital staff having unlawful sexual intercourse with a mentally disordered woman patient or a man having intercourse with such a patient when she is subject to his guardianship, custody or care under the Act).

[1] See also ss. 30-31 and 33-36.

[2] *R.* v. *Howard*, [1965] 3 All E.R. 684, (C.C.A.); [1966] 1 W.L.R. 13.

[3] *R.* v. *Harling*, [1938] 1 All E.R. 307, (C.C.A.). The genuine consent of a girl under 16 is recognised by law to a limited extent, *viz.*, to negative a charge of rape, but the accused in such a case may be guilty of other offences, *infra*, p. 221.

[4] At one time, if the girl was at least 10 years old, proof that the act was against her will was necessary, but if she was under that age the offence was committed whether it was with or against her will; see *infra*.

[5] Sexual Offences Act 1956, s. 37 and Sched. II, (14). For attempted incest with a girl under 13 the penalty is also heavier, namely seven years instead of two; see Indecency with Children Act 1960, s. 2.

[6] *Ibid.*, s. 38(1), as amended by the Family Law Reform Act 1969, s. 1(3) and Sched. I.

220

gested, be for the court to order that she be brought before the juvenile court as being in need of care or control, so that the latter court may make a care order. If the man is the girl's guardian the trial court may also order him to be removed from the guardianship and appoint someone else as guardian during the girl's minority or for any lesser period.[7] The term "guardian" is normally understood to mean a person other than the parent who is appointed to the office by deed, will or order of the court.[8] Because of the definition of incest[9] the only persons who could qualify would be the girl's grandfather or brother. It seems clear, however, that the present provision also applies to the father who, *stricto sensu*, is by law her guardian, at least if she is legitimate. If so, instead of relying on the care or control procedure suggested above, the court could wholly deprive him of his parental rights by appointing a guardian in his place.

The offence of indecent assault on a woman[10] also has special application if the victim is a girl under 16, because, if she is, she cannot give any consent which, in the case of a person of or over that age, would be a defence.[11] To this rule there is one qualification. If the girl has married – which necessarily means that her marriage is void for lack of age,[12] unless both parties have a foreign personal law which recognises the marriage as valid[13] – the man cannot be guilty of the offence because of her incapacity to consent, if he believes her to be his wife and has reasonable cause for his belief. The case of a girl under 16 who is polygamously married will be considered later.[14]

[7] Section 38(2) and (3).
   Any order under s. 38 may be varied from time to time or rescinded by the High Court. Moreover if the girl is defective, the order may, so far as it has effect for the purposes of the Mental Health Act 1959, be rescinded before or after the girl has attained 18; see s. 127(2) of the 1959 Act, as amended by the Family Law Reform Act 1969, s. 1(3) and Sched. I.

[8] *Cf.* the distinction drawn by the C. & Y.P. Act 1933, s. 107(1), between "guardian" and "legal guardian".

[9] Section 10 of the Sexual Offences Act 1956 states that "it is an offence for a man to have sexual intercourse with a woman whom he knows to be his grand-daughter, daughter, sister or mother".

[10] Sexual Offences Act 1956, s. 14.

[11] If she is under 13, the maximum penalty for conviction on indictment is also heavier, namely, five years instead of the normal two; see Indecency with Children Act 1960, s. 2.

[12] Marriage Act 1949, s. 2; Nullity of Marriage Act 1971, s. 1.

[13] See further *infra*, p. 224.

[14] See *infra*, p. 224, and note *ibid.* the question of the defendant's belief that the girl is 16 or over.

221

Special Protection

1. *Unlawful Sexual Intercourse with Girls under Sixteen*

Legislation dealing with the corruption of girls has a long history. It began[15] with the Statute of Westminster I, 1275, which made it an offence, punishable by two years' imprisonment and fine and at the King's pleasure, to ravish "any maiden without age", whether she gave her consent or not. The Statute of Westminster II, 1285, made it a felony punishable by death. The history of these two enactments is not wholly clear. It seems that initially the term "within age" was understood to mean "under twelve years", that being then the age of discretion,[16] but gradually it became established that if the girl was between 10 and 12 it was not the felony of rape if she consented. However, it seems that in the latter case the earlier Statute was invoked and the case was treated as a misdemeanour to which the lesser penalty attached.[17] If this be so, the effect of an Act of 1576[18] which made carnal knowledge of a girl under 10 a felony without benefit of clergy, whether she consented or not, was merely to restate the law with regard to girls under that age without affecting those between 10 and 12. This early legislation was repealed by an Act of 1828[19] which clarified the law by distinguishing between the felony of carnal knowledge of a girl under 10 and the misdemeanour of carnal knowledge of a girl over 10 and under 12. Subsequent legislation,[20] though eventually raising the ages to under 13 and over 13 but under 16 respectively, has preserved the distinction, which is now to be found in ss. 5 and 6 of the Sexual Offences Act 1956. These provisions have, however, been amended by the Criminal Law Act 1967, not only by its abolition of the division of indictable offences into felonies and misdemeanours, but also by amending s. 6 so that the lesser offence applies to any girl under 16,

---

[15] Anglo-Saxon law does not seem to have dealt separately with defilement of girls. One of Alfred's Laws (Cap. 11) was concerned with sexual offences against "young women" but these were not defined, and, although another (Cap. 29) referred to rape of a girl "not of age" (also not defined), the compensation payable was no greater than if she was of age.

[16] See 1 Hale P.C. 631.

[17] 4 Bl. Comm. 212. See also Russell, *Crime*, 12th edn., p. 715, n. 63.

[18] 18 Eliz. I, c. 7.

[19] 9 Geo. 4, c. 31.

[20] See successively the Offences Against the Person Act 1861; Offences Against the Person Act 1875; Criminal Law Amendment Act 1885; Sexual Offences Act 1956.

instead of, as formerly, to a girl over 13 but under 16.[1] This latter change is a minor one, for a man who has unlawful sexual intercourse with a girl under 13 will in practice still be charged with the more serious offence under s. 5, but the amendment enables an alternative verdict to be given[2] on the lesser offence under s. 6, for example, where from the evidence there is doubt as to whether the girl is under 13.[3]

The policy of protection which underlies so much of the Act of 1956 accounts for the rule that the girl's consent is not material to either of the offences under ss. 5 and 6.[4] Nor can it render the girl herself liable for aiding and abetting, or inciting to commit, either offence.[5] The same reason explains the undoubted acceptance of the view that the defendant's belief that the girl was not under age (*i.e.*, not under 13 or not under 16, as the case may be) is no defence. This conclusion is inevitable in view of the fact that such a defence has been firmly rejected in relation to the offences of abduction of a girl under 16[6] and indecent assault of a girl under that age.[7] The Act admits an exception if the offence is under s. 6 and the defendant is under 24, has not previously been charged with a like offence[8] and with reasonable cause believes the girl is under 16,[9] but the effect of the exception is to produce the "grotesque state of affairs"[10] that his belief is a defence to a charge of unlawful sexual intercourse but not to the lesser charge of indecent assault.

Where the defendant is married to the girl but the marriage is invalid under s. 2 of the Marriage Act 1949 because of her

[1] Criminal Law Act 1967, s. 10 and Sched. II, para. 14.
[2] In accordance with the Criminal Law Act 1967, s. 6(3).
It should, however, be noted that this enactment does not enable an alternative verdict of guilt of an offence under s. 5 or under s. 6 to be given where the offence charged is rape; see *R. v. Fisher, Marshall and Mitchell*, [1969] 1 All E.R. 265.
[3] The maximum penalty for an offence under s. 5 is imprisonment for life and for an attempt seven years (Indecency with Children Act 1960, s. 2).
[4] *R. v. Neale* (1844), 1 Den. 36; [1938] 1 All *R. v. Harling*, E.R. 307, (C.C.A.). See similarly s. 14(2), *supra*.
[5] *R. v. Tyrrell*, [1894] 1 Q.B. 710; [1891-4] All E.R. Rep. 1215.
[6] *R. v. Prince* (1875), L.R. 2 C.C.R. 154.
[7] *R. v. Maughan* (1934), 24 Cr. App. Rep. 130.
[8] *I.e.*, an offence under s. 6 or an attempt to commit one.
[9] Reasonable cause is not enough: the defendant must in fact have believed; *R. v. Banks*, [1916] 2 K.B. 621. Therefore it follows that the defendant who wishes to rely on this defence must have directed his mind to the question of age. If he was indifferent to it, the defence is not available to him; *R. v. Harrison*, [1938] 3 All E.R. 134, (C.C.A.).
[10] See *R. v. Laws* (1928), 21 Cr. App. Rep. 45 at p. 46.

non-age, it is still a defence to a charge under s. 6 of the 1956 Act that he believed on reasonable grounds that she was his wife and accordingly had sexual intercourse with her.[11] Section 2 of the Marriage Act applies whether both parties, or only one of them, are domiciled in England, and in the latter case whether it is the party under 16 or the one over 16[12] who has the English domicile. Thus, for example, a man domiciled in England who has married abroad a fourteen-year-old girl whose ante-nuptial domiciliary law permits her to marry will be able to rely on the above defence if charged under s. 6 of the 1956 Act. If both parties are domiciled abroad and their marriage is invalid because the fourteen-year-old girl is under age by her ante-nuptial personal law, and if the parties then come to this country, the defence provided in s. 6 would not, it is submitted, be available, since the marriage would not be invalid under s. 2 of the Marriage Act, but under the foreign law.[13] Nevertheless, it is suggested that, if in such a case the defendant did believe his marriage was valid, a defence by analogy to that in s. 6 should be admitted. Where, on the other hand, the marriage is valid by the parties' foreign personal law, there cannot be any liability under s. 6, because the sexual intercourse, taking place within the bonds of marriage, would be lawful.[14] In *Mohamed* v. *Knott*[15] the Divisional Court expressed the view that this principle would also apply if the parties' marriage were polygamous, providing that it is valid by the foreign law. Nor in this latter kind of case would it make any difference if the man acquired an English domicile while the wife was still under 16. Their union would still be a marriage and there would, it is submitted, be no reason to inquire whether the change of domicile has converted it into a monogamous relationship.[16] A question still to be settled is whether

[11] *Cf.* s. 14 of the 1956 Act, *supra*, p. 221.
[12] *Pugh* v. *Pugh*, [1951] P. 482; [1951] 2 All E.R. 680.
[13] It is, however, noteworthy that, although the long title to the Marriage Act refers to consolidation of "certain enactments relating to the solemnization and registration of marriages in England", this did not prevent the court in *Pugh* v. *Pugh*, (*supra*) from applying s. 2 to a marriage celebrated abroad.
[14] *Cf. R.* v. *Chapman*, [1959] 1 Q.B. 100, (C.C.A.); [1958] 3 All E.R. 143, *post*, p. 229.
[15] [1968] 2 All E.R. 563; [1968] 2 W.L.R. 1446. For the main point of this case see *ante*, Chapter 4, p. 96.

the validity of a foreign marriage of a girl under 13 could also
be invoked as a defence to a charge under s. 5 of the 1956 Act
on the ground that any sexual intercourse would then be lawful.
The answer must depend on how far as a matter of public
policy the English court would be prepared to go in recognising
the incidents of such a marriage. Would it, for example, apply
the factual test of whether the particular girl had attained
puberty, or would it prescribe a minimum age below which it
would refuse recognition.[17]

The current permissive attitude towards teenage sexuality
has raised doubts about the extent to which sexual intercourse
with a girl between 13 and 16 should remain an offence, particularly as the police seem to exercise considerable discretion in
deciding whether to prosecute. It has been questioned[18]
whether it is right that young men should be prosecuted for this
offence. "If a child is born to such a girl, it gives the three
young people a pretty poor start in life if the police prosecute
the father." With great respect, this view is open to objections.
Firstly, there is the general one that the law, having committed
itself to the principle that the age of marriage and the age of
consent to sexual intercourse should be the same, a principle
firmly approved of by the Latey Committee,[19] it should not be
its function, even indirectly, to encourage illicit sexual per-
missiveness. Secondly, it is a truism that, once it is sought to
exempt a class of persons from the operation of a rule, one
invites difficulties. Is it intended that the proposed privilege
should attach to all "young men"? Or is it only to apply where

[16] *Cf. Ali* v. *Ali*, [1968] P. 564; [1966] 1 All E.R. 664, where conversion was
necessary to enable the English court to assume divorce jurisdiction. See
now the Matrimonial Proceedings (Polygamous Marriages) Act 1972.
[17] *Cf.* Dicey and Morris, *Conflict of Laws*, 8th edn., p. 75; Karsten 32
M.L.R. 212.
    The extent to which an English court will take account of foreign ways
of life may also be relevant in cases of unlawful sexual intercourse with
girls under 16 where the accused and the victim are not married, in that
the foreign background may mitigate the gravity of the offence and affect
sentence; see *R.* v. *Byfield* (*Times*, April 19, 1967) where the accused
and the girl, aged 14½, were both Jamaicans and the Court of Appeal
reduced sentence because "it was important to bear in mind that the girl
came from a place where girls of her age reached maturity, and perhaps
greater maturity than English girls of 17 or 18".
[18] By SCARMAN, J., Chairman of the Law Commission, in addressing the
Golden Jubilee Conference of the National Council for the Unmarried
Mother and her Child on 21 November 1968.
    I wish to thank Mrs. Margaret Bramall, the Director of the National
Council, for kindly providing further information on the present topic.
[19] See para. 103 of the Report.

a child is born? If so, the police will have to wait until it is known whether the girl has conceived. Or is it to be limited to the case where the parties are living together in a stable illicit union? And, on any view, what is to be the maximum age of privilege? If the purpose is to encourage the father to take an interest in his illegitimate child, which certainly ought to be done, the solution should, it is suggested, be found not in non-prosecution but in a sympathetic treatment of the defendant once he has been convicted. If, for example, in the light of the social inquiry report he has shown his readiness to accept paternal responsibilities, it might be appropriate to grant him a conditional discharge; or, especially if he is living with the girl and there are signs of domestic problems, a probation order, with its incidental powers of supervision, could well be suitable. For these reasons it is reluctantly suggested that on balance it is better to continue to accept the present uncertainties of enforcement of the law.

2. *Miscellaneous Sexual Offences Involving Girls*

Closely connected with ss. 5 and 6 are ss. 25 and 26 of the 1956 Act,[20] which make it offences for the owner, occupier, or anyone involved in the management or control, of premises to induce or knowingly suffer a girl under 13 or a girl under 16 to use the premises for the purpose of having unlawful sexual intercourse with men or with a particular man.[1] Either offence may be committed by the girl's parent,[2] except where she has already had intercourse with the man and the parent allows him to be brought to the home to have further sexual intercourse, so that he may be trapped into committing an offence under s. 5 or s. 6.[3] It seems that, in accordance with the principle established in the well known case of *R.* v. *Prince*[4] on abduction of girls under 16, a belief that the girl has attained the specified age is no defence.[5] Such a belief would apparently

---

[20] Section 26 is amended by the Criminal Law Act 1967, s. 10 and Sched. II, para. 14.

[1] As with ss. 5 and 6, the maximum penalties under ss. 25 and 26 are respectively imprisonment for life and two years.

[2] *R.* v. *Webster* (1885), 16 Q.B.D. 134.

[3] *R.* v. *Merthyr Tydfil Justices* (1894), 10 T.L.R. 375.

[4] (1875), L.R. 2 C.C.R. 154; see *post*, p. 231, n. 7.

[5] *Cf.* s. 27 of the 1956 Act, which deals with the offence of permitting a woman who is a defective to use premises for unlawful sexual intercourse, where it is expressly provided that it is a defence to show that the accused did not know or have reason to suspect her to be a defective.

also not be available where there is a charge of procuring a girl under 21 to have unlawful sexual intercourse with a third person[6] or a charge of causing or encouraging the prostitution of, or the commission of unlawful sexual intercourse with, or of an indecent assault on, a girl under 16.[7] This last offence[8] may be committed by anyone who is "responsible" for the girl, *i.e.*, any of the following:[9]

(a) Her parent or legal guardian.

In the case of a girl adopted under the Adoption Acts 1958 to 1968[10] the term "parent" refers to her adopters: in the case of an illegitimate girl, to her mother and the adjudged putative father. But the term does not include a person deprived of the girl's custody by order of a court.

Legal guardian has its common meaning of one appointed by deed, will or court order to be guardian.[11]

(b) Any person who has actual possession or control of the girl, or to whose charge she has been committed by her parent or legal guardian or by a person having the custody of her.

(c) Any other person who has the custody, charge or care of her.

This is an even more complicated classification than that which determines the kinds of persons who may be liable for offences against juveniles under Part I of the Children and Young Persons Act 1933[12]. It is suggested that here, too, the law could be simplified, without being made less effective, by imposing liability on anyone who has custody, care or control of the girl.

---

[6] For this offence see s. 23; (maximum penalty is two years' imprisonment). It seems that s. 23 is not impliedly amended by the Family Law Reform Act 1969 so as to reduce the age from 21 to 18. *Cf.* s. 38, *ante*, which is expressly so amended by the 1969 Act.

[7] Section 28; (maximum penalty of two years' imprisonment).

[8] Where a girl has become a prostitute or has had unlawful sexual intercourse or has been indecently assaulted, a person shall be deemed to have caused or encouraged it, if he knowingly allowed her to consort with, or enter or continue in the employment of, any prostitute or person of known immoral character. (s. 28(2)).

For the purpose of s. 28, a girl who appears to the court to have been under 16 at the time of the offence charged shall be presumed to have been so, unless the contrary is proved (sub-s. (5)).

[9] Section 28(3) and (4).

[10] See *post*, Chapter 10.

[11] *Cf.* s. 107(1) of C. & Y.P. Act 1933.

[12] See ss. 1 and 17 thereof, and *ante*, p. 196.

3. *Abduction*

Like child-stealing, abduction of girls is primarily regarded as a wrongful interference with parental rights, but it also invariably involves some harm to the child, which is usually in the form of having unlawful sexual intercourse with her. For this latter reason, if the girl is under 16, proceedings under s. 6 of the Sexual Offences Act 1956 are far more likely than a prosecution for abduction.

As with kidnapping,[13] the common law does not appear to have developed effective rules of criminal liability for dealing with the abduction of women and girls,[14] but this inadequacy was gradually met by legislation. Indeed, the provision in the Statute of Westminster I, to which we referred earlier,[15] was wide enough to cover not only rape but also abduction by force,[16] although doubtless the two invariably went together. An Act of 1487[17] created the distinct offence of abduction of heiresses of property against their will and its policy was extended in 1558 by an Act[18] which made it an offence to take an unmarried child below 16 out of the possession and against the will of her father or mother or the person who at the time lawfully had the order, keeping, education or governance of the child.[19] This and subsequent legislation was repealed but re-enacted and extended during the nineteenth century,[20] and then finally consolidated in the Sexual Offences Act 1956, which contains four[1] offences for abduction. Two of these concern girls of different maximum ages, but, as will be seen, there is considerable overlapping.

(i) *Abduction of girls under sixteen* (s. 20) It is an offence for a person acting without lawful authority or excuse to take an

---

[13] See *ante*, p. 201.

[14] For an isolated reported instance see *R.* v. *Lord Grey* (1682), 9 St. Tr. 127. But even on this case there is a dispute as to whether it is an authority on abduction or criminal conspiracy; see Russell, *Crime*, 12th edn., p. 1479, n. 86.

[15] *Ante*, p. 222.

[16] "The King prohibiteth that none do ravish, nor take away by force, any maiden within age (neigher by her own consent nor without) nor any wife or maiden of full age nor any other woman against her will."

[17] 3 Hen. 7, c. 2.   [18] 4 and 5 Phil. and Mar., c. 8.

[19] For a comparison of this provision with the term "guardian" in the present context see *infra*.

[20] First by an Act of 1828 (9 Geo. 4, c.31) and then by the Offences against the Person Act 1861 and the Criminal Law Amendment Act 1885.

[1] Formerly five, but the Family Law Reform Act 1969, s. 11 (c) has abolished the offence of fraudulent abduction of an heiress under 21.

unmarried girl under 16 out of the possession of her parent or guardian against his will. No sexual motive is required.

(ii) *Abduction of girls under eighteen* (s. 19) This is the offence of taking an unmarried girl under 18 out of the possession of her parent or guardian against his will with the intention that she shall have unlawful sexual intercourse[2] with men or with a particular man.

Certain rules apply to both provisions, others to one or other of them.[3]

Both require the girl to have been *taken* out of possession but it makes no difference whether this was the result of force, fraud or mere persuasion with the girl's consent.[4] The defendant must, however, have taken some active step.[5] His acquiescence is not enough,[6] unless it is shown that he had previously induced the girl to leave,[7] in which case he is liable even if when it comes to her leaving he disapproves of it.[8]

The taking must be out of the *possession* of the parent or guardian. The test of possession here seems to be whether the parent or guardian still has the care and control of the girl.[9] A clear case where he has not is where she is living and working away from home, even if from time to time she spends periods at the parent's home.[10] So, too, she ceases to be in his possession once she leaves home intending permanently or at least indefinitely not to return; but not if her absence is temporary for some specific purpose.[11] It would be absurd if a father were to be held to lose possession of his daughter every time she went out of the house, with the result that if she were

[2] *I.e.*, sexual intercourse outside the bonds of marriage; *R.* v. *Chapman*, [1958] 3 All E.R. 143 (C.C.A.).
[3] Both carry a maximum penalty of two years' imprisonment.
[4] *R.* v. *Manktelow* (1853), 6 Cox C.C. 143 (C.C.C.R.).
[5] *R.* v. *Robins* (1844), 1 Car. & Kir. 456 (bringing ladder to girl's window).
[6] *R.* v. *Jarvis* (1903), 20 Cox 249; *R.* v. *Colville-Hyde*, [1956] Crim. L.R. 117. [7] *R.* v. *Manktelow, supra.*
[8] *R.* v. *Olifier* (1866), 10 Cox C.C. 402.
[9] *Cf.* Jervis C. J. in *R.* v. *Manktelow* (1853), 6 Cox C.C. 143, 147: does the girl continue to be "under the care, charge and control of the parent"?
For criticism of the use of the term "possession" in relation to children see *ante*, p. 195.
[10] *R.* v. *Miller* (1876), 13 Cox C.C. 179; *R.* v. *Henkers* (1886), 16 Cox C.C. 257.
Cf. the Adoption Act 1958, *post*, p. 328, where for the purpose of s. 3 of that Act she may still be in the "care and possession" of her parent.
[11] *R.* v. *Mycock* (1871), 12 Cox C.C. 28.

later picked up in the street that could never constitute abduction.

There is no need, however, for the taking to be permanent.

In *R*. v. *Timmins*[12] a man who, without the father's consent, took the girl away for three days, during that period slept with her at night and then told her to go back home, was guilty. The question is whether the act of taking is "quite inconsistent with the existence of the relation of father and daughter",[13] as it was in *R*. v. *Baillie*[14] where, though absent for only a couple of hours from her home, the girl was during that time induced by the defendant to marry him.

The taking must be against the will of the parent or guardian but positive proof of dissent is not needed. It is sufficient to show that had he been asked he would have refused his consent.[15] On the other hand his past failure to take reasonable care of his daughter, *e.g.*, by allowing her to lead a lax way of life, may be evidence of his consent.[16]

The particular offence is committed if either a parent or guardian is deprived of possession. The latter is defined as the person having the "lawful care or charge of the girl".[17] This is not limited to a legal guardian *stricto sensu, i.e.,* a person so appointed by deed, will or order of the court. It includes anyone in whom the parental rights have been vested by operation of law (for example, a local authority under s. 3 of the Children Act 1948)[18] or to whom care or charge has been delegated by the parent himself.[19] In *R*. v. *Cornforth*[20] it was held under the old Act of 1558[1] that an illegitimate girl may be wrongly taken out of the possession of her putative father. In view of the increasing legal recognition being given to the putative father there is no doubt that the principle of *Cornforth* applies to ss. 19 and 20, but since the term "parent" is not here defined

---

[12] (1860), 8 Cox C.C. 401.   [13] *Ibid.*, at p. 404.
[14] (1859), 8 Cox C.C. 238.
[15] *Per* WIGHTMAN, J. in *R*. v. *Handley* (1859) 1 F. & F. 648, 649.
[16] *R*. v. *Frazer* (1861), 8 Cox C.C. 446; *R*. v. *Primelt* (1858), 1 F. & F. 50.
[17] Compare the wording of s. 56 of the Offences Against the Person Act 1861 (child-stealing), *ante*, p. 201, which refers to the "parent, guardian or other person having lawful care or charge of the child".
[18] See *ante*, Chapter 5.
[19] Compare the wide meaning given by s. 107(1) of the Children and Young Persons Act 1933 to a guardian (as opposed to a legal guardian) so as to include anyone who "has for the time being the charge of or control over the child or young person".
[20] (1742), 11 East 10 n.   [1] *Supra*, p. 228.

to include the putative father, he must be regarded as a "guardian".[2] Obviously he would be if he has been given custody by a court.[3] So, too, it is submitted, if he took possession of the child with the mother's consent or when she died or abandoned the child. But what if his taking was against the mother's wishes? We have seen[4] that that would not be child stealing. It is submitted that in such circumstances for the purposes of ss. 19 and 20 he would *vis-à-vis* any third person (*i.e.*, a person other than the mother) have lawful care or charge.

Section 20, unlike s. 19, does not need a specific wrongful intent, but it does require the defendant to have acted without lawful authority or excuse. A welfare officer acting in pursuance of an order of the court would be a case of lawful authority. An honest but mistaken belief, for example, on the part of a relative that he has a right to the custody of the girl would be a lawful excuse.[5] But intervention based on religious or philanthropic motives is not excusable.[6]

Under s. 19 the defendant may prove that he reasonably believed that the girl was over 18, but a belief that the girl is of the specified age is never a defence under s. 20[7] This strict view has not, however, been adopted where the defendant mistakenly believes that the girl is not in the possession of her parent or guardian. On the contrary, in the case of both sections the onus is on the prosecution to prove that the accused knew or had reason to know or believed that the parent or guardian had possession.[8]

This is an appropriate point to mention another offence which may be grouped with abduction and child-stealing. It concerns children who are in the care of a local authority by virtue of ss. 1 and 2 of the Children Act 1948. It is an offence if anyone knowingly assists or induces or persistently attempts to induce such a child to run away from the accommodation provided by the local authority (whether in a home or otherwise) or takes him away without lawful authority or knowingly

[2] The 1558 Act referred to the "father or mother" and not to the "parent", but *Cornforth* was decided on the basis not that the putative father was a "father" but that he lawfully had the order, keeping, education or governance of the child.   [3] See *post*, Chapter 9.
[4] *Ante*, p. 202.   [5] *R. v. Tinkler* (1859), 1 F. & F. 513.
[6] *R. v. Booth* (1872), 12 Cox C.C. 231.
[7] *R. v. Prince* (1875), L.R. 2 C.C.R. 154.
[8] *R. v. Green* (1862), 3 F. & F. 274; *R. v. Hibbert* (1869), L.R. 1 C.C.R. 184.

harbours or conceals him after he has run or been taken away or prevents him from returning.[9]

Power to Search for and Remove Girls Detained for Immoral Purposes

Where there is reasonable cause to suspect that a woman is being detained at some place in order that she may have unlawful sexual intercourse and that she is being detained against her will or is under 16 or is a defective or is under 18 and is detained against the will of her parent or guardian, a warrant may be issued to search for her and remove her to a place of safety until she can be brought before a justice of the peace.[10] He may then order her to be handed over to her parent or guardian, who for this purpose is defined as the person having lawful care or charge of her.[11] In strict law this is possible so long as she is a minor, since *prima facie* the parent, at least, has the right of custody up to that age, but this is not likely to happen if the girl is 16 or over.[12] Alternatively she may be "dealt with as circumstances may permit and require".[13] The most likely outcome is that she will be brought before a juvenile court as being in need of care or control.

II. PROTECTION OF BOYS

There are no sexual offences concerned exclusively with boy victims, but those dealing with males generally afford special protection to boys by imposing heavier sanctions and by restricting their ability to consent to sexual acts. Thus, if the offence of gross indecency[14] is committed by a man of or over the age of 21 with a male under that age the maximum penalty

[9] See s. 3(8), as substituted by the Children and Young Persons Act 1963, Sched. III, para. 38.
The maximum penalty is a fine of £20 or imprisonment for two months or both.
[10] Sexual Offences Act 1956, s. 43. These powers are additional to those conferred by s. 40 of the C. & Y.P. Act 1933.
A "place of safety" is not defined, but has, it is submitted, the same meaning as it has in the Act of 1933, s. 107(1), (as amended by C. & Y.P. Act 1969, s. 72(3) and Sched. 5, para. 12(2)), namely, a community home provided by a local authority or a controlled home, any police station or any hospital, surgery or any other suitable place, the occupier of which is willing temporarily to receive a child or young person.
[11] *Cf.* definition of "guardian" in s. 107(1) of 1933 Act.
[12] *R.* v. *Lord Grey* (1682), 9 St. Tr. 127.
[13] Sexual Offences Act 1956, s. 43(2). See *ante*, Chapter 3, p. 58.
[14] Sexual Offences Act 1956, s. 13.

is five years' imprisonment instead of the normal two.[15] Where an indecent assault is committed on a boy under 16 his consent to the act is no defence,[16] and the general exemption from criminal liability of homosexual acts between consenting males in private does not apply if one or both parties is under 21.[17]

A surprising statutory omission is that which fails to empower a court convicting a woman of incest, or attempted incest,[18] with a boy to divest her of all authority which she had over him.[19] So, if she is his guardian, that court will not be able to remove her from office and appoint someone else. Separate guardianship or wardship proceedings will have to be instituted. Of course, as with a girl who is the victim of incest, the boy could be brought before the court under care or control proceedings.

III. PROTECTION OF BOYS AND GIRLS

The offence of indecent assault requires some act to be directed towards another person, whether or not it involves a battery. It has, therefore, been held that for a man to invite a child to touch his person is not enough to constitute the offence.[20] But where there is an act and it is against a boy or girl who is under 16 it makes no difference to the defendant's liability that the child willingly participated since, as we have seen, his

---

[15] Sexual Offences Act 1967, s. 3(2). So, too, where a person of or over 21 years of age is a party to or procures or attempts to procure the commission of gross indecency by a male under that age with another man. These age limits are not affected by the Family Law Reform Act 1969. For heavier penalties where buggery is committed with a boy under 16 see *infra* under *Protection of Girls and Boys*.

[16] Sexual Offences Act 1956, s. 15(2).
    A woman, as well as a man, may commit the offence; *R. v. Hare*, [1934] I K.B. 354, (C.C.A.); *cf. R. v. Mason* (1968), 53 Cr. App. Rep. 12, *infra*.

[17] Sexual Offences Act 1967, s. 1(1). The exemption relates to the offences of buggery and gross indecency (s. 1(7)).

[18] If the boy is under 14, *semble* the presumption that he is incapable of sexual intercourse will apply, but the woman may be convicted of the attempt. So it has been held in South Africa; see *The State* v. *A.* 1962 (4) S.A. 679.

[19] For incest by a woman see s. 11 of the Sexual Offences Act 1956, and for the divesting power where a man commits incest see s. 38 and *ante*, p. 220.

[20] *Fairclough* v. *Whipp*, [1951] 2 All E.R. 834, (D.C.); *R. v. Burrows*, [1952] I All E.R. 58, n.
    A woman cannot be guilty of indecent assault on a boy merely by allowing him to have sexual intercourse with her; *R. v. Mason* (1968), 53 Cr. App. Rep. 12.

or her consent is no defence to a charge of indecent assault.[1]

The gap in the law left by the case where there is only an invitation and not an act is largely filled by the Indecency with Children Act 1960,[2] because in such circumstances, if the child is under 14, the invitor, whether male or female, is guilty of the offence of gross indecency with the child under s. 1 of the Act. This offence is also committed by anyone who incites a child under that age to commit such an act with him or her or with some third person and even if the child does not respond to the incitement. It seems that the general principle established by *R. v. Prince*[3] applies, so that it is no defence that the accused reasonably and honestly believed that the child had attained the age of 14. Where both parties to the act are male, proceedings may alternatively be taken, by way of indictment, under s. 13 of the Sexual Offences Act 1956, but there is no point in so doing since no heavier penalty may be imposed.[4] On either alternative the consent of the Director of Public Prosecutions is necessary to institute proceedings,[5] but not where the accused is charged with incitement under s. 1 of the 1960 Act.[6] Where there is no assault, s. 13 is still, however, useful if the boy is between 14 and 16. Neither that section nor s. 1 of the 1960 Act, it should be added, defines gross indecency, but it has been held that actual physical contact is not necessary.[7]

The Sexual Offences Act 1967 also requires the consent of the Director of Public Prosecutions before a man can be prose-

[1] Sexual Offences Act 1956, s. 14(2), *ante*, p. 221, and s. 15(2), *supra*. *R. v. McCormack*, [1969] 3 All E.R. 371, (C.A.).
    This decision must be regarded as overruling earlier cases which held that the act against the child had to be "hostile", *i.e.*, against his will; see *Burrows*, *supra; D.P.P.* v. *Rogers*, [1953] 2 All E.R. 644 (D.C.); *Williams* v. *Gibbs*, [1958] Crim. L.R. 127 (D.C.), and for a criticism thereof Smith and Hogan, *op. cit.*, p. 302.
[2] Passed as a result of the First Report of the Criminal Law Revision Committee, Cmnd. 835.   [3] (1875), L.R. 2 C.C.R. 154.
[4] The maximum under both ss. is two years' imprisonment on conviction on indictment. Section 1 of the 1960 Act, however, allows for prosecution as a summary offence, when the maximum penalty is six months or a fine of £400 (Criminal Justice Act 1967, s. 92(1) and Sched. III, Pt. I, para. 1 (c)) or both.
[5] Sexual Offences Act 1967, s. 8. See *D.P.P.* v. *Burgess*, [1970] 1 Q.B. 432; [1970] 3 All E.R. 266 (D.C.).
[6] *R. v. Assistant Recorder of Kingston-upon-Hull, ex parte Morgan*, [1969] 1 All E.R. 416, (D.C.).
[7] *R. v. Hunt*, [1950] 2 All E.R. 291.

cuted for buggery with another man if either of them is under 21, but consent is, it is suggested, not likely to be withheld if the patient is a boy under 16. No such restriction is imposed where the patient is a female. That Act also imposes the heavier maximum penalties of imprisonment for life and for 10 years where buggery and attempted buggery respectively are committed with a boy under 16 or with a female.[8]

One other offence relating to boys and girls alike is to be found in s. 3 of the Children and Young Persons Act 1933, which forbids anyone having the custody, charge or care[9] of a juvenile who is at least four years old but under 16 to allow him to reside in or to frequent a brothel.

[8] Section 4.
[9] For the meaning of these terms see *ante*, pp. 196 et seq.

CHAPTER 8

Legitimacy

Like most systems of jurisprudence English law has based the legal relationship between the parent and the child not simply upon the fact of parenthood but upon the concept of legitimacy, to be determined by reference to the existence of a valid marriage of the parents. The feudal doctrine which insisted that the parents of a child must be lawfully married at the time of his birth or conception in order to entitle him to inherit an estate in land led to the principle that it was only in respect of such a child that legal rights and duties attached to parents.[1] Otherwise, he was legally *filius nullius* and his exclusion seems to have been complete,[2] until the Poor Law began to impose a duty on the parent to maintain him.[3] Even thereafter parental rights were still denied, until finally, late in the nineteenth century, the mother's legal right to custody was acknowledged.[4] Initially, this denial of legal recognition was counterbalanced by a social tolerance of illegitimacy by mediaeval society.[5] That attitude, which had largely disappeared by the Puritan era (mainly, but not wholly, through the law's rejection of the bastard), is slowly re-emerging, although it would be unwise to be dogmatic about its extent.[6] There has also been a notable improvement in the legal status of the illegitimate child. In public law he now enjoys equality with his legitimate brother.[7] So, too, in respect of claims under the Fatal Accidents Acts 1846 and 1959. If he is the victim of the breakdown of a marriage,

[1] See Graveson, *Status in the Common Law*, pp. 91-92 and the judgments in *Birtwhistle* v. *Vardill* (1840), 7 Cl. and Fin. 895, (H.L.).
[2] See Lord HERSCHELL in *Barnardo* v. *McHugh*, [1891] A.C. 388, at p. 399. But for the earlier view that exclusion was limited to rights of inheritance see Bacon's *Abridgement*, vol. I, p. 758 (cited by James, *Child Law*, p. 37, n. 32).   [3] *Post*, Chapter 14.   [4] *Post*, Chapter 9.
[5] *Post*, Chapter 10. But there were limits; *e.g.*, illegitimacy was a bar to holding ecclesiastical office (see James, *op. cit.*, p. 32).
[6] See the note of warning by SACHS, L. J., in *S.* v. *McC.* (*Orse S.*) *and M.* (*S. intervening*), [1970] 1 All E.R. 1162, 1167. [1970] 1 W.L.R. 672, 678.
[7] *E.g.*, see the protection afforded to both by the criminal law (*ante*, Chapter 6); and the provision of social security benefits (*post*, Chapter 14).

the court will normally have powers to make orders of custody, access and maintenance in respect of him as they would a legitimate child.[8] The legal rights of his mother are the same as those of either parent of the legitimate child,[9] and, comparatively recently, his father has come to acquire some, *viz.*, in relation to custody,[10] guardianship[10] and succession.[11] Further reforms will probably depend on how they may and should proceed without endangering the "legitimate" social unit of the husband, wife and their children.[12]

Reform has been achieved not only by enlarging the legal relationship between the parent and the illegitimate child, but also by broadening the concept of legitimacy.[13] The changes have, however, been cautious.[14] Even after the Legitimacy Act 1926 had introduced legitimation by subsequent marriage, legitimacy with its extended meaning remained a status dependent upon the validity of the marriage of the child's parents, and the same notion is to be found in the rule which preserves the child's legitimacy if the parents' marriage is annulled because it is voidable.[15] The Legitimacy Act 1959, however, has qualified the principle that legitimacy depends upon a valid marriage, since it confers that status in certain circumstances on children born of a void marriage.[16] Notwithstanding these changes, common law legitimacy remains the most extensive form. The Acts of 1926 and 1959 impose time limits from which statutory legitimacy can begin to operate, and there are also some restrictions on the enjoyment of property rights.

A. LEGITIMACY AT COMMON LAW

I. THE SCOPE OF THE PRESUMPTION OF LEGITIMACY

A child conceived before the marriage of his parents but born after his father's death would undoubtedly be treated as legiti-

---

[8] See *post*, Chapter 9, for definitions of "child of the family".
[9] *Post*, Chapter 9.   [10] *Ibid.*   [11] *Post*, p. 255.
[12] Proposals for reform of the law relating to illegitimacy are contemplated by the Law Commission.
[13] For the recognition of legitimacy under a foreign law the reader is referred to text books on the Conflict of Laws.
[14] See, for example, the Report of the Departmental Committee on Human Artificial Insemination, (1960) Cmnd. 1105, paras. 160-171, which declined to recommend that a child should be legitimate if born as a result of A.I.D. to which the husband has consented. Acceptance of the principle "would involve an unprecedented change in the concept of legitimacy".   [15] *Post*, p. 248.   [16] *Post*, p. 246.

mate, but otherwise the common law admits no exception to its rule of legitimacy that the parents must be married when the child is born or conceived.[17] However, within those limits it has until very recently gone to great lengths to ensure the legitimacy of children by an unduly generous application of a presumption in favour of that status.[18] This has been achieved by giving the presumption a wide scope and then by imposing a heavy burden of rebuttal.

The presumption is that a child born of a married woman[19] during the subsistence of her marriage is presumed to be also the child of her husband. It arises even though the child must have been conceived before the marriage, because by marrying the mother the husband is *prima facie* taken to have acknowledged the child as his own. In such a case the strength of the presumption has depended on, *inter alia*, whether at the date of the marriage he knew of her pregnancy.[20] The presumption equally applies where the child is born within the possible period of gestation after the marriage has been terminated by the husband's death[1] or by a final decree of divorce.[2] If, after the termination but before the birth, the mother remarried,

[17] Historically, it seems that the exception stated in the text would not have been regarded as an exception, because in the case where the conception, but not the birth, preceded the marriage, the marriage was deemed to have taken place before the conception; see Lord Brougham in *Birtwhistle* v. *Vardill* (1835), 2 Cl. and Fin. 571 at p. 591.

[18] A secondary factor which contributed to the same result was the old rule, reaffirmed in *Russell* v. *Russell*, [1924] A.C. 687, (H.L.), which excluded evidence by a spouse tending to prove that he had not had sexual intercourse with the other spouse at a time when the child was likely to have been conceived. The rule was abolished by the Law Reform (Miscellaneous Provisions) Act 1949, s. 7. A spouse is now a competent and compellable witness in any civil proceedings; Matrimonial Causes Act 1965, s. 43(1), as amended by the Civil Evidence Act 1968, s. 16(4).

[19] Disputes as to maternity are rare; but see *Slingsby* v. *A.-G.* (1916), 33 T.L.R. 120, (H.L.).

[20] *Gardner* v. *Gardner* (1877), 2 App. Cas. 723, (H.L. (Sc.)); *cp.* the *Poulett Peerage Case*, [1903] A.C. 395, (H.L.).

[1] This rule has a long history; *Alsop* v. *Bowtrell* (1619), Cro. Jac. 541: Co. Litt. 123b: 1 Bl. Comm. 456. For modern authorities see ROMER, J., in *Re Leman's Will Trusts* (1945), 115 L.J. Ch. 89; and WRANGHAM, J., in *Knowles* v. *Knowles*, [1962] P. 161; [1962] 1 All E.R. 659. Although *Re Heath, Stacey* v. *Bird*, [1945] Ch. 417 is also frequently cited in support, COHEN, J., surprisingly declined to decide firmly whether the presumption applied to the posthumous child.

[2] *Re Leman's Will Trusts, supra.*
There is no reason why the presumption should not similarly operate in the rare case where the decree is one annulling a voidable marriage and possibly, within certain limits, even if the marriage were void; see *post*, p. 247.

the better opinion is that the child is presumed to be a legitimate child of the first marriage and not of the second, on the
ground that the mother should be presumed not to have committed adultery.[3]

The scope of the presumption is demonstrated in those cases
where the spouses are living apart. If they do so under a decree
of judicial separation or under a matrimonial order containing
a non-cohabitation clause the presumption is reversed and the
child is *prima facie* illegitimate, on the ground that the spouses
are presumed to have strictly obeyed the order.[4] Otherwise,
the presumption of legitimacy operates. So, it has been held
to apply notwithstanding that at the date of conception (1) the
parties were living apart under a deed or agreement[5] or (2) a
state of desertion existed or (3) a matrimonial order without
a non-cohabitation clause was in force[6] or (4) a petition for
divorce or nullity had been filed or (5) a decree nisi of divorce
or nullity had already been granted.[7] In each of these circumstances the presumption has, however, been readily rebuttable,
and, in so far as a presumption is now needed,[8] there is much
to be said for the view that in all cases where the spouses are
not cohabiting at the relevant date a presumption of illegitimacy
should operate.

II. THE EFFICACY OF THE PRESUMPTION

In the *Banbury Peerage Case*[9] the House of Lords laid down
the limits within which the presumption of legitimacy could
be rebutted. It must be proved that no sexual intercourse took
place between the spouses during the possible period within
which the child must have been conceived, and this burden of

[3] Bromley, *op. cit.*, p. 230. *Cf. Re Overbury*, [1955] Ch. 122; [1954] 3 All
E.R. 308, where the court was able to decide on the facts, without relying
on a presumption, that the child was conceived of the first marriage.
    In continental systems a conflict of presumptions is avoided by
imposing a "waiting period" (*e.g.*, of 300 days) during which the mother
is not allowed to remarry unless meantime the child is born; see Kahn-
Freund, 18 M.L.R. 71.
[4] *Inter the Parishes of St. George and St. Margaret Westminster* (1706),
1 Salk. 123.
[5] *Morris* v. *Davies* (1837), 5 Cl. and F. 163, (H.L.); *Ettenfield* v. *Ettenfield*,
[1940] P. 96, (C.A.); [1940] 1 All E.R. 293.
[6] *Bowen* v. *Norman*, [1938] 1 K.B. 689; [1938] 2 All E.R. 776.
[7] *Knowles* v. *Knowles*, [1962] P. 161; [1962] 1 All E.R. 659.
[8] See *infra*, standard of proof.
[9] (1811), 1 Sim. and St. 153.

proof might be discharged by showing that during that period either (1) sexual intercourse was impossible because (a) the parties were physically absent from one another or (b) one at least of them was impotent, or (2) the circumstances were such as to render it highly improbable[10] that sexual intercourse took place. It is this second main alternative which has produced most litigation.[11] Much of it shows that, where sexual intercourse between the spouses at the time in question was not impossible, all the circumstances surrounding the particular case must be considered including (1) the kind of opportunities which existed for such intercourse to take place,[12] (2) the disposition of the spouses to have intercourse with each other,[13] (3) their conduct towards each other before and during the wife's pregnancy and after the child's birth[14] and (4) the respective attitudes of the wife, her husband and her paramour towards the child.[15]

Where reliance is placed on the husband's impotence for the purpose of rebutting the presumption of legitimacy it might, exceptionally, still be possible to establish his paternity, *viz.*, by proving that the birth was the result of fecundation *ab extra*[16] or of artificial insemination with his seed.[17]

The length to which the courts were prepared to go in upholding the presumption is demonstrated by the rule that once sexual intercourse between the spouses was proved to have taken place at the material time the child must be held to be the issue of that intercourse, even though it was shown that at that time the wife was committing adultery[18] and even though the spouses always practised contraception.[19] But there had to be some eugenic limits even to this extreme conclusion.[20] Thus, it has been widely accepted that dissimilarities in colour (as,

[10] *Cf. infra* the present standard of proof.
[11] See textbooks on the law of evidence.
[12] Compare, for example, *Cotton* v. *Cotton*, [1954] P. 305, (C.A.); [1954] 2 All E.R. 105, with *Sibbet* v. *Ainsley* (1860), 3 L.T. 583.
[13] *Cf. The Aylesford Peerage Case* (1885), 11 App. Cas. 1 (H.L.).
[14] *Aylesford Peerage Case, supra; Burnaby* v. *Baillie* (1889), 42 Ch.D. 282.
[15] *Aylesford Peerage Case, supra; Bosvile* v. *A.-G.* (1887), 12 P.D. 177 (D.C.). [16] *Cf. Clarke (orse, Talbot)* v. *Clarke*, [1943] 2 All E.R. 540.
[17] *Cf. R.E.L. (orse, R.)* v. *E.L.*, [1949] P. 211; *sub nom, L.* v. *L.*, [1949] 1 All E.R. 141.
[18] *R.* v. *Hemmings*, [1939] 1 All E.R. 417, (C.C.A.).
[19] *Francis* v. *Francis*, [1960] P. 17, (D.C.); [1959] 3 All E.R. 206.
[20] As Scots law would recognise; see *Slingsby* v. *A.-G.* (1916), 33 T.L.R. 120 (H.L.).

for example, where the child is a half-caste and the mother and her husband are both white) or the husband's sterility would rebut the presumption.

The principles laid down in the *Banbury Peerage Case* were at one time a realistic recognition of the difficulty which proof or disproof of paternity could cause, but the appearance of new serological techniques has called into question their inflexibility. Two other factors have also led to a dramatic change in the value of the presumption of legitimacy. These are the recent change in the standard of proof needed to rebut it and the difference in social values which are resulting in courts, when dealing with legitimacy issues, being less concerned with determining property rights and more with matters affecting "the ultimate personal and private lives of the litigants",[1] matters which ought not to be determined by the slavish application of presumptions.

Standard of Proof

Since any attempted rebuttal of the presumption necessarily involves the allegation that the mother was guilty of adultery (except for the rare possibility of the child having been conceived by way of artificial insemination), it would have been illogical to have allowed a standard of proof less than that required to establish adultery, *i.e.*, proof beyond reasonable doubt; but *dicta* in *Blyth* v. *Blyth*[2] that adultery could be proved on a preponderance of probabilities left judicial opinion divided as to whether the lesser standard was applicable to rebuttal of the presumption.[3] The uncertainty has been removed by the Family Law Reform Act 1969, which lays down the test of balance of probabilities for the latter purpose:[4]

[1] *Per* ORMROD, J., in *Re L.*, [1968] P. 119, 139; [1967] 2 All E.R. 1110, 1123.

The changing attitude towards the presumption is also reflected in *Blackwell* v. *A.-G.* (1967), 111 S.J. 332 and in *Smith* v. *May* (1969), 113 S.J. 1000 (D.C.). In the former it was held that the bare fact that the petitioner in a legitimacy suit is the child of a person lawfully married at the date of conception is insufficient of itself to establish legitimacy. There must be some evidence that the husband of the mother had access to her at the relevant time. In *Smith* v. *May* the Divisional Court held that the magistrates were entitled to "take a very strong view" that the spouses had not had sexual intercourse, although they shared the same bed, and that therefore the presumption was rebutted.

[2] *Per* Lord DENNING, M. R., and Lord PEARCE; [1966] A.C. 643, (H.L.); [1966] 1 All E.R. 524.

[3] *Re L.*, [1968] P. 144, (C.A.); [1968] 1 All E.R. 20.   [4] Section 26.

"Any presumption of law as to the legitimacy or illegitimacy of any person may in any civil proceedings be rebutted by evidence which shows that it is more probable than not that that person is illegitimate or legitimate, as the case may be, and it shall not be necessary to prove that fact beyond reasonable doubt in order to rebut the presumption."

The new rule will have far reaching effects.

"[It] means that the presumption of legitimacy now merely determines the onus of proof. Once evidence has been led it must be weighed without using the presumption as a make-weight in the scale for legitimacy. So even weak evidence against legitimacy must prevail if there is not other evidence to counter-balance it. The presumption will only come in at that stage in the very rare case of the evidence being so evenly balanced that the court is unable to reach a decision on it. I cannot recollect ever having seen or heard of a case of any kind where the court could not reach a decision on the evidence before it."[5]

One form of evidence which will be materially affected by the change is that relating to the possible period of gestation.[6] The presumption of legitimacy may involve not only a presumption as to paternity but also as to the date of conception, and where there is a legitimacy issue the court will take judicial notice that there is a normal period of gestation and also, *semble*, that that period is not always followed. While no specific maximum and minimum periods of gestation are judicially recognised, it was held in *Preston-Jones* v. *Preston-Jones*[7] that the court could not assume that a child born 360 days after the last act of intercourse between a husband and wife cannot be the child of the husband, but Lord MORTON'S dissenting opinion that an interval of 320 days should be enough to satisfy the court that the husband could not be the father, expressed when the standard was proof beyond reasonable doubt, would, it is submitted, now be sufficient to enable the

[5] *Per* Lord REID *S.* v. *S.*; *W.* v. *Official Solicitor*, [1970] 3 All E.R. 107, 109, (H.L.); [1970] 3 W.L.R. 366, 371. See also Lord MORRIS OF BORTH-Y-GEST *ibid.*, at pp. 120 and 383 respectively. The dictum of Lord REID was applied in *T.(H.)* v. *T.(E.)*, [1971] 1 All E.R. 590, where the court was able to find enough evidence, without relying on the presumption, to hold that the husband of the mother was the father of her child.
[6] The change will also expedite the use of anthropological tests to prove paternity; for example, evidence of the same kind of physical peculiarity in the child and the putative father might be admissible.
[7] [1951] A.C. 391, (H.L.); [1951] 1 All E.R. 124.

court to hold on a balance of probabilities that the presumption of legitimacy was rebutted.

Blood Group Evidence[8]

In the last few years increasing use has been made of blood group evidence in paternity issues. Such is the present state of their scientific reliability that there is on average at least a seventy per cent chance that blood tests can prove that a particular person cannot be the father of a particular child, and where there are uncommon blood factors present in the man or the child the exclusion rate will be much higher.

The admissibility of blood group evidence has raised two basic questions. Have the courts power to order blood tests if the adult parties and the person having custody or care and control of the child do not all consent to them? If so, on what principles should they act in deciding whether to make an order? In *W.* v. *W.* (*No.* 4) the first was answered in the negative by the Court of Appeal in respect of persons *sui juris*,[9] but eventually in *B.* (*B.R.*) v. *B.* (*J.*)[10] it was held that the High Court[11] did have the power to order a *child* to be blood-grouped whenever it was in his best interests,[12] and Part III of the Family Law Reform Act 1969 now confers a general discretionary power on all civil courts to direct adults and children to be blood tested.[13]

The Act enables[14] the power to be exercised by a court in any civil proceedings in which a paternity issue arises, including

---

[8] See Law Commission Paper No. 16, *Blood Tests and the Proof of Paternity in Civil Proceedings;* Hall, [1971] C.L.J. 34; Hayes, *The Use of Blood Tests in the Pursuit of Truth*, 87 L.Q.R. 86.

[9] [1964] P. 67; [1963] 2 All E.R. 841.
  In all the earlier civil cases in which blood group evidence was admitted the parties had consented to undergo blood tests. For earlier academic treatment of the topic see Denton, *Blood Groups and Disputed Parentage* (1949), 27 Can. Bar. Rev. 537; Bartholomew, *Nature and Use of Blood Group Evidence* (1961), 24 M.L.R. 313; and for earlier unsuccessful attempts to introduce a statutory power to order blood tests see the Bastardy (Blood Tests) Bill 1938 and the Affiliation Proceedings (Blood Tests) Bill 1961.

[10] [1968] P. 466; [1968] 2 All E.R. 1023.

[11] But not a divorce county court or a magistrates' court.

[12] Lord DENNING, M. R., had already taken this view in *Re L.*, [1968] P. 119; [1968] 1 All E.R. 20, but the majority of the Court of Appeal there restricted the power to custodial proceedings.

[13] The Act implements recommendations of the Law Commission (Law Com. No. 16, 1968).

[14] Part III is now in operation.

affiliation proceedings.[15] The direction for blood tests to be taken can be given on the application of any party to the proceedings and can relate to the person whose paternity is to be determined, his mother and any party alleged to be his father,[16] or to any one or two of them. A direction is revocable or variable. No test may be carried out on a person aged 16 or over without his consent, and, if he is under that age or is so mentally disordered as not to be able to understand the nature and purpose of blood tests, the consent of the person having care and control of him is necessary.[17] Where a guardian *ad litem* has been appointed his consent is not necessary but he has the right to make submissions against the child's being tested.[18] However, once a direction for testing has been made he is under a duty to support it.

A direction is not compulsory in its effect so as to empower the court to impose a sanction, but a refusal to comply with it will entitle the court to draw such inferences as the circumstances may properly warrant,[19] which usually but not necessarily[20] will be adverse to the refusing party. For example, if a mother for no justifiable reason, such as medical or religious grounds, will not allow herself or her child, whose care and control she has, to be blood tested, the court may conclude that the alleged father is not the father. Moreover, the Act specifically provides that a person, who without reasonable cause fails to comply with a direction after the court has

[15] Section 20. The Blood Tests (Evidence of Paternity) Regulations 1971 provide for the manner in which tests are to be carried out and the making of a report to the court. For the practice and procedure in the High Court, a county court or a magistrates' court see respectively R.S.C., O. 112; County Court Rules, O. 46, r. 23; and the Magistrates' Courts (Blood Tests) Rules 1971. See also Practice Direction, [1972] 1 All E.R. 640.
Tests should be taken promptly; *P.* v. *P.* (1969) 113 S.J. 343, (C.A.); and a welfare report should normally be obtained in cases where a direction to blood test a child is given (*per* SACHS, L.J., in *B.* (*B.R.*) v. *B.* (*J.*), [1968] P. 466, 480-481; [1968] 2 All E.R. 1023, 1029).
[16] If, therefore, it should appear from the evidence that some other person may be the father, that person will first have to be made a party to the proceedings before he can be directed to undergo a test, but it has been pointed out that many proceedings in which the issue of legitimacy is raised do not allow for a third person to be made a party to them; see Bromley, *op. cit.*, p. 236.
[17] See Practice Direction [1968] 3 All E.R. 607.
[18] Section 21. In the case of a mentally disordered person a medical certificate that the taking of a blood sample will not be prejudicial to his proper care and treatment is also necessary.
[19] Section 23.   [20] See *B.* v. *B. and E.*, *infra*, n. 2.

adjourned a hearing in order to enable him to do so, may not be able to rely on the presumption of legitimacy although there is no evidence to rebut it. The main object of this provision is to prevent a refusing wife from relying on the presumption in a claim against her husband for maintenance of the child. As a result of her refusal the court may well draw the inference that she has committed adultery, but her husband may also have had access to her at the relevant time and, as we have seen, the presumption of legitimacy, but for the present statutory rule, would operate.

The Act is concerned with conferring a power to direct the taking of blood tests, but it does not indicate how the court is to exercise its discretion. This is a matter which has given rise to a judicial conflict between the view that the child's best interests should determine whether a blood test should be ordered[21] and that which makes the need to do justice the over-riding consideration and therefore insists on a test so that the best evidence can be available, unless there are exceptional reasons for not admitting it.[22] In *S.* v. *S.* and *W.* v. *Official Solicitor*[1] the House of Lords preferred the latter approach and formulated the principle that a court should allow a blood test of a child to be taken unless it is satisfied that such a course would be actively against the interests of the child: it is not necessary that it should positively be satisfied that the outcome of the test will be for the child's benefit. Save in exceptional cases, as, for example, where a test would be harmful to his health, it will be in the child's interests to resolve paternity doubts on the best available evidence. Better that he should know the truth than that he should be sheltered behind the presumption of legitimacy, especially now that many of the former legal disabilities attaching to legitimacy have been removed. His interests are not likely to be furthered by holding,

---

[21] But there have been differing opinions as to whether those interests should be the sole criterion (*per* WINN, L. J., in *W.* v. *W.*, [1970] 1 All E.R. 1157, 1160; [1970] 1 W.L.R. 682, 685-686) or highly important but not, perhaps, paramount (*per* CROSS, L. J., in *W.* v. *W.*, *supra* at pp. 1161 and 686 respectively).

[22] See Lord DENNING, M. R., in *W.* v. *W.*, *supra* and in *S.* v. *McC.*, [1970] 1 All E.R. 1162; [1970] 1 W.L.R. 672.

[1] [1970] 3 All E.R. 107; [1970] 3 W.L.R. 366. These were the appeals from the decisions of the Court of Appeal *sub nom. S.* v. *McC.* and *W.* v. *W.*, *supra*.

on a presumption of legitimacy, that his mother's husband is his father when the latter is firmly convinced that he is not.[2]

In the above cases the House of Lords thought that the discretion to order tests under the 1969 Act was not unfettered, but it declined to offer guidance on the principles which the courts will have to follow in exercising it. It is submitted that at least the above common law principle will continue to govern it but that it will relate to ordering blood tests of the adults as much as to ordering the child's.

B. STATUTORY LEGITIMACY

I. CHILDREN OF VOID MARRIAGES

Section 2 of the Legitimacy Act 1959 re-introduced into English law the doctrine of the putative marriage, which, while popular in many other legal systems, had been obsolete in England since the Reformation.[3] It provides for the legitimacy of the child of a void marriage if, at the time of the act of intercourse resulting in his birth or of the celebration of the marriage (whichever be the later) both or either of the parties reasonably believed that their marriage was valid. For the section to operate, the father must be domiciled in England at the time of the birth or, if he dies before that date, must have been domiciled here immediately before his death. The first part of this limitation accords with the rules of English conflict of laws, which refer the question of legitimacy exclusively to the law of the father's domicile at the date of the child's birth,[4] but it also has the advantage of avoiding any reference to the domicile of origin of the child. Similar accordance is not, however, to be found in the second part, since the better view is that the law governing legitimacy of a posthumous child is

---

[2] *Aliter* where the husband thinks that he is and it is in the child's interests that the presumption of legitimacy should not be disturbed; *B.* v. *B. and E.*, [1969] 3 All E.R. 1106, (C.A.); Bromley, *op. cit.*, p. 237.

[3] The doctrine was an established part of mediaeval ecclesiastical law; see Tucker 9 I.C.L.Q. 319-320.

[4] Subject to (1) the rule that if a question of heirship is involved the common law test of birth in lawful wedlock prevails and (2) the controversial decision of the House of Lords in *Shaw* v. *Gould* (1868), L.R. 3 H.L. 55 which may be explained as an illustration of the first proviso or is open to other interpretations. See textbooks on the Conflict of Laws.

that of the mother's domicile at the date of birth and not of the father at his death.[5]

The indications are that the section is to be construed strictly. In *Hawkins* v. *Att.-Gen.*[6] it was held that the reasonableness of the belief in the validity of the marriage must be determined objectively. The wording of the section may support the decision but scarcely does its *raison d'être*. This lies in the moral innocence of at least one of the parties, so that the appropriate test ought to be subjective honesty, not objective reasonableness. Did the party at the relevant date honestly believe that his or her marriage was valid? A liberal construction would include not only mistakes of fact but also mistakes of law, but whether they are is doubtful. In Scots law they exclude legitimacy,[7] but possibly some persuasive support for the opposite view can be drawn from the former doctrine of approbation of a voidable marriage, where account is taken of mistakes of law.[8]

The time factor may obviously give rise to problems. Since the burden of proof seems to lie on those asserting legitimacy,[9] it may be very difficult to prove that a party believed the marriage was valid at the relevant date, especially if that party is dead. And where that date is the date of conception (and not of marriage) there may be difficulties about ascertaining it. In such a case the principles relating to the possible period of gestation which are followed in applying the presumption of common law legitimacy[10] should, it is submitted, be adopted. If, for example, the child is born 310 days after the party found out that the marriage was void, it ought to be presumed that the child was already conceived before the discovery, assuming that the parties then had access to each other.

There is also room, in marginal cases, for importing into the section a presumption of legitimacy analogous to that at common law. Supposing, for example, that F. goes through a ceremony of marriage with M., who at the time does not know

[5] Cheshire, *Private International Law*, 8th edn., p. 435.
[6] [1966] 1 All E.R. 392; [1966] 1 W.L.R. 978. For criticism see Samuels 29 M.L.R. 559.
[7] *Purves' Trustees* v. *Purves*, 1895, 22 R.513; *Philp's Trustees* v. *Beaton*, 1938 S.C. 733.
[8] *Slater* v. *Slater*, [1953] P. 235, (C.A.); [1953] 1 All E.R. 246. Compare now s. 3(1) of the Nullity of Marriage Act 1971.
[9] Bromley, *op. cit.*, p. 238.　　　　[10] *Ante*, p. 242.

that F. is already a married person. M., having lived with F. for some time, eventually discovers that her marriage is bigamous. On the same day she ceases to live with F., the last act of sexual intercourse between the parties having occurred on the previous day. A month later M. begins to have regular sexual intercourse with X. M. gives birth to C. 300 days after leaving F. It is submitted that if medical and other evidence fails to show whether F. or X. is the father, it should be presumed that F. is and that C. is therefore legitimate.

The definition of a void marriage for present purposes is perplexing.[11]

"[It] means a marriage, not being voidable only, in respect of which the High Court has or had jurisdiction to grant a decree of nullity, or would have or would have had such jurisdiction if the parties were domiciled in England."

"Marriage" includes not only a voluntary, exclusive union potentially for life of one man and one woman but also a polygamous marriage.[12] But, unless the union is governed by English law, a marriage ceremony ought not to be a prerequisite, if the foreign law does not require it.[13] However, concubinage or a union for a prescribed period is excluded. The reference to past jurisdiction is probably intended to cover the case of the posthumous child, but the inclusion of the words "or had" seem odd, since the death of the father would not deprive the English court of jurisdiction: a decree of nullity in respect of a void marriage can be granted even though one of the parties is dead.[14]

II. CHILDREN OF VOIDABLE MARRIAGES

Section 11 of the Matrimonial Causes Act 1965 provides for the legitimacy of children of all voidable marriages[15] by enacting that:

[11] Section 2(5). See Jones, 8 I.C.L.Q. 725, 726; Tucker, 9 I.C.L.Q. 321, 322; Kahn-Freund, 23 M.L.R. 58, 59.
[12] *Hyde* v. *Hyde*, (1866), L.R. 1 P. D. 130, 133; Matrimonial Proceedings (Polygamous Marriages) Act 1972.
[13] *Cp.* marriage by cohabitation and repute under Scots law.
[14] I am indebted to my colleague, Mr. Raymond Smith, for discussion of this topic.
[15] The rule was first enacted by the Matrimonial Causes Act 1937, s. 7(2), but was limited to marriages avoided on the ground that one of the parties was suffering from unsoundness of mind or epilepsy or that the respondent was suffering from a venereal disease. It was extended by the Law Reform (Miscellaneous Provisions) Act 1949, s. 4(1), to cover all grounds which render a marriage voidable.

where a decree of nullity is granted in respect of a voidable marriage, any child who would have been the legitimate child of the parties to the marriage if it had been dissolved, instead of being annulled, at the date of the decree shall be deemed to be their legitimate child notwithstanding the annulment.

This might seems a circumlocutory enactment, but, so expressed, it provides for legitimacy not only where the child is conceived and born during the subsistence of the voidable marriage but also where only one of those events occurs during that period. It also thereby preserves the legitimacy of the child who is legitimated by his parents' subsequent marriage which is later annulled because it is voidable.

III. LEGITIMATED CHILDREN

The policy of English domestic law before 1926 to refuse to extend legitimacy beyond cases of birth or conception in lawful wedlock was not pursued in the conflict of laws rules. Provided that no question of heirship was involved, the legitimation of a child by the subsequent marriage of his parents was recognised by the common law if the father was domiciled both at the time of the child's birth and at the time of the subsequent marriage in a country whose law recognised the legitimation.[16] The Legitimacy Act 1926 supplemented the common law by providing an alternative rule of recognition which excluded the illogical reference to the father's domicile at the time of the child's birth,[17] but it also introduced legitimation by subsequent marriage into the domestic law,[18] save for the adulterine child who remained unprotected until the Legitimacy Act 1959 removed the injustice.[19]

A question of legitimation may, of course, raise a preliminary issue as to paternity. The fact that the husband married the mother is of limited evidentiary value in proving his paternity, but evidence of recognition by the husband that the child is

[16] The rule was finally established in *In re Grove* (1888), 40 Ch.D. 216.
[17] Section 8. For the conflict of laws aspects of legitimation see textbooks thereon.
[18] Section 1(1). Consistently with the conflict of laws rule, recognition depends on the father being domiciled in England or Wales at the time of the marriage; *i.e.*, the child's status is determined solely by the personal law of the father at that date, without reference to that of the mother.
[19] Section 1. It is too early to assess the extent to which the Divorce Reform Act 1969 will lead to legitimation of illegitimate children of stable unions.

his is much more cogent.[20] So, too, is the fact that the mother has already obtained an affiliation order against him. The existence of the order may be adduced in later civil proceedings whether or not the husband defended the affiliation proceedings.[1]

Subject to certain modifications concerning rights in property,[2] a child who is legitimated by the subsequent marriage of his parents is, from the date of his legitimation,[3] in the same legal position as if he had been born legitimate. In particular he has the same rights and is under the same obligations in respect of the maintenance and support of himself or any other person as if born legitimate, and any claims for damages, compensation and the like apply in respect of him as they would in the case of a legitimate person.[4] This general legal effect, created by the Legitimacy Acts, is specifically supplemented by certain statutory provisions *e.g.*, those relating to nationality[5] and to social insurance.[6]

C. DECLARATIONS OF LEGITIMACY

Issues concerning legitimacy may arise either collaterally in matrimonial causes[7] or property disputes or directly in affiliation proceedings or legitimacy petitions brought under s. 39 of the Matrimonial Causes Act 1965.

Section 39 enables the court to make declarations with regard to the following matters, which are set out in sub-ss. (1), (2) and (4) respectively:

1. *Declarations of Legitimacy or the Validity of a Marriage*
   A British subject or a person whose right to be deemed a

---

[20] See *Battle* v. *A.-G.*, [1949] P. 358.
[1] Civil Evidence Act 1968, s. 12. Strong evidence of paternity would be the fact that the husband had, in accordance with the Births and Deaths Registration Act 1953, s. 10, (as amended by the Family Law Reform Act 1969, s. 27), signed the register of births, even though at that date he and the mother were not married.   [2] See *infra*.
[3] *I.e.*, the date of the marriage or the date of commencement of the particular Legitimacy Act which applies to him, whichever be the later. Thus, an adulterine child whose parents married in 1956 is legitimated from 29 October 1959 when the 1959 Act came into operation.
[4] Legitimacy Act 1926, s. 6.   [5] British Nationality Act 1948, s. 23.
[6] *Post*, Chapter 14.
[7] Where there are children of a void marriage and a decree of nullity is made, the court may pronounce that it was satisfied that a party reasonably believed that the marriage was valid, so entitling the children to be treated as legitimate under s. 2 of Legitimacy Act 1959; *Wynn* v. *Wynn* (1964), 108 S.J. 239.

British subject depends wholly or partly on his legitimacy or on the validity of a marriage may, if he is domiciled in England or Northern Ireland or claims any real or personal estate situate in England, petition for a decree that he is legitimate or that his marriage or that of his parents or grandparents is or was valid.

2. *Declaration of Legitimation*

Anyone claiming that he or his parent or any remoter ancestor[8] has been legitimated in accordance with the Legitimacy Act 1926[9] may petition for a decree to that effect.

Sub-sections (1) and (2) differ in two respects. Sub-section (2), unlike sub-s. (1), does not impose any restriction relating to nationality, domicile or situation of property, and, whereas the High Court alone has jurisdiction to hear a petition under sub-s. (1), a petition under the other sub-section may be heard by that court or a county court.

3. *Declaration of British Nationality*

A person qualified to petition under sub-s. (1) may seek from the High Court a decree that he be deemed to be a British subject.

The court has no power to make declarations with regard to any other matters. Thus, it cannot make a declaration of legitimacy in respect of anyone other than the petitioner[10] or, in dismissing a legitimacy petition, decree that the petitioner is illegitimate.[11] Nor can it determine whether or not the petitioner was heir-at-law to another.[12] The Attorney-General must be made a respondent to the proceedings, and notice must be given to any interested parties who may also be permitted to become parties to the proceedings and oppose the application. The decision of the court is not a judgment *in rem*, but the decree binds the Crown and all persons given notice of the proceedings or joined as parties and their privies, unless it was

[8] "Ancestor" means "lineal progenitor" and so does not include an uncle; *Knowles* v. *A.-G.*, [1951] P. 54; [1950] 2 All E.R. 6.
[9] Either under s. 1 or s. 8; see *supra*, p. 249.
[10] *Aldrich* v. *A.-G.* (*Rogers intervening*), [1968] P. 281; [1968] 1 All E.R. 345.
[11] *B.* v. *A.-G.* (*B. intervening*), [1966] 2 All E.R. 145; [1967] 1 W.L.R. 776.
[12] *Mansel* v. *A.-G.* (1879), 4 P.D. 232.

obtained by fraud or collusion. A petitioner should therefore try to ensure that notice is given to anyone who is likely at any time to challenge his status. Proceedings under s. 39 may be heard in camera,[13] but this protection from publicity does not extend to other proceedings involving questions of legitimacy.[14] In deciding whether to hear a petition in camera the court must take into account in each case the effect of publicity on the petitioner, particularly in relation to his health or occupation and on third parties who might be distressed by the disclosure of family secrets and weigh that against the value of publicity in eliciting further evidence and against the traditional rule of public policy that justice should be administered in public.[15]

D. PROPERTY RIGHTS

I. STATUTORY LEGITIMACY

The Legitimacy Acts 1926 and 1959 impose some restrictions relating to the enjoyment of rights in property.

The legitimate child of a void marriage may only succeed to a dignity or title of honour or to property settled therewith if he was born after the Legitimacy Act 1959 came into operation.[16] The rule of legitimacy also does not affect any rights under an intestacy of a person dying before that date or any disposition (*inter vivos* or testamentary) which came into operation before the date.[17]

The legitimated child is similarly barred from succession to a dignity, title of honour or property devolving therewith.[18] As for his rights to take under any other disposition, the position depends upon whether the disposition was made before 1970 or after 1969. In the former case his rights are determined by the Legitimacy Act 1926.[19] He is to be treated as if he had been born legitimate so as to entitle him, unless a contrary intention is expressed in the disposition,[20] to take an interest under (1)

[13] Domestic and Appellate Proceedings (Restriction of Publicity) Act 1968, s. 2; Matrimonial Causes Act 1965, s. 39(9).
[14] *Prior* v. *Prior (By His Guardian)* (1970) 114 S.J. 72.
[15] *Barritt* v. *A-G*, [1971] 3 All E.R. 1183.
[16] Section 2(3). The date of commencement was 29 October 1959.
[17] Subsection (4).
[18] Legitimacy Act 1926, ss. 3(3) and 10(1).
[19] Section 3(1) (b) and (c).   [20] Section 3(4).

a disposition coming into operation after the date of legitima-tion[1] and (2) an entailed interest created after that date.[2] The rights of his spouse, children and remoter issue to take are to be determined on the same assumption that he was born legitimate. Moreover, the spouse, children and remoter issue of an illegitimate person who died before the marriage of his parents and who would have been legitimated had he been living when they married may similarly be entitled to take *and others may be entitled to claim through them,* provided that the spouse or an issue was alive at the time of the marriage.[3]

Since a disposition by will operates from the date of the testator's death, a person legitimated after that date will not be entitled to take a benefit under the will, unless there is a con-trary intention expressed in the disposition.[4] Moreover, where a will gives a special power of appointment, the will and not the appointment constitutes the disposition and so a child legiti-mated after the will came into operation is not, in the absence of a contrary intention in the will, an object of the power.[5]

Where the disposition is made after 1969 the position of the legitimated child is the same as that of the illegitimate and is dealt with below.

The rights of a legitimated person, or of an illegitimate who would have been legitimated if alive when his parents married, and through him of his spouse and issue, to take under an intestacy are determined by the same principles as those relating to dispositions made before 1969. The intestacy must occur after the date of legitimation or the marriage as the case may be except that where the estate includes an entailed interest the interest must have been created after that date.[6] When a legiti-mated person or his issue dies intestate his property is dis-tributed as if that person had been born legitimate.[7]

---

[1] For the date of legitimation see *ante*, p. 250, n. 3.

[2] For the purpose of ranking children for seniority a legitimated child ranks as if he had been born on the date of his legitimation and where more than one person is legitimated at the same time they rank between themselves in order of seniority (s. 3(2)).   [3] Section 5.

[4] *Re Hepworth, Rastall* v. *Hepworth,* [1936] Ch. 750; [1936] 2 All E.R. 1159.

[5] *Re Hoff,* [1942] Ch. 298; [1942] 1 All E.R. 547.
Where there is a general power of appointment the relevant "disposi-tion" is that whereby the power is exercised and not that conferring it.

[6] Legitimacy Act 1926, s. 3(1) (a) and (c).

[7] Section 4.

II. ILLEGITIMACY

Dispositions of Property

One of the consequences of the common law treatment of the bastard as *filius nullius*[8] was the rule of construction that *prima facie* any reference in an instrument to "children", "issue" and the like was exclusively to those who were legitimate, and, although it was a presumptive and not an absolute rule, it was not easily disturbed. Contrary to the recommendation of the Russell Committee on the Law of Succession in Relation to Illegitimate Persons,[9] s. 15 of the Family Law Reform Act 1969[10] has introduced the contrary rule so that *prima facie* references to children and other relatives include references to, and to persons related through, illegitimate persons. The new presumption extends not only to illegitimate children but also to legitimated, and it applies to any disposition (including an oral disposition) whether *inter vivos* or by will or codicil, which is made on or after 1st January 1970.[11] However, it does not affect the construction of the word "heir" or "heirs" or of any expression which is used to create an entailed interest; and it does not sever property which would (apart from s. 15) devolve along with a dignity or title of honour. Trustees and personal representatives who have distributed property without having ascertained that there is no person who could benefit by reason of the section are protected from personal liability, but anyone with an interest may follow the property into the hands of any person other than a purchaser.[12]

Intestacy

Prior to the Family Law Reform Act 1969 the limits of recognition accorded to the illegitimate child by the law of intestate succession were that he and his issue were entitled to succeed on the intestacy of his mother provided that she left no legitimate issue, and she was entitled to succeed on his intestacy as if she were the only surviving parent.[13]

---

[8] *Ante*, p. 236.   [9] Cmnd. 3051, paras. 57-58.
[10] See Morris, *The Family Law Reform Act 1969, ss.* 14 *and* 15, 19 I.C.L.Q. 328; Samuels, *Succession and the Family Law Reform Act* 1969, 34 Conv. 247, 249.
[11] A codicil executed on or after that date confirming a will or codicil executed before it does not postdate the will or codicil.
[12] Section 17.   [13] Legitimacy Act 1926, s. 9.

The Act of 1969 is a significant event in the legal emancipation of the illegitimate child because it enables him or, if he is dead, his issue to succeed on the intestacy of either of his parents as if he were their legitimate child.[14] Correspondingly, each of them has a right of succession on his intestacy, if they survive him.[15] Nevertheless, there are a number of limits to the section.

It applies to persons dying intestate on or after 1st January 1970, but not to earlier intestacies. It does not affect the right to take an entailed interest. Nor does it entitle the illegitimate child to succeed to a title or dignity of honour. But its most serious defect is that it does not confer on him a right to inherit on the intestacy of any relative other than a parent. It is submitted that he ought to be put on an equal footing with his legitimate brother.

There is a presumption that the child has not been survived by his father unless the contrary is shown, a presumption which reflects the reality that in the vast majority of cases the father is unknown. On the other hand, as has been pointed out,[16] English law does not provide a procedure for formal acknowledgment of paternity, so that there can be practical difficulties of establishing the relationship between the claimant and the deceased. Trustees and personal representatives who distribute without ascertaining whether there is a person entitled under s. 14 are protected as they are in a case under s. 15,[17] but this does not prevent the beneficiary from following the property.

---

[14] For the rights of succession see Administration of Estates Act 1925, s. 47, as amended by Family Law Reform Act 1969, s. 3(2).
[15] Family Law Reform Act 1969, s. 14.
[16] Bromley, *op. cit.*, p. 508.
[17] *Supra.*

CHAPTER 9

Custody

A. LEGITIMATE CHILDREN

I. HISTORY OF PARENTAL RIGHT TO CUSTODY

"Custody" is an ambiguous term. In its primary sense it means the right to physical care and control: it is the correlative of the duty to protect. But in its wider meaning it represents "the whole bundle of rights and powers vested in a parent or guardian".[1] The rights to the services of the child,[2] to exercise disciplinary powers over him, including that of administering reasonable corporal punishment,[3] and to determine his upbringing, especially the kind of education, religious and secular, that he should receive,[4] all stemmed from the parent's being entitled to custody, a right which continues until the child attains 18[5] or until his or her marriage, if earlier.[6]

At common law the right to custody of the legitimate child was vested in the father and was almost absolute. Although his right as the natural guardian has been much attenuated in favour of the mother, its historical strength still has some influence. It accounts for the rule that the child takes his surname and seems to underlie the decision of BUCKLEY, J., in *Re T. (Otherwise H.) (An Infant)*[7] that, if there is a right to change the child's surname, it resides primarily with the father,[8] who may restrain the mother from so doing even if she has been granted custody as the result of divorce proceedings. Only if a change by her is in the child's interests will the father's right

---

[1] Bromley, *Family Law*, 4th edn. p. 268. For a further but narrow meaning see *post*, p. 397. See generally SACHS, L. J., in *Hewer* v. *Bryant*, [1970] 1 Q.B. 357 at pp. 372-373; [1969] 3 All E.R. 578 at p. 585; Hall, *The Waning of Parental Rights*, [1972] C.L.J. 248, especially at p. 261.
[2] See *post*, Chapter 13, p. 451.   [3] See *ante*, Chapter 6, p. 210.
[4] *Post*, Chapter 13.   [5] Family Law Reform Act 1969, s. 1.
[6] See further *post*, Chapter 12, p. 409.
[7] [1963] Ch. 238; [1962] 3 All E.R. 970.
[8] If the child is over 15 and the name is to be changed by deed poll, his consent is required; Enrolment of Deeds Poll (Change of Name) Regulations. 1949, r. 8.

256

not prevail; for example, where his name has acquired notoriety.

So strong was the father's right at common law that he could even enforce it while in prison by insisting on the child being brought to visit him[9] and could even claim from the mother custody of a child at the breast.[10] It was only in exceptional cases, where there was a risk of serious physical or moral harm to the child due to the father's cruelty or to gross corruption of the child resulting from his profligacy,[11] that his right was liable to be forfeited.[12]

Although increasingly during the nineteenth century litigants turned from the common law to the jurisdiction of the Court of Chancery, which was exercised on behalf of the Crown as *parens patriae*, it was not until the last decade of that century that any appreciable change becomes apparent and a more benevolent view is adopted by paying greater attention to the welfare of the child.[13] In 1848 in *Re Fynn* there is no more than a marginal relaxation of the common law rule when Sir James Knight Bruce, V.-C., said that the equitable jurisdiction could only be invoked if:

> "the father has so conducted himself, or has shown himself to be a person of such a description, or is placed in such a position, as to render it not merely better for the children, but essential to their safety or to their welfare, in some very serious and important respect, that his rights should be treated as lost or suspended – should be superseded or interfered with. If the word 'essential' is too strong an expression, it is not much too strong."[14]

[9] *Ex parte Skinner* (1824), 9 Moore C.P. 278.

[10] *R.* v. *De Manneville* (1804), 5 East 221.

[11] *R.* v. *Greenhill* (1836), 4 Ad. and Ei. 624, 640; *R.* v. *Clarke, Re Race* (1857), 7 E. and B. 186, 198.

[12] Proceedings were by way of *habeas corpus*, but could be brought in the Court of Chancery as well as in the Common Law Courts.

[13] For the history of the parental right to custody see especially the judgments of the House of Lords in *J.* v. *C.*, [1970] A.C. 668; [1969] 1 All E.R. 788; DANCKWERTS, L. J., in *Re Adoption Application No.* 41/61, [1963] Ch. 315 (C.A.); [1962] 3 All E.R. 553; and Lord ESHER, M.R., in *R.* v. *Gyngall*, [1893] 2 Q.B. 232 (C.A.).

[14] (1848), 2 De G. & Sm. 457, 474-75. But the interests of the child tended to play a larger part in cases where the father had surrendered custody to another person; see *Lyons* v. *Blenkin* (1821), Jac. 245, *post*, p. 289.

In the earlier case of *Wellesley* v. *Duke of Beaufort* (1827), 2 Russ. 1, (affirmed by H. L. *sub nom. Wellesley* v. *Wellesley* (1828), 2 Bli.N.S. 124), the court refused to remove children from the care of their aunts and hand them over to the father, mainly on the ground that he encouraged them in habits of swearing and keeping low company, but it is arguable that this conduct would equally have justified forfeiture of custody at common law.

Custody

In 1883 in *Re Agar-Ellis*,[15] the Court of Appeal still speaks in strong terms of the father's rights and his being deprived of them only if he has by his conduct shown himself unfit to exercise them. Hence, it is unwilling to interfere with a father who unreasonably refuses to allow free access and free correspondence between his sixteen-year old daughter and her mother from whom he is separated because he is afraid the mother will alienate the daughter's affections from him.

It was under the influence of statutory changes, which conferred on the mother rights to claim custody, that greater attention began to be paid to the child's welfare. Where a father was deprived of custody, whether proceedings had been instituted by way of *habeas corpus* or by petition to the Court of Chancery, the effect of the court's decision might be to allow the mother custody, but neither common law nor equity conferred on her a positive right to seek it. That was first done by the Custody of Infants Act 1839 (Talfourd's Act), which empowered the Court of Chancery to give the mother custody until the child reached the age of 7, provided she had not committed adultery. The Custody of Infants Act 1873, repealing the earlier Act without re-enacting the proviso concerning adultery, extended the right to the age of 16. Meanwhile, the Divorce Court, under the Matrimonial Causes Act 1857,[16] could make custody orders up to the age of 21 on such terms as to it seemed just thus enabling it to give either parent custody, and, when magistrates' courts were first given matrimonial jurisdiction by the Matrimonial Causes Act 1878,[17] their powers included that of awarding the wife custody of those of her children under the age of 10. Much more significant is the Guardianship of Infants Act 1886, because, apart from giving the mother rights concerning guardianship,[18] it not only widened her rights so as to claim custody of a child up to the age of 21, but also directed that in hearing her claim the court was to have regard to, *inter alia*, the welfare of the child.[19]

[15] (1883) 24 Ch. D. 317.   [16] Section 35.
[17] Section 4.   [18] See *post*, Chapter 12.
[19] Section 5. The first reference to the child's welfare was in the Custody of Infants Act 1873, s. 2 of which permits a father by an agreement contained in a separation deed to give up the custody or control of his child to the mother, with the proviso that the agreement is unenforceable if the court considers that it will not be for the child's benefit to give effect to it. See further, *post*, p. 265.

Similarly the Custody of Children Act 1891 referred the court to the child's welfare when it had to decide whether a parent who had abandoned or deserted his child or allowed him to be brought up by another person was now a fit person to have custody.[20] Meanwhile the court when dealing with the custody of orphans was committing itself to the principle that the dominant consideration should be the child's welfare.[1]

As the judgments of the Court of Appeal in *R. v. Gyngall*[2] show, the cumulative effect was to weaken the father's rights, to strengthen those of the mother, but, above all, to lay greater emphasis on the child's welfare at the expense of both. During the earlier part of the present century this emphasis persists "behind the closed doors of the Chancery Division",[3] until the Guardianship of Infants Act 1925 expressly affirmed the paramountcy of the child's welfare. Whether in so doing it took the law further or merely restated it is open to argument,[4] but at least it put the matter beyond doubt.

II. PRINCIPLES ON WHICH THE COURT ACTS WHEN DETERMINING DISPUTES OVER CUSTODY[5]

Section 1 of the Guardianship of Minors Act 1971, which is one of the corner stones of child law, re-enacts the principle of paramountcy, formerly contained in s. 1 of the Guardianship of Infants Act 1925, and provides:

"Where in any proceedings before any court (whether or not a court as defined in s. 15 of this Act) –
(a) the custody or upbringing of a minor; or
(b) the administration of any property belonging to or held on trust for a minor, or the application of the income thereof, is in question, the court, in deciding that question, shall regard the welfare of the minor as the first and paramount consideration,

---

[20] Section 3.
[1] See *Johnstone* v. *Beattie* (1843), 10 Cl. & Fin. 42; [1843-60] All E.R. Rep. 576 (H.L.); *Stuart* v. *Marquis of Bute*, *Stuart* v. *Moore* (1861), 9 H.L. Cas. 440; [1843-60]. All E.R. Rep. 595 (H.L.); *Re McGrath (infants)*, [1893] 1 Ch. 143 (C.A.).
[2] [1893] 2 Q.B. 232. See also LOPES, L. J., in *Re A. an* B. (infants)*, [1897] 1 Ch. 786, 792.
[3] *Per* Lord UPJOHN in *J.* v. *C.*, [1970] A.C. 668, 723; [1969] 1 All E.R. 788, 831.
[4] See, for example, the differing views held in *J.* v. *C.*, *supra*.
[5] See James, *The Legal Guardianship of Infants*, Vol. 82 L.Q.R. 323.

and shall not take into consideration whether from any other point of view the claim of the father, or any right at common law possessed by the father, in respect of such custody, upbringing, administration or application is superior to that of the mother, or the claim of the mother is superior to that of the father."

This provision is applicable to all disputes over the custody, care and control of a child, whether they be between one parent and the other or between a parent and a third party or between two guardians.[6] When giving effect to it the court should consider and weigh all the circumstances that are of any relevance and in so doing the welfare of the child is to be treated as the first and paramount consideration. Since welfare is to be understood in the widest sense so as to include the moral and emotional, as well as the physical and mental, well-being of the child,[7] in most cases all the relevant circumstances will relate to the child's welfare, but the Court of Appeal in *Re L. (infants)*[8] has held that "paramount" does not mean "exclusive" and, therefore, in some cases factors other than those relevant to welfare must be taken into account.[9] The extent to which they are must, as MEGARRY, J., has made clear,[10] depend on judicial discretion and cannot be determined according to any formula. Problems invariably arise with regard to the weight to be attached to the claims and the conduct of the parties.

Claims and Conduct of the Parties

Where the dispute is between the parents the court is directed by s. 1 to disregard from every point of view other than the child's welfare whether the father's claim is superior to the mother's or *vice versa*. In assessing their respective claims their

---

[6] For guardianship see *post*, Chapter 12.
[7] *Cf.* LINDLEY, L. J., in *Re McGrath (infants)*, [1893] 1 Ch. 143, 148.
[8] [1962] 3 All E.R. 1; [1962] 1 W.L.R. 886.
[9] In *J. v. C.*, [1970] A.C., 668, 710; [1969] 1 All E.R. 788, 820-21, Lord MACDERMOTT adopted a rather different view of the words "first and paramount" and thought that they did not simply mean that the child's welfare is to be treated "as the top item in a list of items relevant to the matter in question" but that all the circumstances must be analysed and then the court must follow the course which is most in the interests of the child's welfare.
[10] *Re F. (an infant)*, [1969] 2 Ch. 238, 241; [1969] 2 All E.R. 766, 768; [1969] 3 W.L.R. 162, 165.

conduct is a relevant matter, but its significance is variable.[11] Usually it is not isolated from the question of the child's welfare, but there are marginal cases where it is. The court may be ready so to treat it where one parent is alone responsible for the break-up of the home. This happened in *Re L. (infants)*,[12] where an adulterous mother left the matrimonial home, went to live near her lover and, because of her passion for him, refused to return to her husband and their two daughters, aged six and four. The husband applied to make them wards of court. By that time he and they were being looked after by his unmarried sister in a house provided by him, which was quite suitable for the family; but he was ready to forgive his wife and have her back. The Court of Appeal held that, in the light of the conduct of the parents, it "was a matter of simple justice *between them*"[13] that the father should have the care and control, the girls remaining wards of court.

Even where the unimpeachable conduct of a parent is taken into account as a separate matter, the justice of his claims may be so outweighed by considerations concerning the child's welfare that the court will entrust custody, care and control to the parent whose conduct is impugned.[14] Much will depend on the gravity of the conduct and the risk of future corruption of the child.[15] It is impossible to say, for example, that, because a woman has once committed adultery, she is not a fit person, *vis-à-vis* one who has not, to look after a child;[16] *aliter* if she is promiscuous.[17] Consideration will also be given to the age, sex and health of the child. The courts do not ignore the reality that where children are very young the mother is often at an

---

[11] ". . . in these days guilt or innocence is rarely a determinant as to custody of children". (Sir JOCELYN SIMON, *The Seven Pillars of Divorce Reform*). While this may be true of custody issues in matrimonial proceedings, the parties' conduct tends to play a larger part where the issues arise in wardship proceedings or proceedings under the Guardianship of Minors Act, especially, it is submitted, where a parent of unimpeachable conduct is seeking custody from a third party and not from the other parent. See *Re Thain, Thain* v. *Taylor*, [1926[Ch. 676; [1926] All E.R. Rep. 384.
[12] [1962] 3 All E.R. 1 (C.A.); [1962] 1 W.L.R. 886.
[13] *Per* Lord DENNING, M. R., at pp. 4 and 890 respectively; italics supplied.
[14] But, for the possibility of making a divided order, see *infra*.
[15] *Wellesley* v. *Duke of Beaufort* (1827), 2 Russ. 1.
[16] *Allen* v. *Allen*, [1948] 2 All E.R. 413 (C.A.); *Willoughby* v. *Willoughby*, [1951] P. 184. Compare the former statutory rule in Talfourd's Act, 1839, *ante*, p. 258.
[17] *Cf. Re Witten (an infant)* (1887), 57 L.T. 336; *Re G.*, [1899] 1 Ch. 719.

advantage in the ability to bring them up.[18] It was this factor which weighed heavily with MEGARRY J., when in *Re F. (an infant) F.* v. *F.*[19] he granted care and control of a three-year-old girl, who was a ward of court, to the mother, even though, as in *Re L. (infants)*, she had been responsible for the break-up of the home.[20] Nevertheless, age and sex are no more than relevant considerations. There is no rule of law that a girl under three should normally be with her mother or a boy of eight normally with his father.[1]

However, whenever possible the court tries to relate the parental conduct to the child's welfare and not treat it as a separate and possibly conflicting factor. *Re Thain (Thain* v. *Taylor)*,[2] which was the first authority to consider the relevance of the claims and conduct of the parent in the light of s. 1 of the 1925 Act, and *Re O. (Infants)*[3] both stressed the wishes of an unimpeachable parent but justified giving effect to them on the ground that this would accord with the child's welfare.[4] In the former, the father, a widower who was about to re-marry, was able to recover custody of his seven-year-old daughter from relatives who had brought her up since shortly after her birth. It was only on finding that she would be as happy and well cared for in the one home as the other, that the father's wishes were allowed to prevail.[5] In *Re O. (Infants)*, by taking a longer view than one which unduly emphasised the transient effect of separating young children,[6] the Court of

[18] *Re B.*, [1962] 1 All E.R. 872 (C.A.); [1962] 1 W.L.R. 550.
[19] [1969] 2 Ch. 238; [1969] 2 All E.R. 766.
[20] *Cf. H.* v. *H. and C.*, [1969] 1 All E.R. 262 (C.A.); [1969] 1 W.L.R. 208, where the mother had not only been responsible for the break-up but had not seen her three-year-old child for 20 months.
[1] *Re C. (A.) (an infant), C.* v. *C.*, [1970] 1 All E.R. 309; [1970] 1 W.L.R. 288, where, in relation to the latter proposition, the Court of Appeal disapproved of its earlier view in *W.* v. *W. and C.*, [1968] 3 All E.R. 408; [1968] 1 W.L.R. 1310.
[2] [1926] Ch. 676 (C.A.); [1926] All E.R. Rep. 384.
[3] [1962] 2 All E.R. 10 (C.A.); [1962] 1 W.L.R. 724.
[4] See to the same effect DANCKWERTS, L. J., in *Re Adoption Application No. 41/61*, [1963] 1 Ch. at p. 329; [1962] 3 All E.R. at p. 560 and Lord DONOVAN in *J.* v. *C.*, [1970] A.C. 668, 727; [1969] 1 All E.R. at p. 835; [1969] 2 W.L.R. at p. 580.
[5] See Lord MACDERMOTT in *J.* v. *C.*, [1970] A.C. 668, 711; [1969] 1 All E.R. at p. 821, explaining the judgment of EVE, J.
[6] For another illustration see *Re B. (an infant)* (1966) *Times*, April 5 (C.A.). Nevertheless, the courts are very much aware of the risks involved in removing a child from a stable environment; see CROSS, J., in *Re W.*, [1965] 3 All E.R. 231, 249.

Appeal allowed the father, a Sudanese, to remove his seven-year-old son to the Sudan, leaving his daughter, aged six, with her mother in England. *In Re L. (infants)*[7] one of the reasons for the decision was that by giving care and control to the father there was some hope, albeit a faint one, that the mother might be induced to return to the father for the sake of the children and, if this were to happen, it would ensure "in the best way of all" the children's welfare.[8] In *Re F. (an infant) F. v. F.*,[9] MEGARRY, J., distinguished the case before him on the ground that all possibility of reconciliation of the parents had gone, since the father was intending to re-marry as soon as his marriage to the mother was dissolved, but even there one sees a wish to bring parental conduct under the umbrella of the child's welfare, because, while holding that the two were not directly inter-related in that case, the learned judge recognised that the responsibility for the break-up of the marriage could "[throw] light on the character and behaviour of the parties and thus [assist] . . . in assessing their probable behaviour as parents in the future".[10] In *E. v. E.* the Court of Appeal has further emphasised the need to consider the parent's conduct from the point of view of his or her suitability to look after the children.[11]

Divided Orders

Both *Re L. (infants)* and *Re F. (an infant) F. v. F.* were concerned with wardship proceedings, and, since the court retained custody in the wide sense, the question was whether it would give the care and control to the one or the other parent. But where the proceedings are such that custody is in issue the court may sometimes make a divided order whereby one party is granted day to day care and control, but custody is left with the other, thereby entitling the latter to a voice in the bringing up of the child. Such an order is possible under the Matrimonial Proceedings and Property Act 1970 or the

[7] *Supra.*
[8] See Lord DENNING, M. R., [1962] 3 All E.R. at p. 3; [1962] 1 W.L.R. at p. 890.　　　　　[9] *Supra.*
[10] [1969] 2 Ch. 238, 243; [1969] 2 All E.R. at pp. 769-770.
[11] (1969) 113 Sol. Jo. 721. The mother, who with her two youngest children was living with the co-respondent, successfully appealed against an order giving the husband custody, care and control of the two eldest children, girls aged 10 and 8.

Guardianship of Minors Act 1971, but, for reasons which are later considered,[12] not under the Matrimonial Proceedings (Magistrates' Courts) Act 1960. It is quite common in divorce proceedings; for example, where a wife deserts her husband and takes the children with her and the husband, being the "innocent" party, has no means of bringing them up.[13] It should, however, be regarded as the exception rather than the rule, because normally it is better for a child to have one authority in its daily life,[14] especially if it is the authority of a parent as opposed to a third party.[15] Thus, it is likely to be refused where it would lead to an undesirable conflict, as over the religious upbringing of the child,[16] or where it may prove extremely inconvenient.[17] An illustration of the latter is the father who is going overseas. To award him custody would mean that his consent would be necessary for a surgical operation to be performed on the child.[18] On the other hand, it is arguable that the case of the parent abroad may sometimes be a most appropriate one for a split order so that he may be involved in the long-term upbringing of the child.

In recent years the courts have allowed other permutations of custody, care and control. Thus, while they may refuse to make a split order, it does not follow that all three will be given to one parent. The court may choose to give him or her or even a third party[19] care and control and make no order as to custody, and this, it has been held,[20] will leave both parents with some control over the child's education.[1] The value of such an order may be doubted, because it may give rise to the very problems which a split order may produce.[2] But the risk

---

[12] *Post*, p. 277.
[13] *Wakeham* v. *Wakeham*, [1954] 1 All E.R. 434 (C.A.); [1954] 1 W.L.R. 366.
[14] See SACHS, L. J., in *S.* v. *S.* (*otherwise D.*) (1968), 112 Sol. Jo. 294.
[15] See, for example, *Goodfellow* v. *Goodfellow* (1968), 112 Sol. Jo. 332. See also *D.* v. *D.* (1965), 109 Sol. Jo. 573 (C.A.).
[16] *S.* v. *S. and T.* (1963), 107 Sol. Jo. 475 (C.A.).
[17] *S.* v. *S.* (*otherwise D.*), *supra.*
[18] *I.e.*, if the child is under 16. See Family Law Reform 1969, s. 8.
[19] *Freckleton* v. *Freckleton*, [1966] C.L.Y. 3938.
[20] *Re. M.* (*infants*), [1967] 3 All E.R. 1071 (C.A.); [1967] 1 W.L.R. 1479.
[1] This conclusion impliedly recognises that, until the court otherwise decides, the parents have equal rights with regard to the custody of their child.
[2] In *Re M.* (*infants*), *supra*, it was realised that the order there made could lead to a further dispute between the parties if they could not agree on the course of education that the children should pursue.

should not be overstated. Indeed, where one party is given care and control, the court should not be reluctant to make an order for joint custody,[3] provided that it is clear that both parties have the welfare of their child at heart, that it is reasonably likely that they will co-operate for his well-being and that they are qualified to give wise guidance to him.[4] If the court should decide to postpone the decision as to who should have care and control, it is desirable to give formal custody to one party or the other.[5]

Agreements between Parents relating to Custody

An agreement whereby a parent purports to surrender the custody of his child is contrary to public policy and therefore void.[6] This rule is a particular application of the general principle that an agreement to surrender parental rights is void. Section 2 of the Custody of Infants Act 1873 admits a limited exception.

> "No agreement contained in any separation deed made between the father and mother of an infant or infants shall be held to be invalid by reason only of its providing that the father of such infant or infants shall give up the custody or control thereof to the mother; provided always that no Court shall enforce any such agreement if the Court shall be of the opinion that it will not be for the benefit of the infant or infants to give effect thereto."

The proviso[7] largely removes the value of such an agreement, especially with the current emphasis placed on the child's interests. Moreover, the section is anachronistic in that, designed to curb the common law rights of the father, it fails to take account of the present parity between the husband and wife in claims to custody which s. 1 of the Guardianship of Minors Act 1971 recognises. So, any agreement whereby the mother surrenders her claim to custody is not caught by the section.

---

[3] As it was in *Clissold* v. *Clissold* (1964), 108 Sol. Jo. 220; *cf. S.* v. *S.* (1965), 109 Sol. Jo. 289.   [4] See *Jussa* v. *Jussa*, [1972] 2 All E.R. 600.
[5] *Laxton* v. *Laxton and Eagler*, [1966] 2 All E.R. 977 (C.A.); [1966] 1 W.L.R. 1079.
[6] *Vansittart* v. *Vansittart* (1858), 2 De G. & J. 249, (C.A. in Ch.).
[7] For an illustration of its application see *Re Besant* (1879), 11 Ch. D.508 (C.A.), where it prevented a mother, who promulgated atheistical opinions, refused to allow the child any religious instruction and published, what was then regarded as obscene, a book on birth control, from successfully relying on an agreement which gave her custody of her eight-year-old daughter for 11 months in each year.

It has been suggested that the doctrine of specific performance can be invoked so as to extend the provisions of s. 2 to parol contracts.[8] Even if this were not permitted, the fact that such an agreement has been made would be evidence of the parent's having abdicated his parental authority.[9]

Medical Evidence

Increasing importance is being given to medical evidence in proceedings which involve the possible removal of the child from his present surroundings. The subject is examined later in the chapter on adoption.[10]

Miscellaneous Factors

It is highly desirable that the court should see the parties to the proceedings and everyone else concerned[11] and should not rely only on affidavits or welfare reports,[12] otherwise it cannot properly decide whether a party is a fit and proper person to look after the child.[13] As for seeing the child, the court may do so in order to find out what his wishes are; but practice varies widely.[14] Much will depend on whether the custody is disputed and on the age of the child. Even if he is interviewed, his views will be treated circumspectly for fear that they may have been instilled into him by one of the parents, and they will properly be disregarded if they are contrary to his long term interests.[15] In matrimonial proceedings in the High Court an order may be made for the child to be separately represented by the Official Solicitor, if he consents, or by some other person who has applied to be appointed.[16]

[8] Bromley, *op. cit.*, p. 273. [9] See further *post*, p. 289.
[10] *Post*, pp. 345 *et seq.*
[11] For example, anyone with whom the child is living.
[12] On the other hand, it ought not to reach a decision without a welfare officer's report; *Smith* v. *Smith* (1971), 115 Sol. Jo. 444 (D.C.).
[13] *E.* v. *E.* (1969), 113 Sol. Jo. 721 (C.A.); *H.* v. *H. and C.*, [1969] 1 All E.R. 262 (C.A.); [1969] 1 W.L.R. 208; *P.* v. *P.* (1969), 113 Sol. Jo. 999 (C.A.); *W.* v. *W.* (1971), 115 Sol Jo. 367. With regard to custody disputes arising in matrimonial proceedings in the High Court or a county court, a judge may refuse to admit an affidavit unless the party making it is available to give oral evidence (Matrimonial Causes Rules 1971, r. 92(4)).
[14] For the attitude of divorce courts see the Law Commission's Working Paper, No. 15, pp. 9-10.
[15] See CROSS, J. in *Re S.* (*infants*), [1967] 1 All E.R. 202, 210; [1967] 1 W.L.R. 396, 408. But the judge's suspicions about a parent's conduct may be strengthened by the unsworn evidence of the child, given to him in private; *S.* v. *S.* (1971), *Times*, July 15 (C.A.).
[16] Matrimonial Causes Rules 1971, r. 108.

Disputes over Custody

The rules laid down by the House of Lords in *Official Solicitor* v. *K.*[17] which are to be followed when confidential reports are submitted to the court by the Official Solicitor in wardship proceedings equally apply to his reports and those of welfare officers[18] in custody disputes. They will be considered in relation to wardship.[19]

Problems may arise over the admissibility of further evidence. Where the custody proceedings arise as part of divorce proceedings, evidence which could have been put in at the trial of the petition may be adduced at the subsequent custody hearing if it does not relate to facts on which evidence was given at the trial.[20] If it does so relate, the question is whether the doctrine of *res judicata* applies. In *Hull* v. *Hull* it was held that it did,[1] but this has recently been doubted[2] and is contrary to the present tendency to relax, in the interests of the child and at the expense of the principle of finality of litigation, the normal rules of admitting further evidence. The tendency is demonstrated by the recent ruling that an appellate court concerned with custody may look at material (*e.g.*, a welfare

---

[17] [1965] A.C. 201; [1963] 3 All E.R. 191.
[18] In the provinces probation officers serve as welfare officers, but the Royal Courts of Justice have their own full-time Welfare Officers. For the duty of a probation officer to provide a report at the request of the court see the Probation Rules 1965, r. 31 (b). In the case of an application for an order for custody, care or supervision in matrimonial proceedings in the High Court or a county court, (see *post*, p. 279), in addition to the power of the judge or registrar to call for a welfare report, the applicant may request the registrar to call for such a report before the hearing of the application. The registrar has a discretion so to refer the matter. See Matrimonial Causes Rules 1971, r. 95.
  Courts vary considerably in the use they make of welfare reports; see the Working Paper No. 15 of the Law Commission, referred to *post*, p. 285.
  Where use is made of a report but the court differs from the views of the welfare officer, it is essential to explain the reason for differing; *Clark* v. *Clark* (1970), 114 Sol. Jo. 318.   [19] *Post*, Chapter 12.
[20] *Corbett* v. *Corbett*, [1953] P. 205; [1953] 2 All E.R. 69 (C.A.).
[1] [1960] P. 118; [1960] 1 All E.R. 378.
[2] *F.* v. *F.*, [1968] 2 All E.R. 946 (C.A.); [1968] 1 W.L.R. 1221. *Re F. (W) (an infant)*, [1969] 2 Ch. 269; [1969] 3 All E.R. 595.
  The former case shows that evidence which could not have been reasonably available at the time of the earlier proceedings may certainly be admitted in the custody proceedings provided that it is of a character likely to have a substantial effect on the decision as to custody. But it seems that even if it had been available, it may still be allowed at the later hearing. This is the view with regard to maintenance; *Tumath* v. *Tumath*, [1970], P. 78 (C.A.); [1970] 1 All E.R. 111; *Cp.*, however, *G. (S.D.)* v. *G. (H. H.)*, [1970] 3 All E.R. 844; [1970] 1 W.L.R. 1556.

officer's report) which was not before the court below,[3] and it is likely to lead to acceptance of a similar rule that in an application for variation or discharge of a custody order evidence may be adduced even though it was available at the date of the original order.

All these rules reflect a desire to make the child's interests paramount. The same consideration may be uppermost when it comes to ordering costs. No order will be made if to do so would exacerbate feeling between the parties which would be to the ultimate detriment of the child, and in this respect it makes no difference whether or not the parties are legally aided.[4]

There is yet a further protective rule concerning appeals. If the custody order directs that the child be transferred from one person to another but there is no urgency to do so, the court should order a stay pending appeal, provided that it is satisfied that there is a genuine intention to appeal. It is not in the child's interests to be bandied about from the one person to the other.[5]

III. MEANS OF RESOLVING DISPUTES OVER CUSTODY AS BETWEEN PARENTS OR AS BETWEEN SPOUSES [6]

The appearance of statutory methods of dealing with parental disputes over custody has rendered the writ of *habeas corpus*

---

[3] *B. (B.) v. B. (M.)*, [1969] 1 All E.R. 891, 900; [1969] 2 W.L.R. 862, 872.
  In laying down this rule the Divisional Court did not forget the general rule which limits the powers of an appellate court to interfere with the exercise of the discretion of the trial court to circumstances where the latter has acted on wrong principles, such as where it gave weight to irrelevant or unproved matters or overlooked relevant ones. But the right to interfere has been further extended. If by the time of hearing the appeal the circumstances have so changed that the substratum of the magistrates' decision no longer exists, then, unless the case is such that it ought to be remitted for hearing, the appellate court exercises an unfettered discretion *de novo*, on the facts as they exist at the time of the appeal. If, however, the substratum still exists, the appellate court must put into the scales the facts as found by the magistrates, so far as they have not been falsified by the march of events, together with any relevant new facts, and then seek to exercise a discretion as it seems the magistrates would have done with the full facts before them; (*per* MEGARRY, J., in *Re B. (T.A.) (an infant)*, [1971] Ch. 270; [1970] 3 All E.R. 705). On the powers of an appellate court in custody proceedings see also *Re C. (an infant)* (1970) *Times*, July 23 (C.A.); *Re O. (infants)*, [1971] 2 All E.R. 744; [1971] 2 W.L.R. 784 (C.A.).
[4] *B. (M.) v. B. (R.)*, [1968] 3 All E.R. 170 (C.A.); [1968] 1 W.L.R. 1182.
[5] *Re S.*, [1958] 1 All E.R. 783; [1958] 1 W.L.R. 391.
[6] The alternative is necessitated by the statutory definition of "child of the family".

otiose for this purpose, but a parent may still wish to invoke the inherent jurisdiction of the Family Division by way of wardship proceedings which will enable him to be appointed guardian and given care and control of the ward while the custody (in the wide sense) and, therefore, the supervision of the exercise of the parental rights remain with the court.[7] Otherwise, disputes over custody are usually determined as the result of an application under the Guardianship of Minors Act or as part of matrimonial proceedings.

(1) Guardianship of Minors Act 1971

The relevant provisions conferring jurisdiction are now contained in this consolidating Act. On the application of the mother or father an order granting custody and access[8] may be made by the Family Division of the High Court or a county court or a magistrates' court.[9] The order may be made even though at the time the parents are residing together,[10] but it is not enforceable so long as they reside together and will cease to have effect if the residence continues for a period of three months. Residence apparently means cohabitation.[11]

A county court normally has jurisdiction if the respondent or the applicant or the minor resides within its district,[12] but this rule is qualified where proceedings are to be instituted against a respondent who resides in Scotland or Northern Ireland. Then it only has jurisdiction if the summons can be and is served on the respondent in England.[13] The same rules determine the jurisdiction of a magistrates' court,[14] with this addition, that, where the respondent is resident in Scotland or Northern Ireland and a summons is not served on him in England, a magistrates' court within whose area the mother

---

[7] The High Court also has power to grant an injunction to prevent the immediate removal of the child from the custody of a parent pending the institution of custody proceedings in an inferior court; *L.* v. *L.*, [1969] P. 25; [1969] 1 All E.R. 852, (*post*, p. 299).

[8] For access see *post*, p. 299.

[9] Sections 9(1) and 15(1).   [10] Section 9(3).

[11] See *Naylor* v. *Naylor*, [1962] P. 253; [1961] 2 All E.R. 129. Cohabitation is the test to be applied in deciding whether a state of separation exists between spouses living under the same roof; see *ibid.* It has also been adopted by the Matrimonial Proceedings (Magistrates' Courts) Act 1960 in relation to the operation of orders under that Act; see *post*, p. 278. See also the rules relating to reconciliation in the Divorce Reform Act 1969, s. 3.   [12] Guardianship of Minors Act 1971, s. 15(1) (b).

[13] Section 15(3).   [14] Section 15(1) (c) and (3).

resides has jurisdiction, providing that she and the minor are both resident in England. But this additional jurisdiction only enables the court to make an order in favour of the mother; it cannot give custody to the father.[15]

The High Court and county courts can make custody orders in respect of any minor, *i.e.*, a person under 18,[16] whereas the jurisdiction of magistrates' courts is normally limited to children under 16.[17] Even so, an order once made will, unless varied or discharged, continue in force until the child attains majority. Where the child is physically or mentally incapable of self-support magistrates' courts have the additional powers of the other courts[18] and, like those courts, may at any time vary or discharge the order so long as the child remains a minor. Applications for variation or discharge may be made by either parent or, after either's death, by a guardian[19] or by a third person to whom custody has been granted, if, as seems likely, the court has power to make an order in favour of such a person in proceedings between the parents.[20]

Appeal from a county court or a magistrates' court lies to a judge of the Family Division,[1] with a further appeal to the Court of Appeal, apparently without leave.[2] The High Court may also order an application in a county court (but not in a magistrates' court) to be removed to the Family Division,[3] while a magistrates' court may refuse to make an order on the

---

[15] *Ibid.*, sub-s. (4).
Sub-section (6) also provides that, where a woman resides in Scotland or Northern Ireland and brings proceedings in a magistrates' court for a custody order under s. 9(1) of the Act, the father may make a cross application for custody, but this provision seems unnecessary in view of the court's discretion under s. 9 to make such order as it thinks fit; see Tolstoy, *Divorce*, 7th edn. p. 401.
[16] Family Law Reform Act 1969, s. 1. Previously orders could be made up to the age of 21. But provision for maintenance under the Guardianship of Minors Act 1971 may still be ordered up to that age; see s. 12 of the latter Act and *post*, Chapter 14, p. 457.
[17] Guardianship of Minors Act 1971, s. 15(2).
Also magistrates' courts do not share with the other courts the power to deal with an application involving the administration or application of any property belonging to or held in trust for a minor or the income thereof; see *ibid.*   [18] See *ibid.*   [19] Section 9(4).
[20] There is such a power in proceedings under the Matrimonial Proceedings (Magistrates' Courts) Act 1960; see s. 2(1), *infra*.
[1] Guardianship of Minors Act 1971, ss. 16(2) and (3) and 19 (c); Administration of Justice Act 1970, s. 1 and Sched.
[2] *Re W. (an infant)*, [1953] 2 All E.R. 1337.
[3] Guardianship of Minors Act 1971, ss. 16(1) and 19(c); Administration of Justice Act 1970, s. 1 and Sched. 1.

ground that the matter may more conveniently be dealt with by the High Court.[4]

Failure to obey an order made by the High Court or a county court is punishable with committal until the child is surrendered to the person granted custody.[5] If made in a magistrates' court, the penalty is the payment of up to £1 for every day in default up to £20 maximum or committal until surrender of the child but not exceeding a period of two months.[6] Because there is no power to commit to prison as such and because the order for committal is for civil contempt of court there is no power under s. 39 of the Criminal Justice Act 1967 to suspend the committal, but a stay of execution pending appeal is permissible.[7]

(2) Matrimonial Proceedings in Magistrates' Courts

The Matrimonial Proceedings (Magistrates' Courts) Act 1960 gave to magistrates' courts markedly increased powers with regard to the provisions affecting children which they may include in a matrimonial order when exercising their matrimonial jurisdiction, and thus brought them into line with a similar extension of powers conferred on the Divorce Court.[8]

Unlike the Guardianship of Minors Act, the 1960 Act allows no exception to the rule that a provision for custody can only be made by a magistrates' court if the child is under the age of 16, but in some respects the powers under the latter Act are wider than those exercisable by magistrates' courts under the Guardianship of Minors Act. Apart from that enabling the court to grant the legal custody to one or other of the

[4] Section 16(4).
But the parties cannot insist on the case being transferred to the High Court; *Beaumont* v. *Beaumont,* [1938] Ch. 551; [1938] 2 All E.R. 226.
Quaere a case could be stated on a point of law; see Clarke Hall and Morrison, *op. cit.,* p. 1210.
[5] R.S.C. O.42, r. 7; or County Court Rules O. 25, r. 67.
[6] Magistrates' Courts Act 1952, s. 54. Proceedings in magistrates' courts under the Guardianship of Minors Act are "domestic proceedings" and are governed by the 1952 Act.
[7] *B. (B.)* v. *B. (M.),* [1969] P. 103 (C.A.); [1969] 1 All E.R. 891. As this decision illustrates, these rules of enforcement equally apply to orders made by a magistrates' court under the Matrimonial Proceedings (Magistrates' Courts) Act 1960.
[8] By the Matrimonial Proceedings (Children) Act 1958; see now Part III of the Matrimonial Causes Act 1965, and the Matrimonial Proceedings and Property Act 1970.

spouses or to a third party,[9] there is under the 1960 Act that of committing the child to the care of a local authority up to the age of 18, and, where legal custody is granted to an individual, the court can order the child to be placed under the supervision of a probation officer or a local authority until he is 16.[10] These powers can be exercised even if the court does not make the order for which the complaining spouse asks and even if he or she does not ask for any provision to be made concerning the child.[11] Moreover, the court cannot make its final decision on the complaint until it has decided whether or not, and if so how, to exercise these powers.[12]

We have, for the most part, already considered the scope and effects of the power to commit to the care of a local authority.[13] Committal may only be ordered in exceptional circumstances where it is impracticable "to entrust" the child to an individual. This is commonly taken to, and probably does, mean that committal is an alternative to awarding legal custody to a person, but it might be argued that, since the Act[14] merely speaks of entrusting the child and not of entrusting legal custody, the two are not mutually exclusive and that, for example, legal custody could be given to a father abroad where it is impracticable for the time being to entrust the child to him in the sense of giving him care and control. It is also doubtful whether the Act allows legal custody, as opposed to care, to be given to a local authority.[15] On the other hand, since there is no power under the Guardianship of Minors Act to commit to care, it might be argued that legal custody can be given thereunder to a local authority, but the difficulty about that argument is that there are no statutory provisions defining

---

[9] Under the former Summary Jurisdiction (Separation and Maintenance) Acts 1895-1949, custody could only be granted to the spouse who was the complainant.

[10] See ss. 2 (1) (d) to (f) and 3(9) of the 1960 Act. For access see sub-para. (g) and *post*, p. 301.

[11] *Ibid.*, s. 4(1). See also s. 2(3) which reinforces s. 4(1) by providing that the court may exercise its powers with regard to children even though a separation order or an order for maintenance of a spouse cannot be made because of the complainant's adultery or because, where the complaint is the defendant's adultery, the adultery has been connived at, condoned, or conduced to by the defendant's wilful neglect or misconduct.

[12] *Ibid.*   [13] *Ante*, Chapter 5.

[14] Section 2(1) (e).

[15] *R.* v. *Falmouth Borough Justices, Ex parte Palmer* (1962), 61 L.G.R. 179. (D.C.).

the powers of a local authority to whom legal custody is entrusted, whereas there are where care is given.

Where the court intends to commit to care it must inform the local authority of its intention and give them the opportunity to make representations.[16] These may include representations on the grounds that the authority is not the appropriate authority;[17] that they do not at present have facilities for boarding out or providing accommodation; or that, from their knowledge of the child and the family, committal to care is not likely to be suitable. They are also entitled to be heard on the question of payments for the maintenance of the child if he is committed to their care.[18]

A supervision order, too, must only be made if there are exceptional circumstances making it desirable. Moreover, such an order is not possible if the child is committed to, or is already in, the care of the local authority.[19] Since the policy of the Children and Young Persons Act 1969 is normally not to select probation officers as supervisors of children under the age of 14,[20] it may be that magistrates' courts will take a similar view when making supervision orders under the 1960 Act.[1]

Children of the Family

Whereas the Guardianship of Minors Act is limited, in cases of parental disputes, to a child of both parents, the 1960 Act applies to a child of the family who may, within the meaning of that Act,[2] be either a child of both parties to the marriage or a child of only one of them provided that he has been accepted as one of the family by the other. The term extends

---

[16] Matrimonial Proceedings (Magistrates' Courts) Act 1960, s.3 (1); *R.* v. *Falmouth Borough Justices, supra.* Failure to comply with these requirements will mean that the order for committal will be quashed; see *Ex parte Palmer* (1962), *Times,* December 5.

[17] The appropriate one is that within whose area the child is resident before the order to commit is made; s. 2(1) (e).

[18] Section 3(1).   [19] Section 2(4) (b) and (c).   [20] Section 13(2).

[1] Selection of a probation officer must be in the same way as selection under a probation order; Matrimonial Proceedings (Magistrates' Courts) Act 1960, s. 3(6).

If the child is or will be resident in a petty sessions area other than that to which the selected probation officer has been assigned, the court may substitute an officer assigned to that area. Similarly one local authority may be substituted for another. See *ibid,* s. 3(8) and Magistrates' Courts (Matrimonial Proceedings) Rules 1960, r. 2.

[2] Section 16.

to the illegitimate or adopted child as well as the legitimate child, but the child must be a child of at least one of the parties. Thus, if X, the widower of Y, accepted Y's son, C, as a child of the family when Y was alive, and later marries Z, it is not possible to treat C as a child of the family of X and Z.[3]

Whether a child of one party has been accepted as a child of the family by the other party is a question of fact. Usually there is no difficulty in establishing this. After marrying a woman who already has children of her own the husband "sets up home with his wife, the children come to live there, he treats them as his own and does his best not only to make them members of the family, but also to feel that they are members of the family".[4] The longer this state of affairs lasts the clearer it is that the children have been accepted as members of the family. Difficulties may, however, arise where the parties separate soon after the marriage, especially if they have never set up a home. In *such* cases the question, which is to be answered objectively, is whether the husband married on the basis that he was then accepting the wife's child as a child of the family.[5] He may even accept at that time a child *en ventre de sa mere.*[6] But the court should always be cautious and should insist on clear and unequivocal evidence of accep-

---

[3] *Cf.* the wider definition given to "child of the family" by the Matrimonial Proceedings and Property Act 1970 for the purpose of orders for custody in a divorce court, *post,* p. 280.

    Exceptionally, a child may concurrently be a child of two families; see *Newman* v. *Newman,* [1971] P. 43; [1970] 3 All E.R. 529.

[4] *Per* SALMON, L. J., in *Bowlas* v. *Bowlas,* [1965] P. at p. 451; [1965] 3 All E.R. 40, at pp. 46, 47, and compare *H.* v. *H.* (*H. by his Guardian intervening*), [1966] 1 All E.R. 356; [1966] 1 W.L.R. 187, where the husband had nothing to do with the wife's child.

[5] *Bowlas* v. *Bowlas, supra; Snow* v. *Snow,* [1971] 3 W.L.R. 951, (C.A.). In *Bowlas* SALMON, L. J. seems to have insisted that acceptance must be before or at the time of the marriage ([1965] P. at p. 461; [1965] 3 All E.R. at p. 46), but in *Snow* v. *Snow* the Divisional Court held ([1971] 3 W.L.R. 230) that acceptance *before* the marriage may be withdrawn. The finality of the test which makes the date of the marriage the only relevant one for determining whether there has been acceptance has been questioned (see Bromley, *op. cit.,* p. 285) on the ground that there is no objection in principle to a spouse's changing his mind and accepting a child whom he has previously disowned.

    For an exceptional case where a husband was held to have accepted his wife's child although they had never cohabited see *R.* v. *R.,* [1971] C.L.Y. 3364.

[6] *Caller* v. *Caller,* [1966] 2 All E.R. 754; [1966] 3 W.L.R. 437, where the wife conceived the child by a man other than her husband before she married him, but he, the husband, had even gone so far as to tell his friends before his marriage that he was the father.

tance, because, as ORMROD, J., has warned, "to hold otherwise is to encourage explicit rejection of such children and thus to promote a deal of unkindness to them".[7] The need for strong evidence has been particularly stressed in undefended divorce petitions. The court should not rely on the petitioning husband's statement that a child is not a child of the family because he is not the father and has not accepted the child into the family; the court must see that the interests of the mother and the children are fully protected and that they are given the right to be heard.[8]

Acceptance presupposes knowledge of the material facts. A husband who mistakenly thinks a boy is his son will not be held to have accepted him into the family if, on learning that he is an adulterine child, he disowns him;[9] and, if he learns of the true paternity only after a final break-up of his marriage, it is no longer open to him to accept the child since there is then no family. This is certainly so where the wife separates from her husband and takes the child with her,[10] but it has been suggested that, if she were to leave the child with him, acceptance would still be possible because the husband and the child could be regarded as living as one family.[11] If, however, the husband knows when he marries the mother that the child is not his, its true status, *e.g.*, that it is illegitimate and not the child of a former marriage, is not a material fact, so that the wife's failure to disclose this will not invalidate his ostensible acceptance.[12]

Acceptance of a child of one spouse by the other is not in itself enough. The parent spouse must agree to the acceptance. There must be an arrangement between them that the child

---

[7] *H.* v. *H.* (*H. by his Guardian intervening*), *supra.*

[8] *S.* v. *S.*, [1964] 3 All E.R. 915; [1965] 1 W.L.R. 21; *Bickley* v. *Bickley*, [1964] 3 All E.R. 917 (C.A.); [1965] 1 W.L.R. 600n.; *Hodgkins* v. *Hodgkins*, [1965] 3 All E.R. 164, (C.A.); [1965] 1 W.L.R. 1448.
The petitioner must in his petition give full particulars of the facts relied on in support of his allegation that the child is not a child of the family; see M.C. Rules 1971, r. 9(1) and Form 2, para. 6.

[9] *R.* v. *R.*, [1968] P. 414; [1968] 2 All E.R. 608. The principle was approved by Lord DENNING, M. R., in *Re L.*, [1968] P. 119 at p. 158; [1968] 1 All E.R. 20 at pp. 25-26. See also *B.* v. *B. and F.*, *infra.* Compare the position under the Matrimonial Proceedings and Property Act 1970, *post*, p. 281.

[10] *B.* v. *B. and F.* (*B. and B. intervening*), [1969] P. 37; [1968] 3 All E.R. 232.

[11] Bromley, *Family Law, op. cit.*, p. 284, n. 8.

[12] *Kirkwood* v. *Kirkwood*, [1970] 2 All E.R. 161; [1970] 1 W.L.R. 1042.

should be treated by both of them as the child of both.[13] The fact that the parent is unduly possessive of his or her child does not necessarily exclude such an arrangement; nor, on the other hand, does the fact that the non-parent spouse is not asked to undertake any substantial financial liability; but both are relevant considerations.[14]

Where a child is not a child of both parties and there is no custody order made by an English court in respect of him in force, the court must not make an order under the 1960 Act without taking steps to give notice to a parent who is not a party to the proceedings informing him of the complaint and the venue of the hearing. If he attends he is entitled to be heard. Notice to the father of an illegitimate child need only be given if he has been adjudged by a court to be the father, but, even if an affiliation order has not been made, the father, if he learns of the proceedings, is entitled to attend the hearing and make representations.[15]

The question whether a child is a child of the family is more likely to be raised where there is a dispute over maintenance[16] under the 1960 Act, but it may arise over custody or access. If it is found that the child is not a child of the family and the spouse who is not the parent seeks custody, he cannot proceed under that Act, but will have to do so by way of wardship proceedings.

Divided Orders

The power to make a divided order under the Guardianship of Minors Act or in custody proceedings in a divorce court is due to the wide terms in which the relevant provisions are framed. The court may make such order for custody as it thinks fit.[17] A magistrates' court may therefore make a divided

---

[13] *G.* v. *G.* (1965), 109 Sol. Jo. 831; *Dixon* v. *Dixon*, [1967] 3 All E.R. 659; [1968] 1 W.L.R. 167; *P. (R.)* v. *P. (P.)*, [1969] 3 All E.R. 777; [1969] 1 W.L.R. 898.

[14] *Per* WRANGHAM, J., in *Dixon* v. *Dixon*, [1967] 3 All E.R. at p. 662; [1968] 1 W.L.R. at p. 171.

[15] Matrimonial Proceedings (Magistrates' Courts) Act 1960, s. 4(6).
Before the summons is issued on the complaint the complainant is required to say whether or not there is a child of the family who is not a child of both parties. If there is not, he or she must, if it is known, give the name and address of the parent who is not a party to the proceedings (Magistrates' Courts (Matrimonial Proceedings) Rules 1960, r. 4 (2)).

[16] See *post*, Chapter 14.

[17] Guardianship of Minors Act 1971, s. 9; Matrimonial Proceedings and Property Act 1970, s. 18.

order under the Guardianship of Minors Act,[18] but in *Wild* v.
Wild[19] it was held that this is not possible under the 1960 Act
because the order would be inconsistent with the narrower
provisions of that Act.[20] These do not permit the court to make
an order for access by the person who is given custody by the
matrimonial order, and enable provision for maintenance of
the child to be made only in favour of the person granted
custody. So, if a divided order were allowed, it would mean,
for example, that a husband who is granted the custody could
not by order have access and the wife with care and control
could not claim maintenance.[1] The Divisional Court in *Wild* v.
Wild, however, saw no practical importance in this anomaly,
because it is open to either party to issue a summons under
the Guardianship of Minors Act asking for a split order – provided, of course, that the child is a child of the marriage.

Interim Orders

When a magistrates' court adjourns the hearing of a complaint for more than a week or refuses to make an order because
it considers the case to be more suitable for the High Court[2] it
may make an interim order. So, too, may the High Court, if
after such refusal or on appeal it orders the complaint to be
reheard by the magistrates' court.[3] Courts generally are reluctant to make interim orders, but this is especially so with
regard to custody, because provision for it is only to be included
in an order if special circumstances so require.

An interim order ceases to operate at the end of three months,
unless it is earlier varied or revoked or a specified lesser period
is prescribed by the order or a final order is made.

Operation and Enforcement of an Order Granting Custody

If a matrimonial or interim order is made while the parties
to the marriage are cohabiting, a provision committing the

[18] *Re W. (an infant)*, [1964] Ch. 202 (C.A.); [1963] 3 All E.R. 459.
[19] [1969] P. 33; [1968] 3 All E.R. 608.
[20] In *Smith* v. *Smith*, [1965] C.L.Y. 1249 a magistrates' court made a
divided order, holding that the reasoning in *Re W. (an infant)*, *supra*
applied by analogy to the 1960 Act.
[1] Bromley, *op. cit.*, p. 282, has pointed out that this latter difficulty may
equally arise with regard to a divided order under the Guardianship of
Minors Act, since it enables the mother to obtain maintenance from the
father only if she is awarded custody (s. 9(2)).
[2] Matrimonial Proceedings (Magistrates' Courts) Act 1960, s. 5.
[3] Section 6. An order made by the High Court is to be treated for the
purpose of enforcement as if it were an order of the magistrates' court.

child to the legal custody of one of them will not be enforceable while they cohabit and will cease to have effect after cohabitation has continued for three months.[4] But, otherwise, an order in so far as it contains provisions dealing with custody, care, supervision or access comes into effect when made and remains operative notwithstanding the parties' cohabitation, unless the court otherwise directs.[5]

A copy of the order committing the child to the legal custody of a person or to the care of a local authority may be served on the person presently having actual custody.[6] The order is enforceable in the same way as a custody order made by a magistrates' court under the Guardianship of Minors Act.[7]

Variation and Revocation of Orders

The court has power to vary and revoke provisions relating to legal custody, committal to care, supervision and access, but subject to a number of involved restrictions.[8] If the application is to revoke the whole of a matrimonial order which consists of or includes any provision for legal custody, care or supervision or is to vary the order by revoking any of them or by adding or altering a provision for legal custody, then, if the application is refused, the court may still exercise any of its powers with respect to children and vary the order as it wishes. But, because of the general limitations imposed by the Act,[9] it cannot introduce a provision for custody or for committal to care if another court has already made a custody order, or for committal to care or for supervision or access if the child is already in the care of a local authority. A provision for care also cannot be varied, and neither it nor a supervision provision can be revived once it has ceased to be in force. Nor can the matrimonial order be varied by the addition of either kind of provision.[10]

---

[4] *Cf.* the Guardianship of Minors Act 1971, s. 9(3), *ante*, p. 269.
[5] Matrimonial Proceedings (Magistrates' Courts) Act 1960, s. 7(1). For resumption of cohabitation see *infra*.
[6] Section 13(3); *Pullen* v. *Pullen* (1964), 108 Sol. Jo. 617 (C.A.).
[7] Section 13(3); Magistrates' Courts Act 1952, s. 54(3). Compare *ante*, p. 271. [8] See s. 8(1) read with ss. 4(1) and 2(4).
[9] Section 2(4) (a), (b) and (c).
[10] Proviso to s. 8(1). But this restriction is to be read subject to the overriding provisions of s. 4(1), the effect of which is that if a complaint is made to vary a matrimonial order by revoking a provision granting legal custody, then a provision for committal to care could be added; see *ante*, Chapter 5, p. 155.

Where there is a complaint for revocation on the ground of the complainant's adultery the court is not bound to revoke a provision relating to the children in the order.[11] The same rule applies when the parties resume cohabitation, except that a provision committing custody to either spouse automatically ceases to have effect.[12]

The persons who may be parties to a complaint for variation or revocation are partly determined by the nature of the complaint. The rules are set out in an Appendix.[13]

(3) Matrimonial Proceedings in a Divorce Court
(a) *Nullity, Divorce and Judicial Separation*

In proceedings for nullity, divorce or judicial separation the High Court or a county court having jurisdiction over those matters[14] has power to make orders with regard to custody, committal to the care of a local authority and supervision[15] of a child of the family.[16] As an alternative it may direct that proceedings be taken to make the child a ward of court. Apart from this alternative, these powers are similar to those of a magistrates' court under the Matrimonial Proceedings (Magistrates' Courts) Act 1960, including that of awarding custody to a third person and, like the latter, may be exercised even if the petition is dismissed, providing that this is done forthwith or within a reasonable period after the dismissal. But the jurisdiction of a divorce court is wider in respect of the age of children. Custody and supervision orders may be made so long as the child is under 18,[17] and an order for committal to care if he is under 17.[18] An order is not commonly made once he has attained 16 and, whatever his age when made, will cease to operate when he attains 18.[19]

---

[11] Section 8(2).   [12] Sections 7(1), (2) and 8 (2).
[13] *Post*, p. 308.   [14] Under the Matrimonial Causes Act 1967.
[15] As for access see *post*, p. 299.
[16] Matrimonial Proceedings and Property Act 1970, ss. 17, 18 and 27; Matrimonial Causes Act 1965, ss. 16, 37 and 46. Why these provisions of the latter Act were not repealed and re-enacted by the former is difficult to fathom.
[17] Matrimonial Proceedings and Property Act 1970, s. 18; Matrimonial Causes Act 1965, s. 37.
[18] Matrimonial Causes Act 1965, s. 36(4).
[19] See references in last two footnotes, and for orders already in force on January 1, 1970 see Family Law Reform Act 1969, s. 1(4) and Sched. 3, para. 3(1) (b).
An order for custody is enforceable against the other parent (or spouse)

Custody

With regard to an order for committal to care, it has already been pointed out[20] that, unlike the Act of 1960, there are no express statutory provisions preventing such an order being made where there is already in force a custody order made by an English court or even if the child is already in the care of a local authority. An order for committal cannot also include a provision that the child be placed under supervision[1] or, *semble*, for access to the child.[2] It has, however, already been suggested[3] that the 1960 Act does not prevent the court concurrently making provisions for custody and for committal to care, and it is submitted that this also applies to orders for committal under the Matrimonial Causes Act 1965.[4] Moreover, where a child is already in care under s. 1 of the Children Act 1948 the court may still make a custody order, but may direct that the person to whom custody is given is not to take over the care of the child unless the authority is satisfied that that step would be in the interests of the child.[5]

The Matrimonial Proceedings and Property Act 1970 has widened the definition of "child of the family" so as to include not only a child of both parties to a marriage but also:

"any other child, not being a child who has been boarded-out with those parties by a local authority or voluntary organisation, who has been *treated* by both of those parties as a child of their family".[6]

It is, therefore, no longer necessary for at least one of the parties to be a parent. This extended definition does not, how-

but not against the child, so that if the latter has reached the age of discretion (as to which see *post*, p. 288) and chooses not to live with the party who has been given custody, custody cannot be recovered by *habeas corpus* or otherwise; *Stark* v. *Stark and Hitchins*, [1910] P. 190.
[20] *Ante*, Chapter 5, p. 155.   [1] Matrimonial Causes Act 1965, s. 37(4).
[2] See *ante*, p. 156, n. 11, but see the next footnote.   [3] *Ante*, p. 272.
[4] If both orders are permissible, it is arguable that access could also be ordered, since the Matrimonial Proceedings and Property Act 1970, s. 27(1), expressly provides that custody includes access.
[5] The reason for including such a direction has been that, without it, the person having custody could insist on care being handed over to him, and the local authority, in accordance with its duty under s. 1(3) of the Children Act 1948, would have to comply; see s. 1(3) read with s. 6(2) and see *Rayden on Divorce*, 11th ed., p. 895. But it is submitted that there is no longer the same need for the direction in view of the decision of the Court of Appeal in *Krishnan* v. *London Borough of Sutton*, [1970] Ch. 181; [1969] 3 All E.R. 1367; that there is no absolute statutory duty under s. 1(3) to hand over the child.
[6] Section 27(1); and see *ibid.* for the definition of "child", which includes an illegitimate or adopted child of a party.

ever, apply to proceedings in magistrates' courts.[7] How far case law on the old definition will be relevant to the new is problematical and will depend on the significance which the court will attach to the substitution of a test of "treatment" for one of "acceptance". It is clear that both parties must in fact have treated the child as a member of the family, but it would seem that it is not necessary that one party's treatment should depend upon the other's consenting to it; and it has already been established that knowledge of paternity is not material.[8] It will be seen[9] that, with regard to the making of financial provisions, knowledge that the child is not one's own is relevant in determining what is the appropriate provision, if any, to be ordered, but it is not made an essential element in the definition of a child of the family.

Another notable change made by the 1970 Act is that an order for custody made under it will not affect the rights which any person other than the parties to the marriage in question has over the child, unless the child is a child of one or both of those parties and that person was a party to the proceedings on the application for an order for custody.[10]

Apart from the court's powers in a case of dismissal of the petition, orders for custody, committal to care or supervision may be made before, by or after the decree absolute or, in a case of judicial separation, the final decree.[11] The court's jurisdiction does not depend on the child's being domiciled or resident in England;[12] he may be only temporarily here while in transit to another country or may even be out of the jurisdiction.[13] An order for custody may be made even if one of the parties to the marriage is dead,[14] but *semble* not after the parties have re-married.[15]

---

[7] See *supra*, p. 273.
[8] *W. (R.J.)* v. *W. (S.J.)*, [1971] 3 All E.R. 303.
[9] *Post*, Chapter 14, p. 469.
[10] Matrimonial Proceedings and Property Act 1970, s. 18(2).
[11] Contested custody applications are invariably adjourned into chambers and not dealt with at the hearing of the petition; but *cp. Cooper* v. *Cooper*, [1961] 3 All E.R. 539 (C.A.); [1961] 1 W.L.R. 1369.
[12] *Re C. (an infant)* (1956) *Times*, December 14.
[13] *Philips* v. *Philips* (1944), 60 T.L.R. 395 (C.A.); *Harben* v. *Harben*, [1957] 1 All E.R. 379; [1957] 1 W.L.R. 261.
[14] *Pryor* v. *Pryor*, [1947] P. 64; [1947] 1 All E.R. 381; *B.* v. *B. and H. (L. intervening)* [1962] 1 All E.R. 29; [1961] 1 W.L.R. 1467.
[15] See the Court of Appeal, *obiter, in Grainger* v. *Grainger and Clark*, [1960] P. 99; [1959] 3 All E.R. 51.

Custody

Section 17 of the Matrimonial Proceedings and Property Act 1970
The object of this section, which replaces the narrower provisions of s. 33 of the Matrimonial Causes Act 1965, is to
ensure that due consideration is given to the interests of the
children before the spouse is granted his matrimonial remedy.

The court must not make absolute a decree of divorce or
nullity or pronounce a decree of judicial separation unless it
has by an order declared[16] that it is satisfied on one of the
following matters:[17]

(1) That there are no children of the family to whom s. 17 applies.
The section extends to:
(a) any minor child of the family[18] who at the date of the
order is (i) under 16 or (ii) receiving instruction at an educational establishment or undergoing training for a trade,
profession or vocation, whether or not he is also in gainful
employment,[19]

and (b) any other child of the family to whom the court directs
that the section is to apply because it is of the opinion that
there are special circumstances which make the application
desirable in the interest of the child.

This provision is much wider than its predecessor not
merely because the section may apply to a child over 16 but
also because it admits the principle that a child may need
protecting by a parent or step-parent even after he has attained
majority.[20] Special circumstances which are most likely to move
the court to apply the section are those where the child suffers
a physical or mental disability which impairs his earning
capacity.[21]

---

[16] Section 33 of the 1965 Act did not expressly require a formal order,
and where consideration of the arrangements for the children was
adjourned into chambers, for example where there was a custody issue,
there was the possibility of the court's omitting at the later proceedings
to state formally that it was satisfied about the arrangements; see *B.* v.
B., [1961] 2 All E.R. 396; [1961] 1 W.L.R. 856.

[17] If the court is not satisfied, either party to the proceedings can require
it to make an order to that effect.

[18] *I.e.*, under the age of 18; see Family Law Reform Act 1969, s. 1.

[19] Compare the narrower meaning given to a dependant child for the
purpose of the Matrimonial Proceedings (Magistrates' Courts) Act
1960, where the instruction or training must be full-time and the latter
also for a minimum period of two years; see s. 16(1) thereof.

[20] This principle is also recognised by the Matrimonial Proceedings and
Property Act 1970, s. 8, for the purpose of granting financial provisions
for the child, (*post*, Chapter 14), but otherwise it is scarcely known to
English law. See, however, the protection which exceptionally is afforded
by the criminal law (*ante*, Chapter 6, p. 176), and note the right of an
unmarried daughter of any age to claim maintenance under the Inheritance Family Provisions Acts (*post*, Chapter 14, p. 498).

[21] *Cf.* s. 16(1) of the Matrimonial Proceedings (Magistrates' Courts) Act
1960, *supra*.

or (2) That the only children who are or may be children of the family to whom s. 17 applies are those named in the order and that –

(i) arrangements for the welfare of every child so named have been made and are satisfactory or are the best that can be devised in the circumstances.[22]

or (ii) it is impracticable for the party or parties appearing before the court to make such arrangements.

"Welfare" is defined to include the custody (which in turn includes access) and education of the child and financial provision for him.[23] With regard to this last factor, it should be noted that the 1970 Act enables the court to order financial provision for children who are over 18 both in cases of "special circumstances" and where the child is receiving instruction or training[1] but the requirement under s. 17 to be satisfied about arrangements applies only to the former. Thus, the court may order financial provision for a 20-year-old student without having to be satisfied about arrangements for him, unless perhaps it is prepared to hold in a particular case that his financial circumstances are to be treated as special circumstances.

or (3) That there are circumstances making it desirable that the decree should be made absolute or should be made, as the case may be, without delay notwithstanding that there are or may be children to whom s. 17 applies and that the court is unable to make a declaration in the terms of para. (2). But the court may only make an order in these circumstances if it obtains a satisfactory undertaking from either or both of the parties to bring the question of the arrangements for the children before it within a specified time.[2]

There were conflicting decisions about the effect of not complying with s. 33 of the Matrimonial Causes Act 1965. One view was that any decree nisi of divorce or nullity made absolute

---

For an illustration of special circumstances see the Australian case, *Paull* v. *Paull* (1961) A.L.R. 455 (Q.S.C.) where the son was 19 years old, a spastic and suffering from congenital deafness.

[22] Where proceedings for divorce are contemplated, the court may have already indicated its approval of arrangements for the child when expressing its opinion as to the reasonableness of an agreement which the parties to those proceedings have made or proposed in connection with them; see s. 7(1) of the Divorce Reform Act 1969.

The court should not certify its satisfaction with the arrangements unless they are of a reasonably permanent character; *McKernan* v. *McKernan* (1970), 114 Sol. Jo. 284.

If the child is at school it is generally desirable that the court should have before it a school report on his educational progress and prospects; *Leech* v. *Leech and Dolleman* (1972), 116 Sol. Jo. 274.

[23] Sections 17(6) and 27(1). The former rule under s. 33 of the 1965 Act related less specifically to the "care and upbringing" of the child.

[1] Section 8(3).   [2] See s. 17(2).

Custody

(or decree of judicial separation pronounced) was thereby rendered void,[3] but in *F.* v. *F.*[4] Sir JOCELYN SIMON, P., held that non-compliance only had a voidable effect on the decree. This conclusion was justified partly on the grounds that to treat the decree absolute as void would rarely promote the interests of the child, in some cases would actually do him harm and would sometimes cause hardship to innocent third parties, as in the present case where the husband had remarried.

Section 17 adopts a different approach. On the one hand, it emphasises the importance of the order declaring that the court is satisfied on one of the above related matters by the provision[5] that a decree made absolute (or a decree of judicial separation pronounced) without such an order is void. On the other hand, once an order is made the validity of the decree cannot be challenged on the ground that in making the order the court did not fulfil the conditions prescribed by the section; for example, because the court did not know all the facts.[6]

As the reported cases on s. 33 show, the non-compliance is most often due to a failure to obtain the court's satisfaction in respect of a child born after the filing of the petition but before the decree nisi is made or, as in *P.* v. *P. and J.*,[7] born between the dates of decree nisi and decree absolute. Procedural improvements could reduce the risk of this happening. The present Rules require the petitioner to file with his petition a statement giving full particulars of the arrangements which he proposes for each child, together with a medical report stating whether or not the child is suffering from any chronic disability or illness.[8] But the Rules do not ensure that he or she draws the court's attention to any change of circumstances. It has been suggested[9] that they might be amended, so that when applying for a decree nisi to be made absolute a wife would be required to state that she is neither pregnant nor has given

[3] *B.* v. *B., supra; N.* v. *N.* (1964), 108 Sol. Jo. 99.
[4] [1971] P. 1; [1970] 1 All E.R. 200. The Court of Appeal approved the principle in *P.* v. *P. and J.*, [1971] P. 217; [1971] 1 All E.R. 616.
[5] Section 17(3).
[6] *Cf. Shelton* v. *Shelton* (1965), 109 Sol. Jo. 393, where a certificate made under s. 33 and expressing satisfaction with the arrangements for the children was nullified when it was shown that the judge was not fully aware of the circumstances.   [7] [1970] P. 161; [1969] 3 All E.R. 511.
[8] Matrimonial Causes Rules 1971, r. 8(2) and Form 4.
[9] *Per* Sir JOCELYN SIMON, P., in *F.* v. *F., supra*, at pp. 15, 207-208 respectively, referring to the former Rules (M.C.R. 1968).

birth to any child not mentioned in the petition, while a husband would be required to make such an averment in relation to his wife to the best of his knowledge and belief. This would strengthen an existing Practice Direction[10] which requires any alteration, or proposed alteration, in arrangements already approved by the court to be brought to its notice before application is made for the decree to be made absolute.

A respondent may, without filing an answer, be heard on custody, whether or not he has returned to the court an acknowledgment of service stating that he wishes to be heard on the matter.[11] Moreover, a respondent on whom a statement as to arrangements for children is served may at any time before the court makes an order under s. 17(1) file a written statement of his views on the arrangements.[12]

"Perhaps the greatest weakness of the present procedure is that it sometimes gives the impression of superficiality." This was one of the conclusions drawn in a report by the Law Commission[13] on the operation of the former s. 33. The report reveals considerable variation in the use made by the courts of their powers and recommends a number of valuable improvements in the law and practice. Space does not permit a summary of them, but it must be added that they do take account of the practical difficulties in giving effect to the section; for example, the present limited welfare resources. They also raise the pertinent question of how long the courts should continue to control arrangements for the children's upbringing after decree absolute over and above the general law for the protection of all children. One particularly helpful suggestion is that rather more use could be made of the supervising order.

Variation and Discharge of Orders for Custody, etc. The Court is given a general power to vary and discharge orders relating to custody, committal to care and supervision.[14] These should

[10] [1969] 1 All E.R. 377; [1969] 1 W.L.R. 228.
[11] Rule 49(1) and (3). Under the former Matrimonial Causes Rules 1957 [proviso (a) to r. 33] a respondent who claimed custody normally had to include a statement of proposed arrangements in his memorandum of appearance.   [12] Rule 50.
[13] Working Paper No. 15, p. 38. The report was prepared and written for the Law Commission by Mr. J. C. Hall of the Cambridge Law Faculty.
[14] Matrimonial Proceedings and Property Act 1970, s. 18(5) and (6); Matrimonial Causes Act 1965, ss. 36(7) and 37(6). The first mentioned section also enables a provision in a custody order to be suspended (see s. 18(6)).

be compared with the restricted powers of magistrates' courts under the Matrimonial Proceedings (Magistrates' Courts) Act 1960. On the other hand, unlike that Act and its Rules, the Matrimonial Causes legislation does not explicitly set out who may be parties to proceedings for variation or discharge, except to provide that, without prejudice to the right of any other person entitled to apply for an order as respects a child, the guardian and any other person who, by virtue of an order of the court, has the custody or control of him or his care or supervision [under ss. 36 and 37 respectively] may apply for an order relating to custody, committal to care, or supervision;[15] and except to add specifically that a local authority or a supervising officer may apply for the variation or discharge of orders made under those sections.[16] It is also enacted that, if a child is the subject of a supervision order, variation may be made at the instance of the court itself.[17]

Declaration of Unfitness. In cases of divorce and judicial separation the court may occasionally include in the decree a declaration that either party to the marriage is unfit to have the custody of the children of the family. One effect of the declaration is that if the party to whom it relates is a parent of any child of the family that party will not, on the death of the other parent, be entitled as of right to the custody or guardianship of that child,[18] but will have to satisfy the court that his conduct is now so different that custody or guardianship may be safely entrusted to him. Because of these serious consequences of a declaration a court will want clear evidence of serious misconduct before making it.[1] If, however, it declines to do so, the other parent can take steps to prevent the child from falling into the custody or guardianship of the parent whose conduct

---

[15] Matrimonial Causes. Rules 1971, r. 92 (3).
[16] Rule 93 (4).   [17] Matrimonial Causes Act 1965, s. 37(5).
[18] Matrimonial Proceedings and Property Act 1970, s. 18(3) and (4). Formerly the power to make a declaration related only to children of the marriage; (see M.C. Act 1965, s. 34(2), replacing the Guardianship of Infants Act 1886, s. 7).
  For the right of the surviving parent to guardianship of the child see *post*, Chapter 12.
[1] Declarations were made in *Handford* v. *Handford* (1890), 63 L.T. 256; *Webley* v. *Webley* (1891), 64 L.T. 839; *C.* v. *C.* (1905), 22 T.L.R. 26 and *S.* v. *S.*, [1949] P. 269; [1949] 1 All E.R. 285; but refused in *Woolnoth* v. *Woolnoth* (1902), 86 L.T. 598; *Bagnall* v. *Bagnall and Hobbs* (1910), 26 T.L.R. 659 and *R.* v. *R.* (*No. 2*), [1959] C.L.Y. 949.

is impugned by making the child a ward of court or appointing a testamentary guardian.[2]

(b) *Neglect to Maintain*

When the High Court or a county court with jurisdiction makes an order for maintenance under s. 6 of the Matrimonial Proceedings and Property Act 1970,[3] it is also empowered to make an order for custody of any child of the family who is under 18, but the order can remain operative only so long as the order for maintenance is in force and the child is under that age.[4] The order will not affect the rights which any person other than the parties to the marriage in question has over the child, unless the child is a child of one or both of those parties and that person was a party to the proceedings on the application for an order for custody.[5] The order may be varied or revoked or any provision in it suspended.[6]

If a custody order is made, a provision for supervision may apparently be included, and it seems that alternatively to such an order there is jurisdiction to commit to the care of a local authority.[7]

IV. MEANS OF RESOLVING DISPUTES OVER CUSTODY
AS BETWEEN PARENT AND STRANGER

The term "stranger" is used in this context to mean a person other than a parent, spouse of a parent or guardian of the child.[8]

Although the writ of habeas corpus eventually became obsolete as a means of resolving disputes between parents over custody,[9] it remained the method of enforcing the parental right to custody against a stranger, unless alternatively the parent chose to take wardship proceedings. Indeed, the Custody of Children Act 1891 increased the High Court's powers of dealing with applications for the writ by strengthening its discretion to withhold it where the parent has abandoned or deserted the child or otherwise so conducted himself that the

---

[2] *C. v. C.* (1965), 109 Sol. Jo. 473.   [3] See *post*, Chapter 14, p. 480.
[4] Section 19(1).   [5] Section 19(2).   [6] *Ibid.*
[7] *Cf. ante*, p. 280.
[8] It also includes the rare case of a spouse of a parent whose child is not a child of the family. For disputes between a parent and a guardian or between two guardians see *post*, Chapter 12, p. 407. Note also that an applicant for adoption may by way of an interim order be given custody for up to two years as a probationary period; Adoption Act 1958, s. 8.
[9] See *ante*, p. 268.

Court should refuse to enforce his right to custody.[10] Doubt, however, exists as to how far the writ is issuable once the child reaches the age of discretion.[11] Since the basis of the remedy lies in the illegal detention of a person without his consent, on principle it should no longer be available when the child attains that age and is consenting to be kept in a place away from the parent,[12] but there are dicta[13] to support the view that even in those circumstances the writ may issue if the child's interests so require; for example, where a seventeen-year-old girl is living in a brothel. The point is likely to remain academic in view of other remedies open to the parent.

Apart from wardship proceedings, it seems clear that the parent may seek an order for custody under the Guardianship of Minors Act.[14] If anything, the recent ruling of the House of Lords in *J. v. C.*[15] that the principle of the paramountcy of the child's welfare, formerly embodied in section one of the Guardianship of Infants Act 1925,[16] applies as much to disputes over custody and upbringing between the parents and strangers as to those between parents, tends to strengthen that conclusion.[17]

But in the converse case where a stranger is seeking custody from the parent, the Guardianship of Minors Act, notwithstanding *J. v. C.*, does not enable him to seek an order thereunder.[18] Instead he will have to commence proceedings to

[10] Section 1. See further, *infra.*
[11] In the case of boys *dicta* state this to be 14; *Re Agar-Ellis* (1883), 24 Ch. D. 317, 326 (C.A.); *Thomasset* v. *Thomasset*, [1894] P. 295, 298 (C.A.). For girls it was held in *R.* v. *Howes Ex parte Barford* (1860), 3 E. & E. 332 to be 16; but *cf.* TINDAL, C. J., in *Re Lloyd* (1841), 3 Man. & G. 547, 548, who seems to have regarded 14 as also the age for girls.
  It has been suggested that a court might now fix the age at that at which compulsory education ends; Hall, *Sources of Family Law*, p. 242.
[12] See BRETT, M. R., in *Re Agar-Ellis, ibid. Aliter* if there is no consent.
[13] See *R.* v. *Howes Ex parte Barford* (1860), 121 E.R. 467, 468; *R.* v. *Lewis* (1893), 9 T.L.R. 226, 227; *Lough* v. *Ward*, [1945] 2 All E.R. 338, 348. *Cf.* Bromley, *op. cit.*, p. 281.
[14] See Bromley, *op. cit.*, p. 282. For the contrary view see Clarke Hall and Morrison, *op. cit.*, p. 1204.
[15] [1970] A.C. 668; [1969] 1 All E.R. 788.
[16] See now s. 1 of the Guardianship of Minors Act 1971.
[17] But see Cretney, *Judicial Blinkers* (1969), 119 New L.J. 301, who argues convincingly that neither the parliamentary history of the Guardianship of Infants Act 1925 nor its provisions taken as a whole supported the decision.
[18] See STAMP, J. in *Re P. (infants)*, [1967] 2 All E.R. 229, 232. Were it otherwise, it would not have been necessary to confer on the putative father a specific right to claim custody under the Act; see *post*, p. 305.

have the child made a ward of court and himself appointed guardian.

Where the parent proceeds by way of *habeas corpus*, the Court is directed by s. 3 of the Custody of Children Act 1891 to have regard to the conduct of the parent,[19] and if he has abandoned or deserted his child or allowed him to be brought up by and at the expense of another person, school, institution or public authority for such a length of time and under such circumstances that he must have been unmindful of his parental duties, an order giving him custody of the child cannot be made unless the court considers he is a fit person to have it.[20] This provision fulfilled the dual purpose of extending the common law and equity rules which only allowed intervention with the parental right in cases of very serious misconduct[1] and of reinforcing that which prevented a parent who had surrendered custody of his child to another from recovering it if, to do so, would be prejudicial to the interests of the child.[2] The effect of *J. v. C.* is to make it clear that the common law and equity and the rules of the 1891 Act are superseded by s. 1 of the Guardianship of Minors Act 1971, and that the attitude of the parent is only one of the factors to be taken into account when treating the child's welfare as paramount: there is no rule of law that the wishes of a natural parent presumptively prevail over other considerations. Nevertheless, as we have seen,[3] the court still pays much attention to the wishes of an unimpeachable parent and tries to uphold them on the ground that this will best accord with the child's welfare. This tendency is particularly marked where the dispute is with a stranger and not with the other parent, but exceptionally the welfare of the child may demand otherwise, as happened in *J. v. C.* There the ten-year-old son of Spanish parents who were living in Spain had spent all but 18 months of his life with foster parents in England. He had therefore had little contact with his natural parents, spoke little Spanish and had been brought up in English ways of life, so that his prospects

---

[19] A "parent" includes any person liable to maintain the child or entitled to his custody (s. 5).
[20] Section 3 therefore supplements s. 1 (*supra*). If an order is made, the parent may be required to pay the whole or part of the expenses incurred by the third person or other body in bringing up the child (s. 2).
[1] See *ante*, p. 257.   [2] *Lyons* v. *Blenkin* (1821), Jac. 245.
[3] *Ante*, p. 262.

of education and a career were likely to be substantially better if he were to remain in England. When he was seven he was made a ward of court, and care and control of him were given to the foster parents. The House of Lords dismissed an appeal against the refusal of the trial judge to vary that order in favour of the natural parents, basically on the ground that they would be unable to cope with the problems of adjustment if the child were restored to them, even though their entrusting him to the foster parents had been motivated solely by consideration for his welfare.[4] Their Lordships were also not impressed by the argument of the natural parents that the present order was in effect an adoption order, because there are obvious legal differences in their respective concept, nature and consequences, notably that an order for care and control in wardship proceedings is always open to review and does not sever the child's legal ties with his parents. But the practical value of this distinction in a case like *J. v. C.* has been questioned[5] on the ground that it is doubtful whether the machinery of the Chancery Division was adequate to ensure effective supervision of the terms of such an order.[6] Furthermore, since the order may be "unsettling to the child and his foster parents . . . without any compensating advantage to the parents", it has been suggested[5] that it might be best for the legal relationship of parent and child to be "grafted on" to the *de facto* adoption. The suggestion may eventually gain statutory approval.[7]

V. CONCURRENT ORDERS

The fact that different kinds of courts may exercise custody jurisdiction or that the same court may do so but under different powers may obviously give rise to conflict, although the courts do try to minimise the possibility, as occasionally

[4] Initially the child had been placed with the foster parents when he was four days old because of his mother's illness. Later he returned with his natural parents to Spain for a year or so but because his health deteriorated they requested the foster parents to take care of him again indefinitely.
[5] See Cretney, *Wardship-Parens Patriae* (1969), 119 New L.J. 216 at p. 217.
[6] There is nothing in the Administration of Justice Act 1970 to indicate that the newly constituted Family Division will prove more effective in this respect.
[7] See the provisional proposals of the Departmental Committee on the Adoption of Children (1970), paras. 70-80.

may the legislature.[8] The conflict may arise in the following circumstances.

(i) *Between the High Court and an inferior court*

An order for custody made by a county court or a magistrates' court under its statutory jurisdiction does not, unless the statute expressly provides to the contrary, fetter the powers of the High Court to exercise the jurisdiction of the Crown as *parens patriae*.[9] Nevertheless, the litigant should normally be left either to seek a variation of the original order in the inferior court[10] or to appeal against it,[11] and the prerogative jurisdiction should only be invoked where it is necessary to supplement that order because the inferior court is not competent to do so or where there is some very special reason for invoking the jurisdiction, for example, because of the complexity of the case.[12] A likely instance of High Court intervention is where a mother to whom custody has been granted by a magistrates' court is seeking an injunction to restrain the father from removing their child out of the jurisdiction,[13] since a magistrates' court has no power to make an order against removal[14] or to grant an injunction to prevent it.

Although there is judicial support for the principle that a custody order made by an inferior court, (invariably a magistrates' court) does not oust the matrimonial jurisdiction, any more than the prerogative jurisdiction, of the High Court to make a similar order,[15] nevertheless, there is a similar reluctance to invoke it. In practice the High Court will adopt the same view as it does with maintenance orders,[16] and will only make an order for custody if that of the inferior court is first discharged. Exceptionally, however, it may be willing to supplement a maintenance order of the latter court,[17] and it is sub-

---

[8] See *ante*, p. 278, for the rule that no order for custody or committal to the care of a local authority can be made under the Matrimonial Proceedings (Magistrates' Courts) Act 1960 if an order for custody made by a court in England is currently in force (s. 2(4) (a)).
[9] *Re P. (infants)*, [1967] 2 All E.R. 229; [1969] 1 W.L.R. 818.
[10] *Re K. (K.J.S.) (an infant)*, [1966] 3 All E.R. 154; [1966] 1 W.L.R. 1241.
[11] See COOKE, J., in *Re P. (A.J.)*, [1968] 1 W.L.R. 1976.   [12] See *ibid*.
[13] *Re H. (G.J.) (an infant)*, [1966] 1 All E.R. 952; [1966] 1 W.L.R. 706.
[14] *T. v. T.*, [1968] 3 All E.R. 321; [1968] 1 W.L.R. 1887.
[15] See BATESON, J., in *Vigon v. Vigon and Kuttner*, [1929] P. 157; [1928] All E.R. Rep. 755; but the Court of Appeal declined to decide the point.
[16] *Kilford v. Kilford*, [1947] P. 100; [1947] 2 All E.R. 381.
[17] *Russell v. Russell*, [1956] P. 283 (C.A.); [1956] 1 All E.R. 466.

mitted that it is competent to do the same about a custody
order, for example, by granting an injunction to prevent the
child from being taken out of the jurisdiction.[18]

Where, on the other hand, there is no existing order of a
magistrates' court, it seems clear that the High Court's matrimonial jurisdiction is overriding in that once it is invoked the
magistrates' court is precluded from dealing with any matter
raised in the High Court.[19] If, however, custody is not one of
those matters, there is no ground for restricting the concurrent
jurisdiction of the magistrates' court to deal with it merely
because it is open to a spouse later to take the appropriate
steps to enable him or her to raise the question in the High
Court suit.[20] The reason is that if a spouse does, belatedly,
want the issue of custody decided by the latter court he can
appeal against the decision of the magistrates' court.[1]

(ii) *Between two inferior courts*

Where there is an existing custody order under the Matrimonial Proceedings (Magistrates' Courts) Act 1960 it seems
that another magistrates' court or a county court is not, as a
matter of law, prevented from making a similar order under
the Guardianship of Minors Act, but this should be, and in
fact is, avoided.[2]

(iii) *Within the same court*

Because of the dual powers of a magistrates' court to order
custody under the Matrimonial Proceedings (Magistrates'
Courts) Act 1960 and under the Guardianship of Minors Act,[3]
it is legally possible for two concurrent orders of the same
court to be in force, but this, too, should be, and is, avoided.[4]

---

[18] For the power of the High Court thus to grant an injunction under its
matrimonial jurisdiction see Matrimonial Causes Rules, 1971, r. 94(2).
[19] See the majority of the Divisional Court in *R.* v. *Middlesex Justices,
ex parte Bond*, [1933] 2 K.B.1; [1933] All E.R. Rep. 394. The Court
of Appeal *obiter* expressed qualified approval of the view but refused to
base its decision on it. See also *Craxton* v. *Craxton* (1907), 71 J.P. 399;
Knott v. *Knott*, [1935] P. 158; *Higgs* v. *Higgs*, [1941] P. 27; [1941] 1 All
E.R. 214.
[20] See 115 J.P.N. 676 for a Divorce Registry circular to this effect.
[1] Guardianship of Minors Act 1971, s. 16(3). See also sub-s. (4).
[2] *Quaere* a supplementary order as to access may be made; see Clarke Hall
& Morrison, *op. cit.*, p. 1209.
[3] There is a similar duality in a county court under the latter Act and
by virtue of its matrimonial jurisdiction.
[4] *Heworth* v. *Heworth*, [1948] 2 All E.R. 715 n. (C.A.).

Concurrent Orders

So, if there are two summonses taken out under the respective Acts, the proper course is to make an order under one of them only, especially as there is no longer any practical advantage in having two orders.[5]

Within the High Court, conflict has sometimes arisen between the wardship jurisdiction of the Chancery Division and the matrimonial jurisdiction of the Divorce Division, and it appears that if there were concurrent orders for custody that of the former Division would prevail.[6] Nevertheless since the Divorce Division had almost as much power to safeguard the child's interests as the Chancery Division, there was even less justification for invoking wardship jurisdiction, if the former had already made an order, than there was where an inferior court had done so.[7] Normally it was undesirable to bandy the child from the one Division to the other, and, therefore, as the Court of Appeal stressed in *P. v. P.*, whichever was first seised of the question of custody should retain it.[8] But, exceptionally, there could be good reason for the intervention through wardship jurisdiction; for example, to prevent the child from being taken out of the jurisdiction, since the powers of the Chancery Division in this latter respect seemed wider than those of the Divorce Division.

The appearance of the Family Division in place of the two Divisions will not render such exceptions strictly academic, since the powers of the new Division to make custody orders are still derived from different sources, but it will, it is suggested, be even more unlikely for two judges of that Division to be separately seised of custody matters, and administrative provision could be made to avoid this happening.

The re-organisation of the High Court will, however, have

[5] At one time the maintenance provisions were more favourable under the former Guardianship of Infants Acts.
Until the recent creation of the Family Division of the High Court, (*infra*), there was also the disadvantage that two concurrent orders could lead to conflicting decisions on appeals respectively to the Chancery Division and the Probate, Divorce and Admiralty Division.
[6] *Hall* v. *Hall*, [1963] P. 378 (C.A.); [1963] 2 All E.R. 140.
[7] See *supra*.
[8] (1967), 111 Sol. Jo. 832. See also *Re A-H*, [1963] Ch. 232; [1962] 3 All E.R. 853.
If the child was already a ward of court then "probably as a matter of law but certainly as a matter of comity between judges, no order will be made by a judge of the Divorce Division"; *per* UPJOHN, J., in *Re Andrews (Infants)*, [1958] Ch. 665, 668; [1958] 2 All E.R. 308, 310.

minimal effect on the problem of conflicting custody jurisdiction, which, it is suggested, will not be solved until there is both a uniform system of family courts and a single code of rules for the granting of custody orders.

Foreign Orders

Because an English court must treat the child's welfare as paramount, a foreign order relating to the guardianship or custody of a child does not have the effect of a foreign judgment binding on the English court. As the Judicial Committee of the Privy Council put it in *McKee* v. *McKee*, "comity demands not its enforcement but its grave consideration".[9] If, therefore, the child's interests so demand, the jurisdiction of the English Court may be invoked and a concurrent order made with regard to guardianship or custody. Thus, in *Re B's Settlement, B.* v. *B.*[10] the first case to apply the principle of paramountcy in relation to foreign orders,[11] MORTON, J., refused to entrust the care and control of a boy to his Belgian father so that he might take him back to Belgium, even though he had been granted custody by an order of a Belgium court, which the mother had defied by refusing to return the child to the father in Belgium. She and the child had been living in England for the past two years after the break-up of the marriage, and it was held in the circumstances that the child's interests would best be served by remaining here with her until further order.

But recent cases show that the child's interests are not to bear the same emphasis as they would in a purely domestic case, and instances of a person removing a child from a foreign jurisdiction in defiance of an order of the foreign court have led to some hardening of attitude in favour of the foreign order. In *Re H. (Infants)* CROSS, J., enumerated the various factors to be considered in deciding what the court should do:[12]

---

[9] *Per* Lord SIMONDS, [1951] A.C. 352, at p. 365; [1951] 1 All E.R. 942, 948.   [10] [1940] Ch. 54.
[11] Nineteenth century cases decided before that principle was established show greater respect for the foreign order; see *Nugent* v. *Vetzera* (1866), L.R. 2 Eq. 704; *Di Savini* v. *Lousada* (1870), W.R. 425. But there were already indications of readiness to emphasise the child's interests; see Lord CRANWORTH in *Stuart* v. *Marquis of Bute* (1861), 9 H.L.Cas. 440, 469, ("There is but one object which ought to be kept strictly in view and that is the interest of the infant.").
[12] [1965] 3 All E.R. 906, at pp. 915-916; [1966] 1 W.L.R. 381. See also *Re T. (An Infant)*, 1969, *Times*, September 6 (C.A.).

"When, in what I may call for short a 'kidnapping' case, the judge has to decide whether to send the child back whence he came or to allow the case to be fought out to the end over here, he has to weigh various considerations which may to some extent conflict with one another. On one side there is the public policy aspect, the question of comity and the question of *'forum conveniens'*. Again, on the same side there is the question of the injustice which may be done to the wronged parent if the court delays matters and allows the kidnapped child to take root in this country. On the other side, the court has to be satisfied before it sends the child back, that the child will come to no harm."

Strictly, if s. 1 of the Guardianship of Minors Act 1971 is to be complied with, those several factors other than that of the child's welfare should be subordinated to it, and it might be thought that their respective weight could not properly be assessed without a full inquiry into the merits of the question where and with whom the child should live, but in *Re H. (Infants)* the Court of Appeal affirmed the decision of CROSS, J.,[13] that the English court is not bound to do this if satisfied that the child will not suffer immediate harm by being taken back to the foreign country so that the foreign court may determine the merits. Subsequently in *Re E.(D.) (An Infant)*[14] the same learned judge, whose decision was also affirmed on appeal,[15] further stressed the importance of the foreign order by holding that the English court must pay regard to it unless satisfied "beyond reasonable doubt that to do so would inflict serious harm on the child",[16] and that the reasons for not ordering the return of the child must be compelling.

In *Re H. (Infants)* they were not.[17] A New York court had given the custody of two boys, whose parents were already divorced, to the mother with liberal access to the father. It was a term of the order that the children reside at all times in New York State unless the father otherwise consented, but in defiance of it the mother brought them to England to settle here, and, after refusing to comply with an order of the New York court to return the boys there, she made them wards of

---

[13] [1966] 1 All E.R. 886; [1966] 1 W.L.R. at p. 393.
[14] [1967] Ch. 287; [1967] 1 All E.R. 329.
[15] [1967] Ch. 761; [1967] 2 All E.R. 881.
[16] [1967] Ch. at p. 289; [1967] 1 All E.R. at p. 330.
[17] Similarly see *Re G. (An Infant)*, [1969] 2 All E.R. 1135; [1969] 1 W.L.R. 1001.

court. The New York court then granted exclusive custody to the father who applied to the English court for liberty to take the children back to New York so that that court might fully investigate the custody issue. The application was allowed for various reasons. An investigation by the English court would mean long delay before determination, by which time the children would have taken root in England;[18] as it was, their home had always been in the United States; they and the father were American; and therefore an American court, applying its own law,[19] was the *forum conveniens*. Moreover, in the light of the mother's reprehensible conduct, it would be a grave injustice to the father not to let him take the children back, and such was the relationship between him and them that it was unlikely that they would suffer if that course were permitted.[20]

On the other hand, in *Re E.D. (an Infant)* special circumstances called for intervention by the English court. After initially giving the custody of a baby girl to the mother following divorce proceedings, a New Mexico court transferred custody to the father. Because he considered the mother was unfit to have custody he requested his sister, Mrs. Z, who lived in England, to look after the child in the event of his death. That event occurred some three years later when he was killed in a motor accident. The immediate outcome was that the paternal grandfather took the girl to New York to hand her over to Mrs Z. who had flown out from England. Meanwhile, the mother obtained an order forbidding the grandfather to take the child out of the U.S.A., but before it could be served Mrs Z. and the child left for England where Mrs. Z. made her a ward of court. It was held that her application for care and control should be granted. By her father's death the girl had lost the only effective home she had known in America.

---

[18] *Cf. Re B's Settlement, supra,* where the child had already been living in England for two years.

[19] *Cf. Re Kernot (An Infant),* [1965] Ch. 217; [1964] 3 All E.R. 339, where one of the reasons why the English court went into the merits was that even if the child had been sent back the foreign court would have applied English law to the case. See Webb, *Wardship of Court and the Conflict of Laws,* (1966) 14 I.C.L.Q. 663.

[20] For an illustration of custody proceedings in England being stayed because proceedings pending abroad were more appropriate see *Re S. (M.) (an infant),* [1971] Ch. 621; [1971] 1 All E.R. 459.

Instead she had come to treat her aunt as a second mother and in all the circumstances it would have been disastrous for her to be sent back to the U.S.A.

If there is no foreign order, the justification for the English court's making an order is in principle stronger, since no question of breach of comity could arise.[1] Nevertheless, the court dislikes kidnapping whether there is a foreign order or not, and will not countenance custody or wardship proceedings by the person who has removed the children from the country which has been their home, unless there is a good reason for so doing.[2] However, unlike the case where there is a foreign order, the court may want to hear all the evidence.[3] At least, if there are allegations that the parent who wishes to take the child back to the foreign country is unfit to act as parent, an order must not be made allowing this until the answers to those allegations have been considered.[4]

When an order for custody, care or control is sought in England in the face of a foreign order, it is usually to the prerogative jurisdiction of the High Court that the applicant turns.[5] That jurisdiction is invariably based on the child's presence in England, although there are exceptionally other possibilities, *viz.*, his ordinary residence here or, *semble*, his British nationality.[6] The presence of the child will also normally be the basis for the court's assuming jurisdiction under the Guardianship of Minors Act,[7] but where the issue of custody arises in matrimonial proceedings the jurisdiction of the court depends upon the appropriate rules of domicile or residence

[1] *J.* v. *C.*, [1970] A.C. 668; [1969] 1 All E.R. 788, (H.L.); *Re A. (infants)*, [1970] Ch. 665 (C.A.); [1970] 3 All E.R. 184.

[2] *Re T. (Infants)* [1968] Ch. 704 (C.A.); [1968] 3 All E.R. 411; *cf. Re A. (infants), supra;* and *Re T.A. (Infants)* (1972), 116 Sol. Jo. 78.
It will be particularly reluctant to make an order where foreign proceedings are pending; *cf. X.* v. *X.* (1963), 107 Sol. Jo. 571.

[3] As it did in *Re T. (Infants). Cf. Re H. (Infants), supra.*

[4] *Re M. (An Infant)* (1968), 112 Sol. Jo 94, (C.A.); *Re C. (S.) (An Infant)* 1971, *Times,* June 26.

[5] If the party seeking removal of the child out of England applies for *habeas corpus,* the High Court may stand over that application until the party opposing it is given the opportunity to make the child a ward of court; *Re J.E.T. (An Infant)* (1966) *Times,* October 18 (C.A.).

[6] See further *post,* Chapter 12, p. 418-419.
If proceedings are instituted by way of *habeas corpus,* jurisdiction depends exclusively on the presence of the child within the realm.

[7] Unless maintenance is being sought, an application for custody, care or control is far less likely than wardship proceedings.

of the spouses.[8] This varied jurisdiction of the court, depending as it does upon different connecting factors, has raised particular jurisdictional conflicts within the United Kingdom, especially between the prerogative jurisdiction of the High Court, with its emphasis on the child's presence, and that of the Court of Session, primarily based on the child's domicile.[9] The conflicts have led to the proposal that within the United Kingdom the court of the country in which the child is ordinarily resident at the time of the application for custody should have "pre-eminent jurisdiction", but that in a case of urgency the court of the country in which the child is present could make an order which would then be subject to control and variation by the court of ordinary residence.[10] The proposal has not escaped criticism on the grounds that it would be difficult to apply and would not prevent "legal kidnapping".[11]

Removal of Child out of Jurisdiction

This seems a convenient point to note a matter which may be, though not necessarily is, connected with foreign custody orders or proceedings.

Frequently, when the High Court makes a custody order it also directs that the child is not to be taken out of the jurisdiction. Indeed, where such an order is made by virtue of the court's matrimonial jurisdiction it always includes such a direction that the child is not to be removed before the age of 18, with the proviso that a parent may remove him if he gives a general written undertaking to the court to return him when called upon to do so, and, unless otherwise directed, has the written consent of the other parent.[12] In deciding whether to grant leave to take a child out of the jurisdiction, his best

[8] The reader is referred to textbooks on the Conflict of Laws. But only exceptionally will an order be made if the child is out of the jurisdiction; *Philips* v. *Philips* (1944), 60 T.L.R. 395 (C.A.).
[9] Conflicts may also occur between the inferior courts of the United Kingdom; but rules can help to avoid this; see Guardianship of Minors Act 1971, s. 15, *ante*, p. 269.
[10] See the Report of the Committee on Conflicts of Jurisdiction Affecting Children (1959, Cmnd. 842).
[11] See the note of dissent of Mr. Michael Albery, Q.C., whose own suggestion was that the pre-eminent jurisdiction should lie in "the last joint home in the United Kingdom of the child's parents". See further thereon Gareth H. Jones, (1960) 9 I.C.L.Q. 15.
[12] See *Practice Direction (P.D.A.) Division*, [1966] 3 All E.R. 1008; [1967] 1 W.L.R. 143.

interests should be the primary consideration. In considering them account must be taken of the welfare of the parent having custody, since, if he or she were to become unhappy by not being allowed to remove the child, this might adversely affect the child. Against this, however, should be weighed the wishes of the other parent to continue to have access.[13]

The power restricting removal is also available under the court's parental jurisdiction and where custody is ordered under the Guardianship of Minors Act,[14] but, save where a county court has divorce jurisdiction, neither it nor a magistrates' court has the power,[15] since inferior courts do not have the machinery for enforcing undertakings relating to removal.

A provision in a custody order forbidding removal out of the jurisdiction may be enforced by attachment and committal for contempt of court or by a sequestration order made in respect of the property of the party guilty of the contempt.[16] Either method may be invoked where the child has actually been removed. A threatened removal may be restrained by injunction.[17]

VI. ACCESS

Where there is a dispute over custody between parents or spouses it is usual for the party who is refused custody to be granted reasonable access to the child.

The origins of the power to order access are uncertain. It can scarcely be associated with the writ of *habeas corpus*, since the sole object of that remedy was the removal of the child from his present surroundings. Nor is there evidence of its having been exercised in the earlier part of the nineteenth century by the Court of Chancery or the ecclesiastical courts.

---

[13] *P. (L.M.) (otherwise E.)* v. *P. (G.E.)*, [1970] 3 All E.R. 659 (C.A.); [1970] 1 W.L.R. 1469.

[14] On the other hand, where there is already a foreign custody order, that Act does not give the High Court power to make an order *allowing* the child to be taken out of the jurisdiction. If such an order is sought, the child should be made a ward of court; *Re E. (An Infant)*, [1956] Ch. 23; [1955] 3 All E.R. 174.

[15] *T. v. T.*, [1968] 3 All E.R. 321, (D.C.); [1968] 1 W.L.R. 1887, *ante*, p. 291. n. 14.

[16] *Romilly* v. *Romilly* (1963) *Times*, November 5.

[17] In the case of matrimonial proceedings a petitioner may apply for it at any time after filing his petition; M.C. Rules 1971, r. 94(2). *Cf. R. v. R. and I.*, [1961] 3 All E.R. 461; [1961] 1 W.L.R. 1334, for a similar use of the injunction.

Custody

The first specific reference to it seems to have been in Talfourd's Act in 1839 which enabled the court to give the mother access to her infant children who were in the custody of the father, provided she had not committed adultery. The Matrimonial Causes Act 1857 was silent about access, but the Divorce Court treated Talfourd's Act as a precedent for not granting access to an adulterous mother.[18] However, when the Custody of Infants Act 1873 re-enacted the provisions of the 1839 Act relating to access,[19] it did not include the proviso concerning adultery, and this omission seems eventually to have influenced the Divorce Court to accept the principle that adultery by the wife ought not to be regarded for all time and under all circumstances as sufficient to disentitle her to access.[20] Owing to lack of reported cases it is impossible to state whether the same principle was initially followed in custody disputes heard under the Guardianship of Infants Act 1886[1] or the Summary Jurisdiction (Separation and Maintenance) Acts, but today all questions of access are to be considered in the light of s. 1 of the Guardianship of Minors Act 1971, whose reference to "upbringing" of the child is wide enough to include such questions.

In applying that section the courts have gradually taken the view that reasonable access is "no more than the basic right of any parent"[2] and (perhaps questionably) that granting it normally accords with the child's interests, even where the parent has failed to carry out his parental duties adequately[3]. It will, therefore, only be refused in exceptional circumstances where the parent is not a fit and proper person to be brought into contact with the child, for example, because of his past

[18] *Clout* v. *Clout and Hollebone* (1861), 2 Sw. & Tr. 391.
[19] The 1873 Act also provided that, if the mother was given custody or control of a child up to the age of 16, the father or guardian could be granted access; see, for example, *Re Taylor* (1876), 4 Ch.D. 157, where the paternal grandparents were given access. A similar power seems to be implied in the earlier enactment if the mother was given custody up to the age of 7.
[20] *Stark* v. *Stark and Hitchins*, [1910] P. 190; *B.* v. *B.*, [1924] P. 176 (C.A.), especially POLLOCK, M.R.
[1] See the uncertainty expressed in *Manders* v. *Manders* (1890), 63 L.T. 627.
[2] See WILLMER, L. J., in *S.* v. *S. and P.*, [1962] 2 All E.R. 1 at p. 3; [1962] 1 W.L.R. 445, 448.
[3] In such circumstances, however, the court is more likely to attach conditions to the order; for example, where the parent has committed adultery, that the child shall not come into contact with the person with whom the adultery has been committed.

cruelty to the child[4] or his bad criminal record[5] or because he is so mentally ill that access would be harmful to the child,[6] or where the child's opposition to access is so marked that to allow it would similarly harm him.[7]

The power to order access is expressly given by the Guardianship of Minors Act 1971,[8] the Matrimonial Proceedings (Magistrates' Courts) Act 1960[9] and the Matrimonial Proceedings and Property Act 1970.[10] Both the 1960 Act and the 1970 Act are wide enough to enable custody to be granted to a person other than the parties to the matrimonial proceedings. If this is done under the former Act, access may be given to either or both parties and to any other person who is a parent of the child of the family.[11] There can be no doubt that a divorce court has at least equal powers[12] and, it is arguable, even wider powers so as to allow access to be granted to any person it chooses, *e.g.*, grandparents of the child.[13] If, as has been suggested,[14] custody can be given under the Guardianship of Minors Act to a person other than the parents, either parent, but *semble* no one else, could be given access.[15]

[4] See WILLMER, L. J., in *S.* v. *S. and P.*, *supra*.
[5] *Anon.* (1963), *Times*, October 24, (C.A.), where the father was serving seven years' imprisonment for manslaughter of his brother-in-law whom he killed in the child's presence.
[6] *G.* v. *G.* (1963), *Times*, May 3, (D.C.); *C.* v. *C.* (1971), *Times*, May 28, *Cp. Re R. (an infant)* (1963), *Times*, October 8 (C.A.), where it was held that the father's epilepsy did not justify refusing him access.
[7] *B.* v. *B.*, [1971] 3 All E.R. 682; [1971] 1 W.L.R. 1486 (C.A.); *M. (P.)* v. *M. (C.)* (1971), 115 Sol. Jo. 444 (C.A.).
[8] Section 9(1).
[9] Section 2(1) (g).
[10] Sections 18, 19 and 27(1). Previously, none of the Matrimonial Causes Acts has expressly referred to access and the Divorce Court seems not to have derived its powers relating to access from ecclesiastical jurisdiction.
  Where matrimonial proceedings are pending under the Act and the husband is molesting his wife and abusing his right of access to the children, a summons for an injunction against molestation of the wife should not be combined with an injunction relating to access. The latter matter should be dealt with by summons to a judge in chambers, since it is most undesirable that matters relating to children should be heard in open court; *W.* v. *W.* (1964), 108 Sol. Jo. 504.
[11] See s. 2(1) (g) which expressly so provides.
[12] *Chetwynd* v. *Chetwynd* (1865), L.R. 1 P. & D. 39, where custody was granted to a third party and both parents were given access.
[13] The relevant legislation in Scots law permits this; see *S.* v. *S.*, 1967, S.L.T. 217 (H.L. (Sc.)), affirming the decision of the Court of Session, 1965 S.L.T. 324.
[14] *Ante*, p. 270.
[15] Section 9(1) of the Guardianship of Minors Act 1971 refers only to the "mother or father". But, as Lord CLYDE pointed out in *S.* v. *S.*, *supra*, it would be incongruous if a third person could be given a right of custody but not the lesser one of access.

B. ILLEGITIMATE CHILDREN

I. HISTORY OF PARENTAL RIGHT TO CUSTODY

Prima facie the mother alone has the right to the custody of her illegitimate child, but it took English law an unconscionably long time to accord this recognition. In 1841 it was still being asked on what legal ground she had such a right[16] and as late as 1883 the Court of Appeal was denying any legal relationship between her and her child.[17] But in *Barnardo v. McHugh*[18] the House of Lords eventually recognised that, in view of her duty to maintain her illegitimate child up to the age of 16,[19] it was impossible to deny her a legal right in relation to custody. Once this had been done, the way was open for further recognition both by the judges and by the legislature, and today there is vested in the mother rights similar to those which both parents enjoy in respect of their legitimate child. Thus, because of her right to custody, she has the rights to the services of the child,[20] to exercise disciplinary powers over him, including that of administering reasonable corporal punishment,[1] to determine his upbringing, including his religious and secular education,[2] to consent to his marriage,[3] and to appoint a testamentary guardian for him.[4] Moreover, the rights of intestate succession between the mother and the child are the same as if he were her legitimate child.[5]

Since the tendency of the modern law has been to place the mother in a legal position very much the same as that of the parent of the legitimate child, it seems clear on principle that her right to custody continues until the child attains 18 or until his marriage, if earlier, and that there is no warrant for

[16] *Re Lloyd* (1841), 3 Man. & G. 547, where MAULE, J., doubted whether she was "anything but a stranger" to her child. The earlier decision in *Ex p. Knee* (1804), 1 Bos & P.N.R. 148; 127 E.R. 416; that she was entitled to custody does not seem to have been treated as authoritative.
[17] See LINDLEY, L. J., in *R. v. Nash, Re Carey* (1883), 10 Q.B.D. 454, 456.
[18] [1891] A.C. 388; [1891-4] All E.R. Rep. 825.
[19] At that time, under the Poor Law Act 1834, s. 71.
[20] See *post*, p. 451.
[1] See *ante*, Chapter 6.
[2] *Post*, Chapter 13. The right to determine the child's religion was firstly clearly laid down in *R. v. New* (1904), 20 T.L.R. 583 (C.A.).
[3] Marriage Act 1949, s. 3 and Second Sched.
[4] *Re A., S. v. A.* (1940), 164 L.T. 230; *post*, Chapter 12.
[5] Family Law Reform Act 1969, s. 14, *ante*, Chapter 8.

the view that at common law it ceases at the age of 14.[6]

As for the father, he still has only limited rights, even though he may be required to maintain the child once paternity is established. The law offers him no inducement to assume responsibilities by conferring corresponding rights. So long as the mother is alive he has no substantive right to custody; and the right does not vest in him on her death.[7] Nor does his paternity entitle him to appoint a testamentary guardian.[8] Consequently, he may exercise none of the other rights which flow from custody. In two respects, however, his position has improved. A legal relationship is now recognised between him and his child for the purpose of intestate succession,[9] and, as will be seen[10] his right to *claim* custody has been strengthened. The latter change has had particular implications in relation to the adoption of illegitimate children,[11] but another of its legal effects is to enable him to appoint a testamentary guardian if his claim to custody has been granted by an order made under the Guardianship of Minors Act and is operative at his death.[12] Moreover, if he has actual custody of the child, whether under an order of a court or not, for that reason he acquires certain responsibilities, namely, of seeing that the child receives full time secular education[13] and of protecting him from harm.[14]

II. PRINCIPLES ON WHICH THE COURT ACTS WHEN DETERMINING DISPUTES OVER CUSTODY

Ironically, the absence of any early common law right to custody in the mother comparable to that of the father over his

[6] See DENNING, L. J., in *Re M. (An Infant)*, [1955] 2 Q.B. 479, 488; [1955] 2 All E.R. 911, 912. This view seems to have arisen from the fact that the method of claiming custody was (and still can be) *habeas corpus*, and, as already noted, [*ante*, p. 288] the predominant view is that the remedy cannot issue once the child reaches the age of discretion, which, for boys at least, is 14.

[7] *Ex parte St. Mary Abbotts Guardians* (1887), 51 J.P. Jo. 740.
[8] See *Horner* v. *Horner* (1799), 1 Hagg. Con. 337, 355.
[9] Under the Family Law Reform Act 1969; *ante*, Chapter 8. [10] *Infra.*
[11] *Post*, Chapter 10. [12] Section 14(3).
[13] Education Act 1944, ss. 36 and 114(1); see *post*, Chapter 13.
[14] *Ante*, Chapter 6. But see *ibid.*, p. 198, for the limits of his liability under s. 1 of the Children and Young Persons Act 1933, where he does not have actual custody: liability then depends on whether there is an affiliation order against him.

English Law still has a long way to go in its recognition of the legal status of the putative father. See Lasok, 17 I.C.L.Q. 634.

legitimate child[15] enabled the court to show more latitude when deciding custody issues involving illegitimate children. Undoubtedly much attention was paid to the natural relationship between the mother and her bastard and the court would not countenance the putative father's taking possession by fraud or force.[16] Nevertheless, equity was readier to intervene than it was in cases involving legitimate children, taking account of the child's interests and those of persons other than the mother,[17] and any strengthening of her right to custody following *Barnardo* v. *McHugh* was at once counterbalanced by the discretion given by the Custody of Children Act 1891 to refuse her *habeas corpus* where she had abandoned or deserted the child or otherwise so conducted herself as to justify withholding custody from her. As we have seen,[18] s. 1 of the Guardianship of Minors Act 1971 has in effect superseded the welfare principle embodied in the earlier Act.

That section applies as it does in the case of the legitimate child, except that, where the dispute is between the mother and the father, there is no principle that the parties begin with a parity of claim,[19] since the father has no *prima facie* right to custody at all. Indeed, for that reason the rule that the courts regard it as in the interests of a legitimate child, save in exceptional circumstances, to know both his parents is by no means necessarily applicable in the case of a bastard, and, therefore, if the mother is given custody the father may be refused access, even though he has a genuine affection for the child.[1] The practical importance of the disparity in the legal position of the mother and the father has to some extent been diminished by the principle of paramountcy of the child's interests, so that

---

[15] See *ante*, p. 302.

[16] *R.* v. *Soper* (1793), 5 Term. Rep. 278; *R.* v. *Moseley* (1798), 5 East 224 n.; *R.* v. *Hopkins* (1806), 7 East 579.

[17] In *R.* v. *Nash, Re Carey* (1883), 10 Q.B.D. 454, 456, JESSEL, M. R., observed: "In equity regard was always had to the mother, putative father and relations on the mother's side."

As already noted, [*ante*, p. 258], equity's intervention in respect of the legitimate child was gradually encouraged by legislation between 1839 and 1886 which gave the mother the right to claim custody.

[18] *Ante*, p. 289.   [19] See *ante*, p. 260.

[1] *Re G.* (*An infant*), [1956] 2 All E.R. 876; [1956] 1 W.L.R. 911.

The court may also be reluctant to grant him access where a third party has custody. See *S.* v. *H., Times,* June 12, 1968 (C.A.). There the court refused to approve an arrangement that the father see his young son once a quarter on the ground that it would be unsettling. Would it have similarly disapproved had the child been legitimate?

if they so demand the custody may well be entrusted to the father; but his wishes are not likely to carry so much weight against the mother as they would in a dispute with a third party.[2] As for the mother's wishes, they, like those of a parent of a legitimate child, may be given proper but not undue consideration and should not prevail over the child's welfare, whether the dispute is with the father[3] or a third person.[4] Like the parent of the legitimate child, too, she cannot by agreement surrender custody to a third person.[5]

III. MEANS OF RESOLVING DISPUTES OVER CUSTODY AS BETWEEN PARENTS OR AS BETWEEN SPOUSES

Historically the remedy to which the mother of a bastard turned in order to recover custody was invariably the writ of *habeas corpus*, unless alternatively she chose to commence wardship proceedings, a remedy equally available to the father. Wardship is, of course, always a possibility,[6] but, as in the case of the legitimate child, various statutes have rendered *habeas corpus* unimportant as a method of claiming custody.

(1) Guardianship of Minors Act 1971

The Legitimacy Act 1959[7] conferred on the mother and the father of a bastard the right to apply for an order for custody or access to be made under the Guardianship of Infants Acts, but in so doing expressly created the anomaly that if the mother is granted custody, she cannot be awarded maintenance, as she might if the child were legitimate.[8] These provisions have been re-enacted by the Guardianship of Minors Act 1971.[9]

The Court of Appeal has made it clear that the Act of 1959 did not give the father a *prima facie* right to custody, but only new means for seeking it[10] However, if an order is made in his favour and is operative when the mother dies, he becomes

---

[2] See HARMAN, L. J., in *Re C. (A.) (An Infant)*, [1970] 1 All E.R. 309, 311; [1970] 1 W.L.R. 288; *Re G. (An Infant)*, *supra; Re H. (Infants)* (1965), 63 L.G.R. 396 (C.A.).
[3] As in *Re A. (An Infant)*, [1955] 2 All E.R. 202 (C.A.); [1955] 1 W.L.R. 465; *Re H. (Infants)*, *supra.*
[4] As in *Re E. (An Infant)*, [1963] 3 All E.R. 874; [1964] 1 W.L.R. 51.
[5] *Humphrys* v. *Polak*, [1901] 2 K.B. 385 (C.A.).
[6] See, for example, *Re A.* and *Re G.*, *supra.*   [7] Section 3.
[8] *Post*, Chapter 14.   [9] Section 14.
[10] *Re Adoption Application*, 41/61, [1963] Ch. 315; [1962] 3 All E.R. 553; *Re O. (An Infant)*, [1965] Ch. 23; [1964] 1 All E.R. 786.

guardian either alone or jointly with any guardian appointed by the mother.[11]

(2) Matrimonial Proceedings in Magistrates' Courts

By virtue of the definition of "child of the family" in the Matrimonial Proceedings (Magistrates' Courts) Act 1960[12] the court's powers to make custody orders apply to an illegitimate child of one spouse who has been accepted as a member of the family by the other. In a rare case it could also apply to an illegimate child of both spouses. Normally such a child will be legitimated by the marriage of his parents under the Legitimacy Acts 1926 and 1959, but that would not occur if the father were not domiciled in England at the time of the marriage. In that event legitimation would depend upon the rules of the conflict of laws.[13]

(3) Matrimonial Proceedings in a Divorce Court

(a) *Nullity, Divorce and Judicial Separation*

The powers of a Divorce Court to make custody orders in any of these suits extend to an illegitimate child of both parties to the marriage[14] or to any other illegitimate child who comes within the definition of "child of the family" as defined by the Matrimonial Proceedings and Property Act 1970.[15]

(b) *Neglect to maintain*

A similar power exists when an order for maintenance is made as the result of proceedings under s. 6 of the Matrimonial Proceedings and Property Act 1970.[16]

IV. MEANS OF RESOLVING DISPUTES OVER CUSTODY
AS BETWEEN PARENT AND STRANGER

The same methods are available as in the case of a legitimate child.[17] Unless the mother chooses wardship proceedings, she may rely on *habeas corpus* or, it seems, the Guardianship of Minors Act. An application under that Act and wardship are

[11] And see *supra* the power of the father to appoint a testamentary guardian.
[12] Section 16(1), *ante*, p. 273.   [13] *Ante*, Chapter 8.
[14] Here the possibility of a child's being the illegitimate child of both parties is a real one, because that will be the effect where the marriage is void, unless the Legitimacy Act 1959, s. 2, *ante*, p. 246, operates.
[15] *Ante*, p. 280.   [16] *Ante*, p. 287.
[17] *Ante*, pp. 287 *et seq.*

similarly open to the father, but it is submitted that he may not rely on *habeas corpus* since he does not have a *prima facie* right to custody; *aliter*, if custody has been given to him by the court.

The stranger who seeks custody must commence wardship proceedings, but in a case where an affiliation order is in force providing for payments to the mother and she dies or becomes of unsound mind or is in prison, the magistrates may appoint some person to have custody and to receive the payments under the order.[18]

---

[18] Affiliation Proceedings Act 1957, s. 5(4). The terms of this enactment are such that they seem to preclude the court's granting custody to the father.

APPENDIX

(Matrimonial Proceedings (Magistrates' Courts) Act 1960, s. 10;
Magistrates' Courts (Matrimonial Proceedings) Rules 1960, r. 7)

Nature of Provision in respect of which Complaint is Made	Complainant	Defendants
(1) Custody } (Variation or (2) Access } Revocation)	Any of the following, *viz.:*— (a) A party to the marriage; (b) if the child is a child only of one such party, the parent who is not a party; (c) if the child has been committed by the order to the legal custody of some person other than one of the parents or to the care of a local authority, the person to whom the legal custody is committed by the order or who seeks the legal custody by the complaint; (d) if there is a provision for supervision in force, the supervising officer (*i.e.* the probation officer or the local authority);	All the following, not being the complainant, *viz.:*— (a) A party to the marriage; (b) if the child is a child only of one such party, the parent who is not a party (including the father of an illegitimate child, if he has been so adjudged by a court); (c) any person to whose legal custody the child is for the time being committed by the order; (d) if the child by the order has been committed to the care of, or is under the supervision of, a local authority, that local authority; (e) if by the order the child is under the supervision of a probation officer, that probation officer.
(3) Committal to Care of Local Authority (revocation)	(a) A party to the marriage; (b) the local authority; (c) the person to whose legal custody the child is committed by the order or who seeks the legal custody by the complaint.	The same persons as in sub-paras. (a) (b) (c) and (d) above.
(4) Supervision (variation or revocation)	(a) A party to the marriage; (b) the supervising officer (*i.e.*, the probation officer or local authority); (c) the person to whose legal custody the child is committed by the order or who seeks the legal custody by the complaint.	The same persons as in sub-paras. (a) (b) (c) (d) and (e) above. Also, if the complaint is for variation of the provision, the probation officer or local authority whom it is sought to substitute as the new supervising officer.

CHAPTER 10

Adoption

A. INTRODUCTION

In its First Report, which led to adoption being introduced into English law in 1926, the Tomlin Committee defined it as "a legal method of creating between a child and one who is not the natural parent of the child an artificial family relationship analogous to that of parent and child".[1] That remains its primary purpose, but it has also come to be used as an extension of the natural relationship, *i.e.*, by the mother who adopts her own illegitimate child as a means of escaping the social stigma of illegitimacy and improving the legal relationship between herself and the child.

It is, indeed, the illegitimate child, whether adopted by his own mother or father or by a third party, who has chiefly benefited from adoption. At first, in mediaeval England, his needs were largely met by a society which, reacting against contemporary notions of marriage, showed a kindly tolerance towards illegitimacy.[2] Since marriage was so often a family arrangement and not the result of affection between the parties, breakdown was frequent, and, with no remedy of divorce available,[3] the stable illicit union was widely accepted. Moreover, even where the parents of the adulterine child did not cohabit, there was a marked readiness of members of the mother's family to assume parental responsibility. However, a change in moral and social attitudes by the time of the Puritan era, with a consequent stigma now attaching to illegitimacy, led to parental rejection of the child. Stable unions were less common, and the mother, finding herself abandoned by the father and her own family, was often driven to killing or abandoning the child[4] or, less drastically, submitting to the

---

[1] (1925) Cmnd. 2401, p. 3.
[2] See Ellison, *Adoption and the Deprived Child in History*, pp. 13 *et seq.*
[3] But the use of the nullity decree must not be overlooked.
[4] See *ante*, Chapter 6, p. 176.

severity of the Poor Law. A similar hardship was usually suffered by the orphan and the abandoned legitimate child. Deprived of the care which the mediaeval church had shown for the needy, they, too, were compelled to put themselves upon the parish unless they were one of the few more fortunate who became wards of court or found sympathetic foster parents. During the second half of the 19th century fostering became more common, being sometimes arranged by the voluntary societies then coming into being. It is remarkable that these *de facto* adoptions were so popular as they were. The common law does not allow either parent of the legitimate child[5] or the mother of the illegitimate[6] permanently to divest himself or herself of parental rights and duties by voluntary agreement. However much affection and material benefit the foster parents bestowed upon the child, the arrangement was liable at any time to be upset by the natural parent's asserting his legal rights and claiming back the child, without any regard for the child's welfare or the interests of the foster parents.[7] The readiness of persons to come forward as *de facto* adopters of many orphans and illegitimate children after World War I, notwithstanding the legal risks involved, stirred the public conscience into setting up Committees in 1921 and 1925, whose Reports[8] culminated in the Adoption of Children Act 1926. The object of the Act was, therefore, to provide for the child and the adopters the security of a permanent relationship. Its immediate impact is seen in the fact that there were almost 3,000 entries in the Adopted Children Register for 1927.

The next Act was the Adoption of Children (Regulation) Act 1939, which was mainly directed to the compulsory registration of adoption societies and the regulation of arrangements for placing children for adoption. The changes were the result of an adverse Report by the Horsburgh Committee,[9] which drew attention to the number of bad placements due to lack of

---

[5] *Brooks* v. *Blount*, [1923] 1 K.B. 257; see *ante*, Chapter 9, p. 265.
[6] *Humphrys* v. *Polak*, [1901] 2 K.B. 385.
[7] But, if the parent was forced to take proceedings to recover the child, the High Court had to refuse his application if he had abandoned or deserted the child or allowed him to be brought up by another person at that other's expense for such a length of time and under such circumstances that the parent was unmindful of his parental duties, unless the parent satisfied the Court that, having regard to the child's welfare, he was a fit person to have custody; see s. 3 of the Custody of Children Act 1891.   [8] Cmnd. 1254, 2401 and 2469.   [9] Cmnd. 5499.

skilled inquiries undertaken by some societies. The Act also
dealt with the supervision by welfare authorities of certain
adopted children, prohibited payments and advertisements in
respect of adoptions and restricted the sending of children
abroad for adoption.

Important changes were made by the Adoption of Children
Act 1949 (particularly with regard to rights of succession and
citizenship) and the law was shortly afterwards consolidated,
with minor amendments, in the Adoption Act 1950. Notwithstanding those recent changes, a further Departmental Committee was set up in 1953[10] to review the whole field of legal
adoption and to recommend any changes of policy and procedure thought desirable *in the interest and welfare of children.*
Many of its proposals found their way into the present consolidating Adoption Act 1958.[11] There has been further
amendment by Acts of 1960, 1964 and 1968, which deal
respectively with the revocation of adoption orders in cases of
legitimation, the recognition of certain adoption orders made
outside Great Britain, and the making of "inter-country"
adoption orders by the English court in pursuance of the
Hague Convention on Adoption.

A number of recent inquiries conducted by or with the
support of the Home Office have shown the need for a more
drastic revision of the law. The Report of the Standing Conference of Societies Registered for Adoption, published in
1968[12] directly led to the appointment of a Departmental
Committee which, in considering possible changes, is looking
particularly at the questions of whether the child's welfare
should be made paramount, whether his relatives can apply for

---

[10] Under the chairmanship of Sir Gerald Hurst. For its Report in 1954
see Cmnd. 9248.
[11] They were initially included in Part II of the Children Act 1958, but
before it became operative, Part II was repealed and its provisions re-
enacted in the consolidating Act.
[12] The Conference was commissioned by the Home Office to undertake the
inquiry. Other surveys have been conducted by the Home Office itself
and by the National Bureau for Co-operation in Child Care, and a Report
on Adoption Practice has been published by the Committee of the
Advisory Councils on Child Care.
   For the working of adoption laws in the U.S.A. and England see
Kellmer, Pringle and Dinnage, *Adoption, Facts and Fallacies* and for
general works see Kornitzer, *Adoption* and, by the same author, *Adoption
and Family Life;* Goodacre, *Adoption Policy and Practice;* Rowe, *Parents,
Children and Adoption.*

Adoption

guardianship instead of adoption, the effects of the natural
father's rights to seek custody of his illegitimate child on the
possibility of his being adopted and the rights of long-term
foster parents who want to adopt the child against the wishes
of the natural parent. The Committee has already published a
Working Paper containing far-reaching provisional proposals.

B. THE MAKING OF ADOPTION ORDERS

I. JURISDICTION[13]

(a) Under the Adoption Act 1958

Applications for adoption orders are made under the Adoption
Act 1958 either to the Family Division of the High Court or
to any county court or juvenile court within whose jurisdiction
the applicant or the infant resides at the date of the application,[14] except that a juvenile court has no jurisdiction where the
applicant is not ordinarily resident in Great Britain.[15]

When we were dealing with custody,[16] we referred to some
of the disadvantages arising from different kinds of courts
having concurrent jurisdiction and to the desirability of a
uniform system of family courts. Similar considerations apply
to adoption. The wider the variety of courts the more likely the
variations in interpretation and administration of the law, a
state of affairs which is not helped by having three separate
sets of Adoption Rules[17] which are not uniform.[18] This

---

[13] See McLean and Patchett, *English Jurisdiction in Adoption*, 19 I.C.L.Q.1.
[14] Adoption Act 1958, s. 9(1) and Adoption (Juvenile Court) Rules 1959,
r. 1.
    The date of the application is presumably the date when it is filed with
the court. Where there is a change of residence before the hearing of the
case there is, it is suggested, no obligation to make a fresh application;
cf. the more cautious view of Clarke Hall and Morrison (*op. cit.*, p. 664)
who would also require the guardian *ad litem* to have been appointed
and the date of the hearing to have been fixed before the change of
residence, if proceedings *de novo* are to be avoided.
[15] See s. 12 of the Act, *infra*. But the section does not indicate which
county court has jurisdiction in such a case. It would, it is suggested,
be proper to apply to a county court within whose jurisdiction the
applicant is actually living.   [16] *Ante*, Chapter 9.
[17] Adoption (High Court) Rules 1971; Adoption (County Court) Rules
1959 and 1965; Adoption (Juvenile Court) Rules 1959 and 1965.
[18] See, for example, interim adoption orders, *post*, p. 362; the duties of the
guardian *ad litem* with regard to personal attendance of the infant at the
hearing of the application.

312

diversity and uncertainty in applying adoption law has been amply demonstrated by the Standing Conference of Societies Registered for Adoption [S.C.S.R.A.] in its Report to the Home Office in 1968, and a number of the instances to which the Report refers are mentioned later in this chapter. Moreover, the lack of co-ordination of the records of the various courts weakens the rule[19] that a court, hearing a later application for an adoption order after an earlier unsuccessful one by the same applicant in another court, is not to proceed with it unless satisfied that there has since been a substantial change in the circumstances: there is no guarantee that the court will know of the previous proceedings. The existence of separate systems of courts can also cause delays. This is illustrated by the case where the father of an illegitimate child has already instituted custody proceedings in, say, a magistrates' court and then adoption proceedings are brought, say, in the High Court. Since it is desirable that the issue of custody be decided along with that of adoption,[20] this means an adjournment so that the father may start custody proceedings in the High Court.[1] Another rule which could cause delay is that which enables a county court or a juvenile court to refuse to proceed with an application if, owing to special circumstances, it appears that the application is more fit to be dealt with by the High Court.[2] Fortunately, however, this rule, which is intended only for cases involving difficult points of law, is rarely invoked.

Domicile and Residence of the Parties

(1) *The Applicants*

Jurisdiction under the 1958 Act depends on domicile and residence, but not on nationality.[3] Under s. 1(1) of the Act of 1958 the applicant, or, where there is a joint application by spouses, the applicants, must be domiciled either in England or Scotland and under s. 1(5) must reside in England.[4] Residence is not defined or qualified, but, in view of the fact that

---

[19] See Adoption (H.C.) Rules 1971, r. 5; Adoption (C.C.) Rules 1959, r. 6; Adoption (J.C.) Rules 1959, r. 6.   [20] See *post*, p. 336.

[1] *Re Adoption Application No. 41/61*, [1963] Ch. 315; [1962] 2 All E.R. 833.

[2] Adoption (C.C.) Rules 1959, r. 7; Adoption (J.C.) Rules 1959, r. 7. *Cf.* a similar provision in the Matrimonial Proceedings (Magistrates' Courts) Act 1960, s. 5, and see thereon (1957) 24 The Solicitor 328.

[3] *Cf.* the Adoption Act 1968, *infra*.

[4] A Scottish court correspondingly has jurisdiction if the applicant has an English or Scottish domicile and a Scottish residence.

s. 12 of the Act, which was introduced to supplement s. 1(5), empowers the court to make an adoption order where the applicant is "not ordinarily resident in Great Britain" *prima facie* the irresistible conclusion is that residence in s. 1 must refer to "ordinary" residence.[5] If this is so, and since it has been held[6] that the power under s. 12 is subject to the overriding provision in s. 1(1) that the applicant must be domiciled in England or Scotland, it should follow that so far as concerns the applicant at least (as opposed to the child) his domicile should be the sole factor for determining jurisdiction and that it should not matter whether he is ordinarily resident within or outside Great Britain. Section 12 unhappily does not permit of such a simple solution. For one thing, as already mentioned, a juvenile court does not have jurisdiction under that section; for another, the section modifies the normal rules relating to care and possession of the child prior to the adoption order.[7] What, then, is ordinary residence? The Act itself offers no guidance, but in *Re Adoption Application 52 1951*,[8] a hard case which led to the enactment of s. 12, HARMAN, J., in construing s. 2(5) of the Adoption Act 1950, which s. 1(5) of the 1958 Act replaces, thought that residence in this context denoted "some degree of permanence" and that, while it did not necessarily mean that the applicant had his home in England, it meant that he had "his settled headquarters" here. Accordingly, the wife of a colonial civil servant who lived with him in Nigeria except when they returned to England on leave was held not to be resident in England. It is clear, therefore, that there must be presence in a country over a lengthy period of time, but beyond that it is not possible to lay down firm criteria.[9] HARMAN, J., also concluded that for jurisdictional purposes in adoption proceedings a person cannot have more than one residence at any one time, which further supports the view that residence and ordinary residence are to be treated as synonymous. This, however, can produce difficulties where an

[5] For a criticism of these provisions and other Conflict of Laws aspects of the Adoption Act 1958 see Griew (1959) 8 I.C.L.Q. 569.
[6] *Re R. (an infant)*, [1962] 3 All E.R. 238 (C.A.); [1962] 1 W.L.R. 1147.
[7] See *post*, p. 330.   [8] [1952] Ch. 16; [1951] 2 All E.R. 931.
[9] *Cp.* Scots law where the ruling in *B. Petitioners*, 1949 Sh. Ct. Rep. p. 45, that ordinary residence connotes the place which is the permanent home was subsequently rejected in *M. Petitioners*, 1949 Sh. Ct. Rep. 91. See also *C. Petitioners*, 1949, Sh. Ct. Rep. 93.

applicant is resident in Great Britain. A Scotsman, for example, with a permanent home in Glasgow, whose job compels him to live temporarily in England for, say, 12 months, will not be able to obtain an order in England in respect of a child placed with him with a view to adoption while he is in England, since he is not on the above reasoning resident here. Nor will he be able to turn to the Scottish court, because, though himself resident in Scotland, the child is not.[10] He will have to wait until he returns with the child to Scotland. Adoption agencies would be very reluctant to place children in such cases. It might possibly be argued that as between the English and Scottish jurisdictions residence is to be understood in a "less permanent" sense than that used by HARMAN, J. when distinguishing between residence within and outside Great Britain.[11]

The Act of 1958 does not explicitly state that there must be domicile in England or Scotland and residence in England both at the date of application and at the date of the order,[12] but with regard to residence at least, that is the necessary implication, for, as will be seen later,[13] the legal process from application to order is such as to require continued residence here during that period. As for domicile, s. 1(1) does speak of an "application made . . . by a person domiciled in England and Scotland" which suggests that the date of application is relevant.[14] It follows that, if at that date the applicant is domiciled in England, his continued residence here necessarily means that there will not be a change of domicile before the order is made. It is suggested, however, that an English (or Scottish) domicile at the time of application is not essential provided that it has been acquired by the date of the order. Supposing

[10] See *infra* for the need for the child to reside within the jurisdiction.
[11] This "less permanent" meaning is, it is submitted, the one in which s. 9(1) of the Act (*supra*) may be understood when it requires residence within the local jurisdiction of a county court or juvenile court for the purpose of giving such courts jurisdiction.
[12] Compare, on the one hand, the Adoption Act 1968, s. 3(5), *infra*, which expressly imposes a double qualification and, on the other hand, divorce jurisdiction based on domicile, where an English domicile at the date of commencement of proceedings is enough to confer jurisdiction (*Mansell* v. *Mansell*, [1967] P. 306; [1966] 2 All E.R. 391; *Leon* v. *Leon*, [1967] P. 275; [1966] 3 All E.R. 820).
[13] See under the heading "Care and Possession", *post*, p. 330.
[14] *Cf.* s. 53 for an "application being made by a person who is not domiciled in England or Scotland" for a provisional adoption order.

that a Pakistani domiciled in Pakistan, comes to England in order to obtain a provisional adoption order[15] in respect of his orphaned nephew so as to take him back to Pakistan to be adopted. After applying for that order he decides, and is allowed, to settle in England, where he acquires a domicile. It is submitted that the court would be able to make a full adoption order without his having to make a fresh application.

(2) *The Infant*

The infant's residence in England is also essential,[16] but the Act ignores his domicile for jurisdictional purposes[17] and the courts, notwithstanding their acknowledgement that adoption involves questions of status,[18] have also refused to admit its relevance to the choice of law to govern the application. The result may be a "limping adoption" which is not recognised by the *lex domicilii* of the child.[19] Some concession has, however, recently been made to his personal law in *Re B. (S.) an infant*,[20] where GOFF, J. laid down the principle that where the child is or may be domiciled abroad or is a foreign national or was until recently ordinarily resident abroad the court should consider whether its order will be recognised abroad, unless the case is one in which it is clearly for the child's welfare that an adoption order be made irrespective of its consequences elsewhere; for example, in refugee cases.[1]

(b) Under the Adoption Act 1968

Additional jurisdiction is conferred by the Adoption Act 1968. This Act, which has not yet been brought into force by statutory instrument, implements the Hague Convention on Adoption (1965),[2] to which the United Kingdom Government

---

[15] Under s. 53, *supra.*   [16] Section 1 (5).

[17] Until 1949, under the Adoption Act 1926, s. 2(5), he had to be a British subject.

[18] *Re R. (an infant)*, [1962] 3 All E.R. 238, at pp. 239, 240; [1962] 1 W.L.R. 1147 at pp. 1150, 1151.

[19] Academic opinion is divided on whether account should be taken of the foreign law. See Cheshire, *Private International Law*, 8th edn., pp. 449–450, and Graveson, *Conflict of Laws*, 6th edn., p. 402, and *cf.* Dicey, *Conflict of Laws*, 8th edn., p. 458 and Kahn-Freund, *Treatise on the Growth of Internationalism in English Private International Law*, pp. 62–66

[20] [1968] 1 Ch. 204; [1967] 3 All E.R. 629.

[1] See *Re R. (adoption)*, [1966] 3 All E.R. 613; [1967] 1 W.L.R. 34.

[2] See Cmnd. 2613, and for a comment on the Tenth Hague Conference, which led to the Convention, see Graveson, (1965) 14 I.C.L.Q. 528.

was a signatory, by empowering the High Court (or, in Scotland, the Court of Session) to make "inter-country" adoption orders, *i.e.*, adoption orders in which the applicant does not have the same nationality as, or resides in a different country from, that of the child. In accordance with the following complicated rules jurisdiction is based on nationality and habitual residence, a concept which in recent years has received increasing international recognition.

Qualifications of the Parties

(1) *The Applicants*

A sole applicant is "qualified" to apply if either (a) he habitually resides in Great Britain and is a national of the United Kingdom or of a convention country or (b) he habitually resides in a convention country or a specified country and is a United Kingdom national.[3]

A "convention" country means any country (excluding Great Britain and a specified country) which is designated by statutory instrument[4] as a country in which, in the opinion of the Secretary of State, the Hague Convention is in force. A "specified" country refers to any of the following countries which are designated by statutory instrument for the purposes of any provision of the 1968 Act: Northern Ireland,[5] any of the Channel Islands, the Isle of Man and a colony. If none of these is designated, any of them may be treated as a specified country. Jurisdiction to make orders under the Act is not, therefore, to be limited to persons who are connected by residence with convention countries.

A husband and wife are "qualified" to make a joint application if either (a) both habitually reside in Great Britain and each is a national of the United Kingdom or of a convention country or (b) each habitually resides in Great Britain or in a convention country or in a specified country and both are United Kingdom nationals.[6] There must, therefore, be common nationality or common residence.

The applicant or joint applicants must be qualified both at the time of the application and immediately before the adoption order is made.[7]

---

[3] Sections 1(1) and 11(1).   [4] See s. 12.
[5] Section 13 empowers the Parliament of Northern Ireland to enact legislation similar to the 1968 Act.   [6] Sections 1(1) and 11(1).
[7] Section 3(5). *Cf. supra* the position under the 1958 Act.

(2) *The Infant*

An infant is "qualified" to be adopted if he habitually resides in Great Britain, a specified country or a convention country and is a national of the United Kingdom or of a convention country.[6] The Act is silent about the date to which nationality and residence are to be referred, but it would seem that a double test must be satisfied, as in the case of the applicant.[8]

Nationality

Section 9 of the Act contains a number of rules for determining in doubtful cases whether a person is a national of a convention country. First, the Secretary of State may by order specify, in accordance with information given by the Government of a convention country, kinds of persons who are to be treated as nationals of that country. Secondly, where a person is a national of two or more countries, he is to be treated as a national of one of them according to certain rules of priority. If he is a United Kingdom national,[9] he must always be so treated: if he is not, his convention country of nationality has priority or, where there are two or more convention countries, that with which he is most closely connected: in any other case, where no convention country is involved, it is the country of closest connection. Thirdly, a person with no, or no ascertainable, nationality is to be treated as a national of the country in which he habitually resides.

Habitual Residence

The Hague Convention left each convention country to define for itself "habitual residence". This concept first appeared in English law in the Wills Act 1963,[10] but neither that Act nor the Adoption Act 1968 has provided a definition.

---

[8] However, the chances of a child's changing nationality or habitual residence between the date of application and the date of order are very remote.

[9] This term is qualified by the Act (s. 11(1)) to mean a citizen of the United Kingdom and Colonies satisfying such conditions, if any, as the Secretary of State may specify for the purposes of any provisions of the Act.

[10] Section 1, which provides that a will is to be recognised by an English court as properly executed if executed according to *inter alia* the internal law of the country which was the testator's habitual residence at the time of execution of the will or of his death.

It has been suggested[11] that it should mean a person's "normal dwelling-place where it is his habit to live – or, in one word, his habitation". This seems to be the sense in which "ordinary residence" has been used in the Adoption Act 1958[12] and with regard to wardship jurisdiction,[13] which shows that, although ordinary residence can vary in meaning and emphasis according to the legal purpose for which it is needed,[14] for some purposes it may be impossible to distinguish between it and habitual residence on the basis of the "quality of continuity"[15] of the residence. Whatever the quality essential for habitual residence, English private international law is not prepared to accept the continental doctrine which equates that concept with domicile.[16]

Applicable Law

Where jurisdiction is assumed under the 1968 Act the application and any adoption order subsequently made are governed by the Act of 1958, subject to certain modifications[17] which will be noted when dealing later with particular topics. The application of English internal law thus avoids problems of *renvoi*, but the 1968 Act accords some recognition to the foreign internal law of nationality. As will be seen,[18] the *lex patriae* of the child is relevant to the granting of consents to adoption. Furthermore, if the adopter is not a United Kingdom national, an adoption order must not be made if the proposed adoption is prohibited by a provision of his internal national

[11] Graveson, *The Conflict of Laws*, 6th edn., p. 513. But in his commentary on the Hague Convention on Adoption the learned author did suggest, in relation to adoption at least, that there might be a statutory definition of habitual residence "by reference to a minimum period of time"; see 14 I.C.L.Q. 528, at p. 534.　　[12] See *supra*, p. 314.
[13] *Re P. (G.E.) (an infant)*, [1965] Ch. 568 (C.A.); [1964] 3 All E.R. 977.
[14] With regard to income tax legislation "a very slight connection with the country in question" has been held sufficient to amount to ordinary residence; see Seventh Report of the Private International Law Committee (1963) Cmnd. 1955, para. 11. For a searching analysis of the essentials of residence and ordinary residence see McClean, 11 I.C.L.Q. 1153.
[15] Graveson, *The Conflict of Laws*, 6th edn., p. 196.
[16] See Art. 5 of the Hague Convention to regulate Conflicts between the Law of Nationality and the Law of Domicile (1955) and the Seventh Report of the P.I.L. Committee, para. 16.
[17] These are to be found in involved numerical cross-references in s. 2 of the 1968 Act. Indeed, the general format of that Act, with its own internal cross-references, has produced a complicated piece of legislation. The need for consolidation of the Adoption Acts is all too obvious and one's present sympathies lie particularly with the foreign lawyer who has to interpret them.　　[18] *Post*, p. 351.

law and, in pursuance of the Hague Convention, that provision is notified to the United Kingdom Government and then specified in a statutory instrument.[19] Should the country of nationality contain more than one legal system (*e.g.* U.S.A.) the appropriate legal system is determined according to any rules of selection operating in that country; if there be none, the system is that which appears to the English court to be the one most closely connected with the case.[20]

(c) The Relationship between the Adoption Act 1958 and the Adoption Act 1968

Jurisdiction under the later Act is non-exclusive, but takes precedence in that, if the applicant(s) and the infant come within its provisions, jurisdiction must be assumed under that Act, even though the parties may also be able to comply with the jurisdictional rules of the Act of 1958; for example, the applicant may be domiciled and resident in England, but is a national of a convention country. Since the 1968 Act is concerned with inter-country adoptions involving a convention country, it is expressly enacted that that Act is not applicable where the applicant(s) and the infant are United Kingdom nationals and habitually reside in Great Britain or a specified country.[1] In such a case it is very likely that the applicant(s) will be able to proceed under the earlier Act, but this does not necessarily follow; for example, notwithstanding habitual residence in Great Britain,[2] he (or they) may be domiciled in Northern Ireland.[3]

The inter-relationship of the two Acts may produce difficulties of internal jurisdiction. The reason why jurisdiction is conferred only on the High Court to make "inter-country" adoption orders is that such adoptions may involve problems

---

[19] Section 3(1).

    In accordance with Art. 13 of the Hague Convention the provision may relate to any of the following matters: (a) the existence of descendants of the adopter(s); (b) the fact that a single person is applying to adopt; (c) the existence of a blood relationship between an adopter and the child; (d) the existence of a previous adoption of the child by other persons; (e) the requirement of a difference in age between the adopter(s) and the child; (f) the age of the adopter(s) and that of the child; and (g) the fact that the child does not reside with the adopter(s).

[20] Section 10(1).   [1] Section 3(2).

[2] The residence will, of course, have to be in England in order to confer jurisdiction on the English court; see *ante*, p. 313.

[3] But see the Adoption Act 1964, *post*, p. 372.

of foreign law, especially, as we have just seen, the recognition
of the foreign national law. It may be, however, that when
adoption proceedings are instituted, it will not be realised that
the applicant or the infant is a national of a country which
would let in the 1968 Act. If those proceedings are begun in a
county court or a juvenile court and only later the foreign
nationality comes to light, a new application to the High Court
under that Act will be necessary.

II. CAPACITY OF THE PARTIES

(1) The Applicants

Apart from domicile, residence and nationality, there are
few legal qualifications which the parties must satisfy, although,
since the court must be satisfied that the proposed adoption
will be for the child's welfare, it may well take account of other
"qualifications", notably the religious faith of the parties.[4]

The usual, and normally the most satisfactory, form of
adoption is, of course, that ordered jointly in favour of a
husband and wife, since the child is thereby assured of two
parents; but, apart from a joint adoption by spouses, only one
person is allowed to adopt.[5] On the kind of applicant depends
the requirement of minimum age.[6] Where he (or she) is a sole
applicant and is the father (or mother) of the child there is no
such requirement; if he is a relative,[7] he must be at least 21
years old;[8] in all other cases he must have attained 25. Where
there is a joint application, one of the spouses must comply

---

[4] See *post*, p. 360. Some courts, too, may have their particular prejudices
with regard to disqualifications; for example, concerning adoption of
coloured children by white parents – see S.C.S.R.A. Report, paras.
131-132. The Working Paper has deprecated arbitrary criteria imposed
by courts or adoption agencies (para. 58).

[5] Adoption Act 1958, s. 1(2).   [6] See s. 2(1) and (2).

[7] Relative means "a grandparent, brother, sister, uncle or aunt, whether of
the full blood or half blood or by affinity and includes —

(a) where an adoption order has been made in respect of the infant or
any other person under any enactment (including any enactment of the
Parliament of Northern Ireland) any person who would be a relative of
the infant within the meaning of this definition if the adopted person
were the child of the adopter born in lawful wedlock;

(b) where the infant is illegitimate, the father of the infant and any
person who would be a relative of the infant within the meaning of this
definition if the infant were the legitimate child of his mother and father;"
see s.57(1).

[8] This rule is not affected by the Family Law Reform Act 1969. A person
attains a particular age expressed in years at the commencement of the
relevant anniversary of the date of his birth; see *ibid.*, s. 9(1).

with one of those three conditions, and, if that spouse is not the father or mother, the other spouse must be at least 21 years of age.[8] There is, however, no rule requiring a minimum difference in the ages between the applicant and the child.[9] Nor is there a maximum age beyond which adoption is not lawfully permitted. Nevertheless, the age of the adoptive parents is taken into account by adoption agencies when placing children for adoption, and it is a matter which the court may consider when deciding whether an adoption would be in the child's interests.[10]

An odd restriction is that which forbids an order being made in respect of a girl on the sole application of a man, unless the court is satisfied that there are special circumstances justifying the making of the order as an exceptional measure.[11] Where in such a case an order is made, it ought expressly to refer to the special circumstances, otherwise an appellate or reviewing court may be forced to infer that the lower court did not address its mind to the rule.[12] If there has been a joint application but the wife applicant dies before it is heard, her death may be a special circumstance justifying an order in favour of the surviving husband.[13]

The object of the restriction is apparently to avoid the danger of sexual corruption of the girl, but, if this is so, it is difficult to defend the decision of the Court of Appeal in *Re R.M. (an infant)*[14] that the fact that the applicant is the putative father is not in itself a special circumstance justifying the making of an order. In view, however, of the more sympathetic attitude of the law today towards the putative father,[15] that decision is likely to be narrowly interpreted by a readiness to find special circumstances. Possibly, proof of affection based on the father's past conduct will be enough.[16] Apart from the possible evidence of sexual corruption, it is difficult to see

[9] Formerly, this had to be 21 years.
[10] Courts should be very cautious about allowing an illegitimate child to be adopted by its grandparents; see VAISEY, J., in *Re D.X. (an infant)*, [1949] Ch. 320; [1949] 1 All E.R. 709.   [11] Adoption Act 1958, s. 2(3).
[12] *R. v. City of Liverpool Justices, ex parte W.*, [1959] 1 All E.R. 337; [1959] 1 W.L.R. 149.
[13] *A.B. Petitioner* 1959, 75 Sh. Ct. Rep. 141; *H. Petitioner*, 1960 S.L.T. (Sh. Ct.) 3.   [14] [1941] W.N. 244.   [15] See *ante*, Chapter 9.
[16] The suggestion "that a near degree of relationship might . . . be a proper ground for finding special circumstances", [Clarke Hall and Morrison, *op. cit.*, p. 650], is difficult to support unless *Re R.M. (an infant)* is given narrow scope.

what other purpose the restriction can have. It can hardly be the practical one that account is being taken of the fact that a man, unlike a woman, is not likely to have the time, expertise or facilities for bringing up the child alone, because, if it were, the rule should also apply to boys. A similar objection may be raised against the rationale of danger of sexual corruption, for on that basis the rule should also apply to adoption of a boy by a woman. Indeed, should the sex of the parties really matter, for there might be the danger of a homosexual relationship? It is suggested that the restriction should be abolished and the question of possible sexual corruption should be left to the court to consider along with all the other circumstances of the case when deciding whether the proposed adoption will be in the child's interests.[17]

(2) The Infant

An order can only be made if the child is under 18 years of age and is not and has not been married.[18] Where the application is made under the Adoption Act 1958 the relevant date for determining his age and condition seems to be the date of the adoption order. That has been the view taken in Scotland, at least with regard to age.[19] Under the Adoption Act 1968 the child must be under 18 on such date as the Secretary of State may specify.[20]

English law follows Roman law in allowing a child to be adopted more than once, including his being re-adopted by his natural parents, but the power to order a further adoption depends on whether jurisdiction is assumed under the 1958 Act or the 1968 Act. If under the former, the power relates[1] to a child whose previous adoption was (1) ordered by the English court under the 1958 Act or its predecessor, the Adoption Act 1950, or under the 1968 Act,[2] or (2) the subject

[17] The Working Paper recommends the abolition of this rule and those relating to age limits of adopters.
[18] Adoption Act 1958, s. 57(1), as amended by the Family Law Reform Act 1969, s. 1(3) and Sched. I; Adoption Act 1968, s. 11(1).
The child attains 18 at the commencement of the 18th anniversary of his birthday; see Family Law Reform Act 1969, s. 9(1).
[19] By the Court of Session, Inner House, in *S. Petitioner*, 1953 S.L.T. 220, after it had earlier been held in *Mr. and Mrs. T. B. Petitioner*, 1950 S.L.T. (Sh.Ct.) 74, that the relevant date was that of presentation of the petition.   [20] This has yet to be fixed.
[1] See s. 1(4) of the 1958 Act, as extended by s. 10(3) of the 1968 Act.
[2] This last statement is made on the assumption that the later Act is already operative.

of an order by a court of another part of the United Kingdom,[3] or (3) ordered in a "specified" country, as defined by the 1968 Act,[4] and corresponds to one ordered by the English court under that Act or (4) an "overseas" adoption within the meaning of that Act.[5] Under the 1968 Act, "an adoption order may be made notwithstanding that the infant is already adopted under an adoption order [made under the 1968 Act] *or otherwise*". By virtue of the italicised words[6] the power to make a further order under that Act is wider and extends not only to any of the above cases covered by the 1958 Act, but also to any other case of a previous adoption under a foreign law.

III. ARRANGING ADOPTIONS

Sometimes the prospective adopters are chosen by the parent himself or by a third party, such as a doctor, but the majority of placements[7] are made by an adoption agency, which must be either an adoption society registered under the Adoption Act 1958 or a local authority acting through its social services committee or, as the case may be, a joint committee.[8] It is unlawful for any other body of persons to arrange or negotiate adoptions.[9]

Registration of Adoption Societies

A general control over adoption societies is secured by registration. The responsibility for registering a society lies with the local authority,[10] which must be satisfied that it is a charitable association.[11] The authority may refuse, or cancel, a registration on the ground that (a) there is no committee of the society to control its activities or (b) a particular person

---

[3] See foreign adoptions, *post*, p. 372.   [4] Section 11(1); see *ante*, p. 317.
[5] Section 4(3); see *post*, p. 373.   [6] The italics are supplied.
[7] A Home Office survey of some 3,400 adoption applications to the courts in 1966 shows that about 40 per cent were arranged by adoption societies and 19 per cent by local authorities. There were about 8 per cent direct placements, 4 per cent by third parties and 29 per cent by parents.
[8] See Local Authority Social Services Act 1970, ss. 2-4 and Sched. I, *ante*, Chapter 5, p. 141.
[9] Adoption Act 1958, s. 29.
   Any one concerned in the management or control of such a body is liable on summary conviction to a maximum penalty of six months' imprisonment or £100 fine or both.
[10] Section 30. The application for registration, which must be supported by information explaining the society's activities, is made to the local authority in whose area the society's administrative centre is situated.
[11] Defined for the purpose by s. 57(1) of the 1958 Act.

324

is not a fit person to be employed to make adoption arrangements on its behalf or (c) there are not enough competent persons employed for that purpose or (d) a person taking part in the management or control of the society or any of its members has been convicted of an offence connected with the registration of adoption societies or the placing of children by adoption agencies. In addition registration may be cancelled because the society is no longer a charitable association or because its administrative centre is no longer within the area of the local authority. Appeal against refusal or cancellation lies to the Crown Court.[12] To enable an authority to exercise its powers of cancellation, a society must annually furnish the authority with a statement of its accounts, a return giving details of the cases dealt with and its annual report.[13] The authority also has a general power to inspect the society's books at any time.[14]

The present system is defective because of the inadequacy of the powers to refuse or cancel registration and the disparity in exercising them. The former defect can be cured by more specific criteria for registration being laid down in statutory regulations, as the Houghton Committee recommends,[15] but the question of responsibility for registration is more controversial. A widely held opinion favours entrusting it to the central government, mainly on the ground that it is invidious to ask local authorities to exercise control over adoption societies when they themselves are acting as adoption agencies.[16] If the proposal that local authorities should, as part of a comprehensive national adoption service, ensure a comprehensive service in their own respective areas were implemented,[17] there is much to be said for leaving the responsibility with local authorities, provided that detailed criteria for registration are formulated.

Placements by Adoption Agencies

The Hurst Committee[18] urged a procedure of maximum simplicity and uniformity in placing children for adoption,

[12] Yet another court involved in adoption law.
   For the procedure leading to appeal see s. 31.
[13] Adoption Agencies Regulations 1959, r. 3.
[14] Adoption Act 1958, s. 33.   [15] Working Paper, paras. 37-40.
[16] For the arguments for and against central registration or local registration see *ibid*, paras. 43-46.
[17] See Working Paper, paras. 17-26 and 33.   [18] Cmnd. 9248, para. 4(ii).

provided that their interests were properly secured. The Adoption Agencies Regulations 1959, 1961 and 1965,[19] which apply both to adoption societies and to local authorities,[20] seek to do this in relation to placements by adoption agencies, but they only provide a legal framework and within that a nationally coherent policy has not been developed,[1] even though it is widely recognised that the period before the child is placed can be the most critical stage in the adoption process. It is arguable that a more detailed code of procedure should be laid down.

A number of conditions must, nevertheless, be fulfilled before an adoption agency can place a child with prospective adopters. Firstly, it must see that his parent or guardian is given a memorandum explaining in ordinary language the effect of adoption on his parental rights and calling attention to the process leading to the making of the adoption order and to the statutory provisions relating to parental consent.[2] The parent must then sign a certificate to the effect that he has read and understood the memorandum.[3]

Secondly, the agency must, so far as it is reasonably practicable, investigate a number of matters relating to the child and the proposed adopters.[4] These include matters which determine whether the court has jurisdiction and whether the parties satisfy the statutory qualifications to adopt or be adopted.[5] If these are ignored or not properly investigated with the result that an unlawful adoption is arranged, anyone involved in such an arrangement will be criminally liable.[6] In such a case the convicting court may order the child to be returned to his parent or to the agency.[7] But the main object of the preliminary investigation is to try to ensure that the parties are mutually suitable. Thus, inquiries must be made into such matters as

[19] Made under s. 32 and Sched. III of the 1958 Act. Penalty for non-compliance with a regulation is a fine of up to £25 or, for a subsequent offence, up to £50.
[20] In making these Regulations in so far as they affect local authorities the Secretary of State is not advised by the Advisory Council on Child Care; see s. 43(1) of the Children Act 1948.
[1] See McWhinnie, *Adopted Children, How They Grow Up*, p. 26.
[2] See *post*, p. 335.
[3] Adoption Agencies Regulations 1959, Reg. 4 and Sched. III.
[4] *Ibid.*, Reg. 5(a) and Sched. IV.
[5] See *ante*, p. 313 *et seq.*
[6] Adoption Act 1958, s. 29(3). For the penalties see *supra*, n. 19.
[7] *Ibid.*, sub-s. (5).

the religious persuasion of the parties; their means, including any proprietary interests enjoyed by the child; particulars of all the members of the household of the prospective adopters and the conditions in which they live; their wishes as to the age and sex of the child they wish to adopt; whether they have made any previous applications for adoption or whether they have previously been found unsuitable to act as foster parents.

In addition to these inquiries the agency must obtain a full medical report on the child; it must interview the prospective adopters;[8] it must inspect the premises where they intend that they and the child shall permanently reside; and it must inquire of the local authority in whose area those premises are situated whether the authority has reason to believe that it would be detrimental to the child to be kept there.[9] In the light of all this information the agency must then consider whether to approve the proposed placement. Where the local authority is the adoption agency, these pre-placement duties are carried out by the authority itself through its social services committee, whereas an adoption society must work through a case committee composed of not less than three persons of whom there must be at least one man and one woman.

Third Party Placements

A third party who arranges an adoption does not have to comply with the above conditions. All that he is required to do is to give 14 days written notice to the local authority for the area in which the prospective adopter is living of his intention to place the child.[10] Failure to do so is an offence,[11] but sometimes third parties are unaware of the requirement and prosecutions are rare. Where notice is given the authority may decide to prohibit the proposed placing on the ground that it would be detrimental to the child to be kept by the prospective adopter in the premises in which he proposes to keep him.[12] Appeal against the prohibition lies to a juvenile court.[13]

[8] But the Regulations do not prescribe a minimum number of interviews.
[9] Remarkably, the Regulations fail to require the authority to reply to the agency, but the Hurst Committee suggested that if the local authority does not reply within 14 days the agency should safely assume that there was no objection to the premises, although it ought to notify the authority immediately the child has been placed; see Cmnd. 9248, paras. 27 and 37.
[10] Adoption Act 1958, s. 40(1) and (3).
  If a child is placed as a matter of emergency, notice may be given within one week after the placing.
[11] Section 44. [12] Section 41. [13] Section 42.

Because third party and parental placements fail to ensure proper investigation into the background of the prospective adopter and the child and because they are often motivated by consideration more for the parent who wants to be relieved of the burden of bringing up the child or for the prospective adopter anxious to have a child than for the child himself, there is a widely felt antipathy towards these placements. In recommending their abolition in cases of adoption by non-relatives, the Houghton Committee,[14] unlike the Hurst Committee, does not anticipate unsatisfactory *de facto* adoptions in view of the control which now exists over private fostering.[15] Nor does it see in the abolition an unwarranted infringement of personal liberty, since the argument that people should be free to make their own arrangements wholly overlooks the welfare of the child.

IV. THE PERIOD OF CARE AND POSSESSION

In all cases of proposed adoption, whoever may have arranged to place the child, [16] an adoption order cannot be made unless the child has been continuously in the care and possession of the applicant for at least three months immediately preceding the date of the order.[17] In calculating this period no account is to be taken of the first six weeks of the child's life. The object of this qualification is to discourage placing of a newly born baby until the parent (usually the mother of an illegitimate child) has had the opportunity of carefully considering the matter, but it is of doubtful efficacy since it does not prevent the adoption agency or third party removing the child at any time after the birth. Indeed, some parents wish this to happen as soon as possible and some agencies insist on it.

Continuity of Care and Possession[18]

The term "care and possession" is not capable of precise definition, but the English courts have recognised the absurd consequences of a literal interpretation and have rejected any

---

[14] Working Paper, paras. 64-69.   [15] For fostering see *post*, Chapter 11.

[16] Where adoption is being arranged by an adoption agency it may be necessary for the agency to assume care of the child until he is actually placed with the prospective adopter. If so, the agency will arrange for him to stay at an authorised Home or with foster parents.

[17] Adoption Act 1958, s. 3(1).   [18] See further (1961) 105 Sol. Jo. 220.

need for "continuous physical propinquity with and control of the infant's person".[19] Instead, following the Scottish courts, they have begun to apply the principle that the applicant must stand *in loco parentis* during the relevant three-month period.[20] If this principle is fully applied, continuity of care and possession will not be broken even though the child is away from the applicant's home during the whole of the relevant period, for example, in hospital.[1] In deciding in such a case whether the applicant stands *in loco parentis* much will depend on the earlier relationship between the parties. The Scottish cases suggest a greater readiness to find continuity if the applicant is a relative.

The above principle is possibly qualified by *Re C.S.C. (an infant)*,[2] which was decided before the principle itself had been formulated. There ROXBURGH, J., held that continuity had been broken by the fact that during the relevant period the applicants allowed the mother to take the child away to her own home, on one occasion for two consecutive nights and on the other for a night and a day. It is to be hoped that this ruling is still good law, because although the Adoption Act 1958 does not make the severance of the child from the natural parent a mandatory prerequisite to the making of an adoption order,[3] such severance ought at least to be insisted on during the probationary period. The primary object of that period is to ensure that the applicant and the child are suitably matched and that, therefore, the order will be for the child's welfare. This object is only properly achieved by keeping the child away from the parents (and parents should here include guardians) during the experimental period so that none of the interested parties, particularly

---

[19] See BUCKLEY, J., in *Re B. (an infant)*, [1964] Ch. 1; [1963] 3 All E.R. 125.
[20] *Re B. (G.A.) (an infant)*, *supra*, was the first case to apply the rule. See also *Re A. (an infant)*, [1963] 1 All E.R. 531; [1963] 1 W.L.R. 231.
The Scottish courts, however, have not applied the principle consistently. In *A. Petitioners* 1953 S.L.T. (Sh.Ct.) 45 a probationer nurse who had been brought up by her grandparents, the petitioners, since she was a few weeks old was held to have been continuously in their care even though she had, apart from week-end visits and holidays, been living away from them during her professional training. But in *M. Petitioner*, 1953 S.C. 227, it was held that a grandson on military service who spent his leaves with his grandmother could not be said to be in her care and possession, even though she, too, had brought him up almost from birth.
[1] *Cf. G. Petitioner* 1955 S.L.T. (Sh.Ct.) 27.
[2] [1960] 1 All E.R. 711; [1960] 1 W.L.R. 304.
[3] See *Re G. (D.M.) (an infant)*, [1962] 2 All E.R. 546; [1962] 1 W.L.R. 730.

the child, should suffer any unnecessary emotional disturbance.[4]

Where the applicant is not ordinarily resident in Great Britain and jurisdiction is assumed under s. 12 of the 1958 Act, the question whether the care and possession must also be in Great Britain throughout the statutory three-month period has been related to s. 3(2) of the Act. This requires the applicant to have given, at least three months before the date of the adoption order, notice to the local authority within whose area he was then living[5] of his intention to apply for an order. Once notice is given and the child passes into the applicant's care and possession he becomes a protected child under the supervision of the local authority,[6] but supervision can only be effective if care and possession is exercised in England (or Scotland where jurisdiction is being exercised by the Scottish courts).[7] Section 3(2), however, does not apply where the child is above the maximum compulsory school age or where the applicant is the parent, whatever the child's age. Consequently, it has been held that, since there is no requirement of supervision in either of those cases, the care and possession may then alternatively take place outside Great Britain,[8] although it will still be necessary for the applicant (and the child if old enough) to be available for interview by the guardian *ad litem* and to be present at the hearing of the application.

On the basis of this reasoning the same rules should apply where the applicant is ordinarily resident in Great Britain, but the prevailing judicial opinion is that then in all cases care and

---

[4] The only exception that ought to be allowed is where the applicant is a relative (*e.g.* grandparent) already living with the natural parent and the child. But adoptions of this kind are generally to be discouraged. See *E.O. Petitioner*, 1951 S.L.T. (Sh.Ct.) 11, where it was held that an aunt could not acquire "possession" of the children so long as they and the children's father were living together; *cf. Re D.X. (an infant)*, [1949] Ch. 320; [1949] 1 All E.R. 709, where adoption by grandparents was permitted but considered exceptional. The latter case, it should be noted, was decided under the Adoption of Children Act 1926, and, since the adoption was not being arranged by an adoption society, it was not necessary as the law then stood, for the grandparents to have had continuous care and possession.

For the desirability of securing for the child an assured position vis-à-vis prospective adopters see also *Re B. (M.F.) (an infant)*; *Re D. (an infant)*, [1972] 1 All E.R. 898; [1972] 1 W.L.R. 102, (C.A.).

[5] See s. 12(1) (b) amending s. 3(2).

[6] See *infra*.

[7] But see note 10, *infra*.

[8] *Re W. (an infant)*, [1962] Ch. 918; [1962] 2 All E.R. 875.

possession must take place in England.[9] The conclusion rests on the false premise that residence in a country necessitates physical presence there. What possible objection is there, in the light of s. 3(2), to a parent applicant for example, spending part of the statutory period abroad with his child on holiday?[10]

Joint Applicants

The *in loco parentis* principle similarly operates where there are joint applicants, so that the temporary absence of one spouse from the home, *e.g.*, on a business trip, will not break the continuity of his care and possession. Thus, a regular soldier who has not lived for the statutory three months with his wife and the child (although he has spent his leaves with them) retains care and possession.[11] This doctrine of constructive care and possession operating in favour of an absent joint applicant has wide implications in view of the many kinds of employment which necessitate the husband's temporary absence.[12] These rules will, it is submitted, operate even if the one applicant (*e.g.* a merchant seaman) should be abroad for the whole of the statutory period, provided that they are both still resident in England and the other of them has actual care and possession here.

Where both are (or one of them is) ordinarily resident outside Great Britain either both must have care and possession in Great Britain or it is enough if one has, provided that they have lived together in Great Britain for at least one of the three months of the statutory period.[13] Alternatively, for the reasons already stated, care and possession may take place outside Great Britain if the child is above the maximum compulsory school age or one at least of the applicants is the parent.

Supervision During Care and Possession

When an adoption agency places a child for adoption it must

---

[9] See WILBERFORCE, J., in *Re W.*, *supra* at pp. 925, 877-78 respectively, following HARMAN, J., in *Re Adoption Application* 52/1951, [1952] Ch. 16, 21; [1951] 2 All E.R. 931, 933.

[10] It has been suggested that even in cases where the child is a protected child under s. 3(2) short absences abroad might be possible; see Josling, *Adoption of Children*, 6th edn., pp. 32-33; Bromley, *Family Law*, 4th edn., p. 253.

[11] *A. Petitioner*, 1958 S.L.T. (Sh.Ct.) 61.

So, in Scots law military service presumably precludes one from being adopted (*M. Petitioner*, *supra*) but not from being a joint adopter.

[12] See 105 Sol. Jo. 220.   [13] Adoption Act 1958, s. 12(3).

arrange for him to be supervised until the proposed adopter gives notice to the local authority under s. 3(2), and in particular must see that the child is visited by one of its officers within one month after being placed and thereafter as often as is considered necessary.[14] Reports on visits must be made to the adoption society's case committee or to the local authority, depending on who is the agency. Certain medical tests and reports are also necessary.[15]

As we have seen, once the notice is given under s. 3(2) *and* the prospective adopter has care and possession (whether as the result of direct, third party or agency placement) the child, if under the upper school age limit, becomes a "protected child"[16] and subject to the supervision of the local authority until the adoption order is made or he attains the age of 18, whichever first occurs.[17] The authority must see that the child is visited from time to time by its officers. They in turn must be satisfied about the child's well-being and must give advice about his care and maintenance. They are also authorised to inspect the premises where the child is being kept.[18] The person who maintains the protected child is deemed to have no interest in the child's life for the purposes of the Life Assurance Act 1774.[19]

[14] Adoption Agencies Regulations 1959, regs. 6 and 9. By virtue of the terms of s. 3(2) these regulations apply to a child below the upper school age limit placed with someone other than the parent.

[15] See *ibid.*, reg. 6(2) and (3).

[16] Adoption Act 1958, s. 37(1).
Even if notice of intended adoption is given a child does not come within this term (a) while in the care of any person (i) in premises where a parent, adult relative or guardian of his is for the time being residing or (ii) in any voluntary home within the meaning of Part V of the C. & Y.P. Act 1933 or (iii) in any school in which he is receiving full-time education or (iv) in any hospital or registered or exempted nursing home or (v) in any other home or institution maintained by a public or local authority or (b) while liable to be detained subject to guardianship under the Mental Health Act 1959 or resident in a residential home for mentally disordered persons; see s. 37(1) and (3) as amended by C. & Y.P. Act 1969, s. 52(4) and Sched. 6; Children Act 1958, s. 2(3) and (4) as amended by C. & Y.P. Act 1969, s. 52(2) and Sched. 5, para. 29; and Mental Health Act 1959, s. 19(3) and Sched. VII.
In all these circumstances other persons are responsible for supervision.

[17] Section 37(4). In the event of the child's death the prospective adopter must notify the local authority within 48 hours (s. 40(5)).

[18] Sections 38 and 39. A refusal to allow visits or inspections is an offence (s. 44(1) (b)). It also justifies the issue of a warrant to search for and remove the child (s. 45). Home Office inspectors authorised under the C. & Y.P. Act 1969, s. 58, also have a right to inspect.

[19] Adoption Act 1958, s. 46.

The Period of Care and Possession

Although under the Adoption Agencies Regulations an adoption society is only required to supervise until notice is given under s. 3(2), in practice it continues to do so thereafter, with the result that the child and the prospective adopter find themselves supervised by the society and the local authority. Apart from unnecessary duplication this may lead to conflicting advice and instructions. Indeed,

"... during the three or four months between the placement of a child and the making of an adoption order an adoptive family may well have seven to ten visits from three or four different people; three visits from the society worker, two or three from the child care officer acting as welfare supervisor, one or two from the guardian *ad litem* who may or may not be the same person, and several visits from the health visitor".[20]

The solution is to take out of the protective supervision of local authorities those children who are placed by adoption societies.

A local authority may complain to a juvenile court that the child is being kept or is about to be received by a person who is unfit to have his care or in premises or an environment detrimental to him.[1] The court[2] may order the child to be removed to a place of safety until he can be restored to a parent, relative or guardian or until other arrangements can be made, including the possibility of the local authority receiving him into their care under s. 1 of the Children Act 1948, even if he appears to be over 17.[3] In a case of imminent danger to the health or wellbeing of the child a justice of the peace may make an order for removal on the application of an officer of the local authority.

These supervisory powers of local authorities are exercised not only over children below the upper school age limit who are placed for adoption but also over children under that limit who have been placed, otherwise than temporarily, in the care

---

[20] S.C.S.R.A. Report, para. 63; Working Paper, paras. 127-131.

[1] Adoption Act 1958, s. 43. See also s. 41, *supra*, p. 327, for the power of a local authority to prohibit placing of a child.

[2] The usual restrictions on the sittings of juvenile courts do not apply here and proceedings are held in open court. Appeal lies in the normal way to the Crown Court. See ss. 47 and 48.

[3] The order for removal to a place of safety must be for a specified period not exceeding 28 days, but if alternative arrangements have not meanwhile been made, further interim orders for the child's detention may be made; see C. & Y.P. Act 1963, s. 23.

and possession of someone other than the parent, relative or guardian who *proposes* to adopt him and a person other than a parent or guardian has taken part in the arrangements.[4] Again, however, certain classes of children who are supervised under certain other enactments are excluded.[5]

Termination of Care and Possession

While the application for an adoption order is pending, the parent or guardian, having signified his consent to the proposed adoption, cannot remove the child from the applicant's care and possession without the leave of the court, and in deciding whether to grant this it must have regard to the child's welfare.[6] On the other hand, where the placement has been made by an adoption agency and the applicant later decides either before or after making his application that he does not wish to go on with it, he may give written notice to the agency that he does not intend to retain care and possession. If so, he must return the child to the agency within seven days.[7] The same duty to return arises if his application is refused or if the period specified in an interim order[8] expires without an adoption order having been made or if the agency, with leave of the court, gives him written notice that it does not intend to allow him to continue to have care and possession. Failure to return the child is an offence[9] and the convicting court may order the child to be returned to the parent or guardian or the agency.

These rules also apply where the child has not been placed by an adoption agency but was for the time being in the care of a local authority when notice of intention to adopt was given under s. 3(2).[10] In this kind of case, however, if the application is refused or withdrawn the child need not be returned to the authority unless the authority so require. During the period of care and possession contributions by the father and mother

---

[4] Adoption Act 1958, s. 37(1) as amended by C. & Y.P. Act 1969, s. 52(4). The person taking part in the arrangements must notify the local authority that the child is to be placed (s. 40).
[5] See *ibid.*, sub-s. (2) as amended by C. & Y.P. Act 1969, s. 52(4) and Sched. 6 and especially s. 2 of the Children Act 1958, as amended by the 1969 Act.   [6] Adoption Act 1958, s. 34.
[7] Section 35.   [8] For interim orders see *post*, p. 362.
[9] With a maximum penalty of six months' imprisonment or £100 fine or both (s. 35(6)).
[10] Section 36. If the notice is given to an authority other than that which has the temporary care of the child that other must be told of the notice.

Consents

towards maintenance are not payable[11] and the child may be treated as a child of the family of the prospective adopter for the purpose of Family Allowances; but these rules cease to operate if after 12 weeks from the date of giving notice no application has been made or, if it has, once it has been refused or withdrawn.

V. CONSENTS

The rules governing the granting of consent to adoption are largely to be found in the principal Act, but are in certain circumstances qualified by the Adoption Act 1968, which will be considered separately.

(a) Under the Adoption Act 1958

(1) The Need for Consent

Because adoption results in a complete transfer of parental rights and duties to the adopters the consent of each parent or guardian is essential, unless the court on certain grounds dispenses with it. Subject to a similar power of dispensation, the consent of a spouse is also necessary where the other spouse is alone applying for an order.[12] But, unlike Scots law, English law does not require the consent of the child, although, if he is old enough, his wishes must be considered.[13]

For present purposes a guardian is defined[14] as a person appointed by deed or will in accordance with the Guardianship of Minors Act 1971 or by a court "to be the guardian of the infant". A person who has been granted custody by the court, for example the putative father by virtue of ss. 9 and 14 of that Act,[15] is not as such within the definition.

A parent here means the father and mother of a legitimate child, the mother of an illegitimate,[16] and the adopter of an adopted child,[17] but the term does not include[18] anyone who

---

[11] Under s. 86 of C. & Y.P. Act 1933, see *post*, p. 496.　　[12] See s. 4(1).
[13] Section 7(2); see *post*, p. 360.　　[14] Section 57(1).
[15] See *in Re Adoption Application* 41/61 (No. 2), [1964] Ch. 48, 52; [1963] 2 All E.R. 1082, 1084.
[16] It has been suggested that the rights of the mother of an illegitimate child are not as wide as those of the mother of a legitimate and that in the case of adoption of the former the child's welfare is the main consideration; see James, *Child Law*, p. 61. For a rejection of this view of a "kind of second-class mother" see Samuels, (1963) 107 Sol. Jo. 707, 708.
[17] See *Re R.M. (an infant)*, [1941] W.N. 244, (C.A.).
[18] See Adoption Act 1958, s. 4 (3), as amended by C. & Y.P. Act 1969, Sched. 5.

Adoption

has the rights and powers of a parent by virtue of a care order[19] or a local authority which has assumed them by resolution under s. 2 of the Children's Act 1948.[20] They must, however, be given notice of the hearing of the application.[1] So, too, must a person liable under an order or agreement to contribute to the maintenance of the child,[2] but the Adoption Act 1958 abolished the need for his consent. The person mainly affected by this change was the putative father. It had already been decided that he was not a parent for the purpose of adoption law,[3] a conclusion which was more readily reached by the fact that he is for that purpose classed as a "relative",[4] but at least where he was maintaining the child his consent had been necessary. It was ironic that no sooner had his rights in relation to adoption been further curtailed than the Legitimacy Act 1959 strengthened his right to claim custody.

The result has been that custody proceedings may be used as a means of delaying if not preventing the making of an adoption order, whether in commencing them the putative father is motivated by a genuine desire to bring up the child himself or by a wish to defeat the mother's wishes that the child be adopted. In deciding between the conflicting claims of the putative father and the prospective adopter the paramount consideration is the child's welfare.[5] Where the applications for custody and adoption are made in the same court, these claims are best determined by deferring the decision on either application until both have been heard.[6] If the applications have already been made in different courts it is likely and desirable that the proceedings in one be stayed so that a fresh application can be made in the other which can then hear both

[19] *I.e.*, under s. 24 of C. & Y.P. Act 1969, *ante*, Chapter 5, p. 152.
[20] See *ibid.*, s. 3 and *ante*, p. 149.
On the other hand because of its parental jurisdiction the court's consent is needed if the child is a ward of court.
[1] H.C. Rules, r. 17 (b); C.C. Rules, r. 10 (b); J.C. Rules, r. 12(1) (b).
[2] See *ibid.*, rr. 17 (c), 10 (c) and 12(1) (c) respectively.
Strangely the High Court may direct that notice is not to be served on such a person in High Court proceedings, but there is no corresponding power given to a county court or juvenile court.
[3] *Re M. (an infant)*, [1955] 2 Q.B. 479 (C.A.); [1955] 2 All E.R. 911.
[4] See *ante*, p. 321, n. 7.
[5] See *infra*, p. 360.
[6] *Re O. (an infant)*, (1965] Ch. 23; [1964] 1 All E.R. 786; *Re M. (an infant) (No. 2)* (1964), 108 Sol. Jo. 1031 (C.A.).

Consents

applications together.[7] This inevitably involves some delay and it has been stressed[8] that ordinarily when a putative father learns of the application for adoption there is no reason why he should not put forward his case in adoption proceedings, whether or not he accompanies his intervention with a formal application for custody if the adoption is refused. That still leaves, however, the problem of knowing whether he is aware of the adoption application and how far steps should be taken to inform him. If he is contributing to the child's maintenance, he must be given notice of the hearing,[9] and there should normally be little difficulty in those circumstances in finding him. If he is not so contributing, his identity may remain unknown, especially if the mother is reticent about it. The guardian *ad litem* is under no duty to seek him out or "indeed (in the absence of special circumstances) to make any inquiries as to [his] existence, whereabouts or attitude",[10] but, if he learns of any person claiming to be the father, who wishes to be heard by the court on the question whether an adoption order should be made, he should inform the court,[11] which then has a discretion whether to give notice.[12] Although the law is clear on this point, there is apparently a failure on the part of some courts to recognise its limits.[13] Thus, some of them insist on exhaustive inquiries into the whereabouts of the father and, to facilitate this, often press a mother into reluctantly naming him. Some, too, insist on his giving a signed consent and some require the guardian *ad litem* to interview him. Such measures mean delay in hearing the adoption application. The dilemma facing the courts is on the one hand to minimise the delay but on the other to encourage

[7] *Re Adoption Application No. 41/61*, [1962] 2 All E.R. 833; (on appeal), [1963] Ch. 315; [1962] 3 All E.R. 553. *Re C. (M.A.) (an infant)*, [1966] 1 All E.R. 838 (C.A.); [1966] 1 W.L.R. 646.
Because it is likely that the guardian *ad litem* has already investigated the adoption application and is in a position to provide the court hearing it with information about most, if not all, of the parties, it is better that the court should hear both applications.
[8] Per WILBERFORCE, J., in *Re Adoption Application No. 41/61 (No. 2)*, [1964] Ch. 48; [1963] 2 All E.R. 1082.
[9] *Supra.*
[10] Per WILBERFORCE, J., in *Re Adoption Application No. 41/61 (No. 2)*, [1964] Ch. 48, 58; [1963] 2 All E.R. 1082, 1088.
[11] H.C. Rules, r. 15 and Sched. II, para. 9; C.C. Rules, r. 9 and Sched. II, para. 9; and J.C. Rules, r. 9 and Sched. II, para. 9.
[12] See *ibid.*, rr. 17 (f), 10 (f) and 12(1) (f) respectively.
[13] See S.C.S.R.A. Report, paras. 17, 41-53, 117-120.

the minority of putative fathers who are concerned for the interests of their children to be involved in planning their future and possibly become themselves responsible for bringing them up. A possible compromise is to require investigation in all cases so as to try to determine the identity and attitude of the father, but to impose a time limit on the investigation in order to avoid protracted and futile inquiries, for example, where the father has gone abroad. A possible maximum period might be two months beginning with the date of the application for adoption.[14]

Another difficulty created by simultaneous custody and adoption proceedings is that of preserving the secrecy of the identity of the prospective adopter where that has been his request. The Adoption Rules provide[15] that, if a serial number is given to the applicant, the adoption proceedings must be conducted with a view to securing that he is not seen by or made known to any party who is not already aware of his identity, except with his consent. But if the prospective adopter wishes to be heard on the custody application his identity will have to be disclosed, unless, as HARMAN, L. J., has suggested,[16] affidavit evidence, with names omitted, is relied on and the confrontation of witnesses avoided.

Consents and the Extra-Marital Child

The Standing Conference of Societies Registered for Adoption has drawn attention to the different views held by courts about the need for obtaining the consent of a mother's husband to the adoption of her extra-marital child by third persons.[17] On the one hand, there are those which regard neither consent from nor notification to the husband as necessary and are content to rely on the mother's evidence that the child is not a child of the marriage. Of these some require only her affidavit evidence of non-access by the husband, others insist on her appearing in person. On the other hand, there are those which demand the husband's formal consent in the

---

[14] It should be remembered that, where the child is placed by an adoption agency, the father may have already been interviewed by the agency's officer even before placement; see Adoption Agencies Regulations 1959, reg. 5 (a) and Sched. IV.
[15] H.C. Rules, r. 19; C.C. Rules, r. 14; J.C. Rules, r. 15.
[16] *Re O. (an infant)*, [1965] Ch. 23, 31; [1964] 1 All E.R. 786, 790.
[17] S.C.S.R.A. Report, paras. 99-116.

prescribed form while others insist that he is notified of the adoption application but are usually willing to accept his affidavit of non-access instead of a personal appearance.

Because of this variation in practice it has been recommended that:

> "the adoption law should state unequivocally that if *a child is proved to be illegitimate* so that the mother's husband is not a parent within the terms of the Act, then neither his consent nor notification to him should be required . . ."[18]

So far as the proposal relates to consent it is superfluous, since it is clear from s. 4 of the 1958 Act that the husband's consent is not necessary. As for notification, an express provision as suggested would be as well in view of the power of the court under the Adoption Rules to notify any person who in the opinion of the court ought to be notified of the adoption hearing. But the recommendation begs the real question. What degree of importance is to be attached, for the purpose of adoption proceedings, to the presumption of legitimacy which operates when a married woman gives birth to a child? Normally the presumption has been a strong one[19] and those courts which have called for consent or notification have sought to give it similar effect within the present context,[20] whereas those prepared to rely solely on the mother's evidence have often been willing to rebut it by evidence which would be inadequate to rebut it for other purposes. In view of the fact that there have been a number of cases where consent or notification has produced endless delays in tracing the husband and harmful effects when he is traced, it is suggested that where an extra-marital child is to be adopted there should be a preliminary hearing at which only the mother's evidence is to be heard, with a discretion in the court to bring in the husband if not satisfied of non-access by that evidence.

---

[18] *Ibid.*, para. 116. Author's italics.

[19] As to the future efficacy of the presumption see *ante* Chapter 8.

[20] But only those which require consent and nothing less are logically consistent, because if the husband is presumed to be the father his consent becomes essential under s. 4 of the 1958 Act and notification is not enough.

Several courts maintain that the husband has a right to be notified, because he may then have grounds for divorce, but the S.C.S.R.A. Report (para. 101) points out that there is a "double standard here", since judges do not correspondingly recognise a wife's right to be notified where an illegitimate child of her husband is being adopted.

Adoption

(2) Mode and Time of Giving Consent

The consent of the parent, guardian or spouse must be freely given and not obtained through fraud or improper pressure.[1] It may be given without knowing the identity of the applicant, either unconditionally or subject to conditions as to the religous persuasion in which the child is to be brought up;[2] but, in giving it, a specific applicant for adoption must be in mind.[3]

Consent must be operative at the moment when the order is made,[4] and any consent signified earlier may be withdrawn, subject to the court's power to dispense with it. Where the parent or guardian does not attend the hearing, documentary evidence of consent is admissible under the following conditions.[5] The document must signify the consent and the applicant must be named or identified by a serial number.[6] It may be executed before or after the commencement of the proceedings and if attested is admissible without further proof of signature; but, where it signifies the consent of the mother, it is not admissible unless the child was at least six weeks old when it was executed and attested, the object of this rule being to avoid the risk of the mother's succumbing to pressure (*e.g.* from her parents) to allow adoption, before she has recovered from the child's birth. None of these provisions

---

[1] *Cp. Re P. (an infant)* (1954), 118 J.P. 139, where a statement by the guardian *ad litem* to the mother that if her consent was not given, the prospective adopters would be entitled to claim reimbursement for the cost of maintaining the child during the period of care and protection was held to be unjustifiable but not in the circumstances to have affected her consent.

[2] Adoption Act 1958, s. 4(2). It has been suggested that there should be a similar arrangement for secrecy of identity of the natural mother so as to minimise the risk of inadvertent disclosure of her pregnancy to relatives, *etc.*; see S.C.S.R.A. Report, para. 29.

[3] See SCRUTTON, L. J., in *Re Carroll*, [1931] 1 K.B. 317, 329; Horsburgh Committee Report, Cmnd. 5499, pp. 56-57; Hurst Committee Report, Cmnd. 9248, p. 25. The form of consent prescribed by the Adoption Rules intends a specific applicant.

[4] *Re Hollyman*, [1945] 1 All E.R. 290 (C.A.); *Re F. (an infant)*, [1957] 1 All E.R. 819, esp. at p. 823.

[5] Adoption Act 1958, s. 6 and H.C. Rules, r. 9; C.C. Rules, r. 5 and J.C. Rules, r. 5.

[6] *Cf. Y.Z. Petitioners*, 1954 S.L.T. (Sh.Ct.) 98.
    A prospective adopter wishing to keep his identity confidential may before applying for an adoption order apply for a serial number to be assigned to him; see H.C. Rules, r. 4; C.C. Rules, r. 2; J.C. Rules, r. 2.

Consents

applies to a spouse. Evidence of his consent is admissible in accordance with the general rules of the law of evidence (*e.g.* under the Evidence Act 1938 and the Civil Evidence Act 1968) which, it is submitted, are also alternatively available in the case of the parent or guardian.[7]

(3) Dispensing with Consent[8]
(1) *Consent of the Parent or Guardian—*
Section 5 of the 1958 Act enables the court to dispense with the consent of the parent or guardian if satisfied[9] that —

(1) (a) he has abandoned, neglected or persistently ill-treated the infant; or

(b) he cannot be found or is incapable of giving his consent or is withholding it unreasonably; or

(2) has persistently failed without reasonable cause to discharge the obligations of a parent.

In *Re C. (an infant)* DIPLOCK, L. J., found the basis of each of these grounds, apart from incapacity, in "a callous or self-indulgent indifference on the part of the parent to the welfare of the child, using 'welfare' in the broad sense and not that of mere material advantage, a sense in which it is so often used",[10] but, as will be seen, the House of Lords in *Re W. (An Infant)* has rejected this criterion in relation not only to incapacity but also to the other grounds contained in s. 5(1) (b).[11]

(i) *Abandonment, Neglect or Persistent Ill-Treatment by Parent.*—It seems that the conduct must be such that it would render the parent liable under the criminal law; for example, under s. 1 of the Children and Young Persons Act 1933.[12] So it was held in *Watson* v. *Nikolaisen*[13] with regard to abandon-

---

[7] The Adoption Act 1958 does not say that consent given prior to the hearing must be in writing, but in practice courts rightly insist on this.
[8] For the procedure to be followed in the Family Division when an applicant applies for consent to be dispensed with see Adoption (High Court) Rules 1971, r. 12(2).
[9] It can only do so if satisfied by admissible evidence, and not secret reports, that one of the specified grounds for dispensation exists; *Re E. (an infant)* (1960) *Times,* 24 March (children's officer's confidential report on father who was in prison and was opposed to the proposed adoption was wrongly admitted by juvenile court).
[10] [1965] 2 Q.B. 449, 471; [1964] 3 All E.R. 483, 494.
[11] [1971] 2 All E.R. 49; [1971] 2 W.L.R. 1011. It is doubtful whether DIPLOCK, L. J., intended it to be a necessary criterion; see Lord HAILSHAM, L.C., *ibid.* at p. 54.   [12] See *ante,* Chapter 6.
[13] [1955] 2 Q.B. 286; [1955] 2 All E.R. 427.

341

Adoption

ment, and it is unlikely that a different test would apply to neglect or persistent ill-treatment; but it is arguable that this is a too restrictive view. For example, supposing that a parent deserts his 17-year-old son who is capable of maintaining himself. Cannot it be said, nevertheless, that he has abandoned him?[14]

(ii) *Parent Cannot be Found.*—Consent may only be dispensed with on this ground if the court is satisfied that either every reasonable step by reasonable means has been taken to trace the parent[15] or there are no practical means for communicating with him, because, for example, for political reasons it would be dangerous to him to try to do so.[16]

This ground does not, however, dispense with the need to serve notice at the last known address of the parent.[17] On the other hand, the rule requiring service relates only to practice and procedure and not to the jurisdiction of the court to hear the adoption application and, if necessary, dispense with consent.[18]

(iii) *Parent Incapable of Giving Consent.*—A parent is incapable of giving consent either where he is mentally incapable of understanding what is involved in consenting to the proposed adoption or is ignorant of the proposed adoption and cannot as a practical matter be made aware of it.[18]

(iv) *Parent Withholding Consent Unreasonably[19].*—This ground has become the main cause of contested litigation over adoption. It demonstrates more clearly than any other aspect of

[14] *Cf. dicta* of BUCKLEY, J., in *Re R. (adoption)*, [1966] 3 All E.R. 613, 616, where, in discussing the circumstances in which the infant (who was just under the age of majority) left his parents, the word "abandonment" is used in a non-criminal sense.
[15] *Re C. (an infant)* (1957) *Times*, April 2 (C.A.); *Re F. (R.) (an infant)*, [1970] 1 Q.B. 385; (C.A.) [1969] 3 All E.R. 1101. If an adoption order is made without all reasonable steps having been taken, and the parent later comes forward, he may be given leave to appeal out of time, but the longer the delay in the application the less likely is it to be granted, since it may not be in the child's interests to set aside the order.
[16] *Re R. (adoption)*, supra.
[17] For a full discussion of the point see Clarke Hall and Morrison, *op. cit.*, p. 655, and 132 J.P. 52.
   See also *Re B. (an infant)*, [1958] 1 Q.B. 12 (C.A.); [1957] 3 All E.R. 193, where the mother's address, though in Australia, was known to the court, yet, wrongly, she was not made a party to the proceedings.
[18] *Re R. (adoption)*, supra.
[19] See Blom-Cooper, *Adoption and Parental Responsibility*, (1957) 20 M.L.R. 473.

the parent-child relationship the impossibility of maintaining a fair balance between their conflicting interests.

In *Hitchcock* v. *W.B. and F.E.B.*[20] two basic principles were formulated. First, in exercising its power of dispensation on this ground the court must primarily concern itself with the attitude of the parent, and the welfare of the child is not, as in custody proceedings, the overriding consideration, although it is a matter to be taken into account in deciding whether the parent is being unreasonable in refusing consent. Secondly, since the effect of an adoption order is to destroy parental rights, it is *prima facie* reasonable to withhold consent.

This second principle was firmly accepted in a number of cases immediately following *Hitchcock*, and it was stressed that only in exceptional circumstances could this presumption of reasonableness be rebutted.[1] If, for example, a father is fit to be a father, wants his child and can support him, it is *prima facie* impossible to say that he is acting unreasonably in refusing consent, even though from the point of view of the child's welfare an adoption order is preferable;[2] *aliter* if his refusal is whimsical, arbitrary or made in bad faith[3]. The length to which the courts were prepared to go is indicated by the view expressed by Lord GODDARD in *Watson* v. *Nikolaisen*[4] that even though the parent may have forfeited his or her rights to have the care and custody of a child it was quite another thing to say that, on that account, he or she must give consent to the child being adopted.

---

[20] [1952] 2 Q.B. 561; [1952] 2 All E.R. 119.

[1] See especially JENKINS, L. J., in *Re Adoption Act, Re K. (an infant)*, [1953] 1 Q.B. 117 (C.A.); [1952] 2 All E.R. 877; HARMAN, J., in *Re F. (an infant)*, [1957] 1 All E.R. 819, 825; ("the parents by nature have rights which only in very special circumstances are they to be debarred from using"). The one case which seems inconsistent with the other earlier ones is *W.* v. *D.*, [1955] C.L.Y. 1318. There the mother first gave consent but withdrew it because meantime a child of the same sex had been born to the prospective adopters. The mother, supported by the adoption society, considered that the adoption would then be detrimental to her child, but her refusal was held unreasonable.

[2] See, for example, *Re F. (an infant)*, *supra*, where HARMAN, J., admitted that "but for the attitude of the parents, it seemed a case where adoption was eminently desirable in the infant's interests". See also ORMEROD, L. J., in *Re G. (an infant)*, [1963] 2 Q.B. 73, 91; *Re L. (an infant)*, [1963] C.L.Y. 1771 (C.A.).

[3] See, for example, *L.* v. *M.*, [1955] C.L.Y. 1317, where a father withheld consent to an adoption order in respect of his daughter in favour of his former wife and her present husband because he wanted to spite the wife.

[4] [1955] 2 Q.B. 286, 296; [1955] 2 All E.R. 427.

Adoption

While both of the *Hitchcock* principles remain essentially valid, there has been some shift of emphasis in their application. The first signs of a change appeared in 1962 in *Re L. (an infant)*,[5] where the Court of Appeal moved away from a presumption of reasonableness and clearly laid down an objective test for determining whether the parent's attitude is reasonable. In the words of Lord DENNING, M.R.:

"A reasonable mother surely gives great weight to what is better for the child. Her anguish of mind is quite understandable; but still it may be unreasonable for her to withhold consent. We must look and see whether it is reasonable or unreasonable according to what a reasonable woman in her place would do in all the circumstances of the case."

The case was also significant because it indicated a willingness to pay more attention to the child's welfare. This tendency was even more marked in *Re C. (an infant)*,[6] where, indeed, PEARSON, L. J., held that in applying the test of reasonableness the primary consideration is the parent's attitude to the child's welfare.[7] This approach suffered a temporary set back in *Re W. (an infant)*,[8] when the Court of Appeal held that parental conduct could only be unreasonable if there were some element of culpability (*per* SACHS, L. J.) or if it involved "shutting your eyes to a blameworthy degree to the very serious consequences which your refusal of consent will almost certainly entail for your child" (*per* CROSS, L. J.); but these stricter views were not adopted in *Re B. (an infant)*[9] by a differently constituted Court of Appeal and were rejected by the House of Lords in *Re W. (an infant)*[10] on appeal where the test formulated by Lord DENNING, M. R., in *Re L. (an infant)* was accepted as authoritative and the principle affirmed that a parent may be acting unreasonably even if there is no element of culpability or of reprehensible conduct in his decision to withhold consent.

"In my opinion, besides culpability, unreasonableness can include anything which can objectively be adjudged to be unreasonable. It is not confined to culpability or callous indifference.

[5] (1962), 106 Sol. Jo. 611.
[6] [1965] 2 Q.B. 449; [1964] 3 All E.R. 483 (C.A.).
[7] At pp. 491, 1050 respectively. Compare the more cautious judgment of DIPLOCK, L. J.   [8] [1970] 2 Q.B. 589; [1970] 3 All E.R. 990.
[9] [1971] 1 Q.B. 437; [1970] 3 All E.R. 1008.   [10] [1971] 2 All E.R. 49.

Consents

It can include, where carried to excess, sentimentality, romanticism, bigotry, wild prejudice, caprice, fatuousness or excessive lack of common sense."[11]

In applying the objective test, all the circumstances of the case must be considered, but the child's welfare is a factor of great importance and is "decisive in those cases where a reasonable parent must so regard it".[12]
But in assessing the parental attitude the child's welfare is to be considered in a broad and long-term sense:

". . . one must look at the whole future of the child; not to mere temporary unhappiness or grief, however acute, if it is transient; not to mere material affluence in childhood or a better chance, through educational advantages, to achieve affluence later. . . . Would a reasonable parent regard a refusal to permit the adoption of the child as involving a serious risk of affecting the whole future happiness of the child?"[13]

That is a large question and within the last decade increasing use has been made of medical evidence to help answer it. Previously,[14] when the courts had to consider removing a child, for example, from a foster parent or applicant for adoption and returning him to the natural parent, they seem to have assumed that a very young child was not likely to suffer if the person to whom he was to be handed over was capable of bringing him up and was anxious to do so; and as for a somewhat older child, say of five and upwards, they tended to accept the view of EVE, J. in *Re Thain, Thain v. Taylor*[15] that the effects of partings were "mercifully transient" and that "the novelty of fresh surroundings and new associations [effaced] the recollection of former days and kind friends". Nowadays, however, medical opinion stresses the risks involved in transferring young children from the care of one person to

[11] *Per* Lord HAILSHAM OF ST. MARYLEBONE, *ibid.*, at p. 56.
[12] *Ibid.*, at p. 55. *Cf. O'Connor* v. *A and B*, [1971] 2 All E.R. 1230; [1971] 1 W.L.R. 1227 (H.L.) with *Re P.A. (an infant)*, [1971] 3 All E.R. 522 (C.A.).
[13] *Per* DIPLOCK, L. J., in *Re C. (an infant)*, [1964] 3 All E.R. at p. 495; [1964] 3 W.L.R. at p. 1055.
[14] For these observations on the courts' earlier attitude see CROSS, J., in *Re W. (infants)*, [1965] 3 All E.R. 231, 248-249; [1965] 1 W.L.R. 1259, 1283. See also Michaels, *The Dangers of a Change of Parentage in Custody and Adoption Cases*, Vol. 83 L.Q.R. 547, esp. at pp. 560 *et seq;* Hopkins, *Medical Evidence in Adoption and Custody Cases*, Vol. 9, Medicine, Science and Law, p. 31.   [15] [1926] Ch. 676 at p. 684.

another, especially those aged between six months and three years. Nevertheless, in deciding whether a parent is acting unreasonably by withholding consent to adoption in the face of medical evidence, that evidence must be strong and decisive, as a comparison of the two Court of Appeal cases, *Re C. (an infant)*[16] and *Re W.*,[17] shows. It must be proved that there is a serious risk of severe psychological harm to the particular child if the adoption order is not made, and that the parent is aware of this. Obviously, very much will depend on the length of time the child has been with the prospective adopters. Thus, in *Re L. (an infant)*,[18] where the child was about two years of age by the date of the hearing of the adoption application and had spent almost all his life with the prospective adopters, the court, in dispensing with the mother's consent, took account of medical evidence that removing the child after such a long time would cause him both psychological and physical harm.[19] In view of current medical knowledge about the risks inherent in removing a child from a secure and contented environment, it is suggested that medical evidence should be made compulsory in all contested adoption cases – and if for the purposes of adoption, should it not logically be so in any other type of case where the question of removing the child is in issue, for example, in contested custody proceedings? Certainly, those from whom it is sought to remove the child would be well advised to adduce medical evidence. Its value is indicated by a comparison of these more recent cases with earlier ones where lengthy periods of separation of the child from the parent did not prevent the latter from successfully preventing adoption. In *Re F. (an infant)*[20] and in *Re U.*[1] the separation had gone on for more than four years, yet it was held that the refusal of consent was not unreasonable. In neither case, however, was there medical evidence[2] and it is

---

[16] [1964] 3 All E.R. 483; [1964] 3 W.L.R. 1041.
[17] Unreported but cited in *Re C.*, at pp. 491, 1050 respectively.
Compare also *Re W. (infants)*, [1965] 3 All E.R. 231; [1965] 1 W.L.R. 1259 and *Re B. (S.) (an infant)* (1966), 110 Sol. Jo. 671 (C.A.).
[18] (1962), 106 Sol. Jo. 611 (C.A.), *supra*.
[19] For other instances see *Re C. (an infant)*, *supra*, and *Re W. (infants)*, [1965] 3 All E.R. 231; [1965] 1 W.L.R. 1259.
[20] [1957] 1 All E.R. 819.   [1] [1959] C.L.Y. 1560 (C.A.).
[2] But in *Re U.* a probation officer did state that the child had seen his natural parents while with the foster parents and had been emotionally disturbed.

Consents

questionable whether similar cases would be decided the same way today.[3]

It is clear, therefore, that, in considering the parent's attitude towards the child's welfare, medical evidence is a major factor. Possibly, a court would be entitled to rely solely on it when applying the test of reasonableness, but in *Re C. (an infant)* PEARSON, L. J., recognised the danger in making that a general rule, since it would effectively mean that the issue would be "taken out of the hands of the court and put into the hands of the medical profession".[4] That could lead exceptionally to abuse, with private arrangements being entered into between an unscrupulous doctor and the applicant for adoption. It is desirable, therefore, that the court should look beyond the medical evidence in assessing the parental attitude towards the child's well-being. For example, as in *Re C. (an infant)*, account should be taken of any uncertainty as to where and how the child would be brought up if the adoption order is made. Can the parent himself provide a satisfactory home? If not, what proposals has he for fostering the child? It is also relevant to assess the effect of his refusal to consent on the prospective adopters and their family. His awareness of the likely grief his refusal would cause them would be evidence of an unreasonable attitude.[5] Moreover a court is likely to look unfavourably on a vacillating[6] or a deceitful[7] or a spiteful[8] parent.

[3] On the other hand, there were special features about both cases. Not only in each did the child know who his natural parents were, but also there were sound reasons why they had entrusted the child to foster parents, namely, in *Re F.*, the mother's mental ill-health and in *Re U.* the initial lack of suitable accommodation for bringing up their child. Moreover, in *Re U.* they had never consented to adoption. How far these factors would now outweigh strong medical evidence of likely harm would depend on the extent of the court's wish to emphasise the *Hitchcock* presumption.
[4] [1964] 3 All E.R. 483, 494; [1964] 3 W.L.R. 1041, 1054.
[5] See PEARSON, L. J., in *Re C. (an infant)*, [1964] 3 All E.R. at p. 491; [1964] 3 W.L.R. at p. 1050. DIPLOCK, L. J., preferred to regard the parent's attitude towards the prospective adopters as "perhaps, only of importance in throwing light on her attitude towards the best interests of the child. A selfish disregard of the feelings of others may throw light on the motives of self-indulgence which lie behind her refusal"; see *ibid.*, pp. 495, 1056 respectively.
[6] *Re C. (an infant)*, *supra*; *Re L. (an infant)* (1962), 106 Sol. Jo. 611. Cf. *Re U.*, [1959] C.L.Y. 1560 (consistent refusal to give consent).
[7] *Re W. (infants)*, [1965] 3 All E.R. 231; [1965] 1 W.L.R. 1259.
[8] *L. v. M.*, [1955] C.L.Y. 1317. Cf. *Re L. (an infant)*, [1963] C.L.Y. 1771, where the father genuinely wanted his daughter.

Adoption

There are two rules relating to withholding of consent which the Adoption Act 1958 itself lays down. Both are concerned with the unknown applicant. Firstly, a parent (or guardian) who has initially consented to the proposed adoption without knowing the identity of the applicant and then withdraws his consent for that reason alone is deemed to be unreasonably withholding his consent.[9] But secondly, as we have seen,[10] if in a case of unknown identity the parent gives consent, he is entitled to impose conditions with respect to the religious persuasion in which the child is to be brought up,[11] and this he may do at any time before the adoption order is made. Should the applicant be unwilling to meet these conditions the parent is justified in withdrawing consent. The effect of the rule is that withdrawal of consent on religious grounds where the applicant is not known to the parent can never be unreasonable, even if adoption would be in the interests of the child and even though on the objective test the parent must as a reasonable parent know that to be so. It is an open question whether his powers are as wide where he knows who the applicant is.[12] It is submitted that, since there is no statutory provision, the courts are able and ought to take a more balanced view about the importance to be attached to the child's spiritual welfare.[13] Even where the parent does successfully insist on religious conditions there are, however, no effective means under the Act for enforcing them once the adoption order is made.[14]

Although reported cases indicate that greater attention is being paid to the child's welfare when considering whether to dispense with consent on the ground of unreasonableness, inquiries have revealed considerable variation in the attitude of courts, with some emphasising the child's welfare, but most

---

[9] Section 5(3).   [10] *Ante*, p. 340.   [11] Section 4(2).

[12] In *Re E. (an infant)*, [1963] 3 All E.R. 874; [1964] 1 W.L.R. 51, the mother eventually found out who the applicants had been, but it seems from the Report that this was only in later wardship proceedings which the disappointed applicants brought after their application for adoption had failed because of the mother's withdrawal of consent on religious grounds.

[13] At one time the complaint was that too much emphasis was placed on material welfare.

[14] See *Re G. (an infant)*, [1963] 2 Q.B. 73, 89; [1963] 1 All E.R. 20, 23, *per* ORMEROD, L. J.

Moreover, no other conditions can be attached to an order, *e.g.* access by the natural parent; see PEARSON, L. J., *ibid.*, at pp. 102 and 32 respectively.

still looking primarily to protection of the parent's rights.[15] Much of the dissatisfaction with the present law stems from the rules concerning the time and mode of giving consent, which almost encourage the parent to vacillate. The Working Paper has offered a number of proposals for reform.[16]

(v) *Persistent Failure to Discharge Parental Obligations.* Mindful of the problems created by the ground of unreasonable withholding of consent, but acknowledging that the test for dispensing with consent was not the paramountcy of the child's welfare, the Hurst Committee recommended[17] that that ground should be abolished but a new one added, namely a parent's persistent failure to discharge his parental obligations. The Adoption Act 1958 decided to have the best, or worst, of both worlds by including both grounds. The object of the Hurst proposal was to secure a fairer balance between the interests of the child and the rights of the parent. It was intended to cover the case of a parent who, without abandoning or neglecting his child in a criminal sense, has shown no genuine interest in him and has no reasonable excuse, such as ill-health or lack of suitable accommodation, for his behaviour.

While the high hopes of a liberal interpretation promised by the judgment of PENNYCUICK, J., in *Re P. (infants)*[18] have not been wholly fulfilled, this ground has certainly not been construed in such a restrictive way as have the others. In *Re P. (infants)* it was held that:

"the expression 'obligations of a parent' must include first the natural and moral duty of a parent to show affection, care and interest towards his child; and secondly, as well, the common law or statutory duty of a parent to maintain his child in the financial or economic sense".

Applying that principle to the facts it was found that the mother had failed to fulfil her moral obligations to her two illegitimate children, aged six and four years, whom she had parted with within a few weeks of birth. Apart from having one of them to live with her for three weeks the children had never lived with her, and little interest in their welfare had been shown by her; for example, she seldom visited them. Equally she had failed

---

[15] See S.C.S.R.A. Report, para. 17.   [16] See *infra*, p. 352.
[17] Cmnd. 9248, para. 120.   [18] [1962] 3 All E.R. 789; [1962] 1 W.L.R. 1296.

in her legal duty to maintain them. She had been supported by the putative father, a man earning not less than £12 a week and she drew £94 Family Allowance in respect of the children. Yet, she had paid but £29 towards their maintenance. Moreover, for the past four years she could have had the children to live with her and the putative father. It was held that she had clearly failed to discharge the obligation of a parent and so the court had a discretion to dispense with her consent.[19]

A more cautious approach is, however, discernible in *Re M.* (*an infant*).[20] There an eighteen-year-old mother, anxious to conceal her pregnancy from her parents, arranged for foster parents to take over the care of her baby as soon as it was born, with a view to adopting it. This was done a few days after the birth. Formal consent was later given, whereupon the application for adoption was made; but then the consent was withdrawn. All this happened in less then six months after the birth. In deciding that consent could not be dispensed with on the present ground the case seems to be an authority for the proposition that failure to visit one's child after deliberately placing him for adoption does not *per se* constitute persistent failure to discharge one's parental obligations, and on that basis it should be welcomed,[1] for, as the Court of Appeal recognised, not visiting the child may well be best for him in the circumstances. Moreover, any other view would, it is submitted, be inconsistent with the rationale underlying *Re C.S.C.* (*an infant*),[2] that during the probationary period of care and possession the parent and child should be kept apart to avoid emotional disturbance to the child. On the other hand, if after placement the prospective adopters delay in making their application and the parent is content to do nothing, continued inactivity would be

---

[19] For other instances of persistent failure see *Re G.* (*an infant*), [1963] 2 Q.B. 73 (C.A.); [1963] 1 All E.R. 20; and, a strong case, *Re B.* (*S.*) (*an infant*), [1968] 1 Ch. 204; [1967] 3 All E.R. 629.
[20] (1965), 109 Sol. Jo. 574 (C.A.).
[1] For a different view see Samuels, (1965) 109 Sol. Jo. 799-800, who argues that the mother's "failure to provide emotional fulfilment for the child" during the first six months of its life might be sufficient to justify dispensing with consent. On the other hand, it might be better for the child to be placed for adoption. As the circumstances stood initially in *Re M.* (*an infant*) if the mother had revealed her pregnancy to her parents and sought to keep her baby, it might have led to the child being brought up in an unhappy and unwanted home.
[2] [1960] 1 All E.R. 711; [1960] 1 W.L.R. 304, *ante*, p. 329.

strong evidence of abnegation of parental obligations and if it continued long enough would be persistent.[3]

(2) *Consent of a Spouse*

We have seen[4] that the spouse of an applicant must normally consent to the other's adopting a child, for clearly it would not be in the child's interests to be brought into the spouses' family without the non-adopting spouse being agreeable to it. If the adoption order is made, the effect almost inevitably will be that the child will be a "child of the family" for the purpose of various matrimonial proceedings.[5]

The court may, however, dispense with that consent if satisfied that the spouse cannot be found or is incapable of giving his consent or that the spouses have separated and are living apart and that their separation is likely to be permanent.[6] Whether the separation is by virtue of an order of the court or by agreement or against the wishes of either spouse is immaterial, but, if on the strength of it consent is dispensed with and an adoption order made and the parties later resume cohabitation, it, again, becomes a question of fact whether the child becomes a "child of the family".

(b) *Under the Adoption Act* 1968

The provisions in the Adoption Act 1958 relating to consents[7] will also apply where the adoption order is to be made under the 1968 Act, unless the child is not a United Kingdom national, in which case they are replaced by the rules of the internal law of the country of nationality governing consents and consultations.[8] Any power of dispensing with consent conferred by those rules, will be exercised by the High Court, and for that purpose a rule of the *lex patriae* requiring the personal attendance of any person is treated as having been complied with in respect of a person not residing in Great Britain if (a) he has been given a reasonable opportunity of communicating his opinion on the proposed adoption to the High Court or to an

---

[3] In *Re M. (an infant)* HARMAN, L. J., doubted whether a period of about six months was long enough to satisfy the necessary element of " persistent" failure.   [4] *Ante*, p. 335.
[5] See *ante*, Chapter 9. But exceptionally it may be possible to show that, notwithstanding his consent, the non-adopting spouse did not accept the child as a member of the family.   [6] Adoption Act 1958, s. 5(4).
[7] Sections 4 to 6, *supra*.   [8] 1968 Act, s. 3(3) (a).

appropriate authority of the country of nationality for trans-
mission to that Court.[9]

It is not, however, necessary to seek the consent of or consult with, the applicant for the adoption order or members of
his family, even though the *lex patriae* requires this,[9] except
that, as with adoptions under the 1958 Act, the consent of a
spouse of the applicant is necessary, unless dispensed with on
any of the same grounds as that Act permits.[10]

(c) Proposals for Reform

The Working Paper of the Houghton Committee recommends
several changes concerning consent to adoption.[11] It recognises
that adoption should continue to be possible only with the
consent of the child's parent, unless the court dispenses with it
on specified statutory grounds, but it proposes (a) that the
ground of persistent ill-treatment should be extended to include
serious ill-treatment and, more importantly, (b) that in applying the test of reasonableness to the grounds of unreasonably
witholding consent and persistent failure without reasonable
cause to discharge parental obligations the welfare of the child
should be the paramount consideration. However, the most
important recommendations are those relating to the introduction of a preliminary hearing, distinct from the hearing of the
adoption application, to deal with the giving of parental consent, the procedure depending on whether or not the child is
being placed by an adoption agency.

If he is, the parent should normally be able to give his
general consent to adoption and not, as at present, merely to a
specific application. It should be formally given at the separate
hearing and once that was done the decision would be irrevoc-
able and the rights and responsibilities of the parent would
vest in the agency who would assume a temporary legal guardianship until the adoption order is made. Before declaring the
child legally eligible for adoption the court would also have to
be satisfied that the rights and interests of any other relevant
persons are considered (*e.g.*, the putative father) and opportunity given to them to be heard. Preferably final consent

---

[9] *Ibid.*, sub-s. (4).
[10] See s. 3(3) (b) of 1968 Act, and for the grounds of dispensation s. 5(4)
of the 1958 Act, *supra.*   [11] See Parts VI and VII.

should be given before placement but this should not be a prerequisite.

Where an application for adoption is being made by relatives or foster parents and no agency is involved, the consent should always be to the specific application alone. The giving of it should also be at a court hearing, but this could be held either before or at the same time as the hearing of the adoption application. In either event, the consent would not be final until the adoption order was made.

In cases where consent is withheld, the application to dispense with it should, in agency placements, be made to the court hearing the consent application; in non-agency placements, to that dealing with the adoption application.

VI. THE GUARDIAN AD LITEM

1. Functions

As soon as practicable after the application for an adoption order is made, the court must appoint a guardian *ad litem* of the child.[12] His essential function is to safeguard the interests of the child before the court. To do this he must investigate all the circumstances relevant to the proposed adoption, including the matters alleged in the application[13] and those specified in the Adoption Rules.[14] This involves interviewing the applicant, the parent, every individual who is a respondent to the application, every individual who has taken part in arranging the adoption, and, if old enough to converse with, the child. As an officer of the court he must discharge his duties impartially and must not favour, or bring pressure to bear on,[15] any interested party.

---

[12] Adoption Act 1958, s. 9(7); Adoption (H.C.) Rules, rr. 6 and 7; (C.C.) Rules, r. 8(1); (J.C.) Rules, r. 8(1).

If the parent is himself an infant and is opposed to the application a guardian *ad litem* should also be appointed for him; *Adoption Act, Re K. (an infant)*, [1953] 1 Q.B. 117; [1952] 2 All E.R. 877. But the general principle is that a guardian is not necessary for an infant respondent to adoption proceedings unless the court otherwise directs. For the purpose of such proceedings in a county court the Adoption (C.C.) Rules, r. 29, expressly so provides.

[13] Once appointed he must be given a copy of the application, together with the documents attached thereto.

[14] H.C. Rules, r. 15(1); C.C. Rules, r. 9(1) and J.C. Rules, r. 9(1), and the Second Schedule to each of those Rules.

[15] *Cp. Re P. (an infant)* (1954), 118 J.P. 139, *ante,* p. 340.

353

Much of his investigation relates to the applicant: the circumstances of his home and family;[16] his means; his religious persuasion; any record of serious illness; the reason for wishing to adopt the child and whether he understands the nature of an adoption order; and such other information, including an assessment of his personality and, where appropriate, that of the infant, as has a bearing on their mutual suitability. For this last mentioned reason he must find out whether the child, too, is able to understand the nature of the order, and, if so, whether he wishes to be adopted by the applicant.[17] With regard to the parent or guardian, he must see whether his or her consent[18] has already been freely given and he must ascertain when the mother[19] ceased to have care and possession of the child and to whom these responsibilities were transferred.

On completing his investigations he must make a written confidential report to the court.[20] He must in particular draw its attention to any difference in age between the applicant and the infant which is less than the normal difference in age between parents and their children, and he must also, as we have seen, inform it of any person coming to his notice who wishes, or ought, to be heard on the question whether an adoption order should be made.[1] If he wants to obtain the court's directions on any matter, he can make interim reports to it.

The role of the guardian in cases where the child has been placed for adoption by a registered agency has been criticised by the S.C.S.R.S., mainly on three grounds:[2]

(1) The failure of the law to decide whether he shall be primarily a caseworker or purely a court official.

---

[16] In the case of an application by one only of two spouses, the guardian will want to know why the other does not join in the application.

    If the applicant is not ordinarily resident in Great Britain, the guardian must try to obtain a report on his home from a suitable agency in the country of residence.

[17] The Rules require him to make other inquiries about the child (*e.g.*, whether he has any interest in property) and to inform the applicant accordingly.

[18] Also that of the spouse of an applicant.

[19] Strangely the rules do not mention the father or a guardian.

[20] H.C. Rules, r. 15(2); C.C. Rules, r. 9(2); J.C. Rules, r. 9(2). See further *post*, p. 421.

[1] For the application of this rule to a person claiming to be the father of an illegitimate child see *ante*, p. 336.

[2] See paras. 54-60 of its Report. The Working Paper has taken account of these criticisms.

(2) The lateness of his appointment. By the time the application for an adoption order has been made and he has been appointed the important decisions about the child's welfare have already been taken by the agency.

(3) The duplication of work. The guardian is compelled to cover the same ground as the agency, thus causing delay and subjecting the applicants and the parents to unnecessary distress, which is often exacerbated by a conflict in the casework techniques of the agency and the guardian. If, on the other hand, he tries to minimise duplication and relies on the agency's reports, he cannot be said to be carrying out an independent investigation which is basic to his role as an officer of the court.

It has, therefore, been suggested that "what is needed in agency placements is an assessor, not necessarily a social worker but a court official with special knowledge of adoption to go over all the application papers and reports to make sure that they are in order and that all the information which the court will require is available".[3] This proposal, if implemented, would obviously not apply to direct and third party placings but it would be an added reason for making them illegal and requiring all placements to be made through a registered agency.

2. Appointment

So long, however, as the guardian has to discharge his present functions, the rules governing his appointment will remain inadequate for, while they require certain kinds of persons to be appointed, they do not ensure that those appointed are specially trained for those functions.[4]

Selection depends partly on the court to which the application for an adoption order is made. If this is a county court or juvenile court, the guardian may be[5] –

(a) the director of social services of a local authority or an officer or servant of the authority who assists him in the exercise

[3] *Ibid.*, para. 61.
[4] Indeed, the 1958 Act itself refers only to the appointment of "some person" (s. 9(7)).
[5] See Adoption (C.C.) Rules, r. 8 and Adoption (J.C.) Rules, r. 8.
  The appointment is made by the registrar of the county court or the juvenile court itself.
  References in the Rules to the children's officer must now be understood to mean the director of social services; see the Local Authorities Social Services Act 1970, s. 6.

of his functions,[6] providing that the authority consents;[7] or (b) a probation officer;[8] or (c) if the court considers the appointment of any of those persons is not reasonably practicable or desirable, some other person appearing to be suitably qualified.

But no one can be appointed who has the rights and powers of a parent or has taken part in the arrangements for the adoption or is a member, officer or servant of a local authority, adoption society or other body of persons having such rights and powers or having taken part in such arrangements.[9]

Subject to this disqualifying rule, the director of social services or a welfare officer or a probation officer is usually appointed, but there have been many instances of inexperienced officers being appointed.[10] There has also been some opposition to the use of probation officers as guardians *ad litem*,[11] and the increasing tendency to relieve them of functions connected with children under 14, which is a feature of the Children and Young Persons Act 1969, may well result in their ceasing to fulfil, this role.

In the case of a High Court adoption the Official Solicitor, if he consents, is the guardian.[12] If he does not consent or if the applicant desires someone else to be appointed,[13] the judge may appoint any person appearing to him to be suitably qualified, including the director of social services of a local authority.[14] Where the Official Solicitor is willing to act but the applicant is opposed to this, the court may refuse to accede to his wishes to appoint someone connected with his family, on the ground that the appointment of a guardian is a matter of

---

[6] If the director is appointed, he may carry out his duties through an officer or servant.

[7] Adoption Act 1958, s. 9(8).
 Where an officer is appointed, the court may authorise the authority to incur any necessary expenditure; see *ibid*.

[8] This appointment is also authorised by the Probation Rules 1965, r. 31.

[9] For example, a children's officer whose local authority has assumed parental rights under s. 2 of the Children Act 1948 (see *ante*, Chapter 5, p. 147).   [10] See S.C.S.R.A. Report, para. 57.

[11] See Hurst Committee's Report, Cmnd. 9248, para. 76.

[12] Adoption (H.C.) Rules, r. 6. The applicant must undertake to pay his costs.

[13] In either circumstance the applicant must ask for an appointment in his originating summons, supported by an affidavit stating the facts. This means that he must find out whether the Official Solicitor is willing to act before he takes out a summons; see Josling, *op. cit.*, p. 44.

[14] H.C. Rules, r. 7. Although the rule does not refer to any other officer of the authority, the judge could appoint a child care officer, for example, as a suitably qualified person.

public policy and not only the concern of the family.[15] This procedure, which makes it exceptional for anyone but the Official Solicitor to act as guardian, has been described as obsolete,[16] and is a further illustration of the need for a uniform procedure within a system of Family Courts. The Houghton Committee sees the office of guardian *ad litem* in adoption proceedings depend upon the strengthening of adoption agencies. Once their standards and decision-making procedures are improved they should be made accountable to the court and required to submit a full written report direct to it. When these changes are effected the appointment of a guardian *ad litem* should be discretionary and his duties specified by the court in the particular case.[17]

VII. THE HEARING OF THE APPLICATION

An application for an adoption order must be in a prescribed form giving particulars about the applicant and the child. It usually has to be accompanied by a medical certificate relating to the applicant's health and a medical report on the child, together with any written consent which has been granted.[18]

The procedure for hearing the application is largely governed by the Adoption Rules.[19] In proceedings in a county court or juvenile court the time for the hearing is fixed when the guardian *ad litem* is appointed, but in the High Court the onus is on the applicant to obtain an appointment within 14 days after being notified by the guardian that he has made his report to the Court.[20]

When the time of the hearing has been fixed notice thereof must be given to (i) every person whose consent to the making of the adoption order is required,[1] (ii) any person having the

---

[15] *Re A.B. (an infant)*, [1948] 2 All E.R. 727, where an application by the grandparents of the child for the appointment of the family doctor was refused, because if the child's mother were interviewed by a guardian outside the family circle it might be found that she wanted to keep the child as her own.

[16] Cmnd. 9248, para. 77. For a defence of the High Court procedure see 118 New L.J. 799.

[17] Working Paper, paras. 132-141.

[18] Neither a certificate nor a report is required if the applicant is the father or mother of the child or if the child has reached the upper limit of compulsory school age.

[19] See further thereon Josling, *op. cit.*, pp. 50 *et seq.*

[20] If he fails to do so, the guardian *ad litem* must apply forthwith to the court for directions; see *Practice Direction*, [1966] 1 All E.R. 960; [1966] 1 W.L.R. 706.

[1] *Ante*, p. 335.

rights and powers of a parent by virtue of the Children and Young Persons Acts[2] or s. 3 of the Children Act 1948,[3] (iii) anyone liable under an order or agreement to contribute to the child's maintenance, (iv) the local authority to whom the applicant has given notice of his intention to apply for an order,[4] (v) any local authority or adoption society who has taken part in the adoption arrangements and (vi) any other person who in the opinion of the court ought to be served with notice.[5] With regard to the child, he must be made a respondent to proceedings in the Family Division but not to those in a county court or juvenile court. However, in proceedings in the inferior courts, if the guardian *ad litem* reports that in his opinion the child is able to understand the nature of an adoption order, the court must inform the applicant that the personal attendance of the child is required. If it does, it cannot make an adoption order or interim order unless (a) he attends or it decides that there are special circumstances making his attendance unnecessary[6] and (b) it is satisfied that the child has been informed of the nature of the order.

As for the applicant, his personal attendance is essential, except that where there is a joint application the court may dispense with the personal attendance of one of the applicants provided that he verifies the application by a duly attested declaration. The Court of Appeal has, however, stressed the importance in adoption as well as custody proceedings of hearing oral evidence and not relying solely on affidavits. It ought to hear the applicants and any natural parent opposed to the making of an adoption order.[7]

Proceedings are heard in camera and, where the applicant has had a serial number assigned to him, his identity must not, without his consent, be disclosed to any respondent who is not already aware of it. This applies particularly to the parent or guardian.[7a] To comply with this requirement the court should

---

[2] *Ante*, p. 151.   [3] *Ante*, p. 150.   [4] *Ante*, p. 330.
[5] For example, a putative father who is not contributing to the child's maintenance.
[6] *Cf. Re G. (an infant)*, [1963] 2 Q.B. 73 (C.A.); [1963] 1 All E.R. 20, where this condition was not satisfied but proved to be immaterial since, for another reason, no order was made.
[7] See Vol. 119 N.L.J., p. 962, referring to *Fulton* v. *Barham* (unreported). *Cf.* custody proceedings, *ante*, p.266.
[7a] But he must be given a proper opportunity to answer allegations made against him; *Re M. (An infant)*, [1972] 3 All E.R. 321; [1972] 3 W.L.R. 531, (C.A.).

arrange for the parties to attend at different times.

The Rules provide that any information obtained by a person in connection with his duties is confidential, but the court may call for disclosure. Moreover, where the proceedings are contested a party may request any adoption society or local authority department which has been concerned with placing the child for adoption or with its care or supervision to produce its records or give evidence. Application may be made by or on behalf of the society or department for directions as to what records and information should be made available. If the court is of the opinion that disclosure would be harmful to the child it may instead call for a confidential report.[8]

The parents are not entitled to see the confidential report of the guardian *ad litem*, except insofar as the court thinks fit to disclose its contents.[9] The extent to which it is willing to exercise its discretion is not certain, but one judicial view[10] is that, if a report contains allegations against a party having a direct bearing on whether he should be allowed to adopt the child or to resist its adoption, he should have the opportunity of dealing with them.[11] This view is consistent with what the House of Lords has said about the use of confidential reports in wardship proceedings.[12]

VIII. THE WELFARE OF THE CHILD

It has already been seen[13] that, where the withholding of parental consent is in issue, the question of the child's welfare is inextricably involved and of great importance. However, when that issue has been determined in favour of the applicants, there may still be other matters relating to his welfare

---

[8] See *Practice Direction*, [1968] 1 All E.R. 762; [1968] 1 W.L.R. 373, relating to proceedings in the High Court. The request can also be made in contested proceedings relating to wardship or arising under the Guardianship of Minors Act 1971.

It is suggested that inferior courts should observe the same procedure.

[9] *Re J.S. (an infant)*, [1959] 3 All E.R. 856; [1959] 1 W.L.R. 1218; *Re G. (an infant)*, [1963] 2 Q.B. 73 (C.A.); [1963] 1 All E.R. 20.

[10] See DONOVAN, L. J., in *Re G. (an infant)*, *supra* at pp. 97-98 and 29 respectively.

[11] *E.g.*, where the report contains an adverse comment on a parent which might lead the court to dispense with his consent. See *Re E. (an infant)* (1960) *Times*, March 24 *Re B. (an infant)* (1960) *Times*, March 25.

[12] *Official Solicitor* v. *K.*, [1965] A.C. 201; [1963] 3 All E.R. 191.

[13] *Ante*, pp. 342 *et seq.*

of which the court should take cognisance in deciding whether to make an adoption order. For example, it is statutorily directed[14] to take account of the health of the applicant[15] and, having regard to his age and understanding, the wishes of the child,[16] factors which probably but not necessarily will have been considered in the consent issue. Where no difficulties arise over consent, the court ought to treat the child's welfare as paramount, even though the Adoption Act 1958 does not expressly make it so, since there is no conflict of interests between parent and child which has to be resolved.

The Houghton Committee recommends that the principle of paramountcy should apply to all adoption applications and the question of parental consent subordinated to it.[17] Moreover, because of the permanent effects of adoption, the child's welfare should always be looked at on a long-term view. But that, indeed, is how the courts ought to view it under the present law, even where the principle of paramountcy cannot be applied.[18]

The kinds of matters that may be relevant to welfare may be as varied as they are in custody cases. Some were noted when dealing with parental consent.[19] Others which may be particularly significant in adoption cases are the religious differences between the parent and the applicant,[20] the previous conduct of the applicant towards other children,[1] and the strength of the natural tie between the child and his parent. This last factor soon gained prominence after the putative father's right to claim custody was strengthened.[2] The decision

---

[14] Adoption Act 1958, s. 7(2).
[15] See *supra*, p. 357, for the need in most cases for production of a medical certificate.
  Although s. 7 does not, surprisingly, refer to the child's health, the court ought to have regard to it, and, as seen (*supra*, p. 357), a medical report thereon is also normally necessary. It is submitted that the court should always be under a duty to consider the child's health.
[16] As to the need for his attendance see *supra*, p. 358.
[17] Working Paper, paras. 11-13 and 173. For a different view see Cavenagh and Post, *Adoption Procedure – Views from the Court* in *Social Work Today*, (1970) at p. 33.
[18] See DIPLOCK, L. J., in *Re C. (an infant)*, [1964] 3 All E.R. at p. 495; [1964] 3 W.L.R. at p. 1055.   [19] And see generally Chapter 9.
[20] *Cp., Re G. (an infant)*, [1962] 2 Q.B. 141 (C.A.); [1962] 2 All E.R. 173 where they did not prove decisive. See also *ante*, p. 340, for the right of the parent to impose conditions as to religious upbringing.
[1] But it is not always detrimental to a child to be adopted by a person who has against him a conviction of indecent assault; *Re G. (D.M.) (an infant)*, [1962] 2 All E.R. 546; [1962] 1 W.L.R. 730.
[2] See *ante*, p. 336.

of the Court of Appeal in *Re C. (M.A.)*[3] (commonly referred to as the "blood-tie" case) to award to the father the custody of his 18-month-old child, in spite of the fact that the child had spent all but the first seven weeks of his life with the proposed adopters, aroused much criticism on the ground that it unduly emphasised the blood tie; but it should be treated as a case of exceptional circumstances. Regard should be had to the tie:

> "not on the basis that the person concerned has a claim which he has a right to have satisfied, but only if, and to the extent that, the conclusion can be drawn that the child will benefit from the recognition of this tie".[4]

Thus, since an adoption order in effect legitimises an illegitimate child, that order should be made if the natural father has nothing to offer the child in comparison,[5] even if it should deprive him of a present right to access.[6]

Whatever weight is given to the child's welfare it is not the sole consideration, and, where the purpose of the adoption application is only to secure a collateral advantage, the court will refuse the order. Thus, an application in respect of a child nearing the age of majority, brought solely in order to obtain British nationality, will fail;[7] *aliter* if, apart from that object, the interested parties genuinely want the child to become a member of the family.[8]

Apart from the child's welfare, the court must also be satisfied[9] that (1) every person whose consent is necessary and has not been dispensed with has consented to and understands the nature and effects of an adoption order and (2) the applicant has not received or agreed to receive any unauthorised pay-

---

[3] [1966] 1 All E.R. 838; [1966] 1 W.L.R. 646.
[4] *Per* WILBERFORCE, J., in *Re Adoption Application No. 41/61 (No. 2)* [1964] Ch. at p. 53; [1963] 2 All E.R. at p. 1085. See also Lord DENNING, M.R., in *Re O. (an infant)*, [1965] Ch. 23 at p. 28; [1964] 1 All E.R. 786 at pp. 788–789.
[5] *Re C. (an infant)* (1969), 113 Sol. Jo. 721 (C.A.).
[6] *Re E. (P) (an infant)*, [1969] 1 All E.R. 323; [1968] 1 W.L.R. 1913 (C.A.).
[7] *Re A. (an infant)*, [1963] 1 All E.R. 531; [1963] 1 W.L.R. 231. The application also failed because the proposed adopters did not stand *in loco parentis* to the child; see *ante*, p. 329.
[8] *Re R. (Adoption)*, [1966] 3 All E.R. 613; [1967] 1 W.L.R. 34.
[9] Adoption Act 1958, s. 7(1).

ments or other rewards for the proposed adoption.[10] But what of the burden of proof? It has been strongly argued that, with regard to the child's welfare, there should be a presumption that an adoption order would be for his benefit, that the onus should be on the guardian then to prove otherwise and that the proof must be beyond reasonable doubt.[11] If the argument is valid, there is, it is submitted, no ground for imposing a different burden of proof with regard to the above matters.

IX.   THE ORDER

The court may include conditions in the adoption order,[12] but, except where the parent is entitled to insist on the religious upbringing of the child,[13] it is not likely to do so, because of the practical difficulties of enforcement.

Where the court is doubtful about the suitability of the placement it may make an interim order, giving the custody of the child to the applicant for a period of not more than two years,[14] imposing, if it wishes, conditions with regard to the maintenance, education and supervision of the child. As soon as the period specified expires, the child must be returned to the adoption agency if an adoption order is not made.[15] Although an interim order is not an adoption order, the rules applicable to the latter with regard to jurisdiction, care and possession and consents similarly apply.

[10] For the general prohibition, on unauthorised payments see s. 50. It does not extend to payments made to an adoption agency to meet expenses incurred in connection with the adoption or to those sanctioned by the court.

[11] Freeman, *Adoption and the Burden of Proof*, Vol. 119 N.L.J. 345, criticising the refusal of a county court judge to allow the natural mother and step-father jointly to adopt on the ground that they had failed to prove that adoption would have positive advantages not otherwise obtainable.

[12] Adoption Act 1958, s. 7(3). In particular it may require the adopter by bond or otherwise to make financial provision for the child.

[13] See *ante*, p. 340.

[14] Section 8. If the period specified is less than two years, it may be extended to the maximum.

[15] Section 35(4).

If when the interim order is made no time is fixed for the further hearing and the proceedings are in the High Court, the applicant or the guardian *ad litem* must obtain, at least two months before the interim order is due to expire, an appointment for a hearing. In the juvenile court the date is fixed by the court itself, or in the county court by the registrar, not less than one month before expiration. See H.C.R., r. 20; J.C.R., r. 18; C.C.R., r. 19.

Registration of Adoptions

The adoption must be registered by the Registrar-General in the Adopted Children Register in accordance with the particulars given by the adoption order.[16] These include the date of the child's birth or, if this is not known, the probable date; the country of birth, unless this is not proved to the court's satisfaction;[17] and the name and surname of the child. The names specified in the order must be the name or names and surname stated in the adoption application or, if none is stated, the child's original name or names and the applicant's surname.[18] The order will also direct that the original entry of birth in the Register of Births be marked "adopted", but there is no right to trace the connection between that entry and the entry in the Adopted Children Register, except under a court order. A "full" birth certificate will reveal the date of the adoption order and the court making it, but not the name of the natural parents. A "short" form of certificate will not even disclose that the child has been adopted.

The question whether an adopted person should have, as he has in Scotland once he attains the age of 17, the right to trace his natural parents has been much canvassed. The weight of opinion is against an absolute right and prefers the present rule requiring the court's permission. The Houghton Committee has gone further and proposed that the rules relating to anonymity be strengthened by allowing the parent as much as the applicant to rely on a special number procedure.[19] This retention of the principle of anonymity is not inconsistent with a more open approach towards adoption in which the child is told of his adoption and the background of his former family.

Amendment, Revocation and Quashing of Adoption Orders

The court which made the adoption order may, on the application of the adopter or the adopted person, amend it by

[16] Adoption Act 1958, ss. 20 and 21. Further rules apply to orders made under the Adoption Act 1968; see s. 8.
[17] But if it appears probable that the child was born within the United Kingdom, the Channel Islands or the Isle of Man he is to be treated as born in England (s. 21(2) (b)).
[18] *Semble*, where a child has been baptized its Christian name cannot be changed on adoption, but additional names may be given; see Clarke Hall and Morrison, *op. cit.*, pp. 1056-1057, citing *Re Parrott, Cox v. Parrott,* [1946] Ch. 183; [1946] 1 All E.R. 321.
[19] Working Paper, paras. 230-235.

correcting any error in the particulars;[20] for example, the date of the child's birth.[1] It may also substitute or add any new name which was given to the adopted person within the first year of the order.[2]

There is also power to revoke the order if it was made in favour of the mother or father alone and the child is subsequently legitimated by the marriage of his parents.[3] The obvious advantage of the revocation is that the infant will then be entitled to rights of succession to both parents, but it will not affect the devolution of property under an intestacy occurring, or a disposition made,[4] before the revocation.

This is the only specified ground for revocation and in *Skinner* v. *Carter* the Court of Appeal suggested that probably no other would be recognised, since the finality of an adoption order was likely to work in the child's interests.[5] The importance of this view, if acceptable, should not, however, be overstated, for, apart from the right of appeal,[6] an order made by a county court or juvenile court may be quashed for want of jurisdiction.[7] Nevertheless, until that is done the order must be treated as valid even though the defect in jurisdiction is known. Thus, in *Skinner* v. *Carter* it was held that an order for maintenance could be made by a magistrates' court against a man on the basis that he was the adoptive father although it was now known that he was bigamously married to the joint adopter at the date of the adoption order.

When an application for an adoption order is dismissed on its merits, a further application will not be entertained unless

---

[20] Adoption Act 1958, s. 24.

[1] *R. v. Chelsea Juvenile Court Justices (Re an infant)*, [1955] 1 All E.R. 38; [1955] 1 W.L.R. 52.

[2] For other powers of amendment see s. 24(1) (b); Sched. 5, para. 6(1) and (2).   [3] Adoption Act 1958, s. 26; Adoption Act 1960, s. 1.

[4] A disposition made by will or codicil is made on the date of the testator's death (s. 17(2) of 1958 Act) and the principles established by *Re Gilpin, Hutchinson* v. *Gilpin*, [1954] Ch. 1; [1953] 2 All E.R. 1218 (*post*, p. 370) do not apparently apply.

[5] See Lord GREENE, M.R., and SOMERWELL, L. J., [1948] Ch. 387, at pp. 389, 395 and 397; [1948] 1 All E.R. 917, at pp. 920 and 921.

[6] See *infra*.

[7] *R. v. Leeds City Justices, ex parte Gilmartin*, [1951] C.L.Y. 4853; *R. v. Liverpool City Justices, ex parte W.*, [1959] 1 All E.R. 337; [1959] 1 W.L.R. 149. See also Josling, *op. cit.*, p. 84, who cites other instances of orders being quashed.

In *Re R. (an infant)*, [1962] 3 All E.R. 238; [1962] 1 W.L.R. 1147, an adoption order was quashed and a provisional adoption order substituted.

the court is satisfied that there has since been a substantial change in the circumstances.[8]

Appeals

An appeal from an order of the High Court or a county court lies to the Court of Appeal,[9] but from a juvenile court to a single judge of the Family Division.[10] It may be based on law or fact, but on the latter ground the court will interfere with the findings at first instance only if they are not justified by the evidence or with the discretion only if its exercise was clearly not in the child's interests.[11] Further evidence may with leave be adduced of facts occurring since the date of the order[12] or, in exceptional circumstances, before that date.[13] Unlike the hearing below, the appeal will usually be heard in open court.[14]

The guardian *ad litem* appointed in a juvenile court or county court is the guardian *ad litem* for the purpose of an appeal.[14] His confidential report should be sent to the appellate court, as should the note of evidence taken in the court below.[15]

Where a court does not make an adoption order, it has no power to stay the operation of s. 35(3) of the Adoption Act 1958[16] and authorise the applicants to retain the child pending an appeal,[17] an unfortunate rule if the appellate court should reverse the decision.

C. THE LEGAL EFFECTS OF AN ADOPTION ORDER

The general effect of an adoption order is to create between the adopter and the child a legal relationship almost wholly the

[8] H.C.R., r. 5; C.C.R., r. 6; J.C.R., r. 6.
[9] The Court of Appeal has statutory and inherent jurisdiction.
[10] Adoption Act 1958, s. 10; Administration of Justice Act 1970, s. 1(2) and Sched. I.
[11] *Re G. (D.M.) (an infant)*, [1962] 2 All E.R. 546; [1962] 1 W.L.R. 730.
[12] *Re Adoption Act 1950 (1958) Times*, 29 July.
[13] *Cf.* custody cases, *ante*, p. 267.
[14] *F. & F. v. C. Association* (1955) C.L.Y. 1320. *Cf. Re R. (an infant)*, [1962] 3 All E.R. 238; [1962] 1 All W.L.R. 1147.
[14] *Re S. (An infant)*, [1959] 2 All E.R. 675 n.; [1959] 1 W.L.R. 921.
[15] *Re J. S. (an infant)*, [1959] 3 All E.R. 856; [1959] 1 W.L.R. 1218. If no note was taken a new trial will be ordered; *see ibid.*
[16] Section 35(3) requires the applicant to return the child to the adoption agency; see *ante*, p. 334.
[17] *Re C.S.C. (an infant)*, [1960] 1 All E.R. 711, 716; [1960] 1 W.L.R. 304, 310.

same as that between a parent and his natural child. This result is principally achieved by the Adoption Act 1958, but in addition several statutes expressly include adopted children within their own provisions. As will be seen,[18] most of them are concerned with the financial aspects of the family.

Custody, Maintenance, Education and Cognate Matters

Section 13 of the 1958 Act provides that all rights, duties, obligations and liabilities of the natural parent in relation to the future custody, maintenance and education of the child vest in the adopter as if the child had been born to him in lawful wedlock; and, where there is a joint adoption, the spouses stand to each other and to the child as though they were the lawful father and mother. Consequently, a custody order granted to one natural parent as against the other *ipso facto* comes to an end on the child's adoption.[19]

Notwithstanding the general terms in which the section is enacted, a number of enactments, notably those concerned with the breakdown of marriage, which deal with custody, maintenance and education expressly include the adopted child. Indeed, s. 13 itself feels obliged to refer explicitly to the right of the adopter to appoint guardians for the child. Legislation dealing with such matters as Fatal Accidents claims, taxation, social insurance legislation and various statutory pension schemes[20] make similar express reference to the adopted child. Moreover, for the purpose of various enactments affecting insurance for payment on the death of the parent or child the adopter is deemed to be the parent and, where an insurance policy for the payment for funeral expenses on the death of the child is taken out before the adoption order is made, the rights and liabilities thereunder pass to the adopter.[1] Life assurance policies, effected under s. 11 of the Married Women's Property Act 1882 so as to create a trust in favour of the spouse and children of the assured person, are also expressly extended to adopted children,

---

[18] *Post*, Chapter 14.
[19] *Crossley* v. *Crossley*, [1953] P. 97; [1953] 1 All E.R. 891.
[20] *E.g.*, see the Superannuation Act 1965, s. 99(1).
[1] Adoption Act 1958, s. 14(1) and (2).

The Legal Effects of an Adoption Order

and operate retrospectively if the policy was effected before the adoption order was made.[2]

But for other purposes it may be necessary to rely on the general principle embodied in s. 13. Thus, for the extension of the statutory duty of the parent to maintain his child under the Ministry of Social Security Act 1966[3] reliance must be placed on that principle.

Effect of Adoption Orders on Affiliation Orders and on Children in Care

Except where an illegitimate child is adopted by the mother and she is a "single woman", an adoption order automatically terminates an affiliation order or an agreement by the father to make payments for the benefit of the child; but arrears due under the order or agreement at the date of the adoption order are still payable.[4] Two difficulties arise over the exception, namely, the meaning of the term "single woman" and the relevant time for determining that status. The better opinion seems to be that the term is not confined to a woman not presently married (*i.e.,* a spinster, widow or woman whose marriage has been dissolved or annulled) but that it has the wider meaning given to it for the purposes of affiliation proceedings so as to include also the married woman who is living apart from her husband either (1) by virtue of a decree of judicial separation or a matrimonial order containing a non-cohabitation clause or (2) because she has lost the right to be maintained by him because of her adultery.[5] It is generally recognised that the mother must have this status at the time of the adoption. But the combined effect of these rules can produce, for example, the following consequences.

Supposing that M, the mother of C, obtains an affiliation order against F. M later marries H. Subsequently she decides to adopt C, and, as required,[6] H consents, but does not wish

---

[2] Adoption Act 1958, s. 14(3); but the retrospective effect will not apply to an adoption order made under the Adoption Act 1968.
[3] Section 22.   [4] Adoption Act 1958, s. 15(1).
[5] *Cf.* Josling, *Adoption of Children,* pp. 93-94, who in relation to the present topic supports the wider view for the purpose of an affiliation order but the narrower one for the purpose of an agreement by the father to maintain.   [6] Adoption Act 1958, s. 15(2).

himself to adopt. If M is living with H, she does not come within the terms of the exception and the affiliation order therefore comes to an end. This is a strange result. It has been recognised since the Adoption Act 1958 was enacted that the mother's marriage *after* the date of the adoption order will not affect the continuation of the affiliation order (or agreement). Why, then, should a marriage existing when the adoption order is made do so? The result is also inconsistent with the law relating to the assumption of responsibilities by the step-father. If in the above example there were no adoption and H accepts C as a child of the family, then in any subsequent matrimonial proceedings between H and M it would be relevant in determining H's liability to provide for C to take account of the affiliation order. It is scarcely an encouragement to H to consent to his wife's adopting her child if the father is going to be relieved of financial responsibility by the adoption. It is submitted that the mother's status at the time when she adopts her child should be irrelevant.

It is also the rule that once an adoption order has been made in respect of an illegitimate child, no affiliation order may later be made, but, again, an exception is allowed in favour of the mother wishing alone to adopt her child.

An adoption order also brings to an end a care order made under the Children and Young Persons Act 1969 or a resolution under s. 2 of the Children Act 1948.[7]

Marriage

Adoption affects questions of marriage in two ways. Firstly, the parental right to grant or withhold consent to the child's marrying is transferred to the adoptive parent.[8] Secondly, while it does not affect the prohibited degrees of relationship in which the child stood to other persons before the adoption order is made, it extends the prohibition to intermarriage between the adoptive parent and the child,[9] which continues even if the child is later adopted into another family. However, the Adoption Act 1958 does not expressly go further than this, and it seems that the adopted child is not prevented from

---

[7] *Ibid*, sub-ss. (3) and (4), and see *ante*, Chapter 5.
[8] Adoption Act 1958, s. 13(1).
[9] *Ibid*, sub-s. (3). But the parties are not within the prohibited degrees for the purpose of the law of incest.

marrying either a natural or another adopted child of the adopter.[10] The Houghton Committee would, as a normal rule, extend the prohibition so that an adopted child would be prohibited from marrying anyone whom he would have been debarred from marrying if he had been born rather than adopted into the adoptive family, but the court could give special permission to marry.[11]

Nationality and Domicile

If the adopter, or, in the case of a joint adopter, the male adopter is a citizen of the United Kingdom and Colonies and the child is not, the latter becomes such a citizen from the date of the adoption order.[12] On the other hand a British child who is adopted under a foreign law does not lose his British nationality.

Since the Adoption Acts are silent about the effect of adoption on domicile, it might be argued that the child retains the domicile he has at the date of the adoption order, but the predominant opinion is that he takes, and becomes dependent upon, the domicile of the adopter, although his domicile of origin is probably not affected.[13]

Property

For the purpose of conferring rights of succession on death and *inter vivos* dispositions the adopted person is treated as a member of the adopter's family and not that of his natural parents, but there are time limiting factors.

For the purpose of an intestacy occurring after the adoption order has been made the property devolves in all respects as if the adopted person were a child of the adopter born in lawful wedlock and not the child of any other person, except that this rule does not extend to entailed interests forming part of the estate.[14]

[10] But *cf.* Lord HAILSHAM OF ST. MARYLEBONE, L.C., in *Re W. (an infant)*, [1971] 2 All E.R. at p. 51, where the view is expressed that adoptive brothers and sisters are within the prohibited degrees of intermarriage.
[11] Working Paper, paras. 251-252.
[12] Adoption Act 1958, s. 19(1). The rule applies to anyone adopted since 1 January 1950. Proposed legislation on immigration is likely to create special difficulties for the adopted child; see Bloom, 121 N.L.J. 185.
[13] The position might be different where there is a foreign adoption which the English court recognises, since the foreign law may retrospectively affect his domicile of origin.
[14] Adoption Act 1958, s. 16(1).

Section 16(2) provides:

"In any disposition of real or personal property made, whether by instrument *inter vivos* or by will (including codicil) after the date of an adoption order —

(*a*) any reference (whether express or implied) to the child or children of the adopter shall, unless the contrary intention appears, be construed as, or as including, a reference to the adopted person;

(*b*) any reference (whether express or implied) to the child or children of the adopted person's natural parents or either of them shall, unless the contrary intention appears, be construed as not being, or as not including, a reference to the adopted person; and

(*c*) any reference (whether express or implied) to a person related to the adopted person in any degree shall, unless the contrary intention appears, be construed as a reference to the person who would be related to him in that degree if he were the child of the adopter born in lawful wedlock and were not the child of any other person."

For the purpose of s. 16(2) a disposition made by will or codicil is treated as having been made on the date of the testator's death and not on that of execution of the instrument.[15]

Due to the combined effects of s.16(2), s. 17(2) and Sched. 5, para. 4[16] of the Act of 1958 together with the decision in *Re Gilpin, Hutchinson* v. *Gilpin,*[17] complicated problems can arise in applying to questions of testamentary succession the principle that the adopted child is to be treated as if he were the

---

[15] Section 17(2).

[16] Paragraph 4 reads:

"4.-(1) Subject to the followng provisions of this paragraph, ss. 16 and 17] of this Act apply in relation to an adoption order made under the Adoption Act 1950 or any enactment repealed by that Act or the Adoption of Children Act (Northern Ireland) 1929, as they apply in relation to an adoption order within the meaning of those sections respectively.

(2) Nothing in sub-paragraph (1) of this paragraph affects the devolution of any property on the intestacy of a person who died before the 1st January 1959 or any disposition made before that date.

(3) Subsection (2) of the said s. 17 does not apply in relation to a disposition made by will or codicil executed before the commencement of this Act unless the will or codicil is confirmed by codicil executed after the commencement of this Act.

(4) Notwithstanding any rule of law, a disposition made by will or codicil executed before the date of an adoption order (within the meaning of s. 13 of the Adoption Act 1950) shall not be treated for the purpose of s. 16 of this Act as made after that date by reason only that, before the commencement of this Act, the will or codicil was confirmed by a codicil executed after that date.   [17] [1954] Ch. 1; [1953] 2 All E.R. 1218.

child of the adopter and not of his natural parents. The main rules may be summarised as follows:

(1) Section 16(2) can apply only to dispositions made after 1949.

(2) Section 16(2) can operate only if the disposition is made after the adoption order has been made.

(3) Where the disposition is contained in a will or a codicil executed on or after April 1, 1959, it is deemed to have been made on the date of the testator's death.

(4) Where the disposition is contained in a will or codicil executed before April 1, 1959, it is treated as having been made on the date of execution of the document, unless that document is confirmed by a codicil executed on or after April 1, 1959, in which case r. 3 operates.

(5) Where the will or codicil is executed before the date of the adoption order and is confirmed by a codicil executed after that date but before April 1, 1959, the disposition is not deemed to have been made after the date of the order.

Obviously, with the effluxion of time some of these rules are of diminishing practical importance. Moreover, they must be read subject to any contrary intention of the testator.[18]

In applying ss. 16 and 17 to intestacies and dispositions the child who is adopted by spouses jointly is deemed to be the brother or sister of the whole blood of any natural child or other adopted child of the spouses. In all other cases, *e.g.*, where he is adopted by one person, he is a brother or sister of the half-blood.[19]

Like the legitimate child of a pre-1959 void marriage or a legitimated child,[20] an adopted child cannot succeed to any dignity or title of honour or property devolving therewith.[1]

D. PROVISIONAL ADOPTION ORDERS

It is normally an offence to take or send a child who is a British subject[2] out of Great Britain for the purpose of his

---

[18] The intention may be inferred from surrounding circumstances if the evidence is cogent and convincing; *Re Jones' Will Trusts*, [1965] Ch. 1124; [1965] 2 All E.R. 828; *Re Jebb*, [1966] Ch. 666; [1965] 3 All E.R. 358; *Re Brinkley's Will Trusts*, [1968] Ch. 407; [1967] 3 All E.R. 805.
[19] Section 17(1).   [20] *Ante*, Chapter 8, p. 252.   [1] Section 16(3).
[2] This includes a citizen of the Republic of Ireland (Adoption Act 1958, s. 57(3)).

being adopted (whether in law or in fact),[3] but s. 53 of the 1958 Act admits one exception.

The High Court or a county court may make a provisional adoption order in favour of a person who is not domiciled in England or Scotland giving him immediate custody and allowing him to remove the child from Great Britain so that he may adopt the child under the law of or *within the country of his domicile*.[4] In all cases the English court will require evidence of the foreign law.[5]

Apart from the question of domicile, the requirement that the applicant must have had care and possession for six months instead of three[6] and the need to give the local authority that longer period of notice, the rules relating to the making of an adoption order equally apply. Thus, proper consideration must be given to the child's welfare.[7] Once a provisional order is made it has the same legal effects as a full order except that those concerning the devolution of property and acquisition of citizenship do not apply.[8]

E.   FOREIGN ADOPTIONS

The Adoption Act 1964 enables an adoption order made in Northern Ireland, the Isle of Man or the Channel Islands to have the same effects in England (subject to certain limits as to date of operation)[9] as if it were an adoption order made in England or Scotland under the 1958 Act.

The Adoption Act 1968 will eventually extend similar recognition to other adoptions which take place outside Great

---

[3] Section 52. The restriction does not apply if the child is to be received abroad by a parent, guardian or relative. Note also the power of the Home Secretary to give consent to a child's emigrating (*ante*, Chapter 5, p. 168).

[4] The words italicised probably intend to cover cases where different personal laws operate within the country of domicile.

[5] H.C.R., r. 13; C.C.R., r. 17.

[6] In the case of joint applicants they must, for the purpose of s. 12(3) of the Act, have lived together for at least one of the three months immediately preceding the date of the provisional order and not any month during the six-month period; *Re M. (an infant)*, [1965] Ch. 203; [1964] 2 All E.R. 1017.

[7] *Re G. (an infant)*, [1962] 2 Q.B. 141; [1962] 2 All E.R. 173.

[8] *Quaere* the child retains rights of inheritance to his natural parents' estate under English law in view of the fact that ss. 16 and 17 of the Adoption Act 1958 are excluded; see James, *Child Law*, p. 54.

[9] See s. 1.

Britain.[10] The Secretary of State will be able to specify the kinds of adoption and these "overseas adoptions" need not be confined to "convention adoptions", *i.e.*, adoptions effected in a country in which the Hague Convention (1965) is in force.[11] The High Court will have power to annul any overseas adoption as being contrary to public policy or because the authority which purported to authorise the adoption was not competent to do so.[12] If the adoption is a convention adoption there will be further grounds for annulment or revocation, namely,[13] that (1) the adoption was prohibited by the adopter's internal national law or (2) its provisions relating to consent offended that law or (3) it was contrary to the law of the country in which it was effected or (4) the child has since been legitimated by the marriage of the parents.

When these rules do begin to operate, they will not prevent the court from applying to the overseas adoption the common law rules of recognition[14] and, of course, those will apply exclusively to a foreign adoption which is not an overseas adoption. What they are, however, is another matter.[15] With some uncertainty English law seems to have moved to the point where it will recognise an adoption effected in the country of domicile of the adopter.[16] Whether it is additionally necessary that the child should be resident there, as the Adoption Act 1958 requires an English residence for an English order, is open to doubt. The view that it is[17] accords with the doctrine of reciprocity which was current with regard to the recognition of foreign decrees of divorce when that view was advanced, but, in the light of the wider basis of recognition since given to those decrees,[18] there is a distinct possibility

---

[10] Section 4. [11] See *ante*, p. 317.

[12] Section 6(3) (a). *Any* court in Great Britain may also treat the adoption as invalid for the purpose of the particular proceedings before it (sub-s. (4)).

[13] *Ibid.*, sub-ss. (1) and (2). The powers under these provisions can only be exercised if the adopters or the child reside in Great Britain (s. 7(2)).

[14] Section 10(2).

[15] The reader is referred to textbooks on the conflict of laws. Of the extensive periodical literature see especially Scarman, *English Law and Foreign Adoptions*, 11 I.C.L.Q. 635; Cowen, *English Law and Foreign Adoption*, 12 I.C.L.Q. 168; North, 28 M.L.R. 470.

[16] See *Re Valentine's Settlement, Valentine v. Valentine*, [1965] Ch. 831 (C.A.); [1965] 2 All E.R. 226.

[17] See Lord DENNING, M.R., *ibid.*

[18] Since *Indyka v. Indyka*, [1969] 1 A.C. 33 (H.L.); [1967] 2 All E.R. 689.

that a foreign adoption will be recognised where the adopters or the child or both have a "real and substantial connection" with the country where the adoption took place, even though it is not the domicile of the adopters or the residence of the child.[19]

Whatever may be the proper basis of recognition, the extent of it is not, it seems, exclusively a matter for the foreign law. The point invariably arises in disputes over proprietary rights. Where English law is the *lex causae*, any disabilities or, as the case may be, additional rights relating to property under the foreign law which are not part of English law should be ignored.[20]

---

[19] *Quaere* whether it should also be necessary that the foreign law should provide substantially the same safeguards as English law, *e.g.*, with regard to consents and the child's welfare; see SALMON, L. J., in *Re Valentine's Settlement, supra*.

[20] Compare the differing views of Lord DENNING, M.R. and SALMON, L. J., in *Re Valentine's Settlement*, and see Goodrich, *The Conflict of Laws* (4th edn.), p. 290.

CHAPTER 11

Foster Parenthood

In spite of some attention from the legislature and, recently, the courts and commentators, the foster child is still the Cinderella of English family law. It is the failure to settle basically the legal relationship between the child and the foster parent which accounts for the inadequate treatment. In so far as that relationship exists, it is the product partly of general principles applicable to other children and adults and partly of particular rules which, however, relate only to certain classes of foster children.

In general terms, a foster parent may be described as any person other than a legal guardian[1] who stands *in loco parentis* to a child, *i.e.*, one who takes upon himself the duty of the parent to make provision for the child and assumes the responsibility for his care and control.[2] We have seen that because of the latter assumption the foster parent is under the common law duty to protect the child from physical harm, and similarly certain duties arise under the Children and Young Persons Act 1933.[3] These obligations are incurred whatever may be the reason for assuming responsibility; but, broadly, other rules are applicable only if the foster child falls within one of three categories, namely, (1) those protected by the Children Act 1958; (2) those who are in the care of a local authority or a voluntary organisation and are boarded out; and (3) those in the care of persons who propose to adopt them under arrangements made by adoption agencies.[4]

---

[1] For legal guardianship see *post*, Chapter 12.
[2] See JESSEL, M. R., in *Bennet* v. *Bennet* (1879), 10 Ch. D. 474, citing with approval the definition given by Lord ELDON in *Ex parte Pye* (1811), 18 Ves. 140 and approved and elaborated by Lord COTTENHAM in *Powys* v. *Mansfield* (1837), 3 My. & C.R. 359.
[3] See respectively *ante*, pp. 175 and 188.
[4] See Adoption Act 1958, Part IV, *ante* pp. 331 *et seq.*

375

Foster Parenthood

A. CHILDREN ACT 1958

In 1870 two notable events occurred in the history of child fostering. The Local Government Board began to issue directions for boarding out children who were subject to the Poor Law,[5] and the House of Commons set up a Select Committee on the Protection of Infant Life to investigate baby farming, a pernicious system whereby a person undertook for reward the care and maintenance of children, usually illegitimate, whose parents were anxious to abdicate their responsibilities. The absence of any supervision and the failure to relate the amount of the fee realistically to the child's needs resulted in a high incidence of child neglect and mortality. To combat these evils the Infant Life Protection Act 1872 required anyone who received two or more children under a year old for hire or reward to register with the local authority. Subsequent legislation[6] gradually raised the maximum age and enlarged the powers of control over foster parents, but it only partially succeeded in removing the earlier evils. Indeed, the large number of casual, unsatisfactory placements with foster parents was one of the main reasons for setting up the Curtis Committee in 1946. Neither the Children Act 1948 which amended the earlier law nor the Children Act 1958 which substantially re-enacted it could be said to have solved the problem. The most recent attempt is to be found in the Children and Young Persons Act 1969. This[7] substantially amends the 1958 Act and provides for stricter supervision of foster children by strengthening the powers of local authorities, especially with regard to inspecting, and controlling the use of, premises and by widening the class of children to be supervised.

Foster Children Protected by the Act

For the purposes of the 1958 Act a foster child is now basically defined in wide terms as a child below the upper limit of the compulsory school age whose care and maintenance are undertaken by a person who is not a relative or guardian.[8] "Relative" has the same wide meaning as it has in

---

[5] See post, p. 385.
[6] Infant Life Protection Act 1897; Children Act 1908; C. & Y.P. Act 1932; the Public Health Acts of 1936.
[7] Mainly in ss. 51-57. See also Sched. 7 which sets out ss. 1-6 and 14 of the Children Act 1958 as amended.
[8] Section 2(1), as amended by C. & Y.P. Act 1969, s. 52(1) and Sched. 6.

the Adoption Act 1958,[9] but the term "guardian" is not defined. It is submitted that it is to be interpreted *stricto sensu* as a legal guardian appointed by deed, will or order of the court.[10]

The Children and Young Persons Act 1969 made two basic changes in the definition. Firstly, it is not now necessary for the care and maintenance to be undertaken for reward. A local authority is thus relieved of the need to be satisfied about payment or promise of a reward before being able to intervene and supervise a fostering arrangement.[11]

Secondly, the definition no longer provides that the care and maintenance must be undertaken for a period exceeding one month. Where the period of care does not exceed six days the child was – and still is – protected by the Nurseries and Child-Minders Regulation Act 1948, as amended.[12] The purpose of the former time limit was to exempt from local authority supervision the person who occasionally looked after a child for a week or so while the parent was absent, *e.g.*, on holiday or in hospital. The weakness of the limitation lay in the fact that no supervision could be exercised over the person, who regularly fostered children, during the first month of fostering a particular child. Section 2(3A) of the 1958 Act[13] cures the defect in the following way while still exempting from supervision the casual fostering arrangement of less than a month.

A child is not a foster child for the purpose of the Act if the person undertaking his care and maintenance

(a) does not intend to, and does not in fact, do so for a continuous period of more than six days, the child in those circumstances being protected by the Nurseries and Child-Minders Regulation Act 1948;

or (b) is not a regular foster parent and does not intend to, and does not in fact, do so for a continuous period[14] of more than 27 days.

<hr/>

[9] See *ante*, Chapter 10, p. 321.
[10] See *post*, Chapter 12. Reference in s. 3(7), *infra*, to "every person who is a parent or guardian or *acts as a guardian*" tends to support this interpretation; see also s. 7(5).
[11] The element of reward is, however, still relevant for the purpose of the Life Assurance Act 1774. A policy taken out by a foster parent on the life of a child whom he fosters for reward is void under that Act; see Children Act 1958, s. 9, as amended by C. & Y.P. Act 1969, Sched. 5, para. 30.   [12] See *post*, p. 391.
[13] Inserted by C. & Y.P. Act 1969, s. 52(3).
[14] Continuity is not broken by allowing the child to spend a week-end at the home of his parent; *Surrey County Council* v. *Battersby*, [1965] 2 Q.B.194; [1965] 1 All E.R. 273. *Cf. ante*, Chapter 10, p. 329.

A regular foster parent is defined as a person (other than a relative or guardian) who, during the period of 12 months immediately preceding the date on which he begins to undertake the care and maintenance of a child, has had the care and maintenance of one or more children either for a period of not less than three months (or periods amounting in all to not less than three months) or for at least three continuous periods, each of which was of more than six days.

Having laid down the broad limits of the definition of a foster child, section 2 proceeds to exclude the following categories of children below the upper limit of the compulsory school age who would otherwise come within it, since they are otherwise supervised and protected.

(1) A child who is in the care of a local authority or voluntary organisation[15] or is boarded out by a local health authority or a local education authority (or, in Scotland, an education authority).[16]

(2) A child who is in the care of a person in premises in which a parent, adult relative or guardian is for the time being residing.[17] It is submitted that the appropriate test is whether there is residence in the same household and not merely under the same roof.

(3) A child who is in the care of a person in a voluntary home within the meaning of Part V of the Children and Young Persons Act 1933 or in any residential establishment within the meaning of the Social Work (Scotland) Act 1968.[18]

(4) A child who is in the care of a person in a school where he is receiving full-time education.[19]

A child who is living away from home at a boarding school where he is being educated is not, therefore, a foster child.[20] But if he resides there for more than two

---

[15] Defined as a body whose activities are carried on otherwise than for profit (Children Act 1958, s. 17). A similar definition in the Children Act 1948, s. 59(1), expressly excludes a public or local authority.

[16] Children Act 1958, s. 2(2).

[17] Section 2(3) (a).

[18] Section 2(3) (b), as amended by the Social Work (Scotland) Act 1968. For voluntary homes see *ante*, Chapter 5, p. 165.

[19] Section 2(3) (c).

[20] *Aliter* if he were residing at the school but was being educated at another.

weeks during school holidays he is, subject to certain modifications, to be treated as a foster child.[1]

(5) A child who is in the care of a person in a hospital or nursing home.[2]

(6) A child who is in the care of a person in any other home or institution maintained by a public or local authority.[3]

(7) A child who is in the care of a person in compliance with a supervision order within the meaning of the Children and Young Persons Act 1969 or who is liable to be detained or subject to guardianship under the Mental Health Act 1959 or the Mental Health (Scotland) Act 1960 or who is resident in a residential home for mentally disordered persons within the meaning of those Acts.[4]

(8) A child who is in the care and possession of a person who proposes to adopt him under arrangements made by a local authority or registered adoption society or who is a protected child within the meaning of Part IV of the Adoption Act 1958.[5]

This category has been added by the Children and Young Persons Act 1969[6] to take account of its amendment of the definition of a protected child in the Adoption Act 1958, necessitated by the exclusion from the definition of a foster child of the need for "reward". Until the latter amendment a child placed for adoption could not, prior to notice of intention to apply for an adoption order being given,[7] be a foster child, since the Adoption Act[8] prohibits payment or reward for adopting a child. Now, but for the above amendments, he would come within the definition of a foster child. Instead, he is

[1] Section 12(1), as amended by C. & Y.P. Act 1969, Sched. 5, para. 31. The period was formerly a month, but was reduced because it was found that the staff available to look after children during school holidays was sometimes inadequate and therefore the protection of Part I of the 1958 Act might be necessary; see Home Office Circular No. 261/1969, para. 47.
[2] Section 2(3) (d).   [3] Section 2(3) (e).
[4] Children Act 1958, s. 2(4). This exemption also extends to a child who is in the care of a person as a result of a probation order or a fit person order made before they were abolished in respect of juveniles by the C. & Y.P. Act 1969.
[5] Children Act 1958, s. 2(4A).
[6] Section 52(5).
[7] Once notice is given the child would become a protected child (Adoption Act 1958, s. 37); see *ante*, Chapter 10, p. 332.
[8] Section 50.

expressly taken out of that definition and placed within that of a protected child.[9]

The protection given by the 1958 Act does not come to an end when the foster child attains the upper limit of the compulsory school age. It continues until he would, apart from that limit, have ceased to be a foster child or until he becomes 18 or until he lives elsewhere than with the person with whom he was living when he attained the limit, whichever of those events first occurs.[10]

The Duty and Powers of a Local Authority

The responsibility for ensuring the well being of foster children, as defined by the 1958 Act, falls upon the local authority within whose area the children are.[11] Consistently with its general policy, the Children and Young Persons Act 1969 has widened the authority's discretion, for it is a matter for them to be satisfied about the child's well-being and it is not now necessary for their officers to visit from time to time all foster children, but to do so in "so far as appears to the authority to be appropriate" and to give such advice about care and maintenance as appears to be needed. The authority is thus able to concentrate its resources on those cases which most need supervision, for example, where the foster parents have no previous experience of fostering or the children are young or handicapped.

An authorised officer of a local authority may inspect the whole or part of premises where foster children are kept.[12] If admission is refused or is expected to be refused or if the occupier is temporarily absent, a justice of the peace may issue a warrant authorising an officer to enter and inspect the premises at any reasonable time within 48 hours of the issue.[13] Refusal to allow a visit or inspection of premises or the obstruc-

---

[9] For an admirable comparative summary of the functions of local authorities with regard to foster children and protected children see Leeding, *Child Care Manual for Social Workers*, 2nd edn., pp. 23-43.

[10] Children Act 1958, s. 13.

[11] Sections 1 and 17. The Act avoids any reference to residence.

[12] Section 4(1). See also C. & Y.P. Act 1969, ss. 58 and 59 for the power of the Secretary of State to authorise inspection.

[13] Section 4(1A) (added by s. 54(2) of the C. & Y.P. Act 1969). Compare the similar power made under the Nurseries and Child-Minders Regulation Act 1948, s. 7(2), *post*, p. 395.

tion of an officer acting under a justice's warrant is an offence.[14]

In addition to visits and inspection, the local authority may impose on a foster parent requirements with regard to any one or more of a variety of matters. These relate to the number, age, and sex of the foster children; particulars concerning a particular child and of any change in the number or identity of the children; the accommodation and equipment provided for them (*e.g.*, to ensure the children's safety); fire precautions; medical arrangements; the giving of particulars of the person in charge; the number, qualifications or experience of those employed in looking after the children; and the keeping of records. The power may be exercised even though the home is not used wholly or mainly for keeping foster children, and a requirement may be limited to a particular class of foster children or made applicable only if the number kept in the premises exceeds a specified figure.[15]

A local authority also has power to prohibit the keeping of foster children.[16] The extent of the prohibition will depend on the ground on which it is made. If the premises in which a prospective foster parent intends to keep a foster child are not suitable, the authority may prohibit him from keeping any foster child there. If it is the person and not the premises which are unsuitable,[17] they may prohibit him from keeping any foster child in any premises in their area. Thirdly, however, where they consider that it would be detrimental only to the particular child to be kept in specified premises by the particular person they may limit the prohibition accordingly. The authority may cancel a prohibition either of their own volition or on the application of the person against whom it is made on

[14] Section 14(1) (b). The penalty on summary conviction is imprisonment for up to six months or a fine not exceeding £100 or both.

Refusal to allow a visit or inspection may also be treated as giving reasonable cause for suspecting that a foster child is being ill-treated or that an offence within the First Schedule to the C. & Y.P. Act 1933 has been committed against him, thereby enabling a justice of the peace to issue a warrant under s. 40 of that Act, authorising a constable to search for and remove the child to a place of safety until he can be brought before the juvenile court. (Children Act 1958, s. 8; C. & Y.P. Act 1969, s. 59(3)).

[15] Children Act 1958, s. 4(2), as amended by C. & Y.P. Act 1969, s. 55(1)-(3).

[16] *Ibid.*, s. 4(3), (3A) and (3B), as amended by C. & Y.P. Act 1969, s. 55(4).

[17] The C. & Y.P. Act 1969 removes earlier doubts as to whether this was a distinct ground; see H.O.C. No. 261/1969, para. 34.

the ground of a change in the circumstances in which a foster child would be kept by him.

A requirement or prohibition[18] must be imposed by written notice, which must inform the person of his right to appeal against it to a juvenile court within 14 days.[19] There is also a right to appeal against the local authority's refusal to cancel a prohibition. If it allows the appeal the court may, instead of cancelling a requirement, vary it or allow more time for compliance. Similarly, instead of cancelling an absolute prohibition, it may substitute a prohibition to use the premises after such time as it may specify unless such specified requirements as the local authority could have imposed are complied with.[20] The restrictions on the time and place at which a juvenile court may sit and on the persons who may be present[1] do not apply to sittings in these appeals or to any other proceedings under Part I of the 1958 Act,[2] the reason being that an adult and a local authority, and not the child, are the parties to the proceedings. A further appeal lies to the Crown Court, as does an appeal from any other order made by a juvenile court under Part I.[3]

Notification to the Local Authority

If a local authority are to exercise their powers effectively, it is obviously essential that they know which homes are being used for private fostering. It is now recognised that, to achieve this object, it is not necessary that a foster parent notify the local authority of every child whom he intends to foster and of every foster child who has ceased to be in his care. All that is needed is that a person gives notice when he becomes, and when he ceases to be, a foster parent,[4] and if the local authority should at any time want details concerning foster children in his care they can call for them.[5] However, an infallible method

---

[18] Where a requirement is imposed on a person with regard to any premises he may also be prohibited from keeping foster children there after the time specified for compliance with the requirement unless it is complied with (Children Act 1958, s. 4(4)).

[19] Sections 4(5) and 5(1) and (3).
A requirement does, whereas a prohibition does not, take effect while an appeal is pending.　　[20] Section 5(2).

[1] *Ante*, Chapter 1, p. 65.　　[2] Section 10.

[3] Section 11; Courts Act 1971, s. 8 and Sched. I.

[4] See Children Act 1958, s. 3, as amended by C. & Y.P. Act 1969, s. 53. See also Home Office Circular No. 261/1969, para. 18.

[5] See *supra*, p. 381.

of ensuring that notice, where required, is given has yet to be devised,[6] and the widening of the definition of a foster child will, if anything, mean an increase in the number of instances of non-compliance. Where someone is paid for fostering he is more likely to realise that some public body is going to be interested in the arrangement and will therefore probably make appropriate inquiries;[7] but where the arrangement is informal and without reward he is less likely to be put on his inquiry.

Normally notice must be given not less than two, but not more than four, weeks before the intending foster parent receives the child.[8] The purpose of fixing a maximum period is to dissuade persons from notification where they have only a general intention to begin private fostering at some date in the future if the opportunity should arise but are not immediately committed to the responsibility.[9] But, in the exceptional cases where a person receives the child in an emergency, or the latter becomes a foster child while in his care,[10] the period is only 48 hours from the date of those respective events. This enables the local authority to intervene promptly in case the placement is unsuitable.

Advertising

An advertisement that a person will undertake, or will arrange for, the care and maintenance of a child must not be published unless it truly states the name and address of that person.[11] This is a modest restriction compared with those concerning adoption. They forbid the publication of any advertisement which indicates that the parent or guardian of a minor desires to cause him to be adopted, or that a person desires to adopt a minor or that a person (other than a registered adoption society or a local authority) is willing to make

---

[6] One possibility which would at least partly meet the difficulty would be an administrative arrangement whereby local authorities are informed of family allowances paid to persons other than a parent.

[7] But the fact that failure to notify is an offence (Children Act 1958, s. 14(1)(a)) has not proved an effective sanction; many prospective parents are apparently unaware of it.

[8] Children Act 1958, s. 3(1).

[9] H.O.C. No. 261/1969, para. 20.

[10] For example, where the natural parent has also been living in the premises but has now left them; see *supra*, p. 378.

[11] Children Act 1958, s. 37.

arrangements for the adoption of a minor.[12] Paradoxically, the penalties for breach are more severe under the Children Act 1958 than under the Adoption Act 1958.[13]

Disqualification for Keeping Foster Children

A person against whom any of the following orders or decisions has been made is disqualified from keeping foster children unless he discloses that fact to the local authority and obtains their consent.[14] Contravention of this rule is an offence.[15]

(1) An order under Part I of the Children Act 1958 removing a child from his care;[16]

(2) an order under the Children and Young Persons Act 1933 or the Children and Young Persons Act 1969 resulting in removal;

(3) his conviction of an offence specified in the First Schedule to the Children and Young Persons Act 1933 or his being placed on probation or discharged absolutely or conditionally for any such offence;

(4) a resolution of a local authority (and, where applicable, an order of the court confirming the resolution) under s. 2 of the Children Act 1948 vesting in them his rights and powers with respect to a child;

(5) an order under the Nurseries and Child-Minders Regulation Act 1948 refusing, or cancelling, the registration of premises occupied by him or his registration;[17]

(6) an order under the Adoption Act 1958 removing a protected child who was being kept or was about to be received by him.[18]

The disqualification attaches not only to the person in respect of whom an order is made but also to anyone else living in the same premises as he does or in premises at which he is employed.[19] So, if that other person knows of his disqualification, he, too, must disclose it and obtain the consent of the local authority before he may act as a foster parent. On

---

[12] Adoption Act 1958, s. 51.
[13] For the penalties under the Children Act 1958 see *supra* p. 381, n. 14. Under the Adoption Act the penalty is a fine not exceeding £50.
[14] Children Act 1958, s. 6(1), as amended by C. & Y.P. Act 1969, s.56(1).
[15] Children Act 1958, s. 14(1)(d). For penalties see *supra*, p. 381, n. 14.
[16] See s. 7, *infra*.   [17] Sections 1(3) and (4) and 5.   [18] Section 43.
[19] Children Act 1958, s. 6(2), as amended by C. & Y.P. Act 1969, s. 56(2).

the other hand, anyone who keeps a foster child without knowing or reasonably believing that there is a disqualified person living or employed in the same premises is not guilty of an offence.[20] This is more likely to happen where the disqualified person is a lodger or employee rather than a member of the same family.

Removal of Foster Children Kept in Unsuitable Surroundings
An order may be made removing a child from a foster home and taking him to a place of safety on the ground that the foster parent is unfit to have care or that he is disqualified from keeping foster children or that the local authority have imposed a prohibition on his doing so or that the child is being kept in premises or an environment detrimental to him.[1] Usually the order will be made by a juvenile court on the complaint of a local authority, but, where there is proof of imminent danger to the health or well-being of the child, a justice of the peace may do so on the application of a person authorised to visit foster children. The order must specify a period, not exceeding 28 days, beyond which the child must not be detained in a place of safety.[2] Within that period he can be restored to a parent, relative or guardian or other arrangements can be made with respect to him.[3] One possibility is that he be received into the care of a local authority under s. 1 of the Children Act 1948 and this may be done even though he appears to be over 17.[4] If he still remains in the place of safety at the end of the specified period he must be brought before a juvenile court which must then release him or make an interim order committing him to the care of a local authority.[5] Such an order will afford further opportunity to make arrangements for him, the most likely outcome being that he will be received permanently into care under s. 1 of the 1948 Act.

B. BOARDING OUT

The system of boarding out deprived children is a product of the Poor Law. It first appears in the 16th century when

[20] Children Act 1958, s. 14(1A), as added by C. & Y.P. Act 1969, s. 57(1). The onus is on the person to prove lack of knowledge and belief.
[1] Children Act 1958, s. 7(1).   [2] C. & Y.P. Act 1963, s. 23(1).
[3] Children Act 1958, s. 7(1). Where a child is removed to a place of safety the local authority must, if practicable, inform a parent or guardian of his or anyone who acts as his guardian.
[4] Children Act 1958, s. 7(4).   [5] For interim orders see *ante*, Chapter 3.

orphans and children abandoned by their parents were apprenticed out from workhouses, but it acquired most of its modern characteristics in the second half of the 19th century,[6] when Boards of Guardians began to board out with private individuals children for whom they remained legally responsible. From 1870 onwards the Local Government Board issued Orders with regard to the fostering of Poor Law children. Initially, a distinction was drawn between Guardians boarding out children within their own union and boarding them out with foster parents outside their union, but the distinction virtually disappeared in 1911 and thereafter the system remained essentially unaltered under the Children Act 1948.[7]

One of the main recommendations of the Curtis Committee was that a child deprived of home life should be brought up in a private household rather than in the more impersonal atmosphere of an institutional home. Section 13 of the Children Act 1948, as originally enacted, sought to give effect to this recommendation by requiring a local authority to board out privately a child in their care and it was only where it was not practicable or desirable for the time being to make such arrangements that he was to be accommodated in a local authority home or a voluntary home. We have seen[8] that local authorities are no longer statutorily required to give priority to boarding out.

The Boarding Out of Children Regulations 1955 attempt to ensure the welfare of children under 18 who are boarded out.[9] They apply to children in the care of a local authority,[10] and to those in the charge of a voluntary organisation,[11] but it is an essential requirement that the child is boarded out as *a member of the family*.[12] They do not, however, extend to those who are boarded out for a short holiday not exceeding 21 days, nor to those who are placed with persons who propose to adopt them.

---

[6] See further V. George, *Foster Care*, Chapter 1.   [7] *Ibid.*, p. 13.
[8] *Ante*, Chapter 5, p. 157.   [9] But see *infra*, p. 389.
[10] Children Act 1948, s. 14; Reg. 1.
[11] *Ibid.*, s. 33(3); Reg. 1.
  Some children are received directly into care by a voluntary organisation in a way similar to those received into care by a local authority under the Children Act 1948, but there are others who, being already in care under that Act, are placed by the local authority in the charge of a voluntary organisation who then arrange boarding out. Hence, apparently, the use of the term "charge" in Reg. 1; see also Reg. 11(3).
[12] Compare a 16-year old who is put into lodgings or a hostel.

Boarding Out

In the latter cases the children are protected by the Adoption Act 1958,[13] provided that they are under the upper limit of compulsory school age and the person with whom they are placed is not a parent, relative or guardian. It is submitted that similarly, if a child under that age limit is boarded out with foster parents without adoption in mind but later they give notice of intention to apply for an adoption order, the Regulations by implication cease to apply, since the child becomes a protected child under the 1958 Act.[14]

Restrictions on Boarding Out

Some of the restrictions on boarding out are of general application; others depend on whether it is expected to continue for more than eight weeks. There is, however, no statutory limit on the number of children who may be placed in a foster home.

The only persons who may act as foster parents are a husband and wife jointly or a woman or a grandfather, uncle or elder brother of the child, but if a foster parent dies or, where the sole foster parent is a woman, ceases to live in the household, the child may be boarded out with the other spouse or with another suitable member of the household, as the case may be.[15] Only where the special circumstances of the case make it desirable should a foster home be found outside England and Wales (*e.g.*, with a male relative), and then steps should be taken to ensure that the child's welfare is safeguarded by visits and supervision as it would be if he were boarded out in England or Wales.[16] Except in an emergency, a child must have been medically examined within the last three months before he can be placed with foster parents.[17]

Before a child may be boarded out a social worker must, on behalf of the local authority or voluntary organisation, visit the foster parents and their home and report thereon. But the extent of his inquiry depends on whether the boarding out is likely to exceed the eight-week period. If it is not, all that is necessary to justify placement is a report that it would be suitable to the needs of the child for that short period.[18] Otherwise, a visitor personally acquainted with the child and

---

[13] Section 37, as amended.
[14] See s. 37(1) (b).
[15] Reg. 2.
[16] Reg. 3.
[17] Reg. 6.
[18] Reg. 25.

his needs or fully informed about them before his visit must report on the suitability of the accommodation and domestic conditions of the proposed foster home. He, or another social worker, must also report on the reputation and religious persuasion of the foster parents and their suitability in age, character, temperament and health to have the charge of the child; whether any member of the foster parents' household is believed to be suffering from any illness which might affect the child or to have been convicted of any offence rendering it undesirable that the child should associate with him; and on the number, sex and age of the members of the household. The placement in that household must not be made unless the child's antecedents and the relevant reports indicate that it would be in his best interests.[19] Where the boarding out is for the longer period the foster parents should, where possible, be of the same religious persuasion as the child or give an undertaking that he will be brought up in that persuasion.[20]

Visits, Supervision and Removal

The Regulations provide for regular interviewing of the child and visits to his foster home. These must be made within one month after the commencement of the boarding out; within one month after any change of address of the foster parents; and forthwith after a complaint is made by or concerning the child, unless it is considered unnecessary. The regularity of other interviews and visits depends on the period of boarding out. If the child has been with the foster parents less than two years and he is under the age of five, they must take place once every six weeks and, if he has attained that age, once in every two months. Once he has been with them for two years subsequent interviews and visits are at three-monthly intervals.[1] When he attains the upper limit of the compulsory school age the duty to visit comes to an end, but a visitor must

[19] Reg. 17. If the foster home is in the area of a local authority other than that having care of the child, the latter must inquire of the former whether they know of any reason why boarding out would be detrimental. A voluntary organisation must similarly inquire of the area authority.
[20] Reg. 19. See *ante*, Chapter 5, p. 168.
[1] Reg. 21. For the occasions on which visits must be made where the boarding out is not expected to exceed eight weeks see Reg. 28. If the period is exceeded, Reg. 21 then applies. See also Reg. 29 for visiting of children who, receiving full-time education, are boarded out at intervals with the same foster parents.

still *see* the child within three months of his ceasing to be of compulsory school age and thereafter at least once in every three months, whether he does so by visiting the foster home or otherwise.[2] The Regulations lay down the minimum frequency of interviews and visits. The child's welfare may require more.

On each occasion that he sees a child the visitor must, after considering the child's welfare, health, conduct and progress, report about him to the local authority or voluntary organisation, who must review those matters in the light of reports. The first review must be held within three months after placement and thereafter as often as considered expedient, but not less than once in every six months.[3] The authority or organisation must also see that the child undergoes regular medical examination and receives medical and dental treatment as required.[4]

It is in the light of the visitor's reports that the care authority or voluntary organisation are able to exercise their powers of terminating the boarding out where it no longer appears to be in the child's best interests,[5] but, until they receive adverse reports, they are usually willing to leave to the foster parents a wide discretion as to how the child should be brought up. The delegation is consistent with the written undertaking by the foster parents that they will care for the child and bring him up as their own;[6] but the ultimate decision lies with the care authority or voluntary organisation. For example, one care authority may be ready to allow foster parents to educate the child in a private school, provided that foster parents meet the cost, whereas another authority may, as a matter of general policy, insist on State education of all foster children in their care.

The functions of the visitor are not confined to visiting, supervising and reporting. Where he considers that the conditions in which the child is boarded out endanger his health, safety or morals, he may remove him from the foster parents forthwith.[7]

Although the Regulations go some way to securing the welfare of the foster child, recent investigations have shown that they leave much to be desired in this and other respects. The evidence indicates that they:

[2] Reg. 23.   [3] Regs. 9 and 22.   [4] Regs. 7 and 8.
[5] Reg. 4.   [6] Reg. 20.   [7] Reg. 5.

Foster Parenthood

"are totally unsatisfactory for evaluating performance standards [of child care officers] in foster care. They are vague and obscure regarding the assessment of the foster parents and of the foster child and the matching of the two sides; they make very little mention of preplacement preparations; they are silent regarding the place of natural parents in foster care; and . . . they are outdated regarding the supervision arrangements of foster children".[8]

C. DAY CARE

This is a convenient point to deal with the provisions for day care of young children by persons other than their parents.

The need for preventive and supporting social work is likely to be most acute in the family with pre-school children.[9] Yet, as the Seebohm Committee noted, there is "no direct statutory responsibility on local authorities to provide for the general social care of children [under 5]".[10] There is, of course, their general duty to promote the welfare of children so as to diminish the need to receive them into, or to keep them in, care under the Children Act 1948,[11] but this relates to anyone under 18 and no special obligations in that respect are imposed with regard to younger children. There are, however, some services particularly provided for the latter. Thus, in addition to the general national health schemes available to persons of all ages, there are special local authority health and welfare services provided for their benefit. For example, one of the main functions of health visitors is to visit homes and give advice concerning the care of young children.[12] Again, a local authority, through its social services department, must make arrangements for the care of expectant and nursing mothers and for children under five who are not attending primary schools.[13] The welfare clinic

---

[8] George, *op. cit.*, p. 218.
[9] More than one committee has drawn attention to the fact; see the Plowden Report on *Children and their Primary Schools*, H.M.S.O., 1966, paras. 296-304; the Yudkin Report on *The Care of Pre-School Children*, 1967; the Seebohm Report on *Local Authority and Allied Personal Social Services*, Cmnd. 3703, paras. 191-212 and 447-450.
[10] Cmnd. 3703, para. 193.   [11] C. & Y.P. Act 1963, s. I, *ante*, p. 171.
[12] National Health Service Act 1946, s. 24 (as amended by Health Services and Public Health Act 1968, s. 11). The section does not define "young children". Responsibility for health visitors remains with the local health authority and has not been assigned to social services departments.
[13] National Health Service Act 1946, s. 22. The authority may also, with the approval of the Minister of Health and Social Security, financially assist a voluntary organisation pursuing similar objects.
These functions were transferred from local health authorities to social

is one kind of arrangement. The day nursery is another, but the day care of children is mainly provided in local authority nursery schools and nursery classes in infants' schools under the Education Act 1944[14] or, much more frequently, in private day nurseries or by child-minders.

Private Nurseries and Child-Minders

War-time employment of women popularized the use of private nurseries and child-minders, but the abuse to which the system lent itself led to its being controlled by local health authorities through the Nurseries and Child-Minders Regulation Act 1948. The Act did not diminish the popularity[15] of private care, but it also did not provide an effective system for ensuring registration of nurseries and child-minders,[16] and the number of cases of neglect and lack of proper facilities was reminiscent of Victorian baby-farming. The Health Services and Public Health Act 1968,[17] amending the earlier Act, attempts to remove some of its deficiencies, but it fails to solve the problem of effective registration. The long term solution lies in the creation of a sufficient number of local authority nursery schools and nursery classes in infants' schools, which the Plowden Committee has strongly urged,[18] and in the provision by local authorities of community care facilities for children under five when not attending nursery schools, as the Seebohm Committee recommends.[19]

Registration

The 1948 Act firmly distinguishes between the registration of premises and the registration of persons. Premises must be registered as nurseries where children under the upper limit

---

services departments by the Local Authority Social Services Act 1970, s. 2 and Sched. I. So, too, were those relating to the provision of home help under s. 29 of the National Health Services Act 1946 (for which s. 13 of the Health Services and Public Health Act 1968 is in due course to be substituted). The need for home help where the household includes a child under the upper limit of the compulsory school age is expressly recognised by the section.   [14] See further Chapter 13, *post*, p. 442.

[15] Apart from the increase in the employment of mothers, other factors have accounted for the popularity, such as the incapacity of parents to cope with a young family, especially where it is large or badly housed or where the child creates acute behavioural problems.

[16] Compare the difficulties of ensuring that foster parents are controlled by the Children Act 1958, *ante*, p. 389.   [17] Section 60.

[18] Paragraph 314. See also Sonia Jackson, "*The Illegal Child Minders*".

[19] Cmnd. 3703, para. 204.

of compulsory school age are received, whether or not for reward, to be looked after for the day or for at least two hours as part or parts of a day or for a longer period of not more than six days. Persons must be registered as child-minders when they receive children into their homes for any of the same periods, but registration is necessary only if the children are under five and are received for reward.[20] Where the period of care extends beyond six days the Children Act 1958 will normally operate.[1]

Premises do not have to be registered if they are wholly or mainly used as private dwellings, but the person receiving children into them will have to register as a child minder if the relevant conditions are present. Hospitals, schools, nursery schools, play centres or any institution mentioned in s. 2 of the Children Act 1958[2] are exempted from registration.[3] For example, if school premises are used by a parents' association to provide recreational facilities for children during school holidays, no registration is required.

The responsibility for registration and inspection now rests with the social services department of the local authority (instead of with the local health authority),[4] who may refuse registration or allow it subject to conditions. Registration of premises may be refused on the ground that a person employed there is not fit to look after children or that the premises are not suitable as a nursery because of their condition, situation, construction or size or because of any similar defects in the equipment used. Registration of a child-minder may be refused on similar grounds.[5] Moreover, an application for registration of premises is of no effect unless it contains a statement with respect to each person employed in looking after children at the premises and every other person who has attained the age of 16 and is normally resident there. The statement must declare[6] whether or not (1) the person has been disqualified from keeping foster children,[7] (2) he has been convicted of an offence specified in the First Schedule to the Children and

---

[20] Section, 1 as amended by Health Services and Public Health Act 1968, s. 60(2).   [1] See *ante*, p. 377.   [2] *Ante*, p. 378.
[3] Nurseries and Child-Minders Regulation Act 1948, s. 8.
[4] Local Authority Social Services Act 1970, s. 2 and Sched. 1.
[5] Nurseries and Child-Minders Regulation Act 1948, s. 1(3) and (4).
[6] Health Services and Public Health Act 1968, s. 60(7).
[7] See *ante*, p. 384.

Young Persons Act 1933[8] (3) his rights and powers with respect to a child have been vested in a local authority under s. 2 of the Children Act 1948[9] and (4) an order has been made removing a "protected child" from his care and maintenance in accordance with s. 43 of the Adoption Act 1958.[10] A similar statement has to be made in an application for registration as a child-minder.

On, or at any time after, the registration of a nursery or a child-minder the local authority may impose conditions with regard to the number of children that may be received; the precautions to be taken against the exposure of the children to infectious diseases; the number and qualifications of the persons employed; the safety and maintenance of the premises and equipment; the feeding and diet arrangements; and the records to be kept. For nurseries requirements may also be imposed concerning the qualifications of the person in charge and the medical supervision of the children.[11] There does not seem to be any cogent reason for not allowing the latter requirement to be imposed where the registration relates to child-minding.

Registration may be cancelled for breach of any requirement imposed or on any ground which would have justified refusing the registration initially, but before a local authority may refuse an application or cancel a registration or impose a requirement it must give to the person affected[12] at least 14 days' notice of their intention to do so and allow him an opportunity to show cause why the particular order should not be made. If an order is made, there is a right of appeal within 21 days to a magistrates' court, with a further right to a Crown court.[13] It is suggested that, unless and until family courts are created, the appellate system should follow the same lines as that adopted by the Children Act 1958[14] in that the appeal

[8] For reference to the First Sched. see *ante*, pp. 58 and 215.
[9] *Ante*, p. 147. [10] *Ante*, p. 333.
[11] Nurseries and Child-Minders Regulation Act 1948, s. 2; Health Services and Public Health Act 1968, s. 60(9).
　An order imposing a condition may be varied or revoked.
[12] *I.e.*, to the applicant for registration, the occupier of the premises to which the registration relates or to the person registered as a child-minder, as the case may be.
[13] See Nurseries and Child-Minders Regulation Act 1948, s. 6; Public Health Act 1936, ss. 300-302; Courts Act 1971, s. 8 and Sched. I.
[14] See *ante*, p. 382.

from the order of the local authority should lie to a juvenile court and not an adult magistrates' court.

The Nurseries and Child-Minders Regulation Act 1948 suffers from a defect basically similar to that found in the Children Act 1958. Just as the latter does not ensure that a person who intends to become a foster parent gives notice of that fact to the local authority, so the former fails to guarantee registration of nurseries and child-minders.[15] But at least the Children Act does making the giving of notice obligatory, whereas s. 1 of the 1948 Act appears to make the application for registration of premises or persons discretionary.[16] The fact that failure to register leads to criminal liability might suggest that the distinction is academic, but that conclusion is only valid on the assumption that the person who should apply for registration is the one who is liable if there is failure to register. With regard to registration of nurseries there is some doubt as to whether this is necessarily so. The penalty for failure to register attaches to the occupier of the premises. The person who should register is he who receives or proposes to receive children. If the term "occupier" is intended in this context to mean the person in actual occupation there is no point in the argument, but the better opinion would seem to be[17] that occupation refers to legal occupation, so that the persons may not be the same. As for registration of child-minders, it is clear that exceptionally they may be different persons. On a strict interpretation of s. 1 anyone, including a relative, who receives children into care should apply for registration, but the provisions in s. 4 relating to criminal liability do not extend to a person receiving a child of whom he is a relative. These are untidy and unnecessary discrepancies which a proper correlation between ss. 1 and 4 would remove.

[15] Some tightening up of the requirements of registration was made by the Health Services and Public Health Act 1968, in that the maximum penalties for running unregistered nurseries or operating as unregistered child-minders was increased for second and subsequent offences.

One improvement with regard to registration of child-minders which was proposed but not incorporated into the 1968 Act was that, before accepting advertisements from persons offering child-minding services, newspapers and newsagents should ask for proof of registration.

[16] Section 1(2) provides: "Any person receiving or proposing to receive children . . . may make application . . . for registration . . ."

[17] See Clarke Hall and Morrison, *op. cit.*, pp. 944, 945.

Inspection

The powers of inspection are similar to those conferred on local authorities with regard to foster children. A person so authorised by the local authority may enter without a warrant a registered nursery or the home of a registered child-minder and inspect the premises and the children who are being kept there, the arrangements for their welfare and the records relating to them. Where he has reasonable cause to believe that children are being kept in premises or by persons which or, as the case may be, who have not but ought to have been registered, he may apply to a justice of the peace for a warrant authorising entry and inspection.[18]

Sometimes premises are simultaneously used for the care of foster children in accordance with the Children Act 1958 and for the day care of children under the 1948 Act. Dual supervision under the Acts is avoided by providing that the powers of entry and inspection under the one or the other are to be invoked according to whether the premises are being mainly used for the one purpose or the other.[19] Thus, if the premises mainly accommodate foster children, the occupier is exempted from the penal consequences of non-registration, and the premises from inspection under the 1948 Act. A child-minder and his home are similarly exempted, if in addition to day care he is looking after at least one foster child or a child boarded out with him under a particular enactment. In such a case the powers of entry and inspection under the Children Act 1958 or the enactment are applicable.

[18] Nursery and Child-Minders Regulation Act 1948, s. 7, as amended by Health Services and Public Health Act 1968, s. 60(11).
[19] The Nursery and Child-Minders Regulation Act 1948, ss. 9 and 10.

CHAPTER 12

Guardianship

Mediaeval law, as Pollock and Maitland noted,[1] "never laid down any . . . rule that there [was] or ought to be a guardian for every infant". Had it done so, it might have led to the formulation of a comprehensive definition of guardianship, which, even allowing for the strength of feudal land law, might in turn have checked the proliferation of different kinds of guardianship.[2] In the long run the latter effect has not proved unduly harmful, for many types of guardianship have long been obsolete or of minimal significance – particularly those limited to the estate of the minor, since they have virtually been absorbed into the law of trusts.[3] However, the lack of a unifying definition has had other, serious consequences, which have become increasingly apparent with the growth of "administrative family law".[4] The necessary encroachment of the law upon the privacy of the family has not only undermined parental authority; it has put at risk the liberty of the child. The wide powers of local authorities under the Children Act 1948 and the Children and Young Persons Acts in respect of a child in their care are based upon the need for his welfare, but they also create nice problems of balancing his welfare with his liberty. This is an area where English law still fails adequately to protect the interests of the child, and it has been suggested[5] that this object might be achieved by the creation of a new kind of office, that of the Children's Guardian, who not only could represent the interests of children in care but equally could serve other needs of children for which the law

---

[1] *History of English Law*, 2nd edn., p. 444.
[2] Jowitt, *The Dictionary of English Law*, gives a useful historical summary of them; for a fuller account see Simpson, *Infants*, pp. 149 *et seq.*
[3] Guardianship of the estate may still be relevant where the minor has an interest in property administered abroad. See Johnson, *Family Law*, p. 297.   [4] Friedmann, *Law in a Changing Society*, 2nd edn., p. 287.
[5] Bevan, *Child Protection and the Law*, pp. 23-24. For more drastic proposals see "*Children Have Rights*" (published by the National Council for Civil Liberties) (1971).

does not provide; for example, to act, with the mother's consent, as guardian of her illegitimate child where the father is unknown or shirks his parental responsibilities.

One of the traditional categories of guardianship was that of guardianship by nature, which expressed the relationship between the parent and his legitimate child.[6] It is on this basis that the common law right of the father to custody and the other rights which emanated therefrom are explained.[7] We have seen that this right is very largely of historical interest only, but occasionally it has modern relevance.[8] Today, however, the term "guardian" in its most common meaning describes a person who has been appointed either by a parent under a deed or will or by a court of competent jurisdiction to stand *in loco parentis* to a child. It is so used in this chapter.[9]

A. APPOINTMENT OF GUARDIANS

I. TESTAMENTARY GUARDIANS

A parent may, by deed or will, appoint a guardian or guardians for any of his children who are under the age of 18 and unmarried at the date of his death.[10] Both parents of a legitimate child have the power to appoint.[11] So has the mother of an

---

[6] *Quaere* it included the mother of an illegitimate child, since recognition of a legal relationship between her and her child only appears in the 19th century; see *ante*, Chapter 9, p. 302.

[7] Sometimes custody in this wide sense is treated as synonymous with guardianship of the person; see James, *The Legal Guardianship of Infants* 82 L.Q.R. 323, 324: *Cf.* C. & Y.P. Act 1933, s. 107(1), where it is used to mean *de facto* custody, *i.e.*, charge or control of the child. For a critical analysis of the terminology see Hall, *The Waning of Parental Rights*, (1972) C.L.J. 248, at pp. 261 *et seq.*

[8] See *Re T. (Otherwise H.) (an infant)*, [1963] Ch. 238; [1962] 3 All E.R. 970, *ante*, Chapter 9, p. 256. (Child takes father's surname). See also Bromley, *op. cit.*, p. 271, who points out that "occasionally the old rule [that at common law custody vests exclusively in the father] has a surprising habit of obtruding itself".

[9] This meaning is sometimes expressly adopted by statute; see, for example, Children Act 1948, s. 59(1); Adoption Act 1958, s. 57(1).

There are also the exceptional cases of appointment of a guardian by the minor himself and the customary rights of guardianship exercised by the Lord Mayor and Aldermen of the City of London, through the Court of Orphans, over the orphans of deceased freemen of the City.

[10] Guardianship of Minors Act 1971, s. 4(1) and (2); Family Law Reform Act 1969, s. 1.

For the requirement that the minor is unmarried see *infra*.

[11] Power of appointment was given to the father by the Tenures Abolition Act 1660 (see *infra*), but the mother had to wait until the Guardianship of Infants Act 1886 and then her power was restricted. Whereas a guar-

illegitimate child,[12] but the father is restricted in that an appointment by him is only effective if, by virtue of an order under the Guardianship of Minors Act 1971, he had custody at the time of his death.[13]

The precise scope of the power to appoint is uncertain. This is due partly to the general terms in which it is enacted[14] and partly to the fact that s. 8 of the Tenures Abolition Act 1660 stands unrepealed. The latter, in abolishing military tenures and consequently the incident of wardship, conferred on the father of the legitimate child the power to "dispose of the custody and tuition" of his child. Unlike s. 4 of the Guardianship of Minors Act 1971, s. 8 sets out at length the limits of the father's power. The commonly held view is that the power under the former section is as wide as that under the old enactment.[15] On this basis and in the light of decisions under that enactment the following rules apply.

The parental power extends to the appointment for any child alive at the parent's death, including one *en ventre sa mere*, but some doubt exists as to whether the child must be unmarried at that date. Section 8 so requires, and, if that section is relied on to support the continued application of other rules, there seems to be no overriding reason for not relying on it for this purpose.[16]

A guardian may be appointed conditionally[17] or until the child reaches a specified age which is less than the attainment of his majority or until some other event happens. Provision may also be made for successive appointments, and, although the office of guardian is not assignable,[18] a parent may, in an

---

dian appointed by the father acted alone, without interference by the surviving mother, one appointed by a mother could only act jointly with the surviving father and even then the appointment needed the court's confirmation which could only be granted if the father was considered unfit to be sole guardian. The Guardianship of Infants 1925 extended to the power of appointment, as it did to claims for custody, the principle of parity.   [12] *Re A., S.* v. *A.* (1940), 164 L.T. 230.   [13] Section 14(3).

[14] Section 4(1) of the Guardianship of Minors Act 1971 simply states: "The father of a minor may by deed or will appoint any person to be guardian of the minor after his death." Sub-section (2) correspondingly is in the same terms in respect of the mother's power.

[15] Support for this view may be drawn from the rule in the 1971 Act (s. 8) that a guardian appointed under that Act has all the powers over the estate and person of a minor which a guardian appointed under the 1660 Act has.

[16] As to the effect of marriage after guardianship has come into being see *infra*, p. 409.   [17] *Selby* v. *Selby* (1731), 2 Eq.Cas.Abr., 488.

[18] *Mellish* v. *De Costa* (1737), 2 Atk. 14.

instrument appointing two or more testamentary guardians, authorise the surviving guardian or guardians to nominate a successor to the one who dies.[19]

The general law relating to wills applies to appointments, with some modifications. Thus, no particular form of words need be used in the deed or will, but there must be a clear intention to create guardianship.[20] A parent who is a minor can only appoint a guardian for his child by way of deed. He cannot do so by will since he cannot make a valid will.[1] An exception is allowed in favour of a will made by a soldier or airman on active service or a seaman at sea.[2] An appointment is not invalid if the guardian was a witness to the will or deed,[3] but where made by will it is revoked by the testator's subsequent marriage,[4] unless the will was made in contemplation of the marriage.[5] It was held in *Earl Shaftsbury* v. *Hannam*[6] that an appointment by deed is revoked by a later appointment by will on the ground that the deed is no more than a testamentary instrument in the form of a deed. Logically, on this ground an appointment by will should be revoked by a subsequent appointment by deed and the rule of revocation by subsequent marriage should apply where the instrument is a deed as it would if there were a will, but it seems that the wording of the Wills Act 1837 precludes both conclusions.[7] However, this statutory objection does not, it is submitted, prevent an appointment by deed being revoked by a later appointment by deed.

On the death of the father or, as the case may be, the mother of a legitimate minor, the surviving parent becomes guardian either alone or jointly with any guardian appointed by the deceased parent. If no such appointment has been made or if the appointed guardian dies or refuses to act, the court may, if it thinks fit, appoint a guardian to act jointly with the sur-

[19] *In the Goods of Parnell* (1872), L.R 2. P. & D. 379.
[20] Compare *Miller* v. *Harris* (1845), 14 Sim. 540, with *Bedell* v. *Constable* (1668), Vaugh. 177; *Edwards* v. *Wise* (1740), Barn. Ch. 139; and *Re Lord Norbury* (1875), 9 I.R. Eq. 134.
[1] Wills Act 1837, s. 7.
[2] *Ibid.*, s. 11; Wills (Soldiers and Sailors) Act 1918, ss. 4 and 5(2); Family Law Reform Act 1969, s. 3(1).
[3] *Morgan* v. *Hatchell* (1854), 19 Beav. 86.
[4] Wills Act 1837, s. 18.
[5] Law of Property Act 1925, s. 177.
[6] (1677), Cas. *temp.* Finch 323.
[7] Sections 20 and 18 respectively. See Bromley, *op. cit.*, p. 324.

viving parent.[8] A testamentary guardian who agrees to act will normally do so jointly with the surviving parent, but the latter may object to the former's being a guardian or the former may consider the parent to be unfit to have the custody of the minor. In either event the *guardian* may apply to the court. The court may refuse to make an order, in which case the parent remains sole guardian, or it may make an order that they act jointly or that the testamentary guardian be the sole guardian.[9] Where both parents appoint guardians they act jointly after the death of the surviving parent,[10] and, where a guardian has been appointed by the court to act jointly with a surviving parent,[11] he will continue on the death of that parent to act as sole guardian or, as the case may be, jointly with any testamentary guardian whom the parent has appointed.[12]

Section 14(3) of the Guardianship of Minors Act 1971 cryptically provides that where the minor is illegitimate the natural father is treated as the lawful father for the purpose of the above rules if he has custody by virtue of an order under s. 9 of the Act. It therefore has, for example, the following effects. The father will be entitled to guardianship (either alone or jointly) on the mother's death if he then has custody, and the court's powers of appointment become operative. The rules correspondingly apply where the mother survives if at the date of his death the father has custody. If he has not, his death has no relevance to guardianship. The mother's guardianship, to which she was entitled as sole natural guardian during his lifetime, remains unaffected.

II. GUARDIANS APPOINTED BY THE COURT

The Family Division of the High Court[13] has both inherent and statutory jurisdiction to appoint guardians. The exercise of the former invariably but not necessarily depends upon the minor's being made a ward of court, and is examined later in this chapter. The statutory jurisdiction rests on the Guardianship of Minors Act 1971. The power under s. 3 to appoint a guardian to act jointly with the surviving parent has just been

---

[8] Guardianship of Minors Act 1971, s. 3. Presumably, the parent or anyone interested in being appointed may apply. [9] Section 4(3) and (4).
[10] *Ibid.*, sub-s. (5). [11] See s. 3, *supra.* [12] Section 4(6).
[13] Administration of Justice Act 1970, First Sched.

noted. Section 5 enables the court to appoint a guardian for a minor who has no parent, no guardian of the person and no one else having parental rights with respect to him. Such an appointment may be made even though a local authority has parental rights by virtue of a resolution under s. 2 of the Children Act 1948; but once it is made, the resolution ceases to have effect.

The statutory jurisdiction may also be exercised by a county court or a magistrates' court,[14] but, except for being able to vary or discharge an existing order of appointment, the latter court can only appoint for a minor who is under 16, unless he is physically or mentally incapable of self-support; and it cannot entertain an application involving the administration or application of property or the income thereof belonging to or held in trust for a minor.[15] Neither kind of court has jurisdiction where a respondent resides in Scotland or Northern Ireland, unless a summons can be served on him in England or Wales.[16]

In deciding whom to choose as guardian the court must be primarily guided by the paramountcy of the child's welfare, in accordance with s. 1 of the Guardianship of Minors Act 1971, but, as with disputes over custody, it does consider other factors. It leans in favour of the appointment of blood relations,[17] but the consideration for the child's welfare may demand a complete severance from relations; *e.g.*, where the father has killed the mother.[18] It must be ready to consider the wishes of the parent (including a deceased parent)[19] and, if he is sufficiently mature, those of the minor. It must seek to avoid the creation of religious difficulties between an appointee and the ward and it must try to appoint persons who are likely to get on with each other as joint guardians.[20] When exercising the statutory jurisdiction to appoint a joint guardian with the surviving parent, the sole question is whether the appointment is *per se* desirable for the minor and not whether it can achieve some collateral purpose. In *Re H. (An infant)*[20] a magistrates'

---

[14] *I.e.*, the county court of the district in which or, as the case may be, a magistrates' court having jurisdiction in the place in which, the respondent or the applicant or the minor resides; Guardianship of Minors Act, s. 15(1) (b) and (c).   [15] Sub-section (2).   [16] Sub-section (3) (b).
[17] *Ord* v. *Blackett* (1725), 9 Mod. Rep. 116; *Johnstone* v. *Beattie* (1843), 10 Cl. & F. 42 (H.L.); *Re Nevin*, [1891] 2 Ch. 299, at p. 303.
[18] *Re F.*, [1970] 1 All E.R. 344 (C.A.); [1970] 1 W.L.R. 192.
[19] *Re Kaye* (1866), 1 Ch.App. 387 (C.A. in Ch.).
[20] [1959] 3 All E.R. 746; [1959] 1 W.L.R. 1163.

court appointed the minor's elder sister to act as joint guardian with her father. At the time of the mother's death the minor was in the care and control of the sister and the father was estranged from the family. What the sister wanted was custody, but, since the Guardianship of Infants Acts did not enable her to claim this directly,[1] she first sought appointment as a joint guardian which would then entitle her to apply for custody. The magistrates' order was discharged. The court indicated that the appropriate method of achieving this would have been an application by the sister to make the minor a ward of court.

B. THE RELATIONSHIP BETWEEN GUARDIAN AND WARD

The relation of guardian and ward is "a peculiar relation of trusteeship".[2] With regard to the ward's property the guardian is in the same position as any other trustee of property. The peculiarity lies in the guardianship of the *person*. The rights and duties of the guardian substantially correspond to those of a parent, but in some respects the duties are more onerous and the rights less extensive. For the most part they are examined elsewhere and are merely enumerated here.

I. GUARDIANSHIP OF THE PERSON OF THE WARD

(a) **Duties**

1. *Protection*
The guardian is under the same common law and statutory duties to protect the ward from physical and moral harm as the parent.[3]

2. *Education*

3. *Financial Provision*
His obligations concerning these matters are considered in Chapters 13 and 14 respectively, where it will be seen that in certain respects they differ materially from parental obligations.

4. *Marriage*
A guardian is under a duty to prevent his ward from entering into a marriage which is unsuitable on the ground of age,

---

[1] See *ante*, Chapter 9.
[2] *Per* ROMILLY, M.R., in *Mathew* v. *Brise* (1851), 14 Beav. 341, at p. 345.
[3] See Chapters 6 and 7.

fortune or rank. If he gives consent to it, the court may inter-vene and prevent it on the application of anyone opposed to it. This may be done without making the minor a ward of court, but it is desirable to take that further step, because if the marriage does take place the court is able to invoke its powers of contempt against those involved in bringing it about.[4]

5. *Liability to Third Parties*

The liability of the guardian for the acts of the ward are the same as that of the parent for his child's conduct.[5]

(b) Rights

1. *Custody, Care and Control*

A guardian has the right to the custody of the ward (in the wide sense of the term),[6] but it is not as comprehensive as that of the parent. This is seen in the strength of the right to the care and control of the ward.[7] Where he is sole guardian he will be *prima facie* but not automatically entitled to care and control. Thus, if he is a testamentary guardian and the testator directs that some other person is to have care and control he must comply with the direction, unless he satisfies the court that it would not be in the ward's interests to do so,[8] and, where the court decides that a testamentary guardian is to be the sole guardian,[9] it may, in exercise of its powers to make such order regarding custody as it thinks fit, having regard to the ward's welfare, entrust the care and control to someone else.[10] The Guardianship of Minors Act 1971 omits to confer that power where a guardian is appointed because the ward has no parent, guardian or other person having parental rights,[11] but it is submitted that, if the appointing court is the High Court, it may invoke its inherent jurisdiction so as to grant care and control to a person other than the guardian. If the High Court does not do so or if the court is a county court or magistrates' court, the guardian has the right to care and con-

---

[4] See further *infra*, p. 423.   [5] See textbooks on the law of torts.
[6] See *ante*, Chapter 9, p. 256.
[7] See also the right to services (*infra*) and the right to determine the ward's religious upbringing (*post*, Chapter 13, p. 431).
[8] *Knott* v. *Cottee* (1847), 2 Ph. 192.
[9] Guardianship of Minors Act 1971, s. 4(4), *supra*, p. 400.
[10] Section 10(1). It may also give the parent a right of access.
[11] Section 5(1), *supra*, p. 401.

trol. When care and control is given to someone other than a guardian, the residuary rights which flow from his right to custody (in the wide sense) remain with the guardian.

Where a guardian acts jointly with a surviving parent, it is more likely than not that the latter will have the care and control with the guardian's consent, and in those cases where they are in dispute the court may be more ready to find that the minor's welfare is best served with the parent having care and control rather than the guardian.

While the Guardianship of Minors Act 1971 provides for the determination of custody disputes between a parent and guardian or between two guardians,[12] it does not enable the guardian to invoke that Act to enforce his right against any other person, whereas the Act seems to be available to the parent in a claim against a stranger.[13] The guardian will have to rely on the remedy of *habeas corpus* or institute wardship proceedings. It is suggested that there ought to be a uniform procedure for claiming custody of a child, whether the claimant be a parent, guardian or any other person.

2. *Chastisement*

A right incidental to that of care and control is that which enables a guardian, like a parent, to exercise disciplinary powers over the ward. When the ward reaches the age of discretion the right is almost as tenuous as that of the parent; for example, subject to his duty to see that the ward is protected from physical and moral harm, he cannot prevent him from living wherever he chooses.[14] However, because of the fiduciary relationship he may be under a duty to chastise and control in circumstances where a similar obligation would not be legally demanded of a parent; for example, where the ward is dissipating his personal income.[15]

3. *Change of Ward's Surname*

It seems that if the father of a legitimate minor is dead or is not available the guardian has the power to change the minor's name. It seems also that, even if the father is alive

---

[12] See *infra*.
[13] See *ante*, Chapter 9, p. 288.
[14] *Anon.* (1751), 2 Ves. Sen. 374. A possible exception arises where the guardian has sent the ward away to school.
[15] *Kay* v. *Johnston* (1856), 21 Beav. 536; see Johnson, *op. cit.*, p. 311.

and available, a change is permissible when in the ward's interests.[16]

In the case of the illegitimate child the right to change the name primarily resides with the mother and the above principles would apply *mutatis mutandis* according to whether she is alive and available. It is submitted that this is so even where the father's surname has been entered on the register of births, for it is either with the consent of the mother (as well as his) or at her request (provided he acknowledges paternity) that his name is entered[17] and not by virtue of any right vested in him as natural guardian.

4. *Guardianship Allowance*

A guardian has the right to a guardian's allowance if the ward's parents are both dead and one of them was insured under the National Insurance Acts.[18] Where he is not eligible for the allowance, he may include the ward in his family for the purpose of receiving family allowance.

Apart from the right to care and control a guardian's rights are less extensive than those of the parent in two, if not three other respects. He probably has no right to the services of the ward[19] and he is not entitled to determine his religious upbringing.[20] Whether he can change the domicile of a ward whose parents are dead (or, in the case of an illegitimate ward whose mother is dead) is uncertain. The right of a widowed mother to change her child's domicile so long as it is for the latter's welfare has long been recognised[1] and the court may be ready to extend that principle to the case of the divorced mother who has been granted custody.[2] Early opinions[3] suggested that the guardian does not have a similar right, but

---

[16] See BUCKLEY, J., in *Re T.* *(Otherwise H.)* *(an infant)*, [1963] Ch. 238; [1962] 3 All E.R. 970 *(ante*, p. 256).
     It is submitted that the test of availability is whether the father can be consulted; compare a fugitive from justice.
[17] *I.e.*, entered in accordance with the Births and Deaths Registration Act 1953, s. 10 and the Family Law Reform Act 1969, s. 27.
[18] National Insurance Act 1965, ss. 29 and 42 and Sched. 3, as amended by the National Insurance Act 1969, s. 2.
[19] See *post*, p. 451.
[20] *Post*, p. 431.
[1] *Potinger* v. *Wightman* (1817), 3 Mer. 67; *Re Beaumont*, [1893] 3 Ch. 490.
[2] As Northern Ireland law has, but Scots law has not; see respectively *Hope* v. *Hope* [1968] N.I. 1; *Shanks* v. *Shanks* 1965 S.L.T. 330.
[3] *Potinger* v. *Wightman, supra; Johnstone* v. *Beattie* (1843), 10 Cl. & F. 42 at pp. 66 and 138-140.

Guardianship

these were expressed at a time when the child's welfare did not bear its modern significance and it is entirely open to a court to take a contrary view.[4]

II. GUARDIANSHIP OF THE PROPERTY OF THE WARD

Mention has already been made of the assimilation of the old forms of guardianship into the law of trusts. The property of a ward will be vested in trustees with the usual powers of applying income for maintenance and capital for the advancement, of the ward.[5] But, with regard to the ward's property, the fiduciary relationship between him and his guardian is important in two respects.

Firstly, any transaction between them which benefits the guardian comes under the closest scrutiny.[6] Indeed, the presumption is that the transaction was the result of his having improperly influenced the ward into entering into it and the onus on him to rebut this is a heavy one. If he fails to do so, he must restore any property received (e.g., by gift) to the ward who, if necessary, can recover it from any third person other than a *bona fide* purchaser for value without notice of the original transaction. The presumption of undue influence continues to apply even if the transaction is entered into some time after the ward comes of age, because there is the obvious risk of his still being under the guardian's influence.[7] The likelihood of continued influence and the period for which it lasts will largely depend on the nature of the past relationship between them[8] and on whether they are still residing together. The question has pertinently been asked whether "the reduc-

---

[4] Dicey and Morris, (*Conflict of Laws*, 8th edn., p. 112) offer "speculative possibilities" of change of domicile by guardian, but then cautiously come down against the likelihood of a power to change being allowed (Rule 12 (4)). Compare the provisions in the Domicile Bills, 1958 and 1959, which would have permitted a person having custody of a child to change his domicile.

[5] Trustee Act 1925, ss. 31 and 32.

[6] See especially Lord BROUGHAM, L.C., in *Hunter* v. *Atkins* (1834), 3 My. & K. 113, at p. 135.

[7] *Hylton* v. *Hylton* (1754), 2 Ves. Sen. 547 (attempt by guardian to obtain an annuity out of the ward's estate at the time when he was rendering an account). For other illustrations see *Maitland* v. *Irving* (1846), 15 Sim. 437; and *Maitland* v. *Backhouse* (1848), 16 Sim. 58.
Compare the operation of the presumption in the parent-child relationship after the child attains majority; *Bainbrigge* v. *Browne* (1881), 18 Ch.D. 188; *Lancashire Loans, Ltd.* v. *Black*, [1934] 1 K.B. 380 (C.A.).

[8] *Hatch* v. *Hatch* (1804), 9 Ves. 292.

tion of the age of majority to 18 implies greater maturity and judgment on the part of a person over that age" so that the court will "give correspondingly less weight to the presumption".[9] As a general proposition the answer, it is submitted, must be "yes", but the reduction makes it all the more essential that the court thoroughly investigates the particular relationship and carefully assesses the maturity of the particular ward.

Secondly, when the guardianship comes to an end, the guardian must account to the ward for all the property that has come into his hands and lapse of time does not in itself bar the ward from demanding an account.[10] If, at the ward's request, the guardian continues to manage the ward's property after the latter has come of age and before the accounts for the period of the ward's minority have been settled, he must account on the same principle as if the later transactions had taken place during the minority.[11] An account may always be re-opened on the ground that it contains errors, whether fraudulent or not,[12] or that the ward was not independently advised.[13]

III. DISPUTES BETWEEN GUARDIANS

Disputes between joint guardians over any question affecting the welfare of the minor must be resolved by the court, which may make any order it thinks fit.[14] Matters on which they are most likely to disagree are the question of who is to have custody, care and control of the ward and who is to decide his education, both religious and, less commonly, secular. Where one of them is the father or mother of the ward, he or she may be given right of access to him and there is also the specific power to order the parent to make financial provision for the ward.[15]

C. TERMINATION OF GUARDIANSHIP

Unless the appointment is expressly limited to a shorter period

---

[9] Bromley, *op. cit.*, p. 460, n. 14.
[10] *Mathew* v. *Brise* (1851), 14 Beav. 341.
[11] *Mellish* v. *Mellish* (1832), 1 Sim. & St. 138.
[12] *Allfrey* v. *Allfrey* (1849), 1 Mac. & G. 87.
[13] *Revett* v. *Harvey* (1823) 1 Sim. & St. 502.
[14] Guardianship of Minors Act 1971, s. 7. Jurisdiction resides in any court having power to appoint guardians; see *ante*, p. 400.
[15] Section 11. On maintenance orders see Chapter 14, *post*, p. 456.

or until the happening of some earlier event, a guardianship must come to an end when the ward attains majority. But, apart from these temporal or conditional limitations it will be terminated in any of the following circumstances.

(1) Resignation of the Guardian

A testamentary guardian is entitled to refuse the appointment,[16] but neither he nor a guardian appointed by the court can resign the office once he has accepted it[17] except with the leave of the court. That is likely to be granted, because it is not in the ward's interests to have an unwilling guardian.[18]

(2) Removal of the Guardian by the Court

The High Court may remove a guardian and may, but need not, appoint another in his place, if it considers that the ward's welfare demands this action.[19] The sole criterion, it is submitted, is his welfare,[20] and on this basis it should make no difference whether the guardian is a testamentary guardian or one appointed by the court.[1] The most common ground for removal is misconduct, or the likelihood of misconduct,[2] which is prejudicial to the ward's interests. This may take a variety of forms, but the principle that the court will follow is that any misconduct which would cause it to deprive a parent of custody[3] is equally a ground for removing a guardian. The latter, however, has in some respects heavier responsibilities than the parent, *e.g.*, with regard to the duty to educate,[4] and where this is so failure to fulfil them would also justify removal. But the court's jurisdiction is not limited to cases of misconduct. It may also act where the guardian is otherwise unfit to hold office, *e.g.*, because of mental disorder or even where there is neither misconduct nor unfitness but the circumstances warrant removal so as to ensure the child's welfare, as in *F. v. F.*[5] where by changing her own religion the guardian deprived an

---

[16] *Ex parte Champney* (1762), I Dick 350; Guardianship of Minors Act 1971, s. 3.   [17] *Spencer* v. *Earl of Chesterfield* (1752), Amb. 146.
[18] Bromley, *op. cit.*, p. 332.
[19] Guardianship of Minors Act 1971, s. 6. See also s. 17(1).
    Note only the High Court has this jurisdiction.
[20] For the wide meaning to be given to welfare see LINDLEY, L.J., in *Re McGrath*, [1893] I Ch. 143, at p. 148; see also *ante*, Chapter 9, p. 260.
[1] *Cf.* Johnson, *Family Law*, 2nd edn. p. 306, for the view that the Court will be more willing to remove a guardian appointed by a court, since he is "in effect a mere servant or bailiff of the court".
[2] *Re X, X.* v. *Y.*, [1899] I Ch. 526, at p. 531.   [3] *Ante*, Chapter 9.
[4] *Post*, Chapter 13.   [5] [1902] I Ch. 688.

eleven-year-old ward of the guidance and advice of the religious faith in which the latter had always been brought up.

One of the powers of a court where there is disagreement between joint guardians[6] is to remove one of them if the ward's interests so require.[7]

Note has already been made of the power of a court to remove a male guardian whom it has convicted of incest with the ward,[8] and of the power of a divorce court to declare a parent unfit to have the custody of the children of the family with the consequence that on the death of the other parent the survivor is not entitled as of right to the custody or guardianship of the children.[9]

(3) Marriage of Ward

The effect of the ward's marriage on the guardianship is wholly uncertain. The answer depends upon how much reliance is placed on old cases dealing with guardianship and with the parental right to custody. There are three main views.

The first is that a distinction is to be drawn between a male ward and a female ward. The marriage of the former does not affect the guardianship,[10] whereas in the corresponding case the guardianship is brought to an end. Reliance for this conclusion is placed upon dicta of Lord HARDWICKE, L.C., in *Mendes* v. *Mendes.*[11]

Both the other views reject the distinction but they lead to diametrically opposed conclusions. There is judicial support for the argument that marriage terminates the guardianship of a male as it does that of a female ward. Thus, there is the following observation of ABBOTT, C.J., in *R.* v. *Wilmington*,[12] which by its terms deals with the effect of a son's marriage:

---

[6] *Supra,* p. 407.   [7] *Duke of Beaufort* v. *Berty* (1721), 1 P. Wms. 703.
[8] *Ante,* Chapter 7, p. 221.   [9] *Ante,* Chapter 9, p. 286.
[10] *Eyre* v. *Countess of Shaftesbury* (1725), 2 P. Wms. 103.
[11] (1748) 1 Ves. Sen. 89, at p. 91.
    Johnson, *op. cit.,* p. 303, accepts the distinction but concludes that the effect of the marriage of a female ward depends on the kind of guardianship. It terminates the natural guardianship of parents but not that arising from the appointment of a guardian appointed by the court, and the effect on testamentary guardianship probably depends on whether or not the person she marries is an adult. If he is not, the guardianship of the wife is not affected: if he is, it is terminated or, perhaps, is put into abeyance and capable of being revived in the event of her becoming a widow while still a minor.
[12] (1822), 5 B. & Ald. 525, at p. 526; see also *Lough* v. *Ward,* [1945] 2 All E.R. 338, at p. 348.

". . . during the minority of a child there can be no emancipation unless he marries and so becomes himself the head of a family, or contracts some other relation so as wholly and permanently to exclude the parental control."

Admittedly, that case was concerned with the question whether a child was still a member of a family for the purpose of a poor law settlement and did not directly deal with parental right to custody or guardianship. That comment, however, equally applies to *R.* v. *Rotherfield Greys (Inhabitants)*,[13] at least so far as concerns custody, yet, the latter is often cited in favour of the proposition that parental right to custody is suspended so long as a minor is serving with the armed forces of the Crown. Apart from these dicta, strong persuasive support that the marriage of a minor terminates the right to custody is to be derived from the Marriage Act 1949 in that its rules requiring the consent of a parent or guardian to the marriage do not apply to one who, being a widower or widow, wishes to remarry during minority. There is, therefore, much to be said for the opinion that marriage ends the right to custody and, given that custody is the source of all other parental rights,[14] it can be argued that marriage equally ends the parent's guardianship. On that basis it might further be contended that no distinction is be drawn between the natural guardian and a testamentary guardian or one appointed by the court.

On the other hand it has been pointed out[15] that neither the Tenures Abolition Act nor the Guardianship of Minors Act states that guardianship is to end on the marriage of a ward. Nor, significantly, does wardship of court cease on that event.[16]

(4) Death

Obviously the death of the ward terminates the guardianship. So does the death of a sole guardian, but where there are joint guardians the effect of the death of one of them depends upon whether they are testamentary guardians or guardians appointed by the court. If they are the former, the survivors continue as guardians,[17] whereas in the other case death ends the guardianship of all of them – although the court will be ready to create a new guardianship by re-appointing the survivors.[18]

[13] (1823), 1 B. & C. 345.   [14] See *ante*, p. 286.
[15] Bromley, *op. cit.*, p. 331.   [16] See *infra*, p. 423.
[17] *Eyre* v. *Countess of Shaftesbury* (1725), 2 P. Wms 103, at p. 107.
[18] *Bradshaw* v. *Bradshaw* (1826), 1 Russ, 528.

D. WARDS OF COURT

Wardship of court is one of the oldest institutions connected with English family law. Its origins lay in the feudal obligation of the Sovereign, as liege-lord, to protect his subjects, especially those who were incapable of looking after themselves. Those most affected by it were minors. As *parens patriae* the Crown was responsible for protecting both their person and property. This responsibility was probably delegated initially to the Chancellor,[19] but was taken over in 1540 by the Court of Wards whose function it remained until the Court was abolished in 1660,[20] when it was assumed by the Court of Chancery. In 1875 the jurisdiction passed to the Chancery Division of the High Court and is now exercised by the Family Division.[1]

I. THE PURPOSES OF WARDSHIP

Although in theory this prerogative jurisdiction can be exercised in respect of all minors who are British subjects or are ordinarily resident within the jurisdiction,[2] the kinds of cases in which it has come to be invoked fall into a pattern. The purposes for which it may be sought have appeared in the following chronological order: the protection of the property of the ward; the protection of his person and general welfare; the protection, in his interests, of the parent's rights over him; and the supplementation of the statutory powers and duties of local authorities with regard to children in their care.

After 1660 the feudal associations with wardship were still pronounced in that wardship of court was in practice only sought where the minor had large property interests to protect, but even in these cases his personal interests were not overlooked; for example, through the guardian's duty to educate the ward according to the latter's station or through his control over the marriage of a female ward so as to prevent her property falling into the hands of fortune hunters. However, the emphasis on personal protection does not become prominent until the end of the nineteenth century when the prerogative jurisdiction was being increasingly invoked to settle disputes

[19] See Holdsworth, *History of English Law*, vi, 648.
[20] Tenures Abolition Act.
[1] Administration of Justice Act 1970, s. 1 and Sched. I.   [2] See *infra*, p. 418.

over custody, care and control between the parents or between a parent and a stranger. We have seen[3] that, notwithstanding the growth of the matrimonial jurisdiction of the High Court, county courts and magistrates' courts and of their respective statutory powers to appoint guardians under Guardianship of Infants legislation, wardship of court continues to have much practical relevance. Thus, apart from *habeas corpus*, it is by means of wardship proceedings that a third party must seek care and control against a parent, since he cannot rely on proceedings under the Guardianship of Minors Act 1971 to obtain custody, and, although in the converse case the parent is probably able to rely on that Act,[4] he may certainly choose the prerogative jurisdiction if he wishes. Secondly, the jurisdiction of magistrates' courts is limited in that normally they cannot make custody orders relating to children over 16, and they cannot grant an injunction to prevent the removal of a child from the jurisdiction. Moreover, it has been observed[5] that such a court is

> "a somewhat unsuitable tribunal to deal with cases in which a prolonged investigation into disputed facts is called for or in which the court may have to give and enforce detailed directions as to the upbringing of the children or further applications with regard to care and control or access are likely, for example to take account of changing circumstances".

Just as the shift of emphasis in the nineteenth century to protection of the ward's person was an outcome of the reaction by the mother against the virtually absolute authority of the powers of the father, so, in the modern setting, "teenage wardship"[6] is the result of a reaction by the minor against the authority of the parent. The kind of case where it invariably arises is where a teenage daughter is associating with a man whom she intends to marry and to whom the parents for a variety of reasons are objecting. The difficulty which the court has to resolve is whether enforcement of the parental right to care and control by an order that the man cease the association would be in the ward's interests and, if so, whether the continuance of wardship and the making of such an order would be effective.

---

[3] See *ante*, Chapter 9.   [4] *Ante*, p. 288.
[5] Cross, *Wards of Court*, (1967) 83 L.Q.R. 201, 204.   [6] *Ibid.*, pp. 209-211.

Another modern feature of wardship is the use made of it where a local authority is in dispute with the foster parents or the natural parents over the upbringing of a child who is in the care of the authority in accordance with the Children Act 1948. The dispute may give rise to an issue more commonly associated with the constitutional liberty of the subject,[7] that of the relationship between the prerogative jurisdiction and the exercise of statutory powers and duties. The reasons for minimising in the present context a possible conflict between the Family Division, exercising that jurisdiction, and a local authority, discharging its powers and duties, and the means of achieving harmony were first formulated in *Re M. (An Infant).*[8]

In that case a local authority in April 1956 received an illegitimate child into their care under s. 1 of the Children Act 1948 and immediately boarded out the child with foster parents. In October 1957, after the foster father had died, the authority resolved under s. 2 of the Act that all the rights and powers of the child's natural mother be vested in the authority. In June 1960 the authority decided that boarding out the child with the foster mother was not in the former's best interests and they asked her to return the child to them. This she refused to do, notwithstanding an earlier signed undertaking that she would allow the child to be removed when required by the authority. They then issued a summons for an order of *habeas corpus*,[9] but before the hearing she herself instituted wardship proceedings and the application for *habeas corpus* was adjourned. The authority then applied for an order that the child cease to be a ward of court. In affirming the decision of CROSS, J., that such an order be made, the Court of Appeal established three principles:

(1) The prerogative rights over minors, including that of making an order for wardship, are not ousted or abrogated as the result of a local authority's exercising its powers and duties under the 1948 Act.

(2) But the Act provides a "clear and comprehensive

---

[7] See, for example, *A.-G.* v. *De Keyser's Royal Hotel, Ltd.,* [1920] A.C. 508 (H.L.).   [8] [1961] Ch. 328; [1961] 1 All E.R. 788, (C.A.).
[9] This remedy had already been successfully sought in *Re A.B. (an infant),* [1954] 2 Q.B. 385; [1954] 2 All E.R. 287, but in that case the child was in care under s. 1 of the Children Act and the authority wished the foster parents to hand over the child to the authority so that they in turn could, at the mother's request, entrust the child to a couple named by her.

scheme" for the care of children, which by necessary implication restricts the prerogative jurisdiction.[10] So, where a child is a ward of court the judge will not exercise control in relation to duties or discretions clearly vested in the authority by the Act and properly exercised by them. There might, nevertheless, be exceptional circumstances where it would be proper and competent for him to continue the wardship, even though the court was not seeking to interfere with what the authority had decided should be done.

(3) The court has, however, the right to control the activities of a local authority in those cases where it is acting with impropriety or in breach or disregard of its statutory duties;[11] for example, where their social worker, in recommending (through their social services committee) that the child be removed from the foster parents, is motivated by personal hostility towards the foster parents, or where the authority has failed strictly to observe the procedure laid down in s. 2 of the 1948 Act.[12]

These principles were extended in *Re T. (A.J.J.) (An Infant)*[13] to the case where the child was in the care of a local authority as the result of a fit person order. Now that that kind of order has been superseded by the care order,[14] they will similarly operate where the latter is in force.

In *Re M.* and *Re T. (A.J.J.)* the effect respectively of the resolution under s. 2 of the Children Act 1948 and the fit person order was that the local authority assumed the rights and duties of the parents. Different considerations arise, however, where the minor is in the care of the authority by virtue of s. 1 of the Children Act 1948 and the natural parent notifies the authority of his desire to assume the care of his child.

---

[10] For similar restrictions on prerogative jurisdiction in relation to statutory powers of local education authorities see *Re B. (infants)*, [1962] Ch. 201; [1961] 3 All E.R. 276 (C.A.), *post*, Chapter 13, p. 436.
   Similarly, wardship proceedings may not be used to challenge the powers of an immigration officer to refuse a minor admission to this country, so long as he exercises them fairly and honestly; *Re Mohamed Arif (an infant)*, [1968] Ch. 643; [1968] 2 All E.R. 145, (C.A.).
[11] Compare *Re Mohamed Arif, supra.*
[12] *Re L. (A.C.) (an infant)*, [1971] 3 All E.R. 743.
[13] [1970] Ch. 688; [1970] 2 All E.R. 865 (C.A.); and see Lasok, Judicial or Administrative Decision?, 120 N.L.J. 817; Cretney, 33 M.L.R. 696.
[14] See *ante*, Chapter 5.

Once that happens the right of the authority to keep the child in care under the section comes to an end and the common law rights of the parent revive. It is therefore important, even though there is no absolute obligation on the authority to return the child to the parent,[15] that the prerogative jurisdiction becomes fully effective, thereby enabling any interested person to apply to the court for an order to make the child a ward of court and to issue a directive concerning his care and control.[16] The most likely applicant is the foster parent anxious to keep the child, and his application may be with or without the support of the local authority.[17] In the latter event the court is not precluded from reviewing the decision of the local authority that the foster parent hand over the child to them so that they may hand him over to the parent in accordance with s. 1,[18] but it should only intervene in exercise of its wardship jurisdiction if there are special circumstances justifying encroachment on the statutory duties and discretion of the authority.[19] On the other hand, it should always be ready to supplement the duties and discretion. For example, if a child is in the authority's care under s. 1 and one parent, in order to anticipate attempts by the other parent to remove the child from the jurisdiction, applies to make him a ward of court, the court may order that he remain in the authority's care but that their discretion be supplemented by giving both parents access.[20]

This reliance on wardship *vis-à-vis* the Children Act 1948 is largely explained by the legal insecurity of the long-term

[15] *Re K.R. (an infant)*, [1964] Ch. 455; [1963] 3 All E.R. 337; *Krishnan* v. *Sutton London Borough Council*, [1970] Ch. 181; [1969] 3 All E.R. 1367, (C.A.).
[16] The court may choose to make an interim order placing the child in the charge of any person whom it thinks fit.
[17] There may be a joint application by them; *Re R. (K.) (an infant)*, [1964] Ch. 455; [1963] 3 All E.R. 337.
[18] *Re S. (an infant)*, [1965] 1 All E.R. 865; [1965] 1 W.L.R. 483 (C.A.).
[19] *Re C. (A.) (an infant)*, [1966] 1 All E.R. 560; [1966] 1 W.L.R. 415; see also *Re B.* and *Re M., supra*, on this point.
[20] *Re G. (infants)*, [1963] 3 All E.R. 370; [1963] 1 W.L.R. 1169. See also *C.* v. *Dorset County Council* (1969), 119 N.L.J. 745 where the court confirmed the application of a foster mother for the child to be made a ward of court even though the county council, in whose care the child was, were opposed to the application. It was held that the powers of the local authority were not thereby ousted and they could at any time by leave of the court exercise their powers to remove the child from the foster mother and return her to her natural mother.

Guardianship

foster parent;[1] but wardship jurisdiction has its disadvantages. It means that, if the foster parent is to seek security, he has to apply to the High Court, and, if wardship is ordered, his powers are not precisely defined, especially as the court retains the direct and ultimate control over the child. For these reasons the Working Paper on the Adoption of Children[2] recommends that the foster parent should be given the right to apply for an order for a modified form of "guardianship", *i.e.*, not an order conferring full legal guardianship in place of the natural guardianship of the parent[3] but one which is essentially equivalent to an order for custody under the Guardianship of Minors Act 1971.[4] The effect, therefore, would be that the natural parent would still be parent in law but the foster parent would be given custody, care and control. Certain limits on the rights to apply would be imposed. An application could not be made until the foster parent had cared for the child for at least a year. Subject to that, if the period of care were at least five years the right to apply would be unfettered, otherwise the consent of the local authority would be needed. These proposals would apply to persons who are private foster parents and to those with whom children in the care of a local authority are fostered, but in the latter cases the effect of a "guardianship" order would be that the child would cease to be in care.[5]

II. SCOPE OF THE PREROGATIVE JURISDICTION

When the jurisdiction of the Court of Chancery was mainly being invoked to protect the ward's property, it came to be accepted that any action to administer the trusts of a settlement of property on him or any payment into court of money or securities in which he had interests automatically rendered him a ward of court. Later, when it was recognised that protection

---

[1] In *Re M.*, *supra*, Lord EVERSHED, M.R., referring to the foster mother, said:
"... her position is in truth equivalent to that of a nurse to whom the child has been temporarily committed by the local authority acting *in loco parentis* ..." See Levin, *The Control of Local Authority Powers over Children*, (1971) 1 Fam. Law 101.   [2] Paragraph 106-111, 116-118.
[3] See *ante*, pp. 396 *et seq.*   [4] *Ante*, Chapter 9.
[5] Where the child was not in care merely under s. 1 but by virtue of a resolution under s. 2 of the 1948 Act, the effect of the "guardianship" order would be to revoke the resolution. Similarly it would revoke any order (*e.g.* care order) by reason of which the child was in care.

416

of the person was at least as important, a petition to appoint a guardian for a minor had the same result. Notwithstanding the shift of emphasis towards the protection of the person, the older methods were still mainly relied on for instituting wardship proceedings, even though there were no substantial property interests to protect. The use of the device of settling a small sum on a minor and then bringing an action for administration of the trust so as to make him a ward of court was often unreal and sometimes vexatious. Eventually, a new procedure was introduced by s. 9 of the Law Reform (Miscellaneous Provisions) Act 1949, which enacts that a minor can only be made a ward of court pursuant to an order under the section. The protection begins from the time an application, by way of a summons, for an order is made; but the minor ceases to be a ward of court if no appointment to hear the summons is obtained within 21 days after being issued or if the court does not make the order.[6] Even when occasionally a divorce court exercises its power of directing that proceedings be taken to have a child of the family made a ward of court,[7] the provisions of s. 9 must be strictly observed.

In *Re E. (An Infant)*[8] ROXBURGH, J., concluded that the effect of s. 9 was that the High Court could rely on its prerogative jurisdiction only after an order under the section had been made; but there are earlier dicta which suggest that the jurisdiction does not necessarily depend on a minor being warded.[9] This latter opinion found favour in *Re N.*[10] and in *L. v. L.*[11]

---

[6] See R.S.C., O. 91, r. 2. In order to avoid frivolous or improper applications (see *Re Dunhill* (1967), 111 Sol. Jo. 113) a *Practice Direction*, ([1967] 3 All E.R. 828) requires the applicant to state his relationship to the ward, and, if the master considers the application an abuse of the process of the court, he may dismiss the summons forthwith or refer the point to the judge.

[7] Matrimonial Proceedings and Property Act 1970, s. 18(1). This provision differs from its predecessor (Matrimonial Causes Act 1965, s. 34(1)) in two respects. It is limited to a child of the family who is a minor (*cf. D. v. D.,* [1970] 3 All E.R. 893), and it only enables a divorce court to order that proceedings be taken to make the child a ward of court (*i.e.,* to invoke the prerogative jurisdiction of the Family Division) whereas s. 34(1) allowed for proceedings to be taken "for placing the child under the protection of the court" and thus enabled the High Court to rely on either its inherent or its statutory jurisdiction (*D. v. D., supra*).

[8] [1956] Ch. 23; [1955] 3 All E.R. 174.

[9] See KAY, J., in *Brown v. Collins* (1883), 25 Ch. D. 56, 60-61; NORTH, J., in *Re McGrath*, [1892] 2 Ch. 496, 511.

[10] [1967] Ch. 512, 529-531; [1967] 1 All E.R. 161, 168-169.

[11] [1969] P. 25, 27; [1969] 1 All E.R. 852, 854.

Its advantage is that it enables a court to provide immediate protection to the minor, for example, by the issue of an injunction restraining his removal from the jurisdiction until a summons under s. 9 can be issued. It is therefore of limited practical importance, but it is wholly consistent with the rationale of the inherent jurisdiction.

The same rationale explains the bases on which wardship jurisdiction may be assumed where a foreign element is involved. We have already considered[12] the principles on which the court is prepared to allow wardship where a minor is brought to England in defiance of the wishes of those who have had his care abroad. Because the essence of wardship is the duty of the sovereign to protect the minor arising from the correlative right to his allegiance, in such cases, as in those where there is no "kidnapping",[13] jurisdiction is invariably based on the minor's actual presence in England, even if he is not a British subject or is not domiciled or ordinarily resident here or has no property within the jurisdiction.

But the same reasons of protection and allegiance led the Court of Appeal in *Re P. (G.E.) (An Infant)*[14] to hold that wardship jurisdiction could be exercised over a minor who is ordinarily resident in England but who is not actually present here when the application for an order is made under s. 9. The parents in that case had come to England in 1957 as stateless persons and refugees from Egypt. Eventually they separated and the boy then spent most of each week with his mother and the week-ends with his father, until one week-end in 1962 when, without the mother's knowledge or consent, the father flew with him to Israel, where by the date of the present wardship proceedings instituted by the mother they had been living for almost three months and where the father had acquired for himself and the boy Israeli nationality. It was held that where a minor's parents are living apart and by arrangement between them he is living most of the time with one of them, he is ordinarily resident with that parent, even though the

---

[12] *Ante*, Chapter 9, pp. 295 to 298.
[13] *Re D.*, [1943] Ch. 305; [1943] 2 All E.R. 411, where a German refugee, whose parents were believed to be in a concentration camp, was made a ward of court.
[14] [1965] Ch. 568; [1964] 3 All E.R. 977. See Webb, 14 I.C.L.Q. 663.

other may have the child to stay with him. The boy was therefore ordinarily resident with his mother in England when he was spirited away to Israel and that residence could not be terminated by the unilateral action of the father, especially as the child was still entitled to return to England under a British travel document which had enabled him and the father to leave England. The assumption of jurisdiction on the basis of ordinary residence was essential in such a case as the present one where the minor has been kidnapped and removed from the jurisdiction by force, deception or secrecy.

The interdependence of protection and allegiance also accounts for the rule that the British nationality of a minor will confer wardship jurisdiction over him although he is presently abroad.[15] On the other hand, the Court of Appeal in *Re P. (G.E.)* decisively rejected domicile as a basis of jurisdiction, on the ground that it is an archaic, artificial and unrealistic concept which may be wholly unconnected with allegiance.[16] It is also firmly recognised that property owned by the minor within the jurisdiction is not a sufficient basis,[17] notwithstanding the strong historical association which wardship had with the protection of his proprietary interests.

The reluctance of the English court to invoke its wardship jurisdiction[18] is not confined to cases where minors are kidnapped abroad and brought to England in the face of a foreign custody order or where foreign custody proceedings are pending.[19] A similar attitude is adopted where the minor's presence in England is transient, unless the court's intervention is

---

[15] *Hope* v. *Hope* (1854), 4 De G.M. & G. 328, *per* Lord CRANWORTH at pp. 344-345; *Re Willoughby* (1885), 30 Ch. D 324, *per* COTTON, L.J., at p. 331; *Re Liddell's Settlement Trusts*, [1936] Ch. 365; [1936] 1 All E.R. 239; *Harben* v. *Harben*, [1957] 1 All E.R. 379; [1957] 1 W.L.R. 261.

[16] The Scottish courts have taken the contrary view. This may be due to their treatment of wardship and custody as matters of status, but it has also been suggested (*per* RUSSELL, L.J., in *Re P. (G.E.), (an infant)*, [1965] Ch. 568, 592; [1964] 3 All E.R. 977, 986) that "this approach derives from an attempt to resolve internal conflicts in the United Kingdom" (as to which see *ante*, Chapter 9, p. 298). For the Scottish decisions see *Ponder* v. *Ponder*, 1932 S.C. 233; *Kitson* v. *Kitson*, 1945 S.C. 434; *M'Lean* v. *M'Lean*, 1947 S.C. 79.

[17] *Brown* v. *Collins* (1883), 25 Ch.D. 56.

[18] Or its jurisdiction to make custody orders; see *ante*, Chapter 9, pp. 295 et seq.

[19] *Cp. Re S.M. (an infant)*, [1971] Ch. 621; [1971] 1 All E.R. 459; *ante*, p. 296, n. 20.

needed in an emergency or to support a foreign order or proceedings.[20] Nor will wardship usually be ordered if enforcement is impracticable[1] or is inconsistent with the law of the country in which the minor is present.[2]

Confidential Reports in Wardship Proceedings

In wardship proceedings the court has a discretion to appoint the Official Solicitor (or any other suitable person) as guardian *ad litem*. An appointment is invariably made in "teenage" wardship cases where the dispute is between the parents on the one hand and their child on the other, but is less common where the issue is between the parents over the care and control or upbringing of the child.[3] In the latter kind of case it is part of his functions to investigate the case on behalf of the child, to interview him and the parents and then to make a recommendation to the court with regard to care and control or upbringing. In so recommending he may feel obliged to submit a confidential report to the court, for example, where the child has undergone psychiatric examination.[4] The extent

[20] See PEARSON, L.J., in *Re P. (G.E.), (an infant)* [1965] Ch. 568, 588; [1964] 3 All E.R. 977, 984.

In *Re C. (an infant)*, (1956) *Times*, December 14, an illegitimate child, born in the United States, was passing through England with his putative father who was taking him to Russia. On the application of the mother, who wished to take him back to the United States, he was made a ward of court, but this was subject to the condition that he cease to be so as soon as he arrived back in the United States with her.

[1] *Aliter* if, for example, sequestration of property is available to secure obedience.

In *Re Chrysanthou*, [1957] C.L.Y. 1748, the minor was made a ward of court but the order did not include a direction to the parent to bring him back from abroad, since there was no evidence that the direction would be obeyed.

[2] *Cp. Re Kernot, (an infant)*, [1965] Ch. 217; [1964] 3 All E.R. 339, *ante*, p. 296. [3] Cross, *Wards of Court*, 83 L.Q.R. 201, 207-8.

[4] Increasing use is being made of medical, especially psychiatric, examination of children in wardship and custody proceedings. Where the Official Solicitor has already been appointed guardian *ad litem* it is improper for such an examination to be made without his knowledge or consent. If both parents are intending to call medical evidence and cannot agree on an expert, the Official Solicitor should decide whether an examination is needed, and, therefore, in these cases of parental disagreement he will have to be appointed guardian *ad litem* if this has not already been done. But the parents should co-operate in jointly instructing an expert and then the court will normally approve their choice. See CROSS, J., in *Re S.*, [1967] 1 All E.R. 202, 209; [1967] 1 W.L.R. 396, 407; *Re R. (P.M.), (an infant)*, [1968] 1 All E.R. 691, 693; [1968] 1 W.L.R. 385, 388; *B. (M.) v. B. (R.)*, [1968] 3 All E.R. 170, 174; [1968] 2 W.L.R. 1182, 1185 (C.A.).

to which use should be made of confidential reports and the extent to which they should be protected from disclosure were questions considered by the House of Lords in *Official Solicitor* v. *K*.[5] The criterion applicable is the child's welfare. Since that is the paramount consideration of the Family Division in exercising its inherent jurisdiction over wards of court, disclosure lies within its discretion and overrides the principle that a case should not be decided on information that a party has not seen and cannot challenge. Nevertheless, it should withhold knowledge of the contents of the report from the parties only in rare cases and where fully satisfied that real harm to the child must otherwise result.[6] Even then it may allow disclosure to counsel of the parties, unless either party objects to this procedure. The child's welfare should equally determine whether in the first instance a confidential report should be submitted.

Since these principles rest exclusively on the paramountcy of his welfare, it is submitted that they are not limited to proceedings based on the prerogative jurisdiction of the High Court but equally apply where that Court or an inferior court is exercising its statutory jurisdiction concerning the custody of children.[7] They therefore extend to the reports of the Official Solicitor or other person who represents the child in matrimonial proceedings in the High Court[8] and to the reports of court welfare officers in any custody dispute.[9] In *Re P.A.* (*An Infant*)[10] they were held to apply also to the confidential report submitted by the guardian *ad litem* in adoption proceedings,[11]

---

[5] [1965] A.C. 201; [1963] 3 All E.R. 191.

[6] In *Official Solicitor* v. *K.* the mother objected to the confidentiality of the report, partly on the cogent ground that "she was at least as a 'self-respecting parent' entitled to know what it was in the condition of the infants which called for . . . repeated medical interviews – and that in the absence of such knowledge it would be very difficult for her properly to perform her parental duties and, therefore, would be to the disadvantage of the children themselves" *per* Lord EVERSHED, [1965] A.C. 201, 214; [1963] 3 All E.R. 191, 193.

[7] For a different view, which inextricably relates the principles to the prerogative powers, see Bromley, *op. cit.*, p. 275.

[8] Matrimonial Causes Rules 1971, r. 108.

[9] In *Fowler* v. *Fowler and Sines*, [1963] P. 311; [1963] 1 All E.R. 119, (C.A.) it was held that the oral evidence of a welfare officer, given privately and in the absence and without the consent of the parties, to the judge in custody proceedings in the Divorce Division was inadmissible and the order for custody be set aside. But that decision can, it is submitted, no longer stand in the face of *Official Solicitor* v. *K*.

[10] [1971] 3 All E.R. 522; [1971] 1 W.L.R. 1530 (C.A.).

[11] See *ante*, Chapter 10, p. 354.

a decision which, it is submitted, clearly shows that they are not restricted to cases involving prerogative powers, since the adoption application was heard by a county court.

The above principles are concerned with confidential reports which may properly be presented to the judge. Wholly distinct therefrom is the privilege which precludes reports from being brought even to his notice. In *Re D. (Infants)*[12] it was held that the case records kept by a local authority in respect of children in their care who are boarded out[13] must not, save in rare cases, be disclosed. If welfare officers are to discharge their duty of frankly and fully reporting to their social services committee, it is essential that they should be able to do so without the risk of their reports being later publicly disclosed. A possible exception would be the case where the officer is motivated by personal hostility to an interested party.

III. EFFECTS OF WARDSHIP

When a minor is made a ward of court custody over him, in the wide meaning of that term, vests in the court,[14] and it is therefore able to issue orders concerning various aspects of his upbringing. A parent or guardian of the ward is then subject to those orders and to general supervision by the court, just as a guardian, or any officer, appointed by it would be.[15] Consequently, defiance of any order not only renders him liable to be deprived of powers, such as care and control, which still reside with him,[16] but also constitutes contempt of court.

If the court is to exercise effective control, it is essential that it be kept fully informed of the minor's whereabouts and failure to assist it in this regard is equally a matter for contempt, of which a third party as much as the parent or guardian may be guilty.[17] To ensure control the court also has power to restrict removal of the minor out of the jurisdiction. We have seen[18]

[12] [1970] 1 All E.R. 1088; [1970] 1 W.L.R. 599 (C.A.).
[13] Boarding-out of Children Regulations 1955, reg. 10.
[14] See ORMROD, L. J., in *Re W. (an infant)*, [1964] Ch. 202, 210; [1963] 3 All E.R. 459, 462.
[15] *Johnstone* v. *Beattie* (1843), 10 Cl. & F. 42, 85 (H.L.).
[16] *Eyre* v. *Countess of Shaftesbury* (1724), 2 P. Wms. 103.
[17] Such is the court's insistence, the privilege of confidentiality between solicitor and client is not protected from it; *Ramsbotham* v. *Senior* (1869), L.R. 8 Eq. 575.
[18] *Ante*, Chapter 9, p. 298.

that in exercising this power the governing principle is s. 1 of the Guardianship of Minors Act 1971. If taking the minor abroad is in his best interests, permission will be granted even where the removal is intended to be permanent.

In many cases wardship proceedings are instituted by a parent anxious to secure care and control of his child. Logically the Family Law Reform Act 1969[19] has extended to those proceedings powers which may be exercised in custody disputes arising in matrimonial proceedings. In exceptional cases the court may commit the minor to the care of a local authority or, where care is given to a parent or third person, make a supervision order.

The consent of the court is necessary for the marriage of a ward[20] and, where a marriage or attempted marriage[1] takes place without that consent, the parties to it and any other person who has helped to bring it about, commits a contempt of court.[2] In deciding whether consent should be given the criterion is the ward's welfare. In applying it the court will, *inter alia*, take account of the respective means of the parties, but it is doubtful whether this factor carries the weight it once did. If, with the court's leave, the ward is validly married, his wardship does not cease until he attains majority.[3]

---

[19] Section 7.
[20] Marriage Act 1949, s. 3(6).
[1] *Warter* v. *Yorke* (1815), 19 Ves. 451.
[2] *Re H's Settlement, H.* v. *H.*, [1909] 2 Ch. 260.
[3] See *Re Elwes* (1958), *Times*, July 30.

CHAPTER 13

Education and Employment
of Children

Insofar as it exists, the right of a parent to determine his child's education is not simply a constituent part of the right to custody; it is distinct from it.[1] Nevertheless, in practice the two are usually inextricably involved in the same dispute and they have developed along parallel, though not identical, lines. Where education is an issue it is normally the child's religious upbringing which is involved, and for this reason the relationship between custody and education is here considered with regard to religion, although the same principles apply to secular education. If there is a dispute over the latter, it is likely to be associated with a dispute over religion, since a parent will want the child to attend a school where he will receive instruction in a particular faith. Occasionally, however, the issue may relate solely to secular matters.[2]

It will be seen[3] that certain courts have statutory jurisdiction to make orders concerning education. The term is not defined and, therefore, it is submitted, applies alike to religious and secular education. On the other hand, other provisions, under the Children Act 1948 and the Children and Young Persons Acts, relate only to religious upbringing.

A. RELIGIOUS EDUCATION

I. HISTORY OF PARENTAL RIGHT

1. The Legitimate Child

At common law and equity the right of the father concerning the religious education of his legitimate child was even stronger than his right to custody. Only rarely, where there was grave

---

[1] This is recognised, for example, by s. 4 of the Custody of Children Act, 1891, *infra.*
[2] See, for example, *Re S. (an infant)*, [1967] 1 All E.R. 202; [1967] 1 W.L.R. 396.   [3] *Infra*, p. 430.

misconduct on his part, did he forfeit his right, and it prevailed even in those cases where the child was living with the mother, so that the effect of bringing him up in the father's religion was likely to affect adversely her relationship with the child,[4] and even where the father was dead.[5] We have seen[6] that under the influence of statutory changes, which gave to the mother rights to claim custody of her legitimate child, greater attention began to be paid to the child's welfare in custody disputes and this change is becoming more pronounced by the close of the nineteenth century. It was not, however, accompanied by the same emphasis on the child's welfare *vis-à-vis* the father's right regarding religious education, although there were indications of some undermining of that right.[7]

If there is still a conflict of opinion as to whether s. 1 of the Guardianship of Infants Act 1925 further diminished the father's right of custody or merely declared existing law in making the child's welfare paramount, it was recognised by the Court of Appeal in *Re Collins (Infant)*[8] that the section materially affected his right concerning religious upbringing. The paramountcy of his right was replaced by that of the child's welfare, and this effect operates not only where there is a direct issue between living parents over the religious upbringing but also where there is an issue between the religious views of parents and either or both are dead.

2. The Illegitimate Child

The recognition of the legal right of the mother to custody of her illegitimate child was delayed until the last decade of the last century,[9] but, once accorded, recognition of her right to determine his religion soon followed,[10] and for some time

---

[4] *Hawksworth* v. *Hawksworth* (1871), 6 Ch.App. 539, where, *per* JAMES, L. J., the court was enjoined to have "sacred regard to the religion of the father".

[5] *Andrews* v. *Salt* (1873), 8 Ch.App. 622.

[6] *Ante*, Chapter 9, p. 258.

[7] See *Re McGrath (Infants)*, [1893] 1 Ch. 143 (C.A.); *Re Nevin (Infant)*, [1891] 2 Ch. 299 (C.A.), which should be compared with such cases as *Re Austin, Austin* v. *Austin* (1865), 4 D.J. & SN. 716; *Re Newbery* (1866), 1 Ch.App. 263.

[8] [1950] Ch. 498; [1950] 1 All E.R. 1057.

[9] *Ante*, Chapter 9, p. 302.

[10] *R.* v. *New* (1904), 20 T.L.R. 583 (C.A.), where the mother's religion played a large part in awarding her custody, although the child had lived for 10 years with a married couple as if they were her parents.

after s. 1 of the Guardianship of Infants Act 1925 had been enacted the right remained as strong as ever it had been. Indeed, in *Re Carroll*[11] the majority of the Court of Appeal[12] held that the section did not affect the mother's right so as to make the child's welfare paramount, since it was confined to cases where the dispute was between the mother and father of a legitimate child. This narrow construction of s. 1, which limited it to such parental disputes, having been rejected in *Re Collins*, the way was open for the Court of Appeal in *Re Aster (An Infant)*[13] (where the dispute was between the mother and father) to hold that the section applied to the illegitimate child as to the legitimate and therefore that it was the child's welfare and not the mother's right which was the paramount consideration. The same reasoning prevailed in *Re E. (An Infant)*[14] where the dispute was between the mother and a third person. Finally, in *J. v. C.*[15] the House of Lords disapproved of *Re Carroll*.

II. PRINCIPLES ON WHICH THE COURT ACTS WHEN DETERMINING DISPUTES OVER RELIGION

Although the child's welfare is paramount, there are, as in custody disputes, other matters to be considered. Thus, the court should still pay "serious heed to the religious wishes of the parents"[16] without having "sacred regard"[17] for them as they once did;[18] but, in so doing, it must, in accordance with the express directions of s. 1 of the Guardianship of Minors Act 1971, disregard from every point of view other than the child's welfare whether the father's claim in respect of the religious upbringing is superior to the mother's or *vice versa*.

In considering parental wishes the most relevant factor is the parent's past conduct. For example, a parent may have agreed to his child being brought up in a particular religion. Such an agreement, like one relating to custody, is void on

[11] [1931] K.B. 317; [1930] All E.R. Rep. 192...
[12] SCRUTTON and SLESSER, L. JJ., GREER, L. J., dissenting.
[13] [1955] 2 All E.R. 202; [1955] 1 W.L.R. 465.
[14] [1963] 3 All E.R. 874; [1964] 1 W.L.R. 51.
[15] [1970] A.C. 668; [1969] 1 All E.R. 788.
[16] *Per* UNGOED-THOMAS, J., in *J. v. C.*, [1969] 1 All E.R. at p. 801.
[17] *Per* JAMES, L. J., in *Hawksworth* v. *Hawksworth* (1871), 6 Ch.App. 539, at p. 542.
[18] *Supra*.

the ground of public policy,[19] except where it is contained in a separation deed made between the father and mother[20] and even then it will not be enforced if that is not for the child's benefit.[1] Nevertheless, the fact that the parent entered into the agreement is evidence of his having surrendered his right to determine the child's religion.[2] The same consequence may ensue where there has not been an agreement but the parent by his conduct over a period of time has acquiesced in the child's being brought up in a particular faith, especially if he has shown no interest in his upbringing.[3]

The court may also consult the wishes of the child, without being bound by them, and this is particularly desirable in order to assess the strength of his present religious convictions. There is no minimum age limit imposed by law, but, unless the child is exceptionally mature, he is not likely to be interviewed if he is under 11 or 12 years of age, and almost certainly not if he is under 8.[4] The older the child is the less likely will the court be to allow a change of religion against his wishes, since he may well have acquired firm convictions,[5] but apparently no minor has a legal right to choose his own religion.[6]

[19] See *ante*, Chapter 9, p. 265.
[20] Custody of Infants Act 1873, s. 2; *Condon* v. *Vollum* (1887), 57 L.T. 154.
[1] *Re Besant* (1879), 11 Ch.D. 508 (C.A.), *ante*, p. 265.
[2] *Lyons* v. *Blenkin* (1821), Jac. 245; *Andrews* v. *Salt* (1873), 8 Ch.App. 622, p. 637, *per* MELLISH, L. J.
[3] *Hill* v. *Hill* (1862), 31 L.J. Ch. 505.
[4] See Viscount CAVE in *Ward* v. *Laverty*, [1925] A.C. 101, 109. In that case a child aged 11 was consulted. See also *Stourton* v. *Stourton* (1857), 8 De G.M. & G. 760 (child was nearly 10). Children were not interviewed in *Hawksworth* v. *Hawksworth* (1871), 6 Ch.App. 539, (9); *In Re Newton (Infants)*, [1896] 1 Ch. 740, (11); *Re W., W.* v. *M.*, [1907] 2 Ch.. 557, (11).
[5] For change of religion see *infra*.
[6] *Re May, Eggar* v. *May*, [1917] 2 Ch. 126, where it was held that the child could not determine what his religion could be "until he has reached years of discretion", which the court fixed at 21. The decision is scarcely reconcilable with s. 4 of the Custody of Children Act 1891. This enabled the court to give effect to the parental right that the child be brought up in the parent's religion where custody was granted to some other person, but the court's power was subject to the limitation that "nothing in this Act contained shall . . . diminish the right which any child now possesses to the exercise of its own free choice". Since the Act was apparently concerned only with children who were minors, it impliedly recognised a right of choice at sometime (whatever it might have been) below that age. Although s. 4 has not been repealed, s. 1 of the Guardianship of Minors Act 1971, with its emphasis on the child's welfare, effectively renders it a dead letter. However, there is no modern enactment dealing with the age to choose one's own religion.

In seeking to ensure the child's welfare, a vital factor is the effects which any change of religion would be likely to have upon him, and, where applicable, upon other members of the family.[7] Much will depend upon his age and maturity. The mere fact that he was baptized into a particular faith is of little moment.[8] Far more significant are the fact that he has embarked on a course of religious education and the consequent strength of his existing convictions.[9] Where these are firmly held the court will almost certainly not make any order which is likely to cause him to abandon all religious belief.[10] In *Stourton* v. *Stourton*[11] a Roman Catholic died leaving a widow who gave birth to a posthumous child. About five years later the widow became a member of the Anglican Church and brought up her child, who had been baptized a Roman Catholic, as an Anglican until he was almost ten. Proceedings were then instituted by a relation of the father for making the infant a ward of court with a view to having him educated as a Roman Catholic. It was held that the mother should be appointed sole guardian, without any directions as to the child's religious education, the implication being that the child would continue to be brought up as an Anglican.

Difficulties sometimes arise where the person seeking custody or care and control has no faith or belongs to a religion different from that in which the child has been brought up. Considerations of material welfare may result in the court allowing the person custody or care and control but subject to his undertaking that he will bring up the child in the religion to which he is already committed. Such a solution may not, however, be in the child's long-term interests in that it may give rise to conflict within the family.[12] The court will have to

---

[7] If an older child has acquired strong convictions in a particular faith, it is likely that the court will insist that younger brothers and sisters living in the same family be brought up in the same faith; *Ward* v. *Laverty*, [1925] A.C. 101 (H.L.).

[8] *Stourton* v. *Stourton* (1857), 8 De G.M. & G. 760, *infra;* see also UNGOED-THOMAS, J., in *Re C. (M.A.) (an infant)*, [1966] 1 All E.R. 838; [1966] 1 W.L.R. 646.

[9] *Re M. (Infants)*, [1967] 3 All E.R. 1071; [1967] 1 W.L.R. 1479 (C.A.).

[10] But considerations of material welfare might possibly prove overriding.

[11] *Supra*, n. 8. See also *Re Newton (Infants)*, [1896] 1 Ch. 740 (C.A.); *Ward* v. *Laverty*, [1925] A.C. 101 (H.L.).

[12] The danger was emphasised by the Court of Appeal in *B. (M.)* v. *B. (R.)*, [1968] 3 All E.R. 170; [1968] 1 W.L.R. 1182.

weigh the risks carefully. *J.* v. *C.* illustrates the problem.[13] There foster parents were Protestants and the foster child was the son of Spanish parents who were Roman Catholics. An order was made in 1965, when the child was seven years old, that the foster parents be given care and control on the condition that he was brought up as a Roman Catholic. Later, when the time came for him and P, a natural child of the foster parents, to go to boarding school, P won a place at a Church of England choir school. The foster child failed to gain a place at a Roman Catholic choir school, but was offered a place at a Church of England school. The foster parents applied to the court for him to be brought up in the Church of England. The natural parents were opposed to this and applied for care and control to be given to them. UNGOED-THOMAS, J. could find no justification for disturbing his earlier order concerning care and control, but was equally insistent that there should be no change in the child's religious education.[14]

The courts have consistently declined to discriminate between one faith and another,[15] but they may be ready to hold that a particular form of religious upbringing is inherently harmful to the child. In *Re C (an infant)*[16] both parents were originally members of the Exclusive Brethren but the father later withdrew from the sect. The mother then left the father, taking their child, aged 10, with her. It was held that the requirement of the sect that members should not eat with non-members was intolerable and odious to the vast majority of the people and that the child's welfare demanded that he should live with his father and not his mother. In a case of that kind, therefore, it is better that the child be brought up without any religious belief. Otherwise it may be that the

---

[13] [1970] A.C. 668; [1969] 1 All E.R. 788, (H.L.).
   See similarly *Re E (an infant)*, [1963] 3 All E.R. 874; [1964] 1 W.L.R. 51, where an order was made giving care and control to a Jewish couple on the condition that they bring up a ward of court as a Roman Catholic.
[14] In affirming the decision concerning care and control the House of Lords did not direct itself explicitly to the question of religion.
   For a criticism of the requirement in *J.* v. *C.* that the child be brought up as a Catholic see Samuels, "*Custody and the Welfare of the Child*" (1970), 114 Sol. Jo. 365.
[15] See Lord EVERSHED, M.R., in *Re Collins*, [1950] 1 Ch. 498, at p. 502. For 19th century expressions of opinion to the same effect see, for example, *Re Clarke* (1882), 21 Ch.D. 817, 823 and *Re Newton (Infants)*, [1896] 1 Ch. 740, 752.   [16] (1964), *Times*, August 1.

courts will still take the view, as they did in the last century, that some form of religion is preferable to no religion at all.[17] They are unlikely, however, to show today the positive antipathy they formerly showed towards atheistic beliefs.[18]

III.   JURISDICTION TO MAKE ORDERS RELATING
TO RELIGIOUS EDUCATION

As part of its inherent jurisdiction, the Family Division of the High Court may make orders relating to the education of a minor who is a ward of court. It, and any county court exercising the statutory jurisdiction, has express powers to make similar orders in respect of children of the family under 18 in proceedings for nullity, divorce or judicial separation.[19] However, there are no such express powers in proceedings in those courts based on neglect to maintain[20] or in proceedings under the Matrimonial Proceedings (Magistrates' Courts) Act 1960 or the Guardianship of Minors Act 1971, but the exclusion is, it is submitted, of little practical importance, because in all those cases an order for custody may be made and this power will enable the court to include a provision relating to education,[1] both religious and secular. The only possible significance is that, where there is express reference to education, the court can make an order with regard to it without making one concerning custody.[2] Moreover, a person against whom an order for maintenance is made under the 1971 Act can be required to contribute towards the expense of his child's education, since maintenance includes education.[3] Thus, (1) if the mother is given custody, the father may be required so to

---

[17] The Scottish courts have adopted this line; see *Mackay* v. *Mackay*, 1957, S.L.T. 17; *M'Clements* v. *M'Clements*, 1958 S.C. 286.

[18] See *Shelley* v. *Westbrooke* (1817), Jac. 266n.; *Re Besant* (1879), 11 Ch.D. 508 (C.A.).

[19] Matrimonial Proceedings and Property Act 1970, ss. 18 and 27(1). For the limits of an order as to custody or education see *ante*, Chapter 9, p. 279; and see *ibid.*, for the protective provisions of s. 17 relating to arrangements for the child's welfare, which includes his education and training (ss. 17(6) and 27(1)).

[20] *Ibid.*, ss. 6 and 19.

[1] The power is consistent with a long established rule that the person having custody *prima facie* has the right to determine the child's education; *Hall* v. *Hall* (1749), 3 Atk. 721.

[2] Section 18(1) of the Matrimonial Proceedings and Property Act 1970 speaks of orders for "custody and education", but it is submitted that the term is to be construed disjunctively.   [3] Section 20(2).

contribute; (2) if a person is appointed sole guardian to the exclusion of the parent, the parent may have to contribute; and (3) if there is a dispute between joint guardians, one of whom is a parent, the parent may equally be ordered to contribute.[4] It is submitted that these statutory references to education relate to religious as well as secular education, just as the power to include in a custody order a direction concerning education applies to both forms.

The inherent jurisdiction of the Family Division and the statutory jurisdiction of a court under the Guardianship of Minors Act 1971 have special relevance to guardianship. A guardian is not entitled to choose the ward's religion, but *prima facie* is obliged to bring him up in the religion in which the parents would have brought him up, unless the ward has acquired strong convictions of his own, in which case the guardian should see that those convictions are protected. To impose his own choice of religion on the ward is a ground for removing him from office[5] If he is uncertain about the parental intentions concerning the education of their child or if the parents were in dispute over it or if he is doubtful about the strength of the child's convictions or considers the particular religious upbringing harmful, he should apply to have the child made a ward of court and seek the directions of the court which should act in accordance with the principles already considered.[6] These principles will also operate where there is a dispute between a guardian and a surviving parent or between two guardians.[7]

IV. RELIGIOUS UPBRINGING OF CHILDREN IN CARE OF PERSONS
OTHER THAN PARENTS OR GUARDIANS

It has already been pointed out[8] that a feature of much of the legislation relating to children is the responsibility it imposes on persons looking after them to take account of their religious persuasion. Thus, a local authority who have received a child

---

[4] Sections 9, 10 and 11; and see further Chapter 14, p. 456.
[5] *Di Savini* v. *Lousada* (1870), W.R. 425.
   Moreover, although the guardian may be ready to see that the child continues his past education, a subsequent change of his own faith may also be a ground for removal; *F.* v. *F.*, [1902] 1 Ch. 688.
[6] *Supra.*
[7] See Guardianship of Minors Act 1971, s. 7.
[8] *Ante*, Chapter 5, p. 168.

into their care under s. 1 of the Children Act 1948 and are willing to allow a relative or friend to take over the care must try to see that the person is of the same religious persuasion as the child or undertakes to bring him up in that persuasion.[9] A similar obligation is imposed on an authority who intend to board out a child with foster parents.[10] Where the authority have assumed parental rights under a resolution passed in accordance with s. 2 of the 1948 Act or as a result of a care order they must not cause the person in their care to be brought up in any religious creed other than that in which he would have been brought up but for the resolution or the order.[11] Moreover, when a person in care is placed in a community home or a voluntary home the local authority or other person responsible for carrying on the home must see that facilities for religious instruction appropriate to his persuasion are provided.[12]

B. SECULAR EDUCATION

I. PARENTAL DUTIES

If the common law was not prepared to impose on a parent a direct duty to maintain his child,[13] it would have been surprising if it had imposed a duty to educate him.[14] Moreover, it would have been unrealistic to have done so as long as a comprehensive system of education did not exist. The consequence was that education depended upon the whim of parents who could afford to pay for it. If they could, their children were sent to Charity Schools, most of which appeared, with varying standards of education, in the eighteenth and nineteenth centuries. As with so many other spheres of activity affecting children, the advancement of education owed much to indivi-

---

[9] Children Act 1948, s. 1(3).
[10] Boarding-Out of Children Regulations 1955, reg. 19.
[11] Children Act 1948, s. 3(7); Children and Young Persons Act 1969, s. 24(3).
[12] Community Homes Regulations 1972, reg. 8; Administration of Children's Homes Regulations, 1951, reg. 4.
[13] See *post*, Chapter 14, p. 453.
[14] In *Hodges* v. *Hodges* (1796), Peake Add. Cas. 79, it was recognised that no duty existed.

dual philanthropists and reformers.[15] Yet, it was not until 1870 that a system of public education was introduction. The main cause of the delay was religious dissension. This, for example, was still apparent when the State began in 1833 to assist in the endowment of schools: Treasury grants were carefully divided between the rival National Society (representing the Church of England) and the British and Foreign Schools Society (a non-conformist organisation). Had they been able to agree on the religious tests to be imposed on teachers, legislation might have been enacted earlier than it was. Some impetus to the movement for reform was, however, given by the creation from 1857 onwards of Industrial Schools.[16]

One of the main objects of the Elementary Education Act 1870 was to make education more readily available by enabling schools to be established in districts where there was serious deficiency, but it was the Elementary Education Act 1876 that introduced a compulsory system throughout the country and imposed on the parent the duty to ensure that his child received elementary instruction in reading, writing and arithmetic. The extension of educational facilities gradually assured children of wider instruction, but the scope of the statutory duty remained unaltered until the Education Act 1944.

Duty to Secure Education of Children

The present parental duty is to see that a child of compulsory school age[17] receives efficient full-time education suitable to his age, ability and aptitude by regular attendance at school

---

[15] Bentham, for example, was a strong advocate of a system of public education. So was Colquhoun, who published a Tract on *"A new and appropriate system of education for the labouring people"* (1806).

Such individual interests probably influenced Henry Brougham in 1816 to introduce, though unsuccessfully, a Bill to provide a general education to be financed by local rates.

[16] See *ante*, Chapter 2, p. 19.

[17] The age extends from 5 to 16, the upper limit having been raised from 15 as from September 1, 1972 (Education Act 1944, s. 35; Raising of School Leaving Age Order 1972). For children receiving special educational treatment (*infra*, p. 442) see s. 38.

Under s. 9 of the Education Act 1962 there are two school leaving dates. For the child who attains the upper age limit during the period 1 September to 31 January the date is the end of the spring term following the date when he attains the age; otherwise it is the end of the summer term.

or otherwise.[18] It extends not only to a parent but also to a guardian and every person having actual custody of the child; but where another has custody the parent is not exempted from liability,[19] and where the child is living with both parents either or both may be held responsible.[20] In the case of a guardian, however, he must see that the ward receives not only an education in accordance with s. 36, but also one that accords with the ward's position in life and expectations.[1] This additional obligation is of long standing, but it was laid down at a time when there was no compulsory education and its efficacy may therefore be questioned. Would it be a breach of his duties if the guardian insisted that his wealthy ward's interests were best served by attendance at a comprehensive secondary school and not at a public school? It is a nice point.

Breach of the Duty: School Attendance Order

The responsibility for seeing that the parent fulfils his duty lies with the local education authority. They may, for example, consider that a parent who is himself educating his children at home is not providing adequate facilities for the purpose or that they are not receiving lessons in prescribed courses of study.[2] Whenever it appears to them that there is a failure to perform the duty they must serve a notice on the parent requiring him to satisfy them to the contrary.[3] If he fails to do so, they must serve on him a notice that they intend to serve a school attendance order requiring him to cause the child to

---

[18] Section 36. The parent is relieved of the duty during any period in which it is not practicable for him to arrange for his child to become a registered pupil at a school because the proprietors have refused to admit children during the currency of a school term (Education (Miscellaneous Provisions) Act 1948, s. 4(2)). For the scope of the duty see Dutchman-Smith, 114 Sol. Jo. 921.

[19] *London School Board* v. *Jackson* (1881), 7 Q.B.D. 502.
Subsequent references to a parent include a guardian and anyone having actual custody.

[20] *Plunkett* v. *Alker*, [1954] 1 Q.B. 420; [1954] 1 All E.R. 396, where in such circumstances the mother was alone charged and held liable, under s. 54(6) of the 1944 Act, for her neglect in allowing her son once more to be in a verminous condition after he had already been cleansed under a compulsory cleansing order.

[1] *Powel* v. *Cleaver* (1789), 2 Bro. C.C. 499.

[2] *Cp. Baker* v. *Earl*, [1960] Crim.L.R. 363 where the mother, who had no educational qualifications, merely encouraged her four children, aged between 10 and 14, to follow at home any subject which interested them.
See also *Re B.* (*Infants*), [1962] Ch. 201; [1961] 3 All E.R. 276, (C.A.).

[3] He must be given at least 14 days in which to comply.

become a registered pupil at a specified school, unless within 14 days he himself selects a school. A school selected by him will then be named in the attendance order, unless the Secretary of State otherwise directs or unless the authority consider that that school is unsuitable to the child's age, ability or aptitude or that attendance there would involve them in unreasonable expense, in which case they may, after notifying the parent of their intention, apply to the Secretary of State for a direction as to the school to be named.[4]

The authority must, on the application of the parent, amend an attendance order by substituting a school for that named in the order, unless they consider that the proposed change is unreasonable or inexpedient in the interests of the child. They must revoke an order on the ground that arrangements have been made for the child to receive efficient full-time education otherwise than at school, unless they consider that no satisfactory arrangements have been made.[5]

Failure to comply with an attendance order renders a parent criminally liable,[6] unless he proves that he is causing the child to receive full-time education otherwise than at school.[7] In the event of acquittal the court *may* direct that the order ceases to operate, but a change of circumstances might require the authority to take further action under s. 37.[8] Apart from such a direction an order remains in force so long as the child is of compulsory school age, unless revoked by the authority.[9]

The sanctions for enforcement of a school attendance order are not only the penalties of the criminal law but also the power of a court convicting a parent of an offence under s. 37 to direct that the juvenile be brought before a juvenile court under

[4] Section 37(1)-(3), as amended by the Education (Miscellaneous Provisions) Act 1953, s. 10.
[5] Section 37(4). A parent whose request is not met by the authority may apply to the Secretary of State for a direction on the matter.
[6] For the penalties see s. 40(1).
[7] *Ibid.*, sub-s. (5).
It has been pointed out that the effect of the proviso would appear to be that it would not be a defence for the parent to show that the child was attending a school other than that named in the order; see Taylor and Saunders, *The New Law of Education*, 7th edn., p. 149.
[8] See sub-s. (6).
[9] Sub-section (7).
For the purpose of prosecutions under s. 37 or s. 39 (*infra*), a child is presumed to be of compulsory school age at a material time unless the parent proves otherwise; Education (Miscellaneous Provisions) Act 1948, s. 9(1).

s. 1 of the Children and Young Persons Act 1969 as being in need of care or control.[10] The prerogative jurisdiction of the High Court is not, however, available to assist the local education authority in enforcement of the order. In *Re B. (Infants)*[11] it was held that a child who is the subject of an order cannot be made a ward of court so as to enable the High Court to give directions as to enforcement. The decision follows the principle laid down in *Re M. (An Infant)*,[12] that the court will not intervene in relation to duties or discretions vested by statute in a local authority; but, as we have seen,[13] in other cases the court has been ready to intervene in exceptional cases and to supplement duties and discretions.[14]

Duty to Secure Regular Attendance at School

Distinct from the above duty is that which requires the parent to see that his child regularly attends the school at which he is a registered pupil.[15] If the child fails to attend regularly, the parent is guilty of an offence,[16] whether or not a school attendance order has been served on him and whether or not the parent is aware of the child's absences,[17] unless the child's absence is due to any of the following reasons. The first three listed apply to children who are day pupils and to boarders at school, the remainder only to the former.

(*a*) Leave to be absent was granted by a person authorised by the manager, governors or proprietor of the school.[18]

(*b*) The child was prevented from attending because of sickness or an unavoidable cause.

The cause must be one that affects the child himself and not anyone else.[19]

---

[10] See *infra*, p. 438.   [11] *Supra*, p. 434, n. 2.
[12] [1961] Ch. 328; [1961] 1 All E.R. 788 (C.A.).
[13] *Ante*, Chapter 12, p. 413.
[14] Quaere *Re B.* might have been differently decided had it come up for decision after the courts had considered the relationship between the prerogative jurisdiction and s. 1 of the Children Act 1948.
    For a criticism of the decision see Yale (1961) C.L.J. 137.
[15] Education Act 1944, s. 39.   [16] For the penalties see s. 40(1).
[17] *Crump* v. *Gilmore* (1969), 113 Sol. Jo. 998.
[18] There are strict limits on granting leave to enable a child to undertake employment during school hours or to take holidays during term time. (Schools Regulations 1959, reg. 12, as amended by Schools (Amendment) Regulations 1969).
[19] *Cp. Jenkins* v. *Howells*, [1949] 2 K.B. 218; [1949] 1 All E.R. 942, where the child had been kept at home to look after the home and younger brothers and sisters because of the parent's illness.

(*c*) His absence was on a day exclusively set apart for religious observance by the religious body to which his parent [20] belongs.

(*d*) The school at which the child is a registered pupil is not within walking distance of his home and no suitable arrangements[1] have been made by the local education authority for transport to, or boarding accommodation at or near, the school or for enabling him to attend a school nearer to his home.

"Walking distance" means, in relation to a child under eight, two miles and in the case of any other child three miles. Regrettably the definition has been narrowly construed, for distance is to be determined from the point of view of the shortest route, not of the child's safety.[2] It is unfortunate that financial implications can weigh more heavily than consideration for the child's welfare.

This last ground obviously has no application where the child has no fixed abode, but if proceedings are taken under s.39 against a parent who is engaged in a trade or business which requires him to travel from place to place he is not guilty of an offence if the child has attended a school as regularly as the parent's occupation permits.[3]

In addition to the above reasons, a parent is protected from liability under s. 39 where his child, being suspected of being verminous, has been excluded from attending school pending his examination or cleansing.[4] Otherwise, the list of reasons set out in the section is exhaustive.[5] Thus, in *Spiers* v. *Warrington Corporation*[6] a 14-year-old girl who had had rheumatic fever on two occasions was sent to school dressed in trousers to keep

---

[20] For the meaning of "parent" see *supra*, p. 434, n. 19.
   Difficulties could arise over the interpretation of this provision where a person other than the parent has actual custody and the religion of that person and that of the parent differ.
[1] See *Surrey County Council* v. *Ministry of Education*, [1953] 1 All E.R. 705; [1953] 1 W.L.R. 516.
[2] *Shaxted* v. *Ward*, [1954] 1 All E.R. 336; [1954] 1 W.L.R. 306.
[3] In the case of a child aged six or over there must, however, have been at least 200 attendances during the 12 months ending on the date on which the proceedings were instituted.
   This defence similarly operates where a person is charged under s. 10 of the C. & Y.P. Act 1933 as a vagrant who takes a child from place to place with him and so prevents the child from receiving efficient full-time education.
[4] Education Act 1944, s. 54(7).
[5] Formerly under the Education Act 1921, s. 49 it was open to the parent to put forward any "reasonable excuse"; *London County Council* v. *Maher*, [1929] 2 K.B. 97, (D.C.).
[6] [1954] 1 Q.B. 61; [1953] 2 All E.R. 1052.

her warm. This form of dress was contrary to a school rule, but the headmistress told the parents that she would waive it if a medical certificate were produced saying that trousers were necessary. No certificate was produced, and so whenever the girl appeared at school in trousers she was sent home. It was held that a headteacher had the right and power to prescribe discipline for his school, that to send one's child to school knowing that he would not be admitted amounted to failure to see that he attended regularly and that the father of the girl was therefore guilty of an offence under s. 39.[7]

The effect of the section, therefore, is that the reasonableness of the parent's attitude is irrelevant and the teacher's authority must override his wishes. Not surprisingly it has occasioned sharp criticism in some quarters. Its implications are not confined to questions of whether parents shall have the right to choose the mode of dress or the length of hair that their children shall wear. A parent would not, for example, be legally justified in keeping his child away from school on the ground that he considers that specific contents of a sex-education book used in the school are exposing his child to moral danger. Nor in such a case is the general duty of the local education authority to educate a child in accordance with the parent's wishes likely to be of any avail.[8]

Care Proceedings Concerning Juveniles Not Receiving Proper Education

Proceedings against a parent for an offence under s. 37 or s. 39 of the Education Act 1944 or under s. 10 of the Children and Young Persons Act 1933[9] may be instituted only by a local education authority. Before doing so the authority must consider whether it would be appropriate instead of or as well as instituting those proceedings to bring the juvenile before a juvenile court under s. 1 of the Children and Young Persons Act 1969.[10] For example, if the juvenile is nearing the upper

---

[7] But the scope of the teacher's authority should be carefully noted. It is to refuse admission to a pupil on each occasion when he presents himself at the school. The teacher does not, it is submitted, have the power to issue a general directive that admission is refused until compliance with the school rules.

[8] See s. 76, *infra*.   [9] See *supra*.

[10] Education Act 1944, s. 40(2), as substituted by C. & Y.P. Act 1969, Sched. 5, para. 13; C. & Y.P. Act 1933, s. 10(1A), as inserted by C. & Y.P. Act 1969, Sched. 5, para. 2.

limit of the compulsory school age they should carefully assess the advantage of care proceedings. If the only object is to ensure regular attendance at school for the remaining short period of compulsory education, intervention would scarcely be justifiable. On the other hand, the truancy might indicate a serious risk of delinquency.[11] Apart from the discretion of the authority, the court which convicts the parent of an offence under s. 37 or before which he is charged with an offence against s. 39 may direct the authority to proceed under s. 1 of the 1969 Act.[12]

Care proceedings may be brought under s. 1 where the juvenile of compulsory school age is not receiving full-time education for any of the reasons covered by ss. 37 and 39 of the 1944 Act or s. 10 of the 1933 Act.[13] But, as with all other proceedings under s. 1, it must also be shown that the juvenile is in need of care or control.[14] Where the juvenile is brought before the juvenile court because of non-compliance with a school attendance order made in respect of him, but the relevant condition in s. 1 of the 1969 Act is not satisfied, the court may direct that the school attendance order shall cease to be in force.[15]

II. PARENTAL RIGHTS

In examining the parental duties concerning secular education oblique reference has been made to certain parental rights. Thus, the parent has the basic right to secure his child's education otherwise than by sending him regularly to a school, although the right is rarely exercised. Moreover, when a local authority are compelled to take steps to make a school attendance order the parent has the right, subject to overriding considerations, to choose a particular school. But over and above these there is imposed on the Secretary of State and local

---

[11] If proceedings are taken, similar considerations should weigh with the court in deciding the kind of order to make.

[12] Education Act 1944, s. 40(3), as substituted by C. & Y.P. Act 1969, Sched. 5, para. 13.
    Note that in the case of proceedings under s. 39 a direction may be given whether or not the parent is convicted of an offence.

[13] C. & Y.P. Act 1969, ss. 1(2) (e) and 2(8) (b).   [14] *Ante*, Chapter 2, p. 24.

[15] Education Act 1944, s. 40(4), as substituted by C. & Y.P. Act 1969, Sched. 5, para. 13.

education authorities a general duty to have regard to the wishes of the parents.

Section 76 of the Education Act 1944 states:

> "In the exercise and performance of all powers and duties conferred and imposed on them by this Act the [Secretary of State] and local education authorities shall have regard to the general principle that, so far as is compatible with the provision of efficient instruction and training and the avoidance of unreasonable public expenditure, pupils are to be educated in accordance with the wishes of their parents."

Clearly, the provisos concerning compatibility with efficient instruction and the avoidance of unreasonable public expenditure are themselves marked restrictions on the general principle, but there is the further limitation that the authority is not precluded by the section from taking into account other matters. This point has been considered in connection with the duty of an authority to make sufficient schools available,[16] either by providing them themselves or by making arrangements with the proprietors of direct-grant or independent schools.[17] In *Watt* v. *Kesteven County Council*[18] it was held, *inter alia*, that, provided that they fulfil this general duty,[19] they are not obliged to pay tuition fees at an independent school chosen by the parent but with which they have made no arrangements; and in *Cumings* v. *Birkenhead Corporation*[20] the authority were held entitled to insist on grounds of accommodation that children leaving Roman Catholic primary schools should attend Roman Catholic secondary schools, although the parents objected to this restriction.

The operation of s. 76 in relation to another duty of the local education authority has led to a further restrictive interpretation of the section. Section 11 of the Education Act 1944 empowers an authority to make and revise development plans with regard to primary and secondary schools in its area, and

---

[16] Under s. 8 of the Education Act 1944.
[17] Education (Miscellaneous Provisions) Act 1953, s. 6.
[18] [1955] 1 Q.B. 408; [1955] 1 All E.R. 473 (C.A.).
[19] If they have not, the duty can only be enforced by the Secretary of State (under s. 99 of the 1944 Act) and not by an action in a court of law; see further, Taylor and Saunders, *op. cit.*, p. 90.
[20] [1971] 2 All E.R. 881; [1971] 2 W.L.R. 1458 (C.A.).

disputes with parents may arise over the provision of comprehensive secondary education in place of grammar school education, as occurred in *Wood* v. *Ealing London Borough Council*,[1] where the authority proposed, without any consultation with the parents, to bring in comprehensive schools. The plaintiffs, representing parents' groups, sued for an injunction to prevent the scheme. The action was dismissed, firstly on the ground that s. 11 did not confer any right on parents generally to be consulted as to a plan, and secondly because s. 76 imposed an obligation only to consult individual parents, not local parents as a body; and even then only about the curriculum, religious instruction, co-education and the like and not about the size of a school or conditions of entry.[2] Moreover, the fact that they must have regard to the wishes of parents, does not require the authority to give effect to them.[3]

The one matter on which the wishes of parents are effectively protected is religious instruction. A parent may not only request that his child be excused from attendance at the daily act of collective worship and at classes of religious instruction which schools are obliged to provide,[4] but also, if he wishes him to receive a particular kind of denominational instruction which cannot be provided in the school which the child attends or by his being transferred to another school, he can require the local education authority to make arrangements for the child to receive the instruction elsewhere during school hours, provided that the authority are satisfied that the arrangements will interfere only with his attendance at school at the beginning or end of the daily school session.[5]

---

[1] [1967] Ch. 364; [1966] 3 All E.R. 514.

[2] The implementation of a plan may, however, be defeated by the Articles of the particular school, as in *Lee* v. *Enfield London Borough Council* (1967), 111 Sol. Jo. 772, where parents were granted an injunction to restrain the implementation of a plan to admit children to a grammar school on a non-selective basis because the plan did not accord with the school's articles since it had not taken into account, *inter alia*, the wishes of the parent.

The decision proved to be a Pyrrhic victory for the parents because it was subsequently held in *Lee* v. *Secretary of State for Education and Science* (1967), 111 Sol. Jo. 756 that the Minister may alter school Articles, provided that he allows reasonable time for representations to be made.

[3] See *Cumings* v. *Birkenhead Corporation, supra.*

[4] Education Act 1944, ss. 25 and 26, which apply to county primary and secondary schools. There are special rules for different kinds of voluntary schools (ss. 27 and 28).

[5] Section 25(5).

Education and Employment of Children

III. EDUCATION OF SPECIAL CATEGORIES OF CHILDREN

(1) Children Under Five Years of Age

In fulfilling their duty to provide primary schools a local education authority must have regard to the need for providing nursery schools for pupils aged between two and five. Alternatively, where they consider provision of such schools is inexpedient, they may provide in other schools nursery classes[6] mainly for those aged three to five.[7]

The educational needs of children under five were recognised by the Education Act 1921 which conferred power on local education authorities to provide nursery education. Although the power has been replaced by a duty, it is a qualified duty in that it leaves to an authority a discretion as to the priority it will give to nursery education. Only comparatively recently has greater attention been paid to it. The Plowden Report[8] and the Seebohm Report[9] stressed its importance, but the latter, recognising that there was not an immediate possibility of fully meeting the need, recommended that the social services departments of local authorities should be given responsibility for providing play groups for children under five.

(2) Children Requiring Special Educational Treatment

Local education authorities must also have regard to the need for providing, in special schools or otherwise, special educational treatment for children suffering from any mental or physical disability.[10] Normally provision is made in special schools, but, where that is impracticable or the disability is not serious, arrangements may be made for treatment to be given in another school maintained or assisted by the local education

[6] Education Act 1944, s. 8(2)(b).
[7] School Regulations, reg. 3(1).
[8] Children and their Primary Schools, para. 314.
[9] Cmnd. 3703, paras. 196, 202-210.
[10] Education Act 1944, ss. 8(2) (c) and 9(5).
   The categories of handicapped pupils requiring special educational treatment are: the blind, partially sighted, deaf, partially hearing, educationally subnormal, epileptic, maladjusted, physically handicapped, those suffering from speech defect and those who need a change of environment or cannot, without risk to their health or educational development, be educated under the normal regime of ordinary schools; Handicapped Pupils and Special Schools Regulations, 1959, S.I. 1959 No. 365, as amended by S.I. 1962 No. 2073 and S.I. 1966 No. 1576.

authority,[11] and in extraordinary circumstances a pupil may receive primary or secondary education otherwise than at school.[12] However, a special obligation is imposed on an authority to ensure that pupils suffering from the dual handicap of blindness and deafness or from autism or other forms of early childhood psychosis or from acute dyslexia shall, so far as is practicable, be educated in a school maintained or assisted by the authority.[13]

A pupil registered at a special school must not be withdrawn from it without the authority's consent, but, if the parent's request for that consent is refused, he may seek a direction from the Secretary of State. The latter cannot direct that the child attends another special school unless the parent consents or unless attendance there is expedient because of the nature and extent of the child's disability.[14]

The local education authority must ascertain which children in their area require special educational treatment. They may do this by requiring the parent of any child who has attained the age of 2 to submit the child to medical examination, and, in the light of the medical report and any reports from teachers or others, they must decide whether special educational treatment is required.[15] A weakness of the present duty is that it does not prescribe the extent to which an authority must pursue its investigations. In practice its attention to the fact that a child may need special treatment is most likely to arise from school reports.[16]

Formerly, local education authorities were required to ascertain which children were unsuitable for education at school[17] and arrangements for the special care and training of severely subnormal children fell upon the local health authority, who provided junior training centres for the purpose. In addition there were those children whose condition was so severe that

[11] Education Act 1944, s. 33(2); Education (Miscellaneous Provisions) Act 1953, s. 6(2).
[12] Education Act 1944, s. 56. Note also the right of the parent to arrange for his child to receive education otherwise than at a school (*supra*, p. 434).
[13] Chronically Sick and Disabled Persons Act 1970, ss. 25-27.
[14] Education Act 1944, s. 38(2) and (3).
[15] Education Act 1944, s. 34.
[16] *Cf.* Taylor and Saunders, *op. cit.*, p. 143.
[17] Education Act 1944, ss. 57, 57A and 57B, as substituted by the Mental Health Act 1959.

they were confined to hospital wards. The Education (Handicapped Children) Act 1970 discontinues this classification, and all handicapped children now come under s. 34 of the Education Act 1944, with the responsibility for training centres and their staff being transferred from the Health to the Education service.[18]

A remarkable feature of the relevant law is that it leaves with the local education authority exclusive powers to make arrangements for the educational treatment of handicapped children and gives no power to the juvenile court to make an order certifying a child to be handicapped and to arrange for that treatment.[19] Since the policy of the Children and Young Persons Act 1969 was to expand local authority control over juveniles, it is hardly surprising that the Act did not repair the omission.

C. EMPLOYMENT OF CHILDREN

The history of employment of children has been so frequently and graphically examined that there is little room for fresh comment on it,[20] but one aspect which has largely escaped attention is the influence of parental rights on it. This was exerted in two ways. Firstly, the virtual absoluteness of the father's right of custody[1] was relied on to justify both child slavery, *i.e.*, the right of the father to sell his children to an employer,[2] and "free" child labour, *i.e.*, his right to arrange with an employer for his children to attend for work daily. Secondly, his right to the services of his child indirectly contributed to the wretched conditions which prevailed under the system of apprenticeship. To enable the father to enforce the right against anyone who unlawfully interfered with it, it was essential to impute to him and his child a master-servant relationship, since actions for loss of service could only be founded on that relationship.[3] The temptation to equate the two relationships for other purposes could hardly have been

---

[18] Some 32,000 children were affected by the transfer, 24,000 attending training centres and 8,000 who were confined to hospital units.
[19] See Watson, *The Child and the Magistrate*, p. 139.
[20] A comprehensive account is given by W. Clarke Hall, *The Queen's Reign for Children*.   [1] See *ante*, Chapter 9.
[2] The common law rule that an agreement to surrender custody of one's child is contrary to public policy and void (*ante*, p. 265) seems to have been ignored.   [3] See further *infra*, p. 451.

Employment of Children

resisted. Not until the nineteenth century was it firmly laid down that the father's powers of punishment were limited to those of reasonable chastisement,[4] and it seems that earlier law countenanced excessive powers of paternal control.[5] If, therefore, the father could invoke those powers in relation to his child of whom he could demand the performance of services, why should the master not insist on the same powers in controlling and punishing his apprentice? The analogy was able to give to the barbaric conditions of apprenticeship an aura of respectability.

Attempts to mitigate the severities of child labour appeared from the beginning of the nineteenth century. Broadly, the relevant legislation of the century regulated the hours and conditions of employment of children employed in the textile industry, as chimney-sweeps, in the mines, in non-textile industries, in agriculture and in the entertainment industry – in that chronological order;[6] but its efficacy was variable, partly because of lack of machinery for enforcement and partly because of "restrictive and hostile judicial interpretations".[7] A notable feature of the first Factory Act in 1802, which was concerned, *inter alia*, with children employed in textile mills, was a provision that they were to receive instruction in "reading, writing and arithmetic" but this, like the remainder of the Act, was blatantly ignored by employers. Moreover, the Act only applied to apprentices and this led to increased use of "free" child labour in the industry. The next principal Act, the Factory and Workshops Act 1844, was more far-reaching. It extended to a number of classes of child labour;[8] it raised the minimum age of employment and reduced the hours of employment; it introduced the principle of factory inspection, including safety precautions for children; and it insisted on proper school attendance for them. It remained the principal Act until superseded by the Factory and Workshop Act 1878, which set the pattern for modern factory legislation.

[4] *R. v. Hopley* (1860), 2 F. & F. 202.   [5] See *ante*, Chapter 6, p. 210.
[6] Efforts were also made to regulate the apprenticeship of pauper children. The apprenticeship statutes of Elizabeth I were repealed in 1814 (54 Geo. III, c. 96) and replaced by an Act of 1816 (56 Geo. III, c. 139); see Holdsworth, *History of English Law*, vol. XIII, p. 313.
[7] Hepple and O'Higgins, *Individual Employment Law*, p. 89, para. 9-32.
[8] A major omission was child employment in brickfields, a defect cured by the Factory and Workshop Act 1871.

Education and Employment of Children

The notorious complexity of the modern law governing the employment of minors is partly explained by overlapping classifications of the persons affected, partly by the variety of sources of specific restrictions (many of which have complicated exceptions) and partly by the general restrictions which override them.

(1) EMPLOYMENT OF CHILDREN UNDER SCHOOL-LEAVING AGE

For purposes of employment minors have been basically classified into children under school-leaving age[9] (*i.e.*, formerly under 15) and young persons, but, for certain kinds of employment, a distinction has been drawn between young persons under 16 and those over that age.[10] The classifications need reconsideration now that the school-leaving age is 16.

(a) Specific Restrictions according to Nature of Employment

No child under the upper limit of compulsory school age can be employed in any industrial undertaking (except in those cases where only members of the same family are employed),[11] or below ground in a mine or quarry[12] or in a factory[13] or a shop[14] or on a United Kingdom registered ship.[15] The Children and Young Persons Acts 1933 and 1963 prohibit the employment of children in street-trading, except in so far as local authority byelaws may permit,[16] and only allow children to take part in entertainment performances subject to strict safeguards relating to their health, welfare and education.

Performances by Children
Part II of the 1963 Act and Regulations[17] thereunder provide a comprehensive code.[18] In replacing certain provisions in the

---

[9] Education Act 1944, s. 58.
[10] *I.e.*, over 16 but under 18. Compare the definition in the Children and Young Persons Act 1933, s. 107(1).
[11] Employment of Women, Young Persons and Children Act 1920, s. 1(1).
[12] Mines and Quarries Act 1954, s. 124.
[13] Factories Act 1961, s. 167.
[14] Shops Act 1950, Part II and s. 74(1); but see C. & Y.P. Act 1933, s. 18, *infra*, p. 449.
[15] Merchant Shipping Act 1970, s. 51. Regulations may however permit employment.
[16] See further street-trading in relation to young persons, *infra*.
[17] The Children (Performances) Regulations 1968, S.I. 1968 No. 1728.
[18] The Home Office has published a Guide to the law (*The Law on Performances by Children*, H.M.S.O. (1968)).

1933 Act,[19] they allow for the first time children under 12 to engage in public performances and they take account of the expansion of the film and television industries. The essence of the system is that performances by children under the upper limit of compulsory school age normally depend on the granting of a licence by the local authority.[20] This rule applies to any performance[1] in connection with which a charge is made, any performance in licensed premises or a registered club, any broadcast and any performance recorded with a view to use in a broadcast or film intended for public exhibition.[2] No licence is required, however, when the child has not performed on more than three days in any period of six months, or his performance is given under arrangements made by a school or by a body approved by the Secretary of State or by the local authority and no payment for his performance is made to him or anyone else.[3]

No licence may be granted unless the local authority is satisfied that the child is fit to perform, that proper provision has been made to secure his health and kind treatment and that his education will not suffer.[4] The grant is also subject to restrictions imposed by the Regulations. These include a general limit on the number of performing days in any period of 12 months to 80 days for children aged 13 or over and to 40 for those under that age,[5] and there are further limitations on the number of weekly and daily performances, depending upon whether they are broadcast or recorded performances or other performances.[6] The local authority must approve arrangements for the child's education during the period when he is engaged for performances, for example, the approval of private tuition;[7] and they may also safeguard his financial

---

[19] The changes were largely the result of the Report of a Departmental Committee (Cmnd. 8005).
[20] C. & Y.P. Act 1963, s. 37(1). For offences for breach of s. 37 see s. 40.
[1] This includes the case of a child who is a "stand-in".
[2] C. & Y.P. Act 1963, s. 37(2).
[3] An example of the exemption would be a child performing in an amateur production of a play on more than four days.
[4] C. & Y.P. Act 1963, s. 37(4).
[5] Reg. 6.
[6] See Parts IV and V of the Regulations. Similarly there are limitations on the number and duration of performances for which a local authority licence is not required (Part VI).
[7] Regulation 10. A licence must specify the times when a child may be absent from school (s. 37(7)).

interests, for example, by requiring the whole or part of his earnings to be set aside and a trust fund created.[8] During the period of operation of a licence the child must at all times be in the charge of a "matron", who may be a man or a woman.[9] The local authority must approve the choice of a matron. They must be satisfied that he or she is suitable and competent to exercise proper care and control, having particular regard to the age and sex of the child. The maximum number of children who at any time may be in the care of a matron is 12.

A licence in respect of a child cannot be granted unless (*a*) the licence is for acting and the application for it is accompanied by a declaration that the part cannot be taken except by a child of about his age; or (*b*) it is for dancing in a ballet and there is a similar declaration that only a child of his age can dance the part or (*c*) the nature of his part in the performance is also wholly or mainly musical or the performance consists only of opera and ballet. Now that the school leaving age is raised to 16, this restriction extends to children under 14.[10]

Subject to giving notice to the holder of the licence, the local authority may vary or revoke it for breach of any condition on which it was granted or because they are not satisfied about the child's health, treatment or education. Appeals against refusal, variation or revocation of a licence or against any condition which the authority is not entitled to impose lie to a magistrates' court.[11]

In addition to the above control through local authority licences, there are overriding restrictions on performances. No one under 16 is allowed to take part in a public performance in which his life or limbs are endangered, and anyone who causes or procures, or, being his parent or guardian, allows, the juvenile to participate is guilty of an offence.[12] Children under 12 must not be trained to take part in any performance of a

[8] Regulation 11.
[9] Regulation 12.
[10] C. & Y.P. Act 1963, s. 38 (2).
[11] Section 39.
[12] C. & Y.P. Act 1933, s. 23. The penalties are a maximum fine of £50 for a first offence and £100 for second and subsequent offences (Criminal Justice Act 1967, Sched. 3). Proceedings may be taken only by or with the authority of a chief officer of police.

dangerous nature[13] and those who have reached that age but are under 16 may be so trained only if a local authority grant a licence, which may be made subject to conditions but which cannot be refused if the authority is satisfied that the juvenile is fit and willing to be trained and that proper provision has been made to secure his health and kind treatment.[14] Finally, persons under 18 may only be employed outside the United Kingdom and the Irish Republic in singing, playing, performing or being exhibited for profit if a licence is granted for the purpose,[15] and this can only be granted in respect of a child under 14 within the same limits as apply to licences granted to children under 14 to perform within the United Kingdom.[16]

(b) General Restrictions

No child below the upper limit of compulsory school age may be employed until he has attained the age of 13 years.[17] Those who are outside this prohibition (*i.e.*, those between 13 and 16) are subject to the following restrictions. They must not be employed before the close of school hours on a school day; before 7 a.m. or after 7 p.m. on any day; for more than two hours on a school day; or for more than two hours on a Sunday. They cannot, moreover, be employed to lift or carry anything so heavy as to be likely to cause them injury.[18] These restrictions are all subject to any local authority byelaws affecting employment of children,[19] which may add further restrictions or even prohibit absolutely employment in a specified occupation; or on the other hand, may allow employment of children under 13 in limited circumstances.

[13] Including performances as an acrobat or contortionist (C. & Y.P. Act 1933, s. 30). See also s. 3 of the Hypnotism Act 1952 (as amended by the Family Law Reform Act 1969) which forbids hypnotism of a person under 18 at a public entertainment.
[14] C. & Y.P. Act 1933, s. 24, as amended by C. & Y.P. Act 1963, s. 41. Penalties for breach of the section are maximum fines of £20 for a first offence and thereafter £50.
There is a power to vary or revoke a licence and a right of appeal against refusal, variation or revocation similar to those relating to licences granted under s. 37 of the 1963 Act.
[15] C. & Y.P. Act 1933, s. 25, as amended by C. & Y.P. Act 1963, s. 42.
[16] *Supra.*
[17] C. & Y.P. Act 1933, s. 18(1) (a); Education Act 1944, s. 58; Children Act 1972.
For penalties see C. & Y.P. Act 1933, s. 21, as amended by C. & Y.P. Act 1963, s. 36.
[18] C. & Y.P. Act 1933, s. 18(1) (b)-(f), as amended by C. & Y.P. Act 1963, Sched. III.   [19] *Ibid.*, s. 18(2).

None of them, however, apply so as to prevent a child taking part in a performance under a local authority licence or in a case where no such licence is required.[20]

Local education authorities also have power to prohibit or restrict the employment of children when they are being employed in a manner prejudicial to their health or rendering them unfit to obtain the full benefit of the education they are receiving.[1]

(2) EMPLOYMENT OF YOUNG PERSONS

A mass of varied legislation[2] governs the employment of young persons, especially the maximum number of hours they may work. The protection is given to those over compulsory school age but under 18.

The Employment of Women, Young Persons and Children Act 1920 and the Hours of Employment (Conventions) Act 1936 markedly restrict the employment of young persons in industrial undertakings at night, and the Young Persons (Employment) Acts 1938 and 1964 limit the number of hours they may work in a number of specified occupations, most of which relate to delivery of goods and running of errands.[3] The latter Acts distinguish between young persons under 16 and those over that age. The same distinction is made by the Factories Act 1961 (Part VI) and by the Shops Act 1950 for the purpose of controlling hours of employment in factories and shops. Young persons under 16 are also prohibited from working below ground in a mine, and there are restrictions on employment of all young persons above ground in mines and above or below ground in quarries.[4] Those under 17 may only engage in street trading in so far as local authority byelaws allow,[5] but these provisions do not affect the right to employ young persons or children under maximum school age limit at places where it is customary to carry on a retail trade or business, *e.g.*, in an open air market.

[20] See *supra*.
[1] Education Act 1944, s. 59.
[2] For the detailed provisions see Fridman, *The Modern Law of Employment*.
[3] The provisions in the Act relating to young persons employed on board ship are replaced by the Merchant Shipping Act 1970, s. 51.
[4] Mines and Quarries Act 1954, Part VIII.
[5] C. & Y.P. Act 1933, s. 20, as amended by C. & Y.P. Act 1963, s. 35.

Employment of Children

PARENTAL RIGHT TO CHILD'S SERVICES

This right may briefly and conveniently be noted here.

A parent has the right to the domestic services of those of his children who, being under 18 but old enough to be capable of rendering services,[6] are living with him as members of his family.[7] In those circumstances a master-servant relationship is presumed, whereas, if the child is an adult, proof of a contract of service or actual service is necessary.[8] Against the child himself the right is unenforceable, but it does afford the parent a limited remedy against anyone who wrongfully interferes with the right. In the case of a legitimate child the right resides with the father,[9] but it has been suggested that the increasing recognition accorded by the law to a wife in other respects might lead the court to recognise that the mother also has a cause of action for loss of services.[10] On the other hand it has been held[11] that, although the mother of an illegitimate child is *prima facie* entitled to the services, the right vests in the father if he is living with her, since he is then the head of the household and it is on that basis that services are owed. Since that is the basis, the right is also enjoyed by a person who stands *in loco parentis* (*e.g.*, a foster parent), but in such a case proof of actual service is apparently necessary.[12] However it is very doubtful whether the right extends to a guardian. The fiduciary relationship between him and his ward probably excludes the inference of a master-servant relationship, but it has been argued[13] that the guardian has a right of action where actual services have been rendered.

Interference with the parental right has occasionally been in the form of a tort, such as negligence, committed against the child, in which case both have a right of action, but usually it has been by way of seduction or, less frequently, of enticement or harbouring. In those circumstances the parent alone had a cause of action, but the Law Reform (Miscellaneous Provisions) Act 1970 has abolished the action for loss of services

---

[6] *Hall* v. *Hollander* (1825), 4 B. & C. 660 (child aged two years).
[7] *Cf. Hedges* v. *Tagg* (1872), L.R. 7 Exch. 283.
[8] *Gray* v. *Jefferies* (1587), Cro. Eliz. 55.
[9] *Beetham* v. *James*, [1937] 1 K.B. 527; [1937] 1 All E.R. 580.
[10] Bromley, *op. cit.*, p. 315.   [11] *Beetham* v. *James*, *supra.*
[12] *Peters* v. *Jones*, [1914] 2 K.B. 781.   [13] Bromley, *op. cit.*, p. 329.

due to rape, seduction, enticement or harbouring.[14] Consequently, the action is now limited to those cases where the
loss of service is due to a tort (other than a battery involving
rape) committed against the child. The Act gives effect to proposals of the Law Commission,[15] but it does not implement
the earlier proposal of the Law Reform Committee[16] that there
should be substituted for the action for loss of services a new
action allowing a parent to recover reasonable expenses for
tortious injury to a dependent child.

[14] Section 5. [15] Working Paper No. 19.
[16] Eleventh Report, 1963, Cmnd. 2017, paras. 20-23.

CHAPTER 14

Financial Provisions for Children

A. OBLIGATIONS OF PARENT, SPOUSE OR GUARDIAN

I. AT COMMON LAW

(1) Parent of Legitimate Child

A remarkable feature of the common law was that it imposed no direct civil liability on the father to maintain his legitimate child. Consequently, he was not liable for any debt incurred by the child, even a debt arising from the supply of necessaries, unless he had given the child authority to incur it or had contracted to pay for it:[1] mere knowledge that his child was being maintained by a third party would not render him liable for necessaries supplied by that party to his child.[2] The severity of this rule which denied to the child the benefit of an agency of necessity was partially mitigated by the wife's agency of necessity, because, if she had been deserted by her husband or, for good cause, was living apart from him, she was entitled to pledge his credit for necessaries supplied to the child, at least if she had custody under an order of the court.[3] Even that protection has disappeared,[4] but, if the common law still has any practical relevance, it may possibly be the rule that a liability to pay for necessaries would be implied if the father has deserted the child.[5]

Initially the exemption from liability related only to the father, since he alone was recognised as having custody, but as the mother acquired rights therein the protection seems impliedly to have been extended to her.

---

[1] *Mortimore* v. *Wright* (1840), 6 M. & W. 482.
[2] *A fortiori* if there was no knowledge, *Fluck* v. *Tollemache* (1823), 1 C. & P. 5.
[3] *Bazeley* v. *Forder* (1868), L.R. 3 Q.B. 559.
[4] Matrimonial Proceedings and Property Act 1970, s. 41.
[5] See *Urmston* v. *Newcomen* (1836), 4 Ad. & El. 899, especially *per* Lord DENMAN, C.J., at p. 909. But even if the proposition be valid, it would not apply in respect of a child who has attained majority; see *Coldingham Parish Council* v. *Smith*, [1918] 2 K.B. 90.

(2) Parent of Illegitimate Child

Neither the mother[6] nor the father[7] is liable at common law to maintain the illegitimate child, but, as in the case of the legitimate, either can give the child an authority to incur a debt on her or his behalf or can expressly or impliedly contract to be bound.[8] In *Cameron* v. *Baker*[9] it was held that, though the father:

"is not in the first instance bound to maintain it, unless compelled to do so by an order of magistrates, [yet] if he consents to pay an annual sum for its support he must continue to do so or provide for the child at his own expense or give the most distinct notice of his intention to pay such annual sum no longer";

and shortly after this decision the principle was established that the father can accept liability by contracting with the mother to pay her regular sums for the support of their child.[10] The consideration for his promise to pay may take various forms, such as a promise to have regard to his wishes about the way in which she will bring up their child;[11] it may be a promise not to institute affiliation proceedings;[12] and possibly even a promise to fulfil her own obligation to maintain the child[13] may be adequate.[14] The agreement is, however, no bar to affiliation proceedings by the mother, because any payment thereby ordered to be made to her is for the maintenance of the child and not for her benefit, with the result that she cannot renounce the right to it.[15] This is so even where the consideration for the father's promise to pay is the mother's promise not to take affiliation proceedings, which is "probably a unique example of a promise which is valid for one purpose but contrary to public policy for another."[16]

[6] *Ruttinger* v. *Temple* (1863), 4 B. & S. 491.
[7] *Seaborne* v. *Maddy* (1840), 9 C. & P. 497.
[8] In the light of *Mortimore* v. *Wright, supra,* it seems clear that the father's mere knowledge that the child is being maintained by someone does not disturb the principle of non-liability and the earlier decision of *Nichole* v. *Allen* (1827), 3 C. & P. 36 to the contrary cannot be regarded as good law. Nor can that of *Hesketh* v. *Gowing* (1804), 5 Esp. 131, where the fact that the father had accepted the child as his own was held enough to render him liable for necessaries supplied to the child.
[9] (1824), 1 C. & P. 268.   [10] *Jennings* v. *Brown* (1842), 9 M. & W. 496.
[11] *Cf. Ward* v. *Byham,* [1956] 2 All E.R. 318; [1956] 1 W.L.R. 496 (C.A.).
[12] *Linnegar* v. *Hodd* (1848), 5 C.B. 437.
[13] Under s. 22 of the Ministry of Social Security Act 1966; see *infra.*
[14] So held by DENNING, L. J., in *Ward* v. *Byham, supra,* but not adopted by the majority of the Court of Appeal (MORRIS and PARKER, L.JJ.).
[15] *Follit* v. *Koetzow* (1860), 2 E. & E. 730.   [16] *Bromley, op. cit.,* p. 489.

Unless the terms of the agreement are open to a different construction, it seems that it may be terminated by reasonable notice, that it does not end on the father's death but does so on the mother's.[17]

(3) Guardian and Ward

The guardian is under a common law duty to maintain his ward out of the latter's property but is not obliged personally to do so. So, in the absence of a contract or an authority to incur a debt on his behalf, he is not civilly liable to a third party for a debt incurred by the ward. However, like a parent or anyone else who assumes the care of a person he will be criminally liable at common law as well as under statute if he wilfully neglects to provide the ward with adequate food, clothing, medical aid or lodging.[18]

II. SOCIAL SECURITY

The inadequacy of the common law led to the creation of a statutory duty on the parent to maintain the child as part of the Poor Law of Elizabeth I.[19] This parental obligation was a cardinal principle of the Poor Law and has been embodied in the modern systems of National Assistance and, more recently, of Social Security.

For the purpose of Social Security a man and a woman are each liable to maintain those of their children under the age of 16,[20] whether legitimate, illegitimate or adopted.[1] No similar obligation is imposed on a guardian in respect of his ward. In the case of the illegitimate child the man's liability depends upon his having first been adjudged to be the putative father, whether, it is submitted, as the result of affiliation proceedings or otherwise. As will be seen,[2] the effect of the duty is that the Supplementary Benefits Commission may recover from either or both parents the amount which it has had to pay in the form of supplementary benefit in respect of their child.

[17] *Ibid.*, p. 488.
[18] See *ante*, Chapter 6, especially ss. 1 and 17 of C. & Y.P. Act 1933.
[19] Poor Relief Act 1601.
[20] National Assistance Act 1948, s. 42; Ministry of Social Security Act 1966, s. 22.
[1] Adoption Act 1958, s. 13; see *ante*, Chapter 10, p. 366.
[2] *Post*, p. 505.

III. GUARDIANSHIP OF MINORS ACT 1971

When a custody order is made under this Act in favour of the mother of a legitimate or adopted[3] child, the court[4] may further order the father to pay to her periodical sums, which are usually weekly, for the child's maintenance and education.[5] But the mother who is granted custody of her illegitimate child cannot obtain maintenance under the Act:[6] she is compelled to rely on affiliation proceedings, and there may be obstacles to that remedy[7] and the financial provisions are less favourable. Nor can a maintenance order correspondingly be made against the mother of a legitimate or adopted child when the father has been awarded custody, so long as the child remains a minor.[8] This is a doubly anomalous distinction in view of the power to order either parent to pay maintenance (*a*) in matrimonial proceedings in a magistrates' court and in a matrimonial cause in a divorce court and (*b*) even in proceedings under the Guardianship of Minors Act once the child has attained majority.[8]

Similarly, when a testamentary guardian is appointed sole guardian to the exclusion of the surviving parent[9] or where there is a dispute between joint guardians, one of whom is the parent, the court may order the parent to provide periodical sums for the ward's maintenance.[10]

[3] By virtue of the Adoption Act 1958, s. 13, *ante*, p. 366.
[4] *I.e.*, the High Court (Family Division) or a county court or, subject to certain limits, a magistrates' court. See *ante*, Chapter 9, p. 269.
[5] Guardianship of Minors Act 1971, ss. 9(2) and 20(2). References to maintenance in the Act include education, which is a particularly relevant consideration where orders for maintenance are made in respect of persons between 18 and 21 (see *infra*).
[6] Section 14(2).
[7] See *post*, p. 488.
[8] For the position when he attains majority see *infra*.
[9] Guardianship of Minors Act 1971, s. 4(4), *ante*, Chapter 12, p. 400. "Parent" for this purpose includes the father of an illegitimate child who has custody by an order under the Act (s. 14(3)).
[10] Sections 10(1) (b) and 11 (b).
      There are at least two obscurities about ss. 10 and 11.
   (1) Payments under s. 10(1) (b) must be made to the sole guardian, but s. 11(b) is silent about who the recipient can be, and this suggests that he might be a person other than the joint guardian; *e.g.*, a third person to whom care and control has been granted. But why should this not be possible in a case under s. 10(1) (b)?
   (2) A maintenance order under s. 10(1) (b) is described as a "further" order. *Quaere* this means an order further to one under s. 4(4) appointing the guardian as sole guardian or further to an order regarding custody and access made under s. 10(1) (a). The conjunction "and"

456

Duration of Maintenance

Although a custody order under the Act ceases when the child attains majority, a maintenance order made under s. 9, 10 or 11 may provide for payments by a parent to continue after that date but not beyond the age of 21. It may also provide that when the child becomes 18 payments shall be made directly to him.[11] The extent to which courts are prepared to order payments beyond majority is uncertain. They are most likely to do so where the child is disabled or where it is known that he will still be receiving education or training after he becomes 18, but otherwise they may be disinclined to do so, especially as there is still power, if the circumstances warrant, to make an order for maintenance by a parent after the child has attained majority but is still under 21.[12]

An application for the latter order may be made by either parent or by the child himself requiring either parent to make periodical payments to the other parent or to a third person for the child's benefit or to the child himself. Payments can be ordered up to but not beyond the age of 21. An essential condition is that the child was the subject of an order under the 1971 Act or the Guardianship of Infants legislation (which it replaced) while he was a minor, but since it may be any order it is strange that illegitimate children are wholly excluded.[13] The exclusion logically follows where the original order was a custody order under s. 9, since no accompanying maintenance order could have been made;[14] but it is difficult to see why he is excluded where the original order was made under s. 10 or 11, since those sections do allow for maintenance orders in respect of illegitimate children. One kind of case where an order might be used is where the order made during minority did not provide for continuation of payments after the date of attainment of majority. It seems that the court cannot rely on its powers to vary the original order[15] after that date. Another possible use is where the father alone was required to

---

between the two paragraphs tends to support the latter construction. In s. 11(b) the conjunction does not appear (although it was contained in s. 79 of the C. & Y.P. Act 1933 which s. 11 replaces) which seems to indicate that custody and access orders and maintenance orders under the section are not interdependent.   [11] Section 12(1).
[12] Section 12(2).   [13] Section 14(4).   [14] *Supra.*
[15] Under ss. 9(4), 10(2) and 11(c).

make payments under the original order but by the time the child is 18 the mother is in gainful occupation and able to contribute to maintenance.

Rules of General Application

Certain rules are common to maintenance orders made before majority and those made afterwards.

Regard must be had to the means and obligations of the parent who is to pay in order to determine what is a reasonable sum,[16] but the court is entitled also to take into account the means and obligations of the other parent, usually the mother. However, there may be circumstances where her means should be ignored, as for example, where she is working and it would be in the child's interests for her to give up her employment.[17] Also highly material are the age, health, education and standard of life of the child and the existence of any fund which already provides maintenance for him.[18] Indeed, the court should follow the same principles as it is required to do when making financial orders in a divorce court.[19]

Both kinds of orders may be varied or discharged.[20] They may be made while the parents are residing together, but during that period are not enforceable and no liability may accrue. If the residence continues for three months they cease to have effect.[1] High Court and county court orders are enforced by the usual methods of enforcing orders in those courts.[2] A magistrates' court order is enforceable in the same way as an affiliation order.[3]

IV. MAINTENANCE FOR WARDS OF COURT

Section 6 of the Family Law Reform Act 1969 has imposed on the parents of a ward of court a new duty to provide for his maintenance and education. Either can be ordered by the High Court (Family Division) to make periodical payments to

[16] Sections 9(2), 10(1) (b), 11 (b) and 12(2).
[17] *Re T. (an infant)*, [1953] Ch. 787; [1953] 2 All E.R. 830; *Re W. (Infants)*, [1956] Ch. 384; [1956] 1 All E.R. 368, (C.A.).   [18] *Re W., supra.*
[19] See Matrimonial Proceedings and Property Act 1970, s. 5(2), *post*, p. 467.
[20] See *supra*, n. 15, and, for orders made after majority, s. 12(4).
[1] Sections 9(3) and 12(3). For a criticism of these rules in relation to the right of the adult child to seek maintenance from his parents see Cretney, 33 M.L.R. 662, 678.   [2] *Post*, p. 475.   [3] *Post*, p. 494.

the other parent or to any third person having care and control of the ward, and rules applicable to maintenance orders under the Guardianship of Minors Act 1971 correspondingly apply. Thus, payments can be ordered beyond majority and up to the age of 21; orders can be made after majority within the same limits as those in the 1971 Act; the parents' residence together precludes the operation of the order and the accrual of liability; orders may be varied or discharged, and are enforceable by the same means as other orders for periodical payments are enforced by the High Court.

A serious defect about s. 6, however, is that it does not extend to illegitimate children.[4]

V. MATRIMONIAL PROCEEDINGS (MAGISTRATES' COURTS) ACT 1960

One of the provisions that can be included in a matrimonial order made under this Act is that for the maintenance of any child of the family by either or both spouses.[5]

The meaning of the term child of the family in that Act has already been considered in relation to custody orders,[6] but in the present context it is qualified by the provision[7] that, when the court is determining whether any, and if so what, maintenance is to be paid by a spouse in respect of a child who is not a child of the spouse, it must take into account the extent to which that spouse on or after accepting the child as one of the family assumed responsibility for his maintenance and also the liability of any person other than a party to the marriage to maintain the child. The extent of the spouse's past responsibility is to be assessed not in a temporal sense but according to the amount of his contribution to maintenance,[8] and in an exceptional case he may have accepted the child on the express condition that he would not at all be responsible for his maintenance.[9]

As for third party liability, regard may be had to possible and not only existing liability. So, if the child of the wife is

---

[4] See sub-s. (6).
[5] Section 2(1)(h), as amended by the Maintenance Orders Act 1968, s. 1 and Sched. [6] *Ante*, Chapter 9, pp. 273 to 276.
[7] Section 2(5).
[8] *Roberts* v. *Roberts*, [1962] P. 212; [1962] 2 All E.R. 967. See thereon Samuels, 26 M.L.R. 92.
[9] See *Bowlas* v. *Bowlas*, [1965] P. 450; [1965] 3 All E.R. 40 (C.A.).

Financial Provisions for Children

illegitimate and affiliation proceedings can be, but in fact have not been, taken against the putative father, the hearing of the maintenance claim may be adjourned to allow her to seek an affiliation order before the final determination of the quantum of maintenance to be ordered in the matrimonial proceedings.[10] Should she refuse to do so, she can be asked for reasons, and the putative father can himself be compelled to give evidence in the matrimonial proceedings.[11]

For the purpose of maintenance provisions the Matrimonial Proceedings (Magistrates' Courts) Act classifies children of the family into three categories of "dependants":[12]

(a) those under 16;

(b) those who have attained that age but are under 21 and are either receiving full-time instruction at an educational establishment or undergoing training for a trade, profession or vocation in such circumstances that they are required to devote the whole of their time to that training for not less than two years;[13]

(c) those whose earning capacity is impaired through illness or disability of mind or body and who have not attained the age of 21.

Where an order is made in respect of a child under 16, payments are to be made either to the person having legal custody of the child or, where the matrimonial order commits the child to the care of a local authority, to that authority. Payments in respect of other dependants are made to the person specified in the order; this can be the child himself.[14] In cases of com-

---

[10] *Caller* v. *Callter*, [1968] P. 39; [1966] 2 All E.R. 754.
[11] *Roberts* v. *Roberts, supra.*
But there is a practical difficulty. A parent who is not the complainant or defendant in the matrimonial proceedings may be a party to the proceedings (Matrimonial Proceedings (Magistrates' Courts) Act 1960, s. 4(6)). If he is not present or represented, the court must take steps to give him notice of the proceedings, but it is not obliged to give notice where the child is illegitimate and he is the father, unless he has been so adjudged by a court. If, therefore, the mother does not take affiliation proceedings, there will be no obligation to give notice. That, it is submitted, would not preclude the court from doing so at its discretion, but there would still be no power to compel the attendance of the father to give evidence.   [12] Section 16(1).
[13] *Cf.* the category for the purpose of matrimonial proceedings in a divorce court (Matrimonial Proceedings and Property Act 1970, s. 8(3) (a)).
[14] If the court is satisfied that the child is likely to remain a dependant after attaining the age of 16, it can make an order while he is under that age providing for payments to continue beyond it.

mittal to the care of a local authority, the recipient is the authority. Those payments must terminate when the child ceases to be a dependant.[15] They are enforceable in the same way as payments under an affiliation order.[16] Like any other provision affecting children under the Act, a provision for maintenance can be made even if the court should dismiss the spouse's complaint,[17] and where there is a complaint for revocation of a matrimonial order on the ground of the complainant's adultery, the court is not bound to revoke a maintenance provision relating to a child.[18] The effects of continued cohabitation of the spouses on a maintenance provision are similar to those relating to custody.[19] The order for maintenance is not enforceable and no accrual of liability arises while they continue to cohabit, and it will cease to operate if cohabitation continues for three months.[20] Similarly resumption of cohabitation will terminate an order.[1] These rules of cohabitation apply where payments are to be made by one spouse to the other, but not where a third party is the recipient. The powers to make interim orders and to vary and revoke maintenance and interim orders apply generally as they do to custody orders under the Act.[2]

In assessing the amount of maintenance the court should, it is submitted, follow the same principles as it is statutorily required to do in proceedings for divorce, nullity or judicial separation.[3]

VI. MATRIMONIAL PROCEEDINGS AND PROPERTY ACT 1970[4]

(a) Under Section 3

The powers of the High Court or a divorce county court to make financial provision for children are wider than those of a magistrates' court under the Matrimonial Proceedings (Magis-

---

[15] Compare the powers of a divorce court to order payments beyond 21 (Matrimonial Proceedings and Property Act 1970, s. 8(3)).
[16] Section 13(1); see *post*, p. 494.
[17] See *ante*, Chapter 9, p. 272, for ss. 4(1) and 2(3) respectively.
[18] Section 8(2).
[19] *Ante*, p. 277.
[20] Section 7(1), *ibid.*
[1] Sections 7(1) (2) and 8(2), *ibid.*
[2] But the making of an interim order relating to maintenance, unlike that concerning custody, is not restricted to special circumstances (s. 6(2)).
[3] See Matrimonial Proceedings and Property Act 1970, s. 5(2), *infra*, p. 467.
[4] Subsequently referred to in this chapter as "M.P. & P. Act".

trates' Courts) Act 1960 in respect of the kinds of orders that may be made, their duration and the class of children affected. Orders may be made in proceedings for divorce, nullity or judicial separation[5] at any stage pending suit[6] or when a decree is granted or at any time thereafter. Moreover, as in the case of proceedings under the 1960 Act, financial provision for the children may be ordered even if the spouse's petition is dismissed.[7]

Kinds of Provision

A party to the marriage may be required to make to a specified person (usually the other spouse) for the benefit of the child or to the child himself any one or more of the following, namely, (1) unsecured periodical payments, (2) secured periodical payments, (3) a lump sum payment. It seems that only one lump sum may be ordered,[8] but it may be made payable by way of instalments, either unsecured or secured, and, in particular, it may be made to meet liabilities reasonably incurred by or for the benefit of the child before the application was made for an order; for example, in connection with his education or, where he suffers from a physical disability, to purchase equipment to overcome it.[9]

Section 3 is silent on two matters for which the Matrimonial Proceedings (Magistrates' Courts) Act 1960 expressly provides. Firstly, although it is clear that either spouse, whether petitioner or respondent, may be ordered to provide for the child, it is not stated whether both may be liable where the custody or care and control has been given to a third person.[10] Secondly,

---

[5] For wilful neglect to maintain see *post*, p. 480.

[6] Compare the separate rule needed for dealing with maintenance of a spouse pending suit (M.P. & P. Act, s. 1).

[7] Section 3(1). Further provision may be made from time to time (s. 3(5)).

[8] Compare s. 2(1) (c) which, although it expressly allows for the payment of more than one lump sum to a spouse, means no more than that the court can provide for more than one lump sum in one order; *C. v. C.* (1972), *Times*, July 14.

[9] A lump sum payment may also be made (under s. 2(2)) to a party to the marriage for liability reasonably incurred in maintaining a child of the family before an application for an order under that section.

[10] Bromley, *op. cit.*, p. 474, n. 19, citing *Freckleton* v. *Freckleton*, [1966] C.L.Y. 3938, points out that the former law allowed it.

Persons other than a spouse who may apply for financial provision for the child are: his guardian; anyone having custody or care and control under a High Court or county court order; a local authority to whom care has been committed under s. 36 of the Matrimonial Causes Act 1965 (*ante*, p. 154); anyone who has obtained leave to intervene to apply for custody: the Official Solicitor if appointed guardian *ad litem;* anyone else who has care of the child and who has obtained leave to intervene for the

the section does not prescribe a minimum age limit below which payments cannot be made to the child himself. The choice seems to lie between the age of 16, which is recognised by the 1960 Act[11] and the attainment of majority, which the Guardianship of Minors Act prescribes for maintenance proceedings thereunder.[12]

(b) Under Section 4

One of the advantages of a lump sum payment is that it may be used as a method of permanently adjusting the property interests of members of the family on the breakdown of the marriage. Even if awarded to the spouse[13] and not to the children, it may indirectly benefit the latter, for example, where it is given to enable a wife to purchase a new home for herself and them,[14] or to carry out repairs on the existing one.[15] Another advantage is that it may anticipate the risk of a spouse's taking his assets out of the jurisdiction in order to defeat the claims of his family.[16] These objects can, however, often be achieved by the use of other, wider powers, conferred by s. 4 of the 1970 Act.

Orders may be made in proceedings for divorce, nullity or judicial separation for the transfer or settlement of property by one spouse, whether the petitioner or the respondent, to the other or to or for the benefit of a child or for the variation of a marriage settlement or for extinguishing or reducing an interest under such a settlement. Because they are intended as a permanent property adjustment on the breakdown of a marriage,[17] they cannot be made until a decree is granted, and, in the case of divorce or nullity, cannot come into effect until the decree nisi is made absolute.[18] They may also be made

---

purpose of applying for maintenance for him, (Matrimonial Causes Rules 1971, r. 69). *Semble* the child himself may apply if he has attained majority; but see *post*, p. 472, for the limited circumstances in which orders may be made in respect of adult children.   [11] Section 2(1) (h).
[12] Section 12(1), *supra*, p. 457.   [13] Under s. 2 of the M.P. & P. Act 1970.
[14] *Von Mehren* v. *Von Mehren*, [1970] 1 All E.R. 153; [1970] 1 W.L.R. 56 (C.A.).
[15] *Hakluytt* v. *Hakluytt*, [1968] 2 All E.R. 868; [1968] 1 W.L.R. 1145 (C.A.).
[16] See *Brett* v. *Brett*, [1969] 1 All E.R. 1007; [1969] 1 W.L.R. 487 (C.A.); *Curtis* v. *Curtis*, [1969] 2 All E.R. 207; [1969] 1 W.L.R. 422 (C.A.).
[17] The application of s. 4 to cases of judicial separation is a concession to those spouses who for conscientious reasons do not seek divorce.
[18] Section 24(1).
    The court may direct that the proper instrument be settled by conveyancing counsel and that the grant of a decree be deferred until that instrument has been executed (s. 25).

at any time thereafter, but only with leave of the court.[19]

Section 4 cannot be invoked where the decree has been granted by a foreign court. On the other hand, it may extend to a person domiciled and resident abroad who has property situated within the jurisdiction,[20] and it may be applied to property outside the jurisdiction. The criterion for application is the likelihood of effective enforcement of an order.[1]

Kinds of Provision

(i) *Transfer of Property*

(ii) *Settlement of Property*

These[2] may conveniently be considered together.

The power to order either spouse to transfer property to which he or she is entitled, either in possession or in reversion, is entirely new. That of ordering a settlement of either's property is not wholly so, in that settlement of a wife's property was in very narrow circumstances allowed under the former law.

A transfer order will usually concern primarily the parties to the marriage,[3] but, as with a lump sum payment to a spouse, the children of the family will often benefit indirectly. One of the main purposes of the order is to enable the husband's

---

[19] Section 24(2); Matrimonial Causes Rules 1971, r. 68. For third parties who may apply see r. 69 (*supra*, p. 462, n. 10) and note the apparent right of an adult child to apply.

[20] *Hunter* v. *Hunter*, [1962] P. 1; [1961] 2 All E.R. 121.

[1] Compare *Nunneley* v. *Nunneley* (1890), 15 P.D. 186 and *Forsyth* v. *Forsyth*, [1891] P. 363, where variation of settlements governed by Scots law and relating to property situated in Scotland was ordered, with *Goff* v. *Goff*, [1934] P. 107, where an order for variation of a settlement which in all material respects was connected with New York, was refused on the ground that it would be ineffective in New York. For refusal to order a settlement of property see *Tallack* v. *Tallack and Broekena*, [1927] P. 211.

[2] See s. 4(a) and (b).

[3] When s. 4(a) and (b) first came into operation practitioners seem to have been reluctant to rely on them, and, especially in those cases where a wife had contributed indirectly to the purchase of the matrimonial home, they preferred to continue to rely on s. 17 of the Married Women's Property Act 1882 to determine the interests of each spouse in the home, particularly as the M.P. & P. Act 1970, s. 39, permits actions under s. 17 to be brought up to three years after the marriage has been dissolved or annulled. The advantages of s. 4(a) and (b) are gradually being recognised. Admittedly, under s. 4 as much as under s. 17, the question of ownership has to be determined, but, as has pertinently been pointed out, "it matters less what the decision is if the court can rectify the matter by orders under s. 4 and have regard, as required by s. 5, to the contributions made by each of the parties to the welfare of the family, including contributions made by looking after the home and caring for the family". (Passingham, *Law and Practice in Matrimonial Causes*, p. 196).

interest in the matrimonial home to be transferred to the wife so that she may continue to live there with the children. In this kind of case there will, however, be practical difficulties if the property is subject to a mortgage. Usually it is a term of the mortgage that the mortgagor will not transfer the property except with the mortgagee's consent. So, if the mortgagor complies with an order for transfer and that consent has not been given, the mortgagee may have a right to foreclose. Moreover, if the mortgagor goes out of possession as a result of the transfer order, there is some risk of his not continuing with the mortgage payments. For these reasons a mortgagee should be given the opportunity to be heard on the application for a transfer and to decide whether to give his consent.[4]

An order for settlement, which must be by one spouse for the benefit of the other and the children of the family or either or any of them, has distinct advantages over a transfer. By allowing for a wide variety both in the kinds of interests which may be created and in their duration it enables the court to provide financial assistance for individual members of the family who at any given time will most need it; for example, successive interests for fixed periods may be created to meet the cost of further education of each child as he attains a specific age.

(iii) Variation of a Settlement

(iv) Extinguishing or Reducing an Interest Under a Settlement
A third kind of order is that for the variation of an ante-nuptial or post-nuptial settlement.[5]

Although s. 4 has introduced three important changes[6] with regard to this order, it leaves undisturbed the wide definition of a "marriage" settlement which a mass of case law has firmly established.[7] Dispositions to parties to a marriage have been liberally construed as settlements for the purpose of matrimonial proceedings, even though they are not settlements in the usually accepted sense. This has especially been so where

[4] See Practice Direction (Matrimonial Property: Transfer), [1971] 1 All E.R. 896.
[5] Section 4(c).
[6] Namely, extension of the order to (1) proceedings for judicial separation, (2) settlements made by will (*infra*) and (3) children of the family and not only children of the marriage (*infra*).
[7] The reader is referred to textbooks on matrimonial causes and to Bromley, *op. cit.*, pp. 436 *et seq.*

the transaction relates to the matrimonial home, as where both spouses have contributed to the purchase price and the property has been conveyed to both[8] or one[9] of them upon trust for sale and to hold the proceeds of sale as joint tenants or tenants in common beneficially. In cases of this kind, so long as the power of sale is postponed, the court has power to vary the settlement, for example, by extinguishing the husband's interests. But the introduction of the order for transfer of property can now achieve the same result and the courts are likely to rely on this rather than an order for variation.

Notwithstanding the wide meaning given to a settlement, a disposition must comply with a number of rules if it is to fall under s. 4.[10]

(1) It must be made upon a spouse or both spouses in his or her nuptial capacity, and must provide for the financial benefit of one or both of them in that capacity.[11]

A settlement made solely on the children of the family is therefore outside the section.[12]

(2) It must have been made in contemplation of, or because of the specific marriage which is the subject of the proceedings for divorce, nullity or judicial separation,[13] but not on the basis that the marriage was soon to be dissolved or annulled or the parties judicially separated.[14]

(3) The settlement must be in existence at the date of decree absolute of divorce or nullity or the decree of judicial separation.[15] Thus, where the settlement is made by will, the testator

---

[8] *Brown* v. *Brown*, [1959] P. 86; [1959] 2 All E.R. 266 (C.A.); *Ulrich* v. *Ulrich and Felton*, [1968] 1 All E.R. 67; [1968] 1. WL.R. 180 (C.A.).
[9] *Cook* v. *Cook*, [1962] P. 235; [1962] 2 All E.R. 811 (C.A.).
[10] See especially *Prinsep* v. *Prinsep*, [1929] P. 225.
[11] An absolute transfer of property is not, however, within the definition, except where the transferor is still obliged to make periodical payments (*Prescott* v. *Fellowes*, [1958] P. 260; [1958] 3 All E.R. 55 (C.A.)); but an order for transfer of property could be made under s. 4(a) requiring the transferee to return the property to the transferor.
[12] But see Bromley, *op. cit.*, p. 438, where the possibility of the opposite conclusion is canvassed.
[13] *Burnett* v. *Burnett*, [1936] P. 1; *Hargreaves* v. *Hargreaves*, [1926] P. 42.
[14] *Young* v. *Young*, [1962] P. 27; [1961] 3 All E.R. 695 (C.A.), (maintenance agreement made between decree nisi and decree absolute).
[15] *Dormer* v. *Ward*, [1901] P. 20 (C.A.)
The power to vary can be invoked where the nullity decree relates to a void marriage; see *ibid.*, and *Radziej* v. *Radziej*, [1967] 1 All E.R. 944; [1967] 1 W.L.R. 659; *affd.*, [1968] 3 All E.R. 624; [1968] 1 W.L.R. 1928, (C.A.).

must already be dead at that date, since it is only on his death that the settlement comes into existence. However, since there is power to make an order for variation at any time after granting a decree,[16] it is arguable that the present rule needs qualifying with regard to settlements made by will and that a settlement so made while the marriage subsisted and complying with rules (1) and (2) above may be varied on the testator's death occurring after the date of the decree.[17]

Section 4(d) now allows the court to extinguish or reduce the interest of a spouse under the settlement without conferring any benefit on the other spouse or a child of the family. In practice this power will be relevant where there is no such child.[18] Otherwise, benefit to a spouse or child is a prerequisite to variation.[19]

(c) Matters Relevant to the Making of Orders under Sections 3 and 4

Section 5 of the 1970 Act sets out the matters which must be considered when deciding which orders, if any, are to be made under ss. 3 and 4 in respect of a child of the family. Although the section is substantially declaratory of the former law, there was previously a greater risk of the court's not addressing itself to all the matters that are now prescribed. The express reference to them should help to provide consistency in this regard.

The matters specified by s. 5 are:[20]

(*a*) the financial needs of the child;

(*b*) the income, earning capacity (if any), property and other financial resources of the child;

(*c*) any physical or mental disability of the child;

(*d*) the standard of living enjoyed by the family before the breakdown of the marriage;

---

[16] Section 4.
[17] For the same view see Passingham, *op. cit.*, p. 127, who also points out possible difficulties in settlements by will complying with rules (1) and (2).
[18] For example, where a wife has an interest for life with remainder to the children of the family and, if there be none, to a relative of the wife, her interest could be extinguished, even though there were no children who would thereby benefit.
[19] For example, see *White* v. *White* (1972), *Times*, March 10 (C.A.) where the wife's interest in the equity of the former matrimonial home, which she had left, was extinguished so as to leave the husband and the child of the family undisturbed there.
[20] Sub-section (2).

(*e*) the manner in which he was being and in which the parties to the marriage expected him to be educated or trained.

With regard to (*b*) it seems that only actual income, property and other resources are relevant, and allowance for the future receipt of any funds must be met by later variation of the original order.[1] So, too, only present earning capacity is material, except that, where financial provision is to be made for a child during the period when he will be receiving education or training after attaining the age of 18, account may be taken of any gainful employment in which he will be engaged during that period.[2]

The child's financial needs will obviously depend very largely on the other factors, but the court must have regard to all the circumstances of the case and is not restricted to those specified. For example, a notable omission from them is the age of the child,[3] but this is clearly most relevant to his needs and his earning capacity, especially in deciding whether to order financial provision after he has attained 18. Again, in cases of variation of settlements, the question of which party or his relative settled the funds may be most material.

Having considered the specified matters and any others which it regards as relevant, the court must then take into consideration the income, earning capacity, property and other financial resources of each of the parties to the marriage and their respective needs, obligations and responsibilities. In assessing a spouse's capacity and ability to make financial provision, the court will look at all these matters realistically and thus, for example, will put into the reckoning a husband's ability to make money by the use of bank overdrafts,[4] his receipt of a voluntary allowance, whether in money or in kind,[5] and his potential as well as his actual earning capacity, including his ability to earn more by overtime work.[6] The relevance of

---

[1] Compare s. 5(1) where, for the purpose of assessing financial provision for a spouse, the income, etc., which each spouse has or *is likely to have in the foreseeable future* must be considered.
[2] Section 8(3); see further, *infra*, p. 473.
[3] Compare s. 5(1), which expressly includes the age of the spouses.
[4] *J.-P.C.* v. *J.*, [1955] P. 215; [1955] 2 All E.R. 85, (C.A.).
[5] *Donaldson* v. *Donaldson*, [1958] 2 All E.R. 660; [1958] 1 W.L.R. 827 (husband living rent and board free with mistress); similarly, *Ette* v. *Ette*, [1965] 1 All E.R. 341; [1964] 1 W.L.R. 1433.
[6] *Klucinski* v. *Klucinski*, [1953] 1 All E.R. 683; [1953] 1 W.L.R. 522.

the wife's income and earning capacity will much depend upon the age, health and education of the child, and it may be reasonable in the circumstances to expect her to give up, or not to take up, paid employment.[7]

When the court has to decide whether to make an order against a party in respect of a child who is not his natural or adopted child, it must in addition to all other matters have regard to

    (*a*) whether that party had assumed responsibility for the child's maintenance and, if he had, the extent, basis and length of time of the assumption;

    (*b*) whether in so doing he knew that the child was not his own;

and (*c*) the liability of any other person to maintain the child.[8]

Ignorance of the fact that the child is not one's own is not relevant to the definition of a child of the family, as it was under the Matrimonial Causes Act 1965 and still is for the purpose of proceedings under the Matrimonial Proceedings (Magistrates' Courts) Act 1960,[9] but it is a cogent factor in deciding what is the appropriate financial provision to be ordered under s. 3 and 4. So, too, is the length of period for which financial responsibility was assumed.[10]

This additional rule may, therefore, assist a party to the marriage to limit his financial liability for a child of the family; but it is of no avail to a third party, who has created a settlement, to avoid variation of the settlement in favour of a child of the family whom he did not have in contemplation when he created the settlement, for example, where the beneficiaries are to be children of the marriage. In such a case, however, he and the trustees of the settlement are entitled to notice of the proceedings and their objections heard.[11]

When the court has weighed all the circumstances of the case, it must exercise its powers so as to place the child so far as it is practicable and, having regard to the spouses' respective

[7] See *Attwood* v. *Attwood*, [1968] P. 591; [1968] 3 All E.R. 385, for the principles on which account is taken of a wife's income; and see *Re W.*, [1956] Ch.384; [1956] 1 All E.R. 368 (C.A.).
[8] Section 5(3). For third party liability see *ante*, p. 459.
[9] See *ante*, Chapter 9, p. 275 and 281.
[10] Compare proceedings under the Matrimonial Proceedings (Magistrates' Courts) Act 1960, *ante*, p. 459.
[11] Matrimonial Causes Rules 1971, r. 74(3). See Passingham, *op. cit.*, p. 128.

resources and needs, just to do so, in the financial position in which he would have been if the marriage had not broken down and each party had properly discharged his or her financial obligations towards the child.[12] To achieve this object demands much of any court. The kinds of practical difficulties and the orders eventually made obviously depend considerably on the financial resources of the spouses. Where they are wealthy the court will have a wide discretion in the choice of orders under ss. 3 and 4 and it should not be embarrassed by the fact that the husband is committed to supporting two households, *viz.*, that of his wife and their children and, for example, that of his mistress, with whom he lives, and their children. At the other extreme, where the parties are poor, the court is at most likely to be able to order unsecured periodical payments and even this is only practicable and permissible in so far as payments by the spouse will not reduce his income below subsistence level.[13] Where there are two households to support priority must be given to the children of the family and, if the husband has been the cause of the breakdown of the marriage, to his wife,[14] but the other household cannot be ignored.[14] The court must not draw too sharp a distinction between a man's legal and moral obligations to maintain his dependants and it may, therefore, have to decide, in the light of the husband's financial ability, whether it will make such an order that will wholly relieve the wife and her children of the need to seek supplementary benefits leaving the other household to rely on them or whether to make such provision for the former that both households will have to resort to them.[15] Where the husband is, as the Law Commission has put it,[16] "neither rich nor poor [but] generally has available an earned income, a pension expectancy and a capital asset – a house which may be encumbered with a mortgage", the court may have a reasonably wide discretion in the choice of orders under s. 3,[17] but not,

[12] Section 5(2).
[13] *Ashley* v. *Ashley*, [1968] P. 582; [1965] 3 All E.R. 554.
[14] *Roberts* v. *Roberts*, [1970] P. 1; [1968] 3 All E.R. 479.
[15] The same principles apply in magistrates' courts. Indeed, *Ashley* and *Roberts* were both concerned with proceedings under the Matrimonial Proceedings (Magistrates' Courts) Act 1960.
[16] Law Commission Paper No. 25, Appendix II, p. 154.
[17] Where the capital and income of a spouse are small a lump sum order is inappropriate; *Millward* v. *Millward*, [1971] 3 All E.R. 526; [1971] 1 W.L.R. 1432 (C.A.).

so far as concerns the children of the family, under s. 4.[18] If two households are involved, there may be great practical difficulties in calculating the financial provision to be allowed for the wife and children.

As between the wife and the children of whom she is given custody, or care and control, priority should be given to the latter, but the extent of the priority will depend partly on the degree to which she is responsible for the breakdown of the marriage. Her conduct is directly relevant in determining the amount of financial provision to be allowed to her,[19] but it also indirectly affects the children in that any reduction in the amount she would have received but for her responsibility will be available for their benefit. However, even if she is wholly responsible but is given, say, care and control, it may be necessary to provide some maintenance for her in order to enable her to look after the children. "She must be kept alive and fit in order to perform her function as a mother",[20] although the amount of the maintenance is not to be assessed on the basis of what it would cost to pay a housekeeper to look after them.[1] Quite apart from the question of responsibility, it is well known that magistrates' courts tend to favour provision for the children at the expense of the wife, partly because they are the innocent victims of the breakdown of the marriage, but partly also because this is more likely to persuade the husband to comply with the *whole* of the order, including the provision for the wife.[2] It may be that registrars of divorce courts give similar emphasis.

Where the court is concerned with possible variation of a settlement a different kind of problem sometimes arises between the blameless spouse and the children of the family. The former may want the settlement varied so as to be given a power of appointment to a future spouse or to the children of a subsequent marriage. The principle to be followed in such a

---

[18] An order transferring the matrimonial home to the wife and therefore of indirect benefit to the children may, however, often be appropriate.
[19] Section 5(1).
[20] *Per* HARMAN, L. J.
[1] *Milliken-Smith* v. *Milliken-Smith*, [1970] 2 All E.R. 560; [197c] 1 W.L.R. 973 (C.A.).
[2] Bromley, *op. cit.*, p. 445, n. 5, referring to the tendency, points out that, when the orders relating to the children terminate, the wife can seek variation in her own favour.

case is that the children of the family must not on the whole be placed at a disadvantage.[3] If their present interests are to be affected by admitting third parties to share the settled funds, they must be adequately compensated by alternative pecuniary benefits.[4]

There are two firmly established rules of a negative kind concerning the making of orders for financial provision for children which could with advantage have been included in s. 5. First, the court must not exercise its powers in such a way as to punish the spouse who has caused the breakdown of the marriage.[5] Second, the powers cannot be restricted by any agreement between the parties with regard to the financial provision to be made for a child of the family,[6] for example, by a term purporting to exclude the power to apply to the court for an order;[7] or, *semble*, with regard to the power of variation of a settlement, by any express term in the settlement.[8]

(d) Duration of Orders[9]

The earliest date from which periodical payments, whether unsecured or secured, may be ordered to begin is that of the application for the order. Unsecured, but not secured, payments must (apart from arrears) end on the death of the payer. Neither must, in the first instance, be made to extend beyond the date of the child's birthday following the date when he attained the upper limit of the compulsory school age, unless the court considers it right in the circumstances to specify a later date, and in any case they must normally come to an end when the child attains 18. However, further extension is permissible, and orders for periodical payments, for a lump sum payment and for transfer of property to the child may for the

---

[3] See JEUNE, P., in *Whitton* v. *Whitton*, [1901] P. 348, 353.
[4] For illustrations see *Forsyth* v. *Forsyth*, [1891] P. 363; *Scollick* v. *Scollick*, [1927] P. 205; [1927] All E.R. Rep. 523; *Maxwell* v. *Maxwell and Rognor*, [1951] P. 212; [1950] 2 All E.R. 979; *Best* v. *Best*, [1956] P. 76; [1955] 2 All E.R. 839; *Purnell* v. *Purnell*, [1961] P. 141; [1961] 1 All E.R. 369.
[5] *Attwood* v. *Attwood*, [1968] P.591, 595; [1968] 3 All E.R. 385, 388 (periodical payments); *Brett* v. *Brett*, [1969] 1 All E.R. 1007; [1969] 1 W.L.R. 487 (lump sum); *Ulrich* v. *Ulrich and Felton*, [1968] 1 All E.R. 67, 71; [1968] 1 W.L.R. 180, 187, (variation of settlement; settlement of spouse's property).
[6] *Bishop* v. *Bishop*, [1897] P.138 (C.A.).
[7] *Bennett* v. *Bennett*, [1951] 2 K.B. 572; [1951] 1 All E.R. 1088.
[8] See DENNING, L. J., in *Egerton* v. *Egerton*, [1949] 2 All E.R. 238, 242.
[9] See s. 8.

first time be made after attainment of majority in two kinds of exceptional cases. One of these is where there are special circumstances which justify the further extension or the making of an order, as the case may be: the most likely instance is where the child is ill or disabled. The other is where

> "the child is or will be, or if such an order or [extension] were made would be, receiving instruction at an educational establishment or undergoing training for a trade, profession or vocation, whether or not he is also, or will also be, in gainful employment".[10]

This exception, it will be seen, is much more liberal than that which allows for maintenance of dependants over 18 under the Matrimonial Proceedings (Magistrates' Courts) Act 1960, which obviously needs urgent amendment. One basic distinction between the two enactments is that the exceptions under s. 8 are not subject to any maximum age of the child, whereas no provision may be made for a child beyond 21 under the 1960 Act. It is to be hoped that the divorce court will not be reluctant to make orders under ss. 3 and 4(a) for much older children whose needs justify them. After all, there are no age limits in relation to orders for a settlement of property or variation of a settlement.

(e) Variation and Discharge of Orders

The court can vary or discharge certain orders or suspend, then revive, any terms in them. The scope of its powers is largely determined by the principle that when the marriage is brought to an end there ought to be a final adjustment of property rights. What is subsequently stated with regard to variation applies to the other powers in so far as the context permits.

(*i*) *Periodical Payments*

The powers extend primarily to orders for periodical payments, unsecured and secured.

When an application is made to vary[11] such an order, no order can be made under s. 4. This restriction is understandable and accords with the above principle, but is not, it is submitted, justifiable in a case of judicial separation. A lump

[10] Section 8(3) (a).
[11] The rule applies only to variation.

sum order in favour of a child is, however, permissible, *e.g.*, to meet his educational needs.[12]

Where the order relates to secured payments and the payer dies, the application for variation may be made by the person entitled to the payments or by the payer's personal representatives, but this must be done within six months from the date when representation was taken out, unless the court otherwise directs.

(*ii*) *Lump Sum*

A lump sum order is final in its effect, so that there can be no variation in the amount ordered and no question of repayment; but any provision for payment by instalments is variable, *e.g.*, by extending the period between the payment of instalments.

(*iii*) *Transfer Order*

Like a lump sum order an order for transfer of property is final and not subject to variation whether the order was made on a decree of divorce, nullity or judicial separation.

(*iv*) *Other Orders Under Section* 4

This last rule also applies to orders for settlement of property or for variation of a settlement or for extinguishing or reducing an interest under a settlement if made on or after a decree of divorce or nullity, but if made on or after a decree of judicial separation they may be varied when there is an application for rescission of the decree or for the dissolution of the marriage.[13] This exception recognises that in proceedings for judicial separation a final adjustment of property may be inappropriate because either the parties may later be reconciled or, if divorce does follow, that will be the moment for final adjustment.

In exercising its powers of variation the court must consider all the circumstances of the case, including any change in the

---

[12] A lump sum order is not possible on an application to vary an order for periodical payments in favour of a *spouse;* see s. 9(5). There are also strict limits on the spouse's evading the effects of s. 9(5) by seeking a lump sum order under an original application. While such an application may be allowed if made shortly after the making of the order for periodical payments and on the basis of fresh facts, only in very exceptional circumstances will it be entertained many years after the date of the order for periodical payments; *Powys* v. *Powys,* [1971] P.340; [1971] 3 All E.R. 116; *Jones* v. *Jones,* [1971] 3 All E.R. 1201 (C.A.).

[13] Section 9(2) and (4). Section 9 does not, it is submitted, impliedly allow a lump sum payment to be made on variation of the s. 4 order; for a different view see Bromley, *op. cit.,* p. 450, n. 5.

matters to which it was required to have regard when making the original order, including, therefore, particularly the matters specified in s. 5. In other words, it must act on the same principle as it does when entertaining an original application for an order.[14] Where the party against whom the order was made has died, account must be taken of the changed circumstances resulting from his death. This may be particularly relevant where there is an order for secured periodical payments. If the payer has remarried it may be desirable in the interests of his second wife and their children to relieve his estate of the security; or the release of capital on his death may justify enlarging the security.[15]

Moreover, in the case of an order for periodical payments, where the change of circumstances relates to the person entitled to the payments (*e.g.*, the child receives a windfall) or to the payer (*e.g.*, his reduced earning capacity due to ill-health) or where the latter dies, the court may order the recipient or his personal representative to pay to the payer or his personal representatives a sum which justly represents the excess payments made since the change of circumstances.[16] It is suggested that there will have to be very compelling reasons before a child recipient will be ordered to make repayment.

(f) Enforcement of Orders[17]

(i) Orders for Money Payments

A general restriction is imposed on the enforcement of orders for money payments made under s. 3 of the 1970 Act.[18] The payment of arrears due under an order for periodical payments or of a lump sum payment (or any instalment thereof) can only be enforced with the leave of the court if they became due more than 12 months before the beginning of the proceedings to enforce payment.

---

[14] See s. 5, *supra*, p. 467; *Jones* v. *Jones*, [1971] 3 All E.R. 1201 (C.A.).
[15] See Law Commission, No. 25, para. 91. Prior to the 1970 Act variation of an order for secured payments was not allowed.
[16] Section 11. The order may provide for payment by instalments and it may be varied or discharged.
    See also s. 34 for the jurisdiction of a county court over applications under s. 11.
[17] See generally the Report of the [Payne] Committee on the Enforcement of Judgment Debts (Cmnd. 3909); and for details of the methods of enforcement the reader is referred to textbooks on matrimonial causes.
[18] See s. 10.

Financial Provisions for Children

A variety of methods are available to enforce orders for money payments. Whether the order is made in the High Court or a divorce county court[19] it can be enforced by a judgment summons; an attachment of earnings order; registration in, and enforcement by, a magistrates' court; a charging order;[20] garnishee proceedings; the appointment of a receiver by way of equitable execution; and by a writ of *fieri facias* in the High Court or a warrant of execution in a county court. Additionally, a High Court order is enforceable by writ of sequestration. Arrears due under an order for periodical payments are neither recoverable by action[1] nor provable in bankruptcy;[2] *aliter* a lump sum payment.

Judgment Summons

The power to imprison defaulting civil debtors was abolished by the Administration of Justice Act 1970, following the unanimous recommendation of the Payne Committee, but has been retained by the Act for the purpose of enforcing maintenance orders.[3] A judgment summons may be issued[4] under the Debtors Act 1869 for payment of arrears or a lump sum. If the order for payment was made in a divorce county court or in the High Court, the summons may be issued in a divorce county court; but it is issuable in the High Court only in respect of an order made there. If from an examination of the defaulter's means it appears that he has the ability to pay, he may first be given the opportunity to do so by way of instalments and, in default thereof, may be committed to prison for up to six weeks for contempt.[5]

Attachment of Earnings

Where a judgment summons has been issued the court may

[19] An application can be made for the High Court to enforce a divorce county court order.
[20] BARNARD, J., in *Scott* v. *Scott*, [1952] 2 All E.R. 890, 891 doubted whether this method could be used to recover arrears of maintenance.
[1] *Robins* v. *Robins*, [1907] 2 K.B. 13.
[2] *Re Hedderwick, Morten* v. *Brinsley*, [1933] Ch. 669.
[3] Its retention divided the Payne Committee; see Cmnd. 3909, paras. 1008-1108.
[4] Where the recipient of the payment is a child, his next friend must issue the summons; *Shelley* v. *Shelley* (No. 1), [1952] P.107; [1952] 1 All E.R. 70.
[5] For the application of the procedure to orders under the M.P. & P. Act see the Administration of Justice Act 1970, s. 11 and Sched. 8, as amended by M.P. & P. Act, Sched. 2, para. 8.

instead of ordering committal under the Debtors Act make an attachment of earnings order,[6] but such an order is usually made as the result of an application for it. The relevant law is now consolidated in the Attachment of Earnings Act 1971[7] and extends to, *inter alia*, orders for payments made under the Matrimonial Proceedings and Property Act.[8]

The applicant for an attachment of earnings order will usually be the disappointed payee, but the payer himself can also apply.[9] An order on the application of the payee cannot be made (1) until the debtor has failed to make one or more payments and (2) if the failure is not due to his wilful refusal or neglect. The effect of the order is to direct the payer's employer to make periodical deductions from his "attachable earnings", *i.e.*, from his earnings[10] which remain after the employer has deducted income tax and certain statutory and superannuation contributions.[11] The amounts deducted by the employer must be paid over to the court at such times as are specified in the order.

The scheme for assessing the amount of the deductions is based on the principle of what the payer can reasonably afford, and this is determined by reference to the "normal deduction rate" and the "protected earnings rate".[12] The former is the weekly, monthly or other regular amount which it is reasonable to apply out of the payer's earnings to meet his liability under the original order, but when the attachment of earnings order is sought to secure payments under a maintenance order (not being a lump sum order) account must also be taken of any right or liability of the payer to deduct income tax when making the payments and the rate must not exceed that which appears necessary to secure payment of the sums falling due

---

[6] Attachment of Earnings Act 1971, s. 3(4).
[7] Formerly contained in the Maintenance Orders Act 1958 and Part II of the Administration of Justice Act 1970. It partly implements recommendations of the Payne Committee (Cmnd. 3909, paras. 580-629). See Cretney, 121 N.L.J. 643.
[8] Attachment of Earnings Act 1971, Sched. I.
[9] A debtor also has a general right to apply to a magistrates' court. (See s. 3(1) (d) (i) and (ii)).
[10] For the definition of earnings see s. 24(1). It covers (a) wages or salary, together with such emoluments as fees, bonus or commission and (b) sums payable by way of pension, including an annuity for past services and periodical payments as compensation for loss of office or employment; but it excludes such items as the pay of servicemen or seamen and various social security benefits. [11] Schedule 3, Part I, para. 3.
[12] Section 6(5).

from time to time under the maintenance order and of those already due and unpaid.[13] The protection earnings rate is the weekly, monthly or other regular sum below which, having regard to the payer's resources and needs (including the needs of any person for whom he must, or reasonably may, provide), it is reasonable that the earnings actually paid to him should not be reduced.[14] When on any pay-day the attachable earnings exceed the protected earnings, then, so far as the excess allows, the normal deduction is made, and, if there is still an excess, it can be used to make good deductions which it was not possible to make on another previous pay-day.[15]

In order to administer the system a number of obligations are imposed on the debtor and his employer. For example, both can be ordered to furnish statements of the former's earnings and the payer may also be required to give details of his resources and needs. Both must notify the court of changes of employment and earnings.[16] Such provisions do not eradicate the risk of the debtor's seeking to evade liability by continual change of employment, but it is a risk that can be overstated, particularly in view of the high incidence of unemployment. Possibly a greater risk is that the employer may be tempted to terminate the employment of a person in respect of whom an attachment of earnings order is in force; but the extension of the system beyond enforcement of maintenance orders to that of judgment debts, for which the Attachment of Earnings Act provides, could eventually lead to common acceptance of it by employers as an administrative responsibility.[17] Certainly, there ought to be regular reviews of the working of the system.

Registration of Order in Magistrates' Court

The effect of registering the High Court or county court order in a magistrates' court is that it then becomes enforceable by the magistrates' court in the same ways as an affiliation order may be enforced.[18] That court also has the power to vary

---

[13] Section 6(6).
[14] Section 6(5) (b) and 25(3).
[15] Schedule 3, Part I, para. 6.
[16] Sections 14 and 15; and see s. 7 for the employer's duty to comply with the attachment of earnings order.
[17] Compare the initial opposition of employers to the system of P.A.Y.E.
[18] Maintenance Orders Act 1958, ss. 1-5.
   Correspondingly a magistrates' court maintenance order may be registered and enforced in the High Court.

the rate of payments specified by the original court, provided that it acts on the same principles as the High Court or county court;[19] but it may instead remit the application for variation of the rate to the original court. The magistrates' court has no wider powers of variation and the registration does not otherwise affect those of the original court.[20]

The principle of registration and enforcement in another court is not confined to England and Wales. An order made in one part of the United Kingdom or the Commonwealth may be registered and enforced in another part.[1]

(ii) Orders Other than Money Payments

Orders to transfer or settle property can be enforced by an order for committal in the High Court or by attachment in a divorce county court.

(g) Avoidance of Transactions

The efficacy of an order for financial provision would be seriously undermined if the party against whom it was made, normally but not necessarily the husband, could freely dispose of property which would otherwise be available to meet his obligations under the order. He may be reluctant to do this where the effect would be to deprive his children of direct financial provision given to them by an order, but, even where his action is primarily aimed at his wife, the children are likely indirectly to suffer. Section 16 of the Matrimonial Proceedings and Property Act 1970 affords some protection to the members of the family.

It is an essential condition of the court's intervention that the husband should intend to defeat the applicant's claim for financial provision, *i.e.*, intend to prevent such provision from being granted to her or to her for the benefit of a child of the family or to reduce the amount of the provision which might be granted or to frustrate or impede the enforcement of any order for financial provision.

[19] *Miller* v. *Miller*, [1961] P.1; [1960] 3 All E.R. 115.
[20] Maintenance Orders Act 1958, s. 4, as amended by Administration of Justice Act 1970, s. 48 and Sched. 11.
[1] See Part II of the Maintenance Orders Act 1950 and the Maintenance Orders (Facilities for Enforcement) Act 1920. The latter Act is to be replaced by the Maintenance Orders (Reciprocal Enforcement) Act 1972, which will widen the powers of reciprocal enforcement.

If the court is satisfied that the husband has such an intention it can intervene either by anticipating the husband and restraining him from making any disposition of the property or from transferring it out of the jurisdiction or from otherwise dealing with it or by setting aside a disposition already made. In the latter circumstances the court may act either where the transaction has been completed before any order for financial provision is made or where completed subsequently.

Any disposition made within three years before the date of the application is, unless the contrary is shown, presumed to be intended to defeat the applicant's claim if it would have or, as the case may be, has had that consequence. The same presumption operates where the application is to prevent a disposition being made. Where it is made three years or more before the date of application the wife must positively prove the necessary intention.

There are, however, certain limits to the protection given by s. 16. It does not extend to testamentary dispositions or to any *inter vivos* disposition made more than three years before January 1, 1971, or to any disposition made by the husband for valuable consideration (other than marriage) to a person who acted in good faith and without notice of the husband's intention. Moreover, even if the disposition is set aside, the rights of a purchaser for value arising from a later transaction into which he entered without notice of the invalidity are protected.[2]

VII. WILFUL NEGLECT TO MAINTAIN

Financial provision for a child of the family may be ordered under the Matrimonial Proceedings and Property Act 1970[3] or under the Matrimonial Proceedings (Magistrates' Courts) Act 1960,[4] where a parent or spouse[5] has wilfully neglected to maintain the child. Since there are significant differences in the respective enactments, the topic is treated comparatively. Some aspects of it have been examined elsewhere and therefore require the briefest reference.

---

[2] *National Provincial Bank, Ltd.* v. *Hastings Car Mart, Ltd.*, [1964] Ch. 665; [1964] 1 All E.R. 688. [3] Section 6.
[4] Sections 1(1) (h) and (i) and 2(1) (h).
[5] Subsequent references to a parent include a spouse who is not a parent.

Wilful Neglect to Maintain

(a) Rules of Identical or Similar Application

The following rules apply to both Acts.

(i) Either parent, as party to a valid or voidable marriage,[6] may apply to the appropriate court for an order on the ground that the other has wilfully neglected to maintain the child, but neither the child nor anyone else on his behalf except the parent may do so.

In the vast majority of cases the mother is the applicant and usually she is also alleging the husband's wilful neglect to maintain her.

(ii) Decisions as to the meaning of the expression "wilful neglect to provide reasonable maintenance" are applicable equally to applications under the one Act as to those under the other.[7]

It is questionable whether the parent's liability ought to depend on an element of wilfulness. That is not a requirement of the parent's obligation to maintain his child, or spouse, for the purpose of liability under the Ministry of Social Security Act 1966,[8] where the question is whether there has in fact been neglect which cannot be justified. Since wilfulness involves deliberate conduct, the practical effect of its inclusion as an element is that a parent cannot be guilty of wilful neglect if he is ignorant of the needs of the child; for example, where he is already providing maintenance but because of a change of circumstances, unknown to him, the amount provided has ceased to be a reasonable provision.[9] If the test were made the same for the purposes of the Acts of 1960 and 1970 and the scheme of social security, namely, that liability depends on neglect without good cause, a parent's ignorance would not

---

[6] The marriage must still be in existence at the date when the order is to be made; *Turczak* v. *Turczak*, [1970] P.198; [1969] 3 All E.R. 317; see Karsten, 33 M.L.R. 205.

[7] *Per* BIRKETT, L. J., in *Tulip* v. *Tulip*, [1951] P.378, 385; [1951] 2 All E.R. 91, 95 (C.A.).

[8] See *post*, p. 504.

[9] *Jones* v. *Jones*, [1959] P.38; [1958] 3 All E.R. 410, (ignorance of needs of wife). The dictum of the Court of Appeal in *Lilley* v. *Lilley*, [1960] P.158, 180; [1959] 3 All E.R. 283, p. 289, that "the wrongdoing may . . . consist of the very fact of a failure to maintain" must be read subject to *Jones* v. *Jones*. See Brown, *The Offence of Wilful Neglect to Maintain a Wife*, 23 M.L.R. 1.
The onus of proving that the neglect was not wilful lies on the parent; *cp. Stirland* v. *Stirland*, [1959] 3 All E.R. 891; [1960] 1 W.L.R. 18.

necessarily exclude financial liability for the past, but would be highly relevant in determining its extent, if any.

Neither Act offers guidance as to the factors which the court should take into account in deciding whether there has been a failure to provide, or contribute towards, reasonable maintenance. The 1960 Act is totally silent and s. 6(3) of the 1970 Act merely states that the section applies to any child of the family in respect of whom it is reasonable in all the circumstances to expect the parent to provide or contribute. It is submitted that in proceedings under either Act the court will consider all the circumstances, but will particularly be guided by the criteria which are prescribed by s. 5(2) of the 1970 Act when making financial orders for children in proceedings for divorce, nullity or judicial separation.[10] Case law indicates that this has long been the judicial approach. Thus, regard will be had to the following matters:

(1) The financial needs of the child.
(2) His financial resources.
(3) Any physical or mental disability suffered by him.
(4) The standard of living which he enjoyed before the date when the parent began to neglect to maintain him.[11]
(5) The manner in which he was being educated or trained before that date and in which the parents expected him to be educated or trained.
(6) The financial resources and obligations of the parent against whom an order is sought.

In considering in the present context his potential earning capacity, his wilful abstention from earning to keep his child would be particularly relevant to the question of the wilfulness of his neglect.[12] So, too, would be his refusal to accept the offer of a third party to provide money to enable him to maintain the child.[13] There can, however, be no question of wilful neglect if he does not have resources to provide, or contribute towards, maintenance.

[10] See *ante*, p. 467.
[11] "The word 'reasonable' no doubt has to be interpreted against the background of the standard of life which [the husband] previously had maintained" *per* Hodson, J., in *Scott* v. *Scott*, [1951] P.245, 248; [1951] 1 All E.R. 216, 217.
[12] *Earnshaw* v. *Earnshaw*, [1896] P. 160.
[13] *Walton* v. *Walton* (1900), 64 J.P. 264.

Wilful Neglect to Maintain

All the above matters will be relevant for the dual purpose of deciding whether there has been wilful neglect to maintain, and, if so, the kind of order to be made and its terms. But what relevance have the financial resources and obligations of the other parent, in practice the wife, with whom the child is living? So far as concerns the question of proof of wilful neglect, the answer appears to be, "None". After earlier equivocal dicta to the contrary,[14] the view, was firmly expressed by the Court of Appeal in *Northrop* v. *Northrop*[15] that the husband who is living apart from his wife and child under a separation agreement is not relieved of his duty to maintain the child by the fact that the agreement contains no express or implied term that he should provide for the child or contains an express term that the wife accepts entirely the burden of maintenance. So, even if the child is being wholly maintained by the wife in such circumstances that his present standard of living is far higher than that to which he was accustomed before the parents separated, the husband's liability to the child for neglect is not affected. It is still reasonable, provided that he has the means, to expect him to fulfil his duty by contributing to the child's maintenance, and, where the proceedings are being brought under the 1970 Act, s. 6(3)[16] cannot, it is submitted, assist him. However, having established that there is wilful neglect, the wife's means should not be ignored in deciding what order, if any, is to be made. In the case of proceedings under the 1970 Act the court is directed to make such orders "as it thinks just". It is submitted that it would be just to take into account the wife's means. In a magistrates' court there is not a similar direction, but the terms of an order are, it is submitted, just as much within the court's discretion.[17]

Similar principles apply where the husband is making some financial provision under the separation agreement. A term that the wife will make no further demands on him in relation to the child cannot exempt him from his obligation to the child.

---

[14] *Starkie* v. *Starkie* (No. 2), [1953] 2 All E.R. 1519, 1522; [1954] 1 W.L.R. 98, 104; *Cooke* v. *Cooke*, [1961] P.16, 22; [1960] 3 All E.R. 39, 43; *Young* v. *Young*, [1964] P.152, 158-159, 160; [1962] 3 All E.R. 120, 124-125.

[15] [1968] P.74, 97 and 116; [1967] 2 All E.R. 961, 965, 978-979.

[16] *Supra*.

[17] See DIPLOCK, L. J., in *Northrop* v. *Northrop*, [1968] P.74, 118; [1967] 2 All E.R. 961, 979.

Moreover, a clause restricting her right to apply to a court for financial provision in respect of the child is void.[18] It does not, however, follow that the husband will be guilty of wilful neglect. This will depend upon whether or not the amount of maintenance which he provides under the agreement is held to be reasonable. If it is and payments have been made, there is no wilful neglect.[19] The principles have been laid down where the wife has alleged wilful neglect to maintain her,[20] but apply equally in respect of the child. Where the agreement is in writing and falls within s. 13 of the 1970 Act, the wife may choose to seek variation of it rather than to allege wilful neglect under that Act or under the 1960 Act. The court's powers of variation may be exercised not only to increase the amount of payments where the agreement already contains financial arrangements concerning the child's maintenance or education, but also, where the agreement is a separation agreement and contains no such arrangements, to insert them for the child's benefit.[1]

Where the parent has been providing maintenance for the child in compliance with a maintenance order he cannot be guilty of wilful neglect so long as no change occurs in the financial circumstances of the child.[2] The court must be presumed to have made reasonable provision for him.

(iii) In most applications the wife is alleging wilful neglect of herself and the child. These are two separate offences.[3] Therefore, the wife who has been guilty of desertion[4] or adultery which has not been condoned, connived at or conduced to by the husband[5] or whose conduct has reasonably led him to believe that she has committed adultery[6] has forfeited her

[18] Under s. 13(1) of the 1970 Act if the agreement is within that section (*infra*), at common law on the ground of public policy if it is not (*Bennett* v. *Bennett*, [1952] 1 K.B. 249; [1952] 1 All E.R. 413 (C.A.)).
[19] Equally he would not be liable if he had in fact paid reasonable maintenance, although there was no agreement to pay it.
[20] *Tulip* v. *Tulip*, [1951] P.378; [1951] 2 All E.R. 91 (C.A.); *Dowell* v. *Dowell*, [1952] 2 All E.R. 141.
[1] See s. 14 of M.P. & P. Act 1970 for details of the power to vary or insert.
[2] *Baynham* v. *Baynham*, [1969] 1 All E.R. 305; [1968] 1 W.L.R. 1890 (C.A.).
[3] See the cases cited in footnote 14, *supra*. For a trenchant criticism of the law generally see Brown, *Maintenance and Esoterism*, 31 M.L.R. 121.
[4] *Lilley* v. *Lilley*, [1960] P.169 (C.A.); [1959] 3 All E.R. 283.
[5] In the case of proceedings under the 1960 Act her adultery statutorily precludes an order in her favour (s. 2(3) (b)). There is not a similar rule in the 1970 Act but in accordance with common law principles the effect the same.   [6] *Cooke* v. *Cooke*, [1961] P.16; [1960] 3 All E.R. 39.

right to be maintained and cannot establish his wilful neglect to maintain her. But he can be held liable in respect of the child if the facts warrant it.

If the application is based only on alleged neglect to maintain the wife and not the child but fails for the above reasons, in proceedings under the 1960 Act the magistrates' court may, nevertheless, make an order for provision for the child if it considers it necessary,[7] but there is no corresponding power conferred by the 1970 Act.[8] If an application based on neglect of her succeeds and either it is the only ground alleged or a further allegation of neglect of the child fails, there is nothing to stop the court from making an order in respect of both of them.[9]

Where wilful neglect of the child is proved, the court can not only make an order with regard to him but also order payments to be made to the wife, even if she has been guilty of a matrimonial offence; but the court is not likely to make the amount of the payments to her, especially where she is guilty, greater than is reasonably necessary to enable her in all the circumstances to make proper provision for the needs of the child.[10] Allowances may thus be made for any loss of earnings she suffers through having to look after the child. Alternatively the same result can be achieved by increasing the amount payable to the wife in respect of the child, which is a preferable procedure especially now that the statutory limits on the amount of maintenance awardable by a magistrates' court have been abolished.[11]

(b) Differing Rules

There are a number of detailed points of difference in proceedings under the respective Acts.

(i) A husband's duty under the 1970 Act is to provide

---

[7] Section 4(1). For example, it may think that the amount of the maintenance which the husband has been providing for the child needs to be increased, especially as there will be available additional resources which, had it not been for the wife's conduct, would have been needed to make provision for her. But see *ante*, p. 471: even where the wife can establish a claim, the court may emphasise that of the child at the wife's expense.

[8] There is power where proceedings for divorce, nullity or judicial separation are dismissed (s. 3(1) (b), *ante*, p. 462).

[9] *Ridley* v. *Ridley*, [1953] P.150; [1953] 1 All E.R. 798.

[10] *Northrop* v. *Northrop*, [1968] P.74 (C.A.), [1967] 2 All E.R. 961,WILLMER, L. J., dissenting on this point.

[11] Maintenance Orders Act 1968, s. 1 & Sched.

reasonable maintenance or to make a proper contribution towards reasonable maintenance, whereas the 1960 Act does not expressly allow for the lesser obligation. Nevertheless, it might be implied on the ground that the latter Act does recognise the notion of contribution in that, if any ground of complaint[12] is proved, either party to the marriage may be ordered to make payments for the child.[13]

No problem arises in this respect over the nature of the wife's duty. Under both Acts the alternative obligations are recognised.

(ii) Under the 1960 Act the wife's duty to maintain the child depends on the husband's earning capacity being impaired.[14] There is no such condition precedent in a case under the 1970 Act.

(iii) The class of children of the family is generally wider for the purpose of the 1970 Act, since, unlike its counterpart, the child need not be a child of at least one of the spouses.[15]

Where the child is not a child of the spouse against whom the order is sought, then, in deciding whether there has been wilful neglect and, if so, what order should be made regard must be had to the terms of s. 5(3) of the 1970 Act and s. 2(5) of the 1960 Act, which, it has been noted,[16] differ materially.

(iv) The High Court or a divorce county court has much wider powers with regard to the kinds of orders it may make.[17] It can order periodical payments, unsecured and secured, and [or] a lump sum payment to be made to a person for the benefit of the child or to the child himself. An order for a lump sum may provide for payment by instalments, unsecured or secured. Such an order may particularly be made to enable the applicant to meet liabilities reasonably incurred in maintaining the child before the application was made.[18]

A magistrates' court is restricted to the making of orders for unsecured periodical payments for a weekly sum.[19]

---

[12] Under s. 1. [13] Section 2(1) (h). [14] Section 1(1) (i).
[15] See *ante*, Chapter 9, pp. 273 and 280.
[16] *Ante*, p. 469, and 459 respectively.
  Unlike s. 5(3), s. 2(5) is not expressly related to the question of culpability but only to whether an order should be made and its provisions, but it is submitted that a magistrates' court ought equally to consider it in determining whether there has been wilful neglect.
[17] Prior to the 1970 Act they were more limited.
[18] M.P. & P. Act 1970, s. 6(6). [19] M.P. (M.C.) Act 1960, s. 2(1) (h).

Obviously the financial circumstances of the parent against whom the order is sought will largely determine under which Act it is better to proceed.

(v) The duration of orders beyond the age of 16 may be longer under the 1970 Act than that permitted by the 1960 Act.[20]

(vi) The High Court or a divorce county court may make a temporary order for periodical payments to meet immediate financial needs of the child until the final determination of the application.[1] A magistrates' court can exercise a similar power by making an interim order,[2] but there are certain temporal restrictions[3] which do not apply to an order made by the High Court or a county court.

(vii) Only the respondent can be ordered by the High Court or a county court to make financial provision for the child, whereas either the defendant or the complainant or both can be ordered to do so by a magistrates' court.

(viii) A magistrates' court does not have the power of the other courts to set aside transactions which are aimed at defeating the claims of the child.[4]

(ix) Although an order can, under either Act, be made while the parties cohabit,[5] in the case of proceedings in a magistrates' court continued cohabitation for three months brings the order to an end, except in so far as it provides for payments to be made to a person other than the spouses for the maintenance of the child.[6] Rightly, the 1970 Act does not allow continued cohabitation to affect an order. The sanction of a court order may exceptionally have the salutary effect on, say, the husband of inducing him to discharge the financial responsibilities which he owes to his family with whom he lives.

VIII. AFFILIATION ORDERS

Although the legal gap between the legitimate child and the illegitimate is continually being narrowed,[7] discriminations

[20] See *ante*, pp. 472 and 460.   [1] M.P. & P. Act 1970, s. 6(5).
[2] M.P. (M.C.) Act 1960, s. 6.   [3] *Ante*, Chapter 9, p. 277.
[4] See *ante*, p. 479.
[5] For High Court and county court proceedings see *Caras* v. *Caras*, [1955] 1 All E.R. 624; [1955] 1 W.L.R. 254; and, for proceedings in magistrates' courts, M.P. (M.C.) Act 1960, s. 7(1).   [6] Proviso to s. 7(1).
[7] For a summary of the main changes see *ante*, Chapter 8, p. 236.

remain. Of these the most serious relates to the provisions of maintenance for the illegitimate child by the mother and father. Both may be held liable indirectly by virtue of his or her duty to maintain under the system of Social Security,[8] and exceptionally an order may be made against one of them where the child is involved in matrimonial proceedings as a child of the family.[9] Also, they may enter into an agreement concerning his maintenance. Otherwise, however, financial provision can only be made by the mother's bringing affiliation proceedings, an archaic process which still bears the quasi-criminal marks of the early Poor Law.[10] Under that system recognition of the illegitimate child was initially limited to the duty of the mother or father to maintain him and thereby relieve the community wholly or partly of that duty. Even when a right was eventually given[11] to the mother to seek maintenance from the father, it was permitted only within the narrow confines of the Poor Law system. Consequently, it was only enforceable under the limited jurisdiction of the justices, with the father's financial liability being severely restricted however wealthy he might be. This glaring injustice was not removed until 1968.[12] There are others which equally call for urgent reform.

Under the Affiliation Proceedings Act 1957 the mother may, within certain time limits, apply to a magistrates' court for a summons to be served on the man alleged to be the father. Jurisdiction may certainly be exercised if mother, child and putative father are all in this country,[13] but it is not certain how far all three need to be here and whether mere presence or normal residence is required.[14] Section 3 of the Act supports the test of residence, the jurisdiction of the particular magistrates' court depending on the petty sessional area in which the mother resides. Except where the mother or father resides in Scotland or Northern Ireland,[15] it seems that both of them must

[8] *Ante*, p. 455; *post*, p. 504.
[9] For example, where a wife is seeking provision for her husband's illegitimate child who is a child of their family.
[10] This originated in a statute of 1576 (18 Eliz. I, c.3).
[11] By the Poor Law Amendment Act 1844.
[12] By the Maintenance Orders Act 1968, s. 1 & Sched.
[13] *R.* v. *Bow Road Justices, ex parte Adedigba*, [1968] 2 Q.B. 572; [1968] 2 All E.R. 89 (C.A.).
[14] See von Londauer, 17 I.C.L.Q. 1015.
[15] See Maintenance Orders Act 1950, s. 3.

reside here,[16] but the residence or even the presence of the child may not be essential.[17] The fact that he was born abroad is irrelevant,[18] as is any foreign domicile of the mother or father at the time of birth.[19]

An essential condition is that the mother be a "single woman" either at the time of the birth of her child[20] or at the date of her application.[21] The term "single woman" has been construed liberally and artificially.[1] It covers three main categories:

(1) the mother who was not married at the date of the birth or the application,[2] *i.e.*, was then a spinster, widow or woman whose marriage had been dissolved or, being voidable, had been annulled;

(2) the mother who at the relevant date was married but living apart from her husband by virtue of a decree of judicial separation or a matrimonial order containing a non-cohabitation clause;[3]

(3) the mother who at the relevant date was married but living apart from her husband and had lost the right to be maintained by him because of her uncondoned adultery,[4] or, even if it had been condoned, because of her subsequent desertion. Where they are living in the same house the presumption of cohabitation may be rebutted.[5] Provided that it does not involve merely a short absence from the matrimonial home, the cause of the living apart is apparently immaterial.

---

[16] *Berkley* v. *Thompson* (1884), 10 App.Cas. 45 (H.L.).
[17] See SALMON, L. J., in *Adedigba, supra*, at pp. 581 and 94 respectively.
[18] *Adedigba*, overruling a line of authorities beginning with *R.* v. *Blane*, (1849), 13 Q.B. 769; [1843-60] All E.R. Rep. 397.
[19] *Adedigba.*   [20] Legitimacy Act 1959, s. 4.
[21] *Gaines* v. *W. (an infant)*, [1968] 1 Q.B. 782; [1968] 1 All E.R. 189.
[1] Vividly illustrated by *Kruhlak* v. *Kruhlak*, [1958] 2 Q.B. 32; [1958] 1 All E.R. 154, where a married woman was held to be a "single woman" even *quoad* her own husband in respect of their adulterine child. The necessity for this extended interpretation has almost wholly been removed by the Legitimacy Act 1959, s. 1(1) (*ante*, p. 249) since it provides for legitimation of an adulterine child by the marriage of his parents provided the father is domiciled in England or Wales at the time of the marriage.
[2] These alternative dates are subsequently referred to as "the relevant date".
[3] *Boyce* v. *Cox*, [1922] 1 K.B. 149.
[4] *Jones* v. *Evans*, [1944] K.B. 582; [1945] 1 All E.R. 19; *cf. Marshall* v. *Malcolm* (1917), 87 L.J.K.B. 491.
[5] *Watson* v. *Tuckwell* (1947), 63 T.L.R. 634; *Whitton* v. *Garner*, [1965] 1 All E.R. 70; [1965] 1 W, L.R. 313, *Giltrow* v. *Day*, [1965] 1 All E.R. 73; [1965] 1 W.L.R. 317.

Thus, it may even be due to the husband's serving a term of imprisonment.[6]

There is, it is submitted, no justification for making the putative father's liability turn on the mother's marital or non-marital status. Why, for example, should it depend on whether he has or not condoned her adultery. The requirement that she should be a single woman should be abolished.

So should the time limits on her application.[7] This may be made during pregnancy, but it serves no purpose since no order will be made before birth in case the child is still-born.[8] Otherwise, it must be made:[9]

(1) within 3 years after the birth; or
(2) at any time if the alleged father, whether personally or through his agent (*e.g.*, a parent) whom he authorised,[10] provided maintenance for the child in money or in kind[11] within 3 years after the birth; or
(3) if he ceased to reside in England before the birth[12] or within 3 years after it, then, within 12 months' after his return to England.

Special provision is made for the mother who, before the child's birth, was a party to a marriage which was void because she or the man was under 16 and he had access to her within 12 months before the birth. She may apply at any time.[13] Apart from this exception, the rules are still too restrictive.[14] It is suggested that no statutory limits should be imposed. Any delay in taking proceedings should not operate as an absolute bar, but should be cogent evidence in determining the extent to which the defendant should be financially liable once his paternity is established.

[6] See *R.* v. *Pilkington* (1853), 2 E. & B. 546; Lord GODDARD, C.J., in *Mooney* v. *Mooney*, [1953] 1 Q.B. 38, 41; [1952] 2 All E.R. 812, 813.
[7] For a criticism see Lasok, *Time Factor in Affiliation Proceedings*, 120 N.L.J. 679.   [8] *R.* v. *De Brouquens* (1811), 14 East 277.
[9] Affiliation Proceedings Act 1957, s. 2, as amended by the Affiliation Proceedings (Amendment) Act 1972. The former rules provided for a period of 12 months instead of 3 years. The amendments operate from October 27, 1972.
[10] *G. (A.)* v. *G. (T.)*, [1970] 2 Q.B. 643 (C.A.), [1970] 3 All E.R. 546.
[11] *Roberts* v. *Roberts*, [1962] P.212; [1962] 2 All E.R. 967.
[12] *R.* v. *Evans*, [1896] 1 Q.B. 228.
[13] Alternatively she could bring a nullity suit and seek the far more beneficial orders allowed by the Matrimonial Proceedings and Property Act 1970, *ante*, pp. 461 *et seq.*
[14] Compare the limit imposed where the Supplementary Benefits Commission or a local authority are applying for an affiliation order, *post*, p. 496.

Although affiliation proceedings are domestic proceedings[15] and the burden of proof in civil cases applies, the Affiliation Proceedings Act makes corroboration of the mother's evidence a *sine qua non*, even though corroborative evidence is not an absolute requirement in criminal proceedings. The evidence may take many forms,[16] for example, that the complainant associated with the defendant but not with other men over the relevant period[17] or that he had sexual intercourse with her a short time before the child could have been conceived.[18] The new power to order blood tests[19] will facilitate compliance with the requirement of corroboration.

The rule concerning corroboration is partly explained by the high risk of perjury, but that which has made the giving of evidence by the mother an essential requirement is unjustly restrictive. It is wrong, for example, that a child should be deprived of the benefit of an order because the mother's mental incapacity, which supervenes after the summons has been served, precludes her from giving evidence. That, indeed, would be a case where the need for him to be supported by the father would be all the greater. The Affiliation Proceedings (Amendment) Act 1972 now allows for the possibility of adjudging the defendant to be the putative father on other evidence without requiring the mother's corroborative evidence.[20]

A serious defect is the limit imposed on the kind of financial provisions which the father may be ordered to make. Apart from payments concerning the expenses incidental to the child's birth or, where he has died before the making of an order, his funeral expenses, only unsecured payments by way of weekly sums for the child's maintenance and education are possible.[1] No orders for secured payments, a lump sum

---

[15] Affiliation Proceedings (Amendment) Act 1972, s. 3. But appeal lies to the Crown Court, which is by way of a rehearing, with the same rules relating to the mother's evidence applicable; Affiliation Proceedings Act 1957, s. 8, as amended by the Courts Act 1971.
[16] See Chislett, *Affiliation Proceedings*, pp. 27-32. The following may particularly be noted: *Thomas* v. *Jones*, [1921] 1 K.B. 22 (C.A.); *Jeffery* v. *Johnson*, [1952] 2 Q.B. 8 (C.A.), [1952] 1 All E.R. 450; *Cracknell* v. *Smith*, [1960] 3 All E.R. 569; [1960] 1 W.L.R. 1239.
[17] *Moore* v. *Hewitt*, [1947] K.B. 831; [1947] 2 All E.R. 270.
[18] *Simpson* v. *Collinson*, [1964] 2 Q.B. 80 (C.A.); [1964] 1 All E.R. 262.
[19] *Ante*, Chapter 8.
[20] For the similar position of the Supplementary Benefits Commission or a local authority who provides for the child, see *post*, p. 497.
[1] Sect on 4(2). Where the mother has made her complaint before or within two months after the child's birth, the weekly sum may be calculated from the date of birth (sub-s. (3)).

payment, a transfer or settlement of property may be made, even though one or more of them may be appropriate in view of the father's means. The court must take into account all the circumstances of the case,[2] but the Act does not give guidance as to what specific matters are to be weighed in assessing the amount of the weekly payments. If the child has means of his own, these are relevant. So are his age,[3] health and education and any special circumstances affecting him, such as any disability. *Semble* regard must also be had to any expenses and loss of income incurred by the mother through having to look after the child.[4] As for the standard of living against which the calculation should be made, it is submitted that this should be the standard which the child would reasonably be likely to enjoy were the mother and father married.[5]

There are also restrictions on the duration of the payments. Although they may normally be made until the child reaches 16, they are not required to be made in respect of any period after he has attained 13, unless the order contains a direction that they are to continue until 16.[6] This rule is an unjustified discrimination against the illegitimate child which finds no parallel in provisions for maintenance of legitimate children. Where the child is engaged in a course of education or training, payments may be continued by further orders, but the period for each must not exceed two years, and, in any event, an order must come to an end when the child reaches the age of 21. It will be seen that these provisions differ from the corresponding powers, conferred by the Matrimonial Proceedings (Magistrates' Courts) Act 1960 and the Matrimonial Proceedings and Property Act 1970, to provide for children beyond the ages of 16 and 18 respectively.[7]

Normally, the person entitled to apply for an order to receive the payments thereunder is the mother, but, in the event of her death or unsoundness of mind or imprisonment, magistrates can grant custody of the child to someone else who then becomes entitled to the payments under the order,[8]

[2] Section 4(2).   [3] See *infra*.
[4] See Bromley, *op. cit.*, p. 484, citing *Northrop* v. *Northrop*, [1968] P.74 (C.A.); [1967] 2 All E.R. 961, *ante*, p. 485.
[5] But compare Bromley, *ibid.*
[6] Section 6. This implies that no order can be made in respect of a child aged 13 or over.   [7] *Ante*, p. 460 and p. 472.
[8] Affiliation Proceedings Act 1957, s. 5 (4).

except that if the child is over 18 they can be made to him[9] and he also has the right to apply for extension. A person granted custody in the above circumstances is criminally liable for any misapplication of money paid over by the putative father or for withholding "proper nourishment" from the child or otherwise abusing or maltreating him.[10] This is an inadequate rule.[11] Reliance on the Theft Act 1968 or, as the circumstances may be, on s. 1 of the Children and Young Persons Act 1933[12] is far more appropriate and effective.

A person who has custody of the child either legally or by an arrangement approved by the court can apply for an affiliation order[13] and also can seek extension of payments when the child reaches 16.[14]

The death of the child[15] or of the father[16] automatically terminates the order. An adoption order has the same effect, except where the child is adopted by the mother and she is a "single woman" at the time of the adoption.[17]

The condition that she must have this status at that time is unjustified. Supposing that she is now married and living with her husband, there is no good reason why the father should not remain liable whether she is a sole adopter with her husband's consent or they are joint adopters. The child would be a child of the family and the law recognises the possibility of a third party being liable to maintain him.[18] The rule existed before the concept of the "child of the family" appeared and its abolition to take account of that change seems to have been overlooked. The anomaly is emphasised by the rule that where the mother marries but does not adopt, the affiliation order

[9] Family Law Reform Act 1969, s. 5(2).   [10] Section 11.
[11] The maximum penalty on summary conviction is £10.
[12] *Ante*, Chapter 6, p. 188.
[13] Affiliation Proceedings Act 1957, s. 5(3). For the right of a local authority or the Supplementary Benefits Commission to apply see *post*, p. 496 and 506 respectively.
  Bromley, *op. cit.*, p. 485, doubts whether the person could apply for an order in the first instance. It is, with respect, submitted that the wording of s. 5(3) permits this; but the co-operation of the mother would still be necessary unless the court is willing to make an order without her evidence.
[14] Section 7(6).   [15] Section 6.
[16] *Re Harrington, Wilder* v. *Turner*, [1908] 2 Ch. 687.
[17] Adoption Act 1958, s. 15(1).
  Similarly an affiliation order cannot be made once there is an adoption order except where the mother is the adopter (s. 15(2)).
[18] See *ante*, p. 459 and 469.

does not come to an end, even though her husband accepts or treats the child as a child of the family. In cases of this kind the only question should be whether the change of circumstances justifies a variation of the order.[19]

Enforcement of Orders

The enforcement of affiliation orders is largely regulated by the Magistrates' Courts Act 1952. The same methods are available for the enforcement of money payments provided by a matrimonial order under the Matrimonial Proceedings (Magistrates' Courts) Act 1960.[20] These are (1) attachment of earnings,[1] (2) distress or (3) where there is wilful refusal or culpable neglect to pay and attachment of earnings is inappropriate, committal to prison.[2] Before ordering committal the court may give the defendant a further opportunity to pay off arrears. An affiliation order, like an order under the 1960 Act, may also be registered and enforced in the High Court.[3]

The court may remit the whole or part of the arrears due under an affiliation order.[4]

IX. PARENTAL CONTRIBUTIONS TOWARDS MAINTENANCE
OF CHILDREN IN CARE

The father and mother of a legitimate child, or the mother of an illegitimate child, who has been committed to the care of a local authority by a care order (other than an interim order) or has been received into their care under s. 1 of the Children Act 1948,[5] are under a duty to contribute to his maintenance.[6] The parental duty continues until the child attains

---

[19] The court has wide powers to vary an order; but cannot do so where the party who is not the applicant for variation is out of the jurisdiction; *R. v. Gravesend Justices, ex parte Doodney*, [1971] 2 All E.R. 364; [1971] I W.L.R. 818. However, if the disappointed applicant in such circumstances is the father, the court may be willing to remit arrears; see *ibid.*
[20] Section 13(1).   [1] *Ante*, p. 476.
[2] Magistrates' Courts Act 1952, ss. 64 and 74.
[3] Maintenance Orders Act 1958, s. 21.
[4] Magistrates' Courts Act 1952, s. 76.
[5] The transfer of parental rights resulting from a resolution under s. 2 of the 1948 Act does not affect the parental duty to contribute; see s. 3(6).
[6] Payments are made to the local authority in whose area the contributing parent resides and it is then for that authority to make over the payments to the local authority responsible for the maintenance of the child; Local Government Act 1958, Sched. VIII.

the age of 16. Thereafter the child is personally liable to contribute if he is engaged in remunerative full-time work.[7] The relevant provisions are mainly contained in the Children and Young Persons Acts 1933 to 1969 and the Children Act 1948.[8]

It is obviously preferable that the local authority and the parent should reach agreement about the contribution to be made. The Children and Young Persons Act 1969[9] therefore enables the authority to propose an amount to which the parent may agree. The maximum contribution which may be proposed must not exceed the amount which the authorities would be prepared to pay for boarding out a child of the same age. Only after a written proposal has been made but not accepted within one month or, if accepted, after there has been default in making any contributions can the authority resort to judicial proceedings. Then they may apply to a magistrates' court for a contribution order, which, if granted, provides for the payment by the parent of a weekly sum which must not be greater than that already proposed by the local authority. An order remains in force so long as the child continues in the care of the local authority unless it is earlier revoked. It may also be varied,[10] and it is enforceable in the same way as an affiliation order.

Arrears may be recovered not only where they have arisen under a contribution order but also where there is no order and the parent has defaulted in making the agreed contributions. In the latter circumstances the local authority may apply for an "arrears order", but the aggregate of payments which may be ordered must not exceed the aggregate which would have been payable under a contribution order in respect of the period of default or, if it exceeded three months, the last

---

[7] Subsequent references are to the parent but the rules correspondingly apply to the child who is liable.
   A child over 16 who has been committed to care by virtue of a matrimonial order under the Matrimonial Proceedings (Magistrates' Courts) Act 1960 and is engaged in remunerative full-time work is also liable to make contributions (s. 3(2) (b)); but *quaere* the same rule applies where he has been so committed under the Matrimonial Causes Act 1965 since that Act and the Matrimonial Causes Rules are silent on the matter.

[8] C. & Y.P. Act 1933, s. 86 and 87; C. & Y.P. Act 1963, s. 30; C. & Y.P. Act 1969, s. 62 and Sched. 5 and 6; Children Act 1948, ss. 23 and 24.

[9] Section 62.

[10] Where there is a variation there is a limitation as to the amount which is similar to the rule regulating the amount in the original order. The court cannot order a varied contribution to be greater than that proposed by the local authority.

three months plus any period equal to the time during which the default continued after the making of the application for the arrears order.[11]

Whether or not there is a contribution order no contribution is payable during any period in which the child is allowed by the local authority to be under the charge and control of a parent, guardian, relative or friend.[12] Similarly, if notice is given of intention to apply for adoption of the child, no contribution is payable while he is in the care and possession of the applicants, unless 12 weeks have elapsed since the giving of the notice without the application being made or the application has been refused by the court or withdrawn.[13]

Affiliation Orders

The liability of the father of the illegitimate child to make contributions depends upon there being an affiliation order in force.

During the period when the child, who is already the subject of such an order, is in the care of a local authority as the result of a care order or of being received into care under s. 1 of the Children Act 1948, the affiliation order may be varied on the application of the local authority so that payments are thereafter made to the authority.[14] When the child ceases to be in the care of the local authority or if, while remaining in care, he is allowed to be under the charge and control of a parent, guardian relative or friend, the affiliation order ceases to be operative. However, the mother or the person having custody[15] may apply for it to be revived.

If no affiliation order has yet been made the local authority may themselves apply for it, so that any payments may be made to them.[16] The maximum time limit for making an application is three years from the date when the child was received into care or the care order came into force. It is now possible

---

[11] C. & Y.P. Act 1963, s. 30, as amended by C. & Y.P. Act 1969, Sched. 5.
[12] C. & Y.P. Act 1969, s. 62(2).
[13] Adoption Act 1958, s. 36(2).
[14] C. & Y.P. Act 1933, s. 88; Children Act 1948, s. 23; Criminal Justice Act 1961, Sched. 5; C. & Y.P. Act 1969, Scheds. 5 and 6.
[15] Under s. 5(3) of the Affiliation Proceedings Act 1957, *ante*, p. 493.
[16] Children Act 1948, s. 26, as amended by C. & Y.P. Act 1969, Scheds. 5 and 6; Affiliation Proceedings Act 1957, s. 5(2) (d).

for an order to be made without the authority having to rely on the mother to give evidence.[16a] If the affiliation order is granted but ceases to operate for any of the above reasons, the local authority may later seek revival of it; for example, where they subsequently receive the child back into care or, in a case where they have allowed him to be under the charge and control of a parent, etc., but subsequently terminate that arrangement.

Where there is an affiliation order in force no payments can be required to be made by the father to the local authority once the child attains 16; otherwise his obligation would be heavier than that of the mother or of either parent of a legitimate child.[17] However, payments can be ordered for any period during which the child is permitted by the authority to reside with his mother or the person have custody legally or by any arrangement approved by the court.[18]

X. MAINTENANCE OUT OF THE ESTATE OF A DECEASED PARENT[19]

Because of its insistence on testamentary freedom English law has never been attracted to a system of *legitim* whereby a person's dependants are assured of a certain portion of his estate on his death. Eventually in 1938 it opted for an inadequate and indeterminate system[20] which enables a disappointed dependant to seek the aid of the court by way of an order that reasonable provision be made for him out of the estate. Two of its defects have been removed by the extension of the system to include intestacies and, recently, to benefit the illegitimate child;[1] but there are others.

[16a] Affiliation Proceedings (Amendment) Act 1972, s. 1(4)(a).

[17] But why should liability end at that age? If financial provision is made for a child over 16 either under the Matrimonial Proceedings (Magistrates' Courts) Act 1960 or the Matrimonial Proceedings and Property Act 1970 and he is in care payments are to be made to the local authority so long as he remains in care. See M.P. (M.C.) Act 1960, s. 2(1)(h); M.P. & P. Act 1970, ss. 3 & 4; Matrimonial Causes Act 1965, s. 36(2).

[18] Affiliation Proceedings Act 1957, s. 7(4) (5) and (6); C. & Y.P. Act 1969, Sched. 5.   [19] See Tyler, Family Provision.

[20] See Stone, *The Economic Aspects of Death in the Family*, 8 J.S.P.T.L. 188.

[1] The relevant law is embodied in the Inheritance (Family Provision) Act 1938; the Intestates' Estates Act 1952; the Family Provision Act 1966; the Family Law Reform Act 1969; and the Law Reform (Miscellaneous Provisions) Act 1970, s. 6. The Act of 1938, as amended by those of 1952 and 1966, is printed in Sched. 3 of the 1966 Act.

Children as Dependants

One of these defects relates to the class of children who may be assisted. Apart from the surviving spouse or the survivor of a void marriage entered into with the deceased in good faith,[2] the recognised dependants are:

(i) a daughter of any age who has not been married.

In *Re Rodwell*,[3] *Midgley* v. *Runbold*, it was held that a daughter whose voidable marriage had been annulled qualified as a dependant on the ground that through the retrospective effect of the decree of nullity she had never been married. Such a decision is, however, no longer possible in respect of marriages annulled since the commencement of the Nullity of Marriage Act 1971, because the Act has abolished the retrospective rule.[4]

(ii) a son under the age of 21.

(iii) A son or daughter of any age and whether or not he or she has been married who is, by reason of some mental or physical disability incapable of maintaining himself or herself.

The limitation that a daughter, not suffering a disability, must not have been married is unduly restrictive and excludes, for example, the young widow who might well need parental support.[5] Anomalously, a married son so long as he is under 21 is not similarly excluded. Marriage should be highly relevant in deciding whether to allow maintenance, but it ought not to be a bar to making an application.

It is a pity that the recent legislation amending the Inheritance (Family Provision) Act 1938 did not widen the class of children to accord with the extension made by the Matrimonial Proceedings and Property Act 1970. Thus, while sons and daughters include those who are legitimate, legitimated, adopted and illegitimate,[6] they must be the children of the deceased,[7] so that any other "child of the family", as defined

---

[2] The latest example of recognition of the putative marriage by English Law; Law Reform (Miscellaneous Provisions) Act 1970, s. 6(1).

[3] [1970] Ch. 726; [1969] 3 All E.R. 1363. See also Tiley, 32 M.L.R. 210.

[4] Section 5.

[5] Compare *Re Andrews*, [1955] 3 All E.R. 248; [1955] 1 W.L.R. 1105, a case at the other extreme, where an unmarried daughter, aged 69, who had lived with a man for some 42 years and had children by him, was held entitled to claim against her father's estate, although no order was made in the circumstances.

[6] Inheritance (Family Provision) Act 1938, s. 5(1); Family Law Reform Act 1969, s. 18(1) and (3). Illegitimate children may only be included where the deceased died on or after 1 January 1970.

[7] They include those *en ventre sa mere* when the deceased died.

by the Act of 1970, is left unprotected. Moreover no discretion is given to the court to make provision for the son over 21 who needs it for educational purposes or because of special circumstances other than a physical or mental disability.

Another defect which may prejudice the right of children to claim is the requirement that the deceased must have died domiciled in England.[8] Because of a minor's dependence on his father for his domicile it means that the son or daughter of a deceased person with a foreign domicile cannot invoke the Acts even though he or she is ordinarily resident in England and the deceased has left assets here.[9]

As in the case of financial provision for children where there are matrimonial proceedings, the interests and claims of the children are most commonly bound up with those of the wife. Both she, as the surviving spouse, and they may wish to challenge the will because the whole or substantial part of the testator's estate has been left to a stranger, *e.g.*, his mistress; or the dispute may be between the widow and the children, particularly if the latter are children by a previous marriage of the deceased.[10] This latter dispute may arise either because she or they have benefited under the will at the expense of the other or because the rules of intestacy are operating unfairly against the children.[11] Moreover, it should be noted that disputes may arise between a spouse and a child who is not a dependant; for example, where the widow is complaining against a will in which the sole beneficiary is a son over 21.

Reasonable Provision

The same matters must be considered for the purpose of deciding whether or not reasonable provision has been made for the maintenance of a dependant under the will or the law

[8] Inheritance (Family Provision) Act 1938, s. 1(1).
[9] Because of the unity of domicile of spouses a surviving wife is similarly prejudiced; *Mastaka* v. *Midland Bank Executor and Trustee Co., Ltd.*, [1941] Ch. 192; [1941] 1 All E.R. 236.
[10] *E.g.*, see *Re Howell, Howell* v. *Lloyds Bank, Ltd.*, [1953] 2 All E.R. 604 (C.A.); [1953] 1 W.L.R. 1034; *Re Goodwin, Goodwin* v. *Goodwin*, [1969] 1 Ch. 283; [1968] 3 All E.R. 12.
Conversely there may be a dispute between a former spouse of the deceased and children of a later marriage, since a former spouse, who has not re-married, may apply for maintenance out of the estate (Matrimonial Causes Act 1965, s. 26).
[11] *Sivyer* v. *Sivyer*, [1967] 3 All E.R. 429; [1967] 1 W.L.R. 1482. This is an important decision on several aspects of the subject.

of intestacy or a combination of both and, if not, what reasonable provision should be made,[12] bearing in mind that the powers of the court are to order periodical payments and additionally, or alternatively, a lump sum payment. Regard must be had to the following:

(1) The nature, size and sources of the deceased's net estate.[13]

Thus, the estate may be too small to be able to provide an amount of maintenance which would be reasonable;[14] or it may be just sufficient to justify a lump sum payment whereas the income from it could not support an order for periodical payments; or it may be such that a lump sum order would be inappropriate because it would necessitate an improvident realisation of the assets.[15]

Where there is a dispute between the widow of a second marriage and the deceased's children by a first marriage and the deceased's estate is wholly or partly derived from the former spouse of the first marriage, it may well be reasonable to order maintenance for the children; *e.g.*, where, under the law of intestacy, the widow would otherwise have been solely entitled.[16]

The 1938 Act does not enable an *inter vivos* transaction, made by the deceased and designed to defeat the claims of dependants, to be set aside.

(2) The financial resources of the dependant.[17]

The court must take account of the past, present or future capital or income from any source of the dependant. The extent to which cognisance will be taken of the receipt of State benefits will, however, be very limited. Where the estate is small the court will not make an order if the only effect would be to reduce the amount of the State benefits, *e.g.*, Supplementary Benefits,[18] but where the benefit is in the form of accommodation and maintenance the position is less clear.

---

[12] But see *infra* for the relevance of circumstances arising after the deceased's death.
[13] "Net estate" means all the property of which the deceased had power to dispose by his will (otherwise than by virtue of a special power of appointment) less the amount of his funeral, testamentary and administration expenses, debts and liabilities and estate duty (Inheritance (Family Provision) Act 1938, s. 5(1)).
[14] *Re Vrint, Vrint v. Swain*, [1940] Ch. 920; [1940] 3 All E.R. 470; *Re E.*, [1966] 2 All E.R. 44; [1966] 1 W.L.R. 709.
[15] Section 1(5).   [16] *Sivyer v. Sivyer, supra*, n. 11.   [17] Section 1(6).
[18] *Re E.*, [1966] 2 All E.R. 44; [1966] 1 W.L.R. 709.

In *Re Watkins*[19] it was held that a daughter who was insane and detained in a mental hospital, provided under the National Health Service Act 1946, was not entitled to an order against her father's estate even though it was large enough to justify one being made. The same reasoning was applied:

"... a man cannot be said to be acting unreasonably in not providing for something for which the State will provide and the provision of which by him would only operate to relieve, not the defendant, but the State".[20]

But it is difficult to see why a person should not be said to be acting unreasonably if, having the means, he does not make any of them available to enable a dependant to enjoy comforts and facilities over and above those provided by the State. In such circumstances the moral obligation[1] should carry great weight. With *Re Watkins* should be compared *Sivyer* v. *Sivyer*[2] where a daughter in the care of a local authority was given over half of her father's estate. Nevertheless, the decision may be consistent with the above-reasoning because in such a case the local authority would not, it is submitted, be entitled to claim any of the estate as a contribution towards the expense of maintaining the child and this is so even where she is 16 or over, since her personal contribution only arises where she is in remunerative full-time work[3] and then, it is submitted, is to be made only out of that remuneration.

(3) The conduct of the dependant in relation to the deceased and otherwise.[4]

In weighing this matter a further consideration is whether the deceased owes a moral obligation to the dependant to maintain him, as, for example, where a child has looked after the deceased during a prolonged illness,[5] or whether the child has forfeited any moral claim by his or her conduct, as, for example, where a daughter has been living with a man to whom she is not married.[6]

(4) Any other matter which in the circumstances the court may

---

[19] [1949] 1 All E.R. 695.
[20] *Per* STAMP, J., in *Re E. supra*, at pp. 48 and 715 respectively.
[1] See *infra.*   [2] *Supra.*   [3] *Ante*, p. 495.   [4] Section 1(6).
[5] *Cf. Re Blanch, Blanch* v. *Honhold*, [1967] 2 All E.R. 468; [1967] 1 W.L.R. 987.
[6] *Re Andrews*, [1955] 3 All E.R. 248; [1955] 1 W.L.R. 1105.

consider relevant or material in relation to the dependant, to persons interested in the deceased's estate or otherwise.[7]

Here, too, the moral obligation may be significant. Thus on that ground the deceased's action in leaving his property to a person who is not a dependant may be justified, as where the beneficiary has cared for the deceased over a long period or where he is a child of the family who is not a child of the deceased. Under this head should also be considered the standard of living of the applicant while the deceased was alive and the financial provisions made for the former by the latter during that period.

(5) The deceased's reasons for making the testamentary dispositions which he made, or for not making any, or any further provision for the dependant.[8] The court may accept such evidence of the reasons as it considers sufficient, both written and oral.[9]

In deciding whether reasonable provision has been made for a dependant by a testator the court at one time applied a partially subjective test. His conduct was to be assessed in the light of the circumstances obtaining at his death and the consequences which he ought reasonably to have foreseen.

In *Re Howell*[10] *Howell* v. *Lloyd's Bank, Ltd.* the testator appointed his second wife guardian to his two children by his first marriage and left her all his estate on the assumption that she would look after them. After his death illness compelled her to hand over the children to their mother. It was held that, since he could not reasonably have foreseen her illness, the provisions of the will must stand and the children could have no claim on his estate.

In *Re Goodwin*,[11] *Goodwin* v. *Goodwin* however, MEGARRY, J., preferred the objective test of whether in fact reasonable provision has been made by the testator and not whether he has acted unreasonably; but *Re Howell, Howell* v. *Lloyd's Bank, Ltd.* was not cited, so that there must be some doubt as to

---

[7] Section 1(6).   [8] Section 1(7).
[9] *Re Pugh, Pugh* v. *Pugh,* [1943] Ch. 387; [1943] 2 All E.R. 361; *Re Borthwick, Borthwick* v. *Beauvais,* [1949] Ch. 395; [1949] 1 All E.R. 472; *Re Smallwood, Smallwood* v. *Martins Bank, Ltd.,* [1951] Ch. 369; [1951] 1 All E.R. 372.
[10] [1953] 2 All E.R. 604 (C.A.).
[11] [1969] 1 Ch. 283; [1968] 3 All E.R. 12.

whether the later case will be followed.[12] The vital difference
between the two views is that events subsequent to the
deceased's death must be taken into account both in applying
the objective test and, if it is found that reasonable provision
has not been made, in deciding the terms of an order, whereas
if the alternative test is applied those events only become
relevant for the latter purpose after the testator's unreasonableness has been established.

The Order

Although a lump sum payment may sometimes be appropriate, the order is usually for periodical payments. It may
provide for them to be of a specified amount or to be equal to
the whole or part of the income of the net estate or of the
income of any part of the estate which is to be appropriated
for the purpose of the order.[13] It may be made subject to conditions, and this may be particularly desirable to protect the
interests of children, for example, where receipt of payments
by a widow is to depend on her maintaining the deceased's
children during their minority.[14]

Another useful power is that enabling the court to make an
interim order for one or more payments to meet an immediate
need of financial assistance for an applicant until the making
of a final order.[15] At the court's discretion the latter order may
provide that payments made under the interim order shall be
treated as having been paid on account of maintenance due
under the final order. In deciding whether to make an interim
order the same considerations are relevant as for determining
a final order.

An order for periodical payments in favour of a child dependant must provide for the termination not later than—

(a) in the case of a daughter her marriage or the cesser of
her disability, whichever is the later;

(b) in the case of a son under 21 his attaining that age;

---

[12] For a proposed reconciliation of the two cases see WINN, L. J., in *Re
Gregory, Gregory* v. *Goodenough*, [1971] 1 All E.R. 497, 502 (C.A.);
Cretney 85 L.Q.R. 331.
[13] Section 3(1A).
[14] *Re Lidington, Lidington* v. *Thomas*, [1940] Ch. 927; [1940] 3 All E.R. 600.
See also *Re Franks, infra.*
[15] Section 4A.

(c) in the case of a son under disability, the cesser of his disability or,

(d) in any case his or her earlier death.[16]

An application for an order must normally be made within six months from the date when representation was taken out, but the court may permit a late application, for example, where otherwise there is a risk of hardship or injustice.[17] Once an order has been made, however, there is power to vary it at any time, but only within certain limits.[18] Firstly, variation may be made only in respect of that part of the estate which has already been set aside to provide maintenance for the dependant. Because of this restriction it may be advisable when the court is making the original order to appropriate more than is needed to meet the immediate needs of a dependant with a view to future protection of his interests or those of another dependant, *e.g.*, for the future education of a child.[19] Secondly, the order may be varied either because of non-disclosure of a material fact when it was made or because of a substantial change in the circumstances of the dependant or of a person beneficially interested in the estate under the will or intestacy. Thirdly an order may be made for the maintenance of another dependant.

B. STATE ALLOWANCES FOR CHILDREN

The following is a brief outline of the kinds of allowances provided by the State in respect of children.

I. SUPPLEMENTARY BENEFITS

Persons aged 16 or over who are not in full-time work and whose resources are insufficient to meet their requirements are entitled to claim Supplementary Allowances under the Ministry of Social Security Act 1966,[20] except that where they are still

---

[16] Section 1(2).
[17] *Re Trott, Trott* v. *Miles*, [1958] 2 All E.R. 296; [1958] 1 W.L.R. 604 (posthumous child born just before end of the six-month period).
[18] Section 4.
[19] *Re Franks, Franks* v. *Franks*, [1948] Ch. 62; [1947] 2 All E.R. 638.
[20] Section 4.
   The Family Income Supplements Act 1970 makes available a further benefit to a family with a low income, provided there is at least one child.
   Other benefits relating to children (for the most part those under the age of 15) are free welfare foods and school meals, and free prescriptions and dental treatment under the National Health Service.

at school or otherwise receiving full-time educational instruction[1] they will be treated in the same way as children under 16.[2] The latter cannot themselves claim benefits, but are treated as members of the household in which they live. In the usual case of the married couple living together with dependent children, claims must be made on behalf of all by the husband. Similarly, where a man and woman are cohabiting as man and wife, he is the claimant and the woman will not be entitled to claim in her own right and on behalf of her children, but the onus is on the Supplementary Benefits Commission to prove cohabitation. The test is whether the parties are living together as one household. This can be extremely difficult to establish. Proof of a sexual relationship *per se* is not sufficient. Much more cogent is evidence that the parties pool their resources and that the children are children of both of them or, at least, are treated as such. Even where cohabitation is proved, the woman may be able to make a separate claim in exceptional circumstances, for example, in respect of her children and the man, not being their father, refuses to support them.

Where the Supplementary Benefits Commission has had to provide Supplementary Benefits in respect of a child under 16, it may, by virtue of the duty imposed by the 1966 Act,[3] seek to recover from the parent the cost of the benefits (including those in kind) already provided and to ensure that the parent in future discharges his liability. There is a separate procedure for recovery against the father of the illegitimate child.[4] Otherwise, the Commission applies to a magistrates' court for an order requiring either parent of a legitimate or adopted child or the mother of an illegitimate to pay such sum, weekly or otherwise as the court considers appropriate having regard to all the circumstances and in particular to the resources of the parent.[5] Payments under an order for recovery of the cost of benefits already provided must be made to the Secretary of State and for the future maintenance of the child to "such person as appears to the court expedient in the interests of the

---

[1] In exceptional circumstances even they may claim in their own right.
[2] Section 9.   [3] Section 22, *ante*, p. 455.
[4] See *infra*.
[5] Section 23.

   An order may be varied or revoked and is enforceable in the same ways as any other maintenance order made by a magistrates' court.

child". In practice this will be the other parent or whoever else has custody or care and control of the child.

The right of the Commission to recover from the putative father where benefits have been provided for an illegitimate child is similar to that of a local authority where an illegitimate child is in their care.[6] If there is an affiliation order requiring payments by the father already in force, the Commission may seek variation so that payments be made to the Secretary of State or such other person as the court may direct instead of to the mother or to the person having custody.[7] If there is no such order,[8] the Commission may itself apply for one in order to achieve the same object;[9] and that order may later be varied on the mother's application. The maximum time limit for an application by the Commission is similar to that governing a local authority application, namely, three years from the date when the time when any benefit was paid. The restrictive rule requiring the giving of evidence by the mother no longer applies.[10] Although the right conferred on the Commission is an independent right to obtain an affiliation order,[11] it depends on no such order already being in force for payments by the putative father to the mother.[12] However, once it is made it is not limited to the period during which benefits were being provided, and it has no difference in its effect from one originally obtained by the mother.[13]

II. FAMILY ALLOWANCES

Unlike the scheme of Supplementary Benefits that of Family Allowances is not based upon the resources of the family and the need for support, but is of general application to all families with two or more children. Were it designed only to assist families with low income, there would be every reason for

[6] See *ante*, p. 496.
[7] Ministry of Social Security Act 1966, s. 24(4) and (6); Affiliation Proceedings Act, 1957, s. 5.   [8] See *infra*.
[9] Sub-section (2) and (4) of s. 24 of the 1966 Act.
   Moreover, where the mother brings the affiliation proceedings the Commission may apply for payments to be made to the Secretary of State, (sub-s. (5)).
[10] See Affiliation Proceedings (Amendment) Act 1972, s. 1(4) (b).
[11] *Clapham* v. *National Assistance Board*, [1961] 2 Q.B. 77; [1961] 2 All E.R. 50.
[12] *Oldfield* v. *National Assistance Board*, [1960] 1 Q.B. 635; [1960] 1 All E.R. 524.
[13] *Payne* v. *Critchley*, [1962] 2 Q.B. 83; [1962] 1 All E.R. 619.

applying it to those where there was only child. The scheme could, however, be made selective in favour of those most needing support by "clawing back" the whole or part of the allowances from those claiming tax relief for children, *i.e.*, by reducing the child tax allowances.

For the purpose of Family Allowances, as for that of National Insurance, a family is constituted by one of the following groups:[14]

    (*a*) a man and wife living together,[15] any child being the issue of both or either of them and any child maintained by them;

    (*b*) a man who does not have a wife or does not live with her, any issue of his and any child maintained by him;

    (*c*) a woman who does not have a husband or does not live with him, any issue of hers and any child maintained by her.

A marriage which is potentially polygamous by a foreign law but *de facto* monogamous may be recognised for the purpose of the scheme.[16]

For a child to be included a member of the family as "issue" of the man and wife or a man or a woman,[17] he must be an issue of the first generation. The definition extends to the legitimated child and the child adopted by the head of the family, but an illegitimate child is the issue only of his mother. If the child is the legitimate child of a deceased spouse by an earlier marriage he is treated as issue of the surviving spouse of the second marriage. In similar circumstances, if he is the illegitimate child of the deceased spouse he is treated as issue of the surviving spouse for any period during which he lives with the survivor.[18] To entitle him to be a member of a family as an issue, it is not, however, sufficient for him to come within one of the above categories. He must also either be living with the head of the family[19] or the latter must be contributing not less than a specified weekly amount to the cost of providing for him.[20]

[14] Family Allowances Act 1965, s. 3.
[15] They are deemed to be living together unless permanently separated by an agreement or under an order of a court or because one of them is a deserter (s. 17(1)).   [16] Section 17(9).
[17] Such a person will be referred to as the "head" of the family.
[18] Section 17(2).   [19] Temporary absence is ignored, *e.g.*, at school.
[20] Section 3(2). The current minimum is 90p.

The Family Allowances Act 1965 also defines the circumstances in which a child is a member of a family because he is being maintained by the head, although he is not an issue. If the head is the only person providing for the child or if he contributes more than anyone else, the child falls into his family.[1] It may well be that a child could, in accordance with the above rules, be treated as a member of more than one family, *e.g.*, as an issue of one and because he is being maintained by the other. Where this occurs priority is given to the family of which he is an issue.[2]

A child does not belong to any family while he is being detained under s. 53 of the Children and Young Persons Act 1933 for having committed a grave crime[3] or is in the care of a local authority under a care order or by virtue of a resolution passed under s. 2 of the Children Act 1948, except that where he is in care but is allowed by the authority to be under the control of a parent, guardian, relative or friend he may be treated as a member of a family.[4]

Subject to the above limitations, every child below the upper limit of the compulsory school age comes within the scheme, as does one over that age but under 19 who is receiving full-time education or, as an apprentice, is receiving full-time training for a trade, business or profession and is not earning more than a statutory limit.[5] Formerly a child who had reached the minimum school leaving age of 15 could also be treated as a member of the family until he was 16 if he was unable to work because of disability or prolonged illness. There is, it is submitted, no justification for not allowing benefits to continue to the age of 19 in cases of disability or illness.[6]

Allowances are payable in respect of each child other than the elder or eldest.[7] Where the family includes a man and wife living together, allowances belong to the wife, but they are payable to either spouse and, as in all other cases, they belong

[1] Section 3(3) and Sched.
 But the contribution must be not less than the specified weekly amount (*supra*), unless the child is living with him.
[2] *Ibid.* [3] See *ante*, p. 136. [4] Family Allowances Act 1965, s. 11.
[5] Family Allowances Act 1965, ss. 2(1), (2) and 19(1).
[6] Equally no allowance is possible if there is supervening disability or illness after the child has reached the minimum school leaving age.
[7] The present allowance for the second child is 90p weekly and for each other child £1.00.

to the family as a whole.[8] For this reason they are inalienable.[9]

III. NATIONAL INSURANCE[10]

Under the scheme of National Insurance[11] various allowances are paid in respect of children. For the purpose of the scheme the family unit and the child are defined in the same way as they are for Family Allowances.[12] Where, for example, unemployment benefit, sickness benefit, industrial injuries benefit or disablement benefit are paid to a man, the amount is increased if he has dependant children.[13] Similar increases are paid to a woman where she is entitled to a maternity allowance, widow's allowance or widowed mother's allowance. A child's special allowance is also payable to a mother whose marriage has been dissolved or annulled after the former husband's death, provided that he was still then liable to contribute to the child's maintenance, and in certain circumstances a guardian's allowance may be paid to the guardian of a child where there is no parent to maintain the child because he is dead or cannot be traced.

The National Council for the Unmarried Mother and Her Child has recommended[14] a new kind of benefit for the child of the single-parent family. The main reasons for the proposal are the financial incapacity, or the refusal, of fathers to provide adequately for their children's maintenance, the unwillingness of unmarried mothers to institute affiliation proceedings and the inability of the courts effectively to enforce matrimonial orders and affiliation orders against the husband or father.[15]

---

[8] Section 1. However, either can apply to a magistrates' court for an order that the other should not receive the allowances, a desirable protection against the spouse who will not use the allowances to benefit the family as a whole (s. 4).   [9] Section 10.

[10] See generally Aikin, 8 J.S.P.T.L. 167; and *Forward for the Fatherless, infra.*

[11] National Insurance Act 1965; National Insurance (Industrial Injuries) Act 1965.

Like the Family Allowances Act 1965 these are consolidating Acts, but amendments to social security legislation are so frequent that the need for consolidation is a continual one.

[12] National Insurance Act 1965, s. 114(2).

[13] Since the eldest child does not qualify for Family Allowance, the amount payable in respect of him is larger than for the others.

[14] In its memorandum, *Forward for the Fatherless*, to the Committee on One-Parent Families.

[15] The defects have been convincingly demonstrated by the legal research unit at Bedford College, London; see McGregor, Blom-Cooper and

The proposed benefit would be of two kinds: a Child Allowance for the basic maintenance of the child and a Child Aid Allowance to cover the cost of caring for him. It would be available in respect of the child of a divorced, separated[16] or unmarried mother, but the right to it would vest in the child and where necessary would be enforced on his behalf by the mother or some other person. The cost of such a scheme would be met from three sources, namely, National Insurance Contributions, Contributions by fathers recoverable by the State and an Exchequer grant largely made by a transfer of tax revenue from the Supplementary Benefits Commission.

IV. PROVISION BY LOCAL AUTHORITIES

The preventive powers conferred by s. 1 of the Children and Young Persons Act 1963 on local authorities include the power to make cash payments to families in trouble, but, as already noted, [17] the use made of it is variable, and some authorities seem particularly reluctant to invoke it to help the fatherless family and prevent the separation of mother and child.[18]

A local authority may accommodate in a community home persons over compulsory school age but under 21 who are employed or receiving education or training.[19] They may contribute to the cost of accommodating and maintaining such a person in *any* place near the place of his employment, education or training, if he is, or since ceasing to be of compulsory school age, has been in the care of a local authority.[20] They may also make grants to persons between 17 and 21, who at or after the time when they attained the age of 17 were in the care of a local authority, so as to enable them to meet expenses relating to their education or training.[1]

Gibson, *Separated Spouses;* McGregor, *Social Effects of Matrimonial Jurisdiction of Magistrates,* 118 N.L.J. 41.
    See also the Departmental Committee on Statutory Maintenance Limits, Cmnd. 3587 (1968), which also referred to the possibility of the State's assuming responsibility for the payment and recovery of maintenance.
[16] There could be difficulties over proof of separation; *cf. ante,* p. 505.
[17] *Ante,* Chapter 5, p. 171.   [18] See *Forward for the Fatherless,* paras. 198-200.
[19] Children Act 1948, s. 19, as substituted by C. & Y.P. Act 1969, s. 50.
[20] Children Act 1948, s. 20(1), as amended by C. & Y.P. Act 1963, s. 46(1) and C. & Y.P. Act 1969, Sched. 5.
    The provision is complicated, but its effect is that if the child is no longer in care after reaching the age of 17, the section may be invoked; if he is still in care at that age no assistance can be given until he attains 18.
[1] Children Act 1948, s. 20(2), as amended by C. & Y.P. Act 1963, s. 46(2).

Index

511

Index

JUVENILE COURT—*continued*

care proceedings. *See* CARE PRO-
    CEEDINGS
constitution of, 4 *et seq.*
  Metropolitan area, outside, 6
  panel of justices,
    combinations of, 6
    composition of, 8
    membership of, 7
  Metropolitan area, within, 5
  resumed hearing, at, 92
criminal proceedings in. *See* CRIMI-
    NAL PROCEEDINGS
disclosure of reports by, 84
  power to require withdrawal of
    juvenile or parent, 85
frequency of sittings, 64
jurisdiction of, adoption, over, 15,
    154
  children in care, over, 15, 148, 155
  foster children, over, 15, 154, 385
  generally, 13 *et seq.*
  welfare of minor paramount
    consideration, 15 *et seq.*
origins of, 1 *et seq.*
panel of justices, qualifications, 10
  training, 12
parent or guardian, presence at
  proceedings, 71
persons present, restrictions as to,
  68
premises of, 65
publication of proceedings, restrictions on, 68
summary jurisdiction, of, 40
remand of juvenile by, for psychiatric examination, 83
remission of juvenile to, care proceedings, in, 44
  where finding of guilt by adult
    court, 43
upper age limit, attainment before
  commencement of proceedings,
  45
  attainment during course of
    proceedings, 49

L

LAW REFORM COMMITTEE, 452
LEGITIMACY. *See also* ILLEGITI-
  MATE CHILD
blood group evidence of, consent of
  child over 16 to order, 244
  power of court to order, 243, 245
  refusal by parent to allow, 244
declaration of British nationality,
  251
  validity of marriage, and, 251
historical background, 236

LEGITIMACY—*continued*

legitimation, declaration of, 251
  paternity, proof of, 249
  property, effect on devolution of,
    252
  subsequent marriage, by, 249
presumption of, adoption proceedings, in, 339
  efficacy of, 239
  rebuttal of, 239
  scope of, 237 *et seq.*
  standard of proof of, 241
void marriage, child of, 246
voidable marriage, child of, 248

LOCAL AUTHORITY,

adoption agency as. *See* ADOPTION
adoption societies, registration of,
  324
child in care of, accommodation of,
  community home, in. *See*
    COMMUNITY HOME
  adoption order, effect on, 368
  after-care of, 172
  custody proceedings, resulting
    from, 272, 279, 287
  discharge of care order, 153
  duration of care, 145
  emigration of, 168
  interim care order, 152
  juvenile court, jurisdiction over.
    See JUVENILE COURT
  maintenance of. *See* MAINTENANCE
  matrimonial order, under, 155
  mentally disordered child, 173
  order of High Court, 154, 156
  powers of accommodation of, 167
  powers to receive child, 144
    et seq., 154
  recovery of expenses from another
    authority, 146
  religious persuasion of, 168, 169,
    432
  termination of care by adoption,
    368
  transfer to parent, relative or
    friend, 145
  visits by parents to, 169
  wishes of parent or guardian, 146
community home. *See* COMMUNITY
  HOME
consultation with parents and police,
  53
director of social services, 142
guardian *ad litem* as, 355, 356
foster children, duties towards, 380
  et seq.
health visitor, 390
home provided by, conduct of, 163
  et seq.
  inspection of, 163

517

LOCAL AUTHORITY—*continued*
licence of, for employment of child.
　See EMPLOYMENT
maintenance of young persons by,
　510
matron appointed by, for child
　employees. *See* EMPLOYMENT
notification of, criminal proceedings
　against juvenile of, 52
foster parent, by, 382
parental rights, assumption of, 147
　duration of resolution, 148
　effect of resolution, 149
　religious upbringing, effect on,
　　151
pre-school children, care of, 390
reports on juveniles, duty to provide,
　80
responsibilities towards juveniles,
　generally, 140
social services committee, of, 142
　department, of, 390, 392
supervisor under supervision order,
　as, 98
'visitor', appointment and duties of,
　170
LOCAL EDUCATION AUTHOR-
ITY. *See also* SCHOOL
care proceedings, institution by, 439
handicapped child, duly to provide
　special educational facilities for,
　443
medical examination of child, by,
　443
nursery education, provision of, 442
parents, consultation with, 440
prosecution of, 438, 439
religious education, provision of, by,
　441
report of, 84
school attendance order made by,
　435
　failure to comply with, 435
schools, duty to provide, 440
special schools, duty to provide, 442

M
MAINTENANCE,
affiliation order, adoption order,
　effect on, 367
death of child, 493
duration of order for payment,
　492
enforcement of, 494
financial limits on, 491
local authority's application for,
　496
Supplementary Benefits Commis-
　sion's application for, 506

MAINTENANCE—*continued*
who may apply, 493
affiliation proceedings, evidence
　in, 491
　jurisdiction over, 488
　'single woman' by, 489
　time limit on, 488, 490
child in care of local authority,
　affiliation order, under, 496
parent by, maximum contribu-
　tion, 495
no payment when child placed
　for adoption, 496
recovery of arrears in payment,
　495
parental duty, of, 494
custody order under, parent, pay-
　ment by, 456
duration of maintenance, 457
'dependents' of, 460
estate of parent, from, dependent
　children, 498
form of order, 503
reasonable provision, 499
family allowances, age limits for,
　508
child as member of family, for,
　507
'family', 507
High Court or county court,
　awarded by, 461
avoidance of transactions, 479
duration of order, 472
enforcement of order, attachment
　of earnings, by, 476, 494
judgment summons by, 476
registration in magistrates'
　court, 478
lump sum payment, 462, 463, 474,
　486, 500
relevant matters for court, 467-
　472
transfer and settlement of pro-
　perty, 464
variation and discharge of order,
　473
variation of settlement, 465 *et seq.*
husband's liability to support child,
　483
illegitimate child of, agreement
　between parents, 454
putative father by, 455, 456, 460
See also affiliation proceedings,
　ante.
matrimonial order under, child of
　the family, of, 459 *et seq.*
National Insurance Scheme, under,
　guardian, payment to, 509
parent, payment to, 509